FOURTEENTH EDITION

EFFECTIVE GROUP DISCUSSION
Theory and Practice

GLORIA J. GALANES
Missouri State University

KATHERINE ADAMS
California State University at Fresno

Mc Graw Hill

Connect
Learn
Succeed™

EFFECTIVE GROUP DISCUSSION: THEORY AND PRACTICE, FOURTEENTH EDITION

Published by McGraw-Hill, a business unit of The McGraw-Hill Companies, Inc., 1221 Avenue of the Americas, New York, NY 10020. Copyright © 2013 by The McGraw-Hill Companies, Inc. All rights reserved. Printed in the United States of America. Previous editions © 2010, 2007, and 2004. No part of this publication may be reproduced or distributed in any form or by any means, or stored in a database or retrieval system, without the prior written consent of The McGraw-Hill Companies, Inc., including, but not limited to, in any network or other electronic storage or transmission, or broadcast for distance learning.

Some ancillaries, including electronic and print components, may not be available to customers outside the United States.

This book is printed on acid-free paper.

3 4 5 6 7 8 9 0 DOC/DOC 1 0 9 8 7 6

ISBN 978-0-07-353434-3
MHID 0-07-353434-x

Vice President & Editor-in-Chief: *Michael Ryan*
Vice President of Specialized Publishing: *Janice M. Roerig-Blong*
Publisher: *David Patterson*
Sponsoring Editor: *Debra B. Hash*
Marketing Coordinator: *Angela R. FitzPatrick*
Project Manager: *Melissa M. Leick*
Design Coordinator: *Brenda A. Rolwes*
Cover Designer: Studio Montage, St. Louis, Missouri
Cover Image: © Getty Images RF
Buyer: *Sandy Ludovissy*
Media Project Manager: *Sridevi Palani*
Compositor: *Laserwords Private Limited*
Typeface: *10/12 GaramondStd*
Printer: *R. R. Donnelley*

All credits appearing on page or at the end of the book are considered to be an extension of the copyright page.

Library of Congress Cataloging-in-Publication Data

Galanes, Gloria J.
  Effective group discussion: theory and practice/Gloria J. Galanes,
Katherine Adams.—14th ed.
      p. cm.
  ISBN 978-0-07-353434-3 (alk. paper)
1. Small groups. 2. Communication in small groups. 3. Group problem solving.
4. Discussion. I. Adams, Katherine. II. Title.
  HM736.B75 2013
  302.34—dc23   2011047939

www.mhhe.com

Brief Contents

Contents

PART **II**

Developing the Group   79

PART **III**

Small Group Throughput Processes   143

PART   **IV**

Improving Group Outputs   239

Preface

For this 14th edition, we again confront the ongoing challenge of incorporating important new information without increasing the length of the text. In this edition, we continue the process, which we began in earnest in the 13th edition. We have removed material about the communication process that most students already know, but retained and consolidated information about communication processes as they relate specifically to small groups. We have streamlined many of our discussions and removed redundant information. We believe we have met our goal of updating the text without increasing the length.

One of the most important changes concerns our definition of communication. Starting with this edition, we emphasize the transactional nature of communication as group members simultaneously create, interpret, and negotiate shared meaning through their interaction. While we have always believed this, we bring this process of mutual creation to the forefront as we explain key concepts most relevant to small groups. We continue to highlight bona fide group theory, which we believe has contributed significantly to our understanding of how real-world groups actually work. We also note that the technology available to help groups has become much more affordable and accessible than when we first started writing. To that end, we discuss groups not as *either* face-to-face *or* virtual, but as entities that can use a variety of technologies to assist their work and as existing on a continuum from purely face-to-face to purely virtual. We have added Appendix C, which briefly describes the most important technologies and how group members can use them.

Our primary goal remains the same: to help students become more effective small group members and leaders by giving them the research-based tools—both in terms of theoretical understandings and practical suggestions—for effective participation in groups. When students complete their study of small groups, we hope they will know how to use the information and tools we present to understand why one group is satisfying and another feels like torture. Most important of all, we hope they will understand what they can *do* about it.

Effective Group Discussion focuses on secondary groups, such as work groups, committees, task forces, self-directed work teams, and other small groups with tasks to complete. The text provides practical tips and also serves well as a reference source for advanced communication students, consultants, or group leaders.

Overview

Generally, the chapters move the discussion from systems inputs to through-put processes to outcomes. Instructors have the flexibility to skim or skip chapters or cover them in a different order. For instance, a section in Chapter 2 covers basic communication theory for students without a previous communication course, but this section can be skimmed quickly if it reviews material students already know.

Part I presents an overview of small group and human communication theory. Chapter 1 introduces several ideas developed in subsequent chapters: the importance of small groups in our lives, types of groups, how many groups use technology, what constitutes ethical behavior, and why members should become participant-observers in their groups. Chapter 2 presents the basics of communication theory that serve as the foundation for studying small groups. In Chapter 3, we present systems theory as the organizing framework used throughout the text.

Part II begins the discussion of group developing by focusing on the members, the main small group inputs. Chapter 4 introduces the importance of diversity and the contribution that members' cultures and co-cultures make to that diversity. Chapter 5 discusses how member characteristics contribute to the roles that members play in groups, including a new section about agreeableness, conscientiousness, and openness to experience (three of the "Big Five" personality characteristics from psychology).

Part III focuses on the development of the group as an entity by presenting information about a variety of throughput processes. Chapter 6 consolidates logically the information about norms, fantasy themes, and cohesiveness. Chapters 7 and 8 are companion chapters. Chapter 7 focuses on the theoretical concepts necessary to understanding leadership, and Chapter 8 provides practical suggestions for group leaders.

Part IV discusses the importance of having appropriate problem-solving and decision-making processes to improve the quality of group outputs. As with leadership, Chapters 9 and 10 are paired, with Chapter 9 providing conceptual information for understanding problem solving and decision making and Chapter 10 providing specific suggestions and techniques for improving problem-solving and decision-making processes. Chapter 11 focuses on how conflict, if managed well, can improve group outputs.

In Part V, Chapter 12 presents tools for assessing and improving small groups. Users of the text told us they preferred to have this chapter placed at the end, following discussions of theories and concepts. However, these tools and assessments can easily be used throughout the text to enhance discussion of concepts, if instructors prefer.

There are three appendices to this edition. Appendix A guides members in how to gather and organize their informational resources in preparation for problem solving and decision making. Although this information conceptually precedes Chapters 9 and 10, most upper-division students already know how to gather information. Appendix B discusses the public presentation of a group's work, including how to organize presentations so the information is presented smoothly and seamlessly. Appendix C discusses how groups can use technology to help members accomplish group goals.

New Edition Changes

This 14th edition of *Effective Group Discussion* retains the reorganization of the 13th edition, which fits the way many instructors have told us they prefer to teach.

- We have retained our research base, have consolidated conceptual information where possible, removed material and examples that seemed redundant or out-of-date, and added current theoretical information.

- We have integrated each chapter's opening case more thoroughly with the information presented throughout the chapter.

- Small group techniques are integrated throughout the text so that students can more readily link the concepts to the techniques.

- We have modernized our definition of communication to emphasize its transactional nature, as members mutually negotiate shared meaning.

- We have continued to develop our discussion of technological issues, introducing the idea of a continuum of technological use, from purely face-to-face to purely virtual, and have added an appendix devoted to group use of technology.

- We have enhanced our discussion of diversity and linked cultural and co-cultural differences more closely to that discussion.

- We have sharpened and strengthened our discussion of ethics throughout the text.

- Information about leadership and problem solving/decision making can be overwhelming. We kept the companion chapters devoted to each topic from the 13th edition. The first provides theoretical and conceptual information and the second provides more practical information, techniques, and tips.

- We have added information about three of the "Big Five" psychological personality characteristics relevant to groups in Chapter 5.

- We have retained the Recap boxes placed throughout the chapters.

- As always, we have updated this edition with the most current research available.

Features

Case Studies: Each chapter begins with a case study illustrating that chapter's main points. These are real-life stories designed to help students retain key concepts and understand how that chapter's information is relevant to the real world. We link these case studies explicitly to information presented throughout the chapter.

Recap Boxes: We have placed Recap boxes—internal summaries—throughout each chapter. They provide logical "breathing places" for students to review what they have learned.

Emphasis on Diversity: The importance of diversity and intercultural communication cannot be overemphasized! In addition to a chapter devoted to this topic, relevant information about diversity is distributed throughout the text, and we have provided a more global perspective that reflects our changing world.

Learning Aids: Each chapter includes *learning objectives* and *margin key terms,* which are boldfaced in the text. The end of chapter material includes *Questions for Review* and a *Bibliography* that provides additional reading material. The *Glossary* at the end of the text provides definitions of all key terms.

Online Learning Center at *www.mhhe.com/galanes14e* provides online activities for students that supplement the topics in the chapter. Tools and activities include interactive quizzes, and glossary flashcards. Videos covering Nonverbal Messages, Defensive/Supportive Communication, Aggressive/Assertive Communication, The Employment Interview, Small Group Communication, and Presentation are also available.

Resources for Instructors

Web site: The Online Learning Center at *www.mhhe.com/galanes14e* provides the instructor's manual, (containing sample syllabi, lecture notes, additional exercises, writing assignments,) a testbank of objective and essay questions, and PowerPoint slides, and up-to-date weblinks.

Gloria J. Galanes
Katherine Adams

Acknowledgments

We would like to thank all of the instructors and students who have used *Effective Group Discussion*. We welcome your written reactions to its content and composition. You can send your comments to us via the Department of Communication, Missouri State University, Springfield, Missouri; or the Department of Communication, California State University, Fresno, California.

May all your groups be enjoyable and satisfying!

Numerous people contributed to this book; we can name only a few. First, we acknowledge our debt to instructors and writers Freed Bales, Ernest Bormann, Elton S. Carter, B. Aubrey Fisher, Larry Frey, Kenneth Hance, Randy Hirokawa, Sidney J. Parnes, J. Donald Phillips, M. Scott Poole, Linda Putnam, Marvin Shaw, Victor Wall, and W. Woodford Zimmerman.

Finally, we want to acknowledge the vision and contributions of Jack Brilhart, who died in 2005. Jack wrote the first version of this text in the late 1960s as one monograph in a communication series. For many years, Jack shared his expertise, his passion for understanding and working with small groups, and his vast experience working with a variety of groups. We enjoyed working with him, appreciated his generosity and greatly miss him.

The following instructors were exceptionally helpful in supplying thoughtful, carefully considered suggestions:

Gil Cooper,
Pittsburg State University

Alexia Kolokotrones,
Long Beach City College

Dennis Gouran,
Pennsylvania State University

Bala Musa,
Azusa Pacific University

Douglas Guiffrida,
University of Rochester

Donna Smith,
Ferris State University

Patrizia Hoffman,
Lock Haven University of PA

Barbara Tarter,
Marshall University

The Foundations
of Communicating
in Groups

The three chapters in Part I provide introductory information to focus your study of small group communication. Chapter 1 introduces important terms and concepts used throughout the text. Chapter 2 lays the groundwork for understanding the communicative dynamics of small group interaction. Chapter 3 presents systems theory as a framework for studying and understanding small groups.

STUDY OBJECTIVES

As a result of studying Chapter 1, you should be able to:

1. Explain why you need to understand small group communication and to participate productively in small group discussions.
2. Be familiar with some of the ways technology can help a group be more productive.
3. Use correctly the terms presented in this chapter, particularly *group, small group, small group discussion,* and *ethics.*
4. Describe the difference between primary and secondary groups.
5. Consciously and intentionally become a participant–observer during group discussions.
6. Describe the six ethical principles most relevant to small group communication.

CENTRAL MESSAGE

If you want to succeed in modern organizational and social life, you must understand how to be a productive member of a group and act accordingly, including knowing how technology can benefit a group's work.

Springfield, Missouri, where one of us lives, has a two-day art festival each May, attended by 15,000 to 20,000 people. Typically, more than 130 artists participate in Artsfest, which also offers music and dance performers of all kinds, food vendors, and hands-on activities for children. This combination art show and community festival requires the efforts of hundreds of people. Artsfest is organized by a committee of volunteers working with representatives of the Springfield Regional Arts Council and the Urban Districts Alliance. The large committee of 15 includes LaShonda, an artist whose contacts extend throughout the region. She is mainly responsible for artist recruitment and correspondence. Raj is a technology guru who manages Artsfest's social media campaigns on Facebook and Twitter. Pam is a long-time community volunteer who knows everyone and is a lot of fun to work with. Her extensive lists of contacts provide the core of volunteers who work at the event, handling artist check-in, managing registration, taking gate receipts, selling T-shirts and souvenirs, providing security, and so forth. In addition, Pam encourages a warm and relaxed atmosphere in group meetings—she usually brings cookies. Jerry and Selena, the event coordinators, are both well-organized individuals who are not thrown by the level of detail that must be handled. Selena's planning book keeps details of prior festivals at her fingertips. She knows exactly how many T-shirts were ordered in prior years, how many artists were new to the festival, and how much money was made in soft-drink sales. Jerry's list of corporate sponsors is extensive; if one sponsor decides to drop out, he has three possibilities lined up to replace that sponsor.

The committee meets every other week January through March and weekly in April, with committee members keeping in touch with one another via technology between meetings. For example, committee members used Dropbox to view and make suggestions for wording on artist recruitment letters and other documents. When an issue arose between meetings that needed a quick answer, members voted by e-mail. The committee's normal meeting location was unexpectedly unavailable at one meeting; members were notified by text message of the temporary location. Jerry had to be out of town during one important meeting just before the event; the committee used Skype so he could participate. Members frequently call or text one another between meetings as they think of things that need to be handled.

This example illustrates an important point: one person alone does not have the talent, skill, or ideas to accomplish a complex task. By working together, however, individuals in a group can achieve far more than individuals working alone. And with the advent of easy-to-use technologies, group members can make their participation in groups even more effective.

Small groups, whether in education, business and industry, healthcare, social services, religion, family life, politics, or government work, are the basic building blocks of our society.[1] Lawrence Frey, a leading scholar of small group communication, believes as we do that the small group is *the* most important social formation:

Every segment of our society—from the largest multinational organization to the political workings of federal, state, city, and local governments to the smallest community action group to friendship groups to the nuclear and extended family—relies on groups to make important decisions, socialize members, satisfy needs, and the like.[2]

We spend a tremendous amount of time in formal and informal groups. In the business world alone executives spend on average half of their time in meetings,[3] adding up to an estimated 20 million business meetings a day in the United States,[4] and that this time spent in meetings only increases over time![5] When you add to this the amount of time we spend in groups outside of work, you begin to appreciate how pervasive groups are in our lives. However, poorly managed meetings hurt the very businesses they are suppose to support, wasting valuable time and resources and losing as much as $37 billion in the United States alone each year.[6] Moreover, the ability to function effectively as part of a group requires skills that must be understood and practiced. Over 70 percent of respondents from 750 leading U.S. companies, in a national survey, ranked the "ability to work in teams" as a more essential skill for MBA graduates than knowledge of statistical techniques.[7] Learning to be a good team member is essential to our personal, professional, and social lives.

To get you started learning about effective group membership, we want you to consider three important ideas about groups. First, *the formation of groups is natural to humans*. Why? Groups are a fundamental way humans meet important needs. Schutz explained that we use groups to belong and identify with others (inclusion), find love and esteem (affection), and exercise power over others and our environment (control).[8] Notice that each of these three needs mandates the participation of others and is so significant to us that often we will relinquish our own resources, such as time and energy, to participate in groups and satisfy our basic human needs. For example, citizens of Springfield, Missouri, worked to transform a decaying downtown space into Founders Park, a public green space in the city's center. By assembling in the various groups needed to accomplish their goal, these citizens worked hard because the issue was important to each of them, and they understood it could not happen without their collective efforts.

David Brooks, summarizing research into human behavior in a recent column, speculated that humans are wired to cooperate and collaborate, just as much as they are to compete. Groups provide a vehicle by which we can do this.[9] Stop for a moment and think about all the groups you have participated in this past week, including family and peer groups. College students average about 8 to 10, and sometimes list as many as 24 groups. For example, one student listed the following: family, Bible study, sorority, executive committee of sorority, study group in small group class, project group in marketing class, intramural volleyball team, carpool, and work group of clerks in clothing department. Your professors often list even more groups than these. In fact, Goldhaber found that the average tenured faculty member served on six committees simultaneously and spent 11 hours per week in meetings![10]

Does this seem like a lot of groups? Consider this: Reliance on groups in our society is increasing and expected to increase further, perhaps dramatically. American managers are recognizing the value of participative decision making, with the small group as one important vehicle for encouraging employee participation and improving corporate decision making.[11] Years ago, Ouchi, developer of Theory Z management, warned American managers that their ability to counter Japanese automobile competition depended on how well they learned to work in groups.[12] Waterman identified teamwork as a key element in companies that have kept their competitive edge.[13] Top management teams are recognized as the most influential groups in organizations today.[14]

Why is group work successful? Groups are usually better problem solvers, in the long run, than solitary individuals because they have access to more information than individuals do, can spot flaws and biases in each others' thinking, and then can think of things an individual may have failed to consider. Moreover, if people participate in planning the work of solving the problem, they are more likely to work harder and better at carrying out the solution. Thus, participation in problem solving and decision making helps guarantee continued commitment to decisions and solutions (See Chapter 9).

Second, *just because we often participate in groups, we cannot assume we participate effectively.* Just doing it doesn't mean we do it well! Unless we know something about why a group is unproductive, we won't be able to assess what is happening in our groups or know what to do with that assessment to help the group improve. **Grouphate** captures a negative attitude toward groups that many of us develop that can get in the way of effective participation in groups.[15] In spite of recognizing the central role of groups in our lives, we often have mixed feelings about them, due in large measure to the tradeoffs involved. In return for meeting our needs, we give up autonomy and the ability to do what we want, whenever we want. For instance, students often complain that group grades do not reflect their superior individual performance. Some people may even loathe being a member of a group.[16] Interestingly, Sorensen found that grouphate is partly caused by lack of training in how to communicate effectively as a group member. If you have grouphate, it is in your best interests to get over it because students with negative feelings and attitudes about participating in groups have been less successful academically than those with more constructive and positive orientations toward group work.[17]

Strong communication skills are central to effective discussion and productive teamwork. Donald Petersen, former CEO at Ford Motor Company, learned this during his rise at Ford. At first he envisioned his role as that of a solitary engineer designing cars, but later he discovered that a successful company requires interaction and teamwork: "Communication skills are crucial. And I mean that in both directions—not only the ability to articulate . . . but to listen."[18]

Grouphate
The feeling of antipathy and hostility many people have about working in a group, fostered by the many ineffective, time-wasting groups that exist.

Third, *groups provide the vehicle by which the individual can make a contribution to the organization and the society as a whole.* Larkin postulated that humans have a motivation to give. The basic ingredient cementing social cohesion is not the satisfaction of needs, but rather the availability for contribution. What best binds individuals to groups may not be so much the pressure to obtain necessities as the opportunities to give of oneself to something beyond merely self-interested acquisition.[19] The dignity of individuals, Lawson states, comes from people's contributions to something greater than themselves. People who give of their time, money, energy, and other resources live healthier, happier, and more fulfilled lives; they report that their lives are more meaningful than those who do not.[20] This is confirmed in recent organizational research by Strubler and York, who found that team members felt a greater sense of participation and believed their work within the organization was more meaningful and worthwhile than non-team members.[21] We believe that the success of work-related committees stems largely from this need to contribute collaboratively with others.

Our focus is the communicative dynamics of group members—what people say and do in groups. While we will draw upon findings from other disciplines, we will concentrate on the process of communication among members and how group members can influence this process. The groups we examine will cover a range of group settings: educational, religious, political, corporate, entertainment, health, community, and social services. As you study the central concepts we will be using throughout this text, remember that the complexity of small group interaction among members cannot be reduced to a cookie cutter set of prescriptions. Each element of group interaction influences every other element in the group (see Chapter 3). So while we give you guidelines and suggestions to consider, you have to take into account the group's entire and unique situation as you enact these guidelines.

In the remainder of this chapter, we present definitions of key terms we use throughout the book to reduce the possibility of misunderstanding. We also present information about the types of groups you will encounter in many different kinds of settings. We end with a discussion of ethical behavior important to effective group functioning in Western cultures and centered around a participant–observer perspective.

What Is Small Group Discussion?

Before we define how we view small group communication, we will begin with a big picture, then move to specifics. The first term requiring definition is **group.** What differentiates a *collection* of people from a *group* of people? Don't worry if you have a hard time putting your own definition into words; no single definition of *group* exists among those who study groups for a living. Among the variety of definitions for *group*, we prefer Marvin Shaw's: a group consists of "persons who are interacting with one another in

Group

Three or more people with an interdependent goal who interact and influence each other.

such a manner that each person influences and is influenced by each other person."[22] Shaw argued that, of all the characteristics of groups, none were more important than *interaction* and *mutual influence.*

The Artsfest Planning Committee simply collected in one place does not necessarily constitute a group unless there is reciprocal awareness and influence among members. If, for example, LaShonda, Jerry, and Pam each write separate letters to recruit an artist to apply, Shaw would argue that no group exists yet because Jerry and Pam did not influence LaShonda in recruiting particular artists. However, once the members begin to interact with each other and talk about how to pool their efforts to recruit artists, then we see a group emerging out of their interaction. Interaction assumes coordination of behaviors.[23] More fundamentally, interaction "requires mutual influence."[24]

The Artsfest committee members share a related key feature of a group: an **interdependent goal.** Interdependence exists when all group members succeed or fail together in the accomplishment of the group's purpose—in this case, having a successful festival can be attained only if they coordinate their efforts. In addition, committee members coordinated their actions, so that artists, food vendors, volunteers, and so forth, all showed up at the right times on the right days. This logic extends to group members scattered geographically. If members interact and mutually influence each other by way of newsletters, telephone conversations, computer networks, or closed-circuit TV, they still constitute a group. This occurred with the Artsfest committee. Although not geographically scattered, members influenced each other via their e-mail, phone, text, Skype, and Dropbox correspondence.

The study of groups may include large groupings (e.g., whole societies) or small ones; our focus is on small groups. The notion that "each person influences and is influenced by each other" implies that members are aware of each other, and from this mutual awareness we ground our definition of *small* on perceptual awareness. A **small group,** therefore, is a group small enough that each member is aware of and able to recall each other group member, know who is and is not in the group, and recognize what role each is taking. Attempts to define *small* on the basis of number of members have never worked. At the low end, we can certainly perceive all members in a group of three. At the high end, most of us can take in up to 11 members in a unit and, with training, may learn to handle 12 to 14.[25]

No doubt you have heard and used the word "team" and might wonder whether there is difference between a small group and a team. Some scholars see teams as highly functioning groups with a strong group identity and shared leadership.[26] Others reserve *team* for groups in which leadership is shared, such as the case with self-managed work groups.[27] In a comprehensive review of the research into team dynamics, Salas, Sims, and Burke discovered a recurring theme in all the different definitions of *team*: the recognition of interdependence between members as they strive toward a group goal.[28] Thus, we do not differentiate the two terms—group and team—and use them interchangeably. A small group may be called a team (e.g., top management team), yet function no better than other groups of

Interdependent Goal

An objective shared by members of a small group in such a way that one member cannot achieve the goal without the other members also achieving it.

Small Group

A group of at least three but few enough members for each to perceive all others as individuals, share some identity or common purpose, and share standards for governing their activities as members.

its kind. Like Larson and LaFasto, we are interested in groups that function well, no matter what they are called.[29]

Interaction, mutual influence, and interdependence are all central features of a group. Coordinating behavior requires exchange of messages; thus, the most central feature of human groups is their communication, or interaction. Verbal and nonverbal exchange among group members is where the work of the group gets accomplished. This exchange may be face-to-face or may use computer or audioconferencing equipment. For our purposes, **small group discussion** refers to a small group of people talking with each other in order to achieve some interdependent goal, such as increased understanding, coordination of activity, or a solution to a shared problem. We will now "unpack" this definition, revealing several characteristics of small group discussion:

Small Group Discussion

A small group of people communicating with each other to achieve some interdependent goal, such as increased understanding, coordination of activity, or solution to a shared problem.

1. A small enough number of people for each to be aware of and have some reaction to each other (typically 3 to 7, rarely more than 15).

2. A mutually interdependent purpose, making the success of one member contingent on the success of all.

3. Each person having a sense of belonging, of being part of the group.

4. Interaction involving verbal and nonverbal behaviors, with words conveying the content of the discussion. This definition includes as "verbal" manual languages, such as American Sign Language and typed computer-mediated messages. The *emoticons* used in e-mail messages, such as :) to indicate smiling, count as nonverbal behaviors. Members continuously respond to and adapt their actions to each other. The give-and-take of impromptu communication, rather than prepared speeches, is the essence of small group discussion.

5. A sense of cooperation among members. Although there may be disagreement and conflict, all members perceive themselves as searching for a group outcome that will be as satisfactory as possible to all members.

6. Interaction occurring on a continuum from purely face-to-face to purely computer mediated, or virtual. Traditional definitions of small groups assumed that members meet face-to-face, but all the characteristics mentioned here can occur in a virtual environment where members never meet. Moreover, most group members, these days, use some form of technology in conjunction with their face-to-face group work. Therefore, instead of considering groups to be *either* face-to-face *or* computer-mediated, it is more useful to consider groups on a continuum depending on the extent to which they use computer mediation. Such a continuum is anchored at one end by face-to-face groups that never use computer mediation; followed by groups that use e-mail or texting to touch base between meetings, groups that meet and work virtually using Dropbox, Blackboard, or similar document-sharing software; and anchored at the other end by groups that meet entirely via computers. We will discuss this continuum throughout the text.

Recap: A Quick Review

Human beings are social creatures and form groups naturally. Groups are so pervasive in our lives that we may overlook their importance. Even though negative experiences working in groups can turn many people away from group work, the fact of the matter is that effective small group interaction has profound practical consequences in our personal and professional lives.

1. People use groups to meet inclusion, control, and affection needs. Group participation allows people to make significant contributions to each other and society.

2. Being a group participant does not guarantee effective group behavior; group members have to work to coordinate their actions toward a shared goal.

3. Groups are not merely collections of individuals, but they involve interaction, interdependence, and mutual influence.

4. Small groups are not defined by the number of people in a group but by their limits of perceptual awareness.

5. Small group discussion highlights the key role communication plays in defining a collection of people as a small group with a sense of belonging, purpose, and collaboration.

Types of Small Groups

There are two major categories of small groups, *primary* and *secondary*. Each meets different human needs.

Primary groups exist chiefly to satisfy *primary* needs—needs for inclusion (affiliation, belonging) and affection (love, esteem). They are usually long term. Examples include a nuclear family, roommates, several friends who meet daily around a table in the student center, and coworkers who regularly share coffee breaks. Although such groups may tackle particular tasks, they exist mainly to provide personal attention and support for the members. Members' talk, which appears disorganized and informal, is the end in itself. More than any other forces in our lives, primary groups socialize and mold us into the people we become; their importance is tremendous. For most of us, the family is our first group, where we learn communication patterns, functional and dysfunctional, that can last generations and affect all aspects of our lives.[30] Primary groups are not the main focus of this book; typically, primary groups are studied in interpersonal communication, sociology, and psychology courses. However, the interpersonal relationships at the heart of primary groups are very important to understanding small groups in general.

Secondary groups, like our Artsfest committee in the opening story, focus on task accomplishment and are formed for the purpose of doing work—completing a project, solving a problem, making a decision. Secondary groups, such as most work teams and problem-solving groups,

Primary Group

A group whose main purpose is to meet members' needs for inclusion and affection.

Secondary Group

A group whose major purpose is to complete a task, such as making a decision, solving a problem, writing a report, or providing recommendations to a parent organization.

meet secondary needs for control and achievement. Such groups enable members to exert power over their environment and others. For example, the teams that worked to create Founders Park in downtown Springfield were secondary groups with a specific performance objective to be attained, and members had to coordinate their efforts in order to achieve that objective. While all groups formed to accomplish some task are more secondary than primary, many task groups also help members achieve primary needs for socialization and affection.

As you may have discerned by this point, there are no *pure* primary or secondary groups. Although groups are classified as primary or secondary according to their major function, primary groups also engage in work, and secondary groups also provide affection and belonging to their members. In fact, Anderson and Martin demonstrated that secondary group members are motivated by a number of factors that are more primary than secondary, including desires for pleasure and to escape. Such factors strongly influence secondary group members' communication behaviors, feelings of loneliness, and satisfaction with the group and are worth examining.[31]

In addition to the two major classifications just described, there are many other ways to categorize groups. The four categories described next exhibit both primary and secondary characteristics in varying degrees, with the fourth more purely secondary than the first three.

Activity Groups

Activity groups enable members to participate in an activity, both for the sake of doing the activity and for the affiliation provided by doing the activity with others. The following are examples: a book club whose members meet regularly to discuss a book, bridge and poker clubs, recreational vehicle clubs, hunting and bird-watching groups, video gaming clubs, and numerous other interest groups. Members of such groups solve problems and make choices—when and where to meet, how to pay for their activities, how group membership is determined—but enjoyment of the activity and fellowship with others whose interests are similar are the main purposes.

> **Activity Group**
>
> A group formed primarily for members to participate in an activity such as bridge, bowling, hunting, and so forth.

Personal Growth Groups

Therapy and support groups are called **personal growth groups.** They are composed of people who come together to develop personal insights, help themselves and others with personal problems, and grow as individuals from the feedback and support of others. Goal interdependence is low because no purely group goal is sought; rather, members meet their individual needs for personal learning, awareness, and support in the context of the group. Examples include local chapters of 12-step programs such as Alcoholics Anonymous and Al-Anon, mutual support groups such as Parents without Partners, cancer survivors support groups, and therapy groups for people with eating disorders.

> **Personal Growth Group**
>
> A group of people who come together to develop personal insights, overcome personality problems, and grow personally through feedback and support of others.

Educational Groups

Small groups occur in educational contexts for a variety of purposes. Common **learning groups,** often called study groups, form so that members can understand a subject better by pooling their knowledge, perceptions, and beliefs. These tend to be voluntary and coordinated by interested students. Others, including cohorts, cooperative learning groups, and collaborative learning groups, are used by educators and often are not voluntary.[32] Cohorts, sometimes referred to as learning communities, are used by universities to group selected students around a program of study. Students often take a set of courses together. California State University, Fresno, uses them extensively. Cooperative learning groups are composed of students selected by teachers to work on a class assignment or topic. The group's output, often a report and presentation, is evaluated at the group level. Such assignments characterize a major component of many small group communication courses. Collaborative learning groups, similar to cooperative ones, are used to enhance individual achievement. For example, students may be grouped to work on course papers where they tutor each other in an effort to improve their individual writing skills. In addition to learning about specific subject matter, members of such groups also learn skills of effective speaking, listening, critical thinking, and effective interpersonal communication.

Problem-Solving Groups

Problem-solving groups formed to address some condition or problem vary widely in their composition and functioning. Examples we have already mentioned include the Artsfest Planning Committee and the various Founders Park committees. There are many ways of describing subtypes of problem-solving groups. In this book, we deal with major subtypes prevalent in our modern organizational and social life: committees, quality control circles, self-managed work groups, and top management teams.

Committees   **Committees** are groups that have been assigned a task by a parent organization or person with authority in an organization. Committees may be formed to investigate and report findings, recommend a course of action for the parent group, formulate policies, or plan and carry out some action.

Committees can be classified as either *ad hoc* or *standing*. An **ad hoc committee,** established to perform a specific task, normally ceases to exist when that task has been completed. Ad hoc committees address all kinds of problems, such as evaluating credentials of job applicants, drafting bylaws, hearing grievances, planning social events, conducting investigations, devising plans to solve work-related problems, advising legislators on what to do about statewide problems, and evaluating programs and institutions. A *task force* is a type of ad hoc committee with members appointed from various

---

Learning Group

A group discussing for the purpose of learning about and understanding a subject more completely.

Problem-Solving Group

A group whose purpose is finding ways to solve a problem or address a particular condition.

Committee

A small group of people given an assigned task or responsibility by a larger group (parent organization) or person with authority.

Ad Hoc Committee

A group that goes out of existence after its specific task has been completed.

A committee discusses the content of a report.

departments of an organization or political body and usually charged with investigating a broad issue. For example, in 2007 the president of California State University, Fresno, appointed a task force of faculty, students, staff, and community members to study how the university manages its athletic finances and to make recommendations for improving the management of those finances. Once the task force reported its action or recommendations, it disbanded.

Standing committees are ongoing committees established through the constitution or bylaws of an organization to deal with recurring types of problems or to perform specific organizational functions. The most important standing committee of most organizations is called the executive committee, board, or steering committee. Usually, this group is charged with overall management of the organization and can function for the entire organization when general membership meetings are not feasible. Other common standing committees have names such as membership committee, personnel committee, parking and traffic committee, program committee, bylaws committee, and so forth. These groups continue indefinitely, even though the membership changes.

Quality Control Circles

A **quality control circle** consists of workers (usually five to seven) in a company who either volunteer or are selected to meet regularly on company time to discuss work-related problems. Sometimes called *continuous improvement teams, cycle time reduction groups,* or just plain *quality circles,* their purpose is to improve some aspect of work life—efficiency, quality of finished products, worker safety, and so forth.

Standing Committee

A group given an area of responsibility that includes many tasks and continues indefinitely.

Quality Control Circle

A group of employees who meet on company time to investigate work-related problems and to make recommendations for solving these problems (also called a quality circle).

Self-Managed Work Groups

Self-managed work groups, also called *autonomous work groups* or *peer-led work teams,* are groups of workers given a defined area of freedom to manage their productive work within certain preset limits established by the organization. For example, an automobile assembly team may be responsible for assembling a car from start to finish. Members may be given a deadline by which the car must be fully assembled, but within that limit the team members are free to elect their own leaders, plan their work procedures, and schedule individual assignments for the members. Members of self-managed work groups are often cross-trained, so each member can perform several jobs competently. This permits human and other resources to be allocated efficiently and effectively, gives workers the chance to develop a variety of skills, and reduces boredom. It has been estimated that 81 percent of manufacturing organizations and 79 percent of *Fortune* 1000 companies use self-managed teams.[33]

Top Management Teams (TMTs)

Top management teams, compared to self-managed work groups, encompass the upper echelon of management.[34] Their goal is not to deliver goods or services but to lead an organization. Many of today's organizations are so diversified that they cannot succeed using the typical chief executive officer (CEO)–chief operating officer (COO) model of managing. Instead, a team is formed because members' pooled talent exceeds that of the CEO and the COO. In other cases, a CEO may not want to select a COO, so he or she forms a team of managers to do the job of operating a company. TMTs have substantial power because they comprise some of the most influential members of the larger organization. They make highly complex strategic decisions with far-reaching consequences to the entire organization and themselves. For example, the Caterpillar TMT's decision to provide the U.S. government with heavy equipment during World War II resulted in the development of a worldwide distribution network that even today is central to Caterpillar's corporate success.[35]

In the same way that no group is purely primary or secondary, most small groups you encounter will combine elements of all four group types just described—activity, personal growth, learning, and problem solving. Several years ago, the Springfield City Council established an ad hoc task force to investigate and recommend solutions to the city's solid waste disposal problem. Members had to educate themselves about solid waste, various disposal options, and pros and cons of the options before they could make their recommendations to the city council. They also had to manage their own resources of time and information and be concerned with the comprehensive quality of life in the Springfield area. Thus, this group comprised elements of a learning group, problem-solving group, quality circle, and self-managed work group.

Recap: A Quick Review

Groups are pervasive in our everyday lives. They can be classified by purpose.

1. Primary groups, like family and friends, help us meet our needs for belonging and affection.

2. Secondary groups, those commonly referred to as task groups, help us meet our needs for control and achievement.

3. Subtypes of primary and secondary groups often mix the purposes of both. These include activity, personal growth, educational, and problem-solving groups such as committees, quality control circles, self-managed work groups, and top management teams.

Ethical Behavior of Group Members

We have learned that groups are a necessary and natural part of our lives. Effective and rewarding group experiences require knowledge of group dynamics and the ability to behave in ways that facilitate, not thwart, group efforts. Groups do not just happen because people are thrown together! Nor will groups be effective if they are composed of people who are members in name only. These **social loafers** only watch and contribute little to the group, letting others carry the load. Central to everything we discuss in this text is a willingness by every group member to be a **participant–observer:** someone who *both* actively participates *and* critically reflects on group interaction in order to make the adaptations necessary for success. The ability to participate, observe, and think rests at the heart of ethical group interaction.

Ideally, everyone wants to be someone others can count on. Groups require collaborative, cohesive behavior, not social loafing, from their members; thus, you need to know the kind of behavior that is expected from responsible and ethical members. **Ethics** refers to the "rules or standards for right conduct or practice."[36] In describing principles of ethical behavior for group members, we are guided by appropriate standards of behavior from our general culture and the code of ethics provided by our professional association, the National Communication Association. This code stems from several key values, five of which we believe are directly relevant to small group members: integrity, professional/social responsibility, equality of opportunity, honesty/openness, and respect for self and others.[37] These values—involving the treatment of people, speech, and information—underpin the following six ethical principles for group members. Each principle requires you to consider how you choose to participate as a group member and asks you to reflect on the consequences of your choices. Learning effective communication in groups is about not only what you *can* do in groups, but what you *should* do. You cannot answer

Social Loafer

A person who makes a minimal contribution to the group and assumes the other members will take up the slack.

Participant-Observer

An active participant in a small group who at the same time observes and evaluates its processes and procedures.

Ethics

The rules or standards that a person or group uses to determine whether conduct or behavior is right and appropriate.

the *should* part unless you observe and reflect.[38] The following principles will guide you:

1. **Members should be willing to speak.** Groups work because several heads perform better than one. However, this advantage is sabotaged when members won't speak up. Your first obligation as a group member is to speak up and share your perspective. Communication has a long and distinguished tradition, dating from Aristotle, that supports the value of free speech.[39] For a group to be effective, members' unique perspectives must be shared.

2. **Members must contribute their fair share to the group's effort.** Along with speaking up, you need to contribute your fair share of work. Social loafers drag everybody down and hurt the group's product. They also represent the main reason many of our students hate group work: they do not want their grades and assignments to depend on people who fail to contribute to the group. As an ethical group member, you must do your share. If you find you cannot, you should either leave the group or negotiate with the other members how you can contribute enough so they do not resent your presence.

3. **Group members should embrace and work with diversity within the group.** Member diversity should be encouraged and supported. Diversity stems from various factors that include, but are not limited to, race, ethnicity, age, religion, sexual orientation.[40] These factors contribute to differences in members' perspectives—the very differences that have the potential to enrich and enhance a group's performance. Groupings such as race, ethnicity, gender, and so forth, form what Orbe calls *co-cultures,* smaller groups that exist "simultaneously within, as well as apart from, other cultures"[41] in the United States. However, group members from such co-cultures run the risk of being marginalized, their perspectives and opinions ignored by members of the dominant culture. Orbe argues that co-culture members have to work harder to be included and have their opinions considered than do members of the dominant culture. The challenge to group members, particularly ones representing the dominant culture, is to make it possible for *all* members—regardless of co-culture—to contribute equally. Members who marginalize fellow group members both behave unethically and defeat the purpose of the group.

4. **Group members must conduct themselves with honesty and integrity.** Honesty and integrity take various forms. First, and most obviously, group members should not intentionally deceive one another or manufacture information or evidence to persuade other members to their points of view. It follows from this that members must not falsify data and must document the sources of information they share with the group.

    Integrity implies that members should support group decisions, which may present challenges for the individual member. Sometimes you may be asked to do something for a group that violates your own personal values, beliefs, morals, or principles. For example, what if a group on which you serve decides to suppress information that is contrary to a decision the group wishes to make and pressures you to go along? What will you do? Only you can answer that question. You may try your best to persuade the group to see things your way; you may decide to leave the group. But if you choose to stay with the group, make sure you can support, or at least live with, the group's actions and decisions.

Integrity also suggests that you are willing to place the good of the group ahead of your own individual goals. A team orientation is a core component of successful teams.[42] Focusing on the team involves being willing to hear alternatives offered by other members and assessing those in an effort to determine which one is best for the team. It also involves willingness among members to offer feedback about each other's actions and to accept suggestions from one another about how to behave better for the good of the group. Individuals who are not willing or able to become part of a team and adopt a team orientation make poor team members, and the group is better off without them.

5. **Group members should always treat one another with respect.** They should not disconfirm, belittle, or ridicule other members and should make sure they understand other members before agreeing or disagreeing with them. Deetz stresses that ethical interpersonal behavior should strengthen one's personal identity and should have mutual understanding as its goal.[43] Our first goal, as we interact, should be to strive to understand others to their satisfaction. If this happens, we will confirm and support each others' self-concept and identity, even when we disagree strongly. Communication that confirms rather than disconfirms helps build trust within a group and the expectation that group members look out for each other's interests. When disagreements do occur, members who trust each other will interpret those disagreements more constructively than if they do not trust each other.[44]

6. **Group members should be thorough in gathering information and diligent in evaluating it.** Members should make a conscientious effort to find and present to the group all information and points of view relevant to the group's work. They should also set aside personal biases and prejudices when evaluating that information, and refrain from doing anything that short-circuits this process. Many consequential decisions are made in groups, from how best to get children to read to whether it is safe to launch a space shuttle in cold weather. These decisions will be only as good as the information on which they are based and the reasoning that members use to assess the information. It is absolutely crucial that group members consider all relevant information in an open-minded, unbiased way by employing the best critical thinking skills they can; to do otherwise can lead to tragedies such as the fatal decision to launch the space shuttle *Challenger*.

Group members who choose to be both effective participants in group interaction and thoughtful observers of everyone's behaviors, including their own, are competent, ethical communicators and have extensive knowledge about groups. Broome and Fulbright found that in real-life groups, among other things, members wanted stronger guidance about group methods, procedures, and techniques as well as fellow members skilled in the communication process.[45] To be an all-around valuable member of the group, you need both a participant–observer focus and information and expertise essential to completing the group's task. This is what *Effective Group Discussion* is designed to teach you.

Recap: A Quick Review

1. Effective group members remember they not only behave in groups but also must observe the group processes and make any changes necessary to ensure the success of the group.
2. Successful groups depend on members acting ethically and understanding that how they choose to act and speak has consequences for themselves and others.
3. Ethical members treat speech, information, and others honestly, respectfully, carefully, and open-mindedly.

QUESTIONS FOR REVIEW

 Go to self-quizzes on the Online Learning Center at mhhe.com/galanes14e to test your knowledge of the chapter concepts.

The Artsfest Planning Committee reinforces a critical theme of this text: Small groups provide people with an invaluable way to solve complex problems. Reviewing the story, we learn that individual skills, well coordinated, can produce amazing results.

1. What individual needs are likely being met by being a member of this group of volunteers?
2. What do these members gain by devising a plan, together, as opposed to separately?

3. How are the unique features of a group evident in this story? Which ones are not evident?
4. Does this group meet the requirements to be defined a "small" group?
5. How might this initial secondary group evolve into a primary one?
6. Select one of the members mentioned. How might the member have behaved as a participant–observer in this group?
7. Which ethical principles are most evident in this story?

KEY TERMS

 Test your knowledge of these key terms by visiting the Online Learning Center Web site at mhhe.com/galanes14e.

Activity group	Ethics	Learning group
Committee	Group	Participant–observer
Ad hoc committee	Grouphate	Personal growth group
Standing committee	Interdependent goal	Primary group

Problem-solving group	Self-managed work group	Social loafers
Quality control circle	Small group	Top management teams
Secondary group	Small group discussion	

BIBLIOGRAPHY

Frey, Lawrence R., ed. *New Directions in Group Communication*. Thousand Oaks, CA: Sage, 2002.

Larson, Carl E., and Frank M. J. LaFasto. *TeamWork: What Must Go Right/What Can Go Wrong*. Newbury Park, CA: Sage, 1989.

NOTES

1. Kurt W. Back, "The Small Group: Tightrope between Sociology and Personality," *Journal of Applied Behavioral Science,* 15 (1979): 283–94.
2. Lawrence W. Frey, "Applied Communication Research on Group Facilitation in Natural Settings," in *Innovations in Group Facilitation: Applications in Natural Settings,* ed. Lawrence R. Frey (Cresskill, NJ: Hampton Press, 1995): 1–26.
3. Diane Cole, "Meetings That Make Sense," *Psychology Today* (May 1989): 14.
4. Bill Lawren, "Competitive Edge," *Psychology Today* (September 1989): 16.
5. Sayed M. Elsayed-Elkhouly, Harold Lazarus, and Volville Forsythe, "Why Is a Third of Your Time Wasted in Meetings?," *Journal of Management Development,* 16 (1997): 672–76.
6. Ibid., 672.
7. Charles C. DuBois, "Portrait of the Ideal MBA," *The Penn Stater* (September/October 1992): 31.
8. William C. Schutz, *FIRO: A Three-Dimensional Theory of Interpersonal Behavior* (New York: Rinehart, 1958).
9. David Brooks, "Nice Guys Finish First," *The New York Times*, The Opinion Pages, May 16, 2011. Retrieved May 16, 2011, at http://topics.nytimes.com/top/opinoin/editorialsandoped/oped/columnists/davidbrooks/index.html?inline=nyt-per.
10. Gerald Goldhaber, "Communication and Student Unrest" (Unpublished report to the president of the University of New Mexico, undated).
11. Eduardo Salas, Dana E. Sims, and C. Shawn Burke, "Is There a 'Big Five' in Teamwork?," *Small Group Research*, 36 (2005): 555–99.
12. William Ouchi, *Theory Z: How American Business Can Meet the Japanese Challenge* (Reading, MA: Addison-Wesley, 1981).
13. Robert H. Waterman, Jr., *The Renewal Factor: How the Best Get and Keep the Competitive Edge* (New York: Bantam Books, 1987).
14. Theodore E. Zorn and George H. Thompson, "Communication in Top Management Teams," in *New Directions in Group Communication,* ed. Lawrence R. Frey (Thousand Oaks, CA: Sage, 2002): 253–72.
15. Susan Sorensen, "Grouphate" (Paper presented at the International Communication Association, Minneapolis, May, 1981).
16. Joann Keyton and Lawrence R. Frey, "The State of Traits: Predispositions and Group Communication," in *New Directions in Group Communication,* ed. Lawrence R. Frey (Thousand Oaks, CA: Sage, 2002): 109.
17. K. A. Freeman, "Attitudes Toward Work in Project Groups as Predictors of Group Performance," *Small Group Research*, 27 (1996): 265–82.
18. Quoted in Lisa Stroud, "No CEO Is an Island," *American Way* (November 15, 1988): 97.
19. T. J. Larkin, "Humanistic Principles for Organization Management," *Central States Speech Journal*, 37 (1986): 37.
20. Douglas M. Lawson, *Give to Live: How Giving Can Change Your Life* (LaJolla, CA: ALTI Publishing, 1991).

21. David C. Strubler and Kenneth M. York, "An Exploratory Study of the Team Characteristics Model Using Organizational Teams," *Small Group Research*, 38 (2007): 670–95.

22. Marvin E. Shaw, *Group Dynamics: The Psychology of Small Group Behavior,* 3rd ed. (New York: McGraw-Hill, 1980): 8.

23. Donald G. Ellis and B. Aubrey Fisher, *Small Group Decision Making: Communication and the Group Process,* 4th ed. (New York: McGraw Hill, 1994): 5.

24. Shaw, *Group Dynamics,* p. 8.

25. Robert F. Bales, *Interaction Process Analysis* (Cambridge, MA: Addison-Wesley, 1950): viii, 35–39.

26. Gay Lumsden and Donald Lumsden, *Communicating in Groups and Teams: Sharing Leadership* (Belmont, CA: Wadsworth, 1993): 13–15.

27. Thomas E. Harris and John C. Sherblom, *Small Group and Team Communication* (Boston: Allyn and Bacon, 1999): 123–31.

28. Salas, Sims, and Burke, 559–62.

29. Carl E. Larson and Frank M. J. LaFasto, *Team-Work: What Must Go Right/What Can Go Wrong* (Newbury Park, CA: Sage, 1989): 19.

30. Thomas J. Socha, "Communication in Family Units: Studying the 'First' Group," in *The Hand-book of Group Communication Theory and Research,* ed. Lawrence R. Frey (Thousand Oaks, CA: Sage, 1999): 475–92.

31. Carolyn M. Anderson and Matthew M. Martin, "The Effects of Communication Motives, Interaction Involvement, and Loneliness on Satisfaction: A Model of Small Groups," *Small Group Research*, 26 (February 1995): 118–37.

32. Terre H. Allen and Timothy G. Plax, "Exploring Consequences of Group Communication in the Classroom," in *New Directions in Group Communication,* ed. Lawrence R. Frey (Thousand Oaks, CA: Sage, 2002): 219–34.

33. Peg Thoms, Jeffrey K. Pinto, Diane H. Parente, and Vanessa U. Druskat, "Adaptation to Self-Managing Work Teams," *Small Group Research*, 33 (2002): 3–31.

34. Zorn and Thompson, "Communication in Top," 254–56.

35. J. Barney, "Looking Inside for Competitive Advantage," *Academy of Management Review,* 9 (1995): 49–61.

36. *The Random House Dictionary of the English Language,* 2nd ed. unabridged (New York: Random House, 1987): 665.

37. National Communication Association Code of Professional Ethics for the Communication Scholar/Teacher, Retrieved May 16, 2011 at www.natcom.org/Default.aspx?id=135&terms=Code%20of%20Ethics.

38. See Rob Anderson and Veronica Ross, *Questions of Communication: A Practical Introduction to Theory,* 2nd ed. (Boston, MA: Bedford/St. Martin's, 1998), Chapter 10.

39. Ronald C. Arnett, "The Practical Philosophy of Communication Ethics and Free Speech as the Foundation for Speech Communication," *Communication Quarterly*, 38 (Summer 1990): 208–17.

40. Brenda J. Allen, "'Diversity' and Organizational Communication," *Journal of Applied Communication Research,* 23 (1995): 143–55.

41. Mark P. Orbe, "From the Standpoint(s) of Traditionally Muted Groups: Explicating a Co-cultural Communication Theoretical Model," *Communication Theory*, 8 (February 1998): 2.

42. Salas, Sims, and Burke, 584–87.

43. Stanley Deetz, "Reclaiming the Subject Matter as a Guide to Mutual Understanding: Effectiveness and Ethics in Interpersonal Interaction," *Communication Quarterly*, 38 (Summer 1990): 226–43.

44. Salas, Sims, and Burke, 568–70.

45. Benjamin J. Broome and Luann Fulbright, "A Multistage Influence Model of Barriers to Group Problem Solving: A Participant-Generated Agenda for Small Group Research," *Small Group Research,* 26 (February 1995): 25–55.

Human Communication Processes in the Small Group Context

STUDY OBJECTIVES

As a result of studying Chapter 2, you should be able to:

1. Explain the special features of the small group context.
2. Explain communication as a symbolic, personal, transactional process that is not always intentional.
3. Describe the content and relationship dimensions of communication.
4. Identify and describe the four general listening preferences.
5. Identify and describe the four habits of effective listeners.
6. Explain the process of active listening by paraphrasing.
7. Explain the major characteristics of nonverbal behavior.
8. Name and give examples of eight types of nonverbal behavior and explain how each contributes to communication among small group members.

CENTRAL MESSAGE

Communication is a complex, symbolic process that group members must both observe and understand so they can coordinate their efforts to achieve the group goal.

Lam, Tamika, Ryan, Tyler, and Kelli were students in a small group communication course. Their major semester assignment was a service learning project in their community. These students shared an interest in the animal overpopulation of their city. For five weeks, they studied the animal overpopulation problem and were looking forward to their first class presentation. They were eager to share the work they had accomplished so that they could actually begin to work for a local animal shelter as part of their solution to this problem. Their spirits were high because, for the most part, they had bonded and were working well together. Lately, though, Tyler had missed some meetings but seemed to have good excuses. The first sign of major trouble happened when they met to discuss their plan for the presentation. Tyler had not arrived and, after 20 minutes, Tamika, usually laid back, seemed on edge. She asked as she pulled away from the table, "Man, what time is it already? Tyler is so late. We're 20 minutes into this meeting and need his stuff. I'm tired of this. And while I'm at it, I'm tired of meeting in this old stuffy room." Kelli, in frustration, declared, "I'm tired of waiting for this jerk, too," and started to pick up her things. Ryan defended Tyler by reminding everyone that he had sick parents and tried to come to meetings. Kelli shot back, "I have things I have to deal with, too, and this is getting old. We're down to the wire and need his stuff. He didn't even notify us this time, and I'm out of here!" Lam, sensing everyone was going to leave, switched directions with, "Let's just go ahead and get started and try to finish tonight. If we need another meeting, we can meet at my place to give us more room. Is that okay, Tamika? Ryan, did you bring the visual aids we all need?" Tamika and Kelli then unpacked their things and pulled their chairs back into the circle. The meeting proceeded without Tyler.

Chapter 1 made the case for recognizing small groups as our most important social formation and emphasized that interaction is central to the life of a group. Other disciplines also explore this important social unit. Psychologists direct their attention to the nature of individual members and the effects of factors such as personality on group dynamics. Sociologists focus on groups' social organization by studying such things as status and norms. Communication scholars explore members' message behavior. As our student group shows, what and how we communicate with each other in groups create the nature of the small groups we participate in. Communication is like the nerve network of the small group; it is the verbal and nonverbal message processes by which members forge themselves into a group, maintain the group, and coordinate their efforts. "Communication is the lifeblood that flows through the veins of the group. Communication is not just a tool that group members use; groups are best regarded as a phenomenon that emerges from communication."[1] No communication, no group!

Small group communication refers both to the study of interaction among group members and to the large body of communication theory yielded by such study. We examine this body of theory and principles in detail, and communicative behavior of group members will be the focus of this text. Early communication researchers, extending their interest in public speaking, began to explore the communication within groups and to link members' communication to such group outcomes as the effectiveness of decisions and group climate. As our field has matured, researchers have extended their interests into how ideas are developed, how communication creates and sustains group structure, how leadership is enacted by what people say and do, and how groups can best be studied. These trends will continue and are perceived as appropriate directions for small group *communication* scholars.[2]

This chapter addresses the general nature of small group communication processes. We will first talk about the unique features of the small group context so that you can better appreciate the contextual constraints small groups place upon your communicative efforts compared with other contexts, such as dyads or organizations. Then we will review central principles of communication in small groups and discuss how those principles may be altered in computer mediated communication in groups. Listening, an often neglected component of communication, will be examined. Finally, we will conclude this chapter with a discussion of nonverbal behaviors and how they affect your group interactions.

The Small Group Context

Communication occurs within specific situations that have particular constraints.[3] You communicate, for instance, at work as part of a larger organization, with a friend in a dyad, to an audience giving a speech, and in small groups. These are commonly referred to as **contexts** of communication. Contexts all pose constraints on our communication, some common to several contexts, but many peculiar to a specific context.[4] In order to understand small group communication better, we must appreciate the unique situational constraints that occur in the small group context.

Four factors affect communication across all contexts and pose unique communicative challenges for small groups.[5] The first contextual factor is the number of communicators involved. This alone has the most impact on our communication.[6] For example, consider what happens to your communication when you are talking with a close friend and a third party enters the conversation. Groups, by virtue of involving more than two people, take on a complexity that is a theme running through this text. In Chapter 5, we will explore further how increasing group size increases the amount of coordination and energy members must expend when they work in groups.

Second, while feedback in face-to-face small groups is immediate, as it is in interpersonal relationships, it becomes much more psychologically complex, due to the number of people involved.[7] We talk one on one in interpersonal contexts, but in small group contexts we talk one on one,

Context

The situation or environment that influences the dynamics of communication.

one to other subgroupings, one to the group as a whole—we have much more choice about whom we address. Our small student group of five in the opening case involves 90 potential relationships! Wilmot argues that a group's leadership, to be discussed in Chapters 7 and 8, is what helps us manage these multiple relationships by reducing them into manageable smaller groupings. For example, Lam, in our case, was trying to quell the discontent between two coalitions: Kelli/Tamika and Ryan/Tyler.

Third, the roles among participants become more formalized in small groups compared to the informal, less specified roles in the interpersonal context. When the number of communicators increases, formality becomes necessary to coordinate the communication better. Thus, in small groups, member roles (discussed in Chapter 5) are more explicitly negotiated and member pressure to conform to role expectations is more obvious.[8] Both Kelli and Tamika are not happy that Tyler has failed to meet their expectations and have publicly criticized him. In addition, you cannot split a dyad or pair—if you lose one party, the dyad disappears. But this is not the case in a small group, which makes groups more stable than dyads. We saw in our opening case that the group did not cease to be because Tyler was not. The group dynamics may have changed but the group did not disappear or fail to finish its task. Tyler's behavior also showed us that in small group contexts, coalitions emerge (Ryan and Tyler) as well as deviants (Tyler), which is not possible in dyads. Not only do deviants and coalitions emerge, they change throughout the history of the group as power, leadership, and status evolve. We explore these issues in later chapters, but for now, we remind you to be prepared for the consequences of membership change.

Fourth, again due to the challenges posed by the sheer number of communicators, the goals and purposes of small groups become more defined and are accompanied by pressure to manage individual versus group goals. Fisher claimed that member identification with a larger social unit (the group) was probably the single most important distinction between the interpersonal and small group contexts.[9] The fact that members in a group need each other to accomplish group goals is enough to produce stress among group members. Students report several sources of stress, such as lack of teamwork, problem coordinating the task, dissension among members, and power struggles.[10] Stress in turn impacts group communication because it can undermine a group member's sense of control—when under stress, we tend to act to regain control. This is what Tamika and Kelli were trying to do in our student group.

We do not mean to imply that the nature of communication found in small groups is so unique that you will not find it anywhere else. "The basic process of communication operates in every context in fundamentally the same way, even though each context requires slightly different skills or special applications of general communicative principles."[11] As you read about small group interaction, you should consider how the situational constraints of the small group affect how generally accepted principles of communication work.

Small Group Communication

Many definitions of the term *communication* exist. We define **communication** as the transactional process by which people simultaneously create, interpret, and negotiate shared meaning through their interaction. They do this by creating and sending verbal and nonverbal messages that are received, interpreted, and responded to by other people. In the small group, meaning must be shared sufficiently for the members to accomplish the group task, but is never completely shared between two people, let alone among the four or five who typically constitute a small group. However, for group members to achieve their interdependent goal, at least *some* shared meaning must occur.

Communication

A transactional process by which people simultaneously create, interpret, and negotiate shared meaning through their interaction.

Principles of Communication

We now present five principles of communication. Different authors emphasize different communication principles, but the following are the ones generally accepted by scholars and to us seem particularly important for understanding communication in small groups.

1. **Human communication is symbolic.**

   This is the most widely accepted and probably most important principle of communication. We do not send our meanings directly to people; rather, our messages have to be interpreted because messages are symbolic. **Symbols** are arbitrarily created by people to represent experiences, objects, or concepts. This arbitrariness means that there is no inherent or automatic reason why we call a collection of people a *group*. Our languages are systems of words or symbols and the rules for their use and can be used to identify who is in a particular linguistic community and who is not. While obvious on the surface, people often forget the implications of the symbolic nature of communication when they assume everyone has the same meaning for a word or when they try to freeze meaning and deny its changing nature. The mutual understanding group members seek is complicated. Members must work to negotiate the myriad of symbolic meanings they bring to a group. Members can end up laughing about misunderstandings, such as when a Canadian colleague of ours asked for reports in "point form," confusing his colleagues until they learned he meant "outline form." However, misunderstandings can be deadly. When an air traffic controller in Madagascar said, "Clipper 1736 report clear of runway," the Clipper's American pilot thought he had been given clearance to take off. Instead, the controller meant, "Report that you have cleared the runway." Six hundred people died in the plane crash that followed.[12] Reliance on symbols is central to human communication and is a major reason why meaning can never be shared exactly.

Symbol

An arbitrary, human creation used to represent something with which it has no inherent relationship; all words are symbols.

2. **Communication is personal.**

   The symbolic nature of communication renders communication arbitrary and thus very personal. The same word can have different meanings to different people and different words can mean the same thing. Moreover, those meanings change as the world changes. We poke fun at linguistic arbitrariness to make our point: Remember when a *window* was something you hated to clean and a *ram* was a male sheep? *Meg* was the name of your sister, and *gig* was a job for the night. *Memory* was something you lost, *CD* was a bank account, *log on* was adding fuel to a fire, and *backup* happened to your toilet. Now they all mean different things and that really *mega bites!* The symbolic and personal nature of communication makes *perfect* understanding impossible. Your backgrounds, experiences, and the cultures from which you identify all affect the meanings you give to the words you use and the way you understand those of others. We discuss in detail the effects of member characteristics, diversity, and culture on the communication process in Chapters 4 and 5.

3. **Communication is a transactional process.**

   This principle follows from the previous two. **Transactional** implies that participants in communication must cooperate and negotiate shared meaning and understanding. If we know that the verbal symbol (i.e., word) *excellent* has different connotations to different people, and we want to make sure we understand each other about our project, then we must work together, communicatively, to determine what we jointly mean by *excellent*. In addition, *transactional* implies that the sender-receiver roles occur simultaneously, not alternately. While I am describing what an excellent project means to me, I simultaneously see your frown and guess that you don't agree with my description. Thus, communication is *both* a sender *and* receiver phenomenon simultaneously for each person involved in the process. Both sender and receiver then must negotiate to create mutually understood messages. Thus, *both* have to share responsibility for misunderstandings and stay away from blame games such as "I didn't misunderstand him, he misunderstood me." Instead, they must work together to improve future transactions. The difference between the linear, back-and-forth view of communication and the simultaneous, transactional view is depicted in Figure 2.1. Finally, the concept of *process* implies that communication is an ongoing event with no clear beginning or end. If we argue about how excellent our project will be, then the next time we meet, we will carry the memory of that argument with us. Thus, communication is ever changing, not static.

   In our opening story, Lam, Tamika, Ryan, and Kelli believe that Tyler has a problem being "on time." Note Tamika's exclamation, "Tyler is so late." But what does it mean to be late? "Being on time" and "late" are interpretations of behavioral events (e.g., they agreed

Transactional Process

All interactants mutually and simultaneously define both themselves and others during communication.

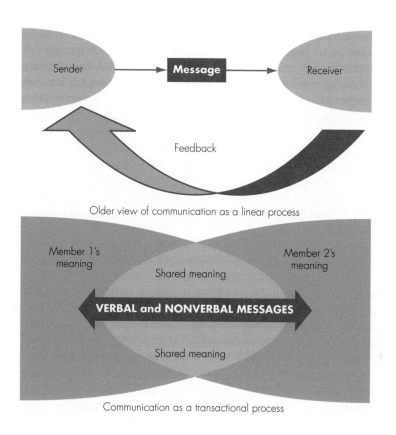

FIGURE 2.1
Picturing
communication
as a transactional
process

Older view of communication as a linear process

Communication as a transactional process

to meet at 2 PM; it is 2:20 and Tyler has not shown up). In this case, the group members are sharing with each other their own experiences of time and communicating, among other things, their understanding of responsibility.

4. **Communication is not always intentional.**
    This principle is sometimes stated as the communication axiom "You cannot NOT communicate," and not all communication scholars agree with this axiom.[13] For example, Infante et al. believe that for an event to "count" as communication, the sender must have intended to communicate with the receiver.[14] "You cannot NOT communicate" was never meant to imply that *all* behavior is communication, only that all behavior in a social setting has potential communicative value. For instance, when two or more humans are in each other's perceptual awareness, they cannot stop sending nonverbal signals to each other, which they pick up, interpret, and respond to. Tyler's absence from his group communicates various things to his group. Thus, in a social setting, one probably cannot avoid communicating.[15] The way symbols are interpreted may not be the way they were intended; Tyler may not intend to communicate to his colleagues that he does

not care enough for the business to be on time. Moreover, people do not always *know* what they intend, and may have multiple intentions for their words or actions.[16] Nevertheless, in a social setting like a group, your behavior always communicates—even silence will be interpreted by fellow group members.

Message
_____
Any action, sound, or word used in interaction.

5. **Communication involves content and relationship dimensions.** Any **message,** or any action, sound, or word used in interaction,[17] contains both dimensions simultaneously. The *content* or denotative dimension of the message is the subject, idea, or topic of the message—the *what* of the message. The *relationship* dimension of the message refers to what the message reveals about how the speaker views his or her relationship to the other participants—the *how* of the message.

At the content level, Tamika's first remark presents a fact—that Tyler has not arrived at the designated time—and an opinion—that the group could have finished its meeting if members had been able to start on time. Clearly, these colleagues feel angry and frustrated that Tyler has failed them again. Kelli's calling Tyler "a jerk" indicates that his behavior pattern is straining the goodwill of the others. Now notice Lam's final remark: "Let's just go ahead and get started. . . . Ryan, did you . . . ?" This comment clearly illustrates the relationship level of communication, which concerns how the speaker views his or her relationship to the other members. Lam takes charge here by suggesting the group begin without Tyler, then asks Ryan for a report. At the content level, Lam seems to be making a procedural suggestion ("Let's get started") and asking Ryan for information. At the relationship level, however, Lam is saying, "I have enough authority in this group to suggest how to proceed, and I'm taking charge now." The rest of the members accept Lam's relational definition, and the meeting gets under way. Why? Lam is their leader, and he is behaving appropriately for his position. The actions of the others support this behavior and thus Lam's authority is sustained. In this instance Lam does not overstep his relational bounds.

The relationship dimension is often conveyed nonverbally through tone of voice and movement. Attitudes of arrogance, dominance, submissiveness, distrust, superiority, neutrality, or concern are not often stated; rather, members interpret them from nonverbal cues or how a message is expressed. Characteristics such as distrust, dominance, and neutrality convey even subtler distinctions of the relationship dimension of messages: responsiveness, liking, and power.[18] We convey *responsiveness* to others when we show them how much or how little we are interested in their communication through eye contact, posture, and facial expressions. In conversation, interactants who synchronize each other's facial expressions and posture may be expressing comfortableness with each other.[19] *Liking,* or for that matter dislike for others, can be expressed with smiles, friendly touching, and frowns. Considering our case, expressions of anger, frustration, and labeling Tyler a "jerk" are indications of low levels of liking or affection in the group. Finally, relationship-level meaning also contains expressions of *power* as we negotiate our status and influence with others. Perhaps both Tyler and Lam are in a power struggle over leadership. Tyler's absence can be seen as irresponsible, or maybe Tyler is making the group wait for him. Making others wait can be used by people as an expression of status. Remember the last time you went for a doctor's visit or waited on a professor?

In our experience, these relationship-level meanings contribute to many of the misunderstandings we observe in small groups. To illustrate, what if Kelli had turned to Tamika and said, in a commanding tone of voice, "Tamika, you take notes for the meeting." Tamika would probably have wanted to say, "Who died and made you queen?" Group members often react strongly to a peer who seems direct and commanding because the manner suggests superiority to the other members and perhaps dislike.

As you continue to read about the central role of communication in small group dynamics in this text, you will see how these principles apply to the interaction in small group contexts. When you reflect on what is going particularly well and what has gone really badly, these principles, along with your knowledge of features of the small group context, will help you make relevant adaptations. We hope you are willing to study something that may seem obvious to you on the surface instead of thinking, "I understand communication; I've been communicating all my life." Communication processes are complicated; just because you engage in them everyday does not mean you understand the underlying principles at play. In addition, do not also assume that all your problems in a group are *communication* problems. This stance trivializes the very real value differences that differentiate people. Finally, simply because you learn to use good communication techniques does not mean you will automatically be a good communicator. The most important skill you can learn is to *want* to be a better communicator. Communication is a complicated, transactional process; no single behavior guarantees an outcome but instead can only facilitate effectiveness. Good communication is aided by understanding the communication process, taking stock of personal attitudes toward that process and other people, and improving the ability to listen—which we turn to now.

Listening and Responding During Discussions

Communication as a transaction places value on both speaking and listening. On numerous occasions we have noted the significance of listening to effective communication. **Listening** involves hearing and interpreting.

Listening

Receiving and interpreting oral and other signals from another person or source.

Hearing is a physiological process that involves the reception of sound waves by the ear. It is only the first element of listening, which also includes the *interpretation* of those sound waves (and other messages). A person with acute hearing may be a poor listener who does not interpret others' statements accurately or respond appropriately. In contrast, someone with considerable hearing loss may be a good listener who is motivated to understand others the way they want to be understood.

In the corporate world, listening is highly valued. In a recent survey, 73 percent of business leaders rated it as an extremely important skill, but also said that only 19 percent of high school graduates had good listening skills.[20] Purdy found that good listeners are attentive, don't interrupt, ask questions in a nonthreatening way, paraphrase, make eye contact with and show interest in the speaker, provide constructive feedback, and are willing to listen.[21]

It was once estimated that every morning in the United States, 15 million meetings take place. Consider that in a six-person group, every time 5 minutes of information is repeated because of poor listening, a total of 30 minutes is wasted. Multiply that by 15 million meetings and that translates into a lot of wasted time![22] The cost of poor listening is high. Jobs are completed incorrectly, shipments go awry, and people are hurt or killed because they or someone else didn't listen well. A good listener is, sorry to say, a rare commodity of great value to a group. Bechler and Johnson found that group members who were perceived as being good listeners (e.g., stayed focused during discussion, maintained eye contact with speakers, and so forth) were also perceived as being leaders.[23] Unfortunately, listening is often underemphasized in discussions of group communication.

Recap: A Quick Review

Communication is the lifeblood of group dynamics. It creates and sustains the character of any group.

1. Communication is a complex transactional process of negotiating shared meaning through the generation, transmission, receipt, and interpretation of verbal and nonverbal messages.

2. Effective groups share enough meaning to enable members to coordinate their behaviors in order to reach an independent goal.

3. Communication is an inexact process because it is a complex, symbolic, transactional, and often unintentional process. Messages always include a content, or *what*, and relationship, or *how*, dimension. Relational dimensions send messages of responsiveness, liking, and power between members.

4. Learning to be a better communicator involves not taking the process of communication for granted, not assuming that all group problems are communication problems, and realizing that the best skill to learn is a *desire* to want to improve communication.

Poor listening is easier to detect in a dyad than in a small group where one person can "hide" for long periods of time.[24] The social pressure to listen is not felt as intensely in a group as it is in a dyad, and bad listening is easier to disguise. Because people can fake listening, only when someone speaks do other members have a basis for judging that person's listening behavior. Making irrelevant comments, going off in tangents, and asking questions about something that has already been explained are evidence of poor listening.

Complicating the challenge to effective listening is the fact that most of us think we are good listeners, but the evidence tells a different story. Berg found, for instance, that topics were switched about one time per minute in discussions he observed. Members were hardly listening or responding to what previous speakers had said.[25] This finding was confirmed by other investigators in a variety of cultures and situations.[26] Nichols and Stevens reported that students listening to lectures on which they knew they would be tested retained only about half the new information presented.[27] We have found that when members of small groups (whether college students or corporate personnel in training groups) are required to paraphrase what a previous discussant said to that person's satisfaction, they can do so only about half the time. This is true even when participants know that they will be assessed for accuracy in listening. How much, then, must group members misunderstand when they are *not* on guard?

Teams do not suddenly become effective and productive; members must *learn* how to work well together, and a major factor that affects how well members mesh together is how willing they are to listen to one another, to share perspectives, and to integrate their viewpoints.[28] Listening is the key.

Listening Preferences

By now we hope you have gotten the idea that good listening in a group is an invaluable skill and poor listening can produce terrible group outcomes. You should also understand we each bring different listening preferences to our group experiences, which if not recognized, can cause problems for the group. Have you ever thought that perhaps your strengths and weaknesses as a listener are tied to your learned listening preference?

Kittie Watson, a specialist in listening and small group communication, has identified four general listening preferences: people-, action-, content-, and time-oriented listeners.[29] Each preference has its advantages and disadvantages. The trick to managing different listening preferences is to be able to identify the listening preferences of all members, including yourself, in group interaction and shifting your preference to fit the needs of the group.

People-oriented listeners are concerned about how their listening behavior affects relationships. Appearing attentive and nonjudgmental, these listeners are the ones people go to when they want someone to listen

People-Oriented Listener

A listener who is sensitive to others, nonjudgmental, and concerned about how his or her behavior affects others; can become distracted from the task by others' problems.

to them. Behaviors indicative of this preference are the use of "we" more than "I," use of emotional appeals in discussion and debates, and willingness to show vulnerability. These members may be heard telling a personal story to calm down members who may be upset or angry. People-oriented listeners may also become distracted by others' problems, may avoid conflicts to maintain a sense of harmony, and may engage in too many side conversations during meetings.

Action-oriented listeners are focused on the job at hand. They help the group stay on task by remembering details and providing feedback about the goal. They enjoy listening to well-organized material. On the other hand, these members can appear overly critical, may interrupt too much if they believe the group is getting off track, and may lose interest if the discussion appears to be going nowhere.

Content-oriented listeners are the group members who really enjoy analyzing the things they hear and are drawn to highly credible sources. You may observe these members using graphs, quoting sources, bringing research to the group, and dissecting the information and arguments of others. These listeners can also be seen as overly critical and maybe even intimidating to other members. Their analytical skills, while valuable, may also slow the group down and can even serve to devalue information they do not see as important, such as anecdotes.

Time-oriented listeners can be identified by their attempts to schedule group meeting and activity times, their sensitivity to nonverbal cues that may indicate impatience, and their focus on moving the group along in a timely manner. The creative and spontaneous discussions so necessary to problem solving can pose difficulties for these listeners. They also discourage additional discussion as the group nears the end of its scheduled meeting time.

No one preference is the best. Preferences are learned, so you are not locked into one of them. A group member's preference is influenced by many factors, including the nature of the relationships between group members and time constraints. Practice participation–observation and observe how members' behaviors help identify their preferences. Be willing to shift your preference to suit the immediate needs of the group and be willing to encourage the productive use of all the preferences.

Now that you understand better the consequences of poor listening to small group communication and the different listening preferences members bring to a group, we hope that you want to improve your listening. We present for your consideration a tested technique to help you take responsibility for your listening choices.

Effective Listening in the Small Group

Listening effectively is an *active* process requiring as much effort as speaking; it involves the choice to listen. No matter how great the speaker is, it

---

Action-Oriented Listener

A listener who focuses on the task, remembers details, and prefers an organized presentation.

Content-Oriented Listener

A listener who enjoys analyzing information and dissecting others' arguments; can be seen as overly critical.

Time-Oriented Listener

A listener sensitive to time; may be impatient or try to move the group prematurely to closure.

is the listener who chooses how to listen, to whom, and when. Thus it is the listener who holds the power in the small group interaction. Therefore, it is to your advantage to understand what a good listener does and to use effective listening techniques yourself.[30]

Good listeners keep in mind four important things.[31] ***Good listeners pay attention to the context of what is said.*** Have you ever been "quoted out of context"? If so, you know that context can change the entire meaning of what is said. ***Good listeners pay close attention to the feelings of the speaker.*** Remember the relationship dimension of a message? Good listeners "read between the lines" of what is said and interpret how messages are said for information about how others feel. Kelli's agitated mood in our opening case frames what she has to say about Tyler, and Lam understands that. ***Good listeners help facilitate understanding in a group*** by actively helping speakers clarify confusing behavior. And finally, ***good listeners interpret silence carefully.*** Nonverbal behavior is ambiguous, and we must be careful how we interpret it. Silence may mean that someone does not understand, disagrees, is apathetic, or is holding back information for all kinds of reasons. Silence can even be a sign of respect to others. If you are listening carefully and do not understand the silence, you should ask for clarification.

One of the best techniques for increasing understanding is **active listening.** Active listening virtually forces the listener to understand a speaker before replying or adding to a discussion. It is a way to practice empathy in listening and avoid premature responses and defensiveness. Here the motivation to receive information is greater than the motive to evaluate and criticize.[32] The main rule is that you must state in your own words, or **paraphrase,** what you understand the previous speaker meant, then ask for a confirmation or correction of your paraphrase. Active listeners paraphrase; they do not repeat word for word. After all, a parrot can repeat, but that doesn't mean that the parrot has understood! A paraphrase in the listener's own words forces the listener to process the information cognitively, allowing the original speaker to determine whether the message was understood as intended. The original speaker can then reply to the paraphrase by accepting or revising it or asking the listener to try again. Only when the original speaker is fully satisfied that the listener has understood what was intended does an active listener proceed with agreement, disagreement, elaboration, change of topic, or whatever. The following dialogue illustrates the technique:

Ed: Requiring landowners to farm in such a way that topsoil is not lost is absolutely necessary if we really want to protect the Earth for our children. (opinion)

Gail: If I understand you, you think we should require that farming practices prevent possible erosion of the topsoil because erosion destroys the Earth for living things? (paraphrase of Ed's opinion)

Active Listening

Listening with the intent of understanding a speaker the way the speaker wishes to be understood and paraphrasing your understanding so the speaker can confirm or correct the paraphrase.

Paraphrase

Restatement in one's own words of what one understood a speaker to mean.

Ed: Right, Gail. (confirmation and acceptance of the paraphrase)

Another example:

Consuelo: If every college graduate were required to demonstrate some competence in using a computer, that might help right at graduation. But computers are changing so rapidly that grads would be no better off in a few years, unless they kept up to date or had to use a computer all along. (opinion)

Taylor: Do I understand you right? Are you saying that a computer science course should *not* be required to get a degree? (attempted paraphrase of Consuelo's opinion)

Consuelo: No, just that it should be more than just how to use a computer. You ought to understand computers and what they do and don't do. (rejects the paraphrase and attempts to clarify)

Taylor: So you think there should be a requirement for a graduate to be able to explain what computers can and can't do, as well as be comfortable with a computer. (second attempt at paraphrasing Consuelo's opinion)

Consuelo: Yes, more than a course as such. (confirms Taylor's paraphrase)

Taylor: I agree with that idea and think we should also have a requirement for ability to investigate, organize, and write a term paper. (His paraphrase confirmed Taylor is now free to add his opinion, on a new topic, to the discussion.)

Every idea proposed in a discussion should be evaluated, but only when you are sure you understand it to the satisfaction of the speaker. Active listeners confirm their understanding *before* they express their positive or negative evaluation. Only at that point is critical listening in order, when the listener evaluates whether the statement is relevant, defensible, likely to be effective, was carefully thought through, and so forth.

Sometimes active listeners cannot hear adequately or are not confident of their understandings. If so, they will say so quickly, asking the speaker to repeat or clarify. Only then will they disagree, add more information, or express whatever is their honest reaction.

Active listening slows the pace of interaction. If you are not used to listening actively, you may at first find yourself with nothing to say for a moment after the other finishes speaking. Keep practicing; soon you will find yourself making spontaneous responses instead of preplanned or irrelevant remarks. Above all, don't fake listening, which often damages trust and cooperation.

Computer-Mediated Communication and Face-to-Face Communication in Small Groups

So far, we have discussed communication that occurs in real time when members meet face-to-face. But since the advent of computers and the explosion of Internet capabilities, groups typically supplement their face-to-face meetings using a variety of technological tools. **Computer-mediated communication,** or CMC, is the formal phrase used to refer to the use of computers to interact with others. CMC can take a variety of forms, including e-mail or electronic mail, chat rooms, electronic bulletin boards, List-servs, videoconferencing, wikis, discussion boards, and decision-making software. Group members often use computer technology to communicate with each other between and during meetings. A question to ask is: "How different is computer-mediated communication from face-to-face communication?" Before we address this question, let's look at the variety of technology-related communication tools available to groups.

As we mentioned in Chapter 1, groups range in the degree to which they use technology—from "not at all" to "that's the only way we meet." Generally, there are three broad functions technology can serve. First, it allows members to keep in touch between meetings. Phone calls, e-mails, and text messages serve this function well. They can help group members connect socially, as when a member calls or texts another to see if everything is OK, and they can help facilitate task accomplishment, as when the chair sends out the meeting notice and agenda in advance. Second, technology allows members to work collaboratively on projects and documents. Devices such as virtual Dropbox allow members to upload documents so others at different locations can access them, respond, suggest changes and so forth. Wikis allow members to work both virtually and collaboratively and allow tracking so everyone can see which member suggested which changes. Such virtual access to projects and documents can supplement regular face-to-face meetings but also may be the only way some groups work on projects. Third, technology may actually allow members to meet in real time, although they may be geographically distributed. For instance, Skype, which requires a computer, Internet connection, and a webcam (many computers now have them build in), allows someone to attend a meeting on video. If a member cannot be present for a key meeting, this is an ideal way to let that person contribute.

Other conferencing possibilities exist, also. The simplest of these is the telephone conference call, or audioconference, where members interact simultaneously on telephone. **Net conference** is a general term that refers to conferences electronically mediated by networked computers and takes two forms, *videoconferences* and *computer conferences*.[33] Videoconferences involve both audio and video communication, which allows members to observe more nonverbal communication in real time. In computer conferences, members actually sit in front of their computers and type messages to one another. Many classes that use Blackboard and similar online course management systems allow for real-time discussions like this, with classmates or group members typing instead of talking. The ability to net conference gets easier, more functional, and less expensive each year and can save a group considerable time and money.

Computer-Mediated Communication (CMC)

Group members' use of computers to communicate with one another.

Net Conference

A conference that takes place electronically over networked computers.

Although this kind of computer technology has its advantages, the question remains: "Do computer-mediated meetings have disadvantages in comparison to face-to-face group meetings?" Depending on the kind of net conference, participant nonverbal messages like facial expressions and body language are missing or exaggerated.[34] For example, during a videoconference participants can see each other, but only to the extent that the camera allows. Proximity is only simulated, *not* duplicated—members are not actually in each other's physical presence. Turn taking is harder because there is often a delay of half a second, which causes participants to overlap each other. Because participants are tied to their computers, gestures are restricted. The sense of sharing, involvement, and team spirit can be low. This could be harmful if the group is trying to build consensus about something, but it may not matter if participants are just trying to generate a list of ideas.[35]

Social Presence

The extent to which group members perceive that a particular communication medium is socially and emotionally similar to face-to-face interaction.

This comparison raises the issue of **social presence,** which refers to how much group members perceive the communication medium is like face-to-face interaction socially and emotionally. This perception depends on the degree to which members perceive that other members are actually *there* during interaction.[36] *Asynchronous* communication, where there is a delay between when a message is sent and when it is received (e.g., e-mail), promotes less social presence than synchronous, more simultaneous communication. One factor that can influence the need for social presence is the complexity of the group's task. The tougher the task, the less adequate some CMC can become because the medium's channels are not adequate.

However, individuals using CMC can become very creative when it comes to replicating the social presence of face-to-face communication. Walther and his associates have challenged the view that computer-mediated communication lacks social presence.[37] Walther's theory of social information processing stems from the premise that individuals are motivated to learn about one another, whether they communicate face-to-face or by computer. Thus, people adapt to the particular medium they are using. If nonverbal cues are unavailable or limited, as with CMC, they will use words instead. Group members can self-disclose, ask about one another, and form close relationships via CMC, although such relationships may take longer. Walther says that relationships formed by CMC can be just as personal and intimate as those formed in face-to-face relationships. In fact, sometimes CMC relationships can be of higher quality than face-to-face relationships, perhaps because with asynchronous communication, people access their messages when it is convenient for them and when they can actually pay attention to the person on the sending end of the message. Social presence *is* important in a group, but members find ways to create social presence with words when other avenues are restricted.

Several factors can improve the effectiveness of net conferences.[38] For example, sandwiching the conference between face-to-face meetings can enhance the sense of groupness between members. Using a trained moderator can improve the process. So will making sure that members know how to use the technology and will abide by the guidelines for speaking. Tasks such as routine meetings and information sharing can be very effective via a net conference. For more complex tasks in which disagreement is likely to occur, face-to-face meetings are still preferable. Research suggests that CMC and face-to-face groups are similar in *potency*—members' belief that a group will be effective—and effectiveness, although the pattern of development may differ. For example, in the groups Lira and her associates studied, group potency remained stable in computer-mediated groups but increased in face-to-face groups.[39] The researchers speculated that more time might be needed for CMC groups to work together and evaluate their potency than the month allotted in the study. In addition, the more effective a group actually is, the greater the group's potency becomes, and this relationship was stronger in CMC groups than face-to-face ones. The researchers recommend providing adequate training for CMC groups to ensure effectiveness and increase potency. However, computer conferences have been used effectively to help members in conflict achieve consensus. Table 2.1 compares the strengths of face-to-face and net conferences or what used to be called teleconference meetings.

Although CMC may appear to be a different kind of communication, the communicative processes involved are still symbolic, personal, transactional, and not always intentional, and they involve content as well as relationship dimensions. We will elaborate on CMC in later chapters.

TABLE 2.1 Comparison of Strengths

Teleconferences	Face-to-Face Meetings
• They can be useful for information sharing, routine meetings.	• Face-to-face meetings are better when group cohesiveness and interpersonal relationships are important.
• Quantity and quality of ideas are equal to face-to-face meetings.	• Group organization is easier to maintain.
• In negotiations, evidence is more persuasive than personality.	• Participants can exchange more messages quicker.
• Participants may pay more attention to what is said.	• Important nonverbal information (facial expressions, uses of space) is available.
• In conflict, more opinion change may occur than in face-to-face meetings.	• People generally prefer face-to-face meetings.
• Audioconferences/computer conferences are cost-effective.	• Participants are more confident of their perceptions in face-to-face meetings.

Source: Adapted from Gene D. Fowler and Marilyn E. Wackerbarth, "Audio Teleconferencing versus Face-to-Face Conferencing: A Synthesis of the Literature," *Western Journal of Speech Communication* 44 (Summer 1980): 236–52.

Nonverbal Behavior in Small Group Communication

Although discussion is the heart of group interaction, verbal *and* nonverbal messages operate together to create meaning; they are indivisible. We have mentioned several times throughout this chapter the importance of non-verbal behaviors. We *artificially* separate them only to help you assess the contribution each makes to create meaning during small group interaction. At different times and for various reasons we may attend more to verbal behavior or more to nonverbal behavior but always keep in mind almost no group communicating is entirely verbal or nonverbal.

Nonverbal Behavior

Messages other than words to which listeners react.

Nonverbal behavior includes all behavior *except* the actual words them-selves. It is vital to small group communication and the meaning negotiated between members. Group members cannot stop engaging in nonverbal behavior in a small group. In the presence of others, any member's non-verbal behavior can be received and interpreted by others, which affects the mood, climate, cohesiveness, and interpersonal relationships among the members—regardless of whether those messages are intended. The myriad of nonverbal behaviors in a group are highly ambiguous as well, and members have to be careful how they are interpreted, as we pointed out earlier with respect to silence. Nonverbal behaviors can contradict verbal behaviors, and often their message is believed over the message of the verbal behaviors. If Tamika, in our opening case, had criticized Tyler's absence in a more laid-back tone, other members might have thought she was joking rather than upset, giving more credence to the laid-back tone. In our case, however, her remarks were matched by an agitated tone and thus her nonverbal behavior supplemented her verbal message of irritation over Tyler's absence.

Nonverbal behaviors not only may contradict verbal behaviors and supple-ment them; they also work to express emotions and regulate our interaction.

Both Tamika and Kelli expressed strong emotions with respect to Tyler's absence by tone of voice, volume, posture, and bodily movement away from the group. In computer-mediated communication, social presence is conveyed by **emoticons,** or typographical emotional.[40] The most popular emoticon, the smiley face ☺, is about 30 years old. While useful in informal group CMC, emoticons are considered inappropriate for business communications.[41] In our student group, members pushed back chairs from the table and also picked up their belongings, nonverbal behaviors that function to guide how the interaction is to proceed—in this case they were signaling a desire to leave the meeting. **Regulators** direct the flow of interaction among group members. Turn-taking in groups is fast and furious and its mechanisms go unnoticed. However, members subtly cue each other as to when conversational turns are ending, when someone else can take a turn, or when a member is not giving up a turn with body motions, eye contact, and audible breaths. Typically, for instance, when a member tries to keep a turn but is being interrupted by others, his or her volume rises, as if to hold the turn with loudness. During CMC, turn-taking processes are more problematic. In net conferences, for instance, the synchronous interaction between members is delayed even though members are "talking to each other." This half second delay between speaking and hearing is enough to affect the humor in net conferences (less humor compared to face to face) and the sheer amount of interaction (monologues are common in net conferences).[42]

Effective group members are aware of and understand these nuances and functions of nonverbal behavior; they use this understanding to improve the process of creating shared meaning. For example, one of us observed a normally quiet group member fold his arms in a closed gesture in response to a statement made by the group's chair. The chair, recognizing that this gesture could be interpreted in a number of different ways, asked the member to share his opinions directly with the group. It turned out that the member strongly disagreed with the emerging group consensus for several excellent reasons the others had not considered. The chair's alertness and sensitivity helped make this member's information available to the entire group.

Emoticons

Symbols and combinations of characters used in computer-mediated communication to help convey relational messages and social presence.

Regulators

Nonverbal behavior used to control who speaks during a discussion.

Recap: A Quick Review

Nonverbal behaviors are vital to small group communication.

1. Nonverbal behaviors are ever present, ambiguous, and generally more trusted if there is a conflict between nonverbal and verbal behaviors.
2. Individuals use nonverbal behaviors with verbal behaviors in several ways. Nonverbal behaviors can supplement, regulate, and contradict words.
3. Nonverbal behaviors also function to express emotions.

Nonverbal behaviors supplement the words.

"Are you sure?" Nonverbal behaviors help us express emotions.

Types of Nonverbal Behaviors

Interpreting nonverbal behavior appropriately requires that we look at the *pattern* of behavior rather than at just a single cue. At the same time, we need to be aware of the various types of nonverbal behavior to avoid overlooking any. Those listed next are especially relevant to communication among group members. Proceed with caution; there is considerable cross-cultural variation in the types of nonverbal behavior exhibited by people from different cultures, and, as we mentioned earlier, behavior can be highly ambiguous and must not be interpreted out of context.

Physical Appearance Members of a new group react to each other's appearances long before they begin to judge each other's expertise and competencies. We attribute factors such as intelligence and likability to people on the basis of what we initially observe of them. Of course, we may change our judgments later, but we form them initially from a variety of nonverbal messages.

Sex, body shape, and ethnicity particularly affect how group members interact with each other initially.[43] Interestingly, given how much American culture pays attention to physical attractiveness, no research to date has examined the impact of relative physical attractiveness of group members to group dynamics or outcomes.[44]

Cultural factors influence our responses to physical appearance as well. Americans apparently have a clear picture of what a leader should look like. We tend to be prejudiced against endomorphs (heavy bodies), whom we often perceive as lazy, sloppy, stupid, and undependable, but also as jolly and easy to get along with. Ectomorphs (tall and skinny) are perceived as frail, studious, and intelligent. Mesomorphs (muscular types) are more likely than others to be perceived as leaders. Height is particularly important. The taller a person is, the more likely she or he is to be looked up to, literally, as a leader; short people have to try harder to be seen as potential group leaders.[45] It is especially important that we teach ourselves to respond to what a person does, *not* his or her physical appearance.

The appearance of group members matters to outsiders as well. Groups do not operate in a social vacuum; how group members appear to others can affect their credibility and even their success during group presentations. The most famous rock band of all time, The Beatles, used black clothes early in their career to mimic the color of beetles.[46] When John Lennon was asked how much of their success was due to their sound rather than their appearance, he replied, "We could have managed, looking like we look and making worse records, or we could have managed, looking like the average pop singer and making our noise. But the combination makes a better impact. We have always looked different from the rest of the mob."[47]

Space and Seating There have been many studies of how we use **proxemics,** or personal space and territory, to communicate. We signal our

Proxemics

The study of uses of space and territory between and among people.

need to be included by how we orient our bodies to the group. A person who sits close to other members, directly in the circle in a flexible seating space, close to a circular table, or at a central point at a square or rectangular table signals a need to belong or a sense of belonging; a member who sits outside the circumference, pushed back from a table, or at a corner may be signaling a desire to withdraw. Sitting within range of touch indicates that we feel intimately or personally involved, whereas sitting from just outside touch distance to several feet away signals a more formal, businesslike relationship.[48] Patterson found that group members making collective (group) decisions sit closer together and in more of a circle than when making individual judgments.[49] Stacks and Burgoon discovered that closer distances (18 inches) make group members more persuasive and credible than distances of 36 or 54 inches.[50]

What is a comfortable distance varies from one individual or one culture to another. In South America, southern and eastern Europe, and Arab countries, people prefer to stand close, whereas in northern Europe, North America, and Japan, people prefer more space.[51] In fact, members of Arabic cultures feel reassured when they stand close enough to be able to smell their conversational partners. Westerners, however, are usually uncomfortable with such close contact and tend to back away, causing Arabs to mistrust their intentions.

In small groups, individuals usually try to place themselves at a comfortable conversational distance according to the norms of their own cultures. Naturally, this can cause problems if the participants are members of cultures with divergent norms about appropriate distance; they may interpret unexpected behavior of others as rudeness or aggressiveness. One of us had a friend from Alabama who kept moving closer to her co-workers in Ohio, who kept backing away. Finally, they began to joke about her "invasion of their personal space," and both she and her co-workers learned something about their own co-cultural rules.

Females tend to sit closer than males and tolerate crowding better. People of the same age and the same social status sit closer together than people of different ages and statuses. The better acquainted people are, the closer they tend to sit. Thus, members of a long-standing group characterized by high interpersonal trust would be comfortable sitting close together in a small room, but people just beginning to form into a group would need more space. Even so, humans are highly adaptable, so when a room or other constraint violates our preferred distances, we adjust, at least for a short time.

A member's status affects how others react to violations of space norms. Burgoon et al. found, for instance, that if low-status group members violated the group's norm regarding space, other members saw them as less persuasive, sociable, and attractive. In contrast, high-status members enhanced their status by moving closer than the group norm specified, and even more if they moved farther away.[52] Thus, it is generally advisable for you to follow group space norms rather than violate them, but if you are a high-status group member, you may have some leeway.

Leadership emergence in a group is related to space. Dominant people and designated leaders usually choose central positions in the group, such as at the head of a rectangular table or across from as many others as possible. Other members frequently avoid sitting next to a designated leader so the arrangement looks like a leader sitting facing a horseshoe.[53] This reinforces the leader's position, allows the leader a comprehensive view of the group, and facilitates the leader's coordination and control.

People sitting across from each other speak more often to each other than people sitting side by side.[54] However, when a group has a dominating leader, "sidebar" conversations tend to break out between people sitting next to each other. Thus, we can conclude that conversation normally flows across the circle, and leaders should sit where they can maintain eye contact with as many group members as possible.

Seating preferences have been found to vary across cultures. Summarizing research in this area, Ramsey explains that Americans show liking with close interpersonal seating, a forward lean, direct orientation toward the other, and eye contact.[55] Leaders seem to gravitate to head positions, with high-status individuals sitting nearby. Similar behaviors occur in Japan, where the leader sits at one end of a rectangular table, and, the lower the rank, the farther away the seat. In some cultures, teachers and others need to be careful in assigning seats for fear of inadvertently violating cultural taboos about who may sit next to whom. In a few cultures, people sit opposite each other when they have differences to settle, but sit side by side in rows when eating or enjoying one another's company. Most of what we know about seating patterns comes from research on Westerners; it may not hold true for people of other cultures.

Seating and spatial features of the group's environment, such as fixed-space permanent features like walls and doors and movable features like furniture, influence the group's interactions.[56] In a large room, group members may choose to sit closer together than normal. If a group is meeting in a space normally used for another activity, the normal use of that space may change the group's interaction; for example, meeting in a member's living room may encourage informality. Sometimes, simply rearranging a group's meeting place can turn a chaotic group into a productive one. One of us advised a student committee whose meetings were characterized by general disorganization, repetition, and sidebar conversations. The room used by the group was normally set up for large assemblies, with a head table on a raised platform at the front, which the members used for their discussions. The president sat at the center of the long table, with the rest of the members sitting on either side of her along one side of the table. Only the members directly next to the president could both see and hear her without great difficulty. The group was advised to stop using the table and instead to rearrange the chairs in a circle. After just one meeting, members reported substantial improvement.

Issues of proxemics take on a different meaning when group members are using some form of computer-mediated communication. *Paraproxemics* refers to the illusion of proximity individuals may have when they are using videoconferences for group business.[57] If the camera zooms in on a person, that may create intimacy; however, if that camera gets too close, members may become threatened. Remember too that being tied to your computer can limit the space you have to gesture or move. Keep in mind that while proximity can be simulated in computer-mediated communication, it cannot be duplicated.

Eye Contact   Eye movements can signal relational messages of disgust, dislike, superiority, or inferiority, as well as liking; the rules for eye contact are highly culturally dependent. For most middle-class white Americans, establishing eye contact is the first step to conversing. Americans use eye contact when they seek feedback, when they want to be spoken to, and when they want to participate more actively.[58] For many middle-class Americans, lack of eye contact is perceived as dishonesty, rudeness, apathy, or nervousness.[59] Burgoon reported that students given free choice of seating arrangements in small classes chose to sit in a circular or U-shaped pattern for their meetings so that they could maintain eye contact with as many other members as possible.[60] Although a stare may indicate competitiveness, in a cooperative group it shows friendship and cohesiveness.[61] Eye contact is important, but must be interpreted carefully in context with other verbal and nonverbal behaviors.

Americans prefer direct eye contact with their conversational partners, but in some cultures (e.g., most Native American cultures) this is perceived as rude, and in still others (e.g., Arabic cultures) intense staring is the norm.[62] Hispanic children are taught to lower their gaze to indicate respect, but this can backfire in cases where Hispanic children interact with members of the dominant American culture.[63] For example, white American teachers and police officers sometimes misinterpret a lowered gaze as sullenness. Many African Americans, too, tend to avoid eye contact, especially with someone of higher status.[64]

Facial Expressions   Facial expressions indicate feelings and moods. Without a word being spoken, you can perceive anger, support, disagreement, and other sentiments. Eckman et al. found that at least six types of emotion could be detected accurately from facial expressions.[65] People with poker faces, who change facial expression very little, tend to be trusted less than people whose expressive faces signal their feelings more openly. But even poker-faced people leak their feelings by physiological changes they can't readily control, such as sweating or blushing.[66] If group members show few facial expressions, watch for other revealing physiological signs.

The face is quick! Some expressions last a mere 200 milliseconds and your eye blinks are over in even less time. A webcam connected to a good

Internet connection can transmit 30 frames every minute, but this drops during a bad connection. The consequence to group discussion is that many facial microexpressions are lost.[67]

Be careful assuming that facial expressions, such as smiling, mean the same in all cultures. For example, a smile in Japan may be a spontaneous expression of pleasure, but it may also represent the desire not to cause pain for someone else.[68] A smiling Japanese may say to you, "I just came from my mother's funeral." According to Japanese rules of etiquette, it is extremely bad form to inflict unpleasantness on someone else; thus, no matter how bad someone feels inside, a cheerful face must be presented to the world.

Movements   The study of how we communicate by movement is called **kinesics.** We reveal our feelings with bodily movements and gestures. We show tension by shifting around in a chair, drumming fingers, swinging a foot, or twitching an eye. Such behavior may signal frustration, impatience with the group's progress, or annoyance. Alert group members will attempt to track down the source of tension by pointing out the kinesic cues and asking what may be producing them.

According to Scheflen, body orientation indicates how open to and accepting of others a group member feels.[69] Members turn directly to those they like and away from those they do not like. Leaning toward others indicates a sense of belonging, whereas leaning away signals a sense of rejection. Members who sit at angles tangential to the rest of the group may not feel included or want to belong. In fact, group members do change their body orientation significantly from one meeting to the next.[70] As they get to know, like, and trust each other, they tend to increase their eye contact and angle their bodies more directly toward each other.

When members are tuned in to each other, they tend to imitate each other's posture and movements, creating a *body synchrony.* Scheflen observed many instances of parallel arm positions, self-touching behavior, and leg positions indicating congruity.[71] Several studies found that group members are more likely to imitate the movements and gestures of members with high status and power than those with low status.[72] We can infer who has power and status in a group by observing which members are mimicked by others.

In discussion groups, body movements often regulate the flow of discussion. For example, speakers often signal that they are finished speaking by relaxing and stopping hand gestures.[73] Scheflen reported that a speaker who is concluding a point makes a noticeable postural shift.[74] A listener can bid for the floor by leaning forward, waving a hand, and simultaneously opening the mouth.

Vocal Cues   Vocal cues, or **paralanguage,** are any characteristics of voice and utterance other than the words themselves. Included are variables such as pitch, rate, fluency, pronunciation variations, force, tonal quality, and

Kinesics

Study of communication through movements.

Paralanguage

Nonverbal characteristics of voice and utterance, such as pitch, rate, tone of voice, fluency, pauses, and variations in dialect.

pauses. Extensive research since the 1930s indicates that listeners attribute certain characteristics to speakers based on these vocal cues,[75] including such things as attitudes, interests, personality traits, adjustment, ethnic group, education, and anxiety level and other emotional states.[76] Tone of voice is an excellent indicator of a person's self-concept and mood. For instance, frightened people tend to speak in tense, metallic tones; anxious people have nonfluencies such as interjections, repetitions, hesitations, sentence correction, and even stuttering in their speech.

How we react to statements such as "I agree" or "Okay" depends much more on the pitch patterns and tone of voice than on the words themselves. For example, sarcasm and irony are indicated primarily by a tone of voice that suggests the words should be taken *opposite* to what they seem to mean. Children generally do not understand sarcasm, and even one-third of high school seniors take sarcastic statements literally.[77] Sarcasm in a group is easily misunderstood.

In both movement and voice, animation tends to increase status within the group. People who speak quietly in a low key have little persuasive impact. They seem to lack much personal involvement with what they say. However, members whose vocal qualities change too extensively may be seen as irrational, not to be trusted as leaders or credible sources. Taylor found, however, that excessive vocal stress was judged more credible than a monotonous vocal pattern.[78] You are advised to vary your vocal tone and use vocal cues to emphasize the verbal content of your remarks.

Cultural differences have been observed in the use of the **backchannel,** which refers to vocalizations such as *mm-hmmm, uh-huh,* and *yeah-yeah-yeah* that are uttered while another is speaking to indicate interest and active listening. In addition, Caucasian Americans do not give such backchannel responses as frequently as African Americans, Hispanics, and people of southern European origins.[79] This can lead to friction if members who use the backchannel frequently think those who do not are not really attuned and listening well, whereas the less active backchannel responders perceive their fellow members as being rude for interrupting so often.

Dialect may also cause misunderstandings. **Dialect** entails regional and social variations in pronunciation, vocabulary, and grammar of a language. Because dialect influences perceptions of a speaker's intelligence and competence, it can seriously affect employability and performance,[80] as well as credibility. Most countries, including the United States, Canada, Great Britain, and Japan, have regional and social class language deviations to the "standard" dialect. We tend to stereotype individuals with nonstandard dialects. People who use *dees* and *dose* instead of *these* and *those* are identified as lower-status speakers and accorded lower credibility ratings. Speakers of the general American dialect are rated higher than Appalachians and Bostonians on sociointellectual status, dynamism, and being pleasant to listen to. Those who speak a French-Canadian dialect are rated as poor and ignorant in comparison with those who speak an English-

Backchannel

Nonverbal vocalizations such as *mm-hmm* and *uh-huh* that are uttered while another is speaking; partly determined by one's culture, can indicate interest and active listening.

Dialect

A regional variation in the pronunciation, vocabulary, and/or grammar of a language.

Canadian dialect. Teachers tend to rate students who use dialects other than general American as less confident and more ignorant. It is important to be aware of judgment errors that result from such perceptions.

Time Cues   Few of us think of time as a nonverbal dimension of communication. Perceptions of time are highly culturally dependent. Americans think of time as a commodity to be spent or saved. People in Western cultures tend to regulate their activities by the clock, but people in many other cultures act according to inner biological needs or natural events.

In the fast-paced culture of the American business world, being considerate of group members' time is important; Americans usually will allow only about a five-minute leeway before they expect an apology.[81] People who come late to meetings (except because of absolutely unavoidable circumstances) are judged to be inconsiderate, undisciplined, and selfish. Likewise, it is considered improper to leave a meeting before the announced ending time, unless some prior arrangement or explanation has been made. Forcing others to keep to your time schedule is the prerogative of high-status individuals.[82] It implies that your time is more important than that of the other members, and marks you as inconsiderate and arrogant.

Let's take a closer look at time and culture to understand better why individuals from different cultures may treat time differently. Hall describes the Spanish culture of New Mexico as *polychronic,* whereas the Anglo culture is *monochronic.*[83] The Spanish do several things at a time; the Anglos tend to do one thing at a time. The Spanish are casual about clocks and schedules; they are frequently late for appointments and meetings. Anglos are offended by such behavior. The cultures of Latin America, the Middle East, Japan, and France are polychronic, whereas the cultures of northern Europe, North America, and Germany are monochronic.[84] In these cultures, time is treated as a tangible *thing* that can be spent, killed, and wasted; time is perceived as more relational in communal cultures, which integrate task and social needs and hold more fluid attitudes about time.

Time also is a commodity in the group's interaction (i.e., "air time"). People can abuse this resource by talking too much or too little. Harper et al. found that persons who talked somewhat more than average were viewed favorably on leadership characteristics. Those who talked an average amount were the most liked. Extremely talkative members were regarded as rude and selfish, members the group could do without.[85] Derber refers to excessive talking as *conversational narcissism.*[86]

Touch   **Haptics** is the study of this important nonverbal dimension in interpersonal communication. It is vital to group maintenance in most primary groups and athletic teams, but may be nonexistent in many American work groups and committees. Studies of touch in group communication are sparse; most information about touch comes from work in interpersonal communication. The kind of touching people expect and enjoy depends

Haptics

The study of the perception of and use of touch.

on their acculturation and the type of relationship they share with others. For instance, touch between strangers, other than a handshake, tends to threaten most Americans.

Touch between individuals may occur to show play, positive feelings, or control, to get a job done, as part of a greeting or farewell; and of course we touch each other accidentally. Jones and Yarbrough found that *control touches* occur most often followed by positive affect touches.[87] *Control touches* are efforts to gain attention or request compliance and are most often accompanied by some sort of verbalization such as "Scoot over." *Positive affect* touches are most often signs of affection and associated with our primary groups but can occur in business settings. They found that some work teams may engage in spontaneous and brief touches to show support.

Touch among group members can strengthen unity and teamwork. Families join hands to say grace before a meal; football players pile on hands in a huddle; actors hug each other after a successful performance. The type of touch and its setting determines the reaction. Pats are usually perceived as signs of affection and inclusion. Strokes are generally perceived as sensual, inappropriate in a small group meeting. A firm grip on an arm or about the shoulders is usually a control gesture, interpreted as a "one-up" maneuver; among a group of equals, this may be resented. A gentle touch may be a means of getting someone to hold back and not overstate an issue. Many a group member has been restrained from saying something hostile by a gentle touch on the arm during a heated argument.

As with other nonverbal behaviors, people vary widely in the extent to which they accept and give touches. Andersen and Leibowitz found that people range from those who enjoy touch to those who react negatively to being touched.[88] For example, the handshake, a standard American greeting, is by no means universal. The willingness to touch hands suggests a belief in the equality of people.[89] This typically Western notion contrasts with the Hindu belief in a hierarchical society. Hindus greet each other by bringing their own palms together at the chest. Muslims, who according to the Koran are all brothers, hug each other shoulder to shoulder. The Japanese bow in greeting, but prefer to avoid physical contact. You can see how a culture's power distance (such as a belief in equality versus a belief in hierarchy) influences such things as the appropriate nonverbal form for a greeting, and also how easy it is for misunderstandings to occur in small groups with members of different cultures.

Often, the unconscious nonverbal behaviors we have discussed determine how much we like or trust someone. We all have a tendency to like people we perceive as similar to us, but we are unaware that our feelings are often based on *nonverbal* similarity.[90] It is important for us to recognize this normal tendency and consciously suspend judgments of others in intercultural settings where the same nonverbal behaviors have different meanings.

Recap: A Quick Review

Nonverbal behavior not only functions in multiple ways but can also be categorized in numerous ways, each with its own cultural implication. Several categories are relevant to group communication.

1. Group member appearance is one of the first nonverbal behaviors judged by members.
2. Proxemics, or use of space and territory, can indicate things such as status, belonging, and comfort.
3. Eye contact is central to managing conversational dynamics.
4. Facial expressions indicate the feelings and moods of group members.
5. Kinesics involves body orientation and vocal characteristics.
6. The experience of time culturally can influence the rules of "being on time" and how members define the duration of speaking turns.
7. Touch, most important to interpersonal communication, also has serious implications to small group communication.

QUESTIONS FOR REVIEW

 Go to self-quizzes on the Online Learning Center at mhhe.com/galanes14e to test your knowledge of chapter concepts.

This chapter elaborates on the central feature of a group: its communication. Whether members function smoothly or experience problems, like our student group, verbal and nonverbal communication processes influence the character of a group.

1. Among other things, communication is personal. What conclusions might be drawn about the personal attitudes of the students in our opening case toward each other and toward group processes?

2. Besides the obvious symbolic meanings of "late," what other meanings can be read into the remarks and the nonverbal behaviors of the students?

3. What are the obvious content dimensions communicated in the students' remarks? What are they communicating to each other about how they perceive their relationships, including responsiveness, power, and liking?

4. Do these students give any hints about their listening preferences? If so, what are they?

5. How would you rewrite some of Lam's comments to show how he could have paraphrased what Kelli, Ryan, and Tamika said?

6. Which of the eight major categories of nonverbal behaviors are most relevant to this student group?

7. How might computer-mediated communication been used by our student group? What precautions might they take should they choose to use it to compensate for absences from meetings?

8. Given your understanding of communication principles, including nonverbal messages, what advice would you give to this student group?

KEY TERMS

 Test your knowledge of these key terms by visiting the Online Learning Center Web site at mhhe.com/galanes14e.

Action-oriented listener
Active listening
Backchannel
Communication
Computer-mediated
    communication (CMC)
Content-oriented listener
Contexts
Dialect

Emoticons
Haptics
Kinesics
Listening
Message
Net conference
Nonverbal behavior
Paraphrase
Paralanguage

People-oriented listener
Proxemics
Regulators
Social presence
Symbol
Time-oriented listener
Transactional process

BIBLIOGRAPHY

Anderson, Peter A. "Nonverbal Communication in the Small Group." In *Small Group Communication: A Reader*, 6th ed. Robert S. Cathcart and Larry A. Samovar, eds. Dubuque, IA: Wm. C. Brown, 1992, 272–86.

Burgoon, Judee K. "Spatial Relationships in Small Groups." In *Small Group Communication: A Reader*, 7th ed. Robert S. Cathcart, Larry A. Samovar, and Linda D. Henman eds. Dubuque, IA: Brown & Benchmark, 1996, 242–53.

Mader, Thomas E., and Diane C. Mader. *Understanding One Another: Communicating Interpersonally*. Dubuque, IA: Wm. C. Brown, 1990.

Roach, Carol A. and Nancy J. Wyatt. "Successful Listening." In *Small Group Communication: A Reader*. 6th ed. Robert S. Cathcart and Larry A. Samovar, eds. Dubuque, IA: Wm. C. Brown, 1992, 301–25.

NOTES

1. Lawrence R. Frey, "The Call of the Field: Studying Small Groups in the Postmodern Era," in *Group Communication in Context: Studies in Natural Groups,* ed. Lawrence R. Frey (Hillsdale, NH: Erlbaum, 1994): ix–xiv.
2. Richard Sykes, "Imagining What We Might Study If We Really Studied Small Groups from a Speech Perspective," *Communication Studies,* 41 (1990): 200–11.
3. Sarah Trenholm, *Human Communication Theory,* 2nd ed. (Englewood Cliffs, NJ: Prentice Hall, 1991): 20–23.
4. Ibid.
5. Gerald R. Miller, "The Current Status of Theory and Research in Interpersonal Communication," *Human Communication Research,* 4 (1978):165; David L. Swanson and Jesse G. Delia, "The Nature of Human Communication," in *Modules in Speech Communication* (Chicago, IL: Science Research Associates, 1976): 37–38.
6. Miller, "The Current Status of Theory and Research in Interpersonal Communication," 165.
7. William W. Wilmot, *Dyadic Communication,* 2nd ed. (Reading, MA: Addison-Wesley, 1980): 18–33.
8. Trenholm, *Human Communication Theory,* 23.
9. Aubrey B. Fisher, *Small Group Decision Making,* 2nd ed. (New York: McGraw-Hill, 1980): 25.

10. Charles R. Franz and K. Gregory Jin, "The Structure of Group Conflict in a Collaborative Work Group During Informational Systems Development," *Journal of Applied Communication Research,* 23 (May 1995): 108–27.

11. Swanson and Delia, "The Nature of Human Communication," 36.

12. "Englishes Are an International Language," *Michigan Today* (June 1995): 17.

13. See especially Michael T. Motley, "On Whether One Can (Not) Communicate: An Examination via Traditional Communication Postulates," *Western Journal of Speech Communication,* I54 (1990): 1–20.

14. Dominic A. Infante, Andrew S. Rancer, and Deanna F. Womack, *Building Communication Theory* (Prospect Heights, IL: Waveland Press, 1990): 8–10.

15. Janet B. Bavelas, "Behaving and Communicating: A Reply to Motley," *Western Journal of Speech Communication,* 54 (1990): 593–602.

16. Glen H. Stamp and Mark L. Knapp, "The Construct of Intent in Interpersonal Communication," *Quarterly Journal of Speech,* 76 (1990): 282–99.

17. Richard West and Lynn H. Turner, *Introducing Communication Theory: Analysis and Application,* 2nd ed. (New York: McGraw-Hill, 2004).

18. Alfred Mehrabian, *Silent Messages: Implicit Communication of Emotions and Attitudes,* 2nd ed. (Belmont, CA: Wadsworth, 1981).

19. Joseph Capella, "The Biological Origins of Automated Patterns of Human Interaction," *Communication Theory,* 1 (1991): 4–35.

20. Michael Purdy, "The Listener Wins," *Monster.com,* http://career-advice.monster.com/in-the-office/workplace-issues/the-listener-wins/article.aspx, accessed May 18, 2011.

21. Ibid.

22. Kittie W. Watson, "Listener Preferences: The Paradox of Small Group Interactions," in *Small Group Communication: Theory and Practice,* 7th ed., eds. Robert S. Cathcart, Larry A. Samovar, and Linda Henman (Madison, WI: Brown & Benchmark, 1996): 268–82.

23. Curt Bechler and Scott D. Johnson, "Leadership and Listening: A Study of Member Perceptions," *Small Group Research,* 26 (February 1995): 77–85.

24. Watson, "Listener Preferences," 270.

25. David M. Berg, "A Descriptive Analysis of the Distribution and Duration of Themes Discussed by Task-Oriented Groups," *Speech Monographs,* 34 (1967): 172–75.

26. Ernest G. Bormann and Nancy C. Bormann, *Effective Small Group Communication,* 4th ed. (Minneapolis. MN: Burgess, 1988): 120.

27. Ralph G. Nichols and Leonard Stevens, "Listening to People," *Harvard Business Review,* 35 (1957): 85–92.

28. Chantal M. J. H. Savelsbergh, Beatrice I. J. M. van der Heijden, and Rob F. Poell, "The Development and Empirical Validation of a Multidimensional Measuring Instrument for Team learning Behaviors," *Small Group Research,* 40 (October 2009): 578–607.

29. Watson, "Listener Preferences," 271–75.

30. Ibid., 269.

31. Carol A. Roach. and Nancy J. Wyatt. "Successful Listening," in *Small Group Communication: A Reader.* 6th ed., eds. Robert S. Cathcart and Larry A. Samovar. (Dubuque, IA: Wm. C. Brown, 1992): 301–25.

32. Charles M. Kelley, "Empathic Listening," in *Small Group Communication: A Reader,* 6th ed., eds. Robert S. Cathcart and Larry A. Samovar (Dubuque, IA: Wm. C. Brown, 1992): 296–303.

33. Tyrone Adams and Normal Clark, *The Internet: Effective Online Communication* (Forth Worth, TX: Harcourt, 2001): 112–19.

34. Ibid.

35. S. R. Hiltz and M. Turoff, "Virtual Meetings: Computer Conferencing and Distributed Group Support," in *Computer Augmented Teamwork: A Guided Tour,* eds. R. P. Bostrom, R. T Watson, and S. T. Kinney (New York: Van Nostrand Reinhold, 1992): 67–85.

36. Everett M. Rogers, *Communication Technology: The New Media in Society* (New York: Free Press, 1986).

37. Information about social information processing is synthesized from the following sources: Joseph B. Walther, Tracy Loh, and Laura Granka, "Let Me Count the Ways:

The Interchange of Verbal and Nonverbal Cues in Computer-Mediated and Face-to-Face Affinity," *Journal of Language and Social Psychology*, 24 (March 2005): 36–65; Joseph B. Walther and Malcolm R. Parks, "Cues Filtered Out, Cues Filtered In: Computer-Mediated Communication and Relationships," in *Handbook of Interpersonal Communication*, 3rd ed., eds. Mark Knapp and John A. Daly (Thousand Oaks, CA: Sage, 2002): 529–61; and Em Griffin, "Social Information Processing Theory of Joseph Walther," in A First Look at *Communication Theory*, 7th ed. (New York: McGraw-Hill, 2009): 138–50.

38. Compiled from Larry L. Barker, Kathy J. Wahlers, Kittie W. Watson, and Robert J. Kibler, *Groups in Process: An Introduction to Small Group Communication,* 3rd ed. (Englewood Cliffs, NJ: Prentice-Hall, 1987): 208; and Robert J. Johansen, J. Vallee, and K. Spangler, *Electronic Meetings: Technical Alternatives and Social Choices* (Reading, MA: Addison-Wesley, 1979): 113–15.

39. Eva M. Lira, Pilar Ripoll, Jose' M. Peiro' and Ana M. Zornoza, "The Role of Information and Communication Technologies in the Relationship Between Group Effectiveness and Group Potency: A Longitudinal Study," *Small Group Research*, 39 (December 2008): 728–45.

40. Adams and Clark, *The Internet.*

41. Ibid.

42. J. Tang and E. Isaacs, "Studies of Multimedia-Supported Collaboration," in *Information Superhighways: Multimedia Users and Futures,* ed. S. Emmott (San Diego, CA: Academic Press, 1995): 123–60.

43. Sandra Ketrow, "Nonverbal Aspects of Group Communication," in *The Handbook of Group Communication Theory & Research,* ed. Lawrence R. Frey (Thousand Oaks, CA: Sage, 1999): 251–87.

44. Ibid.

45. J. B. Cortes and F. M. Gatti, "Physique and Propensity," in *With Words Unspoken,* eds. L. B. Rosenfeld and J. M. Civikly (New York: Holt, Rinehart and Winston, 1976): 50–56.

46. Robert Freeman, *The Beatles: A Private View* (New York: Barnes & Noble, 1990): 46.

47. Ibid., p. 46.

48. Edward T. Hall, *The Silent Language* (Garden City, NY: Doubleday, 1959).

49. M. L. Patterson, "The Role of Space in Social Interaction," in *Nonverbal Behavior and Communication,* eds. A. W. Siegman and S. Feldstein (Hillsdale, NJ: Erlbaum, 1978): 277.

50. Don W. Stacks and Judee K. Burgoon, "The Persuasive Effects of Violating Spatial Distance Expectations in Small Groups." Paper presented at the Southern Speech Communication Association Convention, Biloxi, MS (April 1979).

51. William B. Gudykunst and Stella Ting-Toomey, *Culture and Interpersonal Communication* (Newbury Park, CA: Sage, 1975): 124–28.

52. J. K. Burgoon, D. W. Stacks, and S. A. Burch, "The Role of Interpersonal Rewards and Violations of Distancing Expectations in Achieving Influence in Small Groups," *Communication,* 11 (1982): 114–28.

53. R. F. Bales and A. P. Hare, "Seating Patterns and Small Group Interaction," *Sociometry, 26* (1963): 480–486; G. Hearn, "Leadership and the Spatial Factor in Small Groups," *Journal of Abnormal and Social Psychology, 54* (1957): 269–72.

54. B. Steinzor, "The Spatial Factor in Face to Face Discussion Groups," *Journal of Abnormal and Social Psychology, 45* (1950): 552–55.

55. Sheila J. Ramsey, "Nonverbal Behavior: An Intercultural Perspective," in *Handbook of Intercultural Communication,* eds. Molefi K. Asante, Eileen Newmark, and Cecil A. Blake (Beverly Hills, CA: Sage, 1979): 129–31.

56. Judee K. Burgoon, "Spatial Relationships in Small Groups," in *Small Group Communication: A Reader,* 6th ed., eds. Robert S. Cathcart and Larry A. Samovar (Dubuque, IA: Wm. C. Brown, 1992): 289–90.

57. Adams and Clark, *The Internet.*

58. James McCroskey, C. Larson, and Mark Knapp, *An Introduction to Interpersonal*

Communication (Englewood Cliffs, NJ: Prentice Hall, 1971): 110–14.

59. Peter A. Andersen, "Nonverbal Communication in the Small Group," in *Small Group Communication: A Reader,* 6th ed., eds. Robert S. Cathcart and Larry A. Samovar (Dubuque, IA: Wm. C. Brown, 1992): 274.

60. Burgoon, "Spatial Relationships in Small Groups," 295.

61. R. V. Exline, "Exploration in the Process of Person Perception: Visual Interaction in Relation to Competition, Sex, and the Need for Affiliation," *Journal of Personality,* 31 (1963): 1–20.

62. Donald Klopf, *Intercultural Encounters: The Fundamentals of Intercultural Communication (*Englewood, CO: Morton 1987): 177.

63. Stewart Tubbs and Sylvia Moss, *Human Communication,* 5th ed. (New York: Random House, 1997): 414.

64. Dorothy L. Pennington, "Black-White Communication: An Assessment of Research," in *Handbook of Intercultural Communication,* eds. Molefi K. Asante, Eileen Newmark, and Cecil A. Blake (Beverly Hills, CA: Sage, 1979): 387.

65. P. Eckman, P. Ellsworth, and W. V. Friesen, *Emotion in the Human Face: Guidelines for Research and an Integration of Findings* (New York: Pergamon Press, 1971).

66. R. W. Buck, R. E. Miller, and W. F. Caul, "Sex, Personality, and Physiological Variables in the Communication of Affect via Facial Expression," *Journal of Personality and Social Psychology,* 30 (1974): 587–96.

67. Adams and Clark, *The Internet: Effective Online Communication,* 119.

68. Branch Lotspiech, personal conversation, June, 1990.

69. Albert. E. Scheflen, "Quasi-Courtship Behavior in Psychotherapy," *Psychiatry,* 28 (1965): 245–56.

70. Mabry, "Development Aspects of Nonverbal Behavior in Small Group Settings," 190–202.

71. Albert. E. Scheflen, *Body Language and the Social Order: Communication as Behavioral*

Control (Englewood Cliffs, NJ: Prentice Hall, 1972): 54–73.

72. Judee K. Burgoon and T. Saine, *The Unknown Dialogue: An Introduction to Nonverbal Communication* (Boston: Houghton Mifflin, 1978).

73. S. Duncan, Jr., "Some Signals and Rules for Taking Speaking Turns in Conversations," *Journal of Personality and Social Psychology,* 23 (1972): 283–92.

74. Scheflen, *Body Language and the Social Order.*

75. N. D. Addington, "The Relationship of Selected Vocal Characteristics to Personality and Perception," *Speech Monographs,* 35 (1968): 492; Ernest Kramer, "Judgment of Personal Characteristics and Emotions from Nonverbal Properties of Speech," *Psychological Bulletin,* 60 (1963): 408–20.

76. Davitz and Davitz, "Nonverbal Vocal Communication of Feeling."

77. P. A. Andersen, J. F. Andersen, N. J. Wendt, and M. A. Murphy, "The Development of Nonverbal Communication Behavior in School Children Grades K–12" Paper presented at the International Communication Association Annual Convention, Minneapolis, (May, 1981).

78. K. D. Taylor, "Ratings of Source Credibility in Relation to Level of Vocal Variety, Sex of the Source and Sex of the Receiver" (M.A. thesis, University of Nebraska at Omaha, 1984).

79. Peter A. Anderson, "Nonverbal Communication in the Small Group," 278.

80. Klopf, *Intercultural Encounters,* 178.

81. Hall, *The Silent Language.*

82. Martin Remland, "Developing Leadership Skills in Nonverbal Communication: A Situational Perspective," *Journal of Business Communication,* 3 (1981): 17–29.

83. Edward T. Hall, "The Hidden Dimensions of Time and Space in Today's World," in *Cross-Cultural Perspectives in Nonverbal Communication,* ed. Fernando Poyatos (Toronto: C. J. Hogrefe, 1988): 145–252.

84. Edward T. Hall, *The Dance of Life,* summarized in Gudykunst and Ting-Toomey, *Culture and Interpersonal Communication,* 128–30.

85. R. G. Harper, A. N. Weins, and J. D. Natarazzo, *Nonverbal Communication: The State of the Art* (New York: Wiley, 1978).

86. C. Derber, *The Pursuit of Attention* (New York: Oxford University Press, 1979).

87. Stanley E. Jones and A. Elaine Yarbrough, "A Naturalistic Study of the Meanings of Touch," *Communication Monographs,* 52 (1985): 19–56.

88. P. A. Andersen and K. Leibowitz, "The Development and Nature of the Construct 'Touch Avoidance,'" *Environmental Psychology and Nonverbal Behavior,* 3 (1978): 89–106.

89. Klopf, *Intercultural Encounters,* 178.

90. Walburga von Raffler-Engle, "The Impact of Covert Factors in Cross-Cultural Communication," in *Cross-Cultural Perspectives in Nonverbal Communication,* ed. Fernando Poyatos (Toronto: C. J. Hogrefe, 1988): 96.

The Small Group as a System

STUDY OBJECTIVES

As a result of studying Chapter 3, you should be able to:

1. List and explain the major input, throughput, and output variables in a small group system and provide examples of their interdependence.

2. Define the main terms and types of variables pertaining to systems.

3. Explain how these variables can be evaluated for effectiveness.

4. Describe the main concepts of the bona fide group perspective.

CENTRAL MESSAGE

All components of a small group operate interdependently with one another, and the group itself is interdependent with its environment. To understand a group fully, we must examine the components in relationship to one another, not in isolation.

During one traumatic week, the church board—one minister and three lay people—of a new church faced nearly insurmountable challenges. On Monday the board chair suffered a stroke; on Wednesday the minister died. The remaining members, in shock, recruited three other members to help carry on the work. The board had been working to establish a second church of that denomination in Springfield, Missouri, following an unpleasant church split two years earlier. The new church had just gotten off the ground when these tragedies occurred, but members, committed to the project, decided to keep the church going. The board elected Bill, a lawyer, as chair. Sally, a widow whose husband had been a minister, agreed to serve as secretary. The other members included Marina, a college professor; Sunni, director of a university speech and hearing clinic; and Norm, a massage therapist who was also an accomplished musician. No paid employees worked for the church—all the work was accomplished by volunteers, including board members.

Among the challenges board members faced were how to handle Sunday services without a minister, how to pay for the lease they had recently signed on an older building, and how to overcome opposition to the new congregation from the denomination's headquarters and the original church's minister. The board quickly decided they needed additional expertise so they soon added two more members: Don, a retired business owner, and Gary, a maintenance worker. The members had diverse experiences and expertise, but they all shared a similar vision for the church and common values to guide them in their work. The board met every week for two years. At the end of that time, members could point to several important accomplishments: Sunday services were held every week and attendance had increased from about 40 members to about 90 members per Sunday; bylaws had been approved by the congregation; the board, originally an informal, self-selected board, was voted in by the congregation; enough money had been set aside to cover a minister's salary for six months; and, most important of all, the formerly renegade congregation had received official approval from the denomination's headquarters and was now "legal."

We have already discussed how pervasive small groups are in our daily lives and why we should study them. In this chapter we will use the church board we just introduced to illustrate the basic principles of general systems theory, a framework for understanding small groups. We periodically present dialogue from the church board to illustrate how various principles of systems theory may appear communicatively. Once you have a communication-based model for understanding systems principles, you can recognize the principles operating in any group.

The Systems Perspective

When a new person joins a group, the group changes in some ways. For example, when a new baby is brought into a family, all family relationships will change, including between the parents, among the other children, and among the parents and the children. In addition, new relationships must be accommodated—between everyone else and the new baby. This illustrates the idea of a **system**—a set of relationships among interdependent, interacting components and forces. General systems theory is built upon an analysis of living entities—including groups and organizations—as they attempt to remain in dynamic balance with the environment by making constant adjustments.

The systems framework helps you keep track of all the individual components of a small group as they interact in a complex whole. The "group as system" metaphor has long been dominant among small group communication scholars because, in part, its key premise is that *communication* links the relevant parts of a system together.[1] We like the approach because it brings the role of communication to the forefront of what we study and helps students manage the complexity of small group communication. Even when we focus on a small part of the puzzle (e.g., leadership or problem solving), the systems framework reminds us that each piece of the puzzle interacts with every other piece.

However, the systems perspective has been criticized by some scholars. For instance, some have questioned how useful the perspective is because it appears to be a philosophical framework rather than a useful explanatory framework.[2] Others have said that the systems approach focuses too much on a group's dynamic balance, or *homeostasis*. In other words, systems theorists assume that a system's goal is to maintain stability; thus, the systems framework calls more attention to how groups stay the same rather than how they change. Our point here is not to elaborate on or refute these specific concerns, but to let you know that this is one of several theories used to understand small group communication. In the previous chapter we explained the fundamentals of communication. We now begin the process of examining how communication helps shape the small group system.

Principles of a System

The central system principle, **interdependence,** states that the parts of a system do not operate in isolation but continuously affect each other, as well as the system as a whole. The new baby affects every other family member. Similarly, if the usually cheerful chair of a committee comes to a group meeting in a grouchy mood, the other members may feel uneasy and the group's normally effective decision-making processes may be impaired. In the church board we described, every decision was accomplished through open discussion that emphasized member interdependence. For example, for Sunday services to proceed without a hitch, the worship coordinator had to book the speaker and print the programs; the decorator had to make sure that the flowers were in place and the hymnals distributed; and the

System

An entity made up of components in interdependent relationship to each other, requiring constant adaptation among its parts to maintain organic wholeness and balance.

Interdependence

The property of a system such that all parts are interrelated and affect each other as well as the whole system.

hospitality coordinator had to unlock the building and make the coffee. If anyone failed to do his or her job, the service as a whole would be hurt.

Simply put, competent group members understand that this interrelatedness among all the components of a group, including group members, compels group members to be accountable to each other as they work *together,* not separately, toward their goal. The consequences of their choices during the process of group deliberation reverberate throughout the entire group system.[3]

George Will, a *Newsweek* columnist, dramatically illustrates the principle of interdependence and also reminds us that, because we are all interdependent, actions we take sometimes have unanticipated consequences.[4] When the Lincoln Memorial was illuminated at night, the lights attracted insects, which attracted the spiders that fed on them, which then attracted the birds that fed on the spiders. To keep the monument beautiful for visitors, workers scrubbed the bird droppings and the spider webs that accumulated, but the act of scrubbing the marble made it susceptible to the exhaust fumes from the traffic in Washington, DC. Lighting the monument, intended to have a positive effect, also set in motion a chain of events that is contributing to the monument's deterioration. We cannot know in advance all the effects our actions will cause.

Nonsummativity

The property of a system that the whole is not the sum of its parts, but may be greater or lesser than the sum.

Another key principle is the system property of **nonsummativity** (nonadditivity), which states that the whole system is not just the sum of its parts. It may be either greater or less than the sum of its parts, with either positive synergy or negative synergy operating. Sports fans know they will lose money on a basketball or football game if they add up the statistics for each player, arrive at team totals, and bet on the team with the higher total. On any given day, a so-called poor team can play beyond its apparent potential (positive synergy), or a terrific team can have an off day (negative synergy). Why? Because each team or group is a living system in which everything is interdependent, and no one can predict precisely how the new system will function during any particular time or how the parts will affect one another.

A team takes on a life of its own and becomes a real, living entity that is *based* on members' abilities, but is not simply a totaling up of their skills. For example, the then–Southwest Missouri State University Lady Bears basketball team, whose players were shorter, slower, and less experienced than many top-tier women's teams, won the National Invitational Tournament in 2005. On the other hand, the knowledgeable, intelligent, and dedicated scientists and managers at NASA collectively made a flawed decision in 1986 to launch the space shuttle *Challenger,* which exploded just after liftoff.

No one can predict with certainty whether a group will experience positive or negative synergy. In our classes, we have often had groups composed of bright students whose final products disappointed us. Salazar has posited that the amount of ambiguity a group faces and how it handles the ambiguity play major roles.[5] Ambiguity determines the types of obstacles a group will encounter. Whether the obstacles are dealt with in a helpful or disruptive way determines whether a process loss (negative synergy) or gain (positive synergy) will occur. Another factor is team learning, or the extent to which members have learned "how to play the game together."[6] Savelsbergh and her associates found that, through interaction with one another, members listen to others' perspectives, integrate these with their own views, and collectively learn. Teams whose members explored different perspectives and developed collective meaning performed better than teams that did not. In any case, the communication behavior of the members is the principal determining factor for process gains or losses.

The principle of **equifinality** (literally, *equal ends*) suggests that different systems can reach the same outcome even if they have different starting places; the related principle of **multifinality** states that systems starting out at the same place may reach different end points. Both principles refer to the same idea: It is impossible to predict where a system will end up by knowing only where it starts out.

Odds were against the church board's success. A splinter group from the same original congregation had tried to start a new church years before; it had failed. But this church board, composed of ordinary yet dedicated individuals, succeeded. We have observed similar outcomes in many contexts: government, community and voluntary organizations, business, and education. For example, one group of students turned in, at the last minute, a mediocre final paper because members had not been able to find a way to handle their interpersonal conflict. By the end of the semester, none of them ever wanted to see the others again. Early in the semester, though, we predicted that this group of individual A students would turn in an A paper. In the same class, another group of average students had "jelled"—members liked each other, wanted to do a good job, and were willing to put in extra effort toward the task. They turned in a draft of the paper a week early, so we could pregrade it with comments. They then took those comments and put the final finishing touches on what was an outstanding paper. They had a party to celebrate their success. As you can imagine, the communication among members is the key to where a group ends up.

The systems perspective helps keep us from oversimplifying our understanding of how a group functions and perhaps missing something important. For example, systems theory emphasizes **multiple causation,** the fact that whatever happens in a system is not the result of a single, simple cause, but is produced by complex interrelationships among multiple forces. For example, several factors contributed to the church board's successful efforts, including the board's shared leadership, Bill's democratic coordination, the commitment and expertise of the members, the fact that creation of a new congregation filled a need in the community, and probably some fortuitous factors, such as the availability of an affordable location.

Equifinality

The system's principle that different systems can reach the same end point.

Multifinality

The system's principle that systems starting out at the same place can reach different end points.

Multiple Causation

The principle that each change in a system is caused by numerous factors.

Recap: A Quick Review

Groups are living systems that operate under the following principles:

1. A system is a set of relationships among interdependent components.

2. Two advantages of the systems perspective for examining small groups: It helps organize the complexity of small group communication and places communication at the center of what links all the components together.

3. Groups, as systems, exhibit interdependence—each component affects each other component.

4. Groups and other systems are nonsummative—as with sports teams, sometimes systems perform better than expected (positive synergy) and sometimes worse (negative synergy).

5. Groups exhibit equifinality and multifinality—you cannot predict where a system ends from where it starts.

6. What happens in a group or other system has multiple causes—you cannot point to one factor as being the one and only reason why something happens.

Variables of a System

We earlier defined a system as a set of relationships among interdependent, interacting components and forces. A system is not only about the parts it comprises but just as importantly about how those parts become interrelated. In this section we will look at three of the most common system **variables,** which are its characteristics or dimensions summarized in Figure 3.1. As we identify those characteristics we will also discuss how best to enact them in an ideal system. Good participant–observers in a group understand what these variables are and how best to use them to facilitate positive rather than negative synergy.

A small group system works when members use communication to transform information and other resources into outcomes that are tangible (e.g., a written report; a group presentation) or intangible (e.g., a decision; a team orientation; trust). We can begin to examine in detail how this process works by looking at those system variables: *input, throughput,* and *output.*

Input variables are components from which a small group is formed and that it uses to do its work, including the members; the reasons for the group's formation; resources such as information, expertise, money, and computer technology; and environmental conditions and forces that influence the group. In the church committee, members with their diverse areas of expertise were inputs. For instance, both Sunni and Sally had examples of bylaws from other churches, and Bill knew what to do to incorporate and receive tax-exempt status. All this information, possessed by individuals and shared with the group, served as resource input variables

Variables

Observable characteristics or qualities that can vary.

Input Variables

The energy, information, and raw material used by an open system that are transformed into output by throughput processes.

FIGURE 3.1   Model of a small group as a system

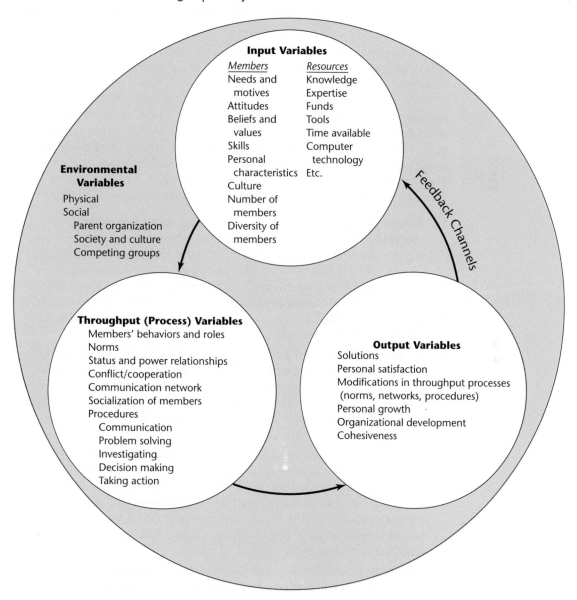

Input Variables

Members   *Resources*
Needs and   Knowledge
  motives   Expertise
Attitudes   Funds
Beliefs and   Tools
  values   Time available
Skills   Computer
Personal   technology
  characteristics Etc.
Culture
Number of
  members
Diversity of
  members

Environmental Variables

Physical
Social
   Parent organization
   Society and culture
   Competing groups

Throughput (Process) Variables
   Members' behaviors and roles
   Norms
   Status and power relationships
   Conflict/cooperation
   Communication network
   Socialization of members
   Procedures
      Communication
      Problem solving
      Investigating
      Decision making
      Taking action

Output Variables
Solutions
Personal satisfaction
Modifications in throughput processes
   (norms, networks, procedures)
Personal growth
Organizational development
Cohesiveness

Feedback Channels

that ultimately affected both the group's deliberations and its success. Consider this exchange, after the minister died:

Sunni: I'm in shock from the past week, but I don't want to give up.

Norm: Me, neither. We're just on the verge of creating something that people have been wanting for two years, and I want to see us keep going.

Marina: Me, too. It's really important for me to have a church where I feel comfortable, so I'm willing to give whatever time is necessary to pull this off!

Members communicated the high level of commitment they brought to this daunting task and their willingness to see it through—important input variables.

Just recognizing group input variables is not enough to ensure group success. Group members must regularly assess how effective those variables are and determine how best to enact them as they strive toward their goal. The following standards for input variables are the ideal. Even though many groups rarely meet these standards, they should strive to meet them. You will note that paying attention to the standards and working to come closer to achieving them reflects a participant-observer perspective.

1. **Members share basic beliefs and values about the purpose of the group.** The church board members made their commitment to the group and its purpose clear: "It's really important to me to have church where I feel comfortable" and "I'm willing to give whatever time necessary to pull this off!" Furthermore, the board members, while bringing different perspectives and information to their problem, shared central group values and goals—they demonstrated an invaluable team orientation.[7]

2. **Members understand and accept the group's purpose.** If half of the church congregation thought that its purpose was to emphasize the split from the original church and the other half thought the purpose was to create a self-sustaining congregation, both parties would have been pulling the church in different directions. Goal clarity is important.

3. **The number of members should be as small as possible, so long as the necessary variety of perspectives is represented.** We discuss group size in Chapters 1 and 5. The challenge to any group, including our church board, is to strive for diversity of perspectives yet not become so large that group members find it impossible to process information, listen to multiple views, find opportunities to participate, and so forth.

4. **Group members know what the group's relationship is to other groups and organizations and what resources they can count on from those groups and organizations.** The church board knew that the original church from which it split would not supply resources, information, or help, but that compatible denominations would provide speakers and consultation to help the new board. The board had a good sense of where it fit into a bigger picture and that it did not operate in an isolated vacuum.

5. **The group has enough time to do its work.** Failure to prepare for the task ahead will only prepare a group to fail. One factor is careful

consideration of the time frame within which a group has to work and how best to organize the work within the time frame. Another factor is whether members will commit to give the time needed to see the job through. Our church board met every week for two years before it considered its main goals met.

6. **The group's meeting place, whether physical or virtual, is comfortable for participants and allows discussions without distractions.** A committee, for instance, that has no adequate space in which to meet regularly will expend too much energy and time just finding and changing meeting sites and trying to get members to those sites. Groups must also consider the aesthetics of the meeting sites, such as noise levels and privacy. For instance, during a search for an athletic director, California State University, Fresno's search committee flew to Las Vegas for its final deliberations in order to hide from the media.

Throughput variables of a group involve how the group actually transforms inputs into final products—how the system functions, what it actually does. Examples include the development of roles, rules, and norms; procedures the group follows; the group's leadership; communication among members; and all the other elements that are part of the process as the group works toward completing its task. In our church board, observe below how certain rules and procedures evolved. First, the members complimented each other and affirmed their commitment to the group's task. This led to a pattern of expressing cohesiveness and mutual respect, which later made it easier for members to contribute freely and frankly. Bill operated as a democratic chair who supported the group's norms of equality and shared leadership. This helped other members feel comfortable to jump in with suggestions or comments.

Throughput Variables
The actual functioning of a system, or how the system transforms inputs into outputs.

Bill: Well, here's draft one of the bylaws! They aren't carved in stone. I suggest that everybody take them home, read them carefully, and come prepared with changes next week. Then we can make the changes and have them copied and distributed for the congregation to look at. Sound OK?

Norm: Hang on a second, Bill. We said we were going to give these to Reverend Lacy [minister of another congregation who agreed to give the denomination's perspective] for feedback. That will take longer than one week.

Bill: You're right; I forgot. Let's schedule our discussion of the bylaws after Norm gets Reverend Lacy's perspective.

In this exchange, chair Bill's original suggestion is challenged, politely, by Norm. Bill acknowledges that he made a mistake and backtracks. This illustrates a throughput process in which members can contribute without fear of repercussion and the leader has no more power to control events than the others do.

As with input variables, the standards to judge the throughput pro-cesses are grounded in how best to sustain effective group interaction. Group members must consistently reflect upon and assess the effectiveness of these processes in order to transform their input variables into positive synergy that promotes viable outcomes. These especially reflect the ethical standards for group behavior.

1. **Members are dependable and reliable.** Interdependence requires group members to accept that they are accountable to each other, and a climate of trust must be created in order to manage the risk involved in such interdependence. Acting toward each other in dependable and reliable ways reinforces this ethic. During their two years, church board members learned they could count on each other to attend meetings, gather information, type reports, schedule speakers, argue with respect, and so on.

2. **Members express themselves competently and are considerate of other members.** Although Gary felt insecure about his ability to express his ideas, he was willing to share his opinions; he did so clearly, and he was encouraged by the other church members. Bill, although he was the chair, often followed his own suggestions with "Sound, OK?" or "Is that all right with the rest of you?"

3. **Members' roles are relatively stable, understood, and accepted by all.** Sufficient role definitions allow members to predict each other's behavior. Marina, for instance, was consistently task focused and organized while Bill was consistently democratic in his actions as chair. Roles also need to be sufficiently flexible so that *any* group member, not just Marina and Bill, could be organized, task focused, or democratic. Role behavior is sufficiently predictable and flexible to allow the group to adapt and change as need be.

4. **Members have relatively equal status.** Bill's external status as a lawyer was relatively high, but that did not stop Norm, the massage therapist, from saying, "Hang on a second Bill, . . .That will take lon-ger than a week," when he reminded Bill of the need for Reverend Lacy's perspective. Equal status promotes teamwork, which means that energy and time is spent on achieving the goals of the group, not competing against each other for power and position.

5. **Norms and rules are understood and followed or are discussed openly and changed when they do not work.** The church board had the habit of searching for diverse opinions, which is why Marina supported Bill when he suggested putting one or two people on the bylaws committee who were most vocal about limiting the power of the minister. Their norm was one of open discussion and consensus.

6. **Communication flows freely in all directions.** There is a balanced distribution of remarks made to the group as a whole and to individual

members. Side-bar conversations between members are minimal during group discussion and members feel safe to talk to each other outside of meetings. Members build on each other's comments rather than ignore or continually disconfirm comments.

7. **Procedures are efficient and members contribute to developing them.** Marina, for instance, had experience with focus groups, and she offered to organize some during a congregational meeting so that the board could learn how the congregation thought things were going. Furthermore, when procedures needed to be changed, the church board decided together how to do that. When the board reduced its meetings to every other week, Norm questioned this procedure by noting the problems it created ("Things really pile up in two weeks . . .") and requested others' opinions: "Does anyone else feel bothered by this or is it just me?" The board discussed the change together before returning to weekly meetings.

A group's **output variables** of a group are the results or products of the group's input variables and throughput processes, including the tangible work accomplished (such as written reports, items built, and policies developed), changes in the members (such as increases in commitment and increased self-confidence), the group's effect on its environment, and changes in the group's procedures. The church board's most obvious tangible output *to its environment* was the formation of a church now serving many people in southwest Missouri. *Within the group,* though, strong bonds of affection, cohesiveness, and pride at a job well done are examples of intangible outputs that developed. In one meeting, after the group had been together for over a year, members articulated their feelings:

> **Output Variables**
>
> Anything that is produced by a system, such as a tangible product or a change in the system; in a small group, includes such things as reports, resolutions, changes in cohesiveness, and attitude changes in members.

Don: As much as we complain about how much work we have to do, look at our finances! We have nearly half a year's salary in the minister's fund.

Bill: I know. At times when I'm swamped and feel like giving up, I think about what we've created and I'm energized again.

Marina: When I get discouraged about all that we *haven't* done and all the things that have fallen through the cracks, I think about how enthusiastic the congregation is, and how wonderful you all are, and I'm overcome with gratitude!

Gary: Speaking of gratitude, I haven't told you all how hesitant I was to be part of this group at first. You all have a lot more education than I do, and I didn't feel like I could express myself as well. But this has been one of the best experiences of my life, and I'm grateful for your encouragement and support.

Clearly, this is a cohesive, supportive group. Could Gary admit something like this if he didn't trust the others?

Several standards exist for judging a group's output variables. These should be used regularly once you are well underway in your group. Regular reflection on the quality of a group's outputs allows a group to better adjust its behaviors and change what is necessary rather than ignoring what is needed or changing behavior that is not warranted and thus creating a whole new set of problems.

1. **Members perceive that the group's purpose has been achieved.** The church board talked about several accomplishments they had achieved, including receiving bylaws approval and saving enough money to pay for half a year's salary for a minister. Group solutions should be accepted by most or all of the people involved.

2. **Members are personally satisfied with their respective roles in the group, the discussion and group work process, and their relationships with other members.** In Bill's remark, "I think about what we've created and I'm energized again" you see this kind of satisfaction. The fact they considered meeting more frequently, not less, indicates a high degree of satisfaction.

3. **Cohesiveness is high.** "This has been one of the best experiences of my life" reflects a strong identification with the church board. Its members, in spite of competing demands on their time, prioritized this board's work.

4. **The group's leadership is stable and reliable.** Bill emerged as the group's designated leader because he organized well, was democratic, and put in considerable work. Yet other members shared in leading the board when their expertise was relevant to the task. If asked, board members could identify this leadership structure.

5. **The group creates a culture that reflects its unique qualities and values.** Each group emerges into its own culture or personality. Effective groups have positive cultures that support the values of members and reflect to the members what is important in that group. Church board members would sometimes stop a discussion for a brief prayer, particularly if a disagreement was under way. The prayer reminded members that disagreement over ideas was acceptable, but being disagreeable to other people was not. In other kinds of group cultures, prayer breaks would not have been appropriate or welcomed.

6. **The parent organization (if one exists) is strengthened as a result of the small group's work.** In the case of the church board, this standard was met. They helped create a viable church that grew, received the approval of its denomination, and eventually hired its first minister.

Environment

The context or setting in which a small group system exists; the larger systems of which a small group is a component.

A System and Its Environment

A system may be either *open* or *closed,* depending on the degree to which it interacts with its **environment,** or the setting in which the group exists.

A group that is an **open system** interacts freely with its environment, with resources, information, and so forth, flowing freely between the environment and the group. For example, a classroom group that solicits relevant information from the instructor, other classmates, friends outside class, and media or news sources is an open system. The church board had a high degree of interchange between itself and the congregation that constituted the main part of its environment, which made it an extremely open system. The board meetings were open to anyone from the congregation. In addition, the board held "town meetings" once every couple of months, at which congregation members were invited to share their opinions about the running of the church. Input was sought in other ways, too, including suggestion boxes in the foyer, e-mail, and through the church's Web site. In contrast, a **closed system** has relatively little interchange between the group and its environment. Its boundaries are more solid and it is limited in its ability to adapt to the environment. A cloistered monastery, where monks interact with each other but have little contact with outsiders, illustrates a closed system. However, there is no completely closed human system.

One specific type of interchange between a group and its environment is **feedback,** which is the environment's response to output it has received from the group. It can come in the form of information or tangible

Open System

A system with relatively permeable boundaries, producing a high degree of interchange between the system and its environment.

Closed System

A system, such as a small group, with relatively impermeable boundaries, resulting in little interchange between the system and its environment.

Feedback

A response to a system's output; it may come in the form of information or tangible resources and helps the system determine whether or not it needs to make adjustments in moving toward its goal.

Recap: A Quick Review

A group system can be described by examining its characteristics, or variables:

1. Input variables are the raw materials a group uses to do its work; they include such things as information, ideas, resources, and members and their attitudes.

2. Throughput variables involve how a group actually functions, what members actually do with the inputs they receive. Communication is the key throughput process; by communicating, members make decisions, manage conflict, establish leadership and roles, and do the work of the group.

3. Output variables are what the group produces; they may be tangible (a report, a policy) or intangible (increased cohesiveness among members, increased self-confidence).

4. The environment is the setting in which a group operates and strongly influences how successful a group can be.

5. Open systems (such as classroom groups) have free interchange between themselves and their environments, with information and resources flowing freely back and forth. Closed systems (such as cloistered monasteries) do not have such free exchanges. No human system is completely closed.

6. Feedback is the environment's response to a group's output. Feedback lets the group know whether and how it must adjust to achieve its goals, such as the outside minister's response to the church board's bylaws, which suggested a few changes.

resources and helps the system determine whether it needs to make adjustments to reach its goals. For instance, a car company that sells many cars (outputs) receives money for those cars (response to the outputs). This positive consumer response to the cars also provides the company with the information that it will likely reach its profit goals. One goal of the church board was having its bylaws approved by its denomination's Ministerial Association. To achieve this goal, the board actively sought feedback:

Sally: I used to know people at the Association, but everyone I knew has moved on. The Association's approval is critical—if they don't like our bylaws, we won't get official approval as a church.

Sunni: Is there any way we can get a preliminary reaction, before we send our final draft?

Norm: Yes—remember Reverend Lacy, from Columbia? She said she'd help us however she could, and she's on a couple of committees at the Association. She could look at the bylaws and tell us how the Association is likely to react.

Reverend Lacy did have several suggestions for modifying the bylaws. Her reaction (feedback) to the draft of the bylaws (the output) produced several changes in the bylaws that strengthened them and enhanced their chances of being approved. This is similar to the student group mentioned earlier, in which members asked one of us to pregrade their paper so that they could improve it. This feedback from the professor helped them achieve their goal of receiving an A.

As you can see, input, throughput, and output variables are not separable; everything influences and is influenced by everything else. For example, attitudes affect interaction, which in turn affects the outcome, which then returns to affect attitudes.

Just as input, throughput, and output variables are interdependent, so is a group highly interdependent with its environment or the setting in which the group exists. Many small group researchers have criticized small group research for ignoring the effect of the group's environment on the group.[8] Some group researchers have implied that the quality of a group's output is entirely or largely within a group's control. They have suggested that as long as the group has skilled and knowledgeable members (inputs) and effective leadership with helpful norms such as a conscientious attitude and good listening behaviors (throughputs), then the group will produce high-quality outputs. This oversimplifies the case because most groups are *not* self-contained entities but in fact are highly dependent on their environments. For instance, Broome and Fulbright asked real-life group members what factors hurt their efforts.[9] They found that organizational factors beyond a group's control often had strong negative effects on a group's performance.

Hirokawa and Keyton asked members of actual organizational groups what factors helped and hindered their groups' progress.[10] Several factors fell into an organizational category—whether the group got assistance from the parent organization, including continuing informational support as needed. Support for this finding was provided by Kennedy and her associates.[11] Team members whose teams were supported by their organizations—through such things as making needed resources available, offering recognition and rewards, and providing helpful training—believed more strongly in their teams' potency, or general ability to get the job done. They also performed better.

These three studies strongly support the view that the group's environment—not just input and throughput variables—substantially influences a group's success. This interface between the group and its larger environment should also be evaluated against a set of standards, just like those for input, throughput, and output variables, in order to foster effective problem solving.

1. **The environment (usually an organization) should publically recognize the accomplishments of the group and reward the group as a group.** Several times during their two years working on a new church, the church board was publicly recognized and thanked by the congregation. Praise and recognition for one's efforts, not only within the group but also by a group's parent organization, are highly motivating.

2. **The environment should supply whatever informational resources the group needs.** Nothing is more frustrating to a group than to be given a task but not the information or data needed to complete the task. You often hear of juries asking the court for more information or the particulars of a case while deliberating. Just imagine what would happen if they were denied such requests!

3. **The environment should supply whatever resources and expertise the group needs.** Groups often receive initial training and orientation prior to beginning their task. When Kathy was a part of her university's NCAA certification, a representative from the NCAA came to Fresno State's campus and briefed members of the certification teams on the certification process. This same kind of help should be available throughout the entire time the group is working on its task.

4. **The environment should provide a supportive atmosphere for the group.** When a parent organization consistently second-guesses or interferes with a group's efforts, members can become demoralized. In addition, sometimes a parent organization can load up a successful group with too many priorities to handle well. Parent organizations should nurture and support their groups and give them room to work without stifling them.

The reality is that for many groups environmental factors are often beyond the control of the group. We explore the complex, interdependent relationship between a group and its environment in the following section.

The Bona Fide Group Perspective   You have probably participated in a classroom group assigned to complete a project. To what extent do you think your classroom group is similar to or different from a "real" group in an organization? Do you think those differences are important? Communication scholars Linda Putnam and Cynthia Stohl developed *bona fide group theory* in large part to correct what they perceived as naïve assumptions about groups; in particular, they wanted to call attention to the importance of a group's context, or environment, which they believed most group scholars failed to acknowledge.[12] The **bona fide group perspective** states that bona fide (i.e., genuine, naturally occurring) groups have stable but permeable boundaries and borders and are interdependent with their environments. Earlier group studies seemed to imply that what happened inside a group—the internal process—was the appropriate focus for small group communication inquiry, but Putnam and Stohl demonstrated that, if we really want a richer understadig of a group, we must understand that group's relationship with its environment.

   First, bona fide groups have stable but permeable boundaries. The boundaries must be recognizable (otherwise, there would not be a group), but they are not rigid—they shift due to four factors. First, group members have multiple group memberships—they belong to several groups at once, and sometimes their roles conflict. For example, you may want to agree with your group on a proposal to distribute organizational resources differently, but if the proposal will cause your department to lose resources, the department members will expect you to argue against it, no matter how you may feel personally. You aren't entirely a free agent as a group member. Second, group members represent other groups, whether they want to or not. We know several female faculty who constantly are asked to serve on committees to ensure that women's concerns are adequately represented. Third, group membership often fluctuates, with old members leaving and new members joining the group. In many cases, these fluctuations are required by the organization's bylaws. For instance, once the church's steering committee became an official board, voted by the members, it was required to hold yearly elections and term limits were imposed. Bill, the original chair, was organized and efficient. Dirk, a newer member who became chair, loved to tell jokes and often got the group off task. Consequently, the board meetings became longer but were more fun (for some people). Finally, group identity formation refers to the varying levels of commitment and belonging members feel to different groups they belong to. New members of the church board, who had not experienced the death of the minister, the anxiety of conforming to the denomination's requirements, and the weekly steering committee meetings, did not bring with them the same intense dedication. However, they did bring in fresh perspectives and creative ideas that ultimately changed the way things were done.

   Second, bona fide groups are interdependent with their relevant contexts, which means that a group both influences and is influenced by

---

Bona Fide Group Perspective

The perspective that focuses on naturally occurring groups with stable but permeable boundaries and are interdependent with their environment.

its environment. Four factors contribute to this interdependence. First, members experience intergroup communication, which means that they interact constantly with members of other groups, exchanging information and ideas. In our church board, Bill, the lawyer, talked to his office partners about the board and vice versa. These interactions simultaneously influenced both groups. Second, groups must coordinate their actions with other groups. Church committees such as the finance committee, building committee, and worship committee had to work with the board for things to go smoothly. Third, members must negotiate their autonomy and jurisdiction. For example, the church's worship committee wanted to make substantial changes in the order of service and the elements included in the service. But it had to negotiate with the board to determine to what extent the committee had the authority to make changes and how to manage those changes in the least disruptive way. Fourth, groups must make sense of their relationships with other groups. Members have perceptions of other people and groups within an organization, and these perceptions may shift over time. For example, one campus department, generally perceived as uncooperative and self-serving, offered to give up a faculty position to another department that was short-staffed. The second department, caught by surprise, had to rethink its perceptions of the first; in subsequent interactions, these two departments began to form alliances and coalitions that would once have been unthinkable.

The bona fide group perspective is consistent with systems theory in its focus on the relationship between a group and its environment. This is an important advantage because most groups are part of a larger organizational structure and must interact with individuals and other groups within that structure. Interestingly, for groups dealing with complex tasks in a very uncertain environment, how often members communicate *within* the group is not as important to their performance as is how often they interact with others *outside the group*.[13] This demonstrates how important it is for groups to match their internal abilities to process information with the external informational demands of the environment they are embedded in. Even nonorganizational groups are also part of an environment. For instance, the environment of a family may be the neighborhood or the region in which it lives.

The *bona fide group perspective's* most recognized contribution is its focus on the embeddedness of smaller groups in larger systems and recognizing that those boundaries are not only permeable but fluid.[14] Identifying a *group* then is not as straightforward as traditional definitions of *group* would lead us to believe. Complicating matters is the reality that many of these smaller groups use computer technology to do their business and interact with their environment. The use of these technologies has prompted even bona fide group theorists to take a second look at this ever complicated relationship between a group and its environment.[15]

Bona Fide Virtual Groups

Most of the research in small group communication has focused on groups whose members meet primarily face-to-face. We began to speculate in previous chapters about how group processes may change in groups whose members do not meet face-to-face. The reality of our global world is that many companies that might not otherwise ever collaborate on tasks now do so with the help of computer technology that allows the members of multiple groups to interact with each other without being on the same site. This represents the virtual end of the face-to-face/virtual continuum described in Chapter 1. For instance, the Boeing 767 airplane is the result of collaboration among Boeing engineers, who designed the fuel and cockpit; Aeritalia SAI engineers, who developed the fins and rudder; and multiple Japanese firms, whose responsibility was the main body of the plane.[16]

Modern-day organizations are rapidly changing. Their employees do not necessarily work in the same place or at the same time. Entire organizations are virtual—that is, they are not an "office" but a network of members connected by computer who may never see each other face-to-face, but contact each other via electronic mail (e-mail) or videoconferencing. The **collaborating group** is one in which its members come from different organizations and form a temporary alliance in order to attain a particular purpose.[17] You will find such groups in the telecommunication, aerospace, motor vehicle, electronic, and computer industries.

Bona fide group theorists have begun to examine virtual groups because, as with face-to-face groups, collaboration is primarily a communicative phenomenon. They ask, *How do virtual collaborative groups manage their roles, tasks, boundaries, and interaction with their environments?* and *How are virtual bona fide groups different from face-to-face groups?* Several differences, particularly in degree, have been observed.[18] For instance, traditional groups usually know where to find information they need, but collaborating virtual groups may be so cutting-edge and multidimensional that no one member has the answer and may not even know whom to ask. In addition, members of virtual groups likely have strong ties to their own organizations and consider their commitment to the virtual group as secondary. Virtual groups often have no clearly defined formal positions of power, so members constantly have to negotiate power. Finally, each virtual group member must answer to his or her own parent organization. The multiple parent organizations that contributed members to the virtual group have their own norms, cultures, expectations, and even demands—and these all affect the internal decision-making processes of the virtual group. For example, UNIX is a computer system that resulted from collaboration between a number of computer companies. At the same time as UNIX was being developed, each of these companies was working on products unrelated to UNIX but that could have affected decision making on UNIX. Virtual collaborating groups will increase in the future, which makes them important to understand.

Collaborating Group
A group whose members come from different organizations to form a temporary alliance for a specific purpose.

Communicating Across Boundaries

In our previous discussion, we emphasized that contemporary groups constantly interact with their environments. Ancona and Caldwell suggest that groups need members who serve as **boundary spanners** by constantly monitoring the group's environment to bring in and take out information relevant to the group's success.[19] Boundary spanners serve three main functions. The first is initiating transactions to import or export needed resources, such as information or support. For instance, in our example of an effective group, Norm contacted Reverend Lacy for advice about organizing the new congregation and help in gaining approval from the association. Second boundary-spanning function consists of responding to initiatives of outsiders. Someone may ask a group member what the group discussed at a particular meeting; that member must then decide whether and what information to relate. The final function involves changes in the membership of the group—new people may be brought into the group either temporarily or permanently. For example, in an unorthodox move, members decided to

Boundary Spanner

A group member who monitors the group's environment to import and export information relevant to the group's success.

invite Gary's wife, Christy, to attend church board meetings in his place as a nonvoting member during a two-month stretch when he was unable to attend meetings. This enabled Gary to keep up with the board information and maintain, through Christy, relationships that he had formed. The management of the group's relationship with the environment is crucial and can spell success or failure for the group. If the church board had decided to be secretive and not share openly with the congregation what was discussed and decided at board meetings, the congregation would have been unlikely to support the church with time, energy, and resources.

Boundary spanning between other groups within an organization—also part of a group's environment—is also important. Drach-Zahavy and Somech suggest that how well an organization performs is largely a function of how well individual groups within that organization perform, with effective boundary spanning between groups a major factor contributing to group effectiveness.[20] Their model describes different ways teams can interact and identifies which boundary activities are likely to occur, depending on particular organizational characteristics. They conclude that when teams have congruent goals and greater interdependence, members are more motivated to cooperate and collaborate, which should improve an organization's effectiveness.

Ancona and Caldwell, in a five-year study of product-development teams, further explored the behaviors of boundary spanners.[21] Their research uncovered key strategies these team members use to carry out their functions as boundary spanners. (See Table 3.1.) When Norm solicited feedback from Reverend Lacy, he was acting in an *ambassadorial capacity* for the church group. Ambassadors check out the environment to see who supports the group; bring in information from the environment in summary form; and may also attempt to persuade outsiders to the desires, goals, and importance of the group. Strategies involving *task coordination* occur when members coordinate technical issues and thus tend to talk laterally across all relevant groups.

TABLE 3.1
Boundary spanner functions and strategies

Boundary Spanner Functions

1. Initiate transactions between the group and its environment to import and export resources.
2. Respond to the initiatives from outsiders.
3. Initiate temporary or permanent group membership.

Boundary Spanner Strategies

1. Ambassador.
2. Task coordinator.
3. Scout.
4. Guard.

Members may address design problems, coordination of schedules and deadlines, and securing resources needed by the group. *Scouting* activities involve general scanning of the outside for relevant information and ideas that can be used by the group, including figuring out what the competition is doing. Ambassadorial, task-coordination, and scouting strategies all involve the group engaging its environment proactively. The last strategy, *guarding,* is characterized by actions by the group to close itself off from the environment. These efforts can be seen as a way the group has of controlling information that may damage its profile.

Ancona and Caldwell argue fervently that a pattern of isolation is not beneficial to productive groups.[22] Successful product teams engaged in consistent communication with their environment. High levels of ambassador activity as well as task coordination are necessary if product teams are to perform well. Groups that remain cut off from their environments are low performers even if they believe they have the necessary information to complete the task or that their output will be judged independent of their process. Although this research involved production teams, any task group should heed Ancona and Caldwell's call for consistent and extensive communication across group boundaries.

The usefulness of the systems perspective should now be clearer to you than when we started this chapter. We can use a systems framework to identify and describe the components of groups, recognizing that each component functions in relation to all the other parts of the system and its environment. The interdependence between group members, the group as a whole, and the group's environment interconnect every person involved to every other person. We are thus obligated to pay attention to our choices and regularly evaluate their consequences if we are to be effective small group communicators.

QUESTIONS FOR REVIEW

 Go to self-quizzes on the Online Learning Center at mhhe.com/galanes14e to test your knowledge of the chapter concepts.

This chapter used the case study of the church board to illustrate many of the concepts discussed in the chapter. Reread the case study and refer to the recap boxes, if necessary, to discuss the following questions:

1. In what ways did the church board demonstrate the system principles of interdependence, nonsummativity, equifinality, multifunality, and multiple causation?

2. The board demonstrated considerable interaction with its environment, particularly with the congregation it represented. How do you see the two main principles of the bona fide group perspective (permeable boundaries and interchange with the environment) operating in the church board? What effects did these exchanges seem to have?

3. In what ways did board members serve as boundary spanners? What boundary-spanning functions and strategies did

members employ, and what were
the effects on the board and the
congregation?

4. In many ways, this board demonstrated
the input, throughput, output,
and environmental factors that are

considered to be ideal. What examples
of the board's inputs, throughputs, outputs, and environmental factors were
particularly striking to you? Were any
of these factors less than ideal? If so,
what effects did this have on the board?

KEY TERMS

 Test your knowledge of these key terms by visiting the Online Learning Center Web site at
mhhe.com/galanes14e.

Bona fide group perspective
Boundary spanners
Closed system
Collaborating group
Environment
Equifinality

Feedback
Input variables
Interdependence
Multifinality
Multiple causation
Nonsummativity

Open system
Output variables
System
Throughput variables
Variables

BIBLIOGRAPHY

Katz, Daniel, and Robert L. Kahn. *The Social
Psychology of Organizations,* 2nd ed. New
York: Wiley, 1978. See Chapter 2.
Mabry, Edward A. "The Systems Metaphor in
Group Communication," in *The Handbook of
Group Communication Theory and Research,*
Lawrence R. Frey, ed. Thousand Oaks, CA:
Sage, 1999, 71–91.
Putnam, Linda L., and Cynthia Stohl. "Bona
Fide Groups: An Alternative Perspective for
Communication and Small Group Decision
Making," in *Communication and Group*

Decision Making, 2nd ed. Randy Y. Hirokawa
and M. Scott Poole, eds. Thousand Oaks, CA:
Sage, 1996, 147–78.
Von Bertalanffy, Ludwig. *General System Theory.*
New York: George Braziller, 1969.
Wood, Julia T., Gerald M. Phillips, and Douglas
J. Pedersen, "Understanding the Group as a
System," in *Small Group Communication: A
Reader,* 6th ed. Robert S. Cathcart and Larry
A. Samovar, eds. Dubuque, IA: Wm. C. Brown,
1992, 5–17.

NOTES

1. Edward A. Mabry, "The Systems Metaphor in
Group Communication," in *The Handbook of
Group Communication Theory and Research,*
ed. Lawrence Frey (Thousand Oaks, CA:
Sage, 1999): 71–91.
2. Stephen W. Littlejohn, *Theories of Human
Communication,* 7th ed. (Belmont, CA:
Wadsworth/Thomson Learning, 2002).

3. Eduardo Salas, Dana E. Sims, and
C. Shawn Burke, "Is There a 'Big Five'
in Teamwork?," *Small Group Research,*
36 (2005): 555–99.
4. George F. Will, "A New Level of Worrying,"
Newsweek (July 22, 1996): 72.
5. Abran J. Salazar, "Understanding the
Synergistic Effects of Communication

in Small Groups: Making the Most Out of Group Member Abilities," *Small Group Research,* 26 (May 1995): 169–99.

6. Chantal M. J. H. Savelsbergh, Beatrice I. J. M. van der Heijden, and Rob F. Poell, "The Development and Empirical Validation of a Multidimensional Measurement Instrument for Team Learning Behaviors," *Small Group Research*, 40 (October 2009): 581.

7. Salas, Sims, and Burke, 584–87.

8. Benjamin J. Broome and Luann Fulbright, "A Multistage Influence Model of Barriers to Group Problem Solving: A Participant-Generated Agenda for Small Group Research," *Small Group Research,* 26 (February 1995): 25–55; Cynthia Stohl and Michael E. Holmes, "A Functional Perspective for Bona Fide Groups," *Communication Yearbook,* 16 (1993): 601–14; Jeremy Rose, "Communication Challenges and Role Functions of Performing Groups," *Small Group Research,* 25 (August 1994): 411–32.

9. Broome and Fulbright, "A Multistage Influence Model."

10. Randy Y. Hirokawa and Joann Keyton, "Perceived Facilitators and Inhibitors of Effectiveness in Organizational Work Teams," *Management Communication Quarterly,* 8 (May 1995): 424–46.

11. Frances A. Kennedy, Misty L. Loughry, Thomas P. Klammer, and Michael M. Beyerlein, "Effects of Organizational Support on Potency in Work Teams: The Mediating Role of Team Processes," *Small Group Research* 40 (February 2009): 72–93.

12. The information about bona fide group theory is synthesized from the following sources: Linda L. Putnam and Cynthia Stohl, "Bona Fide Groups: A Reconceptualization of Groups in Context," *Communication Studies,* 41 (1990): 248–65; Linda L. Putnam and Cynthia Stohl, "Bona Fide Groups: An Alternative Perspective for Communication and Small Group Decision Making," in *Communication and Group Decision Making,* 2nd ed., eds. Randy Y. Hirokawa and M. Scott Poole (Thousand Oaks, CA: Sage, 1996): 147–78; Lawrence R. Frey, "Group Communication in Context: Studying Bona Fide Groups," in *Group Communication in Context: Studies of Bona Fide Groups,* 2nd ed., ed. Lawrence R. Frey (Mahway, NJ: Erlbaum, 2003): 1–20; and Cynthia Stohl and Linda L. Putnam, "Communication in Bona Fide Groups: A Retrospective and Prospective Account," in *Group Communication in Context: Studies of Bona Fide Groups,* 2nd ed. Lawrence R. Frey, ed. (Mahway, NJ: Erlbaum, 2003): 399–414.

13. Deborah G. Ancona and David F. Caldwell, "Bridging the Boundary: External Activity and Performance in Organizational Teams," *Administrative Science Quarterly,* 37 (December 1992): 634–65.

14. Jennifer H. Waldeck, Carolyn A. Shepard, Jeremy Teitelbaum, W. Jeffrey Farrar, and David Seibold, "New Directions for Functional, Symbolic Convergence, Structuration, and Bona Fide Group Perspectives of Group Communication," in *New Directions in Group Communication,* ed. Lawrence R. Frey (Thousand Oaks, CA: Sage, 2002): 3–24.

15. Cynthia Stohl and Kasey Walker, "A Bona Fide Perspective for the Future of Groups," in *New Directions in Group Communication,* ed. Lawrence R. Frey (Thousand Oaks, CA: Sage, 2002): 237–52.

16. Ibid.

17. Ibid.

18. Ibid.

19. Deborah G. Ancona and David F. Caldwell, "Beyond Task and Maintenance: Defining External Functions in Groups," *Group & Organization Studies,* 13 (December 1988): 468–94.

20. Anat Drach-Zahavy and Anit Somech, "From an Intrateam to an Interteam Perspective of Effectiveness: The Role of Interdependence and Boundary Activities," *Small Group Research* 41 (April 2010): 143–74.

21. Deborah G. Ancona and David F. Caldwell, "Bridging the Boundary: External Activity and Performance in Organizational Teams."

22. Ibid.

Developing the Group

The information in Part I provided the foundation for understanding small groups and concluded with a discussion of systems theory, our primary conceptual framework. In Part II, we begin our discussion of how small groups begin to form by focusing on two key factors influencing this process. The first factor is the group's diversity, shaped partly by cultures represented by the members. The second factor involves the members themselves, including how their individual characteristics and interactions help shape their roles in the group. Inputs, including the group's diversity and its members, strongly influence the group's throughput processes.

Diversity and the Effects of Culture

STUDY OBJECTIVES

As a result of studying Chapter 4, you should be able to:

1. Define culture and explain why knowledge of cultural differences in communication is important for effective group discussion.

2. Explain the advantages that can come from diversity in groups and organizations.

3. Describe six major dimensions on which cultures differ.

4. Explain why race, sex, socioeconomic class, and generational differences may be viewed as cultural differences, and describe the differences that have been observed.

5. Know why it is important to understand "deep diversity," the concept that much of a group's diversity is not based on visible characteristics.

6. Describe the ethical principles group members should use to address and embrace cultural differences by acting mindfully.

CENTRAL MESSAGE

The United States is a pluralistic culture composed of many different co-cultures that strongly influence members' communicative behaviors. Diversity in groups is a fact of life *now* and will only increase in the future, which makes it imperative for small group members to recognize, understand, adjust to, and embrace their differences.

Martha, who grew up and attended college in New York City, had always wanted to work in California. During spring semester of her senior year, with her degree in computer science almost in hand, Martha landed a job interview with a software development firm in Silicon Valley. The firm's software development team, a self-managed work group, was responsible for its own interviewing and hiring. Members wanted to have a strong sense of any person they were considering for a position—Would that person be a good "fit" with the rest of the team?—and they had a good track record. Martha would spend an entire day with the team, attending their meetings, shadowing various members, eating lunch with them, and so forth. The team wanted to see how she handled herself in the kinds of work situations that were everyday occurrences for them.

Martha prepared carefully for her interview. She read up on the company, knew the kinds of software it was known for, updated her portfolio of college projects, and selected her clothes for the interview very carefully—new navy blue suit, matching pumps, white shell, discreet jewelry. She was ready!

Martha's first inkling that something might go wrong occurred when team representative Jorge met her at her hotel. Jorge was wearing jeans, a San Francisco 49ers' cap, and a T-shirt with a fish tie handpainted on the front. When they got to the company's building, she noticed that all the workers were similarly dressed—casually, with a certain irreverent style. Team members asked her to talk a bit about her background before they started their meeting, and she relaxed a bit. After all, she had prepared for how to sell herself. About five minutes into her presentation, Jorge interrupted to suggest that he take her on a tour of the building before the next meeting. They left, and the other team members began to talk. "Thinks a lot of herself, doesn't she" said Akimi. "She talks so fast I couldn't follow half of what she said," complained Scott. "She's wired pretty tight," agreed Montana. The group concluded that Martha would probably not be a good fit with the culture of this particular team, in part because she didn't seem like a team player. Within a half hour of first meeting her, they decided not to extend her a job offer.

This story underscores four important points we make in this chapter. First, diversity among group members presents a tremendous challenge to small groups because it forces members to pay more careful attention to their communicative behavior and to give up preconceived stereotypes if the group is to succeed. Second, diversity stems from several sources, including someone's culture, which is the focus of this chapter. Third, cultural differences can exist even among individuals from the same country who speak the same language and have similar educations, as Martha's failed job interview demonstrated. Finally, although diversity is challenging, it represents a potentially valuable group resource and should be embraced, not eliminated.

In this chapter, we consider a member's culture to be an input variable that is a major determinant of that member's behavior. In the following chapter, we consider several personal characteristics that also affect individual behavior.

Information about culture fills textbooks! Our goal is to present you with a framework for understanding cultural influences, but we do not pretend to cover culture in depth. Instead, we hope this framework helps you appreciate the challenges cultural and co-cultural differences create in small groups. We also believe this offers you a tool for diagnosing what has gone wrong and how it can be repaired.

In this century, Americans of Asian, Hispanic, African, Middle Eastern, and eastern European ancestry will outnumber Caucasians of western European ancestry. Called the "browning of America" by *Time* magazine,[1] this phenomenon will have a profound effect on *all* forms of communication. In addition, age differences affect communication behavior in the United States as four different generations must work together.[2] Transactions between people of different ethnic, racial, and age groups require patience and attention to the communication process. And you do not have to leave the United States for these diversity trends to affect you. The workplace in the twenty-first century will be characterized by unprecedented diversity in gender, age, ability, and minority and immigrant status.[3]

We use the term *diversity* to encompass a wide variety of differences, including ethnicity, race, age, social class, education, and sexual preference, among others.[4] Contemporary approaches to diversity go beyond tolerance of differences; they celebrate and capitalize on differences without necessarily trying to force assimilation into the dominant culture of the United States.[5] These approaches demand sensitive and effective communication. A review of how individual and cultural differences can affect a group, conclude that, unless group members are sensitive, groups can experience highly differential rates of participation, poor management of conflict, and factionalism between in-groups and out-groups.[6] Good communication can reduce this so that the potential benefits can be realized. Table 4.1 summarizes the potential competitive advantages that effective diversity management offers an organization. The best teams are able to balance member abilities, so that individual skills and approaches complement one another.[7]

Diversity can enhance a group's performance, if a group's communication process allows members to integrate their diverse perspectives.[8] McLeod and her associates explicitly studied the effects of ethnic diversity on a brainstorming task.[9] They compared ethnically homogeneous (all-Anglo American) groups with ethnically diverse (Anglo, Asian, African, and Hispanic American) groups and found that the diverse groups came up with more creative solutions. However, they also found that the diverse groups had more negative feelings about their groups. To us, these findings highlight the importance of studying the effects of culture; diversity can be an important source of positive synergy and creativity in all areas of American work, but only if we can appreciate and work *with* our differences, not against them.

A person's cultural background profoundly affects every aspect of that person's communication behavior, starting with how we experience and interpret others' behavior and our own. Working with people who have diverse communication patterns is challenging. A first step is recognizing

TABLE 4.1
Competitive Advantages of Effective Diversity Management

Resource acquisition	Companies known for effective diversity management develop reputations as desirable places to work, and thus can recruit a highly skilled labor pool.
Marketing advantage	As markets become diverse, a diverse workforce provides increased awareness and competitive advantage.
System flexibility	Appreciation of varying viewpoints produces greater openness to ideas and helps a company handle challenges and changes.
Creativity	Diverse viewpoints enhance creativity, decision making, and performance.
Problem solving	Diverse viewpoints lead to better decisions because a wider range of perspectives is considered and issues are analyzed more thoroughly and critically.
Cost reduction	Failure to integrate all workers leads to higher turnover, absenteeism, and so forth; effective diversity management saves money.

Source: Information taken from T. H. Cox and S. Blake, "Managing Cultural Diversity: Implications for Organizational Competitiveness," *Academy of Management Executive, 65* (1991): 45–56; cited in Susan Kirby and Orlando C. Richard, "Impact of Marketing Work-Place Diversity on Employee Job Involvement and Organizational Commitment," *Journal of Social Psychology, 140* (June 2000).

Ethnocentric

The belief that one's own culture is inherently superior to all others; tendency to view other cultures through the viewpoint of one's own culture.

our tendency to be **ethnocentric.** People tend to think that their personal native culture is superior and judge everyone else's behavior by the norms of their own culture. Successful communication among culturally diverse individuals requires them to give up their ethnocentricity.[10] The software development team members who interviewed Martha couldn't get past her New York style, with its fast-paced talk and aggressive verbal pattern. In relaxed California, that style says "She thinks she's all that," but in New York, people are taught to promote their accomplishments and talents when given an opportunity. The team concluded, ethnocentrically, that Martha was not a team player because she promoted her accomplishments and spoke fast without pausing for others to jump in. They interpreted her actions through their own cultural filter.

This software development team isn't unusual. Many of us stereotype the behavior of cultural groups different from our own, then negatively evaluate that behavior. Speicher's analysis of a conflict between an African American male and a white female concluded that the participants' failures to recognize cultural differences contributed to the conflict and to each person's negative evaluation of the other person.[11] Leonard and Locke examined stereotypes held by African Americans about Caucasian Americans, and vice versa.[12] Each group evaluated the other negatively on the basis of the group's stereotypical communication behavior. African Americans had worse impressions of the Caucasian Americans than the other way around,

Effective groups, more and more, require sensitivity to cultural differences.

but neither group's evaluations suggested a supportive climate for communication. Perhaps enhanced cultural understanding can begin to undo such negative assessments.

In this chapter we try to sensitize you to how other cultures and co-cultures differ from the "dominant culture" of the United States, thereby improving your communication in groups. Instead of presenting a laundry list of cultures and the characteristics associated with each, we focus primarily on several broad dimensions on which cultures differ. We offer three important caveats. First, from the vast and growing field of intercultural communication, we present information we believe to be most relevant to small group communication. Second, in many instances we are overgeneralizing. For example, when we say that "white, middle-class Americans prefer direct eye contact," we know there is a lot of variation in the preferences of white, middle-class Americans. We urge you to remember that often *there will be as much within-group as between-group variation,* especially for pluralistic cultures such as the United States. Third, small group research into the challenge of intercultural communication within groups is just beginning; however, the results of such research thus far strongly suggest that there is a complex interplay among cultural factors, individual factors, *and* group composition on group problem-solving processes and the quality of a group's output.[13] Although we focus on several factors influencing small group communication, remember that any one factor does not automatically influence member interpretations or behavior—several factors are at play.

We will now define several key terms according to our usage in this book: *culture, co-culture, intracultural,* and *intercultural communication.*

What Is Culture?

Culture

The patterns of values, beliefs, symbols, norms, procedures, and behaviors that have been historically transmitted to and are shared by a given group of persons.

Culture refers to the pattern of values, beliefs, symbols (including language), norms, and behaviors shared by an identifiable group of individuals. When you become part of a culture, you are taught how to perceive the world, to think, to communicate, and to behave. The teaching is done both formally and informally as you learn the lifestyle of the family and community. Small primary groups, starting with the family, are vital to this process and are the chief way individuals become enculturated. Individuals are *taught* such things as language, how and when to speak, how to perceive the world, what is and is not appropriate behavior, and so forth. This process happens so gradually and automatically that our own culture's effect on us is invisible, unless we make a point of looking for it. As with most of us, members of Martha's interview team were oblivious to how their cultural identities affected both their own communication behavior and their interpretation of Martha's behavior. Consider, for example, the culture shock that faced New Orleans natives forced to relocate after Hurricane Katrina's devastation, Originally 9,000 of them fled to Pittsburgh, Pennsylvania, with about 85 families deciding to stay and all with stories about their adjustment to the "Burgh life."[14]

Our definition of *culture* is intentionally broad. *Culture,* as we define it, refers to *any* group of people with a shared identity. For example, a *cultural grouping* can refer to ethnicity (black, white, Hispanic, Greek), a professional grouping (college students, communication professors, nurses, accountants), an interest grouping (hunters, country western dancers), an age group (baby boomers), or even socioeconomic class (working class, middle class). In short, any symbol system that is "bounded and salient" to individuals may be termed a culture.[15]

Co-culture

A grouping that sees itself as distinct but is also part of a larger grouping.

Sometimes a grouping that sees itself as distinct, yet part of a larger culture, is termed a **co-culture.** We use the term *co-culture* rather than the more common *subculture* because we agree with Orbe's argument that *subculture,* which simply refers to size—a smaller grouping within a larger culture—can also imply inferiority.[16] Co-culture, on the other hand, reminds us that "no one culture is inherently superior over co-existing cultures,"[17] although one culture may dominate. Co-cultural groupings can form on the basis of any shared identity. For example, your coauthors consider themselves to be part of the co-culture *professional educators*. We share certain values and beliefs with other professional educators that are very important to us: a belief in the value of education, similar ideas about what does and does not constitute a good education, a desire to place education high on a list of funding priorities, and so forth. When we interact with professional educators (at our universities, at professional conferences, during chance encounters on airplanes, etc.), we take these beliefs for granted—we accept them as "givens."

Each of us belongs to several different co-cultures simultaneously. For example, Gloria is white, middle-class, Greek American; Kathy is white, middle-class, a military brat. Whether a particular co-cultural identification is important in a given circumstance depends on the specific features of that circumstance. Gloria's identification as a Greek American is more salient when she attends the Greek festivals in Springfield and Cincinnati than when she attends professional conferences. Kathy thinks of herself as a military brat when she talks about how much she has moved or when she attends high school reunions with those who went to Wagner High School on Clark Air Force Base in the Philippines.

It is important to understand your cultural identity because it affects *everything* you do, particularly your communication behavior.[18] During **intracultural communication** (among individuals from the same culture or co-culture), much of the communication behavior can be taken for granted. But during **intercultural communication** (among individuals from different cultures or co-cultures), participants must be alert to the added potential for misunderstanding.

Our opening story of Martha was chosen to emphasize that intercultural communication is not limited to encounters between people from different countries. An Anglo American manager talking to an Arabic counterpart certainly represents an instance of intercultural communication, but so does a native of Visalia, California, talking to someone from New York City. In fact, a conversation between people from different countries can be more *intra-* than *inter*cultural (e.g., as between an Anglo American and an Anglo Canadian).

In a sense, *every* act of communication has intercultural elements because each individual is a *unique* blend of learned behaviors.[19] Intercultural communication is a continuum with *intercultural* communication at one end and *intracultural* communication at the other.[20] This is important to small group communication because the more intercultural communication becomes, the greater the potential for communication malfunctions.

Now that we have introduced you to these important terms, we turn to a discussion of five broad characteristics along which group members' communication behaviors differ from culture to culture. This information should be treated as a framework to help you understand where communication differences may originate, diagnose misunderstandings, and decide how you will act.

Intracultural Communication

Interaction between and among individuals from the same culture or co-culture.

Intercultural Communication

Interaction between and among individuals from different cultures or co-cultures.

Recap: A Quick Review

A group member's culture or co-culture has a major influence on that member's communication behavior:

1. The pluralism of U.S. society and the fact that societal diversity is increasing guarantees that groups of the future will be increasingly culturally diverse.

2. The more similar group members' cultures are, making the communication more intracultural, the easier it will be for them to take communication for granted; however, the increase in diversity, making communication more intercultural, demands that members try to understand and embrace their differences.

3. Diversity confers a number of competitive advantages, including creativity and problem solving.

4. Ethnocentricity—judging someone's behavior through the lens of your own culture—creates unnecessary problems in groups.

5. We all simultaneously belong to several co-cultures, smaller cultures within the larger one, whose values and communication patterns may be very important to us.

Cultural Characteristics That Affect Communication

A number of researchers have investigated particular characteristics that differ across cultures.[21] We focus on five that are especially relevant for communication in small groups: *individualism—collectivism; power distance; uncertainty avoidance; masculinity—femininity;* and *high-* and *low-context communication.* As with intra- and intercultural communication, each dimension should be thought of as a continuum. Cultures do not fall exclusively at one end of the continuum or the other; they are complex and exhibit the following characteristics in varying degrees. These characteristics are summarized in Table 4.2.

Individualism–Collectivism

Individualistic Culture

Culture in which the needs and wishes of the individual predominate over the needs of the group.

Collectivist Culture

A culture in which the needs and wishes of the group predominate over the needs of any one individual.

In **individualistic cultures** the development of the individual is foremost, even when this is at the expense of the group, whereas in **collectivist cultures** the needs of the group are more important, with individuals expected to conform to the group.[22] People in the United States admire the person who "marches to a different drummer." The identity of *I* takes precedence over *we,* so they give high priority to *self*-development, *self*-actualization, and individual initiative and achievement. Group members may be encouraged to leave a group if they feel their individual values, beliefs, and preferences are being compromised. This contrasts with most Asian, Native American, and Latin American cultures (including the Mexican American co-culture within the United States). A Chinese proverb states, "The nail that sticks up is pounded down." Thus, if a member is standing out from the group, the group has the

TABLE 4.2   Dimensions of Culture and Associated Characteristics

Collectivism/Individualism	Collectivism	Individualism
	Group is standard of reference; group is valued over individual.	Individual is standard of reference; individual is valued over group.
	Value harmony and conformity.	Value dissent and diversity.
	Value slow consensus building.	Value debate and disagreement.
Power Distance	**High Power Distance**	**Low Power Distance**
	Status differences maximized.	Status differences minimized.
	Status hierarchy based on birth/position in society is normal; people are not created equal.	Status hierarchy based on birth/position in society unfair; people are created equal.
	Prefer authoritarian, directive leadership.	Prefer democratic, participative leadership.
Uncertainty Avoidance	**High Uncertainty Avoidance**	**Low Uncertainty Avoidance**
	Uncomfortable with ambiguity.	High tolerance for ambiguity.
	Prefer clear rules and norms, high structure.	Comfortable with loose, flexible rules.
	Prefer structured leadership.	Prefer democratic leadership.
Masculinity/Femininity	**Masculinity**	**Femininity**
	Value assertive behaviors.	Value caring, nurturing behaviors.
	Value achievement.	Value relationships with others.
	Emphasize objectivity, control.	Emphasize subjectivity.
	Prefer autocratic leadership.	Prefer participative leadership.
High/Low Context	**High Context**	**Low Context**
	Message carried by the context, nonverbal content.	Meaning carried by the words, verbal content.
	Culturally homogeneous; much meaning can be safely assumed. Prefer indirect communication.	Culturally diverse; meaning cannot be taken for granted. Prefer clear, direct communication.

right—even the obligation—to force the individual to conform. Collectivist cultures value cooperation within the group and slow consensus building rather than direct confrontation in which individual opinions are debated.

This distinction between collectivist and individualistic cultures is important to understand because it can lead to communication challenges. For example, members of individualistic cultures, who see themselves as relatively more independent than interdependent, value verbal clarity more than members of collectivist cultures.[23] The mechanics of conversation can be influenced by individualism-collectivism orientations. To illustrate, Oetzel observed different turn-taking patterns in groups of mixed European American and Japanese students versus all-European or all-Japanese student groups.[24] Turn-taking is distributed more unequally in the mixed groups compared to the single-culture groups, with the European American students taking more turns. Equitable distribution of turns is important to group dynamics because it is one communicative characteristic of effective decision making.

Power Distance

Power Distance

The degree to which a culture emphasizes status and power differences among members of the culture; status differences are minimized in low power-distance cultures and emphasized in high power-distance cultures.

Cultures differ with respect to their preferred **power distance,** which is the degree to which power or status differences are minimized or maximized.[25] In low power-distance cultures, such as Austria, Israel, and New Zealand, people believe that power should be distributed equally. The United States is a relatively low power-distance culture; our Declaration of Independence asserts that "all men are created equal." We regard it as unfair for some to receive privileges accorded to them only by accident of birth instead of being earned by hard work or merit. In contrast, high power-distance cultures, such as the Philippines, Mexico, Iraq, and India, generally have a rigid, hierarchical status system and prefer large power distances. In high power-distance cultures, people believe that each person has his or her rightful place, that leaders or others with power should have special privileges, and that the authority of those with power should not be questioned.

Lustig and Cassotta have summarized research that examines how power distance might affect small group communication.[26] They found that power distance is related to leadership styles and preferences, conformity, and discussion procedures. High power-distance cultures value authoritarian, directive *leadership,* whereas low power-distance cultures value participative, democratic leadership. Americans tend to assume, ethnocentrically, that everyone wants a chance to participate in decisions that affect them. That reflects the deeply held cultural values stemming from a relatively low power-distance culture. However, an American group leader trying to use a participative leadership style in a group of Mexicans or Filipinos is likely to be seen as inept or incompetent. Power distance is also related to the *discussion procedures* members prefer. Participation in group discussions and decisions is preferred by persons who believe their individual opinions should be valued regardless of status (i.e., low power-distance cultures), but decision making by the leader, with minimal participation from the group, is the norm in high power-distance cultures. People from high power-distance cultures believe it is appropriate for low-status group members to *conform* to the desires of high-status members; however, in low power-distance cultures, members will be less likely to conform.

Uncertainty Avoidance

Uncertainty Avoidance

The degree to which members of a culture avoid or embrace uncertainty and ambiguity; cultures high in uncertainty avoidance prefer clear rules for interaction, whereas cultures low in uncertainty avoidance are comfortable without guidelines.

Uncertainty avoidance refers to how well people in a particular culture tolerate ambiguity and uncertainty.[27] Does unpredictability make us anxious or eager? Low uncertainty avoidance cultures have a high tolerance for ambiguity, are more willing to take risks, have less rigid rules, and accept a certain amount of deviance and dissent. Great Britain, Sweden, and Hong Kong are such countries. The software group as a whole in our opening case seemed pretty laid back and free of many rules. At the other end of the continuum are countries such as Greece, Japan, and Belgium, where people prefer to avoid ambiguous situations. These cultures establish rules and clear-cut norms of behavior that help individuals feel secure. Members of the culture are expected to behave in accordance with the standards of behavior, and dissent is not appreciated. People from such cultures often have a strong internalized work ethic. The United States is a fairly low uncertainty avoidance culture.

When low and high uncertainty avoidance individuals come together, they may threaten or frighten each other.[28] Uncertainty avoidance affects preferences for leadership styles, conformity, and discussion processes.[29] Cultures high in uncertainty avoidance rely on clear rules, consistently enforced, with the leader expected to structure the work of the group and behave autocratically. They prefer structure and clear procedures. In contrast, low uncertainty avoidance cultures prefer democratic leadership approaches. High uncertainty avoidance cultures value predictability and security; nonconformist behavior threatens this predictability. Conformity to the leader and group opinion is the norm for high avoidance cultures, whereas dissent and disagreement are tolerated, even encouraged, in low avoidance cultures. Lustig and Cassotta postulate that high uncertainty avoidance members should produce groups with greater task orientation, whereas low uncertainty avoidance members should display a more relationship-oriented focus. In part, this may have been a major problem between Martha and the software design group; they wanted someone who would fit with the other members, suggesting that the relationship focus was key, but Martha seemed to be more task (and "me") focused, which violated their expectations.

Masculinity–Femininity

Masculinity refers to cultures that value stereotypical masculine behaviors such as assertiveness and dominance.[30] This is contrasted with **femininity**, referring to cultures that value behaviors such as nurturing and caring for others. Masculine cultures, which include Japan, Austria, Mexico, and Venezuela, prize achievement, accumulation of wealth, aggressiveness, and what we would call "macho" behavior. Feminine cultures, which include the Scandinavian countries, The Netherlands, and Thailand, value interpersonal relationships, nurturing, service to and caring for others, particularly the poor and unfortunate. The United States is a moderately masculine culture.

Lustig and Cassotta observe that masculinity and femininity affect a number of preferences related to small groups.[31] Masculine cultures are

Masculinity (as applied to culture)

The quality of cultures that value assertiveness and dominance.

Femininity (as applied to culture)

The quality of cultures that value nurturing and caring for others.

more comfortable with a controlling, directive leadership. Such cultures value objectivity and control, qualities exhibited by authoritarian leaders. Feminine cultures, which value relationships and subjectivity, prefer a more participative, democratic leadership style. Stereotypical masculinity, with its emphasis on assertiveness and ambition, does not value conformity highly. In contrast, femininity, which stereotypically values cooperation and group-based decision making, expects and values conformity. Finally, social roles between men and women are more clearly differentiated in high masculine cultures. Males are more likely to undertake task-related roles and females, socioemotional ones. This affects the roles performed in small groups, including who will compete for the leadership role and whether women will be accepted in leadership and other high-status positions.

Low- and High-Context Communication

The final cultural characteristic we will consider is low- versus high-context communication.[32] In **low-context communication,** the primary meaning of a message is carried by the verbal, or explicit, part of the message, whereas in **high-context communication,** the primary meaning is conveyed by certain features of the situation. In other words, in a high-context culture, what is *not* said may be more important in determining meaning than what *is* said. In high-context cultures, words aren't needed because members of the culture share the same understandings and can take much for granted. For example, one of our students who is Roman Catholic said she was completely comfortable during a recent trip to Europe when she attended Roman Catholic religious services in Italy and France. Despite the fact that she spoke no Italian or French, she knew from the context exactly what to do and when. In low-context cultures, such as those of Germany, Switzerland, the Scandinavian countries, and the United States, direct, clear, and unambiguous statements are valued. We expect people to state precisely what they mean so that there can be little room for doubt, no matter what the situation (i.e., context) happens to be. The same verbal message given in different contexts means about the same thing. For example, "No, I don't agree with that idea" means much the same thing whether you are in a meeting of co-workers, at the family dinner table, or meeting with your church board. In contrast, high-context cultures such as China, Japan, and South Korea prefer ambiguity, with several shades of meaning possible, because this helps preserve harmony and allows people to save face. In China, instead of "No, I don't agree with that idea," you are more likely to hear, "Perhaps we could explore that option." You would have to be well versed in Chinese communication patterns to know whether that statement means "No, we don't like it" or "We like it very much, but we must build consensus slowly" or "We don't know whether we like it until we explore it more fully." Moreover, you would also have to

Low-Context Communication

Communication wherein the primary meaning of a message is carried by the verbal or explicit part of the message.

High-Context Communication

Communication wherein the primary meaning of a message is conveyed by features of the situation or context instead of the verbal, explicit part of the message.

be astute at reading clues in the situation—for instance, is this in reaction to the boss's suggestion, or to a younger co-worker's? Complicated, isn't it? To Americans, with their low-context bias, it seems as though the Chinese are beating around the bush.[33]

Low-context cultures also tend to be individualistic, and high-context cultures tend to be collectivist.[34] Collectivist cultures operate by consensus of the group; individuals try not to risk offending another member of the group because this might upset a delicate balance of harmony. Ambiguity allows individuals to express opinions tentatively rather than directly without the risk of affronting others and upsetting the balance. Because low-context cultures such as the United States display cultural diversity in which little can be taken for granted, verbal skills are probably more necessary, and thus more valued.[35] But in a high-context culture such as Japan, the high degree of cultural homogeneity means that more can be taken for granted (and thus remain unspoken) during the communication process. In fact, most Japanese value silence more than we do and are suspicious of displays of verbal skills.[36]

Imagine how difficult group communication can be when members from a high-context culture try to interact with members from a low-context culture. One of us observed a student group that included Qing-yu, who was from Taiwan. The American students were used to lively debate and accustomed to speaking out in favor of or in opposition to one another's ideas, but in Qing-yu's culture, disagreement is indicated very subtly. Qing-yu's quiet, subdued behavior in the group irritated the American students, who kept trying to get her to behave more like them. The harder the Americans tried to force her to take a stand, get to the point, and be direct, the more she retreated into her familiar orientation of ambiguity and indirectness. The misunderstanding was severe.

The five dimensions we have just discussed guide what is considered appropriate verbal and nonverbal communicative behavior in a particular culture. In Chapter 2 we talked about several effects of cultural differences on nonverbal communication. In the following section, we focus more on language issues related to cultural or co-cultural orientations. Language and culture *together*, not separately, have a profound impact on shared understanding in group discussions.

Communication Challenges Posed by Co-Cultures

Earlier we described cultural and co-cultural communication rules and patterns as things that are learned, expectations and behaviors that we absorb. The United States contains many co-cultures, some of them more visible than others. We now examine differences in the communication patterns based on race, sex, age, and socioeconomic class. We offer a very important caution to this discussion. When we discuss each co-culture, it will appear as if members from that co-culture display a single, consistent communication pattern, but this is not the case. These differences are broad ones; once you become familiar with them, then you can begin to make more nuanced judgments about how to work better with diversity in your group without overgeneralizing.

Co-Cultural Differences Based on Race

In this section we focus on communication differences observed between African Americans and Caucasian Americans. We do not intend to imply that relationships among other racial and ethnic groups are not equally important. In fact, in the near future, Hispanics will be the largest minority group in the United States as they are now in California, with profound implications for communication. However, we elected to discuss black–white communication because misunderstandings here appear to be among the most serious and volatile at this time. The 2008 United States presidential election will long be remembered for how it brought issues of race to the forefront of American consciousness when Senator Barack Obama ran for and was elected president.

African Americans and Caucasian Americans perceive each other as threatening and have generally negative evaluations of each other;[37] it seems especially important to help each group understand the other.

To some extent we are stereotyping the communication patterns of both groups. However, we take this risk with you because we think it is important that you know and be sensitive to the fact that some communication differences have cultural origins. However, we agree with Orbe, who notes that the considerable diversity *within* the African American community has been largely ignored by researchers.[38]

Foeman and Pressley have summarized research that describes "typical" (although we caution you again that there is no such thing as "typical") black communication, particularly in organizational settings.[39] Black culture in the United States is an oral culture, so verbal inventiveness and virtuosity of expression are highly valued. What many whites perceive as boastfulness Foeman and Pressley call *assertiveness,* which takes both verbal and nonverbal forms (for instance, trying to top someone else's boast, strutting across the street). Black managers are perceived as forthright or overly reactive. In a conflict, for instance, a black is more likely to confront an individual directly, whereas a white manager is more likely to approach the problem indirectly. Consequently, some blacks perceive whites as underreactive, but some whites see blacks as overreactive. Degree of responsiveness (expressiveness) differs; blacks are more likely to respond both verbally and physically (e.g., gesturing often with their hands), whereas whites tend to focus on verbal responses. Blacks make less direct eye contact, but they compensate by standing closer to their conversational partner than most whites. These differences in cultural communication patterns can create serious misunderstandings. For instance, a white expecting more eye contact may be likely to repeat or rephrase statements in order to get the expected signs of understanding (such as eye contact), whereas the black person feels the white person is being condescending.

The black culture is more collective than the more dominant white culture of the United States. For example, Penington examined the interactions of middle-class African American and European American mother–daughter dyads.[40] While both sets of dyads used similar communication strategies to negotiate their relationships, the African American dyads expressed more intensity and greater desire for closeness. The European American dyads expected greater autonomy and preferred more individualism.

African Americans and European Americans express themselves verbally in different ways. Blacks are more playful than most whites in their use of language and relish playing verbal games. Foeman and Pressley explain that blacks *signify* (or hint) at questions rather than asking them directly because they perceive disclosure of personal information to be voluntary; thus, questions are implied so that the person being asked will not feel vulnerable or obliged to answer.[41] In addition, blacks use the backchannel (or *call-response*) to indicate interest and involvement in the discussion. For example, in black churches the services resemble a dialogue, with congregation members freely calling *Amen, Go ahead, Preach* to the minister; such responses would be less frequent in most white churches. Differences in black–white uses of the backchannel, as we discussed earlier, can create misunderstandings and cause hurt feelings.

In the United States, it is often difficult for someone from one co-culture to participate fully in a group dominated by members of a different co-culture. Many African Americans, including some of the most success-ful, say they must behave cautiously and carefully in groups of Caucasian Americans; they can never fully relax.[42] In many ways they have developed bicultural competencies—one set of behaviors for African American groups; another for primarily Caucasian groups. This balancing act can be exhaust-ing, but many African Americans believe that if they do not conform to the communication rules of the dominant European American culture, they will pay a high price.

It also appears that many African Americans and other people of color are accustomed to having their opinions marginalized. Trained facilitators for a series of recent public discussions about democracy were careful to make sure that opinions of all participants were heard respectfully.[43] Participants of color were more satisfied with these discussions and were especially appreciative for the opportunity to speak and be heard. The researchers speculated that white participants took it for granted that they would be able to express their opinions freely and be heard, but partici-pants of color were used to being marginalized, so this represented some-thing unusual. In a small group discussion, such marginalization is harmful on many levels.

Co-Cultural Differences Based on Sex

You will never be able to escape one of the most important influences of culture: the effect of sex roles in a group. Masculine-feminine was one of five dimensions of culture, discussed earlier, that affects small group com-munication. **Gender** refers to the learned characteristics and psychological attributes of masculinity and femininity, whereas **sex** refers to biological characteristics. Reich and Wood found four central themes in their review of research exploring feminine and masculine behavior in small group interaction.[44] These themes do not represent absolute differences between men and women but rather are matters of degree and will help us begin our discussion of sex, gender, and small group communication.

First, men and women differ in *expressive* and *instrumental* behav-iors. Expressive behaviors reflect feelings and relationships. For instance, before the meeting gets under way, Tanya may ask Charlie how he did on the calculus test he was worried about. Instrumental behaviors function to accomplish the group's task. Charlie may tell Tanya he'll talk to her about it after the meeting, but first they need to talk about where they are on the group project.

Gender

Learned and culturally transmitted sex-role behaviors of an individual.

Sex

Biologically determined characteristics of femaleness and maleness.

Second, a related difference is *relationship* versus *task* focus. Feminine expressive behaviors place an emphasis on relationships and are more likely to show that someone cares and wants to help. One effective female leader we know touches base with members of her group between meetings, especially if there has been a disagreement. She fosters harmonious relationships in an effort to help the group run smoothly.

Third, there are differences in *forcefulness*. This kind of behavior concerns how much a member talks, interrupts others, claims personal space, or otherwise calls attention to him- or herself in the conversation. It also reflects the degree of assertiveness and directness in the communication. Men tend to talk more than women, interrupt more, engage in more self-promotion, claim more space, and are more assertive. Men are more likely to say, "OK, here is what I think we should do," versus "This seems like a good idea, but what do the rest of you think?"

Finally, differences have been observed between *individual* and *group* orientations. Women show more collectivist behavior that emphasizes the group as a whole: "We have done a wonderful job of gathering all the information we need." Men tend to spotlight their own accomplishments and personal status with comments like, "I think I did a great job of researching our topic."

We have talked about these dimensions as being differences between men and women—sex differences. However, while there may be tendencies for men and women to demonstrate the behaviors we have presented, these are actually *gender* orientations that can be held by either males and females. Martha, in our opening case, displayed more masculine communication directed at highlighting her abilities, which were read by the others as "thinking highly of herself."

Interestingly, biological sex itself seems to function as a status characteristic in small groups. Propp found that, in mixed sex groups, information provided by women is evaluated more stringently.[45] Information introduced by males was twice as likely to be used by the group in its decision-making process, especially when that information was not known generally by the rest of the group. Propp suggests that biological sex is used as a status cue, and this puts women's expertise at a disadvantage during decision making. Taps and Martin discovered that in all-female groups, women who gave internal accounts for their opinion (e.g., "Based on my previous experience, I think . . .") were more influential and well liked by other members.[46] However, in male groups with one woman, only external accounts (e.g., "Based on research by Dr. Smith, I think . . .") were judged more influential. In sex-balanced groups, the type of account did not matter to the judgments of influence and liking.

This issue of sex balance is an important one. Randel and Jaussi found that when there is only one male or one female in a group, that lone representative will perceive a high level of relationship conflict, particularly if that group member has a strong gender social identity.[47] This finding was more true for men than women. Because relationship conflict can affect both individual and group performance, the authors suggest considering sex balance in assembling a group.

Women appear to understand this relationship between sex and perceptions of status. In a study in which group members interacted anonymously via computer-mediated communication, men were more likely than women to reveal their sex.[48] Women hid identifying information or even represented themselves as men, preferring to remain anonymous during computer-mediated interaction because they believed they had more influence that way.

Generalizing about male and female behavior is misleading for all sorts of reasons. For one, as we have seen, although men and women can and do behave similarly in groups, what might matter most is how those behaviors are perceived. The same action can be evaluated differently depending on whether it was done by a man or a woman in a group context. For example, there appears to be gender bias regarding achievement, with men's performance evaluated as better than their actual performance.[49] In addition, a study of intrusive interruptions in groups found that women who interrupted women were perceived as most dominant (in a negative way) and men who interrupted women as least dominant.[50] Speculation is that women are held to different standards and penalized more for intrusive interruptions, which violate conversational norms. This study suggests that men can use interruptions to control conversation without penalty because they are enacting a more expected, dominant role.

Second, as with any cultural factor, if that factor is not relevant at the time, then other factors will affect behavior more. For example, Canary and Spitzberg found in their study of small group conflict that perceptions of member behavior rested on factors other than sex.[51] They concluded that the *approach* to conflict (e.g., using win-win strategies) not sex, determined effectiveness, with each sex perceived as being equally effective when they used a more win–win strategy.

To complicate our generalizations, multiple factors—such as the nature of the task, group composition, member roles, the behaviors used to cue status, and individual identity preferences—can mediate the influence of gender and sex. As with any cultural variable, we need to stay away from either-or thinking—that is, thinking that men are only *this* way and women are only *that* way, and one way is better. Grob and her colleagues, in studying gender differences in small group communication contexts, make the case that when women and men are treated as being socialized into two different cultures, we tend to stereotype men as instrumental/powerful and women as affiliative/powerless.[52] You can see this dichotomy in the previous themes: expressive/instrumental, task/relationship, and individual/group. However, there are more similarities than differences between men and women.

Typically, women are stereotyped as using powerless speech, such as disclaimers (e.g., "*This could be wrong,* but don't we need to consider the cost before we decide?"), and men as interrupting more and being interrupted less. However, Grob and colleagues found that males and females interrupted others with similar frequency and used disclaimers and tag questions similarly.[53] In fact, they discovered that it was the males in the groups who were interrupted more. However, they also found that when males interrupt others, they are more successful than when females interrupt others.

What are we to make of all this? First, treating males and females only as members of different gender cultures masks other cultural factors that affect communication (e.g., race, ethnicity, age, social class) and also masks the vast similarities. Second, discussing male and female differences within an either-or perspective most often traps us into destructive value judgments—we have to behave *this* or *that* way, but not both ways. We *know* that both men and women communicate in many different ways. Finally, we are studying male and female behavior in groups *not* dyads. In mixed sex groups we see less stereotypical behavior, with members showing different patterns of mutual influence as groups develop over time.[54] Group members are part of a complicated social system, and their focus should not be on whether men and women are behaving as they "should," but on how members together are responsible for a group's success.[55]

Co-Cultural Differences Based on Age

Over our many years of teaching, we have noticed more "nontraditional" (i.e., older) students in our classes than was true 25 or 30 years ago. We have also noticed that events that helped shape us as teachers, such as the assassination of President John F. Kennedy, Vietnam, and Watergate, are things our students know only from their history books. Age and generational differences have produced interesting challenges for us and for our students, who increasingly must participate in multigenerational groups.

Orbe notes that co-cultural patterns come from the lived experiences of members of the co-culture.[56] The significant events people live through together contribute to formation of the worldview and communication preferences co-cultural group members exhibit. Several researchers have examined such events with respect to the four generations that currently predominate in the United States, and have identified a number of key differences that challenge members of different age groups to communicate effectively.[57] The following generational descriptions are, of course, over-generalizations; however, significant happenings—political assassinations, the explosion of the Internet—have influenced each generation's values and approach to life.

The **builder generation,** born from 1901 to 1945, lived through the Great Depression and World War II. They experienced the four-term presidency of Franklin Roosevelt, the polio epidemic, the Japanese attack on

Builder Generation

Individuals born before 1945; key experiences include the Great Depression and World War II.

Pearl Harbor, the U.S. drop of atomic bombs on Hiroshima and Nagasaki, and the Red Scare fear of communism. Most were adults during the 1950s economic boom, when ordinary people could buy houses, appliances, and cars for the first time. This generation tends to be cautious about money, defers gratification, and believes in discipline, self-sacrifice, and working toward the common good. Members tend to value conformity and traditional role relationships between the sexes; they can lack spontaneity, yet can provide loyalty and stability to a group.

Boomer Generation

Individuals born from 1946 to 1964; key experiences include the Vietnam war, the civil rights movement, and Watergate.

The **boomer generation** grew up when television became widely available. Born from 1946 to 1964, boomers experienced the divisiveness of the Vietnam War, political assassinations in the United States, the civil rights movement, the advent of the birth control pill, and the massive mistrust of government precipitated by Watergate. This is a confident generation, willing to challenge authority and tackle big causes. Their sheer size—for a long time this was the largest generation—means that they have been catered to by marketers and producers. Thus, boomers believe they are right all the time, are self-absorbed, and feel free to break rules when they think that's best for them. They also are willing to work hard and expect to be fulfilled in their work. They gave us the concept of *team* in business.

X Generation

Individuals born from 1965 to 1981; key experience includes divorce on a massive scale.

The **X generation** or Gen Xers, born from 1965 to 1981 (dates given sometimes vary), are sandwiched between two very large generations. They were the first to experience divorce on a massive scale and many became latchkey children. They feel abandoned or emotionally neglected, and have a higher suicide rate than the other generations. They believe they are entitled to the good life, and they don't want to wait for it. They want to prove themselves, but feel the boomers aren't giving them a chance to do so. They are flexible, are comfortable with pluralistic points of view, and are used to change. X-ers display commitment to diversity, which they value more than conformity.

Millennial Generation

Individuals born from 1982 to 2000; the first truly "wired" generation, comfortable with technology in all forms.

The final generation, the **millennial generation** or net generation, was born between 1982 and 2000 (dates given sometimes vary). This is the largest generation in terms of numbers, but they are too young yet to have made their influence fully felt. Millennials are the first fully wired generation—they grew up with computers, e-mail, answering machines, cell phones, voice mail, CDs, and DVDs. They have never known a world without AIDS. Major influences include the Internet and the death of Princess Diana. Members of this generation are in touch with their friends constantly through electronics, even though their friends may be widely scattered. Millennials have been doing collaborative work ever since their elementary school days; they are comfortable in group settings, are open minded and tolerant, and are nonlinear thinkers. But they also don't like to conform to bureaucracy and organizational rules.

Generational differences can severely tax the resources of a group if members aren't sensitive to them. When e-mail was just becoming widely used at her university, Gloria chaired a university committee that included builders, boomers, and a millenial student representative. The boomers had become used to using computers and e-mail; the student had grown up with computers. One builder refused to use e-mail for communication; he preferred written memos. Builders, compared to the millenials, resist emoticons and prefer more personal written correspondence instead.[58] Because he was a valuable group member in every other way, Gloria chose to accommodate him by printing out hard copies of all e-mail messages and sending them to him via campus mail. Today, years later, everyone uses e-mail, although some builders and boomers have not learned to navigate the net with the ease of the X-ers and millennials.

One of us observed a classroom group with difficulties caused in part by salient generational value differences. The boomer member, who was the age of the millennials' mothers, attempted to organize the work of the group, to establish regular meeting times, and to coordinate the library research of the group. In her journal, one of the millennial students lamented that she felt "ordered around" by her mother and was having a hard time accepting this boomer student as a peer. She wanted to disagree and to suggest alternative ways of finding information—such as using the Internet for research—but felt uncomfortable about contradicting somebody who reminded her of her mother. Eventually, partly because of the sensitivity of the boomer member, this group was able to talk and joke about their generational differences and to learn from one another. One particularly interesting difference in this group was that the millennial students thought of the Internet *first* as a way to research a topic, whereas the boomer thought first of print sources.

Age or generational differences in small groups have not been investigated much. Studies of media use found generational differences. Kuo found that X-ers in Taiwan used electronic media significantly more than others.[59] Shah et al. found different patterns of media usage for informational purposes, with builders using newspapers, boomers using television, and X-ers using the Internet.[60] Age diversity is likely to be particularly challenging for teams in which task interdependence is high, as in some sports like basketball.[61] These results support further study into the effects of generation-related co-cultural differences.

Co-Cultural Differences Based on Socioeconomic Class

As with generational differences, the effects of socioeconomic class differences in small groups likewise have not been widely investigated. However, numerous studies attest to differences in communication patterns based on socioeconomic class. We like to think we belong to a classless society, but we don't. For example, during the news coverage of Hurricane Katrina's aftermath, it became clear that the disaster plan had been constructed by middle- and upper-class Americans and was based on middle-class assumptions (such as everyone has access to a personal car with which to evacuate). This failure to understand behaviors and life patterns of individuals from lower socioeconomic classes was devastating for the New Orleans poor, who had no way to leave the city before the storm. Socioeconomic class is not based solely on income. Class distinctions are also determined by education, job authority, and skill.[62] In addition, people are readily able to classify others' occupations by socioeconomic class. Furthermore, class differences produce differences in values and communication patterns. Ellis and Armstrong examined television depictions of middle-class and non-middle-class (lower-class and poor) families and found implicit messages about how people of different classes communicate.[63] For instance, middle-class males used longer sentences and generally more complex speaking patterns than non-middle-class males. Middle-class people of both sexes used more adverbs. The word *ain't,* never used by middle-class speakers, served to mark someone as non-middle class.

Communication within the family exhibits class-based communication patterns. Ritchie discovered that families of parents whose jobs entailed a high degree of openness and autonomy in the workplace—in other words, parents of higher socioeconomic class—demonstrated greater conversational orientation within the family, and less conformity.[64] The families that Jordan observed showed relationships among social class, perceptions of time, and media usage.[65] Parents in middle-and upper-class families socialized their children to observe deadlines and structure their time. They used a linear, sequential structure for activities in the home by encouraging their children to do one thing at a time and to complete one task before going on to another. They planned their schedules in advance and adhered to them. The working-class families used looser organizational patterns and tended to do several things at once, such as watch television, eat dinner, and talk to each other at the same time. Schedules were not planned in advance or were changed spontaneously. Middle- and upper-class families perceived time as a scarce commodity that should be managed well and not wasted, and taught their children to perceive time in the same way. Such preferences can produce subtle differences in what individuals from different socioeconomic classes accept as normal or appropriate in a group.

We could find no studies that looked at the effect of class differences within small groups. However, in our own teaching, we have observed the effects (usually bad ones) of communication differences that are class based. A recent book by Payne describes several key communication patterns, related to the co-cultures of class, that can cause problems.[66] Payne, a teacher and principal, has been successful in working with both children and adults from backgrounds of what she calls *generational poverty,* in which a family has experienced socioeconomic poverty for at least two generations. Payne notes that the communicative and daily living rules differ greatly for people from poor, middle, and wealthy classes. Each class experiences its own ethnocentricity, assuming that its rules are both known and appropriate. Middle-class individuals, who include many of the teachers, managers, and professionals in the United States, assume that "everyone knows the rules" for how to do things. But the poor and the wealthy have different values and communicative rules! What are some of those differences?

Payne notes that different classes use discourse in different ways. Individuals from backgrounds of generational poverty use discourse as a form of entertainment. For all discourse, they use the casual register—an informal meandering conversational style the middle class uses only between friends. It is characterized by vague word choice, incomplete sentences, reliance on nonverbal signals to complete thoughts, and a limited vocabulary of 400 to 800 words. The narrative pattern is circular, wherein the speaker talks around an issue before getting to the point. This contrasts significantly with the formal register style middle-class and wealthy speakers use for most conversations. Formal register uses complete sentences, standard sentence construction and syntax, a more extensive vocabulary, and specific words; and the speaker gets right to the point. In Table 4.3, the story of Cinderella, told in both casual and formal discourse, illustrates some of these differences.

The formal register version is told in chronological order, from beginning to end, and demonstrates cause, effect, and conclusion. It follows the typical problem-solving pattern of sequential logic—first one thing happens, then the next, then the next. The casual register version is more entertaining and relies on audience participation. The narrator expects others to jump in and help tell the story. For middle-class readers, the story will appear disorganized. However, and this is an important point to remember, the story has its own logic, an emotionally based one, in which the most important emotional elements are highlighted first.

These differences are interesting, but their point here is to highlight the potential challenges of diverse groups. Imagine how frustrating it can be if you think it is important for a speaker to get right to the point, and you encounter someone in your group with a wandering narrative style. Similarly, can you envision how rude and boring it must seem to someone with a colorful, spiraling narrative style to be paired with a sequential, get to-the-point partner? That is why we think it is important for group members to understand each other's rules and assumptions.

Deep Diversity and Learning to Work Together

Thus far, we have discussed diversity characteristics that are visible: race, age, sex, and so forth. However, these may not be the characteristics that cause group members the most trouble. For example, in our student groups, we have observed that such things as how people approach the group's task causes more problems than the diversity characteristics we

Formal Register Version (abbreviated because of familiarity)

Once upon a time, there was a girl named Cinderella. She was very happy, and she lived with her father. Her father remarried a woman who had three daughters. When Cinderella's father died, her stepmother treated Cinderella very badly and, in fact, made her the maid for herself and her three daughters. At the same time in this land, the King decided that it was time for the Prince to get married. So, he sent a summons to all the people in the kingdom to come to a ball. Cinderella was not allowed to go, but she was forced to help her stepsisters and stepmother get ready for the ball. After they left for the ball, and as Cinderella was crying on the hearth, her fairy godmother came and, with her magic wand, gave Cinderella a beautiful dress, glass slippers, and a stagecoach made from pumpkins and mice. She then sent Cinderella to the ball in style. There was one stipulation. She had to be home by midnight.

At the ball, the Prince was completely taken with Cinderella and danced with her all evening. As the clock began striking midnight, Cinderella remembered what the fairy godmother had said and fled from the dance. All she left was one of her glass slippers.

The Prince held a big search, using the glass slipper as a way to identify the missing woman. He finally found Cinderella; she could wear the glass slipper. He married her, and they lived happily ever after.

Casual Register Version (bold type indicates the narrator; plain type indicates audience participation)

Well, you know Cinderella married the Prince, in spite of that nasty old step-mother. Pointy eyes, that one. Old hag! **Good thing she had a fairy godmother or she never would've made it to the ball.** Lucky thing! God bless her ragged tail! Wish I had me a fairy godmother. **And to think she nearly messed up big time by staying 'til the clock was striking 12. After all the fairy godmother had done for her.** Um, um. She shoulda known better. Eyes too full of the Prince, they were. They didn't call him the Prince for no reason. **When she got to the ball, her stepsisters and stepmother didn't even recognize her she was so beautiful without those rags.** Served 'em right, no-good jealous hags. **The Prince just couldn't quit dancing with her, just couldn't take his eyes off her. He had finally found his woman.** Lucky her! Lucky him! Sure wish life was a fairy tale. Kind like the way I met Charlie. Ha ha. **The way she arrived was something else—a coach and horseman—really fancy. Too bad that when she ran out of there as the clock struck 12 all that was left was a pumpkin rolling away and four mice!** What a surprise for the mice! **Well, he has to find her because his heart is broken. So he takes the glass slipper and hunts for her—and her old wicked stepmother, of course, is hiding her.** What a prize! Aren't they all? **But he finds her and marries her. Somebody as good as Cinderella deserved that.** Sure hope she never invited that stepmother to her castle. Should make her the maid!!

Source: Ruby K. Payne, *A Framework for Understanding Poverty* (Highlands, TX: aha! Process, Inc., 2001): 47–48. (Reprinted by permission.)

just discussed. Larson refers to this as *deep diversity,* which he defines as "differences among members that have at least the potential to affect group performance in a fairly direct way."[67] Deep diversity involves such things as the different types of skills, information, and approaches to problem solving that members bring to the table, which have little to do with sex, race, and other demographic characteristics. For example, regardless of whether a chemical engineer is African American or Caucasian, that engineer is trained to think about things and approach problem solving in specific ways. Deep diversity has the potential to improve group problem solving because it increases the problem-solving approaches and capabilities of the entire team.

However, it can be a challenge for group members who think differently to learn to work together. Yet work together they must, if the team is to succeed. Members must learn to develop a *team* identity that somehow encompasses their individual diversity. One approach is to identify members' diverse features and use the diversity itself as a way of defining the team. This is what the teams studied by Rink and Ellemers did, with members using work-goal and information differences to create positive identities for their teams.[68]

It takes time for team members to mesh and learn to work as a team. Savelsbergh and her associates explain that such learning involves jointly exploring and creating meaning, reflecting on the group's goals and tasks, talking about mistakes and surprises, seeking feedback, and experimenting, or trying out different approaches.[69] Of these factors, having clear goals and task interdependence were most associated with team performance. Moreover, working together is fostered by openness of the members to one another's cognitive differences. Mitchell and her associates suggest that when members value their diverse viewpoints, they will be more willing to share and debate those viewpoints, which enhances knowledge creation and improves decision making.[70]

A number of strategies can help build communicative competence in diverse teams. Jessica Thompson found that when members of the interdisciplinary teams she studied spent time together, talked about trust and the consequences for breaches of trust, talked about the task, talked about the specialized language that their individual disciplines used, and looked for ways to create a common language, they established a solid foundation for building the team.[71] Team communicative competence was further developed when members listened and paid attention (e.g., did not send text messages or act bored), talked about their group processes, and engaged in socioemotional discussions outside of team business. Humor and shared laughter was also important. On the other hand, sarcasm, negative humor, debates related to maintaining someone's ego, jockeying for power, and acting bored hurt team development.

Additional challenges occur when team members are both diverse and distributed. A review of studies looking at distributed multinational groups suggests that developing a safe climate and trust, over time, can overcome difficulties with culture and distribution.[72] This review supports the idea of conceiving of culture as being multifaceted and that cultural differences can cause misinterpretations of messages. However, distance does not automatically hurt team processes because members find creative ways to make personal connections via computer-mediated communication, as Walther noted.

Challenges for Co-Cultural Group Members

Our previous discussion of race, sex, age, and social class has only scratched the surface. It is intended to encourage you to think about your own behavior and be sensitive to ethnocentric behavior that may cause problems in a group. Orbe suggests that members of co-cultures that are not part of the dominant culture can become marginalized in groups and organizations.[73] If they want their views represented, they must expend energy thinking about how their communication affects and is received by members of the dominant culture. There are a number of strategies they use, but they may or may not be successful in being heard.

Kirchmeyer found that minority members of groups are often the lowest contributors.[74] Two plausible explanations for this are that minorities may lack a sense of belonging to the group and that, although they may be skilled in communication within their own culture, they may lack the skills to communicate effectively in groups composed primarily of whites. Because minority status affected contribution levels, Kirchmeyer cautions that multicultural groups may not be using the multiple perspectives of all their members in the final products. This view is supported by Teboul's study of minority hires in organizations.[75] He notes that minority new hires encounter more setbacks in becoming truly part of their organizations, experience more relational isolation, and learn that certain relational doors are closed to them. This represents a significant loss to all of us. Whether we are black or white, young or old, middle class or poor, Protestant or Jewish, urban or rural, we must begin to recognize that differences are just that—differences!

In the film *The Color of Fear*, eight men of different races discuss their personal experiences with racism. Communication scholar Tadasu Imahori, who is Japanese American, discusses his reaction to watching the European American in the film deny that racism is a problem in this country.[76] He observes that he can easily relate with the other men who had experienced racism but were unable to convince the white man of the validity of their experiences. This illustrates a main point we want to convey in this chapter: It is imperative in small groups to invite and acknowledge the experiences, perceptions, and viewpoints of all members. Someone's perspective may be different, but this does not make it invalid, wrong, uneducated, or stupid.

We must learn to work with diversity effectively. When we don't embrace and encourage group diversity, we deprive groups of the ideas, creativity, and problem-solving efforts of *all* members.

Behaving Ethically in Intercultural Interactions

In this chapter we have stressed the value of diversity and have provided information and examples to show how diversity, necessary to a group, also increases the complexity of small group communication. We have pointed out that diverse perspectives do not just happen because group members *look* diverse: Differences have to become salient to the group—and be recognized and deemed relevant to the effectiveness of the group. Stella Ting-Toomey, a respected scholar of intercultural communication, has written extensively on the challenges and complexities of difference. Working with diversity does not happen without **mindful communication.**[77] We have to be alert, open, willing, and reflective if we are to bridge differences. Helpful tips will not work unless group members are the reflective participant-observers we discussed in Chapter 1.

> **Mindful Communication**
>
> Communication in which the participants are thoughtful, paying careful attention to what the other participants' say and also to what they say.

If communication rules can be so culturally diverse, are there any transcending principles that can preserve the integrity of cultural differences, and help members of different cultures work together? We have suggested one overriding principle already—mindful communication. Kale suggests two broad principles that should govern intercultural interactions: We should protect the worth and dignity of all human beings, and we should act in such a way as to promote peace among all people.[78] The following ethical guidelines follow from these broad principles:

1. **Communicate in a way that extends empathy and respect to all members of the group.**

   Similar to the ethical principle described in Chapter 1, this principle requires that you work to understand others as they want to be understood. This is more challenging between group members of different cultures because there are fewer "givens," but there are things you can do. First, remember that all discussions are to some extent intercultural; be aware of and sensitive to cultural differences and view them as potential strengths for a group, not liabilities. Resist making judgments about the intelligence or motives of others. Encourage all members to get to know each other beyond the task demands of the group. Finally, initiate discussion of the differences, especially those "deep" differences that may not be visible. You will help group members move toward greater understanding and empathy if you explicitly acknowledge differences and willingly discuss them, not in a judgmental way but as an opportunity to learn more about your fellow group members and yourself.

2. **Work to incorporate the key cultural values of all members into the group's procedures and outputs.**

    Of course, this is easier said than done, but failure to do this denigrates the cultural values of those members who are ignored. This also means that all members must adjust their normal ways of interacting to accommodate differences. Bantz's work with an intercultural research team provides several specific suggestions for managing cultural diversity.[79] In that team, explicitly establishing common goals and deadlines addressed the needs of members high in uncertainty avoidance, and differences in power distance norms were handled by segregating tasks and varying the leadership styles accordingly. Differing needs for cohesion were addressed by alternating task and social aspects of the work. Notice that these ways of handling the diversity recognized the legitimacy of the differing cultural norms, showed the members' ability to adapt, and demonstrated respect for all concerned—all ethical goals.

    Specific suggestions to help you put these ethical principles into effect in your small groups are summarized in Table 4.4.

TABLE 4.4
Guidelines for ethical intercultural interaction

In intercultural small group communication,

Remember that every discussion is intercultural to some extent. Because we each have unique backgrounds, we do not use verbal and nonverbal signals to mean exactly the same things.

Recognize and accept differences; view them as strengths of the group, not liabilities. Instead of judging others as wrong for behaving in ways different from yours, recognize that each of us is the product of our culture. Resolve to learn from each other, not try to change each other.

Resist making attributions of stupidity or ill intent; ask yourself whether the other member's behavior could have cultural origin. When another member's behavior seems rude, inconsiderate, or unusual, ask yourself whether you could be observing a cultural difference in what is considered appropriate behavior before you decide the other member is worthless to the group.

Be willing to discuss intercultural differences openly and initiate discussion of differences you observe. Instead of being uncomfortable or pretending that differences do not exist, be willing to ask for and share information about cultural norms and rules. When you observe differences, you can enrich everyone's understanding by pointing them out and initiating a discussion about how cultures vary.

Be willing to adapt to differences. Instead of insisting that others follow the prescriptions of your culture, be willing to adapt your behavior to different cultural practices when appropriate. Try to incorporate the key values and needs of each culture into the group's procedures and outputs.

Recap: A Quick Review

We simultaneously belong to several co-cultures that present communicative challenges when we interact in groups with individuals from other co-cultures:

1. African Americans and Caucasian Americans, in general, misunderstand and evaluate each other negatively. In general, the African American co-culture is more collective, expressive, and verbally playful than that of the dominant Caucasian American culture. Blacks seem overreactive to whites, but whites seem underreactive to blacks.

2. Learned gender roles and biological sex differences have been linked to expressive/instrumental, task/relationship, forcefulness, and individual/group patterns, status, power, and conversational mechanics. These differences are too often stereotypical and should be considered cautiously as possible predictors of behavior.

3. For the first time, four different generations (builders, boomers, X-ers, and millennials) must work together in many organizations and groups. Each of these groups was influenced by different experiences and world events, which shaped their view of the world and can make communication between generations challenging.

4. Differences in socioeconomic class have not been widely researched, but there are different communication "rules" for the co-cultures of wealth, middle class, and poverty. In the co-cultures of wealth and the middle class, communication in organizational groups uses formal register, with complete sentences, standard sentence construction, and a linear organizational pattern. Individuals from generational poverty use casual register almost exclusively and tell stories in a circular, meandering style that is negatively evaluated by middle-class listeners.

5. Some of the most important differences are invisible ones, such as how people think, approach work, and solve problems. These deep diversity characteristics may be more difficult to bridge than visible characteristics like sex and race.

6. Two principles govern ethical intercultural communication: communicating with empathy and respect and, as much as possible, incorporating the cultural values of all members into the group's procedures and outcomes.

QUESTIONS FOR REVIEW

 Go to self-quizzes on the Online Learning Center at mbhe.com/galanes14e to test your knowledge of the chapter concepts.

This chapter focused on the types of cultural differences that created challenges for groups composed of members from different cultural and co-cultural groups. One example of those challenges was presented in our opening case of Martha, who lost the job with the software design team.

1. How do the intercultural dimensions discussed in the chapter serve as a framework for assessing the differences in communication pattern between the software design team and Martha? Where were the biggest sources of friction between the two?

2. Martha and the design team were all fairly recent college graduates; all were either from generation X or the net

generation. What are the main differences between these two groups and, if Martha had gotten the job, where would you expect to see the most serious communication challenges?

3. The software team included one Hispanic member (Jorge) and one African American member (Scott). How might these co-cultural differences have created challenges with Martha, if she had gotten the job?

4. If the software team and Martha had been more culturally tuned in, how might they have bridged their initial ethnocentric reactions? If you had been either Martha or one of the members of the team, and you had seen the entire interview disintegrating, is there anything you could have said or done to save it?

KEY TERMS

 Test your knowledge of these key terms by visiting the Online Learning Center Web site at mhhe.com/galanes14e.

Boomer generation
Builder generation
Co-culture
Collectivist culture
Culture
Ethnocentric
Femininity (as applied to culture)

Gender
High-context communication
Individualistic culture
Intercultural communication
Intracultural communication
Low-context communication
Masculinity (as applied to culture)

Millennial generation
Mindful communication
Power distance
Sex
Uncertainty avoidance
X generation

BIBLIOGRAPHY

Allen, Brenda J. *Difference Matters: Communicating Social Identity.* Long Grove, IL: Waveland Press, 2004.

Hicks, Rick, and Kathy Hicks. *Boomers, X-ers, and Other Strangers: Understanding the Generational Differences that Divide Us.* Wheaton, IL: Tyndale, 1999.

Lustig, Myron W., and Laura L. Cassotta, "Comparing Group Communication across Cultures: Leadership, Conformity, and Discussion Processes." In *Small Group Communication: A Reader.* 6th ed. Robert S.Cathcart and Larry A. Samovar, eds. Dubuque, IA: Wm. C. Brown, 1992, 393–404.

Lustig, Myron W., and Jolene Koester, eds. *Among Us: Essays on Identity, Belonging, and Intercultural Competence.* New York: Longman, 2000.

Payne, Ruby K. *A Framework for Understanding Poverty,* new revised edition. Highlands, TX: aha! Process, Inc., 2001, especially Chapters 1 through 4.

Porter, Richard E., and Larry A. Samovar. "Communication in the Multicultural Group." In *Small Group Communication: A Reader,* 6th ed. Robert S. Cathcart and Larry A. Samovar, eds. Dubuque, IA: Wm. C. Brown, 1992, 382–92.

NOTES

1. William A. Henry, "Beyond the Melting Pot," *Time* (April 9, 1990): 29–35.
2. Brenda J. Allen, *Difference Matters: Communicating Social Identity* (Long Grove, IL: Waveland Press, 2004): 5.
3. William B. Johnston and Arnold E. Packer, *Workforce 2000: Work and Workers for the 21st Century* (Indianapolis, IN: Hudson Institute, 1987).
4. C. W. Von Bergen, Barlow Soper, and Teresa Foster, "Unintended Negative Effects of Diversity Management," *Public Personnel Management,* 31 (Summer 2002). Accessed on Internet, July 20, 2002.
5. John M. Ivancevich and Jacqueline A. Gilbert, "Diversity Mavagement," *Public Personnel Management,* 29 (Spring, 2000). Accessed on Internet July 20, 2002.
6. Beth Bonniwell Haslett and Jenn Ruebush, "What Differences Do Individual Differences in Groups Make?" in *The Handbook of Group Communication Theory and Research,* ed. Lawrence R. Frey (Thousand Oaks, CA: Sage, 1999): 115–38.
7. G. M. Parker, *Team Players and Teamwork: The New Competitive Business Strategy* (San Francisco, CA: Jossey-Bass, 1990); R. A. Eisenstat, "Fairfield Systems Group," in *Groups That Work and Those That Don't,* ed. J. R. Hackman (San Francisco, CA: Jossey-Bass, 1990): 171–81.
8. Martha L. Maznevski, "Understanding Our Differences: Performance in Decision-Making Groups with Diverse Members," *Human Relations,* 47 (May 1994): 531–52; Haslett and Ruebush, "What Differences Do Individual Differences in Groups Make?"
9. Poppy Lauretta McLeod, Sharon Alisa Lobel, and Taylor H. Cox, Jr., "Ethnic Diversity and Creativity in Small Groups," *Small Groups Research,* 27 (May 1996): 248–64.
10. Young Yun Kim and Brent D. Ruben, "Intercultural Transformation: A Systems Theory," in *Theories in Intercultural Communication: International and Intercultural Communication Annual,* Vol. 12, eds. Young Yun Kim and William B. Gudykunst (Newbury Park, CA: Sage, 1988): 299–321.
11. Barbara L. Speicher, "Interethnic Conflict: Attribution and Cultural Ignorance," *Howard Journal of Communication,* 5 (Spring 1995): 195–213.
12. Rebecca Leonard and Don C. Locke, "Communication Stereotypes: Is Interracial Communication Possible?" *Journal of Black Studies,* 23 (March 1993): 332–43.
13. See, for example, John G. Oetzel, "Culturally Homogeneous and Heterogeneous Groups: Explaining Communication Processes Through Individualism-Collectivism and Self-Construal," *International Journal of Intercultural Relations,* 22 (May 1998): 135–61; Kim M. Shapcott, Albert V. Carron, and Paul A. Estabrooks, "Member Diversity and Cohesion and Performance in Walking Groups," *Small Group Research,* 37 (December 2006): 701–20.
14. Kacie Axsome, "Uprooted Katrina Evacuees Adjust to 'Burgh life,'" *Pittsburgh Tribune* (September 1, 2007). Retrieved June 11, 2008, from www.pittsburghlive.com/x/pittsburghtrib/s_525237.html.
15. Mary Jane Collier and Milt Thomas, "Cultural Identity: An Interpretive Perspective," in *Theories in Intercultural Communication: International and Intercultural Communication Annual*, Vol. 12, eds. Young Yun Kim and William B. Gudykunst (Newbury Park, CA: Sage, 1988).
16. Mark P. Orbe, "From the Standpoint(s) of Traditionally Muted Groups: Explicating a Co-cultural Communication Theoretical Model," *Communication Theory,* 8 (February, 1998): 1–26.
17. Ibid., 2.
18. Donald W. Klopf, *Intercultural Encounters: The Fundamentals of Intercultural Communication* (Englewood, CO: Morton, 1987): 27–30.

19. Larry E. Sarbaugh, "A Taxonomic Approach to Intercultural Communication," in *Theories in Intercultural Communication: International and Intercultural Communication Annual*, Vol. 12, eds. Young Yun Kim and William B. Gudykunst (Newbury Park, CA: Sage, 1988): 22–38.

20. Young Yun Kim, "On Theorizing Intercultural Communication," in *Theories in Intercultural Communication: International and Intercultural Communication Annual*, Vol. 12, eds. Young Yun Kim and William B. Gudykunst (Newbury Park, CA: Sage, 1988): 12–13.

21. E. Glenn (with C. G. Glenn), *Man and Mankind: Conflict and Communication Between Cultures* (Norwood, NJ: Ablex, 1981); Edward T. Hall, *Beyond Culture* (New York: Anchor Press, 1977); Geert Hofstede, *Culture's Consequences: International Differences in Work-Related Values* (Beverly Hills, CA: Sage, 1980); F. Kluckhohn and F. Strodtbeck, *Variations in Value Orientations* (New York: Row, Peterson, 1961); Charles H. Kraft, "Worldview in Intercultural Communication," in *Intercultural and International Communication*, ed. Fred L. Casmir (Washington, DC: University Press of America, 1978): 407–28; Larry E. Sarbaugh, "A Taxonomic Approach to Intercultural Communication."

22. William B. Gudykunst and Stella Ting-Toomey, *Culture and Interpersonal Communication* (Newbury Park, CA: Sage, 1988): 40–43.

23. Min-Sun Kim and William F. Sharkey, "Independent and Interdependent Construals of Self: Explaining Cultural Patterns of Interpersonal Communication in Multi-Cultural Organizational Settings," *Communication Quarterly*, 43 (Winter 1995): 20–38.

24. John G. Oetzel, "Culturally Homogeneous and Heterogeneous Groups: Explaining Communication Processes Through Individualism-Collectivism and Self-Construal."

25. Hofstede, *Culture's Consequences.*

26. Myron W. Lustig and Laura L. Cassotta, "Comparing Group Communication across Cultures: Leadership, Conformity, and Discussion Procedures," in *Small Group Communication: A Reader*, 6th ed., eds. Robert S. Cathcart and Larry A. Samovar (Dubuque, IA: Wm. C. Brown, 1992): 393–404.

27. Hofstede, *Culture's Consequences.*

28. Myron W. Lustig and Jolene Koester, *Intercultural Competence: Interpersonal Communication across Cultures* (New York: HarperCollins, 1993).

29. Lustig and Cassotta, "Comparing Group Communication across Cultures."

30. Hofstede, *Culture's Consequences.*

31. Lustig and Cassotta, "Comparing Group Communication across Cultures."

32. Hall, *Beyond Culture.*

33. Linda Wai Ling Young, "Inscrutability Revisited," in *Language and Social Identity*, ed. John J. Gumperz (Cambridge, UK: Cambridge University Press, 1982): 79.

34. Gudykunst and Ting-Toomey, *Culture and Interpersonal Communication*, 45.

35. Roichi Okabe, "Cultural Assumptions of East and West," in *Intercultural Communication Theory: International & Intercultural Communication Annual*, Vol. 7, ed. William B. Gudykunst (Beverly Hills, CA: Sage, 1983): 21–44.

36. Donald W. Klopf, "Japanese Communication Practices: Recent Comparative Research," *Communication Quarterly*, 39 (Spring 1991): 130–43.

37. Leonard and Locke, "Communication Stereotypes."

38. Mark P. Orbe, "Remember, It's Always Whites' Ball: Descriptions of African American Male Communication," *Communication Quarterly*, 42 (Summer 1994): 287–300.

39. Anita K. Foeman and Gary Pressley, "Ethnic Culture and Corporate Culture: Using Black Styles in Organizations," *Communication Quarterly*, 35 (Fall 1987): 293–307.

40. Penington, Barbara A. "Communicative Management of Connection and Autonomy in African American and European American Mother–Daughter Relationships," *Journal of Family Communication*, 4 (2004): 3–34.

41. Foeman and Pressley, "Ethnic Culture and Corporate Culture," 295–307.

42. Mark P. Orbe, "Remember, It's Always Whites' Ball."

43. Tarik Abdel-Monem, Shereen Bingham, Jamie Marincic, and Alan Tomkins, "Deliberation and Diversity: Perceptoins of Small Group Discussions by Race and Ethnicity," *Small Group Research* 41 (2010): 746–76.

44. Nina Reich and Julia Wood, "Sex, Gender and Communication in Small Groups," in *Small Group Communication: Theory and Practice,* 8th ed., eds. Randy Hirokawa, Robert Cathcart, Larry Samavar, and Linda Henman (Los Angeles, CA: Roxbury, 2003): 218–29.

45. Kathleen M. Propp, "An Experimental Examination of Biological Sex as a Status Cue in Decision-Making Groups and Its Influence on Information Use," *Small Group Research,* 26 (November 1995): 451–74.

46. Judith Taps and Patricia Y. Martin, "Gender Composition, Attributional Accounts, and Women's Influence and Likability in Task Groups," *Small Group Research,* 21 (November 1990): 471–91.

47. Amy E. Randel and Kimberly S. Jaussi, "Gender Social and Personal Identity, Sex Dissimilarity, Relationship Conflict, and Asymmetrical Effects," *Small Group Research* 39 (August 2008): 468–91.

48. Andrew J. Flanagin, Vanessa Tiyaamornwong, Joan O'Connor, and David R. Seibold, "Computer-Mediated Group Work: The Interaction of Member Sex and Anonymity," *Communication Research, 29* (February 2002): 66–93.

49. Priya Raghubir and Ana Valenzuela, "Male–Female Dynamics in Groups: A Field Study of The Weakest Link," *Small Group Research* 41 (2010): 41–70.

50. Jeff Youngquist, "The Effect of Interruptions and Dyad Gender Combination on Perceptions of Interpersonal Dominance," *Communication Studies* 60 (April-June 2009): 147–63.

51. Daniel Canary and Brian Spitzberg, "Appropriateness and Effectiveness Perceptions of Conflict Strategies, *Human Communication Research,* 14 (1987): 93–118.

52. Lindsey Grob, Renee A. Meyers, and Renee Schuh, "Powerful/Powerless Language Use in Group Interactions: Sex Differences or Similarities?," *Communication Quarterly,* 45 (Summer 1997): 282–303.

53. Ibid.

54. Ibid.

55. Susan B. Shimanoff and Mercilee M. Jenkins, "Leadership and Gender: Challenging Assumptions and Recognizing Resources," in *Small Group Communication: Theory and Practice,* 7th ed., eds. Robert S. Cathcart, Larry A. Samovar, and Linda D. Henman (Madison, WI: Brown & Benchmark, 1996): 327–44.

56. Mark P. Orbe, "From the Standpoint(s) of Traditionally Muted Groups."

57. This information is synthesized from the following sources: Rick Hicks and Kathy Hicks, *Boomers, X-ers, and Other Strangers: Understanding the Generational Differences that Divide Us* (Wheaton, IL: Tyndale, 1999); Therese Kattner, "Best Practices for Working with Millennial Students," *Student Affairs Leader,* 37 (2009): 5; Lynne C. Lancaster and David Stillman, *When Generations Collide: Who They Are, Why They Clash, and How to Solve the Generational Puzzle at Work* (New York: Collins Business, 2002); and Bruce Tulgan, *Not Everyone Gets a Trophy: How to Manage Generation Y* (San Francisco,CA: Jossey-Bass, 2009).

58. Franklin B. Krohn, "A Generational Approach to Using Emoticons as Nonverbal Communication," *Journal of Technical Writing and Communication,* 34 (2004): 321–28.

59. Cheng Kuo, "Consumer Styles and Media Uses of Generation X-ers in Taiwan," *Asian Journal of Communication,* 9 (1) (1999): 21–49.

60. Dhavan V. Shah, Nojin Kwak, and R. Lance Holbert, " 'Connecting' and 'Disconnecting' with Civic Life: Patterns of Internet Use and the Production of Social Capital," *Political Communication,* 18 (April 2001): 141–62.

61. Thomas A. Timmerman, "Racial Diversity, Age Diversity, Interdependence, and Team Performance," *Small Group Research,* 31 (October 2000): 592–606.

62. Mary R. Jackman, "The Subjective Meaning of Social Class Identification in the United States," *Public Opinion Quarterly,* 43 (Winter 1979): 443–62.

63. Donald G. Ellis and Blake Armstrong, "Class, Gender, and Code on Prime-Time Television," *Communication Quarterly,* 37 (Summer 1989): 157–69.

64. David L. Ritchie, "Parents' Workplace Experiences and Family Communication Patterns," *Communication Research,* 24 (April 1997): 175–87.

65. Amy B. Jordan, "Social Class, Temporal Orientation, and Mass Media Use within the Family System," *Critical Studies in Mass Communication,* 9 (December 1992): 374–86.

66. Ruby K. Payne, *A Framework for Understanding Poverty.* Highlands, TX: aha! Process, Inc., 2001.

67. James R. Larson Jr., "Deep Diversity and Strong Synergy: Modeling the Impact of Variability in Members' Problem-Solving Strategies on Group Problem-Solving Performance," *Small Group Research*, 38 (June 2007): 414.

68. Floor Rink and Naomi Ellemers, "Defining the Common Feature: Task-Related Differences as the Basis for Dyadic Identity," *British Journal of Social Psychology,* 46 (2007): 499–515.

69. Chantal M. J. H. Savelsbergh, Beatrice I. J. M. van der Heijden, and Rob F. Poell, "The Development and Empirical Validation of a Multidimensional Measurement Instrument for Team Learning Behaviors," *Small Group Research,* 40 (October 2009): 578–607.

70. Rebecca Mitchell, Stephen Nicholas, and Brendan Boyle, "The Role of Openness to Cognitive Diversity and Group Processes in Knowledge Creation," *Small Group Research*, 40 (October 2009): 535–54.

71. Jessica Leigh Thompson, "Building Collective Communication Competence in Interdisciplinary Research Teams," *Journal of Applied Communication Research*, 37 (August 2009): 278–97.

72. Stacey L. Connaughton and Marissa Shuffler, "Multinational and Multicultural Distributed Teams: A Review and Future Agenda," *Small Group Research*, 38 (June 2007): 387–412.

73. Mark P. Orbe, "From the Standpoint(s) of Traditionally Muted Groups."

74. C. Kirchmeyer and A. Cohen, "Multicultural Groups: Their Performance and Reactions with Constructive Conflict," *Group & Organization Management,* 17 (1992): 153–70; C. Kirchmeyer, "Multicultural Task Groups: An Account of the Low Contribution Level of Minorities," *Small Group Research,* 24 (February 1993): 127–48.

75. J. C. Bruno Teboul, "Racial/Ethnic 'Encounter' in the Workplace: Uncertainty, Information-Seeking, and Learning Patterns among Racial/Ethnic Majority and Minority New Hires," *The Howard Journal of Communication,* 10 (April–June 1999): 97–121.

76. Tadasu Todd Imahori, "On Becoming 'American,'" in *Among Us: Essays on Identity, Belonging, and Intercultural Competence,* eds. Myron W. Lustig and Jolene Koester (New York: Longman, 2000): 68–77.

77. Stella Ting-Toomey, *Communication Across Cultures* (New York: Guilford Press, 1999): 45–54, 261–76.

78. David W. Kale, "Ethics in Intercultural Communication," in *Intercultural Communication: A Reader,* 6th ed., eds. Larry A. Samovar and Richard E. Porter (Belmont, CA: Wadsworth, 1991).

79. Charles R. Bantz, "Cultural Diversity and Group Cross-Cultural Team Research," *Journal of Applied Communication Research,* 21 (February 1993): 1–20.

The Members and Their Roles

STUDY OBJECTIVES

As a result of studying Chapter 5, you should be able to:

1. Know how many members should compose a specific small group.

2. Describe characteristics such as communication apprehension, cognitive complexity, self-monitoring, and preference for procedural order and explain how each can affect problem-solving discussions.

3. Describe personality characteristics, such as those described by the Myers-Briggs Type Indicator®, agreeableness, conscientiousness, and openness to experience, and explain how each can affect group discussion.

4. Differentiate between formal and informal roles and describe how informal roles emerge from within the group.

5. Describe task-oriented, maintenance (relationship-oriented), and self-centered behaviors that constitute members' roles.

6. Explain how group members can manage the conflicts that arise when membership in one group competes with membership in another.

CENTRAL MESSAGE

The number of members, their personal characteristics, and their attitudes are input variables that help shape the group's throughput processes, including the interaction and the development of member roles.

Advertising agencies typically accomplish much of their work in teams. A client—a restaurant, a line of cosmetics, a nonprofit organization—is assigned a team of individuals. One particular agency we know about had an exceptionally productive and successful team of five people. Ben, the team's leader, was the head of retail advertising and handled the meetings. Candi, the account executive, served as liaison between the agency and the client. The others described her as "buttoned down." Marija was the media buyer, Vinnie was the art director, and Toni was the copywriter. The team members took it as a matter of personal pride that they were often given the most demanding clients and toughest assignments. The team also represented a variety of perspectives and work styles. A team can derail if members don't know how to work with others whose styles, perspectives, and approaches are different. But members of this team worked well together. Ben and especially Candi were highly task focused and able to keep everyone on track. Both took seriously their responsibilities for keeping the project within budget. But they both truly appreciated Vinnie and Toni who, although sometimes taking the group's discussion on a tangent, often came up with just the right theme, just the right visual image, or just the right slogan for a particular ad campaign. Marija, the number cruncher, had an excellent command of figures about how much exposure per dollar various media would provide. Toni, although usually fulfilling a creative role, consistently helped the team focus on the project by asking lots of questions about the client, the target market, the product, and the main images the client wanted to project. While other teams might self-destruct over differences in work styles, these open-minded, committed, and competent members had learned to appreciate and work with their differences, and they were highly successful.

Both the individual characteristics of members and their mix affect how a small group functions and how productive it is. LaFasto and Larson, in their study of outstanding teams of all sorts, discovered that excellent team members possessed two overall competencies, a working knowledge of the problem and the ability to work in a team.[1] They found six specific factors that mattered the most: experience, problem-solving ability, communication that was both open and supportive, a desire to act rather than be passive, and a personal style that was positive and optimistic. Members of the advertising team in our story demonstrated all of these characteristics. In Chapter 4 we discussed cultural influences that affect member behaviors. Here, we describe how the number of members and their individual characteristics can help produce a winning team.

Group Size

Theoretically, each member brings some different knowledge, perspectives, and skills relevant to the group's purpose. For complex, nonroutine problems, groups of individuals with diverse skills, information, and perspectives

As groups get larger, they are harder to coordinate, have less equal participation rates, and are less satisfying than smaller groups.

are more effective than homogeneous groups.[2] But that does *not* mean the more, the better. At some point, adding members costs more in coordination time and energy than it benefits. Size becomes a disadvantage if it makes consensus difficult or action impossible.[3] Our guiding rule for group size is Thelen's principle of **least-sized groups:** A group should be as small as possible, so long as it has all the expertise and diverse points of view necessary to complete the task well.[4]

Somehow, we must strike a balance between diversity and size. A tiny group of only three members may feel constrained and tense,[5] but a large group may feel chaotic because it is much more complex. In a three-person group, only three two-person relationships can exist, but in a ten-person group, there can be 45 relationships! Other effects of increased size include unevenness of participation, with a tendency for one person to do more talking.[6] In addition, leadership becomes more centralized and formal, with leaders having to focus on keeping order. Member satisfaction and cohesiveness decrease, but competitiveness, aggression, withdrawal, and fragmentation of work increase.[7] These negative effects can be overcome with a teambuilding program,[8] which we discuss in Chapter 8.

Other factors being equal, a group of three to eight members is best for participant satisfaction and cohesiveness, with some advantage for smaller groups.[9] Groups of three to eight were much more productive and advanced as a team than groups of nine or more members, but smaller groups of three or four members were the most productive and advanced. This size is small enough for informal interaction, gives everyone a chance to speak up, keeps down social loafing (nonparticipation), and makes consensus easier to achieve, yet provides the diverse information and points of view needed for quality decisions. In practice, many groups are larger for reasons that have little to do with efficiency or effectiveness (such as for political reasons). Our advertising group was the perfect size for effective group work.

Least-Sized Group

The principle that the ideal group contains as few members as possible so long as all necessary perspectives and skills are represented.

Personal Traits

A small group's most important resource is its members. Your personal traits are major factors that help determine whether a group succeeds or fails. Hirokawa and his colleagues analyzed stories group members told to explain why groups succeed or fail.[10] Members who helped their groups succeed were knowledgeable and skillful, highly motivated to complete the task well, willing to listen and share information, and expressed pleasure—as well as fear—about the task. On the other hand, group failure was attributed to members who were selfish and resentful, were either overconfident and cocky or demonstrated no enthusiasm for the task, failed to share information, and were poor listeners. Your traits and personality characteristics, discussed later, are the fundamental input variables that contribute to your competence as a group member.

A **trait** is a consistent pattern of behavior or other observable characteristic and is influenced by both genetics and environment. Some traits (e.g., your eye color) are unchangeable, but others can be modified. When we refer to traits in this section, we acknowledge that you may have a predisposition to behave in a certain way, but we also think you have some ability to change your behavior. Our behavior is also determined by our attitudes. An **attitude** is a cluster of values and beliefs someone holds about another person or types of people, an object, or a concept. We infer attitudes from what people say and do. We study individual traits, characteristics, and attitudes in a small group course because research has confirmed that some traits and attitudes are better for groups than others.[11]

A number of personal traits have been shown to influence behavior in groups, including psychological sex type[12] and verbal argumentativeness.[13] We will now discuss four general traits and characteristics that have a significant bearing on the type of group member someone can be: communication apprehension, cognitive complexity, self-monitoring, and preference for procedural order.

Communication Apprehension

Communication apprehension is the anxiety or fear that people experience when they try to speak in a variety of social situations, including in small groups. Sometimes called *shyness* or *reticence,* communication apprehension (CA) has been extensively researched, particularly by James McCroskey and his associates. They note that high CA has far greater negative repercussions in group settings than other settings.[14] For example, high CA group members speak much less than members low in CA, choose seats where leaders can overlook them, make more irrelevant comments, are less likely to become a group's leader, and are more likely to express strong agreement, even when inwardly they disagree. High CAs are perceived as making little contribution to the group, with others seeing them as less desirable

Trait

A relatively enduring, consistent pattern of behavior or other observable characteristic.

Attitude

A network of beliefs and values, not directly measurable, that a person holds toward an object, person, or concept; produces a tendency to react in specific ways toward that object, person, or concept.

Communication Apprehension

Anxiety or fear of speaking in a variety of social situations, including in group settings; reticence; shyness.

members than low CAs. High CAs even have a lower opinion of *themselves* than other members have of them.[15]

Some reticence about speaking has a cultural origin. Porter and Samovar explain that in certain cultures, particularly high-context ones (see Chapter 4), people do not rely on verbal communication to the same extent as people in low-context cultures like the United States and are sometimes suspicious of people who talk a lot.[16] A member from this type of culture may have a very difficult time adapting to the noisy, verbal, direct communication style of most Americans. It is particularly important for others in the group to recognize this possible source of reticence to communicate and to demonstrate patience.

Regardless of where CA originates, group members must be willing to speak up, an important ethical principle described in Chapter 1. People who do not talk actually harm the group by sucking the energy out of it and taking up space that a contributing member might have occupied. How successful would the ad team be, for instance, if Marija decided not to share information about which television show or magazine best matched the target market for a particular ad campaign? High CAs communicate in a **nonassertive,** or passive, way, which frustrates other members. They go along with the majority, even when they disagree, as depicted in Figure 5.1. Some passive members exhibit **passive-aggressive behavior** that appears to be cooperative but sabotages the group. Instead of confronting or disagreeing openly, passive-aggressive members will openly agree with the group, but will sabotage by "forgetting" to do an assignment, being late with a crucial report, or failing to attend a meeting.

Nonassertive Behavior

Nonassertive behavior or passiveness, that allows one's own rights and beliefs to be ignored or dominated, often to avoid conflict; impairs good decision making.

Passive-Aggressive Behavior

Behavior that appears on the surface to be cooperative but subtly sabotages group work, such as when members "forget" to carry out assignment.

FIGURE 5.1
Passive "yessers" do not express genuine agreement

FIGURE 5.2
Assertiveness
lies between
aggressiveness and
nonassertiveness

Aggressive	Assertive	Nonassertive (passive)

Aggressiveness

Behavior designed
to win or dominate
that fails to respect
the rights or beliefs
of others.

Just as bad for group productivity is **aggressive** communication behavior. Aggressive people try to force their ideas and practices on others. They are conversational bullies who name-call, demand, insult, threaten, shout, and frequently drown out others who are trying to speak. Rather than challenging ideas, information, or reasoning, they attack other people. Aggressiveness can come from cultural practices, psychopathology, inability to handle frustration, or just a lack of verbal skills for dealing with conflict.[17] No matter what the cause, aggressive behavior destroys productive discussion and teamwork. It violates the ethical principles we presented in Chapter 1.

Assertiveness

Behavior that shows
respect both for
your own and others'
rights, in contrast to
passive and aggres-
sive behavior.

Ideally, group members should speak in an effective, *assertive* way. **Assertiveness** refers to communication behavior that reflects respect for yourself as well as for other group members. Assertiveness lies on a continuum, illustrated in Figure 5.2. Assertive members communicate to others as equals; they are *both* clear and direct, *and* also sensitive to others. In contrast to aggressors and passive members, assertive members disagree openly and explain why. Even more important, they try hard to understand the perspectives and ideas of the other members so they can help find a mutually satisfactory solution. They are, in effect, ethical participant-observers (see Chapter 1). Consider the following exchange from the ad team:

Ben: I think we should recommend that Ozarks Glass Studio buy a full-page color ad in *417 Magazine* to promote its glassblowing classes.

Marija: Ordinarily, I might agree with you, but Ozarks Glass Studio has a natural demographic—people who like the arts, people who hang out downtown, and people who have plenty of time and disposable income. That matches the demographic of the public radio station, which I think is a better buy. *417 Magazine* hits businesspeople, but public radio hits businesspeople *and* arts-oriented folks. (*Marija went on to provide specific facts and figures.*)

Notice that, in this exchange, Marija neither caved in to Ben nor tried to shout him down. She assertively stated her position and attempted to persuade with facts. That's what she *should* do as a good group member— speak up! And, she should also be open to persuasion by Ben, who may himself have relevant facts about where Ozarks Glass Studio should advertise. If you want to know how assertive you are, complete the Assertiveness Rating Scale in Figure 12.3 in Chapter 12.

If you are relatively high in CA and a passive communicator, what can you do? If you are willing to engage in small group activities, this exposure itself may lessen your anxieties.[18] McCroskey and Richmond add that an in-depth understanding of the communication process and of specific skills can help, too.

Cognitive Complexity

How members act in discussions of complex problems, especially when there are wide differences among members' perspectives and preexisting beliefs, is seriously affected by a trait psychologists call *cognitive complexity*. **Cognitive complexity** refers to an individual's ability to interpret multiple signals simultaneously: how much information someone can absorb, process, and make sense of. Cognitive complexity is a measure of simple-to-complex thinking—do you think in only either/or terms, or can you perceive shades of gray? Compared to people low in cognitive complexity, people high in cognitive complexity use more complex arguments in speaking, can integrate their goals with those of others in these arguments, and do a better job of building on others' feelings and beliefs during discussion.[19] Cognitively complex members ask more questions and provide more objective information during discussions of class policies than do their less developed classmates; they do not presume to know the other's viewpoint and are open-minded. Less cognitively complex members use their own frames of reference as if these were universal. During group decision making, high complexity persons can arrive at consensus much better than less complex persons, who speak as if they already know what their fellow group members believe and have experienced.[20]

If you think you are low in cognitive complexity, you can begin to assume less, ask more questions, and check out what you think others want, feel, and think. For example, Candi, our advertising group's account executive, was highly cognitively complex. She constantly asked questions to understand the client's point of view, she absorbed the massive amounts of information Marija gave her about which media outlets were likely to reach the client's target audience, and she was a master at weaving the client's ideas and suggestions together with the recommendations offered by the advertising professionals.

Self-Monitoring

A third cognitive input variable important to how we interact with others in problem solving is called *self-monitoring*. **Self-monitoring** refers to the degree to which a person monitors and controls self-presentation in social situations: High self-monitors pay careful attention to the social cues other group members send and, from these cues, they infer how their own behavior is being received and interpreted; then, if necessary, they can adapt their behavior so that it is

Cognitive Complexity
How well developed a group member's construct system for interpreting signals is; cognitively complex individuals are able to synthesize more information and think in more abstract and organized terms than are cognitively simple individuals.

Self-Monitoring
The extent to which someone pays attention to and controls his or her self-presentation in social situations; high self-monitors are able to assess how others perceive them and adapt their behavior to elicit a desired response.

more appropriate to the situation.[21] In short, there are two elements to self-monitoring: the ability to perceive how others are responding to you and the ability to adjust your behavior so that others will respond more favorably. In contrast, low self-monitors rely only on their own internal cues and attitudes; thus, they say and do what they want without much consideration about how others are responding to them. High self-monitors, then, are keenly aware of whether others' responses to their behavior suggest approval or disapproval of that behavior. They can adjust their behavior to achieve desired responses better than low self-monitors. In other words, sensitivity to cues from others is not sufficient; flexibility and skill in *adjusting one's behavior* as a small group member is also necessary. In fact, this ability to modify their behavior instead of following their initial inclinations is the main reason why high self-monitors often emerge as group leaders,[22] which we discuss in Chapter 7.

Rhetorical Sensitivity

Speaking and phrasing statements in such a way that the feelings and beliefs of the listener are considered; phrasing statements in order not to offend others or trigger emotional overreactions.

High self-monitors demonstrate **rhetorical sensitivity.** Rhetorically sensitive persons monitor what they say, adapting their statements to how they think other members of the group may react.[23] You might have doubts about the ethical standards of rhetorically sensitive self-monitors, but we do not. The rhetorically sensitive person is not a *reflector* who says what she thinks others want her to say, or a *noble self* who says whatever comes to mind. Rather, before speaking out, rhetorically sensitive people search consciously for the most effective way to express their point in order to help ensure that other members give their points the fairest possible hearing. They are careful not to insult or inflame other members.

Ben, the retail advertising division head who was our advertising team's leader, was good at phrasing suggestions so that clients could give them a fair hearing. For example, a client who owned a chain of shoe stores thought it would be funny to have a cartoon kangaroo (kangaroos have huge feet) wearing women's high heels (an image Ben thought would keep women away in droves). Instead of saying, "Oh, that's a great idea!" (as a reflector would) or "That's one of the dumbest things I've ever heard!" (as a noble self would), he responded in a rhetorically sensitive way: "I think the kangaroo image is really funny, particularly if you think about kangaroos wearing high heels. I'm not sure it will do what you want, though. Our research shows that women are sensitive about their feet sizes—on average, they would rather be wearing a size or two smaller. Calling attention to large feet will send women to other stores." Ben was true to his belief, but didn't insult the client by how he stated that belief.

Preference for Procedural Order

A fourth cognitive trait desirable in members of problem-solving groups is the ability to think critically and systematically. Gouran reported a tendency for most discussion participants to accept inferences without challenging them, even when patently flawed reasoning was involved.[24] For thorough evaluation of proposed solutions, groups need individuals skilled in all aspects of critical thinking along with group procedures that encourage thorough critical evaluation of all solutions. Critical thinking and systematic thinking may be linked in a personality trait referred to as **preference for procedural order** (PPO), the need or desire to follow a clear, linear structure during problem solving. Putnam initially described this characteristic and why it is important to group problem solving.[25] Later research by Hirokawa and associates suggests that high PPO persons do much better in choosing among alternatives when a group follows highly structured problem-solving procedure (such as is presented in Chapter 10). High PPO persons did not seem to think as clearly during loosely structured discussions. However, groups of low PPO persons, who are comfortable with less structured discussion, did equally well whether following a highly structured or loose, procedure. This research suggests that systematic procedures would improve (or at least not reduce) the output quality of most decision-making groups.[26]

Preference for Procedural Order

A trait characterized by need or desire to follow a clear, linear structure during problem solving and decision making.

Recap: A Quick Review

A number of input factors, including size and member characteristics, affect how effective a group will be.

1. Groups need diversity, but too many members make coordination difficult. Groups should be *least-sized:* as small as possible, so long as the necessary diversity of perspective and opinion is represented. Usually, three to eight members are an ideal number.

2. Members with communication apprehension about speaking in groups can impair a group's functioning. They don't contribute to the discussion, make irrelevant comments, express agreement when they don't agree; and they are seen by others as less desirable members. These passive members, along with aggressive members who bully others, impair productivity and cohesiveness. Ideally, members speak assertively, with respect for themselves and others.

3. Group members should be high in cognitive complexity, which helps them handle complex information, weave a variety of perspectives together, and arrive at consensus. Cognitively complex members assume less and ask more questions.

4. Members high in self-monitoring are tuned in to social cues about how others are responding to them and are able to adjust their behavior so that others will respond more favorably. They think carefully before speaking and are rhetorically sensitive.

5. Members high in preference for procedural order prefer a linear, structured process for problem solving and actually perform better when they can use such a process. Members low in preference for procedural order like a looser structure, but can perform well either way.

In the ad team, copywriter Toni and art director Vinnie are low in PPO, but Candi is particularly high, with Marija just behind her. Early in its formation, these differences caused irritation and frustration. Ben, the leader, hoping to prevent a small problem from becoming a major one, facilitated a discussion about work style preferences; the group talked through how structured their meetings would be. While Toni and Vinnie like completely unstructured meetings, which drive Candi and Marija nuts, they can adapt to structure. Once they realized how anxiety-producing the lack of structure was to Candi and Marija, they willingly adapted. Ben now sends an agenda out in advance, and the members have learned to tease each other (with respect!) about their differences ("Candi's stress level just spiked; we'd better get back to the agenda.")

As with the ad team, most groups usually include members with varying preferences for order and structure. Half the students Pavitt surveyed preferred a linear structure during decision making, while the other half preferred a looser "reach testing" process.[27] Groups with similar member preferences will have an easier time working together, but with patience and good communication, members can adjust to each others' preferences, like the ad team, and learn to appreciate their differences. If you want to test your own PPO level, use the scale in Chapter 12.

Personality Characteristics

There are dozens of personality characteristics that affect how you interact in a group. In our experience, personality differences—especially in how members approach work—create the most frustrations for members. Personality differences by themselves are not the problem; the problem is that members do not know how to work with (much less appreciate) others who think and work differently from themselves. For that reason, we have chosen to talk about the Myers-Briggs Type Indicator® (MBTI), one of the most widely known and researched personality classification systems, and three of the so-called Big Five psychological characteristics, agreeableness, conscientiousness, and openness to experience.

The Myers-Briggs Type Indicator®

The **Myers-Briggs Type Indicator®**, based on the work of psychologist Carl Jung, emphasizes how people prefer to relate to the world around them and categorizes people along four dimensions, which we will describe shortly.[28] Each MBTI dimension assesses a particular aspect of how we interact with the world. Each dimension represents a continuum, with opposite descriptors anchoring both ends of the continuum (e.g., extravert and introvert). Each of us has a preference—sometimes strong, sometimes mild—for one end of the continuum or the other. The MBTI measures these preferences along each of the four dimensions, assigns a letter code

Myers-Briggs Type Indicator®

A personality measure based on the work of Carl Jung that categorizes individuals based on how they related to the world around them.

to the preference we reveal, and describes our personality type based on our particular combination of dimensions. No one is a "pure" type—each of us displays some characteristics of anchor points on all the dimensions. However, the anchor points for each dimension display markedly different communication and behavior preferences.

The **extraversion-introversion dimension** assesses whether you focus on the visible outer world or your own inner world. Extraverts focus outwardly. They are sociable, like people, often talk to figure out what they think, and generally enjoy working with others in a group. Not so introverts, who much prefer to work alone. Introverts think things through and don't share ideas unless they've figured out first what their positions are. Extraverts don't mind being interrupted, but introverts do. Extraverts happily collaborate with others to make decisions, whereas introverts are comfortable making decisions independently. It may seem that extraverts are ideally suited for group work and introverts are not, but introverts often thoughtfully and carefully evaluate information and can contribute a great deal to group interaction. Extraverts and introverts operate so differently within a group that they may easily misunderstand one another or fail to appreciate one another's contribution to the group. The MBTI code letter for extraversion is E and the letter for introversion is I.

The **sensing-intuiting dimension** assesses the type of information group members prefer to use. Its code letters are S (sensing) and N (intuiting). Sensing individuals prefer and trust facts and figures. They operate in the here and now and are rooted in what they can actually apprehend through their physical senses. Intuiting individuals, in contrast, prefer to dream about possibilities and make connections between seemingly unconnected ideas and thoughts. They easily make intuitive leaps, which sensing individuals mistrust because they prefer concrete information. Intuitives see the big picture whereas sensors tune into the details, which bore the intuitives. Imagination, invention, and creativity are important to intuitives. In a group, these are the idea people who comfortably leap from idea to idea, but may be short on follow through. Sensing individuals, however, are careful, able to provide specific facts and illustrations to support the big ideas and can provide the grounding that intuitives sometimes lack. Both types provide skills groups need.

The **thinking-feeling dimension,** coded T or F, refers to how individuals prefer to make decisions, whether through careful analysis of objective evidence (thinkers) or empathy and subjective connection with others (feelers). Thinkers are comfortable with a systematic, critical thinking process. They like to analyze data and arrive at verifiable conclusions. They are task-oriented and like holding everyone to a single standard. In contrast, feelers tune in readily to the interpersonal relationships among group members and prefer to adjust the standards to meet individual circumstances. Feelers worry about group harmony and will make sure a group takes individual feelings into account in making a decision. Thinkers may forget to take

Extraversion-Introversion Dimension

The Myers-Briggs Type Indicator® dimension concerned with whether one's focus is the external worlds (extraversion) or one's internal, subjective landscape (introversion).

Sensing-Intuiting Dimension

The Myers-Briggs Type Indicator® dimension concerned with the type of information individuals use; sensers prefer facts and figures, whereas intuiters prefer to dream about possibilities.

Thinking-Feeling Dimension

The Myers-Briggs Type Indicator® dimension concerned with how individuals prefer to make decisions; thinkers are objective and fact-based, whereas feelers are subjective and emotion-based.

others' feelings into account, but will evaluate evidence critically and come to a logical conclusion. Clearly, thinkers and feelers operate by different internal logic systems in making decisions, yet each system is an important one for a group to consider.

The last dimension, the **perceiving-judging dimension,** concerns how people organize the world around them. Perceivers (P) are spontaneous and flexible; they react well to change. They like to gather as much information as they can prior to making a decision. At their worst, they are easily distracted and will postpone making a decision until they've collected every piece of information possible—usually an impossible task. Judgers (J) are decisive and sure in making decisions. They make a plan and can stick to it. However, they don't like to change plans once made and can become stubborn and rigid. Perceivers constantly second-guess decisions they have made, worrying that they have forgotten something important. Judgers are never truly comfortable until the group's work is completed and are excellent at keeping the group focused on the task; however, perceivers can roll with the punches if the group's plan falls through. Perceivers are more excited by starting new projects, whereas judgers are more excited by completing them. You can probably see how perceivers and judgers frustrate each other, yet how each one's strengths balance the weaknesses of the other.

In the MBTI system, the four dimensions combine to form 16 different personality types. For instance, someone assessed as ESTJ is extraverted, relies on facts and figures, likes to think things through objectively, and is decisive. A person with an INFP configuration is likely to be shy and quiet, dreamy, empathetic with other group members, and spontaneous. The most important point to remember about the Myers-Briggs Type Indicator® classifications is that *each* dimension provides a potential benefit to the group—but only if members recognize the potential strengths in having diverse personalities in the group. If members do not recognize this, their frustrations—natural when different personality types try to work together—may escalate into unproductive conflict. The chart in Table 5.1 summarizes the MBTI dimensions.

Agreeableness, Conscientiousness, and Openness to Experience

Psychologists have found that many different individual personality dimensions can be organized into five overarching personality factors,[29] which have been extensively researched and validated over the past two decades. Three of these factors—agreeableness, conscientiousness, and openness to experience—have been found to be particularly important to small groups.

Agreeableness refers to behavior that is generally cooperative and compliant in a friendly way; **conscientiousness** refers to behavior that is reliable, is diligent, shows a strong sense of responsibility, and is well organized.[30] Halfhill, Nielsen, and Sundstrom found that both agreeableness and conscientiousness were related positively to team performance.[31] For agreeableness, both the minimum and average scores were related to

---

Perceiving-Judging Dimension

The Myers-Briggs Type Indicator® dimension concerning how people organize the worlds; perceivers are spontaneous and flexible, whereas judgers are decisive and prefer structure.

Agreeableness

Behavior that is generally cooperative and compliant in a friendly way.

Conscientiousness

Refers to people who are reliable and diligent, have a strong sense of responsibility.

Extraversion-Introversion (Where Is Your Focus?)	
Extraversion (E)	**Introversion (I)**
Focus on external world.	Focus on inner world.
Sociable.	Shy, reserved.
Use talk to clarify your own thinking.	Think things through before sharing verbally.
Enjoy working in a group.	Enjoy working alone.
Don't mind being interrupted.	Hate being interrupted.
Comfortable making decisions collaboratively.	Comfortable making decisions independently.
Sensing-Intuiting (What Type of Information You Prefer to Use)	
Sensing (S)	**Intuiting (N)**
Trust facts and figures, what can be perceived through the senses.	Trust imagination and intuition, what can be imagined.
Prefer concrete information and ideas.	Prefer to dream about possibilities.
Detail-oriented.	"Big picture"-oriented.
Stay in "here and now."	Future-oriented.
Can find specific facts/evidence to illustrate an idea.	Dream about possibilities and make intuitive leaps among seemingly unconnected ideas.
Grounded.	Inventive.
Thinking-Feeling (How You Make Decisions)	
Thinking (T)	**Feeling (F)**
Carefully analyze objective information to make decisions.	Use empathy and subjective feelings to make decisions.
Systematic, critical thinker; like to analyze data to arrive at conclusion.	Tune in to feelings of others and take them into account.
Task-oriented.	Relationship-oriented.
Hold all to a single standard.	Adjust standards to meet individual circumstances.
Use evidence to come to logical conclusion, regardless of individual feelings.	Take others' feelings into account in group decision.
Perceiving-Judging (How You Organize Your World)	
Perceiving (P)	**Judging (J)**
Gather as much information as possible before deciding.	Decisive; can make quick decisions.
Spontaneous and flexible; react well to change.	Stick to a plan once made; dislike change.
Excited by starting new projects.	Excited by finishing projects.
Second-guess decisions you've made yourselves.	Certain; don't second guess.
Make sure group considers all relevant information.	Keep group focused on task.

TABLE 5.1
Characteristics of the Myers-Briggs® Dimensions.

performance. The authors suggest that this dimension is equivalent to the relationship element of group work. This makes sense, because agreeableness intuitively seems like a necessary component for collaborating with other people. By definition, group work emphasizes interpersonal interaction among members. Agreeable people are easy to work with and do not intentionally provoke defensiveness in others.

Halfhill and colleagues suggested that the task element of group work is represented by conscientiousness. The minimum level of conscientiousness correlated with group performance but the average level did not, perhaps because the average level for all groups studied was already fairly high. Interestingly, the more spread out members were on the conscientiousness factor, the worse a group's performance. Group members expect a certain bottom-line level of individual effort and performance. When members are not performing as expected, task conflict is likely to arise, which can hurt a group's overall performance.

Peeters and her associates likewise found agreeableness and conscientiousness positively related to performance.[32] These researchers studied 26 interdisciplinary student design teams charged with creating a robot that would perform certain tasks. In the concept phase of the design process, students had to figure out what they were going to do and agree on the concept. In the elaboration phase, students actually had to develop and build the robot based on the concept. Both agreeableness and conscientiousness were important factors. Agreeable people can more easily understand and combine one another's ideas, which allows the process to go smoothly. Conscientious people pay attention to scheduling, monitoring the group's performance, and making sure everything gets done on time. It is easy to see why both factors are important.

Openness to experience

Refers to individuals who are imaginative and creative, and who are eager to explore unconventional ideas.

Another important factor in team effectiveness is **openness to experience,** which refers to behavior that is imaginative, creative, and intellectually curious.[33] As might be expected, Schilpzand and her colleagues found that openness to experience is significantly related to team creativity.[34] This is important because organizations increasingly rely on teams for innovation. To be creative, teams need to be willing to explore unconventional ideas, challenge their assumptions, and "think outside the box." Teams composed of members open to experience are likely to be more original, to combine ideas in novel ways, and to be more flexible. The researchers found that a diversity of openness was actually more important than having all highly open members in a group. They speculate that the less-open members provide grounding necessary to bring a task to completion.

Having members with a variety of traits and personality characteristics in a group increases the group's challenge. It is a lot easier to work with people who are similar to you—you can take many things for granted and you do not have to work so hard at communicating well. In fact, a recent review of 31 studies of group personality composition found that group effectiveness suffered when members were more dissimilar to one another.[35] This same review found that group members' ability to work collaboratively in real-world, task-oriented groups was improved when members had relationship-oriented personality traits such as agreeableness, emotional stability, and helpfulness. As we noted in Chapter 4, a relationship focus does not cancel out a task focus, and *vice versa*. Relationship and task communication support each other, to the benefit of the S group.

In short, groups need members with a variety of traits and personality characteristics, but this variety makes communication more difficult. But regardless of how different a group's members may be, that group can succeed if members are willing to appreciate and capitalize on each other's differences. The personality characteristics just discussed are not visible, like sex and age. They are examples of the deep diversity described in Chapter 4 and are just as important as the cultural diversity discussed in that chapter.

Traits and personality characteristics are examples of input variables that already exist when a group is formed and that influence members' communication behavior in groups. This behavior—the key element in a group's throughput process—affects the roles that develop within the group. We discuss roles and their development in the next section.

Development of Group Roles

Like a role in a play or movie, member's **role** represents the cluster of behaviors performed by that member and the overall functions those behaviors perform for the group. One actor's role interlocks with the roles of the other actors; so it is with groups, as one member's role interlocks with the other members. And, like Brad Pitt, whose various film roles have included a police detective in Seven, a vampire in Interview with a Vampire, and a harsh father in The Tree of Life, individuals enact many diverse roles in the numerous groups to which they belong. In one group the role might be *daughter* or *son;* in another, *art director;* and in yet another, *church treasurer.* A given individual might be a leader in one group and play a supporting role in another. The role a person enacts in any particular group is a function of that person's personality, abilities, and communication skills, the talents of the other members, and the needs of the group as a whole.

Role

A pattern of behavior displayed by and expected of a member of a small group; a composite of a group member's frequently performed behavioral functions.

Formal Versus Informal Roles

There is a difference between a member's *formal role,* sometimes called a *positional role,* and that member's *informal,* or *behavioral role.* A **formal role** refers to a specific position with a set of expectations for fulfilling that position. For example, a group's *chair* is expected to call meetings, distribute agendas, and coordinate the other members' work. A group's *secretary* is responsible for taking notes, distributing minutes, and handling correspondence. Members who hold these roles are usually elected or appointed to them. Often, the duties associated with formal roles are written into a group's bylaws or operating procedures.

Formal Role

A specific, established position in a group with expectations for fulfilling that position.

The Myers-Briggs Type Indicator® (MBTI) classifies people by how they interact with the world, as measured along four dimensions.

1. Extraverts focus on the outer world and introverts on the inner world. Extraverts talk to figure out what they think, while introverts consider carefully before they speak.

2. Sensing individuals trust facts, figures, and what they can apprehend with their senses; they are well grounded. Perceivers trust imagination and intuition; they are inventive, but may appear flighty.

3. Thinkers make decisions based on objective facts and hold everyone to the same standard. Feelers make decisions subjectively and adjust standards to meet others' needs. Thinkers help groups complete their tasks, and feelers make sure members' feelings are taken into account.

4. Perceivers are spontaneous, flexible, and excited by starting new projects. They may be indecisive because they want to gather all information possible before deciding. Judgers are very decisive and are excited by finishing projects. However, they dislike changing a plan once it has been settled.

5. Member characteristics of agreeableness and conscientiousness correlate with team performance, and the characteristic of openness to experience correlates with team creativity.

6. Diversity of members makes a group's work more challenging because members have to pay more attention to their communication behavior. If they do so, a diverse group can be more successful than a homogenous one.

Informal Role

A unique role resulting from a member's pattern of behavior.

Behavior

Any observable action by a group member.

Behavioral Function

The effect or function a member's behavior has on the group as a whole.

An **informal role** refers to a unique role created as a result of a member's behaviors. Informal roles reflect the traits, personality characteristics, habits, and preferences of the members in a particular group. They are not specified in advance, but emerge from the interaction among members. To understand how informal roles form, we need to distinguish between a *behavior* and a *behavioral function*. A **behavior** is any verbal or nonverbal act by a group member; a **behavioral function** is the effect that behavior has on the whole group. For example, the joke Yukiko tells in her group is the *behavior*. But Yukiko's joke can serve a variety of *functions*, depending on what else has been going on in the group. If her joke relieves tension during an argument, it has a positive function; but if Yukiko's jokes are constantly getting the group off track and members are tired of it, the function is negative. Some behavioral functions are common to all groups and widely shared by members, such as providing information or offering opinions. Others may become the exclusive domain of one member, such as mediating conflicts between members or telling jokes.

Even though formal roles are specified and informal ones are not, members bring their own personalities, preferences, and attitudes to the formal roles they fill. Think about a group you belong to that has a formal designated leader (such as a chair or president). If you have experienced several individuals filling that role, you know that each one brings in his or her special "flavor" to the position. For example, the Curriculum Committee in one of our departments has rotated the chair position for several years. One chair was serious and highly task oriented; his meetings were particularly efficient. Another with a great sense of humor liked to joke around; his meetings took longer but were more fun. A third, who was well connected with other groups in the university, constantly brought in information about the curricular changes occurring in other departments; her focus was, "How do our changes fit in the university's bigger picture?" You can see that, even if a role is formal, each person in that role will enact it somewhat differently.

Role Emergence

The informal role a particular member holds in a small group is worked out in concert with the other members, primarily through trial and error. In a review of how roles develop, Anderson, Riddle, and Martin concluded that members negotiate their roles by observing others and particularly observing how others respond to their behaviors.[36] For example, Ty-isha may have a clear idea of how the group can accomplish its tasks; she will make attempts to structure the group's work: "I suggest we first make a list of all the things we need to do to finish our project." If no one else competes to supply that structuring function, and if the other members see that structuring behavior as helpful to the group, they will reinforce and reward Ty-isha's statements and actions: "Okay, Ty-isha, that sounds like a good idea." This reinforcement, in turn, is likely to elicit more of those structuring behaviors from Ty-isha. On the other hand, if several members are also competent to structure the group's work, the group members collectively will reinforce the actions of the member they perceive to be the most skilled in this performance area. If Ty-isha is not reinforced as the group's "structurer," she will search for some other way to be valuable to, and valued by, the group. For instance, she may help clarify the proposals of the other members ("In other words, are you saying that . . . ?") or become the group's critical evaluator ("I think there are two major flaws with that proposal."). *Every member needs a role that makes a meaningful contribution to the group.*

An individual's role will vary from group to group because roles depend on the particular mix of people in the group. A major principle of small group theory, one that illustrates interdependence, is this: *The role of each group member is worked out in the interaction between the member and the rest of the group* and continues to evolve as the group evolves. Thus, a well-organized person may end up leading one group and playing a supporting role in another, depending on the characteristics and competencies of all members relative to one another.

In addition, members' roles are fluid and dynamic as members respond to others and to shifting conditions in a group. Most people demonstrate flexibility as they enact their roles in a group,[37] a member who supplied information will also support another member's suggestion, for example. Sometimes, consistent with the bona fide group perspective discussed in Chapter 3, external forces in the environment create internal changes in group roles. Apker, Propp, and Zavaba-Ford found that changing societal and professional expectations about the role of nurses led to changes in how nurses actually operated among themselves and with physicians in healthcare settings, particularly with respect to their degree of authority and autonomy.[38]

Classifying Group Roles

Group researchers have developed a variety of systems for classifying group roles. Hare, in a 1994 historical review of research about group roles, says roles should be defined in terms that group members themselves would understand.[39] One such system is the functional role classification system described by Benne and Sheats, who classified members' roles on the basis of the functions those roles performed for the group.[40] These researchers defined three main categories of behavior: task, maintenance (socioemotional), and individual. Task behaviors directly affect the group's task. Maintenance or socioemotional behaviors affect the relationships among members, thus indirectly affecting the task. Individual behaviors are self-centered behaviors that help neither the task nor the relationships, but function to satisfy the individual at the expense of the group.

Although Benne and Sheats's system was first described in the 1940s, current research verifies its usefulness as a classification system. Mudrack and Farrell found that the task, maintenance, and individual distinctions Benne and Sheats described is consistent with members' perceptions and that the system holds up.[41].

To some extent, all classification systems oversimplify group roles by suggesting that a remark or nonverbal behavior performs only one function in a group; in fact, remarks are fluid and affect both task and social dimensions. For example, assume Teresa says to Mona and Melvin, "I think you guys are bypassing each other, and you should listen more carefully." That statement, even though it focuses on the ways members are relating to each other (a socioemotional concern), also has a bearing on the task accomplishment of the group, especially if Melvin and Mona start paying better attention to each other. Moreover, Teresa's statement implies that she has the right to intervene to improve the group's process, which says something about her relationship to the group. Thus, although some researchers consider actions to be *either* task- *or* relationship-oriented, it is more accurate to say that an act may have considerable impact on *both* dimensions.[42] In fact, Mudrack and Farrell found that the gatekeeper role,

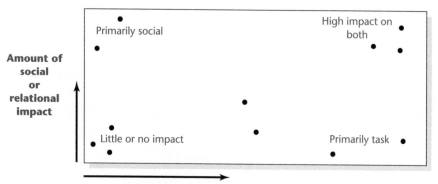

FIGURE 5.3
Task and social/
relational impact
of member
behaviors

a maintenance role we describe later, and the information-seeker role, a task role, straddled both categories.[43] Figure 5.3 depicts these two major dimensions and illustrates how individual acts can affect each dimension to a greater or lesser degree.

Both task and socioemotional needs must be met for a group to be effective. For example, the ad team's members attended to both the task and socioemotional needs of the group. Candi and Marija made sure that the group had all the information it needed to perform well and kept the group on track, but they also participated in the teasing and joking that made meetings fun. Ben provided agendas for the group's meetings, but he also sometimes brought in snacks or treated the group to happy-hour celebrations when something great happened. Toni and Vinnie had a great sense of fun and play, but they made sure their visual and textual images for ad campaigns were done on time and on target. We turn now to a look at the specific kinds of behaviors that contribute to a group's success (or not!). The following list of behavioral functions is based on Benne and Sheats's classification. Figure 5.4 illustrates the roles of three group members who exhibit various combinations of the following behaviors.

Task Functions **Task functions** affect primarily the task output of the group. Some of the most helpful, with statements that exemplify those functions, are:

Task Function

Task-oriented member behavior that contributes primarily to accomplishing the goals of a group.

Initiating and orienting: proposing goals, plans of action, or activities; prodding the group to greater activity; defining position of group in relation to external structure or goal. ("Let's assign ourselves tasks to finish before the next meeting.")

Information giving: offering facts and information, evidence, or personal experience relevant to the group's task. ("Last year, the ad campaign spent $200,000 for TV spots.")

FIGURE 5.4
Roles of three
members of the
advertising group

Candi
IDEA LEADER

Marija
DEVIL'S ADVOCATE

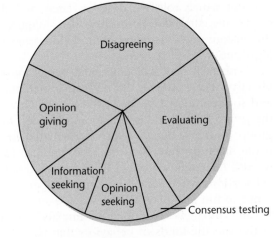

Vinnie
SOCIOEMOTIONAL LEADER

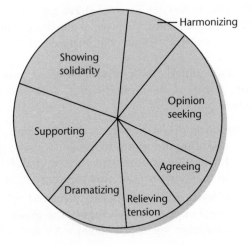

Information seeking: asking others for facts and information, evidence, or relevant personal experience. ("Juan, how many campus burglaries were reported last year?")

Opinion giving: stating beliefs, values, interpretations, judgments; drawing conclusions from evidence. ("I don't think theft of materials is the worst problem facing the library.")

Clarifying: making ambiguous statements clearer; interpreting issues. ("So does 'excellent' to you mean that the report should be perfect grammatically?")

Elaborating: developing an idea previously expressed by giving examples, illustrations, and explanations. ("Another thing that Toby's proposal would let us do is . . .")

Evaluating: expressing judgments about the relative worth of information or ideas; proposing or applying criteria. ("Here are three problems I see with that idea.")

Summarizing: reviewing what has been said previously; reminding the group of a number of items previously mentioned or discussed. ("So, by next week, Marija will have the media research finished and Toni will have the preliminary drawing of the logo for us to see.")

Coordinating: organizing the group's work; promoting teamwork and cooperation. ("If Meagan interviews the mayor by Monday, then Joyce and I can prepare a response by Tuesday's meeting.")

Consensus testing: asking if the group has reached a decision acceptable to all; suggesting that agreement may have been reached. ("We seem to be agreed that we'll accept the counteroffer.")

Recording: keeping group records, preparing reports and minutes; serving as group secretary and memory. ("I think we decided that two weeks ago. Let me look it up in the minutes to be sure.")

Suggesting procedure: suggesting an agenda of issues, or special technique; proposing some procedure or sequence to follow. ("Why don't we try brainstorming to help us come up with something new and different?")

Maintenance (Relationship-Oriented) Functions **Maintenance functions** influence primarily the interpersonal relationships of members. We think the following seven functions, with sample statements, are especially vital to task groups:

Establishing norms: suggesting rules of behavior for members; challenging unproductive ways of behaving as a member; giving negative response when another violates a rule or norm. ("I think it's unproductive to call each other names. Let's stick to the issues.")

Maintenance Function

Relationship-oriented member behavior that reduces tensions, increases solidarity, and facilitates teamwork.

Gatekeeping: helping some member get the floor; suggesting or controlling speaking order; asking if someone has a different opinion. ("Ruben, you look like you want to make a comment. Do you want to say something about the proposal?")

Supporting: agreeing or otherwise expressing support for another's belief or proposal; following the lead of another member. ("I think Joi's right; we should examine this more closely.")

Harmonizing: reducing secondary tension by reconciling disagreement; suggesting a compromise or new alternative acceptable to all; conciliating or placating an angry member. ("Jared and Sally, I think there are areas in which you are in agreement, and I would like to suggest a compromise that might work for you both.")

Tension relieving: making strangers feel at ease; reducing status differences; encouraging informality; joking and otherwise relieving tension; stressing common interests and experiences. ("We're getting tired and cranky. Let's take a 10-minute break.")

Dramatizing: evoking fantasies about people and places other than the present group and time, including storytelling and fantasizing in a vivid way; testing a tentative value or norm through fantasy or story. ("That reminds me of a story about last year's committee . . .")

Showing solidarity: indicating positive feeling toward other group members; reinforcing a sense of group unity and cohesiveness. ("Wow, we've done a great job on this!" or "We're all in this together!")

Whereas the preceding functions are necessary to effective small group functioning, there is another category of functions detrimental to the group. They represent an individual member's hidden agenda.

Self-Centered Function

Action of a small group member, motivated by personal needs, that serves the individual at the expense of the group.

Self-Centered Functions   **Self-centered functions** refer to those member behaviors that serve the performers' unmet needs at the expense of the group. We think the following three are especially harmful:

Withdrawing: avoiding important differences; refusing to cope with conflicts; refusing to take a stand; covering up feelings; giving no response to the comments of others. ("Do whatever you want, I don't care," or not speaking at all.)

Blocking: preventing progress toward group goals by constantly raising objections, repeatedly bringing up the same topic or issue after the group has considered and rejected it. ("I know we already voted, but I want to discuss it again!") It is *not* blocking to keep raising an issue the group has not really listened to or considered.

Status and recognition seeking: stage hogging, boasting, and calling attention to one's expertise or experience when this is not necessary to establishing credibility or relevant to the group's task; game playing to elicit sympathy; switching subject to area of personal expertise. ("I think we should do it the way I did it when I won the 'Committee Member of the Year' award.")

This list is by no means exhaustive; it could be expanded considerably with such categories as *special interest pleading, advocating, confessing,* and similar harmful functions. Self-centered functions manipulate and use other members for selfish goals that compete with what the group needs.

Although researchers believe that both task and maintenance roles are essential to effective group functioning, it is the task roles that seem more important to group members themselves.[44] Members clearly recognized the contributions task roles make to the group effort, but did not seem to value the contributions of the maintenance roles, nor did they *de*value the individualistic roles. We hope group members begin to recognize the importance of social roles and work toward valuing task and social roles equally. We also hope that group members recognize the harm self-centered roles cause and work to minimize those roles. Ideally, group members will display a "benevolent orientation" of cooperativeness and willingness to give back to the team; such members are more likely to engage in good citizenship behavior toward the team.[45] This is behavior that members engage in voluntarily—not because someone told them to—that helps the team function effectively. These behaviors are the opposite of the self-centered actions of some group members.

We cannot emphasize enough how important it is for you to understand that groups need both task and social roles and how you, as a group member, can perform appropriate roles for the group. Plas, writing about the importance of participatory management approaches in American industry, says:

> One of the keys to working well within teams is learning how to differentiate roles—process roles as well as task roles. Successful teams—no matter where you find them—are made up of individuals who know how to define roles for themselves and how to work with the roles that other team members have adopted.[46]

Role Management Across Groups

Just as important to understanding the role structure of your group is the recognition that members bring role expectations into the group from other groups. The bona fide group perspective discussed in Chapter 3 reminds us that group members are often simultaneously members of other groups. One implication of this fact is that our roles in one group may conflict with the time and commitment expectations of our roles in other groups. For instance, the fact that ad team leader Ben was president of the local Public Relations Society of America chapter affected how much time he could devote as a member of his local Rotary Club. How do we manage the roles in our church or community groups with our roles in work and family groups? Michael Kramer studied a community theater group in order to answer such a question.[47]

Most of us belong to what Kramer calls "life enrichment groups" such as church and community volunteer groups. We sometimes experience difficulty in managing our time and commitment in those groups as they clash with the time and commitment demands of our family and work groups. The trick is not only creating but also maintaining, then negotiating, our various roles so we can maintain a balance among all our groups.

Kramer discovered that part of negotiating conflicting intergroup roles involved talking about both roles. First of all, people who knew they couldn't

Recap: A Quick Review

Members bring their various personal characteristics and attitudes into a group as inputs and then begin to interact with one another; in so doing, they shape the group's roles.

1. A role represents the clusters of behaviors a member performs in the group. Formal (positional) roles result from specific positions that members fill and typically are described in a group's bylaws or operating procedures. Informal (behavioral) roles result from members' behaviors and evolve from the group's interactions.

2. A behavior is any action a member performs; a behavioral function is the effect of that behavior on the group. Telling a joke (the behavior) may be positive (e.g., if it relieves tension) or negative (e.g., if it makes fun of another member).

3. Informal roles emerge from the members' interactions with one another. As a member acts, others reinforce (or not) that person's actions. When the actions are reinforced, that member will continue to perform those functions. When the actions are not reinforced, the member will search for behaviors that will be more valued by the others.

4. Members' behaviors can be classified into three categories: task functions, which primarily affect the group's task; maintenance (or relationship-oriented) functions, which serve to strengthen relationships among members; and self-centered functions, which serve the individual member's needs ahead of the group's. Behaviors can have simultaneous effects in more than one category.

5. Members of actual groups readily acknowledge the contributions of task roles to the group's work, but do not always recognize the value of maintenance roles and do not always perceive the negative effects of self-centered roles.

6. Members generally belong to more than one group simultaneously, which can create conflicts in expectations. In managing roles that compete for a member's time and energy, talking about the importance of both sets of roles and demonstrating willingness to make sacrifices help a member balance competing role demands.

balance both sets of roles simply didn't try out for the theater production. Those who did audition and were selected for the theater group expressed how important their home and work commitments were *and* how important the theater group was to them. They talked to their co-workers and family members about their theater participation and they talked to their theater colleagues about their family and work roles.

There are two strategies members can use to manage multiple group commitments, *segmentation* and *integration*.[48] The theater group members *segmented*, or separated, their theater roles from their work/family roles in two ways with respect to time. First, during the day, work and family roles took precedence, but at night, the theater role prevailed. Second, they put clear time boundaries around the theater roles by committing to them for a fixed—in this case, six weeks—time period, after which those roles would end. In the ad team, Marija became the president of her statewide Advertising Club, but she knew this role would last only one year. Members *integrate* their roles by functioning in multiple roles simultaneously. During the year Marija was Ad Club president, she traveled across the state, networked with many people, and learned several new ways of analyzing media markets—which directly related to her function as media buyer on the ad team. Thus, she was able to integrate both roles for a period of time.

QUESTIONS FOR REVIEW

 Go to self-quizzes on the Online Learning Center at mhbe.com/galanes14e to test your knowledge of the chapter concepts.

This chapter used the advertising team to illustrate key concepts and to give you a mental picture of the concepts discussed. Consider the advertising team as you reflect on the following questions:

1. From what you know about the members of the ad team, to what extent do you think each member demonstrated communication apprehension, cognitive complexity, self-monitoring, and preference for procedural order? Give specific examples as evidence for your opinion.

2. From what you know about the members of the ad team in the opening story, what do you think their Myers-Briggs dimensions are? Can you make an educated guess based on the descriptions of their behavior?

3. From what you know about the members, what behavioral functions did each one perform, and how did these behavioral functions merge to shape each member's role? Did there seem to be any roles missing that you think the team should have had? Did there seem to be any competition among members for a particular role?

KEY TERMS

 Test your knowledge of these key terms by visiting the Online Learning Center at mhhe.com/galanes14e.

Agreeableness

Aggressiveness

Assertiveness

Attitude

Behavior

Behavioral function

Cognitive complexity

Communication apprehension

Conscientiousness

Extraversion-introversion
dimension

Formal role

Informal role

Least-sized group

Maintenance function

Myers-Briggs Type Indicator

Nonassertive behavior

Openness to experience

Passive-aggressive behavior

Perceiving-judging
dimension

Preference for
procedural order

Rhetorical sensitivity

Role

Self-centered function

Self-monitoring

Sensing-intuiting dimension

Task function

Thinking-feeling dimension

Trait

BIBLIOGRAPHY

Hare, A. Paul. "Roles, Relationships, and Groups in Organizations: Some Conclusions and Recommendations." *Small Group Research, 34* (April 2003): 123–54.

Keyton, Joann, and Lawrence R. Frey. "The State of Traits: Predispositions and Group Communication." In *New Directions in Group Communication,* Lawrence R. Frey, ed. Thousand Oaks, CA: Sage, 2002, 99–120.

LaFasto, Frank, and Carl Larson. *When Teams Work Best: 6,000 Team Members and Leaders Tell What It Takes to Succeed.* Thousand Oaks, CA: Sage, 2001, 1–32.

McCroskey, James C., and Virginia P. Richmond. "Communication Apprehension and Small Group Communication." In *Small Group Communication: A Reader.* 6th ed. Robert S. Cathcart and Larry A. Samovar, eds. Dubuque, IA: Wm. C. Brown, 1992, 361–74.

NOTES

1. Frank LaFasto and Carl E. Larson, *When Teams Work Best: 6,000 Team Members and Leaders Tell What It Takes to Succeed* (Thousand Oaks, CA: Sage, 2001): 1–32.

2. Susan E. Jackson, "Team Composition in Organizational Settings: Issues in Managing a Diverse Work Force," in *Group Process and Productivity,* eds. Stephen Worchel, Wendy Wood, and Jeffry A. Simpson (Newbury Park, CA: Sage, 1992): 138–73.

3. A. Paul Hare, "Roles, Relationships, and Groups in Organizations: Some Conclusions and Recommendations," *Small Group Research,* 34 (April 2003): 123–54.

4. Herbert A. Thelen, *Dynamics of Groups at Work* (Chicago: University of Chicago Press, 1954): 187.

5. Phillip E. Slater, "Contrasting Correlates of Group Size," *Sociometry,* 21 (1958): 129–39.

6. Robert F. Bales et al., "Channels of Communication in Small Groups," *American Sociological Review,* 16 (1952): 461–68.

7. J. A. Schellenberg, "Group Size as a Factor in Success of Academic Discussion Groups," *Journal of Educational Psychology,* 33 (1959): 73–79; E. B. Smith, "Some Psychological Aspects of Committee Work," *Journal of Abnormal and Social Psychology, 11* (1927):

73–79; Richard B. Powers and William Boyle, "Common Dilemma Choices in Small vs. Large Groups" (Paper presented at American Psychological Association, Anaheim, CA, August 1983).

8. Albert V. Carron and Kevin S. Spink, "The Group Size–Cohesion Relationship in Minimal Groups," *Small Group Research,* 26 (February 1995): 86–105.

9. Susan A. Wheelan, "Group Size, Group Development, and Group Productivity," *Small Group Research,* 40 (April 2009): 247–62.

10. Randy Y. Hirokawa, Daniel DeGooyer, and Kathleen Valde, "Using Narratives to Study Task Group Effectiveness," *Small Group Research,* 31 (October 2000): 573–91.

11. Brian H. Spitzberg, "Interpersonal Competence in Groups," in *Small Group Communication: A Reader,* 6th ed., eds. Robert S. Cathcart and Larry A. Samovar (Dubuque, IA: Wm. C. Brown, 1992): 431.

12. James Joseph A. Diliberto, "A Communication Study of Possible Relationships between Psychological Sex Type and Decision-Making Effectiveness," *Small Group Research,* 23 (August 1992): 379–407.

13. Dean Kazoleas and Bonnie Kay, "Are Argumentatives Really More Argumentative? The Behavior of Argumentatives in Group Deliberations over Controversial Issues" (Paper presented at the Speech Communication Association Conference, New Orleans, LA, November 1994).

14. James C. McCroskey and Virginia P. Richmond, "Communication Apprehension and Small Group Communication," in *Small Group Communication: A Reader,* 5th ed., eds. Robert S. Cathcart and Larry A. Samovar (Dubuque, IA: Wm. C. Brown, 1988): 405–19.

15. K. W. Hawkins and R. A. Stewart, "Effects of Communication Apprehension on Perceptions of Leadership and Intragroup Attraction in Small Task-Oriented Groups," *Southern Communication Journal,* 57 (1991): 1–10.

16. Richard E. Porter and Larry A. Samovar, "Communication in the Multicultural Group," in *Small Group Communication: Theory and Practice,* 7th ed., eds. Robert S. Cathcart, Larry A. Samovar, and Linda D. Henman (Boston: McGraw-Hill, 1996): 306–15.

17. Dominic A. Infant and Charles J. Wigley III, "Verbal Aggressiveness: An Interpersonal Model and Measure," *Communication Monographs,* 53 (1986): 61–67.

18. Rebecca B. Rubin and F. F. Jordan, "Effects of Instruction on Communication Apprehension and Communication Competence," *Communication Education,* 46 (1997): 104–14.

19. Susan L. Kline, Cathy L. Hennen-Floyd, and Kathleen M. Farrell, "Cognitive Complexity and Verbal Response Mode Use in Discussion," *Communication Quarterly* 38 (1990): 350.

20. Ibid., 357–58.

21. Robert J. Ellis and Steven F. Cronshaw, "Self-Monitoring and Leader Emergence: A Test of Moderator Effects," *Small Group Research,* 23 (1992): 114–15; see also Robert J. Ellis, Raymond S. Adamson, Gene Deszca, and Thomas F. Cawsey, "Self-Monitoring and Leadership Emergence," *Small Group Behavior,* 19 (1988): 312–24.

22. Ellis and Cronshaw, "Self-Monitoring and Leader Emergence," 123.

23. Roderick P. Hart, Robert E. Carlson, and William F. Eadie, "Attitudes toward Communication and the Assessment of Rhetorical Sensitivity," *Communication Monographs,* 47 (1980): 2–22.

24. Dennis S. Gouran, "Inferential Errors, Interaction, and Group Decision-Making," in *Communication and Group Decision Making,* eds. Randy Y. Hirokawa and Marshall Scott Poole (Beverly Hills, CA: Sage, 1986): 93–111.

25. Linda L. Putnam, "Preference for Procedural Order in Task-Oriented Small Groups," *Communication Monographs,* 46 (1979): 193–218.

26. Randy Y. Hirokawa, Richard Ice, and Jeanmarie Cook, "Preference for Procedural Order, Discussion Structure, and Group Decision Performance," *Communication Quarterly,* 36 (1988): 217–26.

27. Charles Pavitt, "Describing Know-How about Group Discussion Procedure: Must the Representation be Recursive?" *Communication Studies,* 43 (Fall 1992): 150–70.

28. Synthesized from the following sources: Isabel Briggs Myers, *Introduction to Type:*

A Description of the Myers-Briggs Type Indicator (Palo Alto, CA: consulting Psychologists Press, 1987); Otto Kroeger and Janet Thuesen, *Type Talk: The 16 Personality Types That Determine How We Live, Love, and Work* (New York: Dell, 1988); Otto Kroeger with Janet A. Thuesen, *Type Talk at Work: How the 16 Personality Types Determine Your Success on the Job* (New York: Dell, 1992); Paul D. Tieger and Barbara Barron-Tieger, *Nurture and Nature: Understand Your Child's Personality Type—and Become A Better Parent* (Boston: Little, Brown, 1977): 5–62.

29. John M. Digman, "Five Robust Trait Dimensions: Development, Stability, and Utility," Journal of Personality, 57 (June 1989): 195–214. doi: 10.1111/j.1467-6494.1989.tb00480.x. Accessed May 29, 2011; Paul T. Costa and Robert R. McCrae, "Normal Personality Assessment in Clinical Practice: The NEO Personality Inventory," Psychological Assessment, 4 (March 1992): 5–13. doi: 10.1037/1040-3590.4.1.5. Accessed May 29, 2011.

30. Ibid.

31. Terry R. Halfhill, Tjai M. Nielsen, and Eric Sundstrom, "The ASA Framework: A Field Study of Group Personality Composition and Group Performance in Military Action Teams," *Small Group Research,* 39 (October 2008): 616–35.

32. Miranda A. G. Peeters, Christel G. Rutte, Harrie F. J. M. van Tuijl, and Isabelle M. M. J. Reymen, "Designing in Teams: Does Personality Matter?" Small Group Research, 39 (August 2008): 438–67.

33. Obasi H. Akan, Richard S. Allen, and Charles S. White, "Equity Sensitivity and Organizational Citizenship Behavior in a Team Environment," Small Group Research, 40 (February 2009): 94–112.

34. Marieke C. Schilpzand, David M. Herold, and Christina E. Shalley, "Members' Openness to Experience and Teams' Creative Performance," *Small Group Research,* 42 (February 2011): 55–76.

35. Miranda A. G. Peeters, Christel G. Rutte, Harrie F. J. M. van Tuijl, and Isabelle M. M. J. Reymen, "The Big Five Personality Traits and Individual Satisfaction with the Team," *Small Group Research,* 37 (April 2006): 187–211.

36. Carolyn M. Anderson, Bruce L. Riddle, and Matthew M. Martin, "Socialization Processes in Groups," in *The Handbook of Group Communication Theory and Research,* ed. Lawrence R. Frey (Thousand Oaks, CA: Sage, 1999): 139–63.

37. Hare, "Roles, Relationships, and Groups in Organizations," 128–41.

38. Julie Apker, Kathleen M. Propp, and Wendy S. Zavaba Ford, "Negotiating Status and Identity Tensions in Healthcare Team Interactions: An Exploration of Nurse Role Dialectics," *Journal of Applied Communication Research,* 33 (May 2005): 93–115.

39. A. Paul Hare, "Types of Roles in Small Groups: A Bit of History and a Current Perspective," *Small Group Research,* 25 (August 1994): 433–48.

40. Kenneth D. Benne and Paul Sheats, "Functional Roles of Group Members," *Journal of Social Issues,* 4 (1948): 41–49.

41. Peter E. Mudrack and Genevieve M. Farrell, "An Examination of Functional Role Behavior and Its Consequences for Individuals in Group Settings," *Small Group Research,* 26 (November 1995): 542–71.

42. A. J. Salazar, "An Analysis of the Development and Evolution of Roles in the Small Group," *Small Group Research,* 27 (1996): 475–503.

43. Mudrack and Farrell, "An Examination of Functional Role Behavior."

44. Ibid.

45. Obasi H. Akan, Richard S. Allen, and Charles S. White, "Equity Sensitivity and Organizational Citizenship Behavior in a Team Environment," *Small Group Research,* 40 (February 2009): 94–112.

46. Jeanne M. Plas, *Person-Centered Leadership: An American Approach to Participatory Management* (Thousand Oaks, CA: Sage, 1996): 88.

47. Michael W. Kramer, "Communication in a Community Theater Group: Managing Multiple Group Roles," *Communication Studies,* 53 (2002): 151–70.

48. Ibid., 162–65.

Small Group Throughput Processes

When individuals with diverse backgrounds, personalities, and perspectives begin to interact as members of a small group, they create the group's throughput processes. The three chapters in this section focus on several key throughput processes. Chapter 6 examines the roles of tension among members, group fantasy, member socialization, norms, and group climate in the creation of a group's culture. Chapters 7 and 8 are companion chapters. Chapter 7 focuses on theoretical approaches to group leadership, one of the most important small group throughput processes. Chapter 8 follows up with practical approaches to leadership.

PART

III

Communication and Group Culture: Tensions, Fantasy, Socialization, Norms, and Climate

STUDY OBJECTIVES

As a result of studying Chapter 6, you should be able to:

1. Describe the structuration process whereby member communication creates and maintains the group.

2. Describe primary and secondary tension and explain how members' management of their tasks and social concerns gives rise to the major phases through which most groups pass.

3. Describe how a status hierarchy develops in a group and explain the implications that such a hierarchy has on group dynamics.

4. Describe how fantasy chains help socially construct a small group's culture.

5. Define group socialization and describe the phases of socialization.

6. Explain how group rules and norms develop; be able to recognize, state, and describe their effect on the group.

7. Explain cohesiveness and describe nine techniques for enhancing it in a small group.

8. Differentiate supportive from defensive communication behaviors and explain how they contribute to a group's climate.

9. Describe teambuilding and illustrate how it can be used to increase group cohesiveness, including cohesiveness in virtual teams.

CENTRAL MESSAGE

When individuals collaborating on an interdependent goal begin to interact, their communication shapes them into a group with its own unique culture. This group culture is a function of how group members manage their social and task challenges, the group's fantasy life, status hierarchy, socialization patterns, emergent norms, and climate.

Six medical school faculty members, three psychiatrists with MDs, a psychologist, and two social workers, were selected by their deans to develop an instructional program to teach new methods for identifying psychological disorders.[1] All six members were outstanding teachers and competent in their respective areas. They were given the freedom to develop any program they wished as long as it could be funded by outside grants.

During their first meeting, the members decided to base all group decisions on sound reasoning. Julian was selected leader, perhaps because of his "take charge" nature. The members insisted that he was expected to encourage input by all members and equalize member influence. Julian made solid efforts to meet their expectations because he strongly believed that their best decisions would be those based on input from all members. He even went so far as to consult books on small group communication for ideas about how to equalize participation and influence fairly.

However, the group ran into problems over time. First, group members, strongly entrenched in the medical culture, afforded the MDs greater clout. As a result, the three members without medical degrees found that their comments lacked influence. They talked less and less, did not push for their ideas, and after meetings would complain to each other. Second, the group was under pressure to continue to seek funding or their project would end. This gave Julian even greater influence because his contacts helped him secure funding for two more years.

Soon the group formed into a small clique with Julian as its aggressive leader. He talked more than any other member. When he rephrased others' remarks, he did so in a way that mirrored his own ideas. The non-MDs came to rely on his interpretations and lost influence in the group. Conflicts were not dealt with in a constructive manner and meetings were tense. Despite all their best intentions, Julian found himself the autocratic leader of a clique. How did this group's initial democratic spirit get away from the members? We will look for answers in this chapter and the ones that follow.

Our central theme has been that members' verbal and nonverbal communication is the most important throughput variable of small group dynamics. In this chapter, we describe how communication enables a group to emerge from a collection of individuals. Small group social systems are created in *and* through the communicative behavior of group members to produce output variables such as status hierarchies, norms, and climates. Small groups can change themselves by changing their interactions and, as we saw with our medical group, can stray from their original intentions. Note that a group's throughput processes produce its outputs. For example, the "pecking order" of the medical group emerged out of members' interaction (throughput). Rather than focus on individual characteristics, as we did in Chapter 5, we turn to the effect of member behavior on the group as a whole.

The Interplay Between Communication and Group Culture

In Chapter 4, we discussed culture in general. In this chapter we see that small groups themselves develop unique cultures, just as societies and other larger groupings do. When we talk about culture and small groups, we mean three things: Members bring their own cultural experiences into the group as input variables, each group develops its own unique small group culture (output), and the members' communicative processes both create and maintain the group's culture (throughput and output).

Group culture is the pattern of values, beliefs, norms, and behaviors that are shared by group members and that shape a group's individual "personality." Many factors weave together to create a group's culture, including the content and pattern of interactions, the roles members enact and their interrelationships, and the norms and rules guiding the group's interactions. Each group has a unique, interdependent mix of elements that cannot be duplicated exactly in other groups. For instance, some groups behave informally, with lots of joking and low power distance. Other groups display hostility, aggressive verbal behavior, and divisive conflict. Still others adhere to strict, formal interaction rules with polite, controlled communication. How do these differences come about? We examine some of the processes most important to the development of a group's culture in this chapter.

Group Culture

The pattern of values, beliefs, and norms shared by group members, developed through interaction and incorporating members' shared experiences in the group, patterns of interaction, and status relationships.

Structuration Theory and Group Culture

Communication among members is the means by which members create and sustain their group culture, which is never static. Anthony Giddens's structuration theory and its application to small group dynamics by Marshal Poole and his associates helps us understand the central role communication plays in the emergence of group culture.[2] **Structuration** is the idea that any social system's rules, operating procedures, and resources emerge out of the verbal and nonverbal communication between members. Members' use of those rules and resources sustains the system. *Rules* are guidelines for how actions are to be done. In our opening case, we see the rule that all decisions will be based on sound reasoning. *Resources* are those aspects (e.g., materials and possessions) of a group that are used by members to control the behavior of other members. In our opening case, one resource is the higher status afforded the MDs. Rules and resources are used by group members as they interact with each other.

The theory of structuration embraces three important assumptions.[3] First, the behavior of group members is constrained by such things as the general rules of the society in which they live, the structures of the particular group in which they find themselves, and the behavior of the other

Structuration

The concept that a group creates and continuously recreates itself through member's communicative behaviors; the group's communication both establishes and limits how the group develops.

members. For example, the rules of corporate America frown on executives' settling their differences with a fistfight. The medical group in our opening story was constrained by the status of MDs's within the medical community and the need to secure external funding.

The second important assumption is that people can choose whether or not to follow the rules of the group. Although there may be unpleasant consequences for a member who doesn't follow a group's rules, there is no *law,* like the law of gravity, that forces conformity. In our medical group, despite all attempts by Julian and members' original wishes, a majority of them did not follow the "spirit" of democracy—they caved in to Julian's wishes.

The third important assumption of structuration is that group creation is a process; the group creates itself initially and also continuously *re-creates* itself, changing in incremental ways, always in a state of *becoming,* with communication as the instrument for this creation and constant re-creation. This incrementalism is often the reason groups like our medical group can find themselves "off track" long after the initial changes start happening; the patterns sneak up on you and become entrenched.

The theory of structuration is quite complex. However, the main point remains: The *communication among members* is what creates group rules in the first place; once rules and structures are in place, communication is also what keeps them there, or changes them, as the case may be. Here is an example. Suppose a company appoints a group of several managers to develop a long-range strategy. Two members, Mauricio and Cary, have worked together before and naturally call each other by first names. Mauricio introduces Cary to Carol, an acquaintance of his, by his first name, and pretty soon the rest of the group members are calling each other by first name instead of Mr., Ms., or Dr. As they wait for the meeting to begin, members talk about mutual interests such as sports and jazz music, and several find common outside interests with other members. Norms of informality and friendliness have begun to develop among these members, and these norms will begin to affect other aspects of the members' communication, such as how they deal with disagreement. For instance, assume that, at a later group meeting, Cary says, in a formal and accusing tone of voice, "I respectfully disagree with the proposal offered by my esteemed colleague Mr. Hernandez," and continues to make a formal speech relating his objections. The rest of the members will probably say something like: "When did we get so formal, Cary? What's the big deal here? Why are you sounding like a prosecutor?" What they are saying, in another way, is: "We've developed norms of informality and friendliness,which you are violating. Your behavior seems inappropriate to us."Of course, Cary can choose to continue in his formal, prosecutorial way; if he does, that may either change the informality and friendliness norms to ones more formal and adversarial, or it may cause the other members to ignore Cary and ostracize him from the group.

A variety of internal and external factors influences the types of structures groups create, including member characteristics and preferences, the nature of the group's task, and such structural dynamics as the interplay between important (but perhaps conflicting) values. The members of the medical group valued democratic principles, but the pressure to get the job done and the deference given to a medical degree led members to encourage controlling leadership.[4] This contradiction produced tension within the group and an eventual split. In a study of jury decision making, numerous contradictions existed between internal and external factors.[5] For instance, although the jury was told to use judicial resources should any confusion occur, the jury developed the norm that no jury member could send a note outside the group asking for help before first securing permission from the group. In addition, several members of the jury struggled with reporting inappropriate behavior to the court. The expectations that the law should be followed clashed with the social rule of not ratting on your friends.

Structuration processes can also be found in a group's use of computer technology.[6] **Adaptive structuration theory,** a particular version of structuration theory introduced by Poole and DeSanctis, shows how the rules and resources of computer technology get used during small group decision making.[7] For example, computer-based systems that help groups improve their decision making (called GDSS, for group decision support systems) often are designed so members in a group can give their ideas and opinions anonymously. Such GDSS systems try to force members to pay attention to the *quality* of the ideas themselves, not *who proposed* the ideas. For instance, recent research showed that face-to-face groups with members of dissimilar ages experienced a reduction in trust, but this was not true in computer-mediated groups where members did not know each other's ages; thus, anonymity can be beneficial.[8] However, sometimes group members try to figure out who said what, thereby undercutting the spirit, or intention, of the computer support system. For example, as we learned in Chapter 4, men will often reveal their sex in computer-based discussion, whereas women keep it concealed to offset the status effects of sex. In other words, members *adapt* the technology and tweak it for their own purposes. Poole and DeSanctis suggest that using a GDSS according to its spirit will improve the group's outcomes more than if members adapt the GDSS in a way that is *not* faithful to its intention.[9]

Structuration recognizes that, although human beings are free agents, certain limitations and constraints keep their behaviors in small group systems within certain boundaries while still recognizing that change is possible.[10] Structuration also offers a "way out" for members with little power. Such members can enact small, consistent changes in behavior over time, thereby changing the group's structure. The communicative focus of structuration theory reminds us to look at the *communicative behavior* of members to learn about a group.

Adaptive Structuration Theory

A version of structuration theory that focuses on how the rules and resources of computer technology are used in the structuration process.

Negotiating Task and Social Dimensions of Group Culture

A group's culture emerges from the communicative dynamics of the members as they manage tensions and negotiate status among themselves. As the members handle their dual challenges of getting the job done and managing relationships with one another, their communication begins to assume identifiable patterns.

A number of researchers have studied how groups develop and change over time. This evolutionary process happens gradually, without clear demarcations to separate phases.[11] However, predictable phases of group development can be identified by the types of interactions that occur. Bales was one of the first to investigate a group's progression through these predictable phases.[12] He identified two concerns that group members face and must manage effectively: *socioemotional* and *task* concerns. First, members must develop the kinds of interpersonal relationships that provide stability and harmony, allowing the group to function cooperatively. Second, they must attend to the group's job. Bales noted that groups tend to cycle between these concerns, initially focusing on socioemotional issues and then moving to task concerns; they cycle back and forth between socioemotional and task concerns as they work to finish their charge. This should not be surprising, given our discussion of task and social dimensions in previous chapters.

Primary and Secondary Tension   Early in the group's *formation phase,* the socioemotional dimension predominates as members attempt to negotiate the kinds of relationships they will have with each other. **Primary tension** results from the interpersonal relationships among members and

Primary Tension

Tension and discomfort in members that stems from interpersonal (i.e., primary) sources, including the social unease that occurs when members of a new group first meet or during competition for power among members.

is described as "the social unease and stiffness that accompanies getting acquainted."[13] Primary tension shows up as extreme politeness, apparent boredom, yawning and sighing, frequent long pauses, and tentative statements uttered in soft tones. Members are asking themselves, "Will they like me? Will this be a group I enjoy working with?" The politeness and apparent boredom are only a façade covering the tensions we all feel when we are with people we don't know well. If these tensions are not managed effectively, groups will structure themselves into patterns of over-politeness, formality, and hesitancy to disagree, which can impair their ability to think critically when they attend to their task.

What kinds of actions can group members take to manage their primary tension effectively? First, members can take time to get acquainted with each other. They can talk about themselves, their backgrounds, interests, hobbies, and experiences relevant to the group's purpose, feelings about being groups, and so on. Actively sharing information about each other is a characteristic of cohesive groups.[14] Second, the group may have a social hour or party, with no formal agenda. Joking, laughing together, and having fun can help diminish primary tensions. Third, even if time together seems at a premium, groups can spend a few minutes at the beginning of each meeting getting back in touch. Even groups whose members have worked together over the course of many meetings typically spend a few minutes early in a meeting chitchatting and reconnecting before getting down to work.

Later, in the *production phase* of a group's life cycle, task- or job-related behaviors emerge to present a different set of challenges: the management of secondary tensions. **Secondary tension** is work-related tension found in the differences of opinion among members as they seek to accomplish their task. It is inevitable, because members perceive problems differently and disagree about goals, the means for achieving them, and the criteria they use to evaluate ideas. These tensions are the direct result of the need to make decisions *as a group*.

Secondary tension looks and sounds different from primary tension. Disagreement becomes more direct. Voices become loud and strained. There may be long pauses followed by two or more members' talking at once. Members twist and fidget in their seats, bang fists on the table, wave their arms, interrupt each other, move away from each other, and may even leave the room. They may try to shout each other down, call each other names, or aggressively question each other's intelligence or motives. Some may be very vocal while others may sit stiffly and awkwardly, not knowing what to do.

One of the biggest challenges for a small group is to create and reinforce a culture that manages secondary tension effectively. Too often, group members ignore secondary tension because dealing with it can be uncomfortable, even painful. The medical group at the beginning of the chapter intended to use sound reasoning in its discussions, but granted certain members much higher status than others. This interferred with

Secondary Tension
Work-related tension found in the differences of opinion among members as they seek to accomplish their task.

sound reasoning and ultimately split the group. With different choices, they could have enhanced the quality of their group culture.

Managing secondary tension effectively can lead to three advantages for the group. First, attempts to duck the tension-producing issue don't work. Bormann points out, "The problem . . . if ignored or dodged will continue to . . . impede progress. Facing up to secondary tensions realistically is the best way to release them."[15] Second, groups that find integrative versus divisive ways to manage their secondary tension experience greater cohesiveness. Members teach each other, through their interactions, that they can disagree with each other yet still experience a sense of trust and commitment. In contrast, the medical group members taught each other that it was OK to be told what to do and that talking behind one another's back was acceptable; this fostered distrust between members. Third, group members can learn to welcome the tensions because they force members to look more carefully at task-related issues, which can ultimately help them develop a better final outcome.

Secondary tensions are inevitable; the key to whether they help or hurt a group depends on how they are managed by the group. Three categories of behaviors typically reduced secondary tension among members: agreeing, showing solidarity, and tension release.[16] *Showing agreement* is socially rewarding to the person agreed with, as if to say, "I value you and your opinion." *Solidarity* is shown by indicating commitment to the group. Using *we* to refer to the group, speaking well of members, offering to help, expressing confidence in the group, and talking about the importance of the group and its task are all ways to show solidarity and move members away from an "us versus them" attitude. Humor can help to *release tension*, so long as the humor does not ridicule another member or is used to ignore the disagreement.

The socioemotional and task concerns reflected in primary and secondary tension are interrelated, not independent of one another. The choices that members make as they negotiate these issues affect both dimensions at the same time. At the very first meeting, as a group begins to mesh and create its individual culture, it must *concurrently* deal with its task: what its charge is, how the task should be approached, who is to do what, and so forth. Although interpersonal concerns may dominate the group's early focus, task concerns are still present and are affected by how the group sets its interpersonal tone. As a group matures socioemotionally, more and more time can be devoted to its task. At no time is either issue—task or relationship—absent from the group or unaffected by choices made in the other dimension. This interplay affects a group's status hierarchy.

Status Hierarchy   The six members of our medical group were recognized experts in their fields of study—their individual competence was unquestioned. But the way they chose to interact *with* each other created a culture in which certain members were treated with more value than others. The status hierarchy that emerged did not, in the long run, serve them well.

Status refers to the relative importance, prestige, and power of a member in a small group. As roles emerge, a pecking order forms, like the one that emerged in the medical group. High status members get certain benefits such as feeling important and worthwhile. Other group members defer to them, pay attention to them, agree with their proposals, and seek their advice and opinions. High-status people with titles (e.g., manager or CEO) may be given such tangible signs of status as large offices, private secretaries, and powers not granted to other members.

Effects of status are numerous. High-status members talk more than low-status members; both high- and low-status members talk to them more than they do to low-status members.[17] Low-status members also send more positive messages to high-status members than to other low-status members.[18] Low-status members are interrupted more, and their comments are ignored more often than the comments of those with higher status. High-status members tend to talk more to the group as a whole, whereas low-status members express most of their comments to individuals.

In addition to being granted a number of psychological or material rewards, high-status members are expected to meet certain responsibilities within the group. They are expected to work especially hard to accomplish the group's goals, and to uphold the group's norms. They may lose status by failing to fulfill the group's expectations, although they may be given additional leeway to bend the rules, called **idiosyncracy credit,** that other members do not receive.[19] This means that certain rules can be bent for members who have made an exceptionally valuable contribution to the group. For example, Estrada et al. found a high correlation between idiosyncracy credit and leadership—the group members to whom others awarded idiosyncracy credit also were perceived as leaders.[20] When this was the case, the group's performance was enhanced.

Status within a small group may be *ascribed* or it may be *earned*. At first, before members know each other well, status is **ascribed** on the basis of each member's position outside the small group. It is based on such things as wealth, education, occupation, personal fame, or position in the group's parent organization. For example, a committee composed of a company CEO, the vice president of manufacturing, a senior accountant, two employees from the marketing division, and a college student intern in marketing will initially have that order of ascribed status. However, status can also be **earned** or achieved on the basis of a member's individual contributions to the group. The intern who conducts considerable research on behalf of the group and is a key contributor will have higher earned status than the senior accountant who completes no assignments.

Although status hierarchies are affected by ascribed characteristics such as sex and race, they are also affected by the type of task. Alexander et al. found that open-structured tasks, wherein several solutions are possible and group members are encouraged to develop an array of options, give lower-status members more opportunities to break through the status barriers.[21] Such tasks encourage divergent thinking and allow lower-status

Status

The position of a member in the hierarchy of power, influence, and prestige within a small group.

Idiosyncracy Credit

Additional leeway in adhering to group norms, given to a member for valuable contributions to the group.

Ascribed Status

Status due to characteristics external to the group, such as wealth, level of education, position, physical attractiveness, and so forth.

Earned Status

Status earned by a member's valued contributions to the group, such as working hard for the group, providing needed expertise, being especially communicatively competent, and so forth.

members to provide indirect influence regarding the solutions. Moreover, members need to be careful about violating the group's status hierarchy. Youngreen and Moore found that members who do not behave according to their status in the group (e.g., a high-status member who acts in a deferential or noncommittal way) violates the group's unstated moral code and may lose status and influence in their groups.[22] Furthermore, once a member has lost status, it can be difficult to regain it.

One of the supposed benefits of computer-mediated communication (CMC) in a group is that status differences are minimized because in many CMC groups, members remain anonymous; thus status cues aren't visible. However, Scott's recent review of communication technology and its effects questions this assumption.[23] For one thing, in organizational groups members are not anonymous—they know with whom they work. Influence from the face-to-face context carries over to the CMC context. True anonymity, however, *can* minimize ascribed status social cues.

Ideally, a group's relationships and relative status differences are somewhat flexible so that different members can become more influential as their particular knowledge and skills are pertinent to the issues or problems facing the group at any point in time. Wood found that paying undue attention to ascribed status differences negatively affected a group's ability to accomplish its task.[24] Lower status, however, does not mean *of little value*. Lower-status members are not necessarily unhappy in the group; cohesive groups value the contributions of each member, and each member knows it. Often, everyone in the group might follow the lead of a normally quiet, low-status person who seems to have just the information or ability the group most needs at a given moment. That person might later slip back into a more usual low-profile position, but the contribution will have been noted and appreciated.

Research by Bonito suggests that members take into account both external status characteristics and member behaviors in the group when they make judgments about the value of their own and others' participation in a group.[25] External status characteristics—age, sex, appearance—contribute to expectations about how and how much someone will participate in a group. Although status differences are sometimes related to differential rates of participation, they are not reliable predictors. Members' behavior in the group and contribution to the task also influence others' perceptions of their participation. People differ with regard to which factors they pay more attention to. In any case, rigid status hierarchies based on external status characteristics can diminish the participation of all members.

Fantasy Themes

A continuing theme of ours is that group cultures are socially constructed by the interaction among group members. We turn now to one of the most powerful ways in which group culture is created: through *fantasy*. Technically, **fantasy** refers to "the creative and imaginative shared interpretation

Fantasy

A statement not pertaining to the here-and-now of the group that offers a creative and meaningful interpretation of events and meets a group's psychological or rhetorical need.

of events that fulfill members' psychological or rhetorical need to make sense of their experience and to anticipate their future."[26] Fantasy, in this sense, does not mean fictitious or unreal. It means that during certain periods of the group's interaction, rather than discussing events happening in the here and now of the group, the members are telling stories, relating past events, and sharing anecdotes that have a bearing *at the unconscious level* on the group's process. In other words, group members rarely set out consciously to establish the group's culture. Instead, they just talk. Some of that talk, although appearing tangential to the group's real task, in fact meets psychological and rhetorical needs of the members and helps construct the group's social reality.

When a group member says something not directly related to the present task of the group, that member has introduced a fantasy. This happens often during a discussion, with many fantasies going no further. However, sometimes group members pick up on the fantasy introduced by one group member and elaborate on it. Several members join the fantasy by adding their pieces to the story, in a kind of group storytelling. Bales called a fantasy that members elaborate on a **fantasy chain**[27] During a fantasy chain the speed of the interaction typically picks up, voices become louder, and a sense of excitement can be detected. The mood is electric. A fantasy chain may last from as little as half a minute to as much as half an hour. Eventually, the chain peters out, often when one member pulls the group back on task. Fantasy chaining is a way members create shared images of the group and its environment. This storytelling activity plays a crucial role in structuration of a group's culture.[28]

Fantasy chains develop in a fairly predictable way.[29] First, some form of ambiguity or uncertainty exists in the group. One member begins the fantasy by introducing a core image that somehow relates to the uncertainty. Then, other members spread that core image by adding their own elements to the fantasy, creating a group metaphor, rather than just an individual one. Finally, when the fantasy chain has ended, the group members have converged on a particular picture of the group's reality.

Fantasies are *about* something; the content of the fantasy is called the **fantasy theme.** There is an obvious or *manifest* theme to the fantasy chain, and a *latent,* or below-the-surface theme that, when examined, reveals the culture, values, and norms of the group. Often, fantasies have heroes and villains, plot lines, and a well-developed ethical structure that gives moral or psychological guidance to a group. To interpret the latent meaning of a fantasy, Bales suggests looking for a sudden insight rather than trying to analyze the fantasy systematically.

Fantasy is rooted in the theory of **symbolic convergence,** articulated and developed by Bormann. Symbolic convergence theory acknowledges that humans are storytelling creatures who create and share meaning through talk.[30] *Convergence* refers to the fact that during interaction the private symbolic worlds of individuals often overlap, or converge. When

Fantasy Chain

A series of statements by several or all group members in which a story is dramatized to help create a group's view of reality.

Fantasy Theme

What the actual content of a fantasy or fantasy chain is about.

Symbolic Convergence

The theory that humans create and share meaning through talk and storytelling, producing an overlapping (convergence) of private symbolic worlds of individuals during interaction.

that occurs, as it *must* to some extent in a group or there would be no group, meaning is shared; the symbolic, personal communication of two or more individuals constructs a shared reality that bonds the individuals, helps them discover how they feel about certain events, reveals shared values, and guides them to action. In other words, symbolic convergence theory "accounts for the creation and maintenance of a group consciousness through shared motives, common emotional activity, and consensual meanings for events."[31] We will now turn from this fairly abstract discussion to several specific examples of how fantasy helps shape a group's reality.

In the short and simple fantasy chain below, members of a student group are planning publicity for their annual Career Day seminar.[32] Chris asks Kevin what the previous year's group did for publicity:

Discussion	Commentary
Chris: Kevin, do you know what they did last time?	Chris asks a direct, task-relevant question.
Kevin: Yeah, somewhere I've got a list here. All they really did was put an ad in the school paper and then sent around this tacky memo to the faculty about a week ahead of time asking them to announce it in classes. It was embarrassing!	Kevin answers Chris, but introduces the fantasy about the "embarrassing" performance of last year's group.
Deirdre: I can't believe that's all they did!	Deirdre, animated, picks up on Kevin's criticism of the previous group.
Lori: It was John's fault—he didn't want to do *anything,* and the group didn't do anything!	Lori adds her part.
Tony: What a bunch of lazy wimps!	Tony contributes.
Chris: We've already done more than they ever did, and we've just gotten started.	Chris contributes, and adds the idea that *this* group has already done better than the last one.
Kevin: I know! We're going to look a lot better than they did!	Kevin adds to Chris's idea.
Lori: Okay, I like trashing those guys as much as you do, but we're really getting off track.	Lori stops the fantasy by getting the group back on track.

In this segment, the group starts out addressing its task directly, but quickly gets off task as members enjoy trashing the previous year's group. Kevin introduces the fantasy, with all group members participating in the fantasy chain until Lori, the group's designated leader, stops the chain and returns the group to its task.

What function has this fantasy served? The manifest, or obvious, theme of the fantasy is "Last year's group did a rotten job of publicity." Remember, though, that fantasies help create shared meanings for the *present* group. In this sequence, trashing the previous group builds up the performance of the present group by comparison, as hinted at in Chris's comment, "We've already done more than they ever did." By saying what a lousy group the previous year's group was, this group is not-so-subtly saying, "We're so much better." The group is setting standards of excellence, establishing norms of professionalism missing in the previous group that motivates *this* group to do better.

Fantasies perform several functions for small groups. **First, they help the members create the group's unique identity.**[33] The student group helped define itself as an excellent, hard-working, professional team by comparing itself favorably with the previous group.

Second, fantasies help a group deal with threatening or difficult information that members might feel reluctant to address directly. To illustrate, Morocco related the story of the first meeting of a research group whose student members believed their leaders were not providing them with enough direction.[34] One student recalled seeing a film about an experiment in which baby monkeys were deprived of maternal nurturing. The other members, who had seen the movie in school, began to contribute by adding details and developing a plot and dramatic images associated with the movie. The social and sexual development of the monkeys in the movie had been impaired by the lack of parental care, and this image served to symbolize the reality that these group members were *currently* experiencing. In essence, the group said, "The lack of attention and direction on the part of the leaders will ultimately harm us."

Third, fantasies help direct a group's actions by subtly endorsing or condemning particular courses of action. For example, Putnam and her associates describe a contract bargaining situation between two committees, one of teachers and the other of administrators.[35] The administrators constructed a fantasy chain about one of the teachers, whose constant head nodding reminded them of a woodpecker or a toy bird bobbing up and down on a cup. Their fantasy theme created a shared image of the teachers as well meaning but inexperienced. Later, during the bargaining situation, the teachers appeared to renege on a proposal they had earlier accepted, which is a breach of ethics. The administrators could have shut down the negotiations, but the image of the teachers as inexperienced rather than unscrupulous led them to perceive the teachers' actions as an innocent mistake. This benevolent interpretation by the administrators gave the teachers latitude to err without derailing the bargaining process. The effect was to maintain good feelings all around. The fantasy, in part, inspired this outcome by molding the administrators' perceptions of the teachers' shortcomings.

Finally, fantasies can be entertaining and fun for the group. In the previous example, the administrators' committee kept itself happily entertained by imagining the teacher who nodded constantly as a woodpecker and a whirligig bird. Fantasies help groups exercise their imaginations and creativity. They are powerful shapers of a group's culture and show concretely the interplay between communication and group culture.

The significant role that communication between group members plays in the emergence of a group's culture cannot be overstated. We have used structuration theory to explain this dynamic between communication and culture. In these discussions, we implied that the group maintained a consistent membership. But what happens when new members enter the group? How do individuals and groups socialize new members and become changed themselves in the process?

Recap: A Quick Review

Secondary group dynamics are not just about a group's task. Small groups are composed of human beings; thus, the negotiation of interpersonal relationships is just as important to group dynamics as managing the task.

1. Primary and secondary tensions between group members are to be expected when groups come together for the first time and begin to work on the task. The choices that group members make when facing these tensions affect their success in the long run.

2. Group member interactions around task and social challenges eventually produce a pattern of power relationships that guide, reinforce, and modify the status of each member relative to each other. Uncritical acceptance of the ascribed status of members can harm the group's culture.

3. When groups face the challenges of negotiating task and socioemotional concern, they often engage in creative, often playful fantasizing in the face of uncertainty. These "digressions" are woven together by all group members; this results in a collective new version of their group identity, which in turn redirects how members act toward each other and their task.

Group Socialization of Members

When we hear the word *socialization,* we generally think about someone who is learning to become part of a group or even society at large. Just as children are socialized into families and society, people are socialized into newly formed and established groups. Socialization processes have been studied in organizational research focusing on how the organization molds the newcomer to its culture,[36] but recent research in communication looks at the socialization process in small groups. It also recognizes the active role the new member plays in affecting the existing small group culture.

Carolyn Anderson, Bruce Riddle, and Matthew Martin define **group socialization** as a reciprocal process of social influence and change in which both newcomers and/or established members and the group adjust to one another using verbal and nonverbal communication.[37] Communication plays a central role in all group processes, including the socialization of members.[38] Let's apply this definition to a real-life example. Consider what happened to the following theater group. Actors had been practicing for weeks, but one week before opening night, leading man Richard was told he needed emergency surgery—immediately! The cast was devastated. Of course, cast members were worried about Richard, but they also were concerned about losing six weeks of rehearsals, during which the troupe had developed into a cohesive group. The director thought about canceling the show, but she asked an experienced actor friend of hers to assume Richard's role. Opening night was delayed a week to give Ted time to learn the lines and the troupe time to integrate a new member.

First, the adapting and adjusting that happen when a new group forms or when a new member enters a group occur through group member communication. Such adjustments are often filled with uncertainty, and group members typically communicate with each other in an effort to reduce the anxiety brought on by the uncertainty.[39] Group socialization, when handled effectively, has great potential to help members bond. This is particularly true when members join or leave.[40] If the community theater members do not talk to each other about the new cast member, welcome him into the troupe, and see his presence as a way to move in new directions, then his willingness to replace Richard will be wasted.

Second, effective socialization requires a balance between individual member and group goals and satisfaction.[41] The new cast member, the director, and the rest of the troupe must have similar goals and levels of comfort if his replacing Richard is to be a positive experience.

Third, socialization is an ongoing process involving not only the new member, but also the rest of the group. As a member of the troupe what might you do to help Ted? If you were the director, what might you do to help Ted and the cast negotiate a new formation phase so that they can focus on the play? Socialization is a bi-directional process. Just as new members proactively help socialize themselves into face-to-face groups, so do new members of virtual groups. Burke, Kraut, and Joyce, who studied a variety of online groups, found that new members used three strategies to facilitate their socialization into a group.[42] First, they made direct requests for help from the group (e.g., "Where can I get information about alternative cancer treatments?"). Second, they engaged in group-oriented membership comments, which indicated that they had been keeping up with the posts and were part of the ongoing group discussions, even if

Group Socialization

The social influence and change process during which both newcomers and established members adjust to one another.

they had not posted previously (e.g., "I have been reading the discussion about . . ."). Finally, they made identity-oriented comments, in which the poster discloses personal information showing the connection to the group (e.g., "I am also a breast cancer survivor and . . ."). Members who used these strategies generally got more responses to their posts and more indicators that they were accepted into the group. If you were Ted, what could you do to help others feel comfortable with you? Understanding the phases of group socialization can help you further consider what face-to-face and online groups can do to help socialize new members effectively.

Phases of Group Socialization

Anderson and colleagues describe five phases of group socialization: antecedent, anticipatory, encounter, assimilation, and exit.[43] Each phase has unique communication needs. As you study the phases, remember that groups may move through these phases at different speeds, may revisit one or more of these phases as they accept or reject new members, and that behaviors in one phase have a ripple effect through the other phases.

In the **antecedent phase,** group inputs, including individual characteristics, listening styles, cultural differences, and feelings about group work affect a group's throughput and output variables. All members, including Ted in our previous example, bring to a group their own attitudes, motives, and communication traits, which profoundly influence how ready and able they are to be socialized into a group and to engage in group work and relationship building. For instance, if Ted is verbally aggressive, the socialization process for him and the rest of the cast will be profoundly different than if he is assertive or passive.

The **anticipatory phase** of group socialization involves all the initial expectations members have of each other and the group. These expectations lay the groundwork for what the individual anticipates will happen over the course of the group's life. Suppose the director had enthusiastically talked about Ted's talents, thereby leading the cast to anticipate a master actor and great opening night. In turn, Ted had been told about the great cast he was joining. Both parties would anticipate a successful experience. However, if their expectations were not accurate, socialization could be a disaster. In both examples, the more the expectations differ from the actual experience, the more the members will experience anxiety and perhaps even anger. You can see that socialization involves *two* sets of expectations—Ted's (individual) and the cast's (group).

Group socialization is enhanced when groups systematically have in place ways to welcome new members.[44] In the case of our community theater cast, this could include a meeting with Ted in which members introduce each other and talk about their expectations; an informal dinner with

Antecedent Phase

Prior to group socialization, the phase in which group members' individual characteristics affect their readiness and willingness to socialize members effectively.

Anticipatory Phase

During group socialization, the phase in which members' expectations of each other and the group set the stage for what will occur during socialization.

Ted; and a tour of the theater, stage, and dressing rooms. These kinds of activities or *audition practices* help both the new member and the group draw more realistic expectations and experience less primary tension during socialization.[45]

The third phase of group socialization is the **encounter phase.** This phase, when the expectations of the anticipatory phase meet the realities of the group, lasts for an indefinite period.[46] During this time the individual and the group create or adjust the group's norms, culture, climate, status hierarchy, and leadership structure.

Both the new and old members negotiate their roles in the group in this phase. The addition of a new member can disrupt the roles already established in a newly forming or existing group. Communication about individual role expectations and careful assessment of what the group needs are necessary if socialization is to be a positive experience. For instance, newcomers who proactively seek information about role expectations are socialized more effectively than those who do not seek this kind of information.[47]

The **assimilation phase** is characterized by a member's full integration into the group and its structures.[48] New members are comfortable with the group culture and show an active interest in both the group's task and relationships. In turn the existing members accept the new member. Members blend productively and supportively, enacting the kind of communication necessary to sustain the group's culture. If this integration does not occur smoothly, as is often the case, secondary tension can throw the group back into the anticipatory and encounter phases. Do not let these regressions surprise you because, over a group's life span, members will often have to negotiate the good fit between themselves and the group.

The fifth phase of group socialization is the **exit phase:** Earlier we remarked that group socialization is a process that continues over the course of a group's life. This process is experienced at both the individual and the group level and actually ends when a member leaves or when the group ceases to exist. Exiting a group can be a difficult transition to make and is one group members often minimize.[49] If a member leaves, such as Richard in our community theater example, the group must deal with why he left, how he left, how his departure changes their communication, and what comes next. When an entire group disbands, members deal with variations of the same issues.

Group turnover is common. How many times have you watched as a member left, and then found yourself dealing with the loss and the adjustment to a new member? This process can be filled with uncertainty and resentment or it can be managed quite well. One way a group can effectively manage turnover is to develop a positive group attitude toward turnover—see it as a way to redefine who you are. When an entire group ends, do not treat it lightly—how you disband can and does impact the kind of experiences you take into the next group. Keyton recommends that

Encounter Phase

During group socialization, the phase in which member expectations meet the realities and members begin to adjust to each other in actuality.

Assimilation Phase

During group socialization, the phase in which members are fully integrated into the group and its structures.

Exit Phase

During socialization, the phase that encompasses the process members experience when a member leaves the group or the group disbands.

groups give themselves an opportunity to say goodbye and process their experience.[50]

Our discussions of socialization and structuration of group culture have consistently mentioned the importance of the group's rules. In the following section we take a closer look at rules and norms of group culture.

Recap: A Quick Review

Just as larger social cultures socialize new members, small groups initially socialize each other and do so again when a new member comes into the group.

1. The addition of new members into groups challenges the existing group's way of doing things and how members relate to each other. In socializing a new member, group members teach the new member *how* he or she is expected to behave, thereby reinforcing current group expectations.

2. Group socialization is the responsibility of both the new member and the group; it represents a delicate balance of individual and group goals and satisfaction.

3. The group socialization process is dynamic and can be captured in five interrelated stages: antecedent, anticipatory, encounter, assimilation, and exit stages.

4. How a group ends is just as important as how it begins.

Development of Group Rules and Norms

When individuals begin to interact as members of a group, anything is possible. Somehow, the members must develop a set of rules and operating procedures to coordinate their individual behaviors into a system. Some **rules** are formalized guidelines for behavior. For example, *Robert's Rules of Order*, Newly Revised, is used by many organizations as a guide for governing face-to-face interaction.[51] Robert includes an entire section of rules that apply to any committee of an organization using his parliamentary manual.

However, most of the normal operating procedures for a group are developed gradually, with unspoken consent of the group members. For instance, if Kara comes late to a meeting and other members make a point of chastising her, Kara will likely arrive on time for subsequent meetings and the group has "decided" on a rule that members should arrive on time. Such an informal rule, or **norm,** is seldom written down; instead, it is an unstated expectation about how members should behave, and is enforced by peer pressure. This section focuses on these norms: prescriptions from group behavior that emerge out of group communication and are an important process variable of group interaction.

Norms reflect cultural beliefs about what is or is not appropriate behavior, as we discussed in Chapter 4. Although the norms of an individual group may be specific to that group, chances are they will mirror

Rules

Statements prescribing how members of a small group may, should, or must behave, which may be stated formally in writing, or informally as in the case of norms.

Norm

An unstated informal rule, enforced by peer pressure, that governs the behavior of members of a small group.

general cultural norms. For instance, if physical violence is prohibited by the general culture, with disagreements handled through discussion, then that is what a group established in the context of this larger culture will likely do. Thus, groups do not start out with a blank slate—members bring with them expectations and social rules for how to behave.[52]

Norms are not imposed by an authority outside the group but are imposed by members on themselves and each other through their communication. Various types of peer pressure, ranging from slight frowns to ostracism, enforce them. It is important for group members, particularly new members, to be aware of these norms because to violate them may mean punishment, loss of influence, and perhaps exclusion from the group.

Norms guide and regulate the behavior of group members: how and to whom members speak, how they dress, what they talk about and when, what language may be used, and so on. Rarely do norms specify absolutes; rather, they indicate ranges of acceptable and unacceptable behavior. A particular group may endorse a prompt starting time for its meetings. However, being 4 minutes late may be tolerated without comment, but coming 15 minutes late would not.

Norms develop in virtual groups, too. For example, student groups devise their own ways of using e-mail.[53] Some groups used it to chat, others to coordinate schedules, and others to talk to those who were not present. Further, conformity to the norms increases over time.

Norms often are developed rapidly via the structuration process described earlier, often without members' realizing what is occurring. The group's first meeting is particularly critical in establishing that group's norms. At that time, behaviors typical of primary tension in the formation phase—speaking quietly, suppressing disagreement, making tentative and ambiguous statements—can become norms if not challenged. Norms usually evolve over time and exist below the level of conscious awareness of most members. Often, a norm is brought to a group's awareness only after a member violates it, a new member questions it, or an observer points it out.

The reinforcement of group norms depends on **conformity,** or members going along with emerging norms over time.[54] Conformity to norms helps a group function *as a whole* and confirms members' acceptance of and loyalty to the group. How quickly do group members conform to norms? Five conditions seem to influence conformity to group norms.[55] First are individual characteristics. For example, older people are less likely to conform. Second, members follow well-articulated and well-enforced norms more. Third, the more members who conform to the norm, the more likely it is that others will follow. Fourth, highly cohesive groups tend to generate more conformity to their norms. Finally, members who support the goals of their group are more likely to follow that group's norms.

Conformity

Following group norms and not deviating from them.

General norms direct the behavior of the group as a whole, whereas *role-specific norms* concern individual members with particular roles, such as the designated leader. The medical group discussed in our chapter opening developed a general norm related to rational decision making. Role-specific norms for Julian included his rephrasing and redefining of the others' ideas. He also developed the norm of talking more than the others. Examples of each type of norm follow:

General Norms (Applicable to Every Member)	Role-Specific Norms (Applicable to Specific Members)
Members should sit in the same position at each meeting.	The leader should prepare and distribute an agenda in advance of each meeting.
Members should address each other by first names.	The secretary should distribute minutes of the previous meeting at least three days before the next meeting.
No one may smoke during meetings.	Gulshan may play critical tester of all ideas by asking for evidence.
Members may leave the meeting to get something to drink, but should return to their seats promptly.	Terrell should tell a joke when the climate gets tense during an argument.
Members should arrive on time for meetings.	Julian should restate other members' remarks in his own words.

If norms generally exist below the level of conscious awareness, how can group members discover what their norms are? Norms can be inferred and confirmed by observation. New members, especially, should be sensitive to the group's norms so that they do not inadvertently violate important ones. There are two types of behavior to watch for especially, *behaviors that are repeated regularly* and *behaviors that are "punished."* Repeated behaviors indicate that a norm is operating. For example, do members sit in the same seats? Who sits next to or talks to whom? How is the group brought to order? Perhaps the strongest evidence of a norm is punishment directed at a member who violates the norm. Violations take several forms: nonconformity to a general norm (e.g., consistently coming late to meetings), deviating from the status hierarchy (e.g., a nurse questioning an MD's opinion), or breaking past patterns (e.g., a quiet member suddenly talking a lot).[56] The punishment can take the form of head shaking, surreptitious and disapproving glances passing between members, tongue-lucking, direct negative comments, or even threats.

Listen especially for negative comments, particularly if those comments come from more than one member: "It's about time you got here," and "Maybe you'll have your report ready for our next meeting." Be careful about violating norms! As we noted earlier, norm violators generally lose status and influence in a group and may not be able to recover.

Changing a Norm

Since norms have such a tremendous effect on the processes and outcomes of the group, members should act to change them if they appear to be detrimental. Just because members conform to a norm does not mean the norm is good for the group overall. Small persistent changes can be effective because they are not as noticeable to those who may resist the change.[57] A social worker in our medical group temporarily made the group more democratic when she decided to refuse Julian's attempts to rephrase her comments, which in turn helped him be more aware of his pattern of changing other's ideas to reflect his own. The group managed this new pattern for a while, but when a crisis arose, members, including Julian, fell back into old ways. Had the social worker persisted in her attempts, she might have been successful in changing the autocratic norm.

To change a norm, don't use a full frontal assault that may be perceived as a personal attack and won't work anyway. Follow a few simple, more ethical guidelines:

1. Establish yourself as a loyal member of the group first. The others will perceive you as looking out for the good of the group when you recommend a change.

2. Carefully observe the dysfunctional norm and the effect it has on the group. Be prepared to describe when and how often it occurs and how serious the problem is.

3. Pick an appropriate time and share your observations calmly and clearly, then ask whether other members share your concerns. Don't say, "We never get started on time and I'm sick of it!" Instead, say "For the past four meetings, we have started our work from 15 minutes to half an hour late. We seem to have a rule that we don't have to start on time. But two of us have a class right after this meeting, so we have to miss the conclusion of our business. This means we need to spend more time at the next meeting getting caught up. Does anyone else see this as a problem?" Now the dysfunctional norm is in the open. If you are wrong, the group will correct you; if you are right, members will want to change it.

4. Enlist the other members in changing the norm. Making everyone responsible will help the entire group work for the change.

Central to group structuration is understanding how group members use preexisting general norms of behavior and also create their own norms, often implicitly, which in turn guide group communication until changes occur and new norm(s) alter group interaction.

1. Norms are informal rules that often emerge out of group members' tendencies to conform; they then guide future group task and social expectations.

2. Conformity to group norms is a function of five interrelated conditions: individual tendency toward conformity, number of group members following the norm, how well the norm is articulated and supported, level of group cohesiveness, and degree to which group members support the group goal.

3. Evidence of a group norm can be found in repetitive behavior and the degree to which nonconformity is punished.

4. Changing a group norm should involve thoughtful planning around when to bring up the norm with the group, careful description of the norm and its perceived consequence to the group, and presentation to the group in a manner that shows loyalty to the group identity as a whole.

Development of a Group's Climate

We began this chapter by recognizing that small groups develop their own cultural identities as they meet task and socioemotional challenges, socialize members, and create norms and use fantasy to craft their symbolic realities. We end this chapter with a discussion of group climates, which reflect the emotional tenor of a group's culture and show once again how important it is to recognize the key role that socioemotional dynamics play in shaping the group culture.[58] **Group climate** refers to a group's emotional and relational atmosphere. How well do members work together? Do they seem to like each other? Are members' identity and relational needs being met? Is the atmosphere tense or relaxed? In this section, we discuss two elements that contribute to group climate: cohesiveness and supportiveness.

Group Climate

A group's emotional and relational atmosphere.

Cohesiveness

When the U.S. women's soccer team won the 1999 World Championship, star Mia Hamm said, "Everything I am I owe to this team."[59] By all objective measures, this team presented a stellar example of cohesiveness and teamwork, which drove members to achieve outstanding individual effort. What creates the kind of climate that would lead Mia Hamm to credit her team rather than herself for her performance?

Cohesiveness refers to the common bonds and sentiments that hold a group together. Cohesive teams have a high degree of "stick togetherness" and behave differently from less cohesive groups. They display more characteristics of primary groups.[60] They have higher rates of interaction, express more positive feelings for each other and report more satisfaction with the group, as was demonstrated by the women soccer players choosing to go out to dinner together. Members are willing to cooperate and collaborate with each other.[61] In addition, cohesive groups exert greater control over member behaviors.[62] Highly cohesive teams are better able to cope effectively with unusual problems and handle emergencies. Although in general, highly cohesive groups are more productive,[63] the nature of the task influences the cohesiveness-productivity relationship.[64] If the task is one that requires a high degree of coordination and interdependence among members, with communication an essential factor in the group's task completion, then cohesiveness enhances productivity.

Cohesiveness can involve commitment to personal relationships or to the group's goal.[65] Social cohesiveness from interpersonal attraction and liking produces different results than cohesiveness based on commitment to the task or goal. Too much social cohesiveness can hurt performance.[66] Cohesive groups are productive only when the members have *both* high acceptance of organizational goals implicit in the group's task *and* a strong drive (motivation and enthusiasm) to complete the task.[67] Groups that are highly cohesive but socially oriented rather than task-oriented may end up accomplishing nothing.[68]

Cohesiveness, commitment to the task, and productivity are fostered when members take time to get acquainted and interested in each other as people.[69] In addition, cohesive groups create a dominant sensory metaphor as a group.[70] For example, when a group is first established, various members indicate their understanding by saying, "I see," "I hear you," or "I grasp that." Each of these metaphors for "I understand" concentrates on a different sense—sight, sound, or touch. In cohesive groups, members tend to converge symbolically on one of them. If the visual metaphor is "chosen," for example, members will all start saying, "I see," "I've got the picture," and "I've spotted a flaw." This happens below the level of conscious awareness like fantasy chaining and indicates that the members have influenced each other in subtle but significant ways.

Interestingly, this type of language style matching predicted cohesiveness in both face-to-face and computer-mediated groups.[71] Gonzales, Hancock, and Pennebaker examined language generated during discussions of both face-to-face or text-based computer-mediated communication. They found that when members' speech patterns matched

Cohesiveness

The degree of attraction members feel for the group; unity.

(e.g., use of function words such as articles and conjunctions, verb tenses, pronoun use, word counts, etc.), face-to-face and CMC groups were more cohesive. In addition, linguistic style matching predicted task performance, but only for the face-to-face groups. This information supports the idea that groups mutually create symbolic worlds through their communication.

Interestingly, open disagreement is more frequent in highly cohesive groups, probably because a climate of trust gives each member the security needed to openly disagree on issues, facts, and ideas.[72] On the other hand, if high-status members indicate that they perceive disagreement to be a personal affront and demand compliance, then cohesiveness may become groupthink and be maintained at the expense of high-quality decision making. Cohesiveness, then, is generally desirable. Table 6.1 offers suggestions to enhance cohesiveness:[73]

TABLE 6.1
Creating cohesiveness in a face-to-face team

1. **Help members get to know each other.** You do not have to become best friends, but teams perform better when members spend time getting to know one another.[74]

2. **Set clear, achievable group goals.** High-performing, cohesive teams have a compelling goal that is clear:[75] "We want to win the state debate championship."

3. **Treat members with care and respect.** Group work is not just about the task, but also about member relationships. Follow the ethical guidelines described in Chapter 1.

4. **Develop a group identity.** This may include nicknames, rituals (e.g., Happy Hour Fridays), mascots, insignia, and so forth. Encourage members to develop a rich fantasy life.

5. **Stress teamwork.** Talk about what "we" have accomplished, not what "I" have accomplished.

6. **Recognize member accomplishments.** Look for ways to compliment and praise members. Everybody appreciates attention and recognition.

7. **Reward and celebrate *group* accomplishments.** This can take the form of recognition dinners, public praise, letters of recommendation, and so forth. Outstanding leaders look for ways to celebrate group accomplishments in a variety of ways.

8. **Support both agreement and disagreement.** Highly cohesive groups are comfortable with disagreement. Conflict should be encouraged, not repressed. When conflicts are resolved, group members often feel closer than ever.

9. **Have fun!** Teamwork isn't only about completing the task—it's about enjoying and appreciating your fellow group members. Having fun, either during meetings or during nontask special occasions, can help unify a group.

Building Cohesiveness in Virtual Teams   A **virtual team** is one in which the members' interactions take place primarily through some combination of electronic systems, such as telephone, computer, fax, and videoconferencing, instead of face-to-face.[76] Because virtual team members may never meet face-to-face, building cohesiveness and trust is especially challenging. Actually, because many teams use technology to enhance their face-to-face work, Johnson and her colleagues suggest that it is more accurate to think about computer mediation in teamwork as a continuum, from no computer use to entirely virtual.[77] These researchers found that there was a tipping point—if more than 90 percent of a group's work was conducted via computer mediation, members' positive feelings and perceptions of the team's effectiveness were reduced. They suggest that even a small amount of face time would improve effectiveness.

Being geographically dispersed does not automatically hurt a team. Bazarova and Walther compared entirely dispersed, entirely collocated, and mixed groups with some members together and some members dispersed.[78] They found that members of the dispersed groups were less likely to blame each other and make other negative attributions, perhaps because they assumed that differences in the local conditions were responsible for differences in how members behaved. In addition, Leonardi and his associates found that CMC members found ways to decrease the distance they sometimes feel from their colleagues.[79] They suggest treating distance as a relative concept, with computer mediation having the ability either to increase or decrease the perception of distance, depending on the needs of members.

There are ways to help build trust in virtual teams, including providing for social communication (e.g., setting up a social chat room for a group), showing enthusiasm, making sure members know how to handle the technology, and providing timely feedback.[80] The suggestions in Table 6.2 will help you create a cohesive virtual team.[81]

Virtual Team

A group that meets primarily or exclusively through some combination of electronic means (computers, telephones, videoconferences, and so forth).

TABLE 6.2
Creating a cohesive virtual team

1. **Get acquainted.** All members know who is on the team, where they are located, and how to reach everyone by phone, e-mail, text messaging, etc. Members post short biographies and pictures.

2. **Provide a virtual "social space" and encourage its use.** Create a virtual space for members to chat about non-work-related matters, the way face-to-face teams do.

3. **Manage the team's uncertainty.** The team leader should spell out the team's purpose, specific outcomes, and timeline at the beginning.

4. **Manage technology issues.** Make sure members agree on the technology to use and are trained in and reasonably comfortable with using it.

5. **Meet face to face, if possible.** Although it's not always practical or possible, meeting face to face helps build a team feeling, especially early in a team's life.

6. **Clarify the communication rules to be used for team business.** Because virtual communication lacks social presence, it can seem abrupt. The leader should encourage members to be precise with their language, explain how often members will be expected to check in, and specify what communication forms should be used when (for instance, when to use e-mail and when to use the phone).

7. **Keep the team documents in an easily accessed virtual space.** Set up a bulletin board, wiki, dropbox, or chat room where the team can access minutes, memos, and supporting documents to help keep them on task.

Supportiveness

LaFasto and Larson found that there are significant differences in climate between high-performing teams and ones that are merely OK (or worse).[82] Climates of effective teams are relaxed, warm, and comfortable; members feel accepted, valued, and competent. The climate in poor teams is tense, cynical, political, cold, and overly critical. The members of excellent teams are consistently described as supportive, interested, and willing to help the rest of the members succeed.[83] They bolster other members' confidence, pitch in to help each other, and listen well to each other. Nonsupportive members, in contrast, are "me" oriented, disinterested in the others, and do only the jobs they are assigned.

What LaFasto and Larson observed is consistent with what Gibb observed many years ago.[84] Gibb found that members' communication—how members treat each other—can create a supportive or a defensive group climate. A **supportive climate** is one that values each member. Members know they are wanted and appreciated, that their ideas and opinions are important to the group. Members confirm and support each other. They build each other up. However, in a **defensive climate,** members tear each other down and violate the ethical principle, mentioned in Chapter 1, that states that members should not belittle or ridicule one another. If you have ever worked in a defensive climate, you know that only a portion of your energy is being

Supportive Climate

A group climate in which each member is valued and appreciated.

Defensive Climate

A group climate in which members attack and belittle each other, and where members feel they have to defend themselves from possible attack.

directed to the group's task. Instead, much of it goes to protecting yourself from psychological attack. You can't do your best work that way, so ultimately the group's work suffers.

Gibb described six dimensions of group climate, which we summarize in Table 6.3. Please note that defensiveness and supportiveness are conveyed as much—or more—through nonverbal messages as through verbal ones, particularly tone of voice. When you read the defensive statements we provide as examples, imagine they are being said in a snotty or sarcastic tone of voice.

Supportive Communication	Defensive Communication
Description: Tries to understand other points of view; takes responsibility for one's own opinions and beliefs.	**Evaluation:** Judges and criticizes; blames other people.
"I've noticed that, for the last few meetings, we've started 15 minutes after the announced starting time."	"What's the MATTER with you people? Is there some REASON why we can't get started on time?"
Problem orientation: Tries to solve the problem; enlists others' help; invites others' ideas.	**Control:** Tries to be in charge; dominates; insists on having one's own way.
"What do you all think we should do?"	"Here's what I've decided we're going to do."
Spontaneity: Open, honest, genuine communication.	**Strategy:** Manipulative communication that tries to steer the group in a particular direction.
"I like that idea, but one problem I see with it is . . ."	"Don't you think it would be better if . . .?"
Empathy: Demonstrates caring and understanding; shows members they are valued.	**Neutrality:** Demonstrates lack of understanding and lack of concern; indifference.
"Congratulations! That's a great job, but we're really going to miss you."	"You're leaving? Can I have your office?"
Equality: Minimizes status differences and power distance; encourages members to contribute equally.	**Superiority:** Makes status differences clear; maximizes power distance; pulls rank.
"Nice to meet you, Suzie. Go ahead and call me Gloria, not Dr. Galanes."	"Nice to meet you, Suzie. I'm Dr. Galanes."
Provisionalism: Expresses opinions tentatively; open to others' ideas and opinions.	**Certainty:** Expresses opinions dogmatically and with no room for others' opinions; know-it-all attitude.
"Right now I'm leaning toward Option A, but I'd like to know what you all think."	"Option A is the ONLY thing that will work!"

TABLE 6.3
Supportive and defensive communication

Teambuilding

Sometimes a group needs something out of the ordinary to help it develop or improve its cohesiveness. **Teambuilding** refers to any planned program of activities designed to enhance teamwork, increase cohesiveness, or improve a group's performance in some way: improving decision making, handling conflict, increasing creativity, improving communication skills, and many other group throughput processes. Often, teambuilding activities occur during retreats that take groups out of their normal settings and encourage them to focus on the teambuilding topic.

The best teambuilding programs are tailored to meet the unique needs of each specific group. Tony DiCicco, coach of the U.S. women's soccer team, customized a program especially for the team. He discovered that women respond well to challenges but poorly to chastisement. So, for example, he showed them videos "catching them being good" rather than replays of mistakes. The team participated in trust walks guided by a motivational psychologist. Other common strategies are used in teambuilding sessions (see Table 6.4).

Teambuilding activities can be effective and lasting. A recent analysis of 20 teambuilding studies confirmed that teambuilding improves team outcomes, particularly goal setting, interpersonal relationships, problem solving, and role clarification.[85] Of these, focusing on goal setting and role clarification had the largest effect, with large teams particularly benefited. Another study of the effects of a specific three-day retreat for department leaders found that team improvements still held three years later.[86]

Virtual teams create climates, too, by how members communicate. In one study, Bird found that members in a discussion devoted to the television

TABLE 6.4
Guidelines for teambuilding sessions

A teambuilding session may be planned by a group's leader (see Chapter 8), one of the members, a subgroup within the group, or an outside consultant or facilitator. The following are suggestions for teambuilding planners.[87]

1. **Define the purpose of the teambuilding activity.** The observation and evaluation tools in Chapter 12 can help you pinpoint key areas to address that meet the needs of the group.

2. **Take the group out of its usual setting for the teambuilding activities.** This will enhance concentration on the teambuilding activities and decrease distractions.

3. **Teambuilding sessions must be planned with clear objectives** to give the process focus, yet flexible enough to allow adaptation to the teambuilding process as it unfolds.

4. **Help the group members appreciate the strength in their own diversity.** Often, group members who work with each other day in and day out can lose sight of the fact that their differences can be beneficial to the group rather than frustrating.

5. **Stay tuned to the importance of blending work and meaningful ritual.** The richness of a group's culture is reflected in its rituals, celebrations, and other symbolic activities that serve to coordinate a strong identity.

series *Dr. Quinn, Medicine Woman* created a nurturing online community free of flaming and insults by monitoring their behavior and supporting the list owner in disciplining members who stepped out of line.[88] Members first received a code of conduct when they joined the community and agreed to abide by it. This community has lively disagreements that are respectful, and Bird observed a high level of trust and openness in this virtual community.

Recap: A Quick Review

A group's climate is felt and seen in its emotional and relational atmosphere. Cohesive climates emerge out of patterns supportive group interaction.

1. Group cohesiveness is observed in high member satisfaction, constructive and supportive behaviors, effective coping behaviors in the face of difficulties, and more control over group member behavior.

2. Cohesiveness, while obviously a characteristic of the socioemotional quality of the group culture, is also closely tied to the group's commitment to its goal (or task).

3. Highly cohesive groups, contrary to common assumptions about cohesiveness, show higher rates of open disagreement than do less cohesive groups.

4. Cohesiveness can be facilitated by teamwork, clear goals, allowing time for members to get to know each other, rewarding accomplishments, creating group identity and the rituals to reinforce it, allowing the group time to play, and supporting open disagreement in climates of trust.

5. Virtual groups face the same challenges that face-to-face groups do in creating cohesive climates; in addition, they must consider how their computer technology can both facilitate and impede their cohesiveness.

6. Patterns of supportiveness versus defensive behaviors should be reinforced if a group is to build cohesive climates.

7. Teambuilding is a special set of procedures that group members can use to build cohesiveness; the procedures are out of the ordinary but may be necessary.

QUESTIONS FOR REVIEW

Go to self-quizzes on the Online Learning Center at mhhe.com/galanes14e to test your knowledge of the chapter concepts.

Why do some groups manage to build the kind of group cultures that facilitate success and others fall apart? We argue that the secrets are found in the group's communication among its members and its environment. The medical team of unassailable member competence just could not "get it together." Consider their group and the others mentioned in this chapter when you review these questions.

1. How would you describe the structuration process of the medical group as they try to develop an instructional program? How do they end up creating a group that moves them away from a democratic spirit?

2. How would you describe secondary
   tension to this group and what would
   you recommend to them as ways to
   better negotiate this tension?

3. What are the communicative dynamics
   of both ascribed and earned status in
   Julian's behaviors as well as the other
   members of the medical group? How
   might Julian's idiosyncracy credit help
   and harm the group culture?

4. What might a fantasy chain look like in
   the medical group? How could it have
   helped them move back to their desire
   for a more democratic spirit?

5. Ted graciously agrees to take Richard's
   place in the acting troupe shaken by
   Richard's departure. What are critical
   actions that Ted and the troupe must

   try to make if they are to move through
   the stages of socialization effectively?

6. Consider your responses to question 5. What kinds of norms do your
   responses suggest would help this
   group effectively negotiate a new
   member and change into a more productive group culture?

7. What would a defensive climate sound
   and look like in the acting troupe?
   What are the major norms implied in
   your description, and how would you
   propose that the troupe could change
   any one or more of those norms?

8. Consider the special context and
   challenges to cohesiveness of virtual
   groups. How would you lead a teambuilding activity for this kind of group?

KEY TERMS

 *Test your knowledge of these key terms by visiting the Online Learning Center Web site
at mhhe.com/galanes14e.*

Adaptive structuration theory
Cohesiveness
Conformity
Fantasy
Fantasy chain
Fantasy theme
Group climate
   Defensive climate
   Supportive climate
Group culture

Group socialization
   Antecedent phase
   Anticipatory phase
   Assimilation phase
   Encounter phase
   Exit phase
Idiosyncracy credit
Norm
Primary tension

Rules
Secondary tension
Status
   Ascribed
   Earned
Structuration
Symbolic convergence
Teambuilding
Virtual team

BIBLIOGRAPHY

Bormann, Ernest G. *Small Group Communication:
Theory and Practice,* 3rd ed. New York:
Harper & Rowe, 1990, Chapters 5,
7 and 8.

Clark, Neil. *Teambuilding: A Practical Guide for
Trainers.* New York: McGraw-Hill, 1994.

Ellis, Donald G., and B. Aubrey Fisher. *Small
Group Decision Making: Communication and*

the Group Process, 4th ed. New York: McGraw-
Hill, 1990, Chapter 5.

Feldman, Daniel. "Development and Enforcement
of Group Norms." *Academy of Management
Review, 9* (1984): 47–53.

Larson, Carl E., and Frank M. J. LaFasto.
*Teamwork: What Must Go Right/What Can Go
Wrong.* Newbury Park, CA: Sage, 1989.

Lipnack, Jessica, and Jeffrey Stamps. *Virtual Teams: Reaching Across Space, Time and Organizations with Technology.* New York, Wiley, 1997.

Poole, Marshall S. "Group Communication and the Structuring Process." In *Small Group*

Communication: A Reader, 7th ed. Robert S. Cathcart, Larry A. Samovar, and Linda D. Henman, eds. Dubuque, IA: Brown & Benchmark, 1996, 85–95.

NOTES

1. This story is a modified version of a case found in Marshall S. Poole, "Group Communication and the Structuring Process," in *Small Group Communication: A Reader,* 7th ed., eds. Robert S. Cathcart, Larry A. Samovar, and Linda D. Henman (Dubuque, IA: Brown & Benchmark, 1996): 89–91.

2. Bryan Seyfarth, "Structuration Theory in Small Group Communication: A Review and Agenda for Future Research," in *Communication Yearbook* 23, ed. Michael Roloff (Thousand Oaks, CA: Sage, 2000): 341–79.

3. Marshall S. Poole, David R. Siebold, and Robert D. McPhee, "Group Decision Making and the Structurational Process," *Quarterly Journal of Speech,* 71 (1985): 74–102; Marshall S. Poole, David R. Siebold, and Robert D. McPhee, "A Structurational Approach to Theory-Building in Decision-Making Research," in *Communication and Group Decision Making,* eds. Randy Y. Hirokawa and Marshall S. Poole (Beverly Hills, CA: Sage, 1986): 237–64; and Poole, "Group Communication and the Structuring Process," 85–95.

4. Poole, "Group Communication and the Structuring Process."

5. Sunwolf and David R. Seibold, "Jurors' Intuitive Rules for Deliberation: A Structurational Approach to Communication in Jury Decision Making," *Communication Monographs,* 65 (1998): 282–307.

6. Seyfarth, "Structuration Theory in Small Group Communication."

7. Craig Scott, "Communication Technology and Group Communication," in *The Handbook of Group Communication Theory and Research,*

ed. Lawrence Frey (Thousand Oaks, CA: Sage, 1999): 432–72.

8. Scott A. Krebs, Elizabeth V. Hobman, and Prashant Bordia, "Virtual Teams and Group Member Dissimilarity: Consequences for the Development of Trust," *Small Group Research,* 37 (December 2006): 721–41.

9. Seyfarth, "Structuration Theory in Small Group Communication."

10. Poole, "Group Communication and the Structuring Process."

11. B. Aubrey Fisher and Randall K. Stutman, "An Assessment of Group Trajectories: Analyzing Developmental Breakpoints," *Communication Quarterly,* 35 (Spring 1987): 105–24.

12. Bales, *Interaction Process Analysis.*

13. Ernest G. Bormann, *Discussion and Group Methods: Theory and Practice,* 3rd ed. (New York: Harper & Row, 1990): 132–39.

14. David B. Barker, "The Behavioral Analysis of Interpersonal Intimacy in Group Development," *Small Group Research,* 22 (February 1991): 76–91.

15. Bormann, *Discussion and Group Methods,* 139.

16. Robert F. Bales, *Interaction Process Analysis* (Reading, MA: Addison-Wesley, 1950).

17. J. I. Hurwitz, A. F. Zander, and B. Hymovitch, "Some Effects of Power on the Relations among Group Members," in *Group Dynamics: Research and Theory,* 3rd ed., eds. D. Cartwright and A. Zander (New York: Harper & Row, 1968): 291–97.

18. Dean C. Barnlund and C. Harland, "Propinquity and Prestige as Determinants of Communication Networks," *Sociometry,* 26 (1963): 467–79.

19. E. Hollander, "Conformity, Status, and Idiosyncracy Credit," *Psychological Review,* 65 (1958): 117–27.

20. Michelle Estrada, Justin Brown, and Fiona Lee, "Who Gets the Credit? Perceptions of Idiosyncracy Credit in Work Groups," *Small Group Research,* 26 (February 1995): 56–76.

21. Michele G. Alexander, Alexander W. Chizhik, Estella W. Chizhik, and Jeffrey A. Goodman, "Lower-Status Participation and Influence: Task Structure Matters," *Journal of Social Issues,* 65 (2) (2009): 365–81.

22. Reef Youngreen and Christopher D. Moore, "The Effects of Status Violations on Hierarchy and Influence in Groups," *Small Group Research*, 39 (October 2008): 569–87.

23. Craig R. Scott, "Communication Technology and Group Communication," in *Handbook of Group Communication Theory and Research,* ed. Lawrence R. Frey (Thousand Oaks, CA: Sage, 1999): 432–72.

24. Carolyn J. Wood, "Challenging the Assumptions Underlying the Use of Participatory Decision Making Strategies: A Longitudinal Case Study," *Small Group Behavior,* 20 (1989): 428–48.

25. Joseph A. Bonito, "The Effect of Contributing Substantively on Perceptions of Participation," *Small Group Research,* 31 (October 2000): 528–53.

26. Ernest G. Bormann, "Symbolic Convergence Theory and Communication in Group Decision Making," in *Communication and Group Decision Making,* eds. Randy Y. Hirokawa and Marshall S. Poole (Newbury Park, CA: Sage, 1986): 221. For a thorough review of the development and use of symbolic convergence theory, see Ernest G. Bormann, John F. Cragan, and Donald C. Shields, "Three Decades of Developing, Grounding, and Using Symbolic Convergence Theory," in *Communication Yearbook, 25,* ed. Willam B. Gudykunst (Thousand Oaks, CA: Sage, 2001): 271–313.

27. Robert F. Bales, *Personality and Interpersonal Behavior* (New York: Holt Rinehart and Winston, 1970): 105–8, 136–55.

28. Eric E. Peterson, "The Stories of Pregnancy: On Interpretation of Small-Group Cultures," *Communication Quarterly,* 35 (1987): 39–47.

29. Catherine C. Morocco, "Development and Function of Group Metaphor," *Journal for the Theory of Social Behavior,* 9 (1979): 15–27.

30. Bormann, "Symbolic Convergence Theory."

31. Linda L. Putnam, Shirley A. Van Hoeven, and Connie A. Bullis, "The Role of Rituals and Fantasy Themes in Teachers' Bargaining," *Western Journal of Speech Communication* (Winter 1991): 87.

32. This fantasy chain is a slightly expanded version of the one that occurs near the beginning of the leadership segment, part 1, of the videotape ancillary to this text, *Communicating Effectively in Small Groups.*

33. Morocco, "Development and Function of Group Metaphor," 15–27.

34. Ibid.

35. Putnam, Van Hoeven, and Bullis, "The Role of Rituals and Fantasy Themes in Teachers' Bargaining."

36. Bruce Riddle, Carolyn Anderson, and Matthew Martin, "Small Group Socialization Scale: Development and Validity," *Small Group Research,* 31 (October 2000): 554–72.

37. Carolyn Anderson, Bruce Riddle, and Matthew Martin, "Socialization Processes in Groups," in *Handbook of Group Communication Theory and Research,* ed. Lawrence Frey (Thousand Oaks, CA: Sage, 1999): 139–63.

38. Ibid.

39. Riddle et al., "Small Group Socialization Scale."

40. Larry A. Erbert, Gerri M. Mearns, and Samantha Dena, "Perceptions of Turning Points and Dialectical Interpretations in Organizational Team Development," *Small Group Research,* 36 (February 2005): 21–58.

41. Riddle et al., "Small Group Socialization Scale."

42. Moira Burke, Robert Kraut, and Elisabeth Joyce, "Membership Claims and Requests: Conversational-Level Newcomer Strategies in Online Groups," *Small Group Research*, 41 (February 2010): 4–40.

43. Anderson et al., "Socialization Processes in Groups."
44. Ibid., 149.
45. Stewart Sigman, "The Applicability of the Concept of Recruitment to the Communication Study of a Nursing Home: An Ethnographic Case Study," *International Journal of Aging and Human Development,* 22 (1985–86): 215–33. See also Melanie Booth-Butterfield, Stephen Booth-Butterfield, and Jolene Koester, "The Function of Uncertainty Reduction in Alleviating Primary Tension in Small Groups," *Communication Research Reports,* 5 (1988): 146–53.
46. Anderson et al., "Socialization Processes in Groups," 151.
47. K. E. W. Morrison, "Information Usefulness and Acquisition During Organizational Encounter," *Management Communication Quarterly,* 9 (1995): 131–55.
48. Anderson et al., "Socialization Processes in Groups," 152.
49. Ibid., 164.
50. Joann Keyton, "Group Termination: Completing the Study of Group Development," *Small Group Research,* 24 (1993): 84–100.
51. Henry M. Robert, *Robert's Rules of Order,* Newly Revised (Glenview, IL: Scott, Foresman, 1990): 471–521.
52. Susan B. Shimanoff, "Coordinating Group Interaction via Communication Rules," in *Small Group Communication: A Reader,* 6th ed., eds. Robert S. Cathcart and Larry A. Samovar (Dubuque, IA: Wm. C. Brown, 1992): 255.
53. Tom Postmes, Russell Spears, and Lea Martin, "The Formation of Group Norms in Computer-Mediated Communication," *Human Communication Research,* 26 (July 3): 341–71.
54. J. Dan Rothwell, *In Mixed Company,* 4th ed. (Fort Worth, TX: Harcourt, 2001): 63.
55. Steven Beebe and John Masterson, *Communicating in Small Groups,* 6th ed. (New York: Addison-Wesley, 1999): 82–83.
56. Gay Lumsden and Donald Lumsden, *Communicating in Groups and Teams,* 3rd ed. (Belmont, CA: Wadsworth/Thomson Learning, 2000): 281.
57. Poole, "Group Communication and the Structuring Process."
58. Joann Keyton, "Relational Communication in Groups," in *Handbook of Group Communication Theory and Research,* ed. Lawrence R. Frey (Thousand Oaks, CA: Sage, 1999): 192–222.
59. Information for this story was compiled from several sources. Most information came from Mark Starr and Martha Brant, "It Went Down to the Wire . . . and Thrilled Us All," *Newsweek,* (July 19, 1999): 45–54; with additional information from Bill Saporito, "The New Dream Team," *Time* (July 19, 1999): 60–67; and David Leon Moore, "Goalkeepers: Don't Expect Any Handouts," *USA Today* (Friday, July 9, 1999): 1C–2C.
60. David B. Barker, "The Behavioral Analysis of Interpersonal Intimacy in Group Development," *Small Group Research,* 22 (February 1991): 76–91.
61. Carolyn M. Anderson, Bruce L. Riddle, and Dominic A. Infante, "Decision-Making Collaboration Scale: Tests of Validity," *Communication Research Reports,* 15 (1999): 245–55.
62. Harold L. Nixon II, *The Small Group* (Englewood Cliffs, NJ: Prentice Hall, 1979): 74–76.
63. Charles R. Evans and Kenneth L. Dion, "Group Cohesion and Performance," *Small Group Behavior,* 22 (1991): 175–86; Stanley M. Gully, Dennis J. Devine, and David J. Whitney, "A Meta-Analysis of Cohesion and Performance: Effects of Level of Analysis and Task Interdependence," *Small Group Research,* 26 (November 1995): 497–520.
64. Gully et al., "A Meta-Analysis of Cohesion and Performance."
65. M. E. Johnson and J. G. Fortman, "Internal Structure of the Gross Cohesiveness Scale," *Small Group Behavior,* 19 (February 1988): 187–96.
66. Lynne Kelly and Robert L. Duran, "Interaction and Performance in Small Groups: A Descriptive Report," *International Journal of Small Group Research,* 1 (1985): 182–92.
67. Charles N. Greene, "Cohesion and Productivity in Work Groups," *Small Group Behavior,* 20 (1989): 70–86.

68. Wood, "Challenging the Assumptions."

69. Frederick G. Elias, Mark E. Johnson, and Jay B. Fortman, "Task-Focused Self-Disclosure: Effects on Group Cohesiveness, Commitment to the Task, and Productivity," *Small Group Behavior* 20 (1989): 87–96.

70. William F. Owen, "Metaphor Analysis of Cohesiveness in Small Discussion Groups," *Small Group Behavior, 16* (1985): 415–26.

71. Amy L. Gonzales, Jeffrey T. Hancock, and James W. Pennebaker, "Language Style Matching as a Predictor of Social Dynamics in Small Groups," *Communication Research*, 37 (February 2010): 3–19.

72. Barker, "The Behavioral Analysis of Interpersonal Intimacy."

73. Synthesized from Ernest G. Bormann & Nancy C. Bormann, *Effective Small Group Communication,* 2nd ed. (Minneapolis: Burgess, 1976): 70–76; and Gloria J. Galanes (unpublished research based on interviews with peer-nominated excellent leaders, 2002).

74. Vanessa Urch Druskat and D. Christopher Kayes, "Learning versus Performance in Short-Term Project Teams," *Small Group Research,* 31 (June 2000): 328–53.

75. Larson and LaFasto, *TeamWork;* Frank LaFasto and Carl Larson, *When Teams Work Best: 6,000 Team Members and Leaders Tell What It Takes to Succeed* (Thousand Oaks, CA: Sage, 2001): 65–83.

76. Anthony M. Townsend and Samuel M. DeMarie, "Are You Ready for Virtual Teams?" *HR Magazine,* 41 (September 1996): np; accessed via EBSCOhost on World Wide Web, August 2, 2002.

77. Stefanie K. Johnson, Kenneth Bettenhausen, and Ellie Gibbons, "Realities of Working in Virtual Teams: Affective and Attitudinal Outcomes of Using Computer-Mediated Communication," *Small Group Research*, 40 (December 2009): 623–49.

78. Natalya N. Bazarova and Joseph B. Walther, "Attributions in Virtual Groups: Distances and Behavioral Variations in Computer-Mediated Discussions," *Small Group Research*, 40 (April 2009): 138–62.

79. Paul M. Leonardi, Jeffrey W. Treem, and Michele H. Jackson, "The Connectivity Paradox: Using Technology to Both Decrease and Increase Perceptions of Distance in Distributed Work Arrangements," *Journal of Applied Communication Research*, 38 (February 2010): 85–105.

80. Sirkka Jarvenpas, quoted in Carla Joinson, "Managing Virtual Teams," *HR Magazine,* 47 (June 2002): np; accessed via EBSCOhost on World Wide Web, August 2, 2002.

81. Synthesized from the following sources: Joinson, "Managing Virtual Teams;" Jessica Lipnack and Jeffrey Stamps, *Virtual Teams: Reaching Across Space, Time, and Organizations with Technology* (New York: Wiley 1997); Townsend and DeMarie, "Are You Ready for Virtual Teams?"

82. LaFasto and Larson, *When Teams Work Best;* 68.

83. Ibid., 14–15.

84. Jack R. Gibb, "Defensive Communication," *Journal of Communication,* 11 (1961): 141–48.

85. Cameron Klein, Deobrah DiazGranados, Eduardo Salas, Huy Le, C. Shawn Burke, Rebecca Lyons, and Gerald F. Goodwin, "Does Team Building Work?" *Small Group Research*, 40 (April 2009): 181–222.

86. Susan R. Glaser, "Teamwork and Communication: A Three-Year Case Study of Change," *Management Communication Quarterly,* 7 (February 1994): 282–96.

87. Suggestions synthesized from Neil Clark, *Teambuilding: A Practical Guide for Trainers* (New York: McGraw-Hill, 1994); Glenn M. Parker, *Team Players and Teamwork* (San Francisco: Jossey-Bass, 1991); Glenn H. Varney, *Building Productive Teams: An Action Guide and Resource Book* (San Francisco: Jossey-Bass, 1989); and our own experiences.

88. S. Elizabeth Bird, "Chatting on Cynthia's Porch: Creating Community in an E-mail Fan Group," *Southern Communication Journal,* 65 (Fall 1999): 49–65.

Leading Small Groups: Theoretical Perspectives

STUDY OBJECTIVES

As a result of studying Chapter 7, you should be able to:

1. Define the concepts of *leadership, leader, designated* and *emergent* leaders.

2. Explain the five sources of interpersonal influence (power) in a group and how they are involved in small group leadership.

3. Describe the process of leadership emergence.

4. Explain traits, styles, and function approaches to small group leadership and the strengths and weaknesses of each approach.

5. Describe the unique focus of each of the contingency approaches to small group leadership.

6. Name and describe nine communicative competencies important for small group leaders.

7. Explain how leaders and members are interdependent, describe the LMX model and transformational leadership.

8. Explain *distributed leadership* and why it is an appropriate model for small, task-oriented groups.

9. Explain the "leader as completer" and its relationship to distributed leadership.

CENTRAL MESSAGE

Small group leadership is an interactive phenomenon; it results from, among other things, communicative behaviors appropriate to group task and relational goals, other members' behaviors, and the context.

Jennifer, Robyn, Jiang, and Andreas comprise the broadcast advertising team in the corporate offices of a California-based retail company. Jennifer, with the company for more than 20 years, is the team's designated leader and their broadcast media buyer. Jiang, their promotions coordinator, is responsible for planning and directing promotional events, such as the back-to-school campaign, which coincide with the television and radio advertisements. He also makes sure that all of Jennifer's business records are kept up to date. Andreas, their production coordinator, assists Jennifer in writing, producing, and directing all television and radio commercials. Robyn, their broadcast advertising coordinator and Jennifer's administrative assistant, is primarily responsible for creating and maintaining working relationships with television and radio sales representatives. The company's quarterly profits are directly tied to successful media campaigns, which themselves are directly tied to how well this team works together. Jennifer, although highly regarded by her advertising peers, has a leadership style that does not sit well with the team. She tries to control all their tasks and manage their socioemotional climate. Her style poses problems for the team in the following ways.

High turnover is common in this division. New employees are constantly being trained, often inadequately. New employees are never fully informed about their job responsibilities because Jennifer tightly controls the flow of information to them, but she is often too busy to work with them. Too often, they learn how and what they are supposed to do after being reprimanded by Jennifer for making a mistake. This creates resentment among the team and company time and money. Further resentment is created by Jennifer's desire to control their socioemotional environment. For instance, if Andreas writes a poor advertising script, she expects one of his co-workers to tell him rather than convey the bad news herself. Yet this retail company is successful in part because the broadcast advertising group produces effective advertising. At what point is ineffective leadership considered a problem? Who is responsible for change? Is the character of a group solely determined by one person's behaviors? If you were an outside consultant, what would you say to this division? These and other issues will be touched on in this chapter.

According to Larson and LaFasto, the final ingredient for effective group performance is team leadership, with the right person serving in the leadership role.[1] Serving as a leader in a small group can be a source of self-esteem, recognition, and appreciation; it can also be a nightmare.

Much of the conventional wisdom about what makes a good leader is simply wrong or oversimplified. We hope this chapter and the next one will dispel those beliefs. In Chapter 7 we examine the concepts of *leader* and *leadership,* describe the process of leadership emergence, review traditional and contemporary perspectives about leadership, examine the relationship between leaders and members, and develop an argument in favor of *distributed leadership* for most small task-oriented groups. In Chapter 8 we focus on practical application: The specific duties leaders are expected to perform and how to perform them well.

Leadership and Leaders

Whether your group has a specific person called a leader or not does not matter. What *does* matter, if your group is to function effectively, is that it has *leadership*. Let's look more closely at the relevance of this distinction to small group communication.

Leadership

Hackman and Johnson define **leadership** as a process: "Leadership is human (symbolic) communication which modifies the attitudes and behaviors of others in order to meet group goals and needs."[2] We use their definition because it emphasizes *communication* and thus reflects our definition of communication as explained in chapter 2. Leadership is accomplished through communication—what a leader actually says and does in interaction. Leadership involves persuasion and discussion, not psychological coercion or physical violence. Through communication, leaders *modify* the positions of group members to help the group achieve its goals. Leadership, then, does not exist in a vacuum but is a shared property of the group and is transactionally created through group communication.

Leadership involves power; however, all members of a group can influence group interaction with their power resources.[3]

Sources of Influence (Power)   The ability to influence others stems from **power** that is derived from a particular source, which can include reward, punishment, legitimate, referent, and expert power.[4]

Leaders can *reward* followers by giving them both tangibly and intangibly with special attention, acknowledgment, compliments, personal favors, special titles, money, and material goods. For instance, telling members they were high performers within their work teams (regardless of whether they were) and giving them a high-status job title actually increased their satisfaction, performance, commitment to the organization, and decreased turnover.[5] Jiang, the broadcast advertising team's program coordinator, is in a position to reward Jennifer with up-to-date business records. Jennifer may come down hard on her broadcast-advertising team, but she lets them leave early and gives the team free tickets to social events like concerts and baseball games. Leaders can also *punish* by withholding these same items. For example, Jennifer rolls her eyes when a group member offers what she thinks is a dumb idea. *Coercion* is a special form of punishment power that uses threats or force to "influence" others. Although good leaders may effectively use punishment (especially the fear of losing something important, such as belonging to the group or the respect of the others), they do not use hardball tactics to coerce or force compliance. Coercion breeds resentment, sabotage, and rebellion, which are not desirable small group outcomes. We do not consider coercion to be ethical leadership.

Legitimate power stems from a title or role acknowledged by the followers. Jennifer was manager of the broadcast advertising team, which made

Leadership

Influence exerted through communication that helps a group achieve goals; performance of a leadership function by any member.

Power

The potential to influence behavior of others, derived from such bases as the ability to reward and punish, expertise, legitimate title or position, and personal attraction.

her leadership legitimate. However, legitimate power holds only if requests are accepted as appropriate by followers. Thus, a committee chair does not have the right to tell members how to dress or what kind of car to buy.

Referent power is based on attraction or identification with another person. Robyn's relationships with television and radio sales representatives are built around her referent power; the reps like her and will go the extra mile for her. Some referent leaders have charisma, making others want to associate with them and imitate their behavior. The more leaders are admired and respected, the more members copy their behavior, and thus the greater their power to influence the group.

Expert power comes from what others believe a member knows or can accomplish. The person with expert power is influential because he or she is perceived as having knowledge or skills vital to the group. Jennifer's 20 years of service to the company and the high regard with which she is held by the advertising community help establish her expert power base within the team. If your group is responsible for producing a panel discussion for the rest of your class and you happen to be the only member who has ever participated in a panel discussion, your expertise empowers you in that particular group.

Usually, a leader's power stems from more than one source. The more sources on which a person's power rests, the more that person has the potential to dominate a group. Conversely, the more these bases of power are distributed among members, the more likely leadership will be shared, decision making will be collaborative, and satisfaction will be high. In other words, leadership can be provided by all members' exercising their influence in service to the group goal. We expand on this idea later.

Leaders

Leader

A person who uses communication to influence others to meet group goals and needs; any person identified by members of a group as leader; a person designated as leader by election or appointment.

The term *leader* refers to a person.[6] A **leader** in a small group influences the behavior of others through communication. There are two general types of group leader, *designated* and *emergent*. A person elected or appointed to a leadership position is called a **designated leader.** This person may have the title of chair, coordinator, facilitator, or something similar.

Designated Leader

A person appointed or elected to a position as leader of a small group.

Having a designated leader offers stability to a group. Small groups with stable leadership achieve their goals more often than small groups without it. Energy won't be siphoned off in a leadership struggle, which causes dissatisfaction and low cohesion.[7] Groups with designated leaders *accepted by the members* have fewer interpersonal problems and often produce better outcomes than groups without designated leaders.[8] Thus, even in a group where influence is widely shared, someone must coordinate the flow of communication and the work of the members, and that is the group's designated leader.

Having the title *designated leader* gives someone legitimate power, like Jennifer, but that person must still earn the respect and support of other members. A designated leader's behavior will be evaluated and may

Designated leaders greatly affect small groups.

frequently be challenged by the members. If the designated leader's power rests solely on holding the title, someone else with more broadly based power will likely emerge as a more influential informal leader.

Leadership Emergence An **emergent leader** is a group member who starts out on an equal footing with other members, but emerges as the person others perceive as being the group's leader, charted by Aubrey Fisher (refer to Figure 7.1).[9]

Fisher's three-stage model presumes that all members are potential candidates for emergent leadership. In Stage 1, one or more members drop from consideration right away. They may be uninterested in leading, unable to lead (e.g., too busy), or may communicate in ways others perceive as nonleaderlike (e.g., quiet, uninformed, or dogmatic).[10]

In Stage 2, the members who remain under consideration are supported by other members. In Figure 7.1, A and C are still in contention; B and D have backed out of contention, but support A and C as *lieutenants,* thereby forming two coalitions. Stage 2 can be lengthy, with verbal sparring typical. Eventually, one contender fails at his or her bid for leadership and drops out. The candidate who falls out of contention is usually seen as too directive (bossy) or offensive to the others (for example, talks too much or is manipulative).[11]

In Figure 7.1 Stage 3, C has fallen out and A has emerged as leader, but this may shift. For example, A may be a poor leader and E, B, or D may decide to support someone else.

Emergent Leader

The person who emerges as the leader of an initially leaderless group in which all members start out as equals.

FIGURE 7.1   A model of emergent leadership

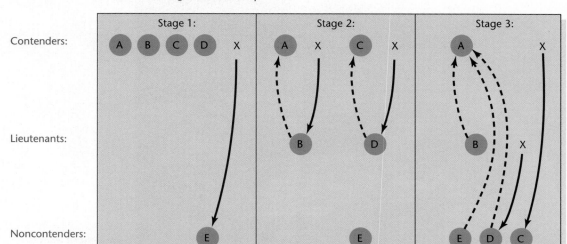

There are several common variations to Fisher's model. One person may quickly secure a lieutenant, with the rest of the group falling into line. Sometimes, an early leader is inadequate in some way and is deposed, throwing the group back into Stage 2. Two final contenders may cooperate as co-leaders, bypassing Stage 3.

While Fisher's model describes general processes, it does not explain *who* will emerge. Several personal characteristics have been linked to leadership emergence, including self-monitoring, verbal style, psychological gender, and task-oriented communication.

Personal Characteristics of Emergent Leaders   Self-monitoring, an input variable discussed in Chapter 5, is associated with emergent leadership. *Self-monitoring* refers to individuals' abilities to monitor social cues and adapt their actions.[12] High self-monitors are sensitive to contextual cues, socially perceptive, and able to respond flexibly according to what seems needed at any given time. Zaccaro et al. found that more than half the variance of leadership emergence was explained by self-monitoring.[13] Ellis and Cronshaw found that male high self-monitors emerged as leaders but women did not,[14] most likely because female high self-monitors, sensitive to subtle clues, sometimes sense that their leadership behavior is perceived as inappropriate. They may then modify their actions to tone down that leadership behavior. High self-monitors are more likely to emerge as leaders across situations, but low self-monitors, who are motivated more by internal than external cues, can also emerge as leaders in situations where they want to express leadership; they will not emerge as leaders if they hold unfavorable attitudes about leadership.[15]

Verbal style, together with the content of a member's communication, also is associated with leadership emergence.[16] Baker found that members whose communication style was quiet, tentative, or vague were perceived as uncommitted to the group and not knowledgeable about the group's task. These members were quickly eliminated as potential leaders because others did not believe they contributed ideas or helped organize the group. Those who did emerge as leaders suggested procedures for the group more often, thereby helping the group get organized. The emergent leader's profile was high in procedure giving, moderate in idea giving, and low in stating opinions. High-status members who were not leaders had a dramatic style that, though unusual, was tolerated because of their perceived helpfulness to the group.

In Chapter 4, we touched upon issues of sex and diversity. Years ago, men were more likely to emerge as leaders than women. However, biological sex has not been a useful predictor of who will emerge as a group leader. *Psychological gender*, on the other hand, may be more useful. Regardless of sex, individuals enacting a masculine communication style (i.e., independent, self-reliant, willing to take a stand) emerged more often as leader than those enacting feminine and nonandrogynous communication styles.[17] Generally, groups appear to choose leaders on the basis of performance, most especially task performance. Hawkins' observations of mixed-sex groups revealed that task-relevant communication, not gender, explained who emerged as leader.[18] Furthermore, she found no significant differences in the amount of task-relevant remarks contributed by men and women. Sex, gender, and leader emergences are difficult processes to unravel. Time and again, research provides evidence that men and women lead equally well, and group members are equally satisfied with both male and female leaders.[19]

Emergent leaders seem to do a good job of focusing on the *task*. Emergent leaders strongly influence the other group members' perceptions about their ability to get the job done, particularly early in a group's life.[20] They seemed to be able to help members make sense of information and events in positive ways, to shape the group's perception about its capabilities, and to set expectations for group success.

The importance of task-focused communication is confirmed by De Souza and Klein, who found that members' individual abilities to contribute to the task and their commitment to the group goal were associated with their emergence as leaders.[21] They also discovered that groups with emerged leaders outperformed those without them. This latter finding is supported by Kurth, who found that group members themselves considered groups with emerged leaders more successful.[22]

What can we learn from this discussion of leadership emergence? First, even if a group has a designated leader, one or more group members can also emerge as leaders. Emergent leaders appear to lead primarily through referent, expert, and reward power. Without a title or a legitimate base of power, they rely on communication skills to lead and, by definition, have the support of other group members. In fact, while this may appear obvious, research has shown that members who see themselves as leaders tend to act in leader-like ways, reinforcing the likelihood others will see them as leaders, thus in turn strengthening their own view of themselves as leaders.[23] Emergent leadership is a combination of acting skillfully and believing you are a leader. Designated leaders, on the other hand, do enjoy the status given them by their legitimate power. In face-to-face groups, their designated status as leader precedes their behaviors—perhaps because they are more aware members are expecting them to act like leaders.[24] Acting contrary to expectation could spell trouble for them. Remember that each group's situation is different. The type of task, the personalities, and the preferences of the members influences the kind of leadership accepted by a group.

Second, if your group does not have a designated leader, one will emerge. Here's what to do if you *don't* want to emerge as your group's leader:[25]

- Miss as many meetings as possible.
- Say very little in group meetings.
- Volunteer readily to be the group's recorder.
- Do what you are told by other members.
- When you do contribute to the group, be dogmatic, verbally aggressive, and act like you know it all—especially early in the group's history.
- When you can, play the role of joker.
- Show disdain for leadership.

Leadership Emergence in Virtual Groups   Most of what we know about leadership emergence and emergent leader behaviors applies only to face-to-face groups. In previous chapters, we have pointed out that groups are increasingly integrating computer technology into their group work, anywhere from partially to completely. This technological reality forces us to question its impact on leadership processes in these groups. What does leadership look like in virtual groups, where members rarely if ever meet face to face?[26]

The old school of thought did not hold much hope for leadership in online task groups because computer-mediated communication lacked the nonverbal behavior believed necessary for the social dynamics of leadership. Designated leaders would not be able to act like leaders, and emergent leaders were unlikely. The physical traits associated with leaders may not be seen online, and certainly, status spatial cues (e. g., seating arrangements) cannot be used to warrant perceptions of leadership. However, we know from the preceding discussion that particular communication behaviors are associated with leadership: amount and kind of communication. These behaviors are certainly accessible for perceptions of leadership online.

In addition, we learned in Chapter 6, that people are able to create a social presence online; they just have to adapt to the textual, linguistic dominance of the medium and give themselves time to build social relationships.

Members, for example, do enact designated roles online and display individuality cues online as well. However, is there empirical evidence that this ability translates into leadership emergence in virtual groups?

In the first study of its kind, Wichham and Walther explored perceptions of leadership in both leaderless virtual groups and designated leader virtual groups.[27] They not only found evidence of emergent leadership, they also discovered that members quite easily could identify their leaders. In fact, often at least two members get identified as emergent leaders, and leaderless groups reported more agreement on who the leaders were compared to groups with designated leaders. In virtual groups, compared to face-to-face groups, the legitimacy of being designated a leader does not carry the same weight. Online behaviors enacted by a member can override their designated position.

What behaviors do members report as important to their perceptions of who is leader? Hands down, the frequency of communication was significant to perceptions of leadership just as it is in face-to-face groups, especially when paired with the trust and liking online members are capable of creating (see CMC and cohesiveness in Chapter 6). In addition to frequency of communication, members who encouraged others rather than ordering them around were perceived as the leaders. These results pertain only to perceptions of leadership in virtual groups and do not apply to groups that use a mixture of face-to-face and online interaction.

The secrets of effective leadership have been sought for years, as you will learn in the next section. As with other social scientific phenomena, the study of leadership has moved from the simple to the complex.

Recap: A Quick Review

Leadership is a process central to small group dynamics. Although a group may not have a leader, it must have leadership to move effectively toward its goal.

1. Leadership is often defined as a process involving communication efforts to influence others toward group goals. The nature of the interpersonal influence may stem from reward, legitimate, referent, coercion, or expert power.

2. *Leader* is a term used to identify a person or position. Groups can have designated or emergent leaders, and sometimes both.

3. Leadership emergence can be described in a general three-stage model depicting how one person can, over time, become perceived as the group's leader. Several kinds of behaviors, such as self-monitoring and verbal style, are related to leadership emergence.

4. Informal leaders who emerge in groups that already have designated leaders usually rely on referent, reward, and expert power.

5. In virtual groups, more than one informal leader usually emerges, and frequency of communication is a key factor in leadership emergence.

Traditional Approaches to Leadership

Many disciplines have studied leadership. Traditional approaches focused almost solely on the *leader* by trying to pinpoint the traits or communicative styles of effective leaders.

Traits Approaches

One of the earliest approaches to studying leadership is the traits approach. A *trait,* as we saw in Chapter 5, is a characteristic of a person. Some traits, such as eye color or height, are unchangeable; others, such as self-monitoring, are subject to some control. The **traits approach** to leadership examines how traits are related to leadership and assumes that leaders are more likely to have certain traits than other group members are.

The earliest studies of the trait approach (from before the Christian epoch through the 1950s) assumed that people were collections of relatively fixed traits, with one leadership situation being much like another. Trait approach researchers believed that leaders were born, not made, and looked for the traits that distinguished leaders from followers. Some studies found that leaders tended to have higher IQs and were taller, more attractive, and larger than nonleaders.[28] As you might guess, there simply is no trait or combination of traits that leaders have but other members don't.

Modern trait approaches examine a variety of complex personality characteristics such as enthusiasm, verbal facility, creativity, critical-thinking ability, and self-confidence. Although they are labeled traits, they seem to represent behaviors that leaders perform rather than invariable, unchangeable characteristics. This approach, although intuitively appealing, is not especially helpful in our attempts to understand complex leadership processes. Personality characteristics are not easily measured and, most important, this approach does not help distinguish between good and bad leaders nor does it explain why leadership changes in a group.[29]

We believe that leadership is not a universal set of traits, but it is clear that people with the ability to adapt their behaviors and who possess communication skills that help clarify the group's task and motivate other members will be influential in groups.[30] Foreshadowing our discussion of other approaches, we believe that appropriate leader behaviors in a group are shaped by the needs of the group.

Styles Approaches

Styles approaches, other early approaches, focus on the pattern of behaviors a leader exhibits in a group. Traditional theorists attempted to discover whether there was one ideal style for small group leaders. More recent style theorists have looked at styles in relationship to member and task characteristics.

Three commonly described styles are *democratic, autocratic,* and *laissez-faire,* summarized in Table 7.1. **Democratic leaders** encourage

---

Traits Approach

The approach to leadership that assumes that leaders have certain traits that distinguish them from followers or members of a group.

Styles Approach

The leadership approach that studies the interrelationship between leader style and member behaviors.

Democratic Leaders

Egalitarian leaders who coordinate and facilitate discussion in small groups, encouraging participation of all members.

TABLE 7.1   Comparison of autocratic, democratic, and laissez-faire leadership styles

	Autocratic	Democratic	Laissez-faire
Characteristics	Theory X assumptions. Directive; controlling. Speaks with certainty. Gives orders; makes assignments. Makes decisions for group.	Theory Y assumptions. Participative; invites input. Speaks provisionally. Makes suggestions; helps structure group time. Involves group in decisions.	Asks group to take charge. Doesn't necessarily voice opinion. Expects group to decide everything.
Typical statements	"I've decided that this is what you're going to do . . ."	"What ideas would you suggest for getting this done?"	"Whatever you decide is okay with me."
Useful when	Group members are unmotivated, uninterested, or unfamiliar with task. Emergency situations occur.	Group members are knowledgeable, interested. Group has time to discuss and deliberate.	Group members are experts, have worked together before, can assume group leadership.

members to participate in group decisions, including policy-making decisions ("What ideas do you have for organizing our task?"). **Laissez-faire leaders** take almost no initiative for structuring a group, but they may respond to inquiries from members ("I don't care; whatever you want to do is fine with me."). **Autocratic leaders** tightly control their groups, making assignments, directing all verbal interaction, and giving orders ("Here's how I've structured your task. First, you will . . . "). They ask fewer questions but answer more than democratic leaders and make more attempts to coerce but fewer attempts to get others to participate.[31]

The autocratic and democratic styles of leadership described here correspond closely with the Theory X and Theory Y assumptions described by management theorist Douglas McGregor.[32] Theory X assumes that people don't like to work and must therefore be compelled by a strong, controlling leader ("boss") who supervises their work closely. In contrast, Theory Y assumes that people work as naturally as they play and are creative problem solvers who like to take charge of their own work. Leaders who accept the assumptions of Theory Y behave democratically by providing only as much structure as a group needs, allowing members to participate fully in decision making and other aspects of the group's work.

Research findings have been consistent about the effects of leadership style on group output.[33] Democratically led groups are generally more satisfied than autocratically led groups in U.S. culture. Autocratic groups often work harder in the presence of the leader, but they also experience more incidents of aggressiveness and apathy. Democratic groups whose leaders

Laissez-Faire Leaders

Do-nothing designated leaders who provide minimal services to the group.

Autocratic Leaders

Leaders who try to dominate and control a group.

provide some structure and coordination are better problem solvers and their members are more satisfied than those in laissez-faire groups without structure. Research continues into the complex relationship among leadership style, satisfaction, and productivity. One meta-analysis found a correlation between style and productivity only when the type of task was taken into account.[34] Democratic leadership is more productive in natural settings and, in laboratory settings, seems to produce higher productivity on moderately or highly complex tasks.

Democratic leadership and satisfaction are not always linked. Members' satisfaction depends on a number of moderating factors.[35] First, the relationship is stronger in artificial laboratory groups than bona fide groups. Second, it is stronger in larger groups, perhaps because inviting member participation counteracts the reduced cohesiveness of larger size. Finally, there is a sex link. Men in bona fide groups prefer autocratic leadership, but men in laboratory groups prefer democratic leadership. This occurs perhaps because artificial groups are composed of college students with more liberal views of what is appropriate leadership, whereas men in the work world are used to more directive leadership. Women prefer democratic groups regardless of setting.

Satisfaction with leadership style is highly culture-dependent. For instance, an autocratic style will be preferred in cultures with high power distance, such as Mexico, the Philippines, and India.[36] Similarly, cultures that demonstrate a stereotypically masculine orientation, including Japan, Austria, and Venezuela, would likewise prefer autocratic leadership.

The issue with styles approaches to leadership is that they oversimplify the complexities of groups as open systems. In the United States a leadership style that provides some degree of structure appears to be the most desirable for both productivity and satisfaction, but several contingent factors (including cultural values) affect how much structure and control a particular group seems to need; that is, you cannot separate any one style from the situation that leaders and followers find themselves in.[37] Even Jennifer, designated leader of the advertising team in our opening story, who typically engages in a controlling leadership style, finds herself adjusting to the situation and to the peculiarities she discovers in each new employee. Group needs do not remain constant over time.

Contemporary Approaches to Leadership

Contemporary approaches to studying leadership acknowledge that leadership is a complex *process* influenced by several factors. These approaches focus on the entire group and assume that group leadership is a shared property of the group as a whole.

Functions Approach

The functions approach sets the stage for viewing group leadership as the property of the group, the responsibility of the leader and other group members together. The **functions approach** is grounded in a common theme found in previous chapters—successful groups recognize both their task and socioemotional needs. This approach rests on two assumptions: (1) For any group to reach its goal, *both* task and social (relational) functions have to be performed, and (2) the performance of these task and social functions is the responsibility of *all* group members.

Task and social dimensions must be performed by someone in the group. The functions approach posits that one or more members must first diagnose what functions are needed and then perform those functions. Designated leaders are expected to do this effectively. If there is no designated leader, then *who* performs these functions is a good predictor of who is likely to emerge as a leader.

Several researchers have attempted to identify specific task and maintenance functions needed for effective leadership. One of the earliest category systems for studying behavioral functions was Bales' Interaction Process Analysis.[38] Later, Benne and Sheats identified a variety of task and maintenance functions productive for the group, along with a set of functions that are counterproductive.[39] Several of the Benne and Sheats functions are included in the lists in Chapter 5.

Fisher believed that a leader mediates, or acts as a go-between, among group events, activities, and the final outcome.[40] To do this, Fisher identified four broad functions of leaders. First, they provide sufficient information and help the group process considerable information. Second, they enact a variety of functions within the group. Third, they help members make sense of what happens in the group by supplying good reasons for actions and decisions. Finally, they stop the group from jumping to unwarranted conclusions or adopting stock answers too quickly.

Consistent with this idea is Weick's metaphor of the leader as medium.[41] Task groups must overcome a variety of task and interpersonal obstacles. To do this well, members must grapple with a vast amount of complex and ambiguous information so they understand it. Weick says that the basic function of leadership is to help the group create an organizing system to aid in problem solving. The leader is the medium, or mechanism, through which this is accomplished. In our opening story, Jennifer does not help her employees narrow down plausible interpretations for many work tasks, especially their job responsibilities. She is an inadequate medium.

Contingency Approaches

All **contingency approaches** assume that group situations vary, with different situations requiring different leadership behaviors. These approaches explicitly acknowledge that factors such as members' skills and experience, cultural values, the type of task, and the time available affect the type of leadership likely to be effective. Contingency approaches acknowledge the complexity of small group systems, with factors such as task, members, and environment affecting each other interdependently.

Functions Approach

The study of functions performed by leaders; the theory that leadership is defined by the functions a group needs and can be supplied by any member.

Contingency Approaches

The study of leadership that assumes that the appropriate leadership style in a given situation depends on factors such as members' skills and knowledge, time available, the type of task, and so forth.

Group members as well as researchers accept contingency-like assumptions. Wood asked members of continuing small groups what they expected of designated leaders. Members expected different behaviors depending on the group's focus, although a moderate degree of team spirit was expected for all types of groups.[42] Griffin found that the amount of structuring and directive behavior expected from supervisors depended on subordinates' growth needs. People with high growth needs (i.e., who enjoy challenging jobs) preferred participative, considerate supervisors, whereas employees with lower growth needs preferred more autocratic leadership.[43] A complex relationship was found among member needs, leadership style, and member satisfaction, supporting the general contingency hypothesis of leadership in small discussion groups.

Downs and Pickett also examined contingencies of leader style and member needs.[44] Groups of participants with high social needs were most productive with task-oriented procedural leaders and least productive with no designated leader. Groups of people low on interpersonal needs did equally well with designated leaders who provided task structuring only, with leaders who provided both task structuring and socioemotional leadership, and with no designated leader. Groups with some members high and some low in interpersonal needs performed somewhat better without a designated leader.

Further work with the contingency approach has revealed that satisfaction involves a complex interaction between leader behavior and work group attitudes.[45] The following traits of followers influence the type of leadership they preferred: degree of authoritarianism, need for achievement, and locus of control (whether one feels in control of one's own life or governed by fate).[46] We can safely conclude that a discussion leader needs to be flexible, adapting to situational contingencies, but that in almost all situations in the United States, a democratic structuring approach will be productive, or will at least not be counterproductive. We would modify this advice for other cultures. We now examine two specific contingency approaches with opposing views of leader adaptability.

Fiedler's Contingency Model   Some contingency approaches assume that there are limits to leaders' abilities to adapt; in other words, people are relatively inflexible and have leadership styles they prefer to use. Fiedler's contingency model reflects this view. Three factors determine how a leader should act: leader-member relations (good or poor), task structure (structured or unstructured), and strength of the leader's position, or legitimate, power (strong or weak).[47] Fiedler's central idea is that individuals' needs and personalities make them suited for leadership only in certain situations, so it is more productive to match a leader to an appropriate situation than to change the leader's preferred style. Fiedler believes that most problem-solving groups are best served by democratic structuring leaders with concerns for people, but that some situations (for example, emergencies or leading primary groups) call for more controlling or relationship-oriented styles.

	Quadrant 3: Supporting	Quadrant 2: Coaching
High	High-intermediate readiness level, requires high relationship/low task behavior	Low-intermediate readiness level, requires high task/high relationship behavior
Relationship Behavior (Supportive Behavior)	Quadrant 4: Delegating High readiness level, requires low relationship/low task behavior	Quadrant 1: Directing Lowest readiness level, requires high task/low relationship behavior
Low	**Low**	**High**
	Task Behavior (Directive Behavior)	

FIGURE 7.2 Task and relationship needs of developing groups

Source: Adapted from Hersey and Blanchard's Situational Leadership Model, in *Management of Organizational Behavior: Leading Human Resources* (8th ed.), by Paul Hersey, Kenneth H. Blanchard, and Dewey E. Johnson, 2001, Prentice-Hall, Upper Saddle River, NJ.

Hersey and Blanchard's Situational Model Other contingency approaches assume that people are flexible enough to adapt their behavior to meet the needs of many groups. Representative of this approach is the situational model developed by Hersey and Blanchard.[48] Leadership behaviors can be located along two dimensions, relationship orientation (giving socioemotional support) and task orientation (coordination efforts, instructions, direction, and so forth). A leader can be high on one, both, or neither dimension (see Figure 7.2). However, whether a leader is effective depends on the ability to adapt to the needs of the members *at all points* during the life of the group. For instance, a new group of inexperienced members who may be unwilling, may be unable or may simply not have the information to complete the task on their own is in low readiness. In this case, *directing* (low relationship and high task) may be an effective leadership style. Through close supervision and direction, group members can improve their readiness; the leader adds in relationship behaviors to exhibit a *supporting* style. As members need less direction about the task, the leader can focus on the relationships among members. *Supporting* (high relationship and low task) styles recognize a high level of readiness in members, with the leader able to facilitate shared responsibility for the group. Any group member may be supported in performing leadership behaviors. The fully ready group is one in which members are both able and willing to perform and need little direction and encouragement. In such groups, leaders can shift to a *delegating* (low relationship and low task) style in which responsibility is turned over to the group as a whole.

Hersey and Blanchard's model places great faith in the leader's ability to adapt to the needs of the group as the group's situation changes over time. Indeed, many leaders are flexible, Wood found, evidence of such behavioral flexibility.[49] The designated leader's communication varied depending on the stated purpose of the discussion. Leaders tended to compensate as needed, depending on what had occurred at previous meetings, by providing more or less structure. Her results have been confirmed. Sorenson and Savage observed greater variety in the effective leaders' communicative styles than in those of ineffective leaders, particularly with respect to the degrees of dominance and supportiveness they exhibit.[50] In addition, leaders covered a wide range of functions, and their interaction was more complex than the interaction of other members.[51]

The Communicative Competencies Approach

No matter what approach you adopt to study leadership, you must acknowledge that *communication* is how a leader gets the job done. Barge and Hirokawa proposed a **communicative competency model** of group leadership, which is based on two assumptions: Leadership involves behaviors that help a group overcome obstacles to goal achievement and communication skills (competencies) are how leaders actually lead.[52] This model maintains the task and relationship distinctions mentioned earlier and assumes that leaders are flexible enough to draw on a repertoire of task and relationship competencies.

Good leaders know which competencies are needed when, and these members use ethical principals to ask whether they should enact these behaviors. Note as you read each of the following competencies how they mirror our five ethical principles from Chapter 1: integrity, personal and social responsibility, encouraging equitable participations, honesty and openness, and respect for self and others.

Communicative Competency Model

The model that assumes that the communication-related skills and abilities of members are what help groups overcome obstacles and achieve their goals.

1. **Effective small group leaders communicate actively, clearly, and concisely.**

   Research consistently finds that emergent leaders are high in verbal participation, although not necessarily the highest in a group.[53] Involvement in group discussion and decision making alone is not enough; group leaders had better communicative skills than other members.[54]

   What are these skills? Leaders were perceived as speaking more clearly and fluently than other members.[55] They were better at verbalizing problems, goals, values, ideals, and solutions. These skills become even more important when the task is complex, member roles are ambiguous and the climate is negative.[56]

2. **Effective group leaders communicate a good grasp of the group's task.**

   Above all else, their communication behaviors reveal extensive knowledge about the task, skills for organizing and interpreting that knowledge, and an understanding of procedures that facilitate task accomplishment. They have technical know-how, are credible to the members, and know when to ask others for help.[57]

3. **Effective group leaders inspire team members' confidence in themselves.**

   Effective leaders set clear expectations and let their members know they have confidence in members' abilities. Empowering members affects both the members' collective confidence and their performance.[58] They bolster members' self-assurance by providing clear performance goals, by assigning responsibilities that demonstrate the leader's trust in them, and by accentuating the positive.[59] Showing confidence in team members increases their desire to achieve, decreases their fear of failure, and can produce extraordinary successes!

4. **Effective group leaders skillfully mediate information and ideas supplied by all members.**

   Such leaders foster critical thinking, which leads to thorough evaluation and integration of information. They structure unorganized information, ask probing questions to bring out pertinent information, and evaluate inferences and conclusions drawn from information. They help all members focus on activities relevant to the group's goal.[60]

5. **Effective group leaders express their opinions provisionally.**

   Most Americans prefer their leaders not to be dogmatic. Groups whose leaders suspended judgment and encouraged full consideration of minority viewpoints produced better solutions than did other groups.[61] Moreover, groups whose leaders withheld their opinions until later in a discussion produced more and better alternatives than groups whose leaders expressed their opinions early.[62] Groups prefer open-minded leaders.[63]

6. **Effective group leaders are not self-centered.**

   Interviews with 90 successful leaders across professions revealed that "there was no trace of self-worship or cockiness in our leaders."[64] They exhibit personal commitment to that goal in both words and deeds.[65] Furthermore, such leaders readily confront members who are more self- than group-centered.[66]

7. **Effective group leaders model a collaborative climate by respecting and supporting others.**

   Excellent leaders establish a collaborative climate and make it safe for group members to communicate.[67] Such leaders are sensitive to nonverbal signals and the feelings these signify. The best leaders perceive the needs and goals of members, then adjust their own behaviors to these needs.[68]

Effective discussion leaders are courteous. This may be particularly important in a virtual environment, where members don't normally (or ever) interact face-to-face. Defensive communication may find a "natural home" in the impersonal atmosphere of a virtual team because members are typically chosen on the basis of their expertise, and thus may be tempted to present opinions and information as "certain and unchallengeable."[69] Team leaders must make a special effort to promote the social aspects of teamwork and to help align members' priorities with organizational priorities in a way that will interest and excite them.

8. **Effective group leaders promote celebration of diversity and sensitive diversity management.**
   Effective group leaders make sure to include *all* members in the team's work and play. Team members perceive them as impartial, not showing favoritism to particular members.[70] Leaders also make time for group members to get to know one another and learn to appreciate one another as individuals. Ethnically diverse teams especially benefit from leadership that focuses on relational aspects of the team.[71]

9. **Effective group leaders share rewards and credit with the group.**
   Leaders are often tempted to take credit for the accomplishments of the group and to consolidate their personal power. But effective leaders share as equals both within the group and when dealing with outsiders. They give credit to the group for accomplishments and work to develop the leadership competencies of all members.[72]

Leadership Competencies in Virtual Groups

Leadership competency in virtual groups is no less complicated, and perhaps more so.[73] Virtual team members are geographically spread out all over, often speak different languages, and work across multiple time zones. Added to this mixture are varying levels of technological experience and the time it takes to build relationships and complete tasks online. Surprisingly, there is some debate over the degree to which virtual groups need leadership: leave them alone with their own talents or give them the leadership appropriate to virtual groups? In a qualitative analysis of virtual group leaders and members across six different organizations, four areas of leadership competence emerged.[74]

1. **Effective leaders are central to the success of virtual groups.**

   Just as members in face-to-face groups expect their leaders to help them gel as a group, so do members of virtual groups. These leaders; however, require a specialized skill set adapted to the unique character of the medium.

2. **Effective virtual group leaders have to thoughtfully manage virtual group meetings.**

   These meetings take on added significance in virtual groups because they are the one time members are "together." They must be organized well and run by a leader who knows the ins and outs of technology, like teleconferencing, in order to ensure equitable, thoughtful participation.

3. **Effective virtual group leaders do not lose sight of the social dimension of virtual groups.**

   Our discussion in Chapter 6 pointed out that computer-mediated communication is heavily task focused due to the lack of nonverbal behaviors in this medium. Social dynamics do occur in CMC, but it takes time to develop. Virtual group leaders have to consciously pay attention to personalizing the work of members or face losing this important dimension of groups.

4. **Effective virtual group leaders use different technologies in their group work.**

   Virtual groups use a variety of media to communicate (e.g., e-mail, teleconferencing, instant messaging, telephones, etc.), and leaders have to know how to use each one effectively.

Recap: A Quick Review

Leadership is one of the most studied processes in the social sciences. Several theories have been developed to explain the secrets of effective leadership.

1. Trait approaches to leadership try to identify personality characteristics of leaders (e.g., self-confidence, creativity). However, these approaches have not found a universal set of traits that guarantees leadership in all situations.

2. Style approaches try to discover those patterns of behaviors that leaders exhibit in groups (e.g., democratic, autocratic, and laissez-faire). However, one style for all situations is not related to effective leadership.

3. The functions approach zeros in on critical task and socioemotional functions that any group member must perform if a group is to reach its goal. However, it does not adequately consider group contingencies.

4. Contingency approaches assume that different group contingencies require different leader behaviors or that a group's situation will change over time, requiring adjustment on the leader's part.

5. The communicative competency model focuses specifically on the task and relationship skills leaders in all kinds of groups need to perform well.

The Relationship Between Leaders and Followers

All contemporary approaches to leadership assume an interdependent relationship between the communication behavior of the leader and the behavior, skills, preferences, and expectations of the members. Although we discuss leaders and members separately, we do so only for convenience; leader-member behaviors form a unit, an interdependent system. Whether a leader's behaviors are effective depends in large part on both the perceptions and behaviors of the other members.

Most people in our culture want their leaders to perform structuring behaviors and to be considerate as well. Members expect leaders to be enthusiastic and organized, to encourage participation from all members, and to suggest procedures for the group.[75] Subordinates like their leaders' communication style to be *affirming* (relaxed, friendly, and attentive) and low in verbal aggressiveness (attacks on others' self-concepts).[76]

One characteristic that affects what members perceive and prefer is sex. Several studies suggest that women enact leadership differently than men, perhaps because members perceive different behavior as appropriate for men and women. Women seem to distance themselves from the label of *leader*[77] and seem to be more comfortable calling themselves *organizer* or *coordinator,* apparently because they perceive a stigma attached to the leader label.[78] Women often become leaders by outworking men in a group, and they use more themes of cohesion.[79]

The expectations of other members affect how male and female leaders are perceived. Women who used a dominant approach to leadership were less influential than women who used a considerate approach, especially with men.[80] And although women gave dominant female leaders higher ratings of effectiveness, they liked female bosses less than men did. Koch found that female leaders received more negative nonverbal signals than male leaders, but were rated as more competent.[81] She also found that in bona fide groups, where members know and have worked with each other, female leaders received more nonverbal displays of all kinds, positive and negative. Interestingly, they received significantly more negative displays from other women. Male leaders were perceived as competent by men and women equally, whereas female leaders were perceived as more competent by men than by women. Clearly, the sex of the leader and the sex of the group members interact in complex ways. As we have noted before, sex is a characteristic that affects groups in numerous, sometimes surprising, ways.

Leader-Member Exchange (LMX) Model

The leadership model based on the finding that supervisors develop different kinds of leadership relationships with their subordinates, depending on characteristics of both the leader and members.

Leader-Member Exchange (LMX) Model

One model that has looked systematically at the nature of the interdependent relationship of leader-member behaviors and perceptions is the **Leader-Member Exchange (LMX) model,** which suggests that supervisory leaders develop different kinds of leadership relationships with different members, depending on leader and member characteristics. Members differ in the amount of *negotiating latitude* they are allowed by leaders; a member with a high negotiating latitude is given a great deal of leeway to design and perform his or her job, whereas a member with low negotiating latitude is not accorded such freedom by the leader. Generally, members with higher negotiating latitude are more satisfied and more committed to the organization or group. The member's degree of negotiating latitude is transacted through a reciprocal interaction process with the leader, whose impression of the member's capabilities helps determine the degree of negotiating latitude permitted.[82]

The best leader-member fit seems to be determined by similarity about the need for power.[83] Leaders with high power needs gave greater negotiating latitude to members with high power needs; likewise, leaders with low power needs gave greater negotiating latitude to members with low power needs. Clearly, leaders with high power needs take a different approach to forming groups than leaders with low power needs; both types of leaders appear to be more comfortable with members who share their assumptions about the appropriate use of power.

Leaders must be careful not to play favorites. McClane compared groups with wide variations in the amount of negotiating latitude and groups with little variation.[84] High differentiation (having some members with high negotiating latitude and some with little latitude in the same group) may have an undesirable effect on a group, particularly if the members accorded high negotiating latitude are seen as an elite core group with the rest feeling like hired hands. Lee found that members with little negotiating latitude perceived less fairness than members with high latitude.[85] Those members who thought things were fair also perceived the work group's communication to be more cooperative. Although it is normal for leaders to interact differently with different members, clearly, they must tread carefully in doing so.

The foregoing discussion is designed to remind us that neither the leader nor the members operate in a vacuum; instead, their interactions are shaped by each other. Even though we isolate leadership and treat it as an individual variable for study purposes, in fact it is a *system-level* variable that is a property of the group as a whole, not of the individual called the group's leader. Contemporary transformational leadership models try to capture this interdependence between leaders and followers in a different way.

Transformational Leadership

The concept of **transformational leadership** emerges out of contemporary organizational and management philosophy.[86] Traditional models of leadership assume that leaders trade rewards for group or team member performance.[87] Leaders use their power to influence group members to do things for the group. However, an inspirational leader can *transform* group members so that they perform beyond original expectations.[88]

Transformational leaders do not use rewards or even punishment to sustain their influence; instead, they use creative and dramatic messages to craft a powerful inspirational vision that motivates members to exceed expectations. Four characteristics define transformational leadership.[89] First, these leaders give the kind of *individual attention* to group members that we discussed in the LMX models. They coach, advise, and treat

Transformational Leadership

Transformational leadership empowers group members to exceed expectations by rhetorically creating a vision that inspires and motivates members.

members as unique individuals who *matter* to the group. Second, these leaders are charismatic, portraying a spirit of confidence that is attractive. Members find them *inspirational* in their communication, which in turn motivates them, through symbols and rhetorical visions, to aim higher. Third, transformational leaders blend their socioemotional skills with an *intellectual stimulation* that is contagious, encouraging members to be sharp critical thinkers and problem solvers. Finally, here is the bottom line: These leaders inspire members of a group or team and thus *empower* them. When people are empowered, they have been given the freedom to discover their own self-efficacy—self-determination and confidence in their ability to perform.[90]

Transformational leadership can elicit extraordinary performance from group members, but it can also trigger higher levels of conflict. Transformational leaders engender greater task involvement among group members, increase members' capacity to debate ideas constructively, and engage members' emotions. However, these factors may prompt members to fight harder to defend their positions, so transformational leadership can be a "double-edged sword."[91]

In addition, how transformational leaders are perceived depends partly on characteristics of the group members. Members whose levels of extraversion and agreeableness are similar to those of the leader perceive more transformational leadership from that leader.[92] Thus, perceptions of a leader are not based only on what the leader does but also on characteristics of members. Do you think members of the broadcast advertising team believe Jennifer is a transformational leader who inspires and empowers them?

Distributed Leadership and the Leader as Completer

Distributed Leadership

The concept that group leadership is the responsibility of the group as a whole, not just of the designated leader; assumes that all members can and should provide needed leadership services to the group.

We have said several times that small group leadership is the property of the group, not the individual who happens to hold the title of leader. We believe strongly that although a group's designated or emergent leader bears a lot of responsibility for coordinating and structuring the group's activities, all members can and should be equally responsible for the leadership of the group. The idea of **distributed leadership** explicitly acknowledges that the leadership of a group is spread among members, with each member expected to perform the communication behaviors needed to move the group toward its goal. Remember, a group may be able to function without a leader, but it cannot function without *leadership*. For example, Counselman described a group that had been active for 17 years without a designated leader.[93] Various leadership functions had been picked up by members of the group. The most important of these were providing structure, gatekeeping, setting group norms, and adhering to the group's task. We know this is unusual; most groups can and should use the services of a designated leader. However, this case verifies the important point that we made earlier: leadership belongs to the group.

Barge provided support for the distributed leadership concept when he compared two models of group leadership—one in which the leader was an active, directive influence in the group and a leaderless model, in which all members engaged in the leadership process.[94] He discovered that the better predictor of group productivity was *overall* leadership activity, as opposed to the activity of the designated leader alone. Barge concluded that although an individual leader's behavior may not necessarily help a group achieve its goals, the overall group leadership behavior does.

Gastil's studies of small group democracy also provide support for distributed leadership. Gastil says that democratic leadership distributes responsibility among members, empowers them by improving their general abilities and leadership skills, and helps the group in its decision-making process.[95]

We hope you agree that it is good for the group *and* good for the members when leadership is distributed among them. But you may be wondering, if members assume leadership duties for the group, where does the leader fit in? The metaphor we suggest is that the members are the bricks that provide support and substance to the group, and the leader is the mortar that binds them together and allows the group to hold its shape, as shown in Figure 7.3. This is the picture of the **leader as completer,** a participant-observer who monitors the group's process, identifies what

Leader as Completer
A leader who functions as a particpant-observer, monitoring the group's process, noticing what is missing, and providing what is needed.

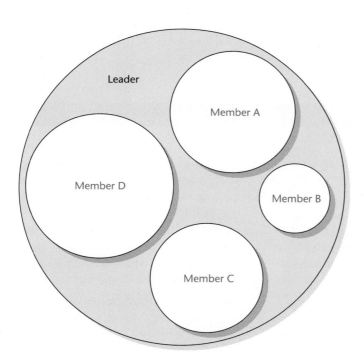

FIGURE 7.3
The leader as "completer" of the group

functions are missing, then either supplies those functions or asks one of the members to do so.[96] For example, one of the things Jennifer does well is notice when group spirits need a pickup; that's when she schedules a happy hour or does something fun, like bringing in a noted chef to cook lunch for the team. One of the things she does *not* do well is clarify information when people are confused. But Andreas is great at that, so he will jump in on his own to make sure people understand everything. This team has been successful not because of Jennifer alone, but because the other team members pitch in as needed. Their strengths compensate, in part, for her weaknesses, and vice versa. This is the advantage that distributed leadership can provide.

Recap: A Quick Review

Leadership involves an interdependent relationship between leader and followers; it is a process that involves all group members.

1. The LMX model of leadership highlights the benefits of the leader's nurturing unique relationships with each group member.

2. Transformational leadership is a contemporary philosophy of leadership stressing the ways a dynamic and creative leader can use rhetoric and powerful symbols to empower group members. A vision is crafted that motivates group members to exceed expectations.

3. Distributed leadership promotes the idea that all members of a group can enact behaviors that effectively move the group toward its goal. The leader then serves as completer, providing whatever is missing.

QUESTIONS FOR REVIEW

Go to self-quizzes on the Online Learning Center at mbhe.com/galanes14e to test your knowledge of the chapter concepts.

This chapter scrutinized the complexity of group leadership. Consider the broadcast advertising team led by Jennifer. Members have problems, in part due to Jennifer's leadership style, but they also produce successful advertisements.

1. Pinpointing the leader of this group is easy. Why? In your own words, how would you describe the leadership of this group?

2. What types of interpersonal influence can you observe in this team? How might the way members use their power explain why they can produce effective advertising, even though they also have leadership problems?

3. Jennifer is this group's designated leader. Could any other member emerge as an informal leader? How?

4. Why are traits and styles approaches inadequate to explaining the leadership of this team, once you examine the team's dynamics?

5. How can functions and contingency approaches help explain why this team is successful, even with its leadership challenges?

6. What communication competencies are found in this group? Which competencies does Jennifer seem to lack?

7. What advice would you give this team to help members move to a more transformational or a distributed model of leadership?

KEY TERMS

 Test your knowledge of these key terms by visiting the Online Learning Center Web site at mbhe.com/galanes14e.

Autocratic leader
Communicative competency model
Contingency approaches
Democratic leader
Designated leader
Distributed leadership

Emergent leader
Functions approach
Laissez-faire leaders
Leader
Leader as completer
Leader-Member Exchange (LMX) model

Leadership
Power
Styles approach
Traits approach
Transformational leadership

BIBLIOGRAPHY

Barge, J. Kevin, and Randy Y. Hirokawa. "Toward a Communication Competence Model of Group Leadership." *Small Group Behavior, 20* (1989): 167–89.

Bennis, Warren, and B. Nanus. *Leaders: The Strategies for Taking Charge.* New York: Harper & Row, 1985.

Cathcart, Robert S., Larry A. Samovar, and Linda D. Henman. *Small Group Communication:* *Theory and Practice.* 7th ed. Madison, WI: Brown & Benchmark, 1996, Section 7.

Hackman, Michael Z., and Craig E. Johnson. *Leadership: A Communication Perspective.* Prospect Heights, IL: Waveland Press, 1991.

Larson, Carl E., and Frank M. J. LaFasto. *TeamWork: What Must Go Right/What Can Go Wrong.* Newbury Park, CA: Sage, 1989.

NOTES

1. Carl E. Larson and Frank M. J. LaFasto, *Team-Work: What Must Go Right/What Can Go Wrong* (Newbury Park, CA: Sage, 1989): 118.

2. Michael Z. Hackman and Craig E. Johnson, *Leadership: A Communication Perspective* (Prospect Heights, IL: Waveland Press, 1991): 11.

3. E. Hollander, "Leadership and Power," in *The Handbook of Social Psychology 3,* vol. II, eds. G. Lindzey and Elliot Aronson (New York: Random House, 1985): 485–537.

4. John R. P. French and Bertram Raven, "The Bases of Social Power," in *Group Dynamics: Research and Theory,* 3rd ed., eds. Dorwin Cartwright and Alvin Zander (New York: McGraw-Hill, 1981): 317.

5. Jeffrey W. Lucas, "Behavioral and Emotional Outcomes of Leadership in Task Groups," *Social Forces,* 78 (December 1999): 747–78.

6. Marvin E. Shaw, *Group Dynamics: Research and Theory,* 3rd ed. (New York: McGraw-Hill, 1981): 317.

7. Ernest G. Bormann, *Discussion and Group Methods,* 2nd ed. (New York: Harper & Row, 1975): 253–69; Nancy L. Harper and Lawrence R. Askling, "Group Communication and Quality of Task Solution in a Media Production Organization," *Communication Monographs,* 47 (1980): 77–100.

8. E. P. Hollander, *Leadership Dynamics* (New York: Free Press, 1978): 13–16.

9. Donald Ellis and B. Aubrey Fisher, *Small Group Decision Making: Communication and the Group Process* (New York: McGraw-Hill, 1994): 203–6.

10. Ernest G. Bormann, *Small Group Communication: Theory and Practice,* 3rd ed.(New York: Harper & Row, 1990): 205–14, 291–292; John C. Geier, "A Trait Approach to the Study of Leadership in Small Groups," *Journal of Communication,* 17 (1967): 316–23.

11. John C. Geier, "A Trait Approach to the Study of Leadership in Small Groups," 316–23.

12. M. Snyder, "Self-Monitoring Processes," in *Advances in Experimental Social Psychology,* vol. 12, ed. L. Berkowitz (New York: Academic Press, 1979).

13. Stephen J. Zaccaro, Roseanne J. Foti, and David A. Kenny, "Self-Monitoring and Trait-Based Variance in Leadership: An Investigation of Leader Flexibility across Multiple Group Situations," *Journal of Applied Psychology,* 76 (1991): 308–15.

14. Robert J. Ellis and Steven F. Cronshaw, "Self-Monitoring and Leader Emergence: A Test of Moderator Effects," *Small Group Research, 23* (February 1992): 113–29.

15. Steven F. Cronshaw and Robert J. Ellis, "A Process Investigation of Self-Monitoring and Leader Emergence," *Small Group Research,* 22 (November 1991): 403–20.

16. Deborah C. Baker, "A Qualitative and Quantitative Analysis of Verbal Style and the Elimination of Potential Leaders in Small Groups," *Communication Quarterly,* 38 (Winter 1990): 13–26.

17. Judith A. Kolb, "Are We Still Stereotyping Leadership? A Look at Gender and Other Predictors of Leader Emergence," *Small Group Research,* 28 (1997): 370–93.

18. Katherine W. Hawkins, "Effects of Gender and Communication Content on Leadership Emergence in Small Task-Oriented Groups," *Small Group Research,* 26 (May 1995): 234–49.

19. Susan Shimanoff and Mercilee M. Jenkins, "Leadership and Gender: Challenging Assumptions and Recognizing Resources," in *Small Group Communication: Theory and Practice,* 7th ed., eds. Robert S. Cathcart, Larry A. Samovar, and Linda Henman (Madison: WI: Brown & Benchmark, 1996): 327–44.

20. Anthony T. Pescosolido, "Informal Leaders and the Development of Group Efficacy," *Small Group Research, 32* (February 2001): 74–94.

21. Gita De Souza and Howard J. Klein, "Emergent Leadership in the Group Goal-Setting Process," *Small Group Research,* 26 (November 1995): 475–96.

22. Lita Kurth, "Democracy and Leadership in Basic Writing Small Groups" (Paper presented at the Annual Meeting of the Conference on College Composition and Communication, March 1995).

23. Cecile Emery, Kim Daniloski, and Ann Hamby, "The Reciprocal Effects of Self-View as a Leader and Leadership Emergences," *Small Group Research,* 42, (2011): 199–224.

24. Kathryn Wickham and Joseph Walther, "Perceived Behaviors of Emergent and Designated Leaders in Virtual Groups," *International Journal of e-Collaboration,* 3 (January–March 2007): 1–17.

25. Ellis and Fisher, *Small Group Decision Making,* 210–12.

26. Wickham and Walther, "Perceived Behaviors," 1–17.

27. Ibid., 1.

28. Ralph M. Stogdill, *Handbook of Leadership: A Survey of Theory and Research* (New York: Free Press, 1974): 63–82; Marvin E. Shaw,

Group Dynamics, 2nd ed. (New York: McGraw-Hill, 1976): 274–75 and Chapter 6.

29. Ellis and Fisher, *Small Group Decision Making,* 182.

30. Charles Pavitt and Pamela Sakaroff, "Implicit Theories of Leadership and Judgments of Leadership among Group Members," *Small Group Research,* 21 (1990): 374–92.

31. Lawrence B. Rosenfeld and Timothy B. Plax, "Personality Determinants of Autocratic and Democratic Leadership," *Speech Monographs,* 42 (1975): 203–8.

32. Douglas McGregor, *The Human Side of Enterprise* (New York: McGraw-Hill, 1960).

33. Ralph K. White and Ronald Lippett, "Leader Behavior and Member Reaction in Three 'Social Climates,'" in *Group Dynamics: Research and Theory,* 2nd ed., eds. Dorwin Cartwright and Alvin Zander (Evanston, IL: Row, Peterson, 1960): 527–53; William E. Jurma, "Effects of Leader Structuring Style and Task-Orientation Characteristics of Group Members," *Communication Monographs,* 46 (1979): 282; Malcom G. Preston and Roy K. Heintz, "Effectiveness of Participatory versus Supervisory Leadership in Group Judgment," *Journal of Abnormal and Social Psychology,* 44 (1949): 344–45; George Graen, Fred Dansereau, and Takau Minami, "Dysfunctional Leadership Styles," *Organizational Behavior and Human Performance,* 7 (1972): 216–36; Norman R. F. Maier and Ronald A. Maier, "An Experimental Test of the Effects of 'Developmental' vs. 'Free' Discussions on the Quality of Group Decisions," *Journal of Applied Psychology,* 41 (1957): 320–23; William E. Jurma, "Leadership Structuring Style, Task Ambiguity and Group Members' Satisfaction," *Small Group Behavior,* 9 (1978): 124–34.

34. John Gastil, "A Meta-Analytic Review of the Productivity and Satisfaction of Democratic and Autocratic Leadership," *Small Group Research,* 25 (August 1995): 384–410.

35. Rob Foels, James E. Driskell, Brian Mullen, and Eduardo Salas, "The Effects of Leadership on Group Member Satisfaction," *Small Group Research,* 31 (December 2000): 676–701.

36. Myron W. Lustig and Laura L. Cassotta, "Comparing Group Communication across Cultures: Leadership, Conformity, and Discussion Processes," in *Small Group Communication: Theory and Practice,* 7th ed., eds. Robert S. Cathcart, Larry A. Samovar, and Linda D. Henman (Boston: McGraw-Hill, 1997): 316–26.

37. Ellis and Fisher, *Small Group Decision Making,* 184.

38. R. F. Bales, *Interaction Process Analysis* (Cambridge, MA: Addison-Wesley, 1950).

39. Kenneth D. Benne and Paul Sheats, "Functional Roles of Group Members," *Journal of Social Issues* 4 (1948): 41–49.

40. B. Aubrey Fisher, "Leadership as Medium: Treating Complexity in Group Communication Research," *Small Group Behavior,* 16 (1985): 167–96.

41. Karl Weick, "The Spines of Leaders," in *Leadership: Where Else Can We Go?* eds. M. McCall and M. Lombardo (Durham, NC: Duke University Press, 1978): 37–61.

42. Julia T. Wood, "Alternative Portraits of Leaders: A Contingency Approach to Perceptions of Leadership," *Western Journal of Speech Communication,* 43 (1979): 260–70.

43. R. N. Griffin, "Relationships among Individual, Task Design, and Leader Behavior Variables," *Academy of Management Journal,* 23 (1980): 665–83.

44. Cal W. Downs and Terry Pickett, "An Analysis of the Effects of Nine Leadership–Group Compatibility Contingencies upon Productivity and Member Satisfaction," *Communication Monographs,* 44 (1977): 220–30.

45. David J. Skaret and Nealia S. Bruning, "Attitudes about the Work Group: An Added Moderator of the Relationship between Leader Behavior and Job Satisfaction," *Group & Organization Studies,* 11 (1986): 254–79.

46. M. L. Chemers, "Leadership Theory and Research: A Systems-Process Integration," in *Basic Group Processes,* ed. P. B. Paulus (New York: Springer-Verlag, 1983): 9–39.

47. Fred E. Fiedler, *A Theory of Leadership Effectiveness* (New York: McGraw-Hill, 1967).

48. Paul Hersey and Kenneth Blanchard, *Management of Organizational Behavior: Utilizing Human Resources,* 7th ed. (New York: Prentice-Hall, 1996).

49. Julia T. Wood, "Leading in Purposive Discussions: A Study of Adaptive Behaviors," *Communication Monographs,* 44 (1977): 152–65.

50. Ritch L. Sorenson and Grant T. Savage, "Signaling Participation through Relational Communication: A Test of the Leader Interpersonal Influence Model," *Group & Organization Studies,* 14 (September 1989): 325–54.

51. Gay L. Drecksell, "Interaction Characteristics of Emergent Leadership" (Unpublished doctoral dissertation, University of Utah, 1984).

52. J. Kevin Barge and Randy Y. Hirokawa, "Toward a Communication Competency Model of Group Leadership," *Small Group Behavior,* 20 (1989): 167–89.

53. Charles G. Morris and J. R. Hackman, "Behavioral Correlates of Perceived Leadership," *Journal of Personality and Social Psychology,* 13 (1969): 350–61.

54. Hugh C. Russell, "Dimensions of Communicative Behavior of Discussion Leaders" (Paper presented to Central States Speech Convention, Chicago, April 1970).

55. Velma J. Lashbrook, "Gibb's Interaction Theory: The Use of Perceptions in the Discrimination of Leaders from Nonleaders" (Paper presented at the Speech Communication Association, Houston, December 1975).

56. Barge and Hirokawa, "Toward a Communication Competency Model."

57. Frank LaFasto and Carl Larson, *When Teams Work Best: 6,000 Team Members and Leaders Tell What It Takes to Succeed* (Thousand Oaks, CA: Sage, 2001): 130–35.

58. Dong L. Jung and John J. Sosik, "Transformational Leadership in Work Groups: The Role of Empowerment, Cohesiveness, and Collective-Efficacy on Perceived Group Performance," *Small Group Research,* 33 (June 2002): 313–36.

59. LaFasto and Larson, *When Teams Work Best,* 121–30.

60. Fisher, "Leadership as Medium," 205–7.

61. Norman R. G. Maier and A. R. Solem, "The Contributions of a Discussion Leader to the Quality of Group Thinking: The Effective Use of Minority Opinions," *Human Relations,* 5 (1952): 277–88.

62. Lance E. Anderson and William K. Balzer, "The Effects of Timing of Leaders' Opinions on Problem-Solving Groups: A Field Experiment," *Group & Organization Studies,* 16 (March 1991): 86–101.

63. Franklyn S. Haiman (From a paper given at the Speech Communication Association Annual Conference, Chicago, December 1984).

64. Warren Bennis and Burt Nanus, *Leaders: The Strategies for Taking Charge* (New York: Harper & Row, 1985): 57.

65. Larson and LaFasto, *TeamWork,* 121–23.

66. Ibid., 135.

67. LaFasto and Larson, *When Teams Work Best,* 108–20.

68. D. A. Kenny and S. J. Zaccaro, "An Estimate of Variance Due to Traits in Leadership," *Journal of Applied Psychology,* 68 (1983): 678–85.

69. Judith G. Oakley, "Leadership Processes in Virtual Teams and Organizations," *Journal of Leadership Studies,* 5 (Summer 1998): 3–17.

70. LaFasto and Larson, *When Teams Work Best,* 121–28.

71. Warren E. Watson, Lynn Johnson, and George D. Zgourides, "The Influence of Ethnic Diversity on Leadership, Group Process, and Performance," *International Journal of Intercultural Relations,* 26 (February 2002): 1–16.

72. Larson and LaFasto, *TeamWork,* 126–27.

73. Laura Hambley, Thomas O'Neill, and Theresa Kline, "Virtual Team Leadership: Perspectives From the Field," *International Journal of e-Collaboration,* 3 (January-March 2007): 40–64.

74. Ibid.

75. Pavitt and Sackaroff, "Implicit Theories of Leadership and Judgments of Leadership among Group Members," 374–92.

76. Dominic A. Infante and William I. Gordon, "How Employees See the Boss: Test of

Argumentative and Affirming Model of Supervisors' Communicative Behavior," *Western Journal of Speech Communication,* 55 (Summer 1991): 294–304.

77. William Foster Owen, "Rhetorical Themes of Emergent Female Leaders," *Small Group Behavior, 17* (November 1986): 475–86.

78. Patricia Hayes Andrews, "Sex and Gender Differences in Group Communication: Impact on the Facilitation Process," *Small Group Research,* 23 (February 1992): 74–94.

79. Owen, "Rhetorical Themes," 475–86.

80. Carol Watson, "When a Woman Is the Boss: Dilemmas in Taking Charge," *Group & Organization Studies,* 13 (June 1988): 163–81.

81. Sabine C. Koch, "Evaluative Affect Display Toward Male and Female Leaders of Task-Oriented Groups," *Small Group Research,* 36 (December 2005): 678–703.

82. G. B. Graen and T. A. Scandura, "Toward a Psychology of Dyadic Organizing," in *Research in Organizational Behavior, 9,* eds. L. L. Cummings and B. Shaw (Greenwich, CT: JAI, 1987): 175–208.

83. William E. McClane, "The Interaction of Leader and Member Characteristics in the Leader-Member Exchange (LMX) Model of Leadership," *Small Group Research,* 22 (August 1991): 283–300.

84. William E. McClane, "Implications of Member Role Differentiation: An Analysis of a Key Concept in the LMX Model of Leadership," *Group & Organization Studies,* 16 (March 1991): 102–13.

85. Jaesub Lee, "Leader-Member Exchange, Perceived Organizational Justice, and Cooperative Communication," *Management Communication Quarterly,* 14 (May 2001): 574–89.

86. Gay Lumsden and Donald Lumsden, *Communicating in Groups and Teams: Sharing Leadership,* 4th ed. (United States, 2004).

87. Bernard M. Bass, "From Transactional to Transformational Leadership: Learning to Share Vision," *Organizational Dynamics* (Winter 1990): 19–31.

88. Lumsden and Lumsden, *Communicating in Groups and Teams: Sharing Leadership.*

89. Bass, "Leadership and Empowerment: A Social Exchange Perspective."

90. Lumsden and Lumsden, *Communicating in Groups and Teams: Sharing Leadership,* 268.

91. Igor Kotlyar and Leonard Karakowsky, "Leading Conflict?: Linkages Between Leader Behaviors and Group Conflict," *Small Group Research,* 37 (August 2006): 397.

92. Birgit Schyns and Jörg Felfe, "The Personality of Followers and its Effect on the Perception of Leadership: An Overview, a Study, and a Research Agenda," *Small Group Research, 37* (October 2006): 522–39.

93. Eleanor F. Counselman, "Leadership in a Long Term Leaderless Group," *Small Group Research,* 22 (May 1991): 240–57.

94. J. Kevin Barge, "Leadership as Medium: A Leaderless Group Discussion Model," *Communication Quarterly,* 37 (Fall 1989): 237–47.

95. John Gastil, "A Definition and Illustration of Democratic Leadership," *Human Relations,* 47 (August 1994): 953–75.

96. William, C. Shutz, "The Leader as Completer," in *Small Group Communication: A Reader,* 3rd ed., eds. Robert S. Cathcart and Larry A. Samovar (Dubuque, IA: Sm. C. Brown, 1979).

Leading Small Groups: Practical Tips

STUDY OBJECTIVES

As a result of studying Chapter 8, you should be able to:

1. Name the three major types of services expected of designated small group leaders and describe specific ways of providing them.

2. Produce written messages essential to the work of small secondary groups, including meeting notices and agendas, minutes, and reports to other groups and organizations.

3. Describe the ethical principles that guide group leaders in both face-to-face and virtual groups.

CENTRAL MESSAGE

Group members expect their designated leaders to perform several administrative, structuring, and developmental activities for the group. They also expect leaders to model ethical participant-observer behavior.

Maureen, an active community volunteer in Springfield, Missouri, was asked by the local Community Foundation to chair a task force charged with producing a community report card. Twenty-seven committee members, who represented numerous community agencies and organizations such as the local health department, the public schools, the city's transportation department, and so forth, had already been selected. Maureen's task was to organize the work of this large group so that, at the end of the eight months of the task force's work, she would have the relevant information to evaluate how the community stacked up in 11 different areas, including business, transportation, housing, economic conditions, education, and recreation. The final professionally designed report would be widely distributed throughout the community by the local organizations that sponsored it: Community Foundation, Chamber of Commerce, United Way, Library System, and Junior League. This high-visibility, high-stakes project had to satisfy a lot of individuals and agencies.

The large group decided to split into 11 subcommittees, each focusing on a different area of the report. The subcommittees added community members with relevant expertise to their ranks; for example, the education committee added the school district's statistician, who supplied (and explained) up-to-date figures about the district's performance. The entire group met monthly, with subcommittees meeting more frequently to gather information, compare Springfield's performance with other cities, explain the data so that normal people could understand it, and meet their deadlines. Maureen faced several leadership challenges: managing the discussion of a group of 27 people, keeping track of the work of the subcommittees ensuring that the subcommittees sections were understandable and could be defended, and promoting buy-in, so that each committee member accepted the format of the report and the information it contained. Her know-how as a group leader helped the group complete the Community Report Card on time, to widespread praise.

Throughout this text, you have been presented with theories, concepts, and advice regarding various elements of the group discussion process. In this chapter, we focus on the *practice* of small group leadership.

This chapter is a type of "leader's manual" for when you find yourself in the leader's role, so you can be the best leader possible. We describe the three major types of duties that leaders are expected to perform and conclude with ethical principles leaders should follow. Remember our theme: *All* group members should perform leadership services for the group, but the leader has the unique responsibility to make sure the group gets what it needs to do its job well.

Responsibilities and Techniques of Discussion Leaders and Chairs

Being leader of a group can be daunting, but if the group has developed along the democratic lines suggested, the tasks will be shared. Even so, your group members will expect you to perform three broad types of functions:

administrative duties, discussion coordination, and group development. Our advice is based on research findings and the democratic philosophy we espouse.

Administrative Duties

Leaders handle numerous administrative duties; the most important ones are assembling the team, planning for meetings, following up on meetings, maintaining liaison with other groups, and managing the group's written communication.

Assembling the Group   Even before the group has its first meeting, the leader (or person to whom the group reports) has spent time thinking about who will be in the group and what the group will do.[1]

1. **Select group members carefully.**
   Group leaders, including Maureen, don't always have the luxury of picking the group members, but when they do, effective leaders carefully consider who should be part of the group. Think through what skills, expertise, and personal characteristics are needed for the group's particular task, then select just the people you need and no more! You want motivated, positive people who will contribute.

2. **Develop a group charter.**
   A **group charter** is a document that describes the purpose of the group, its specific charge, its area of freedom, its membership, what output the group must produce, and other key information such as deadlines. Maureen's committee spent the first four meetings developing the committee's structure, procedures, and work plan. Once that was done, the subcommittees were able to meet on their own with clarity about their tasks.

   Group Charter

   A written document describing a group's purpose, charge, limitations, membership, deadlines, and other key information.

3. **Make sure members commit to the group's goals.**
   Recruit people who are willing to commit to the group's goals. You may have to explain your group purpose to some who are initially skeptical, but that is better than recruiting someone who winds up rejecting the goal.

Planning for Meetings   Once you've selected the group, you will start to hold meetings. To use everyone's time well, make sure that you have your prework finished prior to each meeting. The following checklist can guide your planning:

1. **Define the purpose of the meeting.**
   First, decide whether you need a meeting. Do *not* call a meeting if you can get the job done using other communication avenues (telephone, teleconference e-mail, memo), when there isn't time for participants to prepare adequately, when one or more essential people cannot participate, or when the issues are personal and better handled privately.[2]

Define the purpose of the meeting clearly and formulate *specific* outcomes to be achieved. "To talk about our report" is *not* adequately defined, but "To review the Transportation Subcommittee's draft and make recommendations for change" is specific.

2. **Establish starting and ending times for the meeting.**
   People are busy; respect their time by starting and ending a meeting on time. Running overtime will kill member involvement and attendance.[3] Setting an ending time encourages the group to use its time well. If the work cannot be finished, plan additional meetings. Maureen's committee had to add three extra meetings to its schedule.

3. **If special resource people are needed for the meeting, advise and prepare them.**
   Small groups frequently need to question specialists with unique knowledge and skills or experience. Such invited resource persons need to know in advance what information to prepare and what to expect. For example, Maureen invited the head of the regional Division of Children and Families to present current information about child abuse and neglect rates in Springfield.

4. **Think through the tools you may need for the meeting.**
   There are countless procedures and techniques you can use to help you accomplish what you want to do in a particular group meeting. We describe several of these throughout this book, including brainstorming (Chapter 10), the Procedural Model of Problem Solving (Chapter 10), and Principled Negotiation (Chapter 11).

5. **Make all necessary physical arrangements.**
   Has the meeting room been reserved? Are handouts, notepads, chalk, charts, and possibly beverages ready? Leaders should carefully select and use their meeting space. The room should be comfortable, allow members to see and hear one another and any audiovisual materials presented, and be big enough to hold everyone. It also shouldn't be too big, since that can create psychological distance between members.[4]

6. **Have all the appropriate technology you need and make sure it works.**
   How many times have you waited for someone to fix a computer so that a PowerPoint presentation can proceed?

7. **Prepare a procedure for evaluating the meeting.**
   Groups should regularly evaluate their meetings, even if the evaluation is brief. We describe several such instruments for oral or written evaluations in Chapter 12.

8. **Notify members of the purpose or agenda, necessary preparation, and time and place of the meeting.**
   The chair is responsible for seeing that members are notified and given ample opportunity to prepare for a meeting. Maureen delegated

this duty to the professional secretary at the Community Foundation, who took care of sending meeting reminders and distributing minutes, although Maureen called her to ensure that these would be done.

Following Up on Meetings   Two kinds of follow-up are needed: touching base with group members and making sure the group's reports are getting to the right groups or individuals. Leaders often call or e-mail group members between meetings for a variety of reasons. One important reason is to make sure members are working on their assignments and have all the information and resources they need to complete their individual tasks. For instance, Maureen discovered that the Housing Subcommittee had made almost no progress on its section. She scheduled a meeting with the subcommittee and invited two individuals from an area social service agency who knew the housing situation. Maureen chaired this meeting and tactfully got the group moving forward. She also continued to monitor that subcommittee's work because it seemed to need more guidance than the other subcomittees. Leaders also help maintain good social relationships by interacting with members between meetings. You may want to know what a quiet member really felt about a meeting, or whether a member involved in a disagreement needs to vent to someone. Don't underestimate the value of keeping in regular touch with your group.

In addition, a chair often prepares and sends letters, memoranda, formal reports, notices of group decisions, advice prepared by the committee, and so forth, to appropriate people. This includes getting copies of minutes prepared and distributed, but also involves writing formal resolutions, sending updates to key outside groups, or carrying out whatever decisions for action the group has made. Although the group decides *what* to do, *who* does it is often the group's designated leader.

Liaison   A **liaison** serves as spokesperson for the group to other groups or to the parent organization; usually this is the designated leader's job. In most organizations, the chairs of standing committees coordinate with each other. Whenever you act as liaison, keep in mind that you represent *your group* rather than yourself.

Occasionally, committee chairs will be interviewed by public media. Anticipate this so that you can be prepared to answer reporters' questions. The chair's statements should accurately reflect the group's work, findings, and beliefs. The chair normally does not share internal conflicts outside the group. As one of our friends put it, "Family business is family business, and the group is a family."

Managing Written Communication for a Group   Written messages and records keep members on track. They provide continuity from meeting to meeting; remind members of their assignments; confirm agreements and accomplishments; provide legal documentation of attendance, decisions, and actions; bring

Liaison

Communication between or among groups; interfacing; a person who performs the liaison function.

absentees up to date; and inform the parent organization and others about what the group is doing.

Written messages include personal notes, meeting records, meeting notices and agendas, and reports and resolutions. All (except personal notes) can be circulated to members electronically and made available to the group via e-mail or virtual space for document storage and access. Examples are provided in Appendix C.

Personal Notes   Taking notes focuses group members' listening so that they don't lose sight of the group goal or switch subjects. When you take notes, keep track of the thrust of the discussion by jotting down just a key word or two (see Figure 8.1). Personal notes help leaders summarize discussion when needed, double-check the minutes, and follow up between meetings to ensure that assignments are being completed.

Group Records   All ongoing committees should maintain accurate and comprehensive **minutes** that serve as official summary records of the important content of meetings, especially of decisions made. The leader is responsible for seeing that minutes are recorded, that they are accurate, and that they are distributed to members before the next meeting. An original copy of all minutes should be kept in a safe place as a permanent record of the group's work.

Minutes are legal documents for the group. One of us served on the board of a community theater whose minutes describing an *ad hoc* personnel review contained evidence defending the theater in a former employee's lawsuit for being fired arbitrarily. Lacking this record, the theater probably would have lost the suit.

Minutes prevent wasted time and unnecessary tension. Without them, members often forget important information, fail to complete assignments, or argue about what was decided. For instance, at one meeting of the Community Report Card group, a member questioned why a particular topic was to be included in one section; he thought it should be included in a different section. Maureen referred to the minutes of the meeting (which he had missed) where this topic was discussed and decided. That satisfied the member (and also reminded him to read the minutes more carefully in the future).

Minutes focus on the content, not the process of discussion. They record all task-oriented information shared during the meeting, all ideas proposed as solutions, all decisions and how they were made (majority, consensus, consent), all assignments, and any plans or procedures for future action. Any handouts distributed at a meeting are attached to the official set of minutes.

The format and formality of minutes vary widely, depending on the nature of the group. At the formal end, meetings whose work is subject to public scrutiny (e.g., school boards, city councils and other government bodies, task forces, and so forth) have a required format that they must follow. In addition, once members have had a chance to review the minutes of a particular meeting, they must vote to approve them as is or to correct any

Minutes

A written record of every relevant item dealt with during a group meeting, including a record of all decisions.

FIGURE 8.1 A discussion leader's personal notes

February 10, 2012--- Everyone present

Discussion topic: what topics should we include in our class presentation on group polarization?

Main criteria:

Judy & Bill --- to get an "A" info must be accurate
Bart --- has to have practical application
Bev --- Dr. Brilhart wants innovative presentation
Everybody should have a part in presenting the topic to the class.

Topics

* Definition of group polarization (all agreed)
  Risky shift (Hal says can become a cautious shift w/ cautious members --- this term is outdated)
* Exercises to demonstrate when group takes risks & when it becomes cautious --- Judy says there's a bunch of these in a book she has
* Need to show how this applies in real life.

* Decisions Made
Assignments: Me (applications); Judy & Bill (library research); Hal & Bev (exercises -- w/ Judy's book)

Next meeting --- Wed., February 15

inaccuracies. We provide three examples of minutes. Table 8.1 shows a formal set of minutes from the church board, described in Chapter 3, which was legally required to keep minutes. This particular format makes it easy to see what items were discussed and what actions were taken without combing through a lot of narrative. Table 8.2 shows an informal set of minutes of a student group organizing a project; its main purpose was to remind members of their assignments and the next meeting. Midway between these two in formality are the minutes in Table 8.3, from another student group preparing to make a formal presentation to the Student Government Association. Whatever form minutes take, they should be distributed to members as soon as possible after the meeting. E-mail makes it easy to do this.

Meeting Notices and Agendas. A notice of each meeting should be sent to all members so they can prepare for the meeting. A **meeting notice** normally includes the who, what, when, where, and why of a meeting. It should include the purpose of the meeting; specific outcomes to be achieved; the

Meeting Notice
A written message providing the time, place, purpose, and other information relevant to an upcoming meeting.

TABLE 8.1   Example of formal minutes of the church board

Board of Directors Meeting Minutes
April 18, 2012

Present: Bill Prior, Norm Kerris, Gary Sloane, Don Bowles, Sally Schultz (directors): Sunni Prior, Marina Kerris (invited guests); Jane Simmons, church secretary.

Call to order: Opening prayer was given by Sally. Minutes of the April 11 meeting were approved as presented.

Topic	Discussion	Actions/Recommendations
Attendance/offering	120—Sunday, April 15 Total deposit—$1,552.52 Building fund—$5,858.00	
Founders Sun., May 16	Marina will attempt to get the MSU Gospel Choir to sing for a 30-minute program. Covered dish supper to follow service. Jody (Hospitality Committee) in charge of setup.	
Adult Sun. School	Roy Hackman will be teaching from "Spiritual Economics" starting April 24.	
Rental of facilities	Ada Cole asked cost of renting sanctuary for a workshop. Discussion centered on cost of utilities/wear and tear.	Norm moved, Don seconded, that we establish a policy of charging $30 per half day for all rentals. Passed.
Circle Suppers	Bill shared information about Circle Supper program; it has been very successful at the Columbia church. Discussion followed, and several names suggested to organize.	Sally moved, Gary seconded, that we ask Jean Ames to coordinate; that we hold them monthly on second Saturday. Passed.
Search Committee	Marina reported we have 10 applications; search committee will telephone interview and ask 3 to come for a full interview.	

Meeting adjourned at 8:30 PM Don gave the closing prayer.

Respectfully submitted,

Sally Schultz

agenda listing all items of business to be taken up; and any relevant facts, reading sources, or other preparation members should make prior to meeting. For the first meeting of any group, the notice should also include a list of all group members.

Thursday, April 6
Assignments for project (by April 11)
   Shawna: Research library theft on Internet
   Tyson and Marie: Interview head librarian
   Nate: Reserve a room and computer for PowerPoint presentation on May 3
Next meeting: Friday, April 13, 7 PM, Nate's house

TABLE 8.2
Example of typical informal minutes from a student group

An **agenda** is a list of the items of business, topics, and other matters in the sequence they will be considered in the meeting. For a continuing group, approval or correction of the previous meeting's minutes is usually the first item of business. Table 8.4 is an example of a combined meeting notice and agenda.

Agenda

A list of items to be discussed at a group meeting.

TABLE 8.3 Much more detailed than the previous example, this student group wants to ensure that nothing falls through the cracks.

Report of Third Meeting of Polarization Instruction Group
Date of Meeting: Tuesday, March 20, 2012
Time and Place: 7:30–9:00 PM in Room 8, Craig Hall
Attendance: Bev Halliday, Inez Salinas, Terrell Washington, Bill Miklas, Judy Hartlieb

Report of Second Meeting

Judy distributed copies of the report of the second meeting to all members. It was approved. It was decided that Judy would be responsible for recording and distributing reports of each group meeting.

Goals

A suggested outline for problem solving presented by Terrell was followed. This led to a discussion of group polarization and to determining the actions to be taken involving the group's "problem."

The group goals were identified as 1) understanding group polarization, 2) conducting a presentation with a class exercise on polarization for the class, and 3) each member being able to write a personal essay about the group experience.

Exercise Portion of Presentation

After some discussion of the type of exercise to be used in the presentation, it was decided that Inez would be responsible for trying to locate a book with sample exercises that could be considered by the group at the next meeting. Bill will also have primary responsibility for this portion of the presentation and will see that copies of the test are produced and ready for the class. The other group members will individually brainstorm for exercise ideas, and further discussion of these will take place during our class meeting of Tuesday, March 27.

TABLE 8.3 *continued...*

Criteria for class exercises were discussed. It was concluded that the purpose of the exercise would be to demonstrate the phenomenon of group polarization at work. The exercise would be divided in such a way that each individual in the class would first take it alone and then with a small group, and see what shifts occurred.

Leader and Role

The group determined that the leader would be responsible for developing agendas and outlines for future meetings and should serve as an overall controller and fill-in or backup person for other group members. Bev was selected by unanimous vote to fill this role as group leader.

Structure of Presentation

A structure and time schedule of the presentation was decided on:

5 minutes—Each member of the class takes the exercise individually.

10 minutes—The class is divided into four groups, with four of our small group members serving as observers. Each group will determine how to solve the exercise problem.

5 minutes—One member of our group will present a short report on group polarization research to the class. At the same time, the four observers will be finishing their notes regarding what happened in their respective groups.

5 minutes—The four groups will each discuss what occurred in the group. The observer may start the discussion or serve as a guide/reference person, answering questions and giving insight into what happened with polarization in the group.

5 minutes—The class as a whole will have the opportunity to share what was observed and experienced within the groups. The observers may again start the discussion and open the floor to any class member's contribution.

Additional Member Roles

Bill agreed to present the five-minute oral report on polarization to the class.

Terrell will be responsible for arranging meeting places and will serve as a backup to any member who might be absent.

Adjournment and Next Meeting

The meeting adjourned at approximately 9:00 PM Further planning will take place on Tuesday, March 23, during class time.

Ideally, reports to be distributed to members should be attached to the meeting notice and agenda. Reports might include tables, graphs, duplicated copies of text, lists, and drawings. Likewise, prior to the meeting, the report maker needs to prepare visual aids such as charts, diagrams, and graphs. Such a report is mentioned in the minutes by citing it ("see attached") and a copy stapled to the official set of minutes.

Formal Reports and Resolutions. Many small groups must submit written reports of their work to a parent organization or administrator. Such reports are often the end product of a committee's work and may include

Date: February 8, 2012
To: Curriculum Committee (Berquist, Bourhis, Galanes, King, Morris)
From: Kelly McNeilis, chair
Re: Next meeting of the Curriculum Committee

The next meeting of the Curriculum Committee will be on Friday, February 17, from 1:00 PM to 3:00 PM in Craig 320.

AGENDA (by the end of the meeting we must have an answer for each of the following questions):

1. What will be the focus of our departmental assessment (student outcomes, student perceptions, alumni perceptions, or something else)?
2. What areas of the department should be assessed?
3. Whom will we recommend as members of subcommittees to plan assessment procedures for each area decided under #2?

TABLE 8.4
An example of combined meeting notice and agenda

findings, criteria, and recommendations. Usually, the liaison person submitting the written report also gives a brief oral summary.

The leader submits the report, but the actual writing may be done by one or two members. A draft is circulated to all members, inviting their suggestions for revisions and additions. The group then meets to discuss, amend, and eventually approve the draft report. The final version is signed by all members, copied, and submitted.

Administrative Duties for Virtual Groups Leaders of virtual groups are responsible for the same administrative functions as leaders of face-to-face teams. Face-to-face groups often use technology to enhance their work yet as we have shown in virtual teams most if not all of their work is done online. Leading virtual groups is more complicated than leading face-to-face groups due to the challenges of virtual space. Virtual teams, remember, lack the full complement of nonverbal signals, so text can be easily misinterpreted and the negative consequences of these misunderstandings are amplified in a virtual team.[5] Imagine having to lead a group whose members are spread out all over the country and the globe with different schedules, times when they can work, levels of expertise in the use of technology, personality preferences, energy levels, and so forth. Effective leadership of these teams absolutely makes a different to their moral and performance.[6] Their leaders are expected to have the same kind of skills as face-to-face leaders, yet leading virtual teams as you would a face-to-face team is a mistake. Here, we will take a look at the special nuances of their administrative duties.

Often, virtual team leaders are in charge of assembling their team, and they, too, want to select their team carefully. Especially important to some virtual teams are project managers.[7] Virtual leaders have to delegate this role to someone if they themselves do not take it. Virtual team members report more satisfaction with delegation when it is done well in order to coordinate their efforts and keep them connected.[8] It is recommended that virtual leaders select a strong project manager based on "real" knowledge of his or her capabilities acquired through one-on-one experience with the person or through viable performance measures.

Although virtual teams operate with little to no face-to-face contact, members desire some use of face-to-face communication, especially very early when the team is being assembled.[9] Such face-to-face communications can possibly take place in an initial gathering of the team for a kind of launch event.

A dominant theme to emerge from current research in virtual leadership is the necessity of and respect for team meetings.[10] We mentioned in Chapter 7 that these are often the only time virtual members are "together." Team members report strong preferences for leaders who can plan meetings thoughtfully in order to make the best use of time and talent as possible. Virtual team meetings need occur on a regular basis, they need to be organized, and they should respect the different time zones members are in by rotating meeting times.

Virtual team members expect their leaders to be able to select and use a variety of computer tools that promote team "work." A number of Web conferencing tools are available, for instance. One tool we will highlight here is wiggio (www.wiggio.com/). This platform is designed for people who manage multiple groups and is very user-friendly. Virtual leaders can simply connect their team members; once "grouped," mass e-mails and even voice mails can be sent. Invites to meetings are synched to shared calendars, and reports and other information can be shared and even worked on together. During meetings, members can use conference calls and chats, which allow records of the meetings to be stored and retrieved. You can even poll members using this platform. This service is free and requires no complicated registration process.

Recap: A Quick Review

The administrative duties include those organizational and behind-the-scenes functions that groups need to perform smoothly. Specific duties are:

1. Thinking carefully before the group is assembled about who should be included, choosing members that are committed to the group, and developing a clear charter or statement of purpose for the group.

2. Planning for meetings by knowing and communicating what the meeting's purpose is; when it will start and end; what people, materials, or resources need to be prepared in advance; what tools will be needed, such as instructions for special

procedures or technology; how the meeting will be evaluated; and notifying the members in advance so that they can come prepared.

3. After a meeting, following up to make sure that members are completing assignments and to touch base, especially if a member was unusually quiet or seemed upset at the meeting.

4. Serving as liaison between the group and other groups, individuals, and the parent organization and to represent the group publicly, including to the media.

5. Managing the group's entire written communication is a critical task. This includes keeping personal notes; making sure the group's records, such as minutes, are in good order; sending out meeting notices and agendas in advance; and making sure that the group's outputs, including reports, resolutions, and so forth, are completed and delivered to the appropriate person or place.

6. Effective leadership of virtual groups requires many of the same skills as face-to-face leaders and some that are different. Virtual leaders must respect the importance of virtual meetings and ensure their team has the right tools to work collaboratively online.

Leading Discussions

Administrative duties of designated leaders precede and follow small group meetings. Now we consider what leaders are expected to do *during* actual meetings. In general, leaders must tend to both relational and task goals. The following guidelines will help you balance these broad goals.

Opening Remarks   Opening remarks set the stage for the meeting by creating a positive atmosphere and helping focus the group on its task. They should be brief. Here are several guidelines:

1. **Make sure that members and guests have been introduced.**
   This may seem obvious, but sometimes leaders can become so task focused that they forget this step. Sometimes you may want to provide name tags. If you are in a group whose leader forgets introductions, you should jump in with something like: "I'm not sure I know everyone. Could we take a moment to get introduced?"

2. **Review the group charter at a group's first meeting and go over the specific purpose of the present meeting, including what outcomes should be accomplished.**
   Basically, you are like a band director getting everyone to start on the same page. You may need to allow for discussion of the charter and the meeting agenda, and it's better to do that early rather than late, to prevent misunderstandings.

3. **See that any special roles are established.**
   Will the group need a recorder in addition to the designated leader? Will the group have a member acting as a special observer? The group may choose to rotate such jobs so that various members receive practice performing them.

4. **Distribute any handouts.**
   Handouts may include written materials from the parent organization or administrator, copies of findings, case problems, outlines to structure the problem-solving procedure of the group, or explanations of special discussion techniques.

5. **Establish initial ground rules.**
   Make sure that everyone knows the rules for the group! For instance, you may want to affirm that confidentiality regarding the group's discussions must be maintained. Or, if your meeting involves discussion about a controversial issue, you may want to remind members of the ethical principles for group behavior.

6. **Suggest procedures to follow.**
   If you think the group will benefit from using a particular procedure or technique, such as one of the techniques mentioned in this text, present it to the group as a suggestion. Explain the procedure, give members a copy of the procedure, and make sure the group agrees before you proceed. Also, members should know in advance whether decisions will be by consensus or majority vote.

7. **Focus initial discussion on the first substantive agenda issue with a clear question.**
   Your focus question may require a simple answer: "Tyrone, will you give us last week's sales figures?" Or it may need considerable discussion: "What do we think are the reasons for the dropoff in attendance?" In either case, the right question (see Chapter 9) helps launch the group into the substantive portion of the agenda.

Regulating and Structuring Discussions   Once group members are oriented to each other and the task, the leader helps the group function efficiently by adding structure to the group's deliberations. Group discussion should be orderly so that each person has an opportunity to speak, but it should not be *over*regulated so that members feel handcuffed. Generally, the larger the group, the more formal your procedures should be.

Deciding How Formal You Should Be.   Many large groups and assemblies use *Robert's Rules of Order,* Newly Revised, as their parliamentary code.[11] When an organization has adopted *Robert's Rules of Order,* the committees of that organization *must* use Robert's rules for committees (see Table 8.5). But what many people do *not* know is that these rules for committees are much less formal and detailed than the parliamentary rules you may have encountered. These rules make it unnecessary (and undesirable) for members to

Administrative Matters

- The committee chair can be appointed or elected or is the first person named on the list of members.
- The chair or any two committee members can call a meeting.
- A quorum (the number needed to do official business) is a simple majority of members.
- If a committee cannot reach consensus, the minority can make a report to the parent organization that differs from the majority report.

Chair's Responsibilities

- The chair is responsible for the committee's records, but can delegate that duty.
- The chair can take stands on issues and vote.

Discussing, Making Motions, and Voting

- Members can speak without being "recognized" by the chair, as long as they don't interrupt others.
- Members can discuss anything without having to make a motion.
- Motions, if made, do not need a second.
- Members can speak as often as they want; motions to limit discussion are not allowed.
- Informal discussion without a motion is appropriate; members may want to make a motion for an official vote when a consensus or majority decision seems to be emerging, but motions aren't required to record a vote.
- "Straw" (nonbonding) votes can be taken at any time.
- The chair can ask if members consent or agree, and if no one objects, the decision is made.
- A motion to reconsider a previous vote or decision can be made at any time by any member, even one who voted with the losing side or was absent during the original vote.
- Motions can be amended informally, using consensus rather than voting.

TABLE 8.5
A brief summary of Robert's Rules of Order for committees

utter "question," "point of order," or "We can't discuss this topic because it hasn't been moved and seconded." *Robert's Rules* suggests using parliamentary procedure in groups with over a dozen or so members, but we believe that groups as large as 30 can operate less formally. In Maureen's committee of 27, members raised their hands when they wanted to speak and voted when a particular decision needed to be recorded, but they did not use motions, questions, points of order, and so forth, during their meetings. Discussions in this group were less formal than *Robert's Rules* calls for, but more formal than the free-flowing discussion of most truly small groups.

In actual practice, Weitzel and Geist found that even members of community groups who thought they were experts on parliamentary procedure made many mistakes in its use.[12] What's more important, their problem-solving did not seem to suffer from their selective use of the rules. What does this mean to you? Don't memorize *Robert's Rules of Order*. Use common sense to determine how formal or informal your discussion will be, and talk about it within the group so that everyone knows how the group will operate. Now that you have thought about the degree of formality to use, we present our guidelines for structuring discussions.

1. **Keep the discussion goal-oriented.**

   You have already focused the group with the team charter or the meeting agenda, which helps the group stay on track and uses members' time well. Some digression, such as fantasy, helps establish a group's culture, but if a digression lasts too long, bring the discussion back on track.

2. **Temporarily "park" off-topic items in the "parking lot," to be taken up later.**

   When a member brings up something that he or she thinks is worth discussing, but is off the current topic, place that new topic or item on a separate board, computer file, or piece of notepaper (sometimes referred to as the "parking lot") for consideration later. This accomplishes several things. It acknowledges the member's idea, which is supportive. It helps ensure that potentially important topics are actually considered by the group and aren't dismissed just because they are off the current topic. Finally, it helps keep the group on track by encouraging members to complete one topic before embarking on a new one. After the group works its way through the agenda, it can then discuss the items in the parking lot.

3. **Use summaries to make clear transitions between items.**

   Help the group make a smooth transition from one topic or agenda item to the next by achieving closure on the current issue. You can do this by summarizing what the group has decided or concluded, asking whether the summary is adequate, and then checking to see whether the group is ready to move on: "So, we've decided to add two sections to the Community Report Card, one on Housing and one on Early Childhood, right?" [Maureen paused to make sure she understood correctly.] "Now, let's go on to the next topic, which is how we should address the issue of poverty in our community." [She paused again to give people time to respond and shift gears.] Explicit transitions help keep the group on track.

4. **Help the group manage its time.**

   Ideally, the group will address all or most items on the agenda, but members can get so involved in the discussion that they lose track of time. Nothing is more frustrating than running out of time before you have a chance to discuss an issue important to you! It's up to the designated leader to keep track of time and monitor progress on the agenda: "We are only on our third agenda item, with 15 minutes left. Are we ready to wrap this topic up, or would you rather deal with the remaining agenda items at a special meeting next week?"

5. **Bring the discussion to a definite close.**
   This should be done no later than the scheduled ending time for the meeting, unless all members consent to extending the time. Briefly summarize the progress the group has made and the assignments given to members. Many leaders thank the group, ask for a brief evaluation of the meeting ("How well did this meeting accomplish what you wanted to accomplish today?"), and remind members of the next meeting.

Equalizing Opportunity to Participate   Each member needs a fair share of "air time" in the group. It's up to you to ensure that everyone has an opportunity to speak, with no member stage hogging or withdrawing. There are several things you can do to encourage such equity:

1. **Address your comments and questions to the group rather than to individuals.**
   Unless you ask for a specific item of information or respond directly to what a member has said, speak to the group as a whole. Make regular eye contact with everyone, especially with less talkative members.

2. **Make sure all members have an opportunity to speak.**
   You may have to act as **gatekeeper**, regulating who will speak next so that everyone has a fair, equal chance. Eye contact with less talkative members shows them you expect them to speak, whereas looking at talkative members encourages them to talk more. We suggest you make a visual survey of the entire group every minute or so. If you see a nonverbal sign that a silent member has something to say, help that person get the floor: "Pieta, did you want to comment on John's proposal?" or "Pieta, you seem concerned about John's proposal. Would you share your concerns with us?" That opens the gate to Pieta without putting her on the spot if she has nothing to say. Sometimes reticent members can be assigned roles that *require* their participation. For instance, someone might be asked to investigate an issue and report to the group. If you know a member is well informed but has not spoken out, try encouraging participation without forcing: "Selim, I think you studied that issue. Could you give us any information about it?"

   Controlling long-winded members is often harder than encouraging quiet members, but it *must* be done for the sake of the group. The following techniques range from the most subtle to the most direct:

   a. When feasible, seat talkative members where you can seem to overlook them naturally, and try not to make eye contact when you ask a question of the group.

Gatekeeper

Any group member who controls who speaks during a discussion and who helps others gain the floor.

    b. When a windbag has finished one point, cut in with a tactful comment, such as "How do the rest of you feel about that issue?" to suggest that someone else speak.

    c. Suggest a group rule that each person make one point only, then give up the floor to others, or that each person's comments be held to one minute. You can be lighthearted about this—some groups have used squirt guns, tossed nerf balls, or passed a penny around to remind members when it's time to yield the floor.

    d. In private, tactfully ask the excessive talker to help you encourage quiet members to speak: "Your ideas have been very helpful to the group, but because you are so articulate, I'm concerned that others feel intimidated about participating. How can you help me get Susan and Juan to contribute to the discussions more often?"

    e. Have an observer keep a count of how often or how long each member speaks, and report the findings to the group. If a serious imbalance is apparent, the group can decide what to do.

    f. As a last resort, ask the person to control talking or leave the group: "While your ideas are excellent, your constant talking prevents other members, whose ideas are equally good, from contributing. This hurts both group morale and decision making. For the sake of the group, if you will not control your talking, I will ask you to leave the group."

3. **Listen with real interest to what an infrequent speaker says, and encourage others to do the same.**
Nothing discourages a speaker more than a lack of listening. Yet the evidence is clear that most people ignore comments from a quiet member. Leader intervention can help an infrequent speaker get a fair hearing.

4. **Don't comment after each member's remark.**
Some leaders fall into this pattern, while others do this to overcontrol the group. Listen, then speak when you are really needed, but don't become the constant interpreter or repeater of what others say.

5. **Bounce requests for your opinions on substantive issues back to the group. Leaders can influence members just because they are leaders.**
Encourage independent thinking by members by withholding your opinions until others have expressed theirs. You might reply, "Let's see what other members think first. What do the rest of you think about . . . ?" When you do offer an opinion, give it as only one point of view to be considered, not as *the* point of view.

6. **Remain neutral during arguments.**
When you get heavily involved in an argument, you lose the perspective needed to mediate, to summarize, and to perform well as a leader. If you realize that evaluation is needed, point that out and ask others

to provide it. At most, act as a devil's advocate for a point of view that otherwise would not be considered, and tell the group that you're playing the devil's advocate role. Of course, you are always free to support decisions as they emerge.

Stimulating Creative Thinking   Groups are potentially more creative than individuals, but often group outputs are mediocre or worse. Sometimes creativity must be stimulated deliberately. Leaders can do several things to encourage creativity:

1. **Defer evaluation and ask group members to do the same.**
   The main idea behind brainstorming, described in Chapter 10, is to defer evaluation of ideas until members have no more ideas to suggest. Who wants to suggest an idea that will get shot down? When a group member criticizes a suggestion, gently remind that person of the "defer evaluation" rule.

2. **Try brainstorming and other creativity-enhancing techniques.**
   Brainstorming not only requires deferred judgment, but it also encourages members to be playful with ideas. Brainstorming and other techniques temporarily disable the logical part of the mind so that the creative mind can emerge.

3. **Encourage the group to search for more alternatives.**
   When no one seems to be able to think of any more ideas, you can ask an idea-spurring question: "What *else* can we think of to . . . ?" or "I wonder if we can think of five more ways to . . . ?" Often, the most creative ideas are ones that pop up after the group thinks it has exhausted its possibilities.

4. **Be alert to suggestions that open up new areas of thinking; then pose a general question about the new area.**
   For example, if someone suggests putting up posters in the library that show users how much theft costs them, you might ask, "How *else* could we publicize the costs of theft to the library?"

Stimulating Critical Thinking   After a group has done its creative thinking, it must then subject the various options to rigorous evaluation before it reaches a final position. Sometimes groups develop norms of politeness that make this impossible. Here are ways to encourage good critical evaluation:

1. **If the group gets solution-minded too quickly, suggest more analysis of the problem.**
   Groups typically jump right to discussing solutions too early, which becomes a major source of faulty decision making. Chapter 10 presents a systematic method for helping a group focus on problem analysis.

2. **Encourage members to evaluate information.**
   For example:
   a. To check the relevance of evidence, ask: "How does this apply to our problem?" or "How is that like the situation we are discussing?"
   b. To evaluate the source of evidence, ask: "What is the source of that information?" "How well is Dr. So-and-So recognized in the field?" or "Is this consistent with other information on the subject?"
   c. To check on the credibility of information, ask: "Do we have any information that is contradictory?"
   d. To encourage thorough assessment of a group member's suggestion, ask: "How will implementing that solve our problem?" or "How will the students (union members, secretaries, neighborhood residents, etc.) react to that suggestion?"
   e. To test a statistic, ask how it was derived, who conducted the study, or how an average was computed.
   f. Bring in outside experts to challenge the views of the group.

3. **Make sure all group members understand and accept the standards, criteria, or assumptions used in making judgments.**
   For example, you might ask: "Is that criterion clear to us all?" "Does everyone agree that using our professional association's guidelines is a good idea?" or "Do we all accept that as an assumption?"

4. **Test all proposed solutions thoroughly before accepting them as final group decisions.**
   Encourage the group to apply the available facts and all criteria. Be especially careful to consider possible harmful effects of all proposed solutions.
   a. Ask questions to encourage thorough evaluation:
      - Do we have any evidence to indicate that this solution would be satisfactory? Unsatisfactory?
      - Are there any facts to support this proposal?
      - How well would that idea meet our criteria?
      - Would that proposal solve the basic problem?
      - Is there any way we can test this idea before we decide whether to adopt it?
      - What negative consequences might this proposal produce?
   b. Ask members to discuss tentative solutions or policies with trusted people outside the group.
   c. One or more members can be asked to take the role of devil's advocate so that all ideas are challenged and everyone has a chance to air doubts.
   d. Divide the group into two subgroups under different leaders to evaluate all alternatives; then rejoin to iron out differences.

e. Before reaching a binding solution with far-reaching consequences, hold a "second chance" meeting at which all doubts,
ethical concerns, or untested assumptions can be explored.

5. **Help prevent groupthink.**
Groupthink, described in detail in Chapter 9, can send a group along
a path to disaster. Follow the suggestions for preventing groupthink
in Chapter 10.

Fostering Meeting-to-Meeting Improvement   A group doesn't achieve its
ultimate goal by chance. After each meeting, the designated leader should
assess how well the meeting's goals were accomplished and how the meeting could have been improved. That, then, suggests a road map for improving
future meetings:

1. **Determine how the meeting could have been improved.**
Take a few minutes to reflect on the meeting. Did the group receive
the leadership services it needed at the right time? Were the meeting's
purposes clearly communicated? Did members agree on the goals? Was
the entire agenda covered in a timely fashion? Was the meeting well
structured? Did members stay on the topic, for the most part? Take a
few moments to consider the members. Did everyone participate? Did
anyone talk too much? Not enough? Did you talk too much? Too little?
Were the members allowed to digress too often? Not enough? Did the
members seem to enjoy the discussion? After answering these and
other questions, you can plan your strategy for the next meeting.

2. **Determine the most important changes to be made at the next
meeting and adjust behavior accordingly.**
After examining all the areas in which you could improve the group
meeting, concentrate on improving the two or three that are most
potentially harmful to the group. If one or two members monopolized
the floor, plan ways to curtail their participation. If someone seemed
upset, touch base by calling or e-mailing that member. Maureen said:
"Last week, we got through only half the items on our agenda. This
week, I'm going to pay more attention to our time, and I'll be step-
ping in more often to help us stick to one issue at a time. I'd appreciate your help with this, too."

Leading Discussions in Virtual Groups   As we have mentioned, leading virtual teams is challenging, but not impossible. One area you do not
want to fall down in is the running of meetings—central to the dynamics of
virtual teams and often cited as a problem teams have with their leaders.[13]
You start by being familiar with the technological tools that work well for
virtual groups. Teleconferencing is the most used tool for virtual meetings.
Next, set the rules for use of the teleconference platform, including rules of

instant messaging and chats, if they are used. Members appreciate, especially in this medium, the early establishment and modeling of guidelines and expectations.[14] A general expectation is that contributions during meetings will be equitable. Leaders can use their own checklists to monitor who has spoken and ask members directly for their input. If a virtual meeting involves some members actually together in the same space and others at different location, the ones further from the co-present members need to feel a part of the discussion. Virtual leaders should also look out for members "checking out" of the discussion, which is easy to do in virtual meetings.

Virtual leaders, themselves, need to monitor their own communication.[15] They have to show patience listening in virtual communication to avoid interrupting or dominating. It can be tempting to cut off someone during the lag time in transmission of messages that can occur in asynchronous communication and in some forms of videoconferencing. The nonverbal signals in virtual communication have to be read carefully—silence in an e-mail or a nonresponse to a comment can mean all sorts of things. Promptness in checking with the meaning of a message in computer-mediated communication is key.

Instant messaging and chats are popular in virtual groups.[16] Instant messaging should only be used for short messages and not the "go to" medium for detailed material. It does not provide a recorded history of the meeting but is useful for sales meetings, for instance, because members can talk to each other during the negotiations. Chats do allow for discussions to be recorded and members prefer them because they are more "social" than e-mail and can promote more distributed discussion.

Recap: A Quick Review

Leaders are expected to lead the group's discussions. To do so effectively, they should attend to the following:

1. In their opening remarks, leaders should make sure that members are introduced to one another; review the group's and the specific meeting's purpose and goals; make sure people have been identified to perform special functions, such as taking minutes; have handouts distributed; make sure that ground rules and specific procedures, such as specialized techniques, have been explained and are followed; and start the group off with a focused, substantive question.

2. In regulating and structuring discussions, the leader must decide how formally or informally the group's discussion should be, including whether parliamentary rules or special rules for committees should apply; must keep the discussion moving toward the goal, including by encouraging members to "park" off-topic items in a "parking lot" for later discussion; provide internal summaries to help keep the

group together and provide smooth transitions; keep discussion moving along; and bring the discussion to a definite close.

3. Leaders must equalize members' opportunity to contribute by controlling long-winded members and encouraging quieter members to speak up; by addressing questions to the group as a whole; by not commenting after each member's remarks, so that they don't create a wheel network; by listening with genuine interest; by asking the group for its opinions; and by staying neutral during arguments.

4. Leaders stimulate creative thinking by asking members to refrain from evaluating items right away; using creativity-enhancing techniques, such as brainstorming; and prodding the members to keep thinking about more alternatives and new areas of thinking.

5. Leaders stimulate critical thinking by stopping the group from becoming solution-minded too early, encouraging the critical evaluation of information, making sure that factors such as criteria and assumptions have been discussed and accepted, testing solutions before they are finally adopted, and working to prevent group-think.

6. Effective leaders evaluate their own and the group's performance to determine how the meeting could have been improved and what adjustments need to be made at the next meeting.

7. In virtual groups, because of the increased possibility of misunderstanding, leaders pay particular attention to whether members are following good communication practices, which promote equitable and clear communication.

Developing the Group

Developing the group involves two fundamental processes: helping the group evolve into an effective team, and helping the individual members grow to their potentials so that distributed leadership can work effectively. Few people start out knowing how to be effective team members or leaders; this takes practice. As leader, you can help develop the talent on your team.

Helping Individuals Grow   Effective leaders help develop the members' leadership skills, including the members' abilities to assess the group's throughput processes and suggest appropriate changes. Here are several suggestions:

1. **Encourage members to assess the group's processes and make suggestions. Outstanding teams periodically assess themselves.** Sometimes, just asking, "How are we doing?" can prompt growth. Build self-assessment into the group's processes. For instance, a short evaluation can end each meeting: "How well do you think our meeting went today?" and "How might we make our next meeting more

productive?" The answer to the second question led the church board in Chapter 3 to rearrange its agenda so that "new business" would be discussed early in the meeting before group members became tired and uncreative.

Another suggestion might be to designate someone as a process observer to watch the interactions and share observations with the group as a whole. Rotate the job of process observer among members so that everyone gets practice observing and assessing or bring outside consultants in to evaluate the group and offer suggestions for improvement.

2. **Model the behavior that you want others to adopt.**
As designated leader, model group-centered, thoughtful, responsible behavior. Your own behavior does a lot to promote teamwork and develop the trust needed for collaboration. Encourage others to evaluate your suggestions, and react open-mindedly and nondefensively to others' criticisms.

3. **Give members practice at performing needed group duties.**
Suggest ways for group members to serve the needs of the group. For instance, rotate the job of recorder so that several members get practice. Give members the chance to report on their areas of expertise to the group and to perform special tasks for the group. Let members substitute for you as discussion leader or liaison to other groups. Don't jump in right away when you see that the group needs something; give the other members a chance to respond before you do.

A particularly striking example of this occurred during a Community Report Card group meeting. The Recreation and Leisure Subcommittee resubmitted its section without fixing the problems that the rest of the committee identified. Instead of expecting Maureen to play bad cop, several members of the committee called the subcommittee members to task and explained why their revision was still unacceptable. The message was more compelling because it came from the subcommittee's peers rather than the group leader.

Establishing and Maintaining Trust True collaboration (literally, "working together") is possible only when members trust each other, and is fundamental to working with diversity (see Chapter 4). Larson and LaFasto found four components of trust: honesty (no lies, no exaggerations), openness (a combination of open-mindedness and willingness to share), consistency (predictability, dependability), and respect (treating others with fairness and dignity).[17]

The following suggestions can help you establish and retain a climate of trust:

1. **Establish norms, based on ethical principles, that build trust.**
Trust-building communication is based on three important ethical principles: working to understand others, communicating to enhance

others' identities and self-concepts, and behaving like a responsible group member. Specific behaviors that promote trust are listening actively, encouraging others to explain themselves, helping others with assignments or tasks, maintaining confidentiality, getting assignments done when promised, making sure you understand someone's position before disagreeing, and making others feel free to disagree.

2. **Confront trust violators and other problem members.**

   Two of the most common complaints are that groups tolerate members who put self over group and that leaders fail to confront such team members.[18] If repeated efforts by you and other members don't work, it is far better to remove offenders from the group than to allow trust to erode.

3. **Encourage members to understand and embrace their diversity.**

   Diversity can be a group's greatest strength, but not if members can't capitalize on that diversity. Whether the group's diversity is based on personality characteristics, differences in stage of life, or varying cultural or co-cultural backgrounds, encouraging members to get to know each other at more than a superficial level can help produce understanding and appreciation. The leader should help the team recognize one another's differences and the unique strengths those differences provide.

   It may help to invite an outside trainer in to conduct a workshop about differences and their value. A library staff we know participated in a trainer-led workshop on personality differences revealed by color preference. The staff had fun learning about how different people preferred to approach work. That helped them see that others weren't being contrary; they were just trying to work in the way they felt most comfortable. The staff began to use color vocabulary in a teasing, but friendly, way: "Oh, you're being so green! We blues will never understand you!" The workshop helped improve staff relationships and work efficiency.

4. **Be a principled leader.**

   Principled leaders put the needs of the group ahead of their individual needs and behave in ethical ways consistent with the group's norms.[19] For instance, they do not *say* they want group participation, then squash members' attempts to participate. Good group leaders inspire members to work toward the group's vision. They show personal commitment to the team's goals. Moreover, they develop the talents of the other members. Leaders create leaders by giving members the experience and latitude they need to act with self-confidence.

Promoting Teamwork and Cooperation Establishing a climate of trust will do more than anything else to develop cooperation and teamwork among members. Chapter 6 provided several suggestions for promoting cohesiveness and teamwork both face-to-face and virtual groups in a group, which we won't repeat here. Instead, we provide suggestions specifically geared to leaders:

1. **Plan some fun for the group.**
   Fun could be a party, snacks before a meeting, a celebration when a major task is completed, happy hour after work, and so forth. Relax and allow digressions, which can relieve secondary tension. Let the group chain out fantasies that enrich its climate and contribute to establishing shared beliefs and values. If this is hard for you, enlist the help of members who are good at it. One group leader we know brought an ice cream cart into her team's offices to thank them for reaching an important sales goal.

2. **Promote the group.**
   As one of our friends said, "If the team leader isn't the team's biggest fan, who is?" It's the leader's unique responsibility to make sure that the group is known within the organization for its good work. Let people in the organization, particularly higher-ups, know when the team has accomplished something valuable for the organization, make team members' accomplishments visible to others, and talk about the successes of the group.

3. **Share all rewards with the group.**
   Leaders often receive praise from authority figures for work the group has done. Wise leaders give credit to the group.

4. **Get group input and buy-in about promoting teamwork.**
   Ask team members to recall the best group they've ever been part of, and to identify the behaviors that contributed to that team feeling. Ask them to suggest how that feeling can be recreated in the present group. Their suggestions provide guidelines and norms for the group, with the added advantage that they came from the members themselves.

5. **Confront members whose behavior is hurting the team.**
   One of the worst things you can do is ignore individualistic, selfish behavior that hurts the team. It will not go away on its own, and you must address it constructively. Talk to the member privately first, focusing on the behavior that you believe is problematic. Say, "Roger, when you read your texts while others are talking, we interpret your behavior as lack of interest in the team," not "You jerk! What do you think you're doing, ignoring what people are saying?"
   Sometimes, two members just don't like each other and let their personal feelings erupt in team meetings. In such cases, you may have to have what a friend of ours calls a "Come to Jesus" meeting with them. This friend told two warring women on her team that she wanted them to act with respect and friendliness toward each other in the team meetings, even if they had to fake it. They stopped the offending, harmful behavior because they wanted to stay on her team, but they never came to like one another. You do not have to like someone to work well with him or her.

6. **Keep arguments focused on facts and issues, not personalities.**
   Step in at once if any member starts an attack on another's personality, ethnicity, or character. However, recognize also that members may have strong feelings about some issues, so don't squelch expressions of feeling, as long as those expressions do not denigrate others.

7. **When a group seems to be deadlocked, look for a basis on which to compromise.**
   Perhaps you can synthesize parts of several ideas into a consensus solution or suggest a mediation procedure, such as the *principled negotiation procedure* described in Chapter 11.

Developing Virtual Groups   Virtual leaders face challenges in developing the group, but they are expected to help members gel into a unique team culture with a vision. Central to this challenge is realizing that virtual groups, just like face-to-face ones, rely on effective facilitation of both the task and social dimensions of group life. Paramount to the effective development of virtual groups is leadership that recognizes how swiftly the social dynamics of these teams can be lost given the dominant task nature of computer-mediated communication.[20] Although face-to-face contact with each other may be difficult, leaders need to consider this kind of contact with members when it is available. Face-to-face contact has been found to help virtual leaders speed the process of group rapport and cohesiveness.[21] This kind of contact can occur between the leader and members one-on-one during site visits or even among all members in kick-off celebrations or later in the group's life.

Virtual leaders, no matter their geographic distance, can establish and nurture online relationships.[22] They can personalize e-mails by including personal information to the e-mail or even just by asking how the member is doing. Using the "reply all" function in e-mails, while handy, can send an impersonal message. E-mails should not be used to deal with conflict or difficult relational issues. They can ensure during meetings that social information is also a part of the discussion. They can create virtual space in blogs or chat rooms for members to share only social information.

Virtual team members, just like their face-to-face counterparts, expect principled leadership.[23] Leaders should respect and honor team member work; take the time to connect one on one with each member in e-mails, telephone calls, and site visits; and help members know the ground rules for work procedures and interaction with each other. Modeling best practices goes a long way to facilitating effective member interaction, cohesiveness, and commitment to the team.

Ethical Principles for Group Leaders

The leader's behavior serves as a model for members to follow no matter which medium the group is using, because "Responsible leaders maintain the highest possible standards of ethics."[24] There are six principles for leaders that we believe are relevant for small groups, which mirror the ethical principles in Chapter 1: integrity, professional and social responsibility, equitable participation, honesty and openness, and respect for self and other.

1. **Do not intentionally send deceptive or harmful messages.**
   Tell the truth and hold *truth* as an appropriate standard for the group's decision making. Make sure that *all* relevant information, whether it supports your position or not, is presented to the group and evaluated in an unbiased, fair way.

2. **Place concern for others above concern for personal gain.**
   Don't take advantage of the position you hold for personal gain or advantage and don't harm the self-esteem of members.

3. **Establish clear policies that all group members are expected to follow.**
   Follow the same rules and norms you expect the members to follow.

4. **Respect the opinions and attitudes of members.**
   This encourages equal opportunity for all to participate and supports distributed leadership.

5. **Stand behind members when they carry out policies and actions approved by the group.**
   Support members who carry out the plans of the group. Don't save your own skin by throwing members under the bus.

6. **Treat members consistently, regardless of sex, ethnicity, or social background.**
   Minimize external status differences to encourage participation by all. Value members for their contributions to the group.

As with other desirable behaviors, the leader should model ethical behavior that will serve as a standard for members to follow. By doing so, the leader will help create a climate of trust and a spirit of cohesiveness.

Recap: A Quick Review

Good leaders develop their members' own leadership capabilities and skills and act ethically.

1. They help individuals grow by modeling the behavior they want others to adopt, encouraging members' contributions to the group's process, and giving members the opportunity to perform important functions for the group.

2. Leaders help establish and maintain trust by promoting norms that build trust, confronting members who violate group norms and create problems, embracing the group's diversity, and being highly principled.

3. In promoting teamwork and cooperation, leaders plan fun activities and celebrations for the group; serve as advocates and cheerleaders for the group to outsiders; share rewards, including praise, with the group as a whole; seek group buy-in about how to promote teamwork; confront members who are hurting the team; keep arguments evidence-based, not personal; and look for ways to harmonize and compromise divergent views.

4. For virtual groups, leaders are responsible for creating a cohesive virtual group culture by actively paying attention to both the task and social needs of the group and its members.

5. Ethical leaders tell the truth, put concern for others ahead of individual gain, establish clear policies that everyone is expected to follow, respect others' opinions and attitudes, stand behind members, and do not discriminate or show favoritism.

QUESTIONS FOR REVIEW

 Go to self-quizzes on the Online Learning Center at mhhe.com/galanes14e to test your knowledge of the chapter concepts.

This chapter used the example of Maureen, an experienced community volunteer, and the Community Report Card task force to illustrate a variety of concepts.

1. How did Maureen demonstrate the philosophy of democratic, group-centered leadership? In what ways did she show that she was able to adjust to the needs of the individual members and the group?

2. What administrative duties did she perform? What functions did these serve for the group?

3. How well did she seem to lead the group? What specifics in the story and in other examples throughout the chapter lead you to your conclusion?

4. Did Maureen show evidence of helping develop the skills and leadership abilities of the other members? How so?

5. Do you think Maureen was an ethical group member? Why or why not?

KEY TERMS

 Test your knowledge of these key terms by visiting the Online Learning Center Web site at mhhe. com/galanes14e.

Agenda	Group charter	Meeting notice
Gatekeeper	Liaison	Minutes

BIBLIOGRAPHY

Cathcart, Robert S., and Larry A. Samovar, eds. *Small Group Communication: A Reader.* 6th ed. Dubuque, IA: Wm. C. Brown, 1992, especially Section 8.

Fisher, B. Aubrey. "Leadership: When Does the Difference Make a Difference?" In *Communication and Group Decision-Making.* Randy Y. Hirokawa and Marshall S. Poole, eds. Beverly Hills, CA: Sage, 1986, 197–215.

Hambley, Laura, Thomas O'Neill, and Theresa Kline, "Virtual Team Leadership: Perspectives From the Field," *International Journal of e-Collaboration,* 3 (January–March 2007): 40–64.

LaFasto, Frank, and Carl Larson. *When Teams Work Best: 6,000 Team Members and Leaders Tell What It Takes to Succeed.* Thousand Oaks, CA: Sage, 2001, especially Chapter 4.

Robert, Henry M., III, William J. Evans, Daniel H. Honemann, and Thomas L. Balch. *Robert's Rules of Order,* Newly Revised in Brief. Cambridge, MA: Da Capo Press, 2004.

Schwarz, Roger M. *The Skilled Facilitator: Practical Wisdom for Developing Effective Groups.* San Francisco: Jossey-Bass, 1994.

Tropman, John E. *Making Meetings Work: Achieving High Quality Group Decisions.* Thousand Oaks, CA: Sage, 1996, part 2.

NOTES

1. Gloria J. Galanes, "In Their Own Words: An Exploratory Study of Bona Fide Group Leaders," *Small Group Research, 34* (December 2003): 741–70.

2. Michael Z. Hackman and Craig E. Johnson, *Leadership: A Communication Perspective* (Prospect Heights, IL: Waveland Press, 1991): 129.

3. John Gastil, "Identifying Obstacles to Small Group Democracy," *Small Group Research, 24* (February 1993): 5–27.

4. Roger M. Schwarz, *The Skilled Facilitator: Practical Wisdom for Developing Effective Groups* (San Francisco: Jossey-Bass, 1994).

5. Laura Hambley, Thomas O'Neill, and Theresa Kline, "Virtual Team Leadership: Perspectives From the Field," *International Journal of e-Collaboration,* 3 (January–March 2007): 40–64.

6. Ibid, 55–58.

7. Ibid.

8. Suing Zhang, Marilyn Tremain, Rich Egan, Allen Milewski, Patrick O'Sullivan, Jerry Fjermestad, "Occurrence and Effects of Leader Delegation in Virtual Software Teams," *International Journal of e-Collaboration* (January–March 2009): 47–68.

9. Hambley, O'Neill, and Kline, "Virtual Team Leadership," 55–58.

10. Ibid.

11. Henry M. Robert, III, William J. Evans, Daniel H. Honemann, and Thomas J. Balch, *Robert's Rules of Order,* Newly Revised, 10th ed. (Cambridge, MA: Perseus Publishing, 2000): 464–525.

12. Al Weitzel and Patricia Geist, "Parliamentary Procedure in a Community Group: Communication and Vigilant Decision Making," *Communication Monographs, 65* (September 1998): 244–59.

13. Hambley, O;Neill, and Kline, "Virtual Team Leadership," 55–58.

14. Ibid.

15. Ibid.

16. Ibid.

17. Larson and LaFasto, *TeamWork,* 130–31.

18. Ibid., 136.

19. Ibid., 118–29.

20. Hambley, O'Neill, and Kine, "Virtual Team Leadership," 55–58.

21. Ibid.

22. Ibid.

23. Ibid.

24. Hackman and Johnson, *Leadership:* 205.

Improving Group Outputs

Problem solving and decision making are the reasons most secondary groups exist. Because problems solved by groups affect us all, we need to understand how to make the problem-solving and decision-making processes in groups the best they can be. Part IV focuses on the processes that help this occur. Like Chapters 7 and 8, Chapters 9 and 10 are companion chapters, with Chapter 9 presenting theoretical information about problem-solving and decision-making processes and Chapter 10 providing practical suggestions and techniques for effective problem solving. Chapter 11 describes how group members can make conflict work for them rather than against them.

PART

IV

239

Problem Solving and Decision Making in Groups: Theoretical Perspectives

STUDY OBJECTIVES

As a result of studying Chapter 9, you should be able to:

1. Describe the relative advantages and disadvantages of group and individual problem solving and decision making.

2. Be able to explain why a group should systematically structure its problem-solving process.

3. Describe the key steps to the Functional Perspective of group problem solving and decision making.

4. Explain what a group's charge and area of freedom are and why they are important.

5. Describe the four types of questions groups address during problem solving: questions of fact, conjecture, policy, and value.

6. Understand what criteria are and how they can guide group problem solving.

7. Describe four typical ways groups make decisions: by the leader, the leader in consultation, majority vote, and consensus.

8. Describe the phases many groups experience during decision making and explain several factors that may affect these phases.

9. Define critical thinking and describe how to evaluate information and reasoning, including from the World Wide Web.

10. Describe five common fallacies that inhibit critical thinking.

11. Describe the group polarization effect and how it can affect group decision making.

12. Define groupthink and explain how it can affect group decision making.

CENTRAL MESSAGE

Groups that approach problem solving and decision making with a plan tend to do a better job. Approaching problem solving and decision making systematically helps counteract several things that can go wrong during the process.

241

The city of O'Fallon, Missouri, just west of St. Louis, has experienced phenomenal growth during the last two decades. In the early 1990s, city officials knew they would have to find a long-range solution to the city's water treatment problems.[1] O'Fallon's dropping water table signaled that the city couldn't stay on its deep well system forever. Officials sought a long-term solution that would be both cost-effective and efficient. In a series of meetings, they determined two criteria for an effective solution: Whatever they decided to do had to provide high-quality water to the citizens of O'Fallon and also give the city long-term control over costs. Next, city officials had to investigate what their options were and discovered three realistic possibilities. They could interconnect with other water districts to buy water from them, they could build a traditional-style water treatment plant, or they could build a membrane treatment plant. Finally, in another series of small group meetings, they evaluated these options.

Buying water from the surrounding districts would be easy, but this option left the city at the mercy of other districts in terms of both quality and cost. The traditional water treatment plant would be cheaper to build initially, but required more chemicals to treat the water and was likely to need future upgrades as the Environmental Protection Agency continues to tighten water quality standards. The membrane treatment system, which would be more expensive initially, needed fewer chemicals to provide high-quality water and provided the best long-term control over costs. Officials concluded that the membrane treatment system best met their two main criteria. It was the first membrane treatment system built in Missouri.

In addressing this issue, city officials in O'Fallon demonstrated the problem-solving and decision-making throughput activities central to small groups. In these two chapters, we consider those two critical small group processes: problem solving and decision making. In this chapter, we present theoretical information about group problem solving and decision making, and in the next chapter we follow up with practical tips for improving these processes.

Problem Solving and Decision Making

A **problem** is a discrepancy between the current state—what actually *is* happening—and a desired goal—what *should* be happening. **Problem solving** is the comprehensive, multistep procedure a group uses to move from its current state—which is unsatisfactory in some way—to the desired goal. It involves creating and discovering solutions, evaluating them, choosing among them, and putting them into effect. In O'Fallon, the problem was clear: The city's need for water would soon outstrip the plant's ability to provide it; doing nothing was not an option. The desired goal

---

Problem

The discrepancy between what should be happening and what actually is happening.

Problem Solving

A comprehensive, multistage procedure for moving from a current unsatisfactory state to a desired goal and developing the plan for reaching the goal.

was clear: to secure enough good water for all citizens, affordably, into the foreseeable future. In order to solve the problem, city officials had to figure out what the issues were, determine what they hoped to accomplish, discover what their options were and evaluate them, then select what they thought was the best option. Finally, they had to implement their solution by building the membrane plant. This problem-solving process took many months.

In the course of solving the water problem, O'Fallon officials had to make many different decisions. **Decision making** refers to the act of choosing among alternatives. The most obvious choice the O'Fallon group made was selecting the membrane treatment plant, but, in fact, members made many less obvious decisions along the way. For example, they had to decide who should be involved in the process, what the main issues were, what sort of process they would use to make the decision, where they would meet, what their time frame would be, how they would go about getting the information they needed, and so forth. Thus, although problem solving and decision making refer to different processes, in fact they are so inextricably linked that we have chosen to discuss them together.

Group Versus Individual Problem Solving and Decision Making

Groups can be much better problem solvers and decision makers than individuals. At their best, groups achieve an **assembly effect** in which the decision is qualitatively and quantitatively better than the best individual judgment of any one member or the averaged judgments of all the members. In this kind of synergy, the whole becomes greater than the sum of its parts. A number of studies have found evidence of the assembly effect.[2] However, only when group members interact and work *interdependently* on the task is positive synergy possible; groups whose members work *independently* do not achieve this result.[3] If group members complete individual assignments on their own and just compile their individual products into the final group product without discussing each members' individual work *as a group,* that group will probably not achieve an assembly effect. Communication among members allows this synergy to occur.[4]

However, there are tradeoffs, and the advantages must be balanced against the disadvantages. Let's take note of the advantages. First, members can compensate for each others' weaknesses.[5] By sharing what they know, members give the group a larger pool of information and ideas to draw from. Second, group members can spot each other's errors, recognize fact from opinion, and process more information than individuals can.[6] Third, they also provide different perspectives to a problem. For example, an O'Fallon taxpayer may feel differently about the cost of building an expensive membrane treatment facility than the city manager does,

Decision Making

Choosing from among a set of alternatives.

Assembly Effect

The decision of group members collectively is better, qualitatively and quantitatively, than adding or averaging the individual judgments of the members.

but both perspectives need to be taken into account. Fourth, groups can get much more done than an individual can. Can you imagine the time it would take for *one person* to do just the preliminary research that O'Fallon needed about types of treatment facilities, costs, and so forth? Instead, group members and their staffs spent a lot of time finding the needed information. Fifth, group involvement in decision making increases acceptance of a decision.[7] For instance, when workers have a voice in changing a work procedure, they are more productive than when the change is imposed on them[8] and are more committed to the change.[9] Finally, as we noted in Chapter 1, groups meet our human needs for belonging and affection.

On the flip side, though, groups usually take more time to make decisions than individuals take. One of us participated on a committee revising the *Faculty Handbook;* out of curiosity, a member calculated how many person-hours went into the project, and it was staggering. In addition, group members can experience pressures to conform and may cave in to that pressure, even if they don't agree. Finally, when the group process goes badly, relationships among members can become strained, sometimes permanently, and the parent organization can be harmed.

Factors Affecting Quality of Group Outputs

Several factors affect whether the quality of a group's output will be better than what an individual can produce, including the type of task, the abilities of the members, and the type of communication they engage in. First, groups are better at **conjunctive tasks,** in which each member possesses information relevant to solving a problem, but no one member has all the needed information. However, groups are not better at **disjunctive tasks,** which require little or no coordination and which the most expert member working alone can answer correctly.[10] Often, groups cycle between conjunctive and disjunctive tasks and must know when to switch from individual to group decision making. For instance, teams can be more efficient when members work individually, then pool their insights to create a team-designed solution.[11] The key is to recognize which type of task you are working on and which type of strategy is most suitable.

The abilities of members is another factor that affects output quality. Group potential, as defined by individual members' abilities, strongly influences group performance.[12] Members with high *integrative complexity*—the ability to engage in highly complex reasoning processes—produced group interaction that was more complex and better able to incorporate diverse points of view into the ultimate decision, especially on conjunctive tasks.[13] Similarly when members are predisposed to process information cognitively—that is, they have a high *need for cognition*—decision quality is improved.[14] Overall decision-making performance is hurt by weaker members, whose impaired abilities to reason and hypothesize correctly

---

Conjunctive Task

A task where each member has relevant information, but no one member has all the information needed; thus, a high level of coordination among members is necessary.

Disjunctive Task

A task in which members work on parts of the group problem independently, with little or no coordination and group discussion needed.

affected the entire group.[15] The relationship between member abilities and group performance is an important one.

Communication among members, *the* essential group throughput process, affects the quality of a group's output. Verbal interaction itself, not just a summing of individual members' perceptions of opinions, contributes to the increased quality that groups usually exhibit.[16] Group studies suggest that task-relevant communication is perhaps even more important than originally thought.[17] Communication that is goal directed, with issues handled systematically and assertions documented, produces increased decision quality. Effective groups do a better job of sharing and providing information;[18] focus more of their talk on understanding and establishing criteria for evaluating decisions;[19] and spend more time analyzing the problem, establishing group procedures, and evaluating alternatives.[20] Groups whose members carefully assessed their options produced better decisions.[21]

Bona fide group members themselves were asked which behaviors help or hurt small group decision making.[22] Three factors emerged as being important. By far the most influential factor is the full participation of all group members, and includes such behaviors as encouraging members to contribute, to disagree, and to elaborate on their suggestions. The second two factors pertained to how group members establish the group's climate. Negative socioemotional behaviors—being sarcastic, expressing dislike, personal attacks—hurt decision making, but positive socioemotional behaviors—respecting and supporting others' ideas—improved it. Clearly, *both* input (e.g., members' abilities) *and* throughput (e.g., how members communicate) factors affect a group's output.

In an extensive look at group system dynamics, Losada and Heaphy reconfirm the important relationship among communication, member relationships, and team performance.[23] There is a powerful pull in groups to stay close to tried and true ways of interacting, which does not promote creative "out of the box" risks needed if the benefit of group work is realized. They found that low- to medium-performing teams could not break from negative comments that stifled creativity and promoted self-centeredness. High-performing teams broke the pull of negativity with more positive comments than negative ones that were respectful, supportive, and constructive. This dominant positivity created a "we" emotional climate and sustained an ethic of dialogue—both of which pushed the group into an enthusiasm that allowed them to achieve their work within their working parameters.

The Need for Structure in Group Problem Solving

When you have a problem to solve what do you do? When, philosopher John Dewey asked people this question most people told him they reflected carefully about the problem, thought of options for solving it, evaluated those options, selected one, then implemented their choice. Dewey developed his Reflective Thinking Model of decision making based on individual problem solving. This model serves as the basis for different group problem-solving models we discuss in Chapter 10. Each of these models provides a logical structure for group members to follow as they begin to solve a problem. But why do groups need structure? Why can't they just jump in and start talking about the problem? They can—but without guidelines, group problem solving can be pretty haphazard.[24] Typically, someone mentions a problem, someone else suggests a way to solve it, the group briefly discusses the idea, then it is adopted or something else is proposed, and the group is off on another topic. Groups often flit from idea to idea and this random process is unlikely to produce a good solution. Organizing problem-solving discussions helps groups balance participation, improve reflectiveness, coordinate group members' thinking, and establish important ground rules for proceeding.[25]

There is ample evidence that discussions in groups using a problem-solving structure are rated higher in quality and produce better decisions. In one early study, participants following a highly structured problem-solving procedure made a greater proportion of statements relevant to the issue than when the leader did not use a problem-solving structure to guide the group.[26] Groups not instructed in how to use problem-solving guidelines tended to spiral from discussing problem issues to discussing solutions, a sequence called "reach testing."[27] Observers rate the quality of such discussions lower than unstructured ones.[28] Even participants low in task orientation rate structured discussions higher than those in which the leader fails to help organize the problem-solving procedure.[29] Following a structured procedure often provides logical priorities and reminds group members of something they forgot to do in an earlier stage (such as analyze the problem thoroughly before proposing solutions).[30] As long as the logical priorities are incorporated into a sequence (e.g., problem analysis before proposing solutions), no single structure seems to be better than another. In a study by Brilhart and Jochem, three different problem-solving structural outlines produced decisions of equal quality (although the participants preferred one of the structures to the others).[31] This finding was confirmed by Bayless and Larson, but Larson also found that using *no* structural pattern for problem solving produced distinctly worse solutions.[32]

Some people believe that following a systematic linear procedure is not normal for small groups, but trainers in business and industry invariably recommend teaching corporate personnel systematic procedures before they institute participative management groups such as quality circles or self-managed work teams. For example, researchers associated with a scientific research and development corporation argued forcefully for a highly systematic, structured problem-solving format to prevent scientists from making the kinds of mistakes often attributed to random error.[33]

They note that systematic problem solving is not a rigid set of techniques but "a matter of effective *communication* and data *handling*."[34] Group participants themselves seem to want methods and procedures to help them function more effectively. Experienced group participants can identify "methodological deficiencies" (e.g., gaps in knowing what to do at the right time and how to do it) as significant barriers to effective group problem solving.[35] They asked for tested procedures to help them deal more productively with complex problems. The same expectations around structure are found in virtual groups. While some have questioned the need for structured delegation in virtual groups, research into what works best for virtual groups shows a need for structure and members who are able to identify what they need.[36]

The Functional Perspective of Group Problem Solving and Decision Making

We have noted that procedures improve group problem solving and decision making, but that no particular procedure seems to be superior to another. That is because a procedure itself is not the key factor in determining performance; what procedures *do* is oblige group members to pay attention to the *functions* necessary for a group to do a good job of problem solving or decision making.[37] That is the heart of the **Functional Perspective,** which states that the communicative actions of group members determine decision-making and problem-solving performance.[38]

The Functional Perspective assumes that group members are motivated to make the best choice possible, that the choice isn't obvious, that they have access to the information and other resources they need, and that they have the cognitive ability and communication skills necessary for the task.[39] For many years, Gouran, Hirokawa, and their associates have investigated what communicative functions need to be performed for a group to succeed, and have concluded that groups must meet five fundamental task requirements:

1. Group members must understand the issue to be resolved.
2. Members must determine what minimal characteristics any acceptable alternative must have.
3. They must determine what those relevant and realistic alternatives are.
4. They must carefully examine those alternatives against the previously determined characteristics necessary for an acceptable choice.
5. They must select the alternative that seems most likely to have the characteristics needed.

Productive groups usually address the five essential tasks in a more or less organized sequence, although the sequences may vary from discussion

Functional Perspective

The approach to group problem solving that focuses on the necessary communicative functions group members must perform for the group to do an effective job of problem solving and decision making.

to discussion.[40] Groups that omit one or more of these steps or do not thoroughly discuss them are headed for the single biggest problem-solving mistake they can make.

Both laboratory studies of group problem solving using college students and a field study of committees in a large utility company support the premises of the Functional Perspective.[41] In a Midwestern manufacturing firm, Propp and Nelson discovered continued support for the importance of addressing these issues.[42] The most consistent predictor of group performance was vigilant attention to the nature of the problem or task facing the group. In addition, they found that this particular group addressed another issue: *What procedures should we use to address how we want to solve our problem?* Handling this concern effectively appears to be most important when a group faces several difficult decisions. Finally, groups with the highest quality decisions not only use a vigilant decision-making procedure but also are willing to second-guess their work by retrospectively questioning their previous choices.[43]

Critical thinking, discussed later in the chapter, is at the heart of the Functional Perspective, which encourages vigilance—unbiased and thorough analysis of a group's problem and its possible solutions—in the problem-solving and decision-making processes. In short, the Functional Perspective focuses our attention on the communicative functions necessary for high-quality group outputs.

Recap: A Quick Review

Group problem solving and decision making are key throughput processes that largely determine the quality of a group's output.

1. Problem solving (a multistep procedure that includes analyzing a problem, creating or finding solutions, evaluating the solutions, choosing the best, and implementing it) and decision making (the act of choosing) are intertwined.

2. Groups can achieve an assembly effect when members work interdependently, share what they know, and compensate for one another's mistakes, so usually group decisions are superior to individual decisions.

3. Groups do better than individuals on conjunctive tasks, when members have good cognitive abilities and communication skills, when they all participate, and when they create a positive group climate.

4. Without structure, group problem solving is haphazard and its ultimate products are of lower quality.

5. The Functional Perspective focuses on five key functions that a group must perform to succeed. Structured guidelines help ensure that these functions are fulfilled, but no structured guideline is superior, although using *any* guideline works better than using none.

Starting Out Right: Addressing the Charge, Type of Question, and Criteria

Systematic problem solving works better than random problem solving because the group is less likely to ignore or forget important elements of the problem-solving process. Three such factors help a group focus clearly: the charge (including its limitations), the type of question, and the criteria for evaluating solutions.

Understanding the Charge and Area of Freedom

The **charge** is the assignment given to the group, usually by a parent organization or individual. Sometimes a group develops its own charge; neighbors who band together to try to reduce speeding in their neighborhood streets are not given the charge by an outside body, but develop it out of mutual interests. The charge specifies what a group is to do; it usually includes the group's **area of freedom,** or amount of authority it has, along with any limitations it faces. Are there budget restrictions? Is the recommendation to be kept private or shared? Are there things the group should *not* do? For example, a Student Services Committee was charged by the vice president for Student Affairs with recommending improvements to services for evening students. Ignoring their charge and area of freedom, committee members produced a report recommending that two individuals be fired and that the budget be reallocated, with more money for student services. They distributed their report to the entire administrative staff of the college, including the two whose positions they wanted to eliminate. Needless to say, their actions were not well received.

Make sure that all members of your group understand the charge: What is the group supposed to do? By what time frame? What resources does the group have (e.g., money, computer time, secretarial help)? What should the group *not* do? What will the final product be (e.g., a written report, an oral recommendation)? Who receives the final product?

Understanding the Type of Questions to Be Addressed

A second important factor is making sure the group understands the type of question it must address. Four common types of questions that groups address are *questions of fact, questions of conjecture, questions of value, and questions of policy.*[44] You must know which type of question you face because each question requires a different discussion emphasis. A **question of fact** asks whether something is true, whether something actually happened. For example, O'Fallon's city officials needed to determine whether the water table in the area was actually falling. They relied on objective, credible experts to help make that determination. A **question of conjecture** asks a group to speculate, or make an educated guess, about what might or could happen in the future. O'Fallon officials asked, *Based on what we know*

Charge

A group's assignment or task, often given by a parent organization or individual.

Area of Freedom

The amount of authority and limitations a group has.

Question of Fact

A question that asks whether something is true, or actually happened.

Question of Conjecture

A question that asks a group to speculate or make an educated guess about something.

is true right now about the water table and the population growth, how long do we think the current water treatment facility will be able to handle the demand? As you can see, making a *good* educated guess depends on having accurate information and facts. A **question of value** refers to what is right, good, preferable, or acceptable. In O'Fallon, the group had to decide how much members valued local control of their water supply. One of the cheapest alternatives, in the short run, was to buy water from neighboring districts—but that would put O'Fallon at the mercy of others! *How important is it, officials asked, to keep control of our water supply and pricing?* A **question of policy** asks what course of action a group will take: *What are we going to do, recommend, decide about something?* The bottom line for O'Fallon was a decision about which option to choose: buying water from another district, building another treatment plant, or building a state-of-the-art membrane plant.

As you can see, it is usually easier to decide questions of fact because their answers can usually be verified. This is not the case with questions of conjecture or value. Sometimes, members' perspectives and values are so different that they will answer questions of conjecture or value differently. And, of course, if those are answered differently, members will likely decide things differently. You can also see from the O'Fallon examples that, with complex problems, groups have to deal with all four types of questions. Groups need to understand what questions they must address so that members know where to put their efforts. For instance, if the group must come to consensus about a question of value, then members must share what they believe and be willing to look for common values they all agree on, so they can recommend a solution that does not violate those mutual values. That isn't always possible.

Discussing Criteria for Evaluating Solutions

The group must establish and agree on **criteria,** or standards against which to evaluate the various options before they can begin to evaluate their options. Criteria establish the group's standards and express the values shared by members. Two people with different values will use different criteria to evaluate options, thereby arriving at quite different solutions. For example, Rubenstein asked Arab and American students whom they would save if their boat capsized and they could save only one other person beside themselves: wife, child, or mother. *All* the Arabs chose the mother (your mother holds a unique and irreplaceable position in your life), but *none* of the Americans did—they split about evenly between the child and the wife.[45] In this case, Arab values and American values supported widely divergent criteria for deciding whom to save. Without agreement about criteria, consensus may be impossible.

Some criteria *must* be met and are *absolute,* but with *relative* criteria, the group has some leeway. (Examples of absolute and relative criteria are shown in Table 9.1.) For example, O'Fallon city officials held water quality

---

Question of Value

A question that asks whether something is right, good, preferable, or acceptable.

Question of Policy

A question that asks what course of action a group will take.

Criteria

Standards against which alternatives are evaluated.

Absolute (*Must* Be Met)	Relative (*Should* Be Met)
Entertainment must not cost over $400.	Location should be convenient, that is, within 30 minutes' driving time for all members.
Must be enjoyable to members and their families. (*Enjoyable* means provide a variety of activities designed to appeal to people ranging in age from 3 to 80.)	Facilities should be comfortable; for example, shelter in case of rain, electrical outlets, hot and cold running water, restroom facilities, and so on.

TABLE 9.1
Absolute versus relative criteria to guide plans for a club's annual picnic

as an absolute standard—whatever solution they developed, the water had to be of "high quality." But criteria should be measurable, if possible; criteria such as "high quality" are abstract, so a group should quantify its criteria. For example, "high-quality water" may mean water that has certain specified maximum levels of heavy metals, particulates, and bacteria. Water quality engineers and the Environmental Protection Agency helped the O'Fallon officials specify what "high quality" meant to them.

Theorists have argued about whether and when a problem-solving discussion should include a step for establishing explicit criteria. Many people place it early in the problem-solving process, before talking about solutions. Others suggest that criteria are better discussed after the group has accumulated all possible solutions first. There is no simple, single answer to this. Brilhart and Jochem found that decision quality was not affected by *when* criteria were discussed, or whether discussion of criteria was a separate step in the problem-solving outline. However, significantly more participants wanted criteria discussed explicitly and preferably *after* brainstorming, not before.[46]

If criteria have high evaluation clarity, they may not need to be discussed at all.[47] Evaluation clarity is high when criteria are clearly presented to the group as part of the charge and are understood by all members. Evaluation clarity is low when standards are not presented to the group, are fuzzy, or are understood differently by different members. When evaluation clarity is high, decision quality is not affected much by whether members discuss or use evaluation criteria; but when evaluation clarity is low, decision performance is strongly related to whether members establish and use explicit criteria.

Advice from the research is mixed, and if the criteria are part of the group's charge or otherwise clearly understood, you do not have to discuss them; however, we think it's never wrong to discuss criteria. For one thing, group members may have misjudged their degree of understanding of and agreement about criteria! Discussing criteria explicitly, even briefly, may save you from unnecessary misunderstanding or disagreement when you begin to evaluate options. *When* you discuss criteria is up to you, although members seem to like brainstorming options before discussing criteria.

Understanding How the Group's Decision Will Be Made

Groups may use a number of different methods to make decisions. Among the most common are the four described here, with their advantages and disadvantages outlined in Table 9.2. Group members should know at the outset how the decision will be made. Hurt feelings—or worse—will occur if group members think they will make the ultimate choice but the group leader actually ends up choosing, so clarify this at the beginning of the process.

Decision Making by the Leader

Sometimes a designated or emergent leader thinks the problem through alone and announces a decision. Group members are then given instructions for executing the decision. The resulting solution may or may not

TABLE 9.2   Comparing advantages and disadvantages of four common decision-making methods

Decision-Making Method	Advantages	Disadvantages
By the Leader	• Can be high-quality decision if leader is an expert. • Is fast. • Group avoids anxiety/responsibility of decision making.	• Lacks others' input, so may not be high quality. • Members may not support decision. • May cause resentment, reduced cohesiveness, lack of motivation for future.
By the Leader, with Consultation	• Can be high-quality decision. • Can be faster than having group decide. • Especially useful if group cannot come to consensus. • Members appreciate opportunity to participate.	• Members may resent decision if their input isn't used. • "Losing" side may not support decision. • May encourage members to duck hard work of developing consensus.
By Majority Vote	• Familiar procedure for Americans. • Each vote counts equally. • Decision can be reached quickly.	• Minority side may stay silent out of fear. • Minority may resent outcome and not support it. • Majority is not always right; decision may be flawed.
By Consensus	• All members support decision. • Members more satisfied and committed to decision. • Decision can be high quality, because all viewpoints are taken into account.	• Usually takes more time. • Members may feel pressured to conform. • May be hard or impossible to achieve.

be a high-quality one, but other outcomes of such control by the leader may be resentment, lowered cohesiveness, half-hearted support for the decision, and unwillingness to contribute to subsequent decisions. Members may even sabotage the decision. We once observed a group of faculty members who became furious that their designated leader had made an important decision without consulting them. They called a special meeting to overturn his decision. After discussing their options, they proceeded to make *exactly the same* decision that he had made. Clearly their distress was not about the *content* of the decision but about the *process* and their anger at being left out.

Decision Making by the Leader in Consultation with Members

Often, a group leader reserves the right to make a decision, but wants input from the group. The leader consults with members, individually or as a group, then decides based on that consultation. This is appropriate when the leader alone is responsible for the decision, such as a department head who must determine annual budgets, but who wants to broaden his or her base of knowledge. It is also effective when a group cannot come to consensus. One of us was responsible for deciding which teaching area a new faculty position should represent. The broadcast journalism, print journalism, and media production faculty each argued that the new position should fill teaching needs in those individual areas; the group could not achieve consensus. The various arguments helped your coauthor make the decision, and even though some faculty were disappointed, they all believed they had been heard.

Decision Making by Majority Vote

Making a **majority decision** through voting by a show of hands, saying *aye,* or written or electronic ballots is probably the procedure used most often to settle a difference of opinion in democratic groups. On the plus side, everyone has an equal opportunity to influence the decision by speaking, each vote counts equally, and the decision is reached more quickly than if the group's norms require a consensus decision. The numerical power of the majority wins But usually the vote is split, with minority members (losers) sometimes doubting that their ideas have been understood fully and treated fairly. People in a minority may even remain silent for fear of being ridiculed for opinions that deviate from the majority opinion. Not only does the quality of the decision sometimes suffer, but the group's cohesiveness and commitment to the decision may be lowered. When a group's bylaws *require* that a vote be taken, the group may want to discuss an issue until consensus has been reached, then vote to confirm it "legally."

Majority Decision
Decision made by vote, with the winning alternative receiving more than half the members' votes.

Decision Making by Consensus

A **consensus decision** is one that all members agree is the best that everyone can support. It is not necessarily the alternative most preferred by all members. When a true consensus has been reached, the output is usually better and members are more satisfied and likely to accept the outcome. However, reaching consensus may take much more time than other procedures. Furthermore, unanimity—the state of perfect consensus in which every group member believes that the decision achieved is the best that could be made—is not at all common. Sometimes a true consensus cannot be achieved, no matter how much time is spent in discussion.

More than just the merit of the decision is involved when a group strives for consensus. Certain personality traits, values, and other characteristics of the members affect a group's ability to achieve consensus, as we mentioned in Chapter 5. For example, groups with members similar in decision-rule orientation were more likely to achieve consensus.[48] Three common decision-rule orientations are attempts to minimize losses (a conservative, pessimistic approach), attempts to maximize gains (a risk-taking, optimistic approach), and the maximum expected utility approach (an attempt to derive the highest average payoffs no matter whether a pessimistic or optimistic future is envisioned). The degree of comfort that members felt with the decision was more important in achieving consensus than the quality of the decision itself. Groups with members whose decision-rule orientations were similar had an easier time achieving consensus. Thus, more than just the merit of the decision is involved when a group strives for consensus.

Consensus may be superficial when some members accommodate to higher-status members, including "experts" who express their opinions with exceptional force, a designated leader, or a large majority. One of us once completed "Lost on the Moon," a group decision-making exercise in which the group is asked to rank the usefulness of several items to astronauts lost on the moon. Her group included several electrical and mechanical engineers with considerable scientific and technical expertise. She readily conceded to these experts. Interestingly, her individual ranking of the items was better than the group's ranking, but she was swayed by the engineers' confidence in their knowledge. Even though it may be uncomfortable to be the group's opinion deviate, do not suppress your opinions because divergent opinions can lead to better decisions.

Understanding Phasic Progression During Decision Making

Groups often cycle through predictable phases as they attempt to solve problems and make decisions. Bales and Strodtbeck were among the first to identify this **phasic progression**.[49] During the *orientation* phase, members orient themselves to the task and to one another, if they do not already know each other. In the *evaluation* phase, they decide what they collectively think about the problem or decision. Finally, during the *control* phase, the group has reached enough socioemotional maturity for members to concentrate on completing their task. For each new problem they confront, groups will tend to cycle through all three of these stages, returning to an orientation stage for a new problem once a decision has been reached about a previous problem.

Fisher's Model of Group Phases

Later, Fisher observed that experienced decision-making groups pass through four phases as they work toward deciding among a group of alternatives.[50] These phases are orientation, conflict, decision emergence, and reinforcement. They can be identified by the kinds of interactions that occur in each.

Orientation   During the orientation phase, members develop a shared understanding of their task, the facts about available options, and how to interpret them. Signs of disagreement are minimal; ambiguous and favorable remarks are common. This makes sense because, when group members are uncertain about the facts or concerned about how others will perceive them, they will not make strong statements of disagreement that might offend another member. In this early stage, a member is more likely to say, "Well, that idea sounds like it might work, but maybe we should take time to think about it some more," than to say, "That's not going to work at all—we're going to have to try a lot harder if we are to come up with a decent solution." The first remark is ambiguous and tentative; the second is clear and definite.

Conflict   During the conflict phase, members offer initiatives, take stands, disagree, offer compromises, argue for and against proposals, and generally discuss ideas in a more open manner than during orientation. Ambiguous remarks fall to a low level in this phase, but disagreeing and agreeing remarks are common. For instance, Selena says, "I think we should get more information about the impact this might have before we proceed much further." Andrew replies, "Naw, we have all the information we need right now to decide." Then Tina supports Selena: "I agree with Selena. We need to know a lot more or we might really mess things up." Members argue for and against proposals, with most people taking sides. Wishy-washy behavior disappears as opinions are expressed clearly and forcefully.

Decision Emergence   For a group to achieve its goal, it must move, somehow, from a position where each member argues a particular point of view to a position where members are willing to be influenced by one another. This movement is signaled by the reappearance of ambiguity in the group. Whereas the earlier ambiguity served as a way of managing primary tension, now it helps resolve secondary tension by allowing the members to back off from staunchly held positions and save face at the same time. It would be hard on a member's self-image to switch suddenly from "I think we should accept the first proposal" to "OK, let's reject the first proposal." A transition is needed; the ambiguity provides this transition, which allows the member to move from "I think we should accept the first proposal" to "*Maybe* you are right. There might be some problems with the first proposal that I hadn't considered. Let's look at it more closely before we decide." Members move gradually toward a common group position. Near the end of this phase a consensus decision emerges, sometimes suddenly. The members usually know when this point is reached, and they all indicate support for the decision. If members do not reach this point, they may need to resolve the disagreement by majority vote.

Reinforcement   After a group has accomplished its primary objective, it doesn't just immediately move on to a different problem or disband. Members reinforce each other and themselves for a job well done. They say such things as, "Wow, it took a long time, but we got some really important things done," or "I really like the proposal. It's going to work beautifully," or "I'm proud of us for coming up with this. You are super and this has been a rewarding experience." Members pat each other on the back and reinforce the positive feelings they have toward the decision and toward each other.

Fisher believed that unless some outside factor (like severe time pressure) interferes with the group's natural decision-making process, these phases will follow each other in a predictable way, although the proportion of time spent in each phase may vary from decision to decision. It is important to recall, however, that he studied interaction in previously developed groups that had already passed through their formation stage.

Poole's more recent investigations have called into question the idea that most groups experience exactly the same phases, in the same order.[51] Group decision making is more complex than unitary sequences suggest. A number of factors influence not only what phases groups experience, but also in what order the phases occur.[52] For example, some groups experience long, drawn-out conflict phases with little socioemotional integration after the conflict. Others experience lengthy periods of idea development with no overt conflict.

Poole's contingency model of group decision making describes three types of factors that affect phasic progression: objective task characteristics, group task characteristics, and group structural characteristics.[53] *Objective task characteristics* include such factors as goal clarity and potential impact of the decision. For example, if the group's goal is clear at the beginning of the process, members may be able to shorten the orientation phase. *Group task characteristics* include such factors as time and population familiarity. Members are more likely to spend extra time orienting themselves to the task and arguing the merits of various options for a novel task that is unfamiliar to them than for a familiar one. Finally, *group structural characteristics* refer to how members of the group work together and include such factors as cohesiveness, conflict, and history. Members who have experienced divisive conflict may either run away from potential arguments in the group or may approach group meetings with their defenses up and boxing gloves on.

As you can see, group decision making is complicated, with numerous factors potentially influencing phasic progression. Thus, from our review of work on phasic progression and from our own experience, we envision a group cycling repeatedly through phases like those Fisher described while moving gradually forward from early formation to full and efficient production. This movement is captured in the spirals of Figure 9.1.

This back-and-forth spiral movement is typical of many continuing groups. Scheidel and Crowell observed the spiral-like progression of a group's problem-solving process and noted that a group does not move in a clear, straight line toward a decision.[54] This spiral-like effect has been observed by others. Sabourin and Geist described the collaborative nature

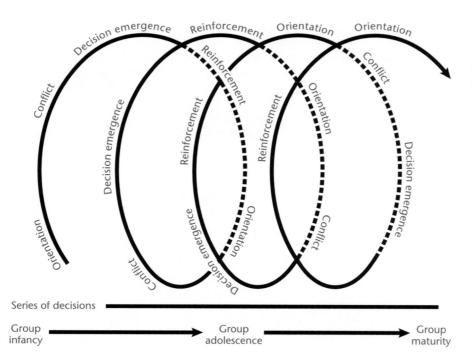

FIGURE 9.1
Decision making within the development of a small group

of group decision making as a process in which group members build on each other's proposals.[55] Fisher and Stutman also observed the messy, but ultimately progressive, nature of the spiral model.[56] However, a recent investigation by Pavitt and Johnson suggests that this spiraling movement is not universal.[57] There was great variation in the spiraling exhibited by the groups that these authors analyzed, ranging from little or no spiraling to much more than the spiral model indicates. Even so, it may be especially helpful for members high in preference for procedural order to know that such messy cycling between problem analysis to a decision and solution discussion is normal; they can better endure the frustration they feel when a group's progress seems to be "two steps forward, one step back."

Recap: A Quick Review

There are several factors that will help a group succeed if members carefully consider them early in the problem solving process, and they must know how a decision will be made:

1. Members must be clear about their charge and area of freedom, or limitations.

2. Members must know whether they are dealing with questions of fact, conjecture, value, or policy.

3. Members must understand and agree on the criteria they will use to evaluate their options. Whether members discuss criteria explicitly depends on evaluation clarity; when clarity is high (meaning that criteria are already clear to all), it isn't essential to discuss criteria explicitly.

4. Members must know and agree about how the group will decide: by the leader, by the leader in consultation, by majority vote, or by consensus. If this is not understood at the beginning, misunderstandings and hurt feelings may occur.

5. The leader can choose, but members may resent it; they are less likely to resent it if the leader consulted with the members first (unless the leader ignores their input).

6. Members can use majority voting, but those in the minority may not feel heard or understood.

7. In consensus decision making, members believe the option they selected was the best they could all agree to, but the process may be long and consensus may be impossible.

8. Many groups experience phases during decision making; Bales first identified phasic progression with three phases he often observed: orientation, evaluation, and control.

9. Fisher described four phases, orientation, conflict, decision emergence, and reinforcement; later, Poole noted three types of factors affected whether the phases occurred and in what order: objective task characteristics, group task characteristics, and group structural characteristics.

Promoting Critical Thinking

Earlier, we mentioned that the Functional Perspective emphasizes the importance of critical thinking to effective problem solving. **Critical thinking** is the systematic examination of information and ideas on the basis of evidence and logical reasoning, rather than intuition or hunch. Unfortunately, many groups do not encourage critical thinking skills. For instance, Meyers et al. found that group arguments in undergraduate groups consisted of simple assertions almost half the time and that members seldom cited rules of logic or used criteria as standards.[58] But to evaluate options thoroughly, you must make critical thinking a team effort. Groups evaluate both information and reasoning.

> **Critical Thinking**
>
> The systematic examination of information and ideas on the basis of evidence and logic rather than intuition, hunch, or prejudgment.

Evaluating Information

Information—facts, ideas, opinions, data—is the raw material from which a group's decision is made. A group's final decision can be only as good as the information inputs used by the group. Members must evaluate information for accuracy, credibility, and relevance to the group's decisions.

Distinguishing Between Facts and Inferences   Distinguishing between facts and inferences, opinions, and preferences is very important. Often, group members state opinions as though they were facts, thus leading other group members to accept what may be erroneous conclusions.

A **fact** can be verified as *true* or *false*. Facts either exist or do not exist; they are not open to argument. A *statement of fact* is a declarative statement that describes an observation of some event. "It is raining outside" is a statement of fact if it really is raining and someone could verify that fact (e.g., by looking out the window). Present events are relatively easy to verify. If the statement of fact refers to a past event, that past event must have actually been observed by somebody. If several independent sources report the same information as fact, you can be more confident than if it comes from only one source.

> **Fact**
>
> A verifiable observed event; a descriptive statement that is true.

An **inference** is an opinion that goes beyond what was actually observed; it makes a leap from a fact to a conclusion based on that fact. A *statement of inference* contains an opinion, preference, or conclusion. For example, "The Springfield metropolitan area is growing rapidly" is a statement of inference that goes beyond the *fact* that the area's population was 325,721 in the 2000 census and 436,712 in the 2010 census. *Rapidly* is a relative term; whether this inference is valid depends on what we compare the growth rate to: average growth rate for metropolitan areas in the United States, average growth rate for Missouri metropolitan areas, recent growth rate for areas of similar size, and so on. Thus, inference *is arguable*. Table 9.3 provides examples and further descriptions of facts and inferences.

> **Inference**
>
> A statement that goes beyond fact, involves some degree of uncertainty or probability, and cannot be checked for accuracy by direct observation.

TABLE 9.3
Comparing
statements of fact
and statements
of inference and
opinion

Statements of Fact	Examples
• Are limited to description.	• The population of the Springfield metropolitan area recorded in the 2010 census was 436,712.
• Can be made only *after* observation.	• On August 9, 2008, Gloria Galanes lived with two cats.
• Are as close to certain as humans can get.	• The university library's catalog contained 2,437,532 volumes on July 8, 1996.
• Only a limited number of facts exist.	• After instituting lotteries, three states reduced their tax rates.
Statements of Inference and Opinion	**Examples**
• Go beyond what was observed directly.	• Springfield is growing rapidly.
• Can be made at any time without regard to observation.	• Gloria Galanes likes cats.
• Can be made by anyone, observer or not.	• The heart of a good university is its library.
• Entail some degree of probability, inferential risk, or uncertainty.	• We should legalize casino gambling to reduce the state income tax.
• An unlimited number can be made about anything.	

Evaluating Survey and Statistical Data Factual-type statements, including statistics or the results of surveys, need to be evaluated carefully for dependability. Surveying is a sophisticated operation. The questions and who asks them can make a big difference in the results. Ask the following questions when evaluating statistics: Who commissioned the study? How were the data gathered and analyzed? How were questions phrased? You may need the help of an expert to evaluate and interpret statistical data properly, especially if you are basing an important conclusion on those data.

Evaluating the Sources and Implications of Opinions When first introduced to the differences between facts and opinions, some students act as if statements of opinion are less valuable in a discussion. Hardly so! Facts provide the basis for discussion and debate. As we discussed regarding types of questions, groups must deal not only with what has already been verified but also determine priorities of values, ethics, goals, and procedures acceptable to all. Members make inferences about what will probably happen *if* they adopt each possible alternative. For example, facts regarding AIDS and how it is spread are fairly well known, but what a particular board of education will *do* about it depends on the values, opinions, and judgments about policies that will be acceptable to the community.

All people have an equal right to express their opinions, but opinions themselves are not all equal. Opinions *can* be evaluated for their validity and appropriate use of fact. First, consider the source of the opinion.

1. Is this person (or other source) a recognized expert on the subject? How do other experts in the field regard this person? If their opinions are different, how might this be explained?

2. Does the source have a vested interest that might have influenced the opinion? For example, a flood victim, insurance agent, politician, and taxpayer will have different opinions about whether government should reimburse victims of natural disasters for all their losses.

3. How well does the source support the opinion with documented evidence? Is the evidence well organized, with supporting statistics and tables and clear reasoning?

4. How consistent is this opinion with others expressed by the source? If not consistent, is there an acceptable explanation for the person's inconsistency?

Second, consider the implications of the opinion. Where does the conclusion lead, and is that acceptable to the group? For example, a writer may argue that outlawing private ownership of handguns would protect us from accidents and murderers. What are the implications of this statement? That dangerous devices should not be allowed in the hands of citizens at large? That only nonessential dangerous tools that could potentially be used as murder weapons should be restricted? That eventually all potential murder weapons should be restricted? When a group decision depends on opinions, it is important to test these opinions for what they assume and imply.

Evaluating the information available to the group is only the first element of critical thinking. It is equally important to evaluate both information sources and group members' reasoning from this information.

Evaluating Reasoning

Valid reasoning connects information with conclusions in an appropriate and defensible way. Once you have evaluated the information (raw data), you must also look at how speakers and writers reason from that information. Are their conclusions logical and plausible? Here is where *group* decision making can be clearly superior to individual decision making, because one member is usually able to spot a flaw or a reasoning error, called a **fallacy,** that another member missed. We now discuss five common fallacies observed in group discussions.[59]

Overgeneralizing   An **overgeneralization** is a conclusion that is not supported by enough data. Because something is true about one or a few

Fallacy

A reasoning error.

Overgeneralization

An assumption that because something is true about one or a few items, it is true of all or most items of the same type.

instances, someone claims it is true of all or most instances of the same type. For example, when a person concludes that because *some* college students have defaulted on their government-guaranteed loans, *most or all* college students are irresponsible, that person has overgeneralized. Generalizations are not automatically wrong. After all, that is what statistics do—help us generalize appropriately from a relatively small sample to a large population. The problem occurs when we *overgeneralize*. To test generalizations, ask whether evidence other than personal testimony is being offered to support the generalization and how many cases the generalization is based on.

Ad Hominem Attack

An attack on a person rather than his or her argument.

Ad Hominem Attacks   An ***ad hominem* attack** is a statement that attacks a person instead of pointing out a flaw in the person's argument. The attack diverts the group's attention so that members debate the merits of the person rather than his or her position on the issue. *Ad hominem* attacks may be explicit ("You can't trust women or minorities to evaluate affirmative action laws fairly!") or veiled ("Why do you think someone *like that* could help our group?"). In any case, they are a subtle form of name-calling. Determining the credibility of the person supplying information is important, but *ad hominem* attacks condemn individuals on the basis of characteristics irrelevant to the validity of opinions or accuracy of information they provide. And they do *not* help evaluate the arguments advanced by the person for or against some proposal.

Suggesting Inappropriate Causal Relationships   Sometimes people assume that because two events are related or occurred close to each other in time, one must have caused the other. Common sense suggests that events usually have multiple and complex causes. To suggest that one single event causes another almost always oversimplifies a relationship among numerous variables. For example, we overheard a newscaster say that because female graduates of women-only colleges were more likely to serve on the boards of *Fortune* 500 companies than graduates of coeducational schools, attendance at women's colleges probably caused greater career achievement. This is a preposterous statement! Numerous factors influence career achievement. For instance, many women's colleges are both highly selective and expensive; their students are often bright, grew up in families who own or are connected to Fortune 500 companies, and can afford to attend expensive schools. Attendance at women-only colleges may indeed provide women with greater opportunities for engaging in leadership activities. More likely, native ability, economic resources, and family connections "cause" both attendance at women-only colleges and career achievement. Whenever you see causal connections being posited, look for other reasons why the events might be linked. Only when alternative explanations have been eliminated can a causal connection be accepted as probably true, and then only tentatively.

False Dilemmas   A **false dilemma** poses an either–or choice that implies, wrongly, that only two courses of action are possible. For example, either the university builds a new parking lot *or* students have to walk miles to get to class. Either sex education is taught by the parents *or* by the schools. Each of these statements ignores the fact that other options exist to accomplish both goals—in other words, the dilemma is false. The university could provide a shuttle bus service to transport students from faraway parking lots, schedule classes early or late to alleviate parking crunches at certain times, or set up a car-pooling service to improve the parking situation. Children can be taught sex education by their parents; their teachers; their ministers, priests, or rabbis; committees composed of teachers and parents working together; teams of clergy and parents; and so forth. Just because a writer or speaker does not offer you alternatives should not blind you to their existence. Whenever you are offered an either–or choice, look for additional options.

Faulty Analogies   A **faulty analogy** is a comparison that stretches a similarity too far. Comparisons help us understand issues more vividly, but all comparisons have limitations. Author Gloria's orange tabby cat may look and act like a tiger, but he does not eat 10 pounds of meat per day and cannot hurt you if he jumps on your lap. We have heard many students complain (we have even complained ourselves!), "You can't really learn how to be a public relations professional in college. It would be like trying to learn to swim from a book, but never getting in the water." At first glance, this remark hits home because there *are* limitations to what you can learn in school. Examining the analogy more closely, however, reveals that many classroom activities and assignments prepare students for professional practice. Public relations majors practice writing for a variety of audiences, learn principles of graphic design and use them to design materials for a variety of clients, put together dynamic oral presentations, write job specifications and budgets for proposed projects, and so on. All of these are activities that public relations professionals carry out in professional practice. Whenever you hear an analogy being offered as an argument, ask yourself three things: (1) What two things are being compared? (2) How are they similar? and, more important, (3) How are they different or where does the comparison break down? Always ask, "Is the conclusion warranted by *this* analogy?"

The fallacies we have just presented are among the most common, but by no means are they the only ones you will encounter. The important thing is for you and your fellow group members to be alert to mistakes in reasoning.

Evaluating Information and Reasoning from the World Wide Web

The foregoing information pertains to all sources of information, regardless of the method you used to acquire the information. But because anyone can post virtually anything on the World Wide Web, evaluating Web-based

False Dilemma

Either–or thinking that assumes, incorrectly, that only two choices or courses of action are possible.

Faulty Analogy

An incomplete comparison that stretches a similarity too far; assuming that because two things are similar in some respects, they are alike in others.

sources poses unique problems In a 2009 study of information found on the Internet, 2,814 web pages covering a variety of topics were evaluated for whether they contained essential information about a given issue. Only 11 percent were rated good or excellent.[60]. Adams and Clark suggest using six evaluation criteria that look at accuracy, authority, audience, purpose, recency, and coverage.[61]

Accuracy   How do you know information from the Web is accurate? You can't know beyond any doubt, but three factors can help you. First, be suspicious of information that has not passed through any editorial checks. Some Web-based sources, such as those maintained by credible news organizations like CNN, carry information that has been screened. Second, determine whether multiple sources verify the same information. Finally, use your common sense. If something seems too good or too incredible to be true, don't accept it automatically. We found a Web site that advertised manbeef—human meat for food consumption. It was a spoof, but some people accepted it as true.

Authority   Ask what the source of the information is, and determine whether you would trust that source. Collective or corporate authority, such as the National Communication Association or the American Medical Association, adhere to stricter standards for information than most individuals do. Find the information's home page to determine who is providing it and whether there may be bias. Look for names of directors or contributors to the site and investigate their backgrounds.

Audience   For whom is the information being offered? Web designers have particular audiences in mind. Information is tailored to reach particular audiences. It may be too technical, too jargon-filled, or too simplistic for your purposes. It may also be slanted to appeal to a particular audience. What do the links provided on the Web site tell you about the agenda of the site?

Purpose   Why is this information being offered? It may be intended to inform, persuade, entertain you, or advocate for something. A good clue is what comes after the dot. A .gov ending is sponsored by the government, for instance, and is probably intended to inform. A .com signifies a commercial enterprise and is probably trying to sell you something. Organizational sites (.org) are probably advocating a cause or course of action. Be careful, though, because there are no restrictions for registering with these endings, so you can be misled.

Recency   How current is the site? The Internet allows information to be placed instantly, but some sites are not monitored or updated frequently. A site's date may be the date it was created or the date it was last modified—it isn't always clear. Many sites have an e-mail address that allows you to ask questions or give feedback to the site owners. Use this to find out more.

Coverage Is your topic covered in enough depth? The Internet's speed can work against depth of coverage, but, often, you can link to additional sites that touch on your topic. Use a variety of sources to get sufficient information.

These suggestions aren't foolproof, but they will help you gauge the value and usefulness of Web-based information. Don't just accept something because it's on the Web. Remember, that while the information on the Web is vast and accessible, most of the knowledge in the world is still found in print!

Recap: A Quick Review

How well a group evaluates the pros and cons of its alternatives affects how good its solution or decision will be:

1. Critical thinking—the systematic examination of ideas based on evidence and reasoning—is crucial to effective group problem solving and decision making.

2. In evaluating information, members must distinguish between facts, which are not arguable, and inferences (or opinions), which are.

3. Evaluating survey and statistical data may require the help of an expert, since how the questions are asked and the data gathered can influence the results.

4. When members evaluate sources and opinions, they try to determine whether the source is credible unbiased, supports his or her opinion with evidence, and whether that opinion is consistent with those of other experts.

5. When members evaluate reasoning, they look for fallacies, which are reasoning errors.

6. Five common fallacies are *overgeneralizing* (drawing a conclusion based on one or just a few cases); *ad hominem* attacks (attacking the person instead of the argument); suggesting *inappropriate causal relationships* (assuming that because two events are related, one caused the other); a *false dilemma* (acting as if only two choices exist, when likely there are several); and making a *faulty analogy* (stretching a comparison too far).

7. Because anyone can post something on the World Wide Web, members need to evaluate information from the Web carefully.

8. Ask if Web information is accurate (has the information passed some kind of screening or review before being posted?); whether the source is a credible authority; who the audience is for the information; what its purpose is (paying attention to the ending helps—you can guess that .com represents a site that wants to sell something); how recent or current the site is; and coverage of the topic (is the topic covered in depth?).

Understanding What Can Go Wrong During Decision Making

Groups *can* make better decisions than individuals, but they don't always reach their potential, even when they achieve consensus. Of 10 groups that achieved consensus, Burleson found that eight of them made better decisions than their individual members acting alone, but two of them produced worse decisions.[62]

Wood observed several factors that impede decision making, including members who don't have the needed skills or information and members whose social needs prevent them from attending to the task.[63] Poor operating procedures, including the failure to provide structure for the decision-making process and failure to test for consensus, hurt decision quality. Finally, adhering to ascribed (external) status characteristics impaired open and honest communication, which prevented critical thinking. Very cohesive groups with high-performance expectations perform well,[64] and groups that approach decision making systematically make better decisions than groups that do not.[65] Group interaction itself can promote collective inferential error if members accept unusual cases as representative (i.e., overgeneralizing), passively accept specialized knowledge without questioning it, or create hypothetical scenarios with no basis in fact.[66]

Three phenomena pose particular problems for effective decision making: hidden profiles, group polarization and groupthink.

Hidden Profiles

Sometimes, group members may not actually exchange the information they have as individuals[67] or do a good job of using the information they *do* share.[68] A **hidden profile** occurs when members collectively hold the information they need to make the best decision, but the information they hold in private, as individuals, favors a less effective solution.[69] In other words, if members chose to share all the relevant information they hold privately, the group would find the best solution. Unfortunately, members freely discuss information they *already* know in common, but tend to hold onto their own unique information without sharing it. As groups move away from hidden profiles and become willing to share what each member knows separately, they make better decisions.[70]

This is consistent with Klocke's findings. Klocke noted that groups tend to experience two information-processing biases: a preference bias (in favor of the initial preferences of members) and a shared information bias (in favor of information all members hold).[71] When members appreciated their own and the other members' unique information, as well as information that was inconsistent with their initial preferences, the quality of the group decision was higher. Information-sharing seems to improve when groups are smaller and members have little common information. Apparently, this forces members to share what they have.[72]

Hidden Profile

When the information members hold collectively favors the best decision, but the information they hold in private, as individuals, favors a less effective solution.

Group Polarization

Group members can and should influence each other, but such influence can produce the **group polarization** tendency, which refers to the finding that group members often make decisions that are more extreme (either more risky or more cautious) than the individual members' initial preferences.[73] Group members push themselves *further* in a particular direction than where they initially started. Two explanations have been proposed for this.[74]

Social Comparison Theory (SCT) focuses on psychological factors; it suggests that as members get to know each other's values, they want to appear "correct" and may exaggerate opinions in the direction that they believe the group values positively. For example, if you are mildly liberal politically and you are in a group that seems to value liberal thought, then you might be tempted to exaggerate how liberal you are. Thus, if the group or cultural norm favors risk (as with many business decisions in our culture), the group will shift toward risk; if caution is the cultural norm (as with a decision affecting a child's life), the group shifts toward caution.

The second explanation for group polarization focuses on cognitive factors. *Persuasive Arguments Theory* (PAT) says that the number, salience, and novelty of arguments in a particular direction persuade members to move in that direction. Thus, if members initially favor risk (or caution), there will be more and stronger arguments presented in favor of risk (or caution); the persuasive power of these arguments shifts the group in that direction.

Studies have found support for both SCT and PAT. Whether SCT or PAT better explains choice shift in a specific group may depend on conditions within the group. For example, when the task becomes more ambiguous, SCT seems to explain shifts better, but as task ambiguity decreases, PAT makes more sense.[75] The type of task matters; SCT explanations prevail for tasks requiring judgment, but PAT explains the choice shifts better for intellective tasks that have correct answers.[76]

An intriguing study of burglar behavior by Cromwell et al. supports the concept of group polarization and confirms that both cognitive and emotional factors come into play during group decision making.[77] Burglars themselves believe they take more risks when working with others, but the evidence suggests otherwise. Burglars normally rate potential targets on the basis of the risks associated with those targets. When burglars work in groups, one burglar may point out risks the others miss, so they collectively take into account risk cues they may not have noticed working alone. For example, in one group of three burglars, two rated a particular house a 6 (with 10 the lowest risk), but the third burglar, a woman, pointed out that the time was nearly 3 PM, school would soon be out, and many children were likely to be playing nearby. The burglars collectively reassessed the risk as 2.

At the same time, burglars working together apparently increase each other's excitement and egg each other on. In the same study, burglars in groups were more likely to go on multiple burglary sprees, hitting multiple targets, something that individual burglars did not and would not do. These

---

Group Polarization

The tendency for group members to make decisions that are more extreme (more risky or cautious) than they would make individually.

findings about burglar risk and caution, which seem incompatible, can be reconciled as follows. Burglars deciding to commit a crime experience high rates of arousal, which is increased by the presence of others. This social facilitation effect can lead to increased risk taking. However, assessing a particular site for degree of risk is actually a low-arousal state that requires cognitive information-processing skill, which is helped by the presence of others. Thus, both cognitive and psychological factors appear to be involved in decision making, and both are affected by the participation of others. It is interesting to note that one of the major advantages for group decision making—that several heads are better than one—is distinctly helpful during the information-processing phase of decision making, even for burglars.

Thus, decision making can be impaired or improved by the particular norms and arguments that prevail in a group. Being aware of these normal group tendencies can help group members guard against bias in decision making.

Groupthink

Groupthink

The tendency of some cohesive groups *not* to subject information, reasoning, and proposals to thorough critical analysis.

A factor that can significantly impair critical thinking in a small group is groupthink. Coined by Irving Janis, **groupthink** occurs when a highly cohesive group wants to maintain consensus so much that it suppresses confrontation and disagreement, so that the group's decisions are not carefully thought through.[78] The group's balance tilts toward maintaining cohesiveness and harmony rather than toward thinking critically. Janis compared two decisions by President John F. Kennedy's National Security Council. The first, a disastrous one, occurred when the United States decided to invade Cuba at the Bay of Pigs shortly after Fidel Castro had established a communist government there. The second is considered a model of effective group decision making; it was the 1963 decision to blockade Cuba when missile sites were discovered there and ships with nuclear warheads to arm them were photographed on their way from the Soviet Union. Janis was intrigued by the fact that essentially the same group of people made decisions of such divergent quality. He found the reason *not* in the individual decision makers' personalities or intentions, but in the *throughput processes* they used. Groups making effective decisions and proposing high-quality alternatives are willing to engage in open conflict, challenge one another's reasoning, and test all information and ideas for soundness. Janis found that Kennedy's advisers did not thoroughly test information before making the Bay of Pigs decision, which explains how such well-educated, intelligent individuals, in the face of evidence to the contrary, *as a group* allowed such a stupid decision to be made.

Please note that just because a group decision turns out badly does not automatically mean groupthink is the culprit. Sometimes decisions go awry because of factors over which the group has no control or can't have known about. What makes a decision faulty because of groupthink is the group's failure to consider all the information available *at the time of the decision* in a thorough and unbiased way. Highly cohesive groups are particularly vulnerable to the groupthink trap because that very cohesion creates a general desire to keep the members together on a decision. This then leads to pressure for consensus and touches off a fear of anything that seems to threaten the cohesion, particularly conflict. The pressure to achieve consensus is particularly acute in groups experiencing time pressures and with leaders who have a preferred alternative that they attempt to promote, and may even support the hidden profile biases we discussed earlier.[79]

Groupthink is revealed in members' communication. Cline compared the conversations of groupthink and non-groupthink groups and found several surprising differences.[80] Although levels of disagreement were similar in both sets of groups, the groupthink groups exhibited significantly higher levels of *agreement,* and these agreements were simple, unsubstantiated ones. Group members ended up making statements and agreeing with themselves. In contrast, the agreements exhibited in the non-groupthink groups were substantive in nature, with different speakers providing different evidence and lines of reasoning to support their assertions. In groupthink, concern for positive relationships and cohesiveness seem to override critical thinking.

Groupthink is a common phenomenon in government, business, and educational groups. It has been implicated in a number of disastrous policy decisions, including NASA's 1986 decision to launch the space shuttle *Challenger,* which exploded just after takeoff.[81] Swissair, also known as the "Flying Bank" because of its financial stability, rode off into bankruptcy due to faulty business decisions attributed to groupthink actions.[82] In a recent analysis, the U.S. invasion of Iraq was faulted for groupthink actions that dramatically shifted U.S. foreign policy toward Saddam Hussein.[83] Even in the area of sports, organizations have been faulted for groupthink actions that lead to poor decisions. Major league umpires, in negotiation with Major League Baseball (MLB), decided to enact a huge walkout in 1999, believing they had the power to sway MLB. Their walkout failed miserably.[84] In all these decisions, group members had information that should have forewarned them of impending failure, but biases affected how they processes the information: Beliefs in their invulnerability, overestimation of their strength, self-censorship, desire for harmony, and cohesiveness, among other things, sabotaged the decision-making process. It seems that when informational and normative pressures (pressures stemming from group norms) compete, the influence of norms supporting agreement outweighs the pressure to share and evaluate information carefully.[85]

Groupthink is not inevitable in a cohesive group. Antecedents of groupthink, such as high cohesiveness and directive leadership, do not inherently produce dysfunctions in a group.[86] High socioemotional cohesiveness is most likely to produce groupthink symptoms, especially when it is paired with low task-oriented cohesiveness.[87] A meta-analysis of cohesiveness confirmed that cohesiveness based on interpersonal attraction among members can produce the kinds of problems associated with groupthink, but cohesiveness based on commitment to the task has the opposite effect.[88] The effects of cohesiveness are magnified when a group must decide unanimously instead of by majority rule.[89]

A revised model of groupthink that takes these and other factors into account has been proposed by Neck and Moorhead, who add time pressure and importance of the decision as factors contributing to groupthink.[90] These authors believe that two moderating factors, the role of the leader and how methodical the group's decision-making processes are, determine whether the antecedent conditions of cohesiveness, time, and importance will actually produce groupthink. The leader's behavior is particularly important. A leader with a closed communication style minimizes member participation in decisions, discourages diverse opinions, states his or her opinions at the outset of a discussion, and does not emphasize the importance of making a wise decision. When groupthink conditions are present, this style is more likely to produce groupthink than an open style that encourages participation.

There are many things that can go awry during problem solving and decision making. In the next chapter, we give you specific suggestions to help ensure that your groups stay on track.

Recap: A Quick Review

Many things can affect the processes of problem solving and decision making, which require vigilance on the part of group members.

1. Among the factors that can impair decision making are the facts that members often do not share the information they have with each other, do not use a systematic process for decision making, fail to test for consensus, and pay too much attention to ascribed (external) status.

2. Hidden profile conditions, where members together have the information they need to make the best decision, but individually do not have what they need, can be overcome if members appreciate their diversity of opinion and seek out opinions contrary to their initial preferences.

3. Group polarization, the tendency of groups to make decisions that are more extreme than the individuals in the group would make on their own, can hurt decision making by shifting members too far toward either risk or caution.

4. Social Comparison Theory explains polarization by noting that members want to look good to each other on the values important to the group, so they exaggerate their opinions in those directions.

5. Persuasive Arguments Theory explains polarization by noting that the number, novelty, and salience of the arguments members hear from each other pushes them in a particular direction.

6. Groupthink, the failure of group members to think critically and evaluate information thoroughly, has been blamed for several disastrous decisions, including the the launch of the shuttle *Challenger and the U.S. invasion of Iraq.*

QUESTIONS FOR REVIEW

 Go to self-quizzes on the Online Learning Center at mbhe.com/galanes14e to test your knowledge of the chapter concepts.

The opening case in this chapter concerned a group of officials in O'Fallon, Missouri, who were faced with finding a long-term solution to the city's water treatment problems. Reread the case, if necessary, to answer the following review questions:

1. How systematic in its problem-solving approach did the O'Fallon group seem to be? Do you think they achieved the assembly effect?

2. How well did they seem to meet the functions identified by the Functional Perspective as being necessary for good problem solving?

3. What types of questions did the group have to deal with in the course of solving its problem? Do some types of questions seem harder to resolve than others? If so, which ones?

4. What were the criteria against which the group compared its three realistic options? Why do you think the solution chosen—the membrane treatment facility—met the criteria better than the others? Where were the others weaker?

5. How critical was the O'Fallon group's thinking? What examples in the story lead you to that conclusion?

6. Is there any evidence that the O'Fallon group's problem-solving process experienced polarization or groupthink?

KEY TERMS

 Test your knowledge of these key terms by visiting the Online Learning Center Web site at mbhe.com/galanes14e.

Ad hominem attack	Fact	Overgeneralization
Area of freedom	Fallacy	Phasic progression
Assembly effect	False dilemma	Problem
Charge	Faulty analogy	Problem solving
Conjunctive task	Functional Perspective	Question of conjecture
Consensus decision	Group polarization	Question of fact
Criteria	Groupthink	Question of policy
Critical thinking	Hidden profile	Question of value
Decision making	Inference	
Disjunctive task	Majority decision	

BIBLIOGRAPHY

Adams, Tyrone, and Norman Clark. *The Internet: Effective Online Communication.* Ft. Worth, TX: Harcourt, 2001.

Gouran, Dennis S., and Randy Y. Hirokawa. "Effective Decision Making and Problem Solving in Groups: A Functional Perspective."

Randy Y. Hirokawa, Robert S. Cathcart, Larry A. Samovar, and Linda D. Henman, eds. *Small Group Communication, Theory and Practice: An Anthology.* Los Angeles, CA: Roxbury, 2003, 27–38.

Hirokawa, Randy Y., and Marshall S. Poole, eds. *Communication and Group Decision Making.* Beverly Hills, CA: Sage, 1986, 81–111.

Larson, Carl E., and Frank M. J. LaFasto. *TeamWork: What Must Go Right/What Can Go Wrong.* Newbury Park, CA: Sage, 1989.

Shaw, Marvin E. *Group Dynamics.* 3rd ed. New York: McGraw-Hill, 1981, Chapter 10.

Worchel, Stephen, Wendy Wood, and Jeffry A. Simpson, eds. *Group Process and Productivity.* Newbury Park, CA: Sage, 1992.

NOTES

1. Patrick Banger, personal interview, March 18, 2002.
2. Francois Cooren, "The Communicative Achievement of Collective Minding: Analysis of Board Meeting Excerpts," *Management Communication Quarterly,* 17 (May 2004): 517–51; Brant R. Burleson, Barbara J. Levine, and Wendy Samter, "Decision-Making Procedure and Decision Quality," *Human Communication Research,* 10 (1984): 557–74; Herm W. Smith, "Group versus Individual Problem Solving and Type of Problem Solved," *Small Group Behavior,* 20 (1989): 357–66.
3. Patricia Fandt, "The Relationship of Accountability and Interdependent Behavior to Enhancing Team Consequences, *Group & Organization Studies,* 16 (1991): 200–12.
4. Charles Pavitt and Kelly Kline Johnson, "An Examination of the Coherence of Group Discussions," *Communication Research,* 26 (June 1999): 303–21.
5. Mark F. Stasson and Scott D. Bradshaw, "Explanations of Individual-Group Performance Differences: What Sort of 'Bonus' Can Be Gained through Group Interaction?" *Small Group Research,* 26 (May 1995): 296–308.
6. Patrick Laughlin, Scot W. VanderSteop, and Andrea B. Hollingshead, "Collective versus Individual Induction: Recognition of Truth, Rejection of Error, and Collective Information Processing," *Journal of Personality and Social Psychology,* 61 (1994): 50–67.
7. M. L. Chemers, "Leadership Theory and Research: A Systems-Process Integration," in *Basic Group Processes,* ed. P. B. Paulus (New York: Springer-Verlag, 1983): 19–20; Randy Y. Hirokawa, "Consensus Group Decision Making, Quality of Decision and Group Satisfaction: An Attempt to Sort Fact from Fiction," *Central States Speech Journal,* 33 (1982): 407–15.
8. Lester Coch and John R. P. French, Jr., "Overcoming Resistance to Change," *Human Relations,* 1 (1948): 512–32.
9. Myron W. Block and L. R. Hoffman, "The Effects of Valence of Solutions and Group Cohesiveness on Members' Commitment to Group Decision," in *The Group Problem Solving Process,* ed. L. Richard Hoffman (New York: Prager, 1979): 121.
10. Herm W. Smith, "Group versus Individual Problem Solving and Type of Problem Solved," *Small Group Behavior,* 20 (1989): 357–66.
11. Michael Pacanowsky, "Team Tools for Wicked Problems," *Organizational Dynamics,* 23 (Winter 1995): 36–51.
12. Abran J. Salazar, Randy Y. Hirokawa, Kathleen M. Propp, Kelly M. Julian, and Geoff B. Leatham, "In Search of True Causes: Examination of the Effect of Group Potential and Group Interaction on Group Performance," *Human Communication Research,* 20 (June 1994): 529–59.
13. Deborah H. Gruenfeld and Andrea B. Hollingshead, "Sociocognition in Work Groups: The Evolution of Group Integrative Complexity and Its Relation to Task Performance," *Small Group Research,* 24 (August 1993): 383–405.
14. Joseph N. Scudder, Richard T. Herschel, and Martin D. Crossland, "Test of a Model Linking Cognitive Motivation, Assessment of Alternatives, Decision Quality, and Group Process Satisfaction," *Small Group Research,* 25 (February 1994): 57–82.

15. Laughlin et al., "Collective versus Individual Induction."

16. Burleson et al., "Decision Making Procedure and Decision Quality."

17. Salazar et al., "In Search of True Causes."

18. Michael E. Mayer, Kevin T. Sonoda, and William B. Gudykunst, "The Effect of Time Pressure and Type of Information on Decision Quality," *Southern Communication Journal,* 62 (Summer 1997): 280–92.

19. Elizabeth E. Graham, Michael J. Papa, and Mary B. McPherson, "An Applied Test of the Functional Communication Perspective of Small Group Decision-Making," *Southern Communication Journal,* 62 (Summer 1997): 269–79.

20. Kathleen M. Propp and Daniel Nelson, "Problem-Solving Performance in Naturalistic Groups: A Test of the Ecological Validity of the Functional Perspective," *Communication Studies,* 47 (Spring/Summer 1996): 35–45.

21. Scudder et al., "Test of a Model."

22. Michael E. Mayer, "Behaviors Leading to More Effective Decisions in Small Groups Embedded in Organizations," *Communication Reports,* 11 (Summer 1998): 123–32.

23. Marcial Losada and Emily Heaphy, "The Role of Positivity and Connectivity in the Performance of Business Teams: A Nonlinear Dynamics Model," *American Behavioral Scientist,* 47 (2004): 740–65.

24. Irving L. Janis and Leon Mann, *Decision Making: A Psychological Analysis of Conflict, Choice, and Commitment* (New York: Free Press, 1977); Irving L. Janis, *Groupthink: Psychological Studies of Foreign-Policy Decisions and Fiascoes,* 2nd ed. (Boston: Houghton-Mifflin, 1983).

25. Susan Jarboe, "Procedures for Enhancing Group Decision Making," in *Communication and Group Decision Making,* 2nd ed., eds. Randy Y. Hirokawa and Marshall Scott Poole (Thousand Oaks, CA: Sage, 1996): 345–83.

26. John K. Brilhart, "An Experimental Comparison of Three Techniques for Communicating a Problem-Solving Pattern to Members of a Discussion Group," *Speech Monographs,* 33 (1966): 168–77.

27. Thomas M. Scheidel and Laura Crowell, "Developmental Sequences in Small Groups," *Quarterly Journal of Speech,* 50 (1964): 140–45.

28. Dennis S. Gouran, Candace Brown, and David R. Henry, "Behavioral Correlates of Perceptions of Quality in Decision-Making Discussions," *Communication Monographs,* 45 (1978): 62; William E. Jurma, "Effects of Leader Structuring Style and Task Orientation Characteristics of Group Members," *Communication Monographs,* 46 (1979): 282–95.

29. Jurma, "Effects of Leader Structuring Style."

30. Marshall S. Poole, "Decision Development in Small Groups II: A Study of Multiple Sequences in Decision Making," *Communication Monographs,* 50 (1983): 224–25; Decision Development in Small Groups III: A Multiple Sequence Model of Group Decision Development," *Communication Monographs,* 50 (1983): 321–41.

31. John K. Brilhart and Lurene M. Jochem, "Effects of Different Patterns on Outcomes of Problem-Solving Discussions," *Journal of Applied Psychology,* 48 (1964): 175–79.

32. Ovid L. Bayless, "An Alternative Model for Problem-Solving Discussion," *Journal of Communication,* 17 (1967): 188–97; Carl E. Larson, "Forms of Analysis and Small Group Problem Solving," *Speech Monographs,* 36 (1969): 452–55.

33. Charles M. Kelly, Michael Jaffe, and Gregory V. Nelson, "Solving Problems," *Research Management,* 30 (1987): 20–23.

34. Ibid.

35. Benjamin J. Broome and Luann Fulbright, "A Multi-Stage Influence Model of Barriers to Group Problem Solving: A Participant-Generated Agenda for Small Group Research, *Small Group Research,* 26 (February 1995): 25–55.

36. Laura A. Hambley, Thomas A. O'Neill, and Theresa J. B. Kline, "Virtual Team Leadership: Perspectives from the Field, International Journal of e-Collaboration, 3 (2007): 40–64; Joseph B. Walther and Ulla Bunz, "The Rules of Virtual Groups: Trust, Liking

and Performance in Computer-Mediated Communication, *Journal of Communication*, (2005): 828–846.

37. Randy Y. Hirokawa, "Why Informed Groups Make Faulty Decisions," *Small Group Research*, 18 (1987): 3–29.

38. The principles of the Functional Perspective are summarized succinctly in Dennis S. Gouran and Randy Y. Hirokawa, "Effective Decision Making and Problem Solving in Groups: A Functional Perspective," in *Small Group Communication, Theory and Practice: An Anthology,* eds. Randy Y. Hirokawa, Robert S. Cathcart, Larry A. Samovar, and Linda D. Henman (Los Angeles, CA: Roxbury, 2003): 27–38. Other relevant sources include Dennis S. Gouran and Randy Y. Hirokawa, "Functional Theory and Communication in Decision-Making and Problem-Solving Groups: An Expanded View," in *Communication and Group Decision Making,* 2nd ed., eds. R. Y. Hirokawa and M. S. Poole (Thousand Oaks, CA: Sage, 1996): 55–80; Randy Y. Hirokawa, "Communication and Group Decision Making Efficacy," in *Small Group Communication: A Reader,* 6th ed., eds. Robert S. Cathcart and Larry A. Samovar (Dubuque, IA: Wm. C. Brown, 1992): 165–77; Randy Y. Hirokawa and Kathryn Rost, "Effective Group Decision Making in Organizations: A Field Test of the Vigilant Interaction Theory," *Management Communication Quarterly,* 5 (February 1992): 267–88; Randy Y. Hirokawa, "Group Communication and Decision-Making Performance: A Continued Test of the Functional Perspective," *Human Communication Research,* 14 (1988): 487–515; Dennis S. Gouran, "Inferential Errors, Interaction, and Group Decision Making," in *Communication and Group Decision Making,* eds. R. Y. Hirokawa and M. S. Poole (Beverly Hills, CA: Sage, 1986): 93–111; Randy Y. Hirokawa, "Discussion Procedures and Decision-Making Performance: A Test of the Functional Perspective," *Human Communication Research,* 12 (1985): 59–74. Randy Y.

Hirokawa, "Group Communication and Problem-Solving Effectiveness II: An Exploratory Investigation of Procedural Functions," *Western Journal of Speech Communication,* 47 (1983), 59–74.

39. Gouran and Hirokawa, "Effective Decision Making and Problem Solving in Groups."

40. Randy Y. Hirokawa, "Group Communication and Problem-Solving Effectiveness II;" Marshall S. Poole and Joel A. Doelger, "Developmental Processes in Group Decision-Making," in *Communication and Group Decision Making,* eds. R. Y. Hirokawa and M. S. Poole (Newbury Park, CA: Sage, 1986): 35–61.

41. Hirokawa and Rost, "Effective Group Decision Making," 20–22.

42. Kathleen M. Propp and Daniel Nelson, "Problem-Solving Performance in Naturalistic Groups: A Test of the Ecological Validity of the Functional Perspective," *Communication Studies,* 47 (1996): 35–45.

43. Randy Y. Hirokawa, "Why Informed Groups Make Faulty Decisions, "*Small Group Behavior,* 18 (1987): 3–29.

44. Types of questions and their relationship to effective problem solving and decision making are discussed in detail in Dennis S. Gouran and Randy Y. Hirokawa, "Effective Decision Making and Problem Solving in Groups."

45. Moshe F. Rubenstein, *Patterns of Problem Solving* (Englewood Cliffs, NJ: Prentice Hall, 1975): 1–2.

46. Brilhart and Jochem, "The Effects of Different Patterns."

47. Randy Y. Hirokawa, John G. Oetzel, Carlos G. Aleman, and Scott E. Elston, "The Effects of Evaluation Clarity and Bias on the Relationship between Vigilant Interaction and Group Decision-Making Efficacy" (paper presented at the Speech Communication Association Convention, November, 1991).

48. Michael J. Beatty, "Group Members' Decision Rule Orientations and Consensus," *Human Communication Research,* 16 (1989): 79–96.

49. Robert F. Bales and Fred L. Strodtbeck, "Phases in Group Problem-Solving," *Journal*

of Abnormal and Social Psychology, 46 (1951): 485–95.

50. For a complete summary of Fisher's work on decision-making phases, see B. Aubrey Fisher and Donald G. Ellis, *Small Group Decision Making: Communication and the Group Process,* 3rd ed. (New York: McGraw-Hill, 1990), especially Chapter 6.

51. Marshall Scott Poole, "Decision Development in Small Groups I: A Comparison of Two Models," *Communication Monographs,* 48 (1981): 1–24; "Decision Development in Small Groups II: A Study of Multiple Sequences in Decision Making," *Communication Monographs,* 50 (1983): 206–32; "Decision Development in Small Groups III: A Multiple Sequence Model of Group Decision Development," *Communication Monographs,* 50 (1983): 321–41; M. Scott Poole and Jonelle Roth, "Decision Development in Small Groups IV: A Typology of Group Decision Paths," *Human Communication Research,* 15 (1989): 322–56; "Decision Development in Small Groups V: Test of a Contingency Model," *Human Communication Research,* 15 (1989): 549–89.

52. Poole, "Decision Development II" and "Decision Development III."

53. Poole and Roth, "Decision Development V."

54. Thomas M. Scheidel and Laura Crowell, "Idea Development in Small Discussion Groups," *Quarterly Journal of Speech,* 50 (1964): 140–45.

55. Teresa C. Sabourin and Patricia Geist, "Collaborative Production of Proposals in Group Decision Making," *Small Group Research,* 21 (1990): 404–27.

56. B. Aubrey Fisher and Randall K. Stutman, "An Assessment of Group Trajectories: Analyzing Developmental Breakpoints," *Communication Quarterly,* 35 (1987): 105–24.

57. Charles Pavitt and Kelly Kline Johnson, "Scheidel and Crowell Revisited: A Descriptive Study of Group Proposals Sequencing," *Communication Monographs,* 69 (March 2002): 19–32.

58. Renee A. Meyers, David R. Siebold, and Dale Brashers, "Argument in Initial Group Decision-Making Discussions: Refinement of a Coding Scheme and a Descriptive Quantitative Analysis," *Western Journal of Speech Communication,* 55 (Winter 1991): 47–68.

59. Much of the following information is distilled from M. Neil Browne and Stuart M. Keeley, *Asking the Right Questions: A Guide to Critical Thinking,* 7th ed. (Englewood Cliffs, NJ: Prentice Hall, 2004).

60. Chuanfu Chen, Qiong Jung, Xuan Huang, Zhiqiang Wu, Haiying Hua, Yuan Yu, and Song Chen, "An Assessment of the Completeness of Scholarly Information on the Internet," *College and Research Libraries,* 70 (July 2009): 386–401.

61. The following information is taken from Tyrone Adams and Norman Clark, *The Internet: Effective Online Communication* (Fort Worth, TX: Harcourt, 2001): 166–75.

62. Brant R. Burleson, Barbara J. Levine, and Wendy Samter, "Decision-Making Procedure and Decision Quality," *Human Communication Research,* 10 (1984): 557–74.

63. Carolyn J. Wood, "Challenging the Assumption Underlying the Use of Participatory Decision-Making Strategies: A Longitudinal Case Study," *Small Group Behavior,* 20 (1989): 428–48.

64. Paul Miesing and John E. Preble, "Group Processes and Performance in Complex Business Simulation," *Small Group Behavior,* 16 (1985): 325–38.

65. Randy Y. Hirokawa, "Consensus Group Decision Making, Quality of Decision and Group Satisfaction: An Attempt to 'Sort Fact from Fiction,'" *Central States Speech Journal,* 33 (1982): 407–15.

66. Dennis S. Gouran, "Inferential Errors, Interaction, and Group Decision Making," in *Communication and Group Decision Making,* eds. R.Y. Hirokawa and M. S. Poole (Beverly Hills, CA: Sage, 1986): 93–111.

67. Alan R. Dennis, "Information Exchange and Use in Small Group Decision Making," *Small Group Research,* 27 (November 1996): 532–50.

68. Michael G. Cruz, Franklin J. Boster, and Jose I. Rodriguez, "The Impact of Group Size and

Proportion of Shared Information on the Exchange and Integration of Information in Groups," *Communication Research,* 24 (June 1997): 291–313.

69. David Dryden Henningsen and Mary Lynn Miller Henningsen, "Examining Social Influence in Information-Sharing Contexts," *Small Group Research,* 34 (August 2003): 391–412.

70. Ibid., 407–09.

71. Ulrich Klocke, "How to Improve Decision Making in Small Groups: Effects of Dissent and Training Interventions," *Small Group Research,* 38 (June 2007): 437–68.

72. Cruz, Boster, and Rodriguez, "The Impact of Group Size."

73. Marvin E. Shaw, *Group Dynamics,* 2nd ed. (New York: McGraw-Hill, 1976): 70–77.

74. Daniel J. Isenberg, "Group Polarization: A Critical Review and Meta-Analysis," *Journal of Personality and Social Psychology,* 10 (1986): 1141–51.

75. Jerold Hale and Franklin J. Boster, "Comparing Effects-Coded Models of Choice Shifts," *Communication Research Reports,* 5 (1988): 1880–86.

76. Martin F. Kaplan and Charles E. Miller, "Group Decision Making and Normative versus Informational Influence: Effects of Type of Issue and Assigned Decision Rule," *Journal of Personality and Social Psychology,* 53 (1987): 306–13.

77. Paul F. Cromwell, Alan Marks, James N. Olson, and D'Aunn W. Avary, "Group Effects on Decision-Making by Burglars," *Psychological Reports,* 69 (1991): 579–88.

78. Irving L. Janis, *Groupthink: Psychological Studies of Policy Decisions and Fiascoes,* 2nd ed. rev. (Boston: Houghton Mifflin, 1983).

79. Gregory Moorhead, Richard Ference, and Chris P. Neck, "Group Decision Fiascoes Continue: Space Shuttle *Challenger* and a Revised Groupthink Framework," *Human Relations,* 44 (1991): 539–50.

80. Rebecca J. Welsh Cline, "Detecting Groupthink: Methods of Observing the Illusion of Unanimity," *Communication Quarterly,* 38 (1990): 112–26.

81. Dennis S. Gouran, Randy Y. Hirokawa, And Amy E. Martz, A Critical Analysis of Factors Related to Decisional Processes Involved in the *Challenger* Disaster," *Central States Speech Journal,* 37 (1986): 119–35.

82. Aaron Herman and Hussain G. Rammal, "The Grounding of the Flying Bank," *Management Decision,* 48 (2010): 1048–62.

83. Diana Badie, "Groupthink, Iraq, and the War on Terror: Explaining US Policy Shift Toward Iraq," *Foreign Policy Analysis,* 6 (2010): 277–96.

84. Charles P. Koerber and Christopher P. Neck, "Groupthink and Sports: An Application of Whyte's Model," *International Journal of Contemporary Hospitality,* 15 (2003): 20–28.

85. Michael G. Cruz, David Dryden Henningsen, and Mary Lynn Miller Williams, "The Presence of Norms in the Absence of Groups? The Impact of Normative Influence under Hidden-Profile Conditions," *Human Communication Research,* 26 (January 2000): 104–24.

86. Ronald J. Aldag and Sally Riggs Fuller, "Beyond Fiasco: A Reappraisal of the Groupthink Phenomenon and a New Model of Group Decision Processes," *Psychological Bulletin,* 113 (3) (1993): 533–52.

87. Paul R. Bernthal and Chester A. Insko, "Cohesiveness Without Groupthink: the Interactive Effects of Social and Task Cohesion," *Group and Organization Management,* 18 (March 1992): 66–87.

88. Brian Mullen, Tara Anthony, Eduardo Salas, and James E. Driskell, "Group Cohesiveness and Quality of Decision Making: An Integration of the Groupthink Hypothesis," *Small Group Research,* 25 (May 1994): 189–204.

89. Tatsuya Kameda and Shinkichi Sudimori, "Psychological Entrapment in Group Decision Making: An Assigned Decision Rule and a Groupthink Phenomenon," *Journal of Personality and Social Psychology,* 65 (August 1993): 282–92.

90. Christopher P. Neck and Gregory Moorhead, "Groupthink Remodeled: The Importance of Leadership, Time Pressure, and Methodical Decision-Making Procedures," *Human Relations,* 48 (May 1995): 537–57.

Problem Solving and Decision Making in Groups: Practical Tips and Techniques

STUDY OBJECTIVES

As a result of studying Chapter 10, you should be able to:

1. Explain the steps in the Procedural Model of Problem Solving (P-MOPS), the Single Question Format, and the Ideal Solution Format.

2. Describe and use a problem census, problem mapping, brainstorming, brainwriting, and electronic brainstorming.

3. Distinguish between problem questions and solution questions and be able to state a problem appropriately.

4. List suggestions for achieving consensus.

5. Describe the symptoms of groupthink and list suggestions for preventing groupthink.

6. Describe and be able to use the RISK technique to second-guess a group's tentative choice and the PERT technique to keep track of implementing a solution.

7. Describe how to modify a problem-solving procedure based on the seven characteristics of problems.

8. Describe various technologies that help groups and explain how netconferences and group support systems, in particular, can both help and hinder group problem solving.

CENTRAL MESSAGE

A number of specific suggestions and small group techniques can help groups organize their problem-solving and decision-making processes to make them more systematic, including several technological aids. These procedures can often be tailored to fit the specific problem facing the group.

At a university where one of us worked, registration staff members calculated that they were spending thousands of dollars processing all the courses that students dropped and added during a single quarter. In the days before computerized registration and fee payment, each of these drop-adds had to be processed by hand—a time-consuming and expensive process. The registration staff discussed ways to cut the number of drop-adds. Staff members concluded that students were scheduling classes without careful planning and forethought, so they decided to penalize "frivolous" drop-adds by imposing a fee on each one. But because they realized that some drop-adds were "legitimate," they included a procedure whereby the student's academic adviser could waive the drop or add if the student's reason was a legitimate one (such as failing a prerequisite course!). Before computerized scheduling, that meant that a paper form had to be completed for *each course* dropped or added, and if the fee was to be waived, another form was needed for *each course* whose fee was waived. It turned out that most students had legitimate reasons for dropping and adding courses, often because their work schedules changed from one quarter to another. The bottom line was that the Registration Office processed nearly twice as many paper forms as before, at greater cost than the old, free drop-add system. After a couple of years, this new system was abandoned in favor of the old one.

To us, this example suggests at least three flaws in the registration staff's problem-solving and decision-making processes. First, the staff made assumptions about *why* students dropped and added classes, and the assumptions (students are irresponsible and don't plan ahead) were flat out wrong! This indicates that the staff didn't do its homework to learn why students dropped and added classes. Second, it seems as if the staff didn't do a thorough job of developing its options to reduce the numbers of drop-adds. Staff members seemed to latch onto the first "solution" that fit their preconceived ideas about why the students were drop-adding. Finally, staff members didn't pretest their solution first, either by asking the advisers for their opinions or by trying the process on a limited scale or as a pilot project before they involved the entire university. This group would have benefited from using a systematic procedure that focused on problem analysis.

Using Problem-Solving Guidelines

In this chapter, we present a number of tools and techniques to help you improve your group problem-solving and decision-making processes. We noted in Chapter 9 that all groups, face-to-face to virtual ones, that use systematic procedures generally do a better job of problem solving. Even if they aren't given a procedure to follow, many groups develop one anyway because they sense, intuitively, that they need one.

Do not think, because we stress systematic problem solving, that we dismiss the value of intuition! Each of us has often gotten inspiration from an intuitive "ah-ha" moment, and we value those flashes of insight. Use your intuition—but don't rely on it alone, particularly when your decision will affect others. That's when you really need to assess your problem systematically and evaluate potential solutions thoroughly.

The first tools we present are three different procedures to give you an idea of what is available to help groups organize their problem solving (summarized in Table 10.1). Each addresses the functions of the Functional Perspective, although in slightly different ways. We then use one of those procedures—the Procedural Model of Problem Solving (P-MOPS)—as an extended example of how groups can use structured guidelines.

TABLE 10.1   Comparison of the questions addressed by three problem-solving guidelines

The Procedural Model of Problem Solving (P-MOPS)	The Single Question Format	The Ideal Solution Format

1. What is the nature of the problem facing the group?
2. What might be done to solve the problem we've described?
3. What are the probable benefits and possible negative consequences of each proposed solution?
4. What seems to be the best possible solution that we can all support?
5. How will we put our decision into effect?
	1. What is the single question that, when answered, means that the group knows how to accomplish its purpose?
	2. Collaboration
	  A. What principles should we agree on in order to maintain a reasonable and collaborative approach throughout the process?
	  B. What assumptions and biases are associated with the single question identified in step 1, and how might they influence the discussion?
	3. What issues or subquestions must we answer to fully understand the complexities of the overall problem?
	4. What are the two or three most reasonable answers to the subquestions?
	5. Among the possible solutions, which one is most desirable?
		1. Does everyone agree on the nature of the problem?
		2. What would be the ideal solution from the point of view of all interested people or groups involved?
		3. Which conditions within the situation could be changed to achieve the ideal solution?
		4. Of all the solutions available, which one best approximates the ideal solution?

The Procedural Model of Problem Solving (P-MOPS)

The **Procedural Model of Problem Solving (P-MOPS)** is a general procedure, modeled according to the sequence originally described by Dewey,
that can be adapted to fit any group problem-solving situation. The acronym P-MOPS has a double purpose: It helps us remember the full name
of the model and, as a pun, it reminds us that the purpose of this (or any)
model is to "mop up" all the details or logical necessities for high-quality
problem solving. We call this a *general* model because it can be adjusted to
fit all the contingencies facing a group.

The following are the major steps:

Step 1: Problem description and analysis: *What is the nature of the
problem facing the group?*

Step 2: Generating and elaborating on possible solutions: *What
might be done to solve the problem we've described?*

Step 3: Evaluating possible solutions: *What are the probable benefits
and possible negative consequences of each proposed solution?*

Step 4: Consensus decision making: *What seems to be the best possible solution we can all support?*

Step 5: Implementing the solution chosen: *How will we put our
decision into effect?*

The model assumes that the leader has formulated a written outline containing specific questions about all the issues the group must consider.
For complex problems, the group should participate in identifying all the
subquestions so that no important contingency is overlooked. This linear
procedure's focus is equally distributed, in sequence, on the critical functions identified in the Functional Perspective.

The Single Question Format

The **Single Question Format** is less highly structured than P-MOPS, but also
addresses the functional issues critical to effective decision making. This technique has been developed and tested over the last 30 years by Larson and
LaFasto.[1] One thing that differentiates it from other formats is its focus on solution or issue analysis, thereby helping prevent a group from becoming prematurely solution-minded. Individuals who are low in preference for procedural
order may prefer this slightly less-structured format. The steps are as follows:

Step 1: Identify the problem: *What is the single question that, when
answered, means that the group knows how to accomplish its purpose?*

Step 2: Create a collaborative setting

2A: Agree on principles for discussion: *What principles should
we agree on in order to maintain a reasonable and collaborative
approach throughout the process?*

2B: Surface any assumptions and biases: *Which assumptions and biases are associated with the single question identified in step 1, and how might they influence the discussion?*

Step 3: Identify and analyze the issues (subquestions): *Before individuals respond to the single question in step 1, what issues or subquestions must be answered in order to fully understand the complexities of the overall problem?*

Step 4: Identify possible solutions: *Based on an analysis of the issues, what are the two or three most reasonable solutions to the problem?*

Step 5: Resolve the single question: *Among the possible solutions, which one is most desirable?*

A group using the Single Question format may spend considerable time in step 1, but after that, the group's attention is focused and the goal is clear. The Single Question format is the only procedure we describe that explicitly addresses issues of group climate and how members will interact with one another and requires members to discuss, in advance, how they plan to establish a collaborative climate.

The Ideal Solution Format

The **Ideal Solution Format,** also developed by Larson, focuses the group's attention on what the ideal solution would look like, and it recognizes that different groups likely have different ideal solutions.[2]

> **Ideal Solution Format**
> A problem-solving format that takes individual perspectives into account by asking a group to focus on what the ideal solution would do.

Step 1: Identify the nature of the problem: *Does everyone agree on the nature of the problem?*

Step 2: Identify the ideal solution: *What would be the ideal solution from the point of view of all interested people or groups involved?*

Step 3: Identify the conditions that must change: *Which conditions within the situation could be changed to achieve the ideal solution?*

Step 4: Select the most ideal solution: *Of all the solutions available, which one best approximates the ideal solution?*

The Ideal Solution format acknowledges the different perspectives that individual members and groups may have and encourages open discussion of what would look ideal from each of these perspectives. A simple procedure to follow, it is particularly useful when members and the groups they represent must accept the solution.[3] It also can capture group members' imaginations, as they envision the possibilities of what an ideal solution could do.

All three of the guidelines presented are easy to follow and address the functions important to effective problem solving and decision making. Each requires problem analysis. The Single Question Format focuses on the goal and the climate that members create, the Ideal Solution Format focuses on what the solution can do for the group, and P-MOPS distributes members' attention fairly evenly to the key functions. Each technique is adaptable to suit a group's particular situation.

Recap: A Quick Review

A number of techniques exist to help groups organize their problem-solving process:

1. The Procedural Model of Problem Solving (P-MOPS) is a general, all-purpose procedure, based on Dewey's work on reflective thinking, that can be adjusted to fit a variety of problems.

2. The Single Question Format asks, What is the single question that, when answered, means that the group knows how to accomplish its purpose? Its simpler structure appeals to those who may prefer a looser order, and it focuses explicitly on building collaborative climates.

3. The Ideal Solution Format engages members' imaginations by asking them to envision what the perfect solution would do and is particularly useful when members and the groups they represent must accept the group's solution.

Using P-MOPS to Address Complex Problems

We turn now to an in-depth discussion of P-MOPS, which we believe is one of the most flexible procedures available to groups tackling any type of problem. In this discussion, we identify the main goal for each step of P-MOPS and offer techniques helpful to accomplish the goal.

Step 1 of P-MOPS: Problem Description and Analysis

In many ways, this is a deceptively simple step. Why? For complex problems, this step alone can take up quite a bit of time. In addition, regardless of the complexity of the problem, if groups shortchange this question, their subsequent work can be grounded in misleading assumptions. The question to be addressed in step 1 is *What is the nature of the problem facing the group?* Subquestions to think about are listed here.

Problem Census

A technique in which group members are polled for topics and problems that are then posted, ranked by voting, and used to create agendas for future meetings.

Identify Problems to Work On   How do groups find problems to address? Often, someone—another group, a parent organization—gives the group the task of solving a problem. Or, the group became aware of the problem and decided on its own to tackle it. Sometimes, particularly in organizations or continuing groups, pro-active leaders anticipate what problems loom on the horizon rather than waiting for them to become obvious. The **problem census** is a "posting" technique used to identify important issues or problems. Thus, it is often used to build an agenda for future problem-solving

TABLE 10.2
Steps in the
problem census

1. Group members sit in a semicircle facing a board or flip chart.
2. The leader (or person designated to conduct the census) explains the purpose and procedures.
3. Members present problems one by one, in round-robin fashion, until all problems have been presented.
4. The leader posts each item as the member presents it. The leader or members can ask for clarification and elaboration, but cannot argue. The problem statement may be condensed so that it is concise enough to fit on the chart. Chart pages are removed and fastened to the wall so that all items are visible.
5. Some questions may be easily answered then and there; if so, they are removed from the list.
6. Members establish a priority order for the remaining items. Sometimes, members have a sheet of 5 or 10 stickers to place on the items they think are most important. All items remain on the list, but voting or attaching stickers prioritizes the list.
7. Each remaining item is dealt with in turn over the course of the group's deliberations. Often, a member will volunteer to do the legwork of preparing the discussion guideline for a particular problem.

meetings or discovering problems encountered by organization members. The steps are listed in Table 10.2.

The group makes a list of all concerns, problems, questions, or difficulties that any member would like to discuss. The group thus establishes a priority order for which issues to take on first; some of the issues or problems may be minor and can be answered or handled right away. The remaining problems are developed into an agenda for the group to work on over time, with individual members usually taking the lead for particular issues. A university department where one of us worked conducted, at the beginning of the school year, a problem census that developed into the department's agenda for the year. Faculty members first listed all the problems they thought should be addressed and assigned themselves to research and present an outline of each problem for eventual problem solving by the entire group.

Focus on the Problem   After you have identified or been assigned problems to solve, you must focus on the problem before jumping in to try to solve it. What would you think if you drove your car to a mechanic, who said, "You need new valves," before even looking under the hood? Focusing on the problem is the equivalent of looking under the hood. Getting solution-minded too quickly is a common problem; writers concerned with business groups have noted this tendency and the harm it can cause.[4] Questions to guide your analysis of a problem are presented in Table 10.3.

State the Problem Appropriately   One thing that will help prevent you from getting solution-minded too quickly is stating the group's problem in the form of a single, unambiguous **problem question**, which focuses on

Problem Question

A question that focuses the group's attention on the issue or problem; does not suggest any particular type of solution in the question itself.

TABLE 10.3
Questions to guide problem analysis

What does this problem question mean to us?

What are our charge and area of freedom?

What is unsatisfactory at present?

   Who (or what) is affected?

   When, where, and how?

   How serious do we judge the problem to be?

   How long has the problem existed?

   Do we need to gather any additional information to assess the nature and extent of the problem adequately?

What conditions have contributed to the problem?

   What appear to be causative conditions?

   What precipitated the crisis leading to our discussion?

What exactly do we hope to accomplish (the goal, desired situation)?

   What obstacles to achieving the desired goal exist?

What information do we need before we can find a satisfactory solution?

   What additional subquestions must we answer?

   How might we find answers to these subquestions?

   What are the answers to these subquestions?

How can we summarize our understanding of the problem to include the present and desired situation and causal conditions?

Solution Question

A question in which the solution to a problem is implied in the question itself.

the issue or the goal. In contrast, a **solution question** implies or suggests the solution within the question itself. What if the university registration staff had asked themselves, "How can we cut the number of illegitimate drop-adds?" instead of "How can we penalize students for dropping and adding during the quarter?" The first, a problem question, leaves the door open for many different options, but the second channels group members' thinking into only one option, penalizing drop-adds. Examples of solution versus problem questions are shown in Table 10.4.

Map the Problem   We describe mapping a problem in Appendix A. Group members should take the time to share what each person knows about the issue or problem so that if one person knows something, the others do as well. Mapping the issue tends to minimize the potential problem of hidden profiles (see chapter 9), encouraging members to pool their information, as is demonstrated in Figure A.1 in the Appendix A.

Step 2 of P-MOPS: Generating and Elaborating on Possible Solutions

The question we ask here is, *What might be done to solve the problem?* Our use of "might" not "should" is intentional; at this stage, you don't want to squash members' creative ideas by getting too focused on trying to decide

Solution Questions	Problem Questions
How can I transfer a man who is popular in his work group but slows down the work of other employees in the group?	How can I increase the work output of the group?
How can we increase the publicity for our club's activities so that attendance will be increased?	What can we do to increase attendance at our club's activities?

TABLE 10.4
Solution versus problem questions

something. You want good ideas to choose from. Ultimately, you will need to evaluate all the ideas you identify to assess how good they are, but for now, try to capture as many ideas as possible so you have plenty to choose from. This process may be lengthy, but members should guard against adopting the first solution that seems to solve the problem.

Using Brainstorming to Discover Alternatives   One technique to help you find or create good ideas is **brainstorming,** developed in the advertising industry, whose business it is to create innovative advertising campaigns.[5] Its use has spread to areas such as banking, engineering, medicine, education, and government—any place where creative ideas are desired. In order for a group's creativity to be released, members must feel safe in a nonthreatening environment free of judgment.[6] Because critical evaluation kills creativity, the main principle behind brainstorming is "no evaluation" during the brainstorming process. Evaluation of ideas—a necessary component of critical thinking—takes place *after* group members have listed all the ideas they can think of.

Effective brainstorming is harder than it looks because staying nonjudgmental is not easy! We have a tendency to comment on suggestions: "That sounds great!" or "Where did you get *that* idea?" Some organizations have creatively used squirt guns and nerf balls to stifle this tendency, sending water or a ball in the direction of the offender.[7] After years of research into brainstorming, two measures have emerged that help ensure both quantity and quality of ideas: If you have the time, allow members to generate ideas initially alone and then offer them to the group. This is especially helpful for generating quantity of ideas. Second, the less said the better. Avoid storytelling tangents and explanations of the ideas—the gist of the idea is your priority.[8] Follow wisely the steps of brainstorming (see Table 10.5) by staying focused and minimizing evaluation. Brainstorming steps are briefly described in Table 10.5.

Brainstorming has several variations, including **brainwriting,** which capitalizes on the fact that group members are sometimes more productive when they work alone initially, but in the presence of others. During brainwriting, members are given a specified time limit—10 or 15 minutes—to

Brainstorming

A technique for stimulating creative thinking by temporarily suspending evaluation of alternatives.

Brainwriting

Individual brainstorming in writing before group discussion of items.

TABLE 10.5
Steps in
brainstorming

1. Members are presented with the problem, which can range from specific (*What should we name our new microbrew?*) to abstract (*How can we improve living conditions in the residence halls?*)
2. Members are encouraged to generate as many solutions as possible, under the following rules:
   A. No evaluation is permitted. No one is allowed to criticize, laugh at, or negatively react to any idea.
   B. Quantity is sought. Members should try to generate as many solutions as they can, initially alone if time allows. The facilitator should prod them to think of more if there is a lull.
   C. Innovation is encouraged. Wild and crazy ideas are encouraged—you never know which one will spark just the right solution for the group.
   D. Hitchhiking on previous ideas is encouraged, but tangents and explanations should be curtailed; just focus on the gist of the idea.
3. All ideas are written down so that the entire group can see.
4. All ideas are evaluated, but at another session or after a substantial break.

write down as many ideas as they can generate about the problem. They are encouraged to write as fast as they can without stopping and, as with brainstorming, to piggyback on their own ideas. When the time is up, members share their ideas, round-robin, and proceed as with regular brainstorming. Brainwriting can overcome some drawbacks of traditional brainstorming, including the inhibition of some participants, having one or two dominant speakers monopolize the session, or the group's fixating on just a few ideas.[9]

Electronic Brainstorming

Brainstorming on computers linked to a large screen that displays all responses, but no one knows who contributed which items.

Electronic brainstorming (EBS) is another variation; it capitalizes on the fact that anonymity can remove inhibitions. Members sit at computer terminals and type in their ideas, which are sent via computer to a large screen visible to all. No one knows who contributed which idea. EBS groups often generate more ideas, and more high-quality ideas, than oral brainstorming groups or members working alone.[10] Members were less fearful of being evaluated and were more satisfied with EBS than with oral brainstorming. Anonymous EBS is an excellent method to use in a large group in particular.[11]

Interestingly, a facilitator can influence how group members use the technology.[12] When facilitators tried to stimulate creativity with comments such as "Remember to be innovative when offering our views" and "Let's understand each other's views" the creativity was actually *negatively* affected. Apparently the comments, even in anonymous EBS groups, introduced an element of judgment too early in the process, which hurt the generation of ideas. Even though the comments were offered in an effort to spur creativity, they were perceived as judgmental. Leaders and facilitators must be carefully trained in how to use the technology so that they don't misuse it.

Step 3 of P-MOPS: Evaluating Possible Solutions

Once the problem has been thoroughly analyzed, with alternatives accumulated and criteria clearly understood by all members, the group is ready to evaluate alternatives. The pros and cons of each solution must be explored, as members ask, *What are the probable benefits and possible negative consequences of each proposed solution?* Group members must employ their sharpest critical thinking skills to ensure thorough evaluation of all options.

Establish a Collaborative Climate for Evaluation   Your critical thinking task will be facilitated if you engage in some preparation work first. Members are more willing to think critically when the group's climate is collaborative and supportive and when that climate explicitly supports critical thinking. Use the best communication skills you can—listen to understand, help other group members make their points, and encourage everyone to participate. We discussed the factors that contribute to a supportive climate in Chapter 6; here is the place to be particularly mindful of the way you interact with others.

Some groups discuss explicitly the type of atmosphere they want to create and how they will do that. An acquaintance of ours who works in marketing for a *Fortune* 500 company asks group members to think of the best group or team they've ever been part of, then to think of how the present group could become as good as their "best" group. This prompts members to establish their own norms of mutual respect, careful listening, and commitment to the task. The Single Question Format explicitly allows for this kind of discussion. While the other two do not, nothing prevents *any* group from having this discussion.

Establish Norms That Promote Critical Thinking   We explained in Chapter 9 how important it is for group members to be the best critical thinkers they can, and we described groupthink as a potential problem when a group fails to think critically. Here, we show you how you can spot the symptoms of groupthink and what you can do to prevent it.

Symptoms of Groupthink   How can you recognize groupthink? The symptoms of groupthink, fall into three main categories:

1. **The group overestimates its power and morality.**
   A group may be so optimistic that it overestimates the chances for its programs to succeed. For example, Swissair, known as the "Flying Bank," was one of the top 10 airlines in the world and the darling of Switzerland's corporate successes.[13] Its collapse came out of nowhere and dealt a huge national blow to Switzerland. Previous successes and a reputation for outstanding corporate practices lulled the company into a sense of invulnerability that overshadowed poor financial and administrative decisions, leading to its collapse.

The Major League Baseball umpires, as well, came to believe they were irreplaceable to the game of baseball.[14] They had benefited from highly successful past contract negotiations with MLB. With impending contract negotiations upon them and ill will between them and MLB, they decided to deliver the first punch—resign en masse. Their negotiation strategy failed miserably.

2. **The group becomes closed-minded.**
   Either a high-status leader or the group has a preferred solution, and the group closes itself off to any information contrary to this preference. This sounds like the registrar staff proposing its "solution" for drop-adds. A group may also stereotype outside figures who disagree so that it doesn't have to pay attention to what they might have to say. The MLB umpires signed their letters of resignation without having talked to lawyers or even family members. Reportedly, their leader pounded the table three times, calling for them to sign their letters.[15] The umpires commonly referred to MLB officials as the "enemy."

3. **Group members experience pressures to conform.**
   Pressure to conform manifests itself in a variety of ways. First, members censor their own remarks, exemplified in Figure 10.1. If you think everyone else in the group favors a proposal, you will tend to suppress your own doubts and fears. Self-censorship and the illusion of vulnerability were the two most significant factors contributing to the failure of the umpires' chosen negotiating

FIGURE 10.1   Groupthink in action

Reprinted with permission of King Features Syndicate.

strategy.[16] Second, the group members have a shared illusion of
unanimity, manifested by the amount of simple agreement discovered by Cline.[17] Because individuals do not express doubts openly,
the members think they all agree. Consensus is assumed rather than
obtained.[18] Third, a member who *does* venture a contradictory opinion will experience direct pressure from the rest of the group to conform: "Why are you being so negative, Jim? The rest of us think it's
a good idea." The group may also have a number of self-appointed
mindguards who "protect" the group by deliberately preventing dis-
sonant information from reaching the group—by stopping outsiders
from addressing the group, failing to mention contrasting points of
view contained in research materials, and so forth. Finally, in groups
with rigid status hierarchies, lower-status members are less likely to
contradict higher-status members and will avoid issues they think
may produce conflict.[19] These conformity pressures are especially
dangerous when a group *must* achieve consensus. The need for
consensus can lead to an "agreement norm," which curtails disagreement, ultimately causing the decision to suffer.[20]

Preventing Groupthink   Critical thinking is the responsibility of all group
members. Here are specific suggestions to help prevent groupthink:

1. **Each member should assume the role of critical evaluator.**

    Every member should use his or her best critical thinking skills on
    behalf of the group. Occasionally, the group may assign a specific
    individual to serve as a *devil's advocate* or *reminder,* who is charged
    with constructively criticizing the ideas brought to the group. Ideally,
    this role rotates among members so that the criticism doesn't become
    associated with a particular individual.

2. **Independent subgroups can be formed to work on or evaluate
    the same issue.**
    The competition of rival subgroups, even friendly ones, can make the
    subgroups more careful and thorough in their work. In addition,
    the clash between subgroups can spark novel or creative solutions.

3. **The group should prevent its own insulation from outside
    information.**
    Members who serve as mindguards keep what they perceive as con-
    tradictory information away from the other members of the group,
    but sometimes this information is exactly what can benefit the group
    and prevent a disastrous decision! The registration staff didn't seek
    feedback from anyone but themselves in making the decision. The
    MLB umpires never once consulted with their spouses or lawyers.
    Their chosen strategy neglected the fact that legally, they could not
    rescind their resignations once MLB received them.[21]

Leaders, in particular, can take steps to offset insularity. They can encourage members to get feedback on tentative proposals from trusted associates outside the group, then report back to the group. Leaders can also arrange for outside experts to discuss their views with the group, thereby helping to ensure a broadly based foundation for making the decision.

4. **Leaders should refrain from stating their preferences at the beginning of a problem-solving or decision-making session.** Richard Phillips, leader of the umpire's union, was highly respected and known for his previous contractual successes with MLB. He was so popular that some umpires believed their union was really his, not theirs. He made it clear that resigning was the umpires' best choice.[22] Group members may want to defer to or please the leader, but this can impair decision making. Leaders should hold off sharing their views.

5. **Group members can suggest and use appropriate technology to encourage thorough problem solving.** There are many relatively inexpensive computer programs, which we will discuss later in the chapter, designed to keep a group focused on the task. Some systems allow members to react anonymously so that the effects of conformity pressure and strong leadership can be minimized. Miranda found that even when a group is predisposed to groupthink, group support systems helped prevent groupthink and promoted effective decision making.[23]

Step 4 of P-MOPS: Consensus Decision Making

The group's entire work comes down to making the actual decision. The question the group must address is: *What seems to be the best possible solution that we can all support?*

Suggestions for Achieving Consensus   The process of reaching consensus gives all members an opportunity to express how they feel and think about the alternatives, and an equitable chance to influence the outcome. For important decisions, it is worth the time. Here are some discussion guidelines outlined by Hall for making consensus decisions[24]:

1. **Don't argue stubbornly for your own position.** Present it clearly and logically. Listen actively to others and consider all reactions carefully.

2. **Avoid looking at a stalemate as a win–lose situation.** Rather, see whether you can find a next best alternative acceptable to all.

3. **When agreement is reached too easily and too quickly, be on guard against groupthink.** Through discussion, be sure that everyone accepts the decision for similar or complementary reasons and really agrees that it is the best that can be reached. Don't change your position just to avoid conflict.

4. **Avoid conflict-suppressing techniques, such as majority vote, averaging, coin tossing, and so forth, except as a last resort.** Although they prevent destructive interpersonal conflicts, they also suppress constructive substantive arguments.

5. **Seek out differences of opinion, which are helpful in testing alternatives and evaluating reasoning.** Get every member involved in the decision-making process. The group has a better chance of selecting the best alternative if it has a wider range of information and ideas.

Even when you reach consensus and group members are satisfied with the solution, others may see problems the group has missed. It's a good idea to second-guess your choice.

Second-Guess the Tentative Choice Before Fully Committing to It After consensus has emerged in a group or a group has chosen an alternative in another way, members should, if possible, consider that choice a tentative one and second-guess it, perhaps in a meeting held especially for that purpose. Hirokawa's research shows that one of the most crucial functions a group should perform is assessing the potential negative consequences of a decision.[25] This can be especially difficult toward the end of a group's problem-solving process because, when groups sense closure, they begin reinforcing their hard work, and it's difficult to switch gears. Hirokawa found that when members of effective groups begin to screen the alternatives, they first spot the serious defects.[26] Once they find an alternative they like, they switch strategies and begin to detail the positive aspects of the alternative. It can be really hard at this point to revisit their choice, but that is exactly what members should do to ensure they haven't overlooked a fatal flaw. The RISK technique can help them do that.

Using the RISK Technique to Second-Guess the Choice The **RISK technique** is designed specifically to allow a group or organization to assess how a proposed policy or change might negatively affect the individuals and groups involved.[27] The six basic steps in the RISK technique are summarized in Table 10.6.

Using the RISK procedure can benefit the entire organization as well as the group. If the registration staff had used this procedure, especially if they had invited others to the meeting who would be affected by the change in drop-add procedures, they would have discovered the downsides of the proposal in terms of cost and loss of goodwill from the students. The Major League umpires not only insulated themselves and followed an overzealous and misinformed leader, they never collectively talked about the risks of resigning or formulated any contingency plans should their strategy fail.[28]

Once the group has developed its solution and made its choice, it is ready for the final phase of this problem-solving discussion: implementation.

RISK Technique

A small group procedure for identifying and dealing with all risks, fears, doubts, and worries that members have about a new policy or plan before it is implemented.

TABLE 10.6
Steps in the RISK technique

1. The leader describes the proposed solution or change in policy in detail and asks for any concerns they might have about the proposal.
2. Members brainstorm, to discover all potential problems with the solution or change in policy.
3. Problems are posted, round-robin fashion, so they are accessible to all members. Members can add to the list as they think of new problems. They may also seek clarification or elaboration, remembering to be constructive; otherwise, others may feel threatened, and other risks may not come forward for consideration.
4. A master list of all problems is compiled and distributed to all participants, who can add additional problems to the list. This list can also be distributed to others outside the group who may be affected by the proposal for their input.
5. Risks are discussed one at a time in a subsequent meeting. Minor risks or ones easily handled are removed from the list.
6. Serious risks are compiled into an agenda for future problem-solving discussions. These can be handled in another problem census.
7. Look for possible modifications of the proposal in the discussion of risks in step 6. If the risks cannot be resolved, the group needs to reconsider the proposal and possibly discard it.

Step 5 of P-MOPS: Implementing the Solution Chosen

Once a group has made its choice, it is now ready to implement its solution. Members must now decide *What will we do to put our solution into effect?* Sometimes a group will hand this task off to a different group or individual, but here we are assuming that the same members who made the choice are responsible for carrying it out. Sometimes the implementation process is almost as complex as the entire problem-solving process; someone needs to see that the group has worked out all necessary details. The group must answer the following questions: *Who will do what, when, and by what date? Do we need any follow-up evaluation of how well our solution is working? If so, how will we do that?*

Program Evaluation and Review Technique (PERT)

A procedure for planning the details to implement a complex solution that involves many people and resources.

Use PERT to Keep Track of Implementation Details   For complex problems involving the entire group, the **Program Evaluation and Review Technique (PERT)** can help members keep track of implementation details. Sometimes a solution is very complicated, involving a variety of materials, people whose work must be coordinated, and steps that must be completed in a specific sequence. Think of what is involved in remodeling a large building on campus or constructing something like a space station. PERT was developed to expedite such detailed operations so that they can be done efficiently and so that people can keep track of each step of the process. The procedure can be simplified to help even a student project group keep track of who is responsible for what. The main points of PERT[29] are summarized in Table 10.7, and an example of a simple PERT chart for a student project group is provided in Table 10.8.

1. Describe the final step (how the solution should appear when fully operational).
2. Enumerate any events that must occur before the final goal is realized.
3. Order these steps chronologically.
4. If necessary, develop a flow diagram of the process and all the steps in it.
5. Generate a list of all the activities, resources, and materials needed to accomplish each step.
6. Estimate the time needed to accomplish each step; then add all the estimates to get a total time for implementing the plan.
7. Compare the total time estimate with deadlines or expectations and correct as necessary (by assigning more people or less time to a given step).
8. Determine which members will be responsible for each step.

TABLE 10.7
Steps in the PERT procedure

TABLE 10.8   Sample PERT chart for a student group project

Date	Aretha	Barney	Candy	Denzil	Entire Group
Tues Sep. 8	Report on pre-lim observ.		Report on prelim observ.		Decide group to observe; decide variables
Thu Sep. 10		Prelim report, conflict	Prelim report, Leadership	Prelim report, roles	Discuss prelim reports; decide methods of analysis
Tues Sep. 15		Complete library research, Conflict	Complete library research, Leadership	Complete library research, Roles	
Thu Sep. 17		Observe group, 8 PM	Observe group, 8 PM	Have observation materials ready; survey, SYMLOG (see Chapter 12)	
Tues Sep. 22		Complete SYMLOG of group	Complete SYMLOG of group		Meet after class, discuss preliminary findings
Thu Sep. 24			Observe group, 8 PM	Observe group, 8 PM Have tape recorder ready	
Tues Sep. 29					Discuss overall observations; listen to tape
Thu Oct. 1		Complete first draft, Conflict	Complete first draft, Leadership	Complete first draft, Roles	
Mon Oct. 5	Begin overall editing and typing	Final draft, Conflict; Intro done	Final draft, Leadership; Conclusion done	Final draft, Roles	Look at each other's sections to improve style

(continued)

TABLE 10.8   *(continued)*

Date	Aretha	Barney	Candy	Denzil	Entire Group
Tues Oct. 6					
Wed Oct. 7					
Thu Oct. 8					
Fri Oct. 9	Editing and typing done	Tables and charts to Aretha (conflict)	Table/Charts to Aretha (leadership)	Tables/Charts to Aretha (roles)	
Sat Oct. 10	Proof; make copies			Proof; make copies	
Sun Oct. 11	Distribute copies to all by 8 PM	Assemble full report by 5 PM	Assemble full report by 5 PM	Make large charts for class presentation	
Mon Oct. 12		Read full paper	Read full paper	Read full paper	Rehearsal at Aretha's 7 PM
Tues Oct. 13					Final presentation to class

We have just described all the P-MOPS steps. P-MOPS, as with any problem-solving procedure, is not meant to provide rigid steps that group members must blindly follow. P-MOPS is meant as a guide—a flexible, adaptable sequence of things to consider. For instance, a group may realize they forgot to think about something in an earlier step. They should then recycle and take care of the work that was forgotten instead of risking a poor decision later. Throughout our discussion of P-MOPS, groups are asked at each step to reflect on the goals of that step and make whatever adjustments are needed to correct their path to success. A team's success is intimately connected to both how well it reflects on its work as well as how it practically makes changes to adapt appropriately to those reflections.[30] This responsibility falls not just on one individual in a group, but on *everyone*. With proper amounts of reflection and adaptation, both team performance and group collaboration improve.

Tailoring P-MOPS to Fit a Specific Problem

Reflection and adaptation are central to using P-MOPS effectively; otherwise, P-MOPS is just a list of steps. P-MOPS is meant to remind you of the important functions that need your attention during problem solving. Tailoring this procedure is easy. For example, if your group is charged with solving

Recap: A Quick Review

Understanding how to use guidelines such as P-MOPS can be useful to groups, whether the problem is simple or complex.

1. Many groups and organizations deliberately seek out problems to work on; the problem census technique helps group members identify issues that can be built into the group's working agenda.

2. During step 1, problem description and analysis, members must focus on the problem before they begin to identify solutions; they can help ensure this by starting with a good problem question as opposed to a solution question, which narrows members' thinking.

3. Group members should map the problem by sharing what they each know individually about it so that they will hold in common as much information as possible.

4. During step 2, generating and elaborating possible solutions, the group's goal is to identify as many relevant and realistic options as it can without evaluation. Techniques such as brainstorming—and its variants brainwriting and electronic brainstorming—can help members achieve this goal.

5. Step 3 requires a group to evaluate all the options it has identified, while mindfully creating a collaborative climate for doing so.

6. Critical thinking is important in step 3. Members need to identify symptoms of groupthink, such as members overestimating their power and morality, becoming close-minded, and experiencing pressures to conform; they then must work to prevent groupthink, in part by assigning every member the role of critical evaluator.

7. During step 4, achieving consensus, members are encouraged to share their divergent views, avoid reaching consensus to easily and avoid conflict-suppressing techniques such as voting.

8. When consensus is achieved, members should second-guess their tentative choice by using procedures such as RISK, which asks members and others to help identify any potential problems they may see.

9. Step 5, implementing their solution, can be coordinated with tools such as. PERT charts that help group members keep track of the many details involved in that implementation.

a problem that is complex, touches a lot of people, may be costly, and affects quality of life (such as figuring out how to negotiate a fair salary and benefit package with Major League Baseball), you need to make sure that you make the most carefully thought-out decision possible. Very likely, you will want to use all the steps of P-MOPS. But if your group is charged with planning a party for your service club, you don't run a big risk of making a mistake. You can skip or shorten some of the steps. How do you know the best way to adjust? You can consider the characteristics of your particular problem.

Problem Characteristics

In his classic synthesis of group dynamics, Shaw described five characteristics of problems that small groups tackle: *task difficulty, solution multiplicity, intrinsic interest, cooperative requirements,* and *population familiarity.*[31] To these we add *acceptance requirements* and *technical requirements.* Only the most general steps in the problem-solving procedures will be the same for all problems.

Task difficulty refers to the problem's complexity—hence, the effort, knowledge, and skill needed to achieve the goal. Groups generally are asked to tackle complex problems, those for which a number of different perspectives must be considered. For instance, consider recent government task forces assigned to recommend improvements in the U.S. healthcare system, reduction of the budget deficit, or improvement in high school graduation rates—problems beyond the capacity of any single person. Thorough problem analysis and mapping will be needed.

Solution multiplicity refers to the number of conceivable alternatives for solving the problem. There are usually only a few useful ways to get from your residence to your classroom, but there are innumerable ways to decorate your living room. Structured procedures like *brainstorming* help us think of more possible alternatives when solution multiplicity is even moderately high.[32]

Ideally, groups would discuss only intrinsically interesting problems. In actuality, people are assigned to committees that deal with a variety of problems, some of little interest to them. **Intrinsic interest** is "the degree to which the task in and of itself is interesting, motivating, and attractive to the group members."[33] When group members are highly interested in their task, they want to share control of the group's procedures, but when interest is low, they are happy to let the discussion leader assume control.[34] If interest is high, members at first want to express opinions and feelings and will resist strict procedural control. After they have vented their feelings, they are more likely to accept procedural control of the problem-solving procedure.

Cooperative requirements reflect the degree to which coordinated efforts are essential to satisfactory completion of a task. In other words, the task is conjunctive. Increased complexity requires members to talk to each other, share information, and cooperate—to be competent communicators.

The **population familiarity** dimension of the problem is the level of members' knowledge about and previous experience with the task. Groups with experienced members tend to perform better than groups with inexperienced ones.[35] When population familiarity is low to start, the problem-solving procedure should concentrate on analysis of the problem. But sometimes very knowledgeable people become smug and unwilling to think of new approaches. Then procedures to increase innovation may be essential.

The **acceptance requirements** of a problem refers to the extent to which a proposed solution must be acceptable to people whom it will

---

Task Difficulty

Degree of problem complexity and effort required to solve a problem.

Solution Multiplicity

Extent to which there are many different possible alternatives for solving a particular problem.

Intrinsic Interest

Extent to which the task itself is attractive and interesting to the participants.

Cooperative Requirements

The degree to which members must coordinate their efforts for a group to complete its task successfully.

Population Familiarity

The degree to which members of a group are familiar with the nature of a problem and experienced in solving similar problems.

affect. Legislation enacted to solve public problems has often backfired when acceptance requirements were overlooked. A task force recently created a planning and zoning ordinance for a county near where one of us lives, but citizen groups, although acknowledging a need for some such law, refused to accept it. The United States has experienced epic struggles over laws controlling guns, marijuana, and cell phone use while driving. Sometimes a group must give heavy consideration to the acceptability of a solution; at other times, little or none.

The **technical requirements** characteristic of a problem's solution refers to whether it must match some standard of technical excellence or technical feasibility. For instance, Toyota has had to rethink its quality control procedures, due to several disastrous recalls.

Use common sense when you modify P-MOPS. One of us spent two hours in a staff meeting trying to decide what would be the most appropriate thank-you gift for a college's outgoing board of trustees. What a waste of time! Heavy problem analysis, which the group leader insisted on, was unnecessary—there was no possibility of making a mistake because all the options were appropriate. In fact, the staff would have been happy to have the leader select the gifts, with or without consultation. Examples of P-MOPS modifications suggested by a problem's characteristics are shown in Table 10.9.

Acceptance Requirements

The degree to which the solution for a given problem must be accepted by the people it will affect.

Technical Requirements

The degree to which the solution for a given problem is technically feasible or must meet standards of technical excellence.

Problem Characteristic	Adaptation of Problem-Solving Procedure
1. Intrinsic interest is high.	A period of ventilation before systematic problem solving.
2. Task difficulty is high.	Detailed problem mapping; many subquestions.
3. Solution multiplicity is high.	Brainstorming.
4. Cooperative requirements are high.	A criterion step, creating and ranking explicit criteria.
5. High level of acceptance is required.	Focus on concern of people affected when evaluating options.
6. High level of technical quality is required.	Focus on evaluating ideas, critical thinking; perhaps invite outside experts to address group.
7. Population familiarity is high.	Focus on criteria and creation of multiple options.
8. Need only one or a few stages of the problem-solving process.	Shorten procedure to only steps required.

TABLE 10.9
How problem characteristics suggest ways to adapt P-MOPS

Examples of discussion outlines are provided to give you a mental model of how a leader might structure the group's problem-solving process. Examples of two leaders' outlines adapting P-MOPS are presented in Tables 10.10 and 10.11. In Table 10.10, the outline deals with all the complexities of parking on an urban campus. From the outline, you can see how major criteria were arrived at and used to evaluate proposals. Table 10.11 is a leader's simple outline for structuring discussion of a problem with few solutions and for which discussion time was limited. Table 10.12 uses the Single Question Format for a discussion about the Springfield area's solid waste disposal problem, and Table 10.13 shows

TABLE 10.10
Using P-MOPS to structure a complex question about student parking

PROBLEM QUESTION: What should be done to improve student parking at Missouri State University?

I. What is the nature of the problem that students encounter with parking at MSU?

   A. What is the scope of our concern with student parking?

      1. Do any terms in the question need to be clarified?

      2. What authority do we have?

      3. Do we need to determine the authority and duties of departments involved with campus parking?

   B. What is now unsatisfactory about student parking?

      1. What have we found to be unsatisfactory?

         a. Have any studies been done?

         b. What complaints have students been making?

      2. Does any other information exist about student parking that we need to consider?

   C. What goals does the committee hope to achieve by changes in parking that we need to consider?

   D. What obstacles may stand in the way of improving parking for students?

      1. What do we know about what is causing the problem(s) we've described?

      2. How much interest do involved persons have in this problem?

      3. What limits are there on resources that might be needed?

         a. Funds?

         b. Space?

         c. Personnel?

         d. Other?

      4. Are there any other obstacles to changing student parking?

   E. How shall we summarize the problem(s) with student parking at MSU?

      1. Do we all perceive the problem the same?

      2. Should we subdivide the problem?

Used with permission of Greg Gravenmeier, student in John Brilhart's class.

I. What sort of written final exam should we have for our class?
   A. How much authority (area of freedom) do we have?
   B. What facts and feelings should we take into account as we seek an answer to this question?
II. What are our objectives (criteria) in deciding on the type of exam?
   A. Learning objectives?
   B. Grades?
   C. Type of preparation and study?
   D. Fairness to all?
III. What types of written final exams might we have?
IV. What are the advantages and disadvantages of each?
V. What will we recommend as the form of our written exam?

TABLE 10.11
Using P-MOPS to structure a simple question with limited discussion time about a final exam in a college class

1. *What is the single question . . . ?*
   What is the most environmentally benign, politically acceptable, and economically feasible way to dispose of solid waste from Springfield and the surrounding counties?
2. *Collaboration*
   A. *What principles should we agree upon in order to maintain a reasonable and collaborative approach throughout the process?*
      • We will solicit all viewpoints and treat them with respect.
      • We will listen carefully to each other and not interrupt.
      • We will treat each other with respect.
      • We will do what we think is best for the citizens of O'Fallon and not for ourselves personally.
   B. *What assumptions and biases are associated with the single question identified in step 1, and how might they influence the discussion?*
      • We assume that there are better methods than our current method.
      • We believe that sometimes new technology isn't necessarily tested well.
      • We tend to be biased in favor of low-cost alternatives so that rates won't rise.
      • We don't like being vulnerable to surrounding communities for water or for reasonable rates.
3. *What issues or subquestions must we answer to fully understand the complexities of the overall problem?*
      • How could the solid waste of Springfield be disposed of?
        ◦ How much will each feasible method cost?
        ◦ What will facilities and start-up cost?
        ◦ What will continuing operation cost?
        ◦ Will the method generate enough revenue to pay its costs?

TABLE 10.12
Using the Single Question Format to structure discussion about solid waste disposal methods

(continued)

TABLE 10.12
(continued)

- What might be the harmful effects of each method?
  - How will each method affect water, air, land, and the environment?
  - What health hazards might each method create?
- What problems might we have getting voters to accept each method?
  - What group or groups opposed each method?
  - How well has this method been accepted elsewhere?
- How well has this method worked in other places?
  - How dependable has it been?
  - What personnel training is required?
  - How long will this method serve Springfield?

(The task force engaged in extensive research efforts, including paying consultants, hiring an engineering consulting firm, and making several trips to observe facilities used by other cities.)

4. *What are the two or three most reasonable answers to the subquestions?*
   - The Materials Recovery Facility (MRF) emerges as the best choice.

(The task force recommended the MRF with composting and limited landfill usage to voters. After an extensive information campaign, voters approved the MRF.)

TABLE 10.13
Using the Ideal Solution format for O'Fallon's problem about water treatment

1. *Does everyone agree on the nature of the problem?*
   - Geologists have evidence that the water table is dropping.
   - Construction of new deep wells is not feasible due to the dropping table.
   - The problem will become a crisis in about 10 years.
2. *What would be the ideal solution from the point of view of all interested people or groups involved?*
   - What do the geologists prefer? (protection of the water table)
   - What do voters prefer? (low cost with high quality)
   - What do elected officials prefer? (not raising taxes; long-term solution)
   - What does the health department prefer? (safety)
   - What do surrounding cities and counties prefer? (ability to sell water for profit)
   - What do environmentalists prefer? (no degradation of the environment)

(Analysis of the preferences of interested parties revealed three main criteria that emerged: The solution must provide high-quality water; it must be cost-effective and efficient; it must give the city long-term control over costs.)

3. *Which conditions within the situation could be changed to achieve the ideal solution?*
   - The current system cannot be expanded safely or reliably.
   - Voters could be educated about the long-term benefit of building a membrane treatment plant and would likely support it when they see the eventual cost savings.
4. *Of all the solutions available, which one best approximates the ideal?*
   - The membrane treatment facility best meets all criteria.

how O'Fallon city officials might have used the Ideal Solution Format to discuss their water treatment problem, discussed in Chapter 9

Using Technology to Help a Group's Problem Solving and Decision Making

In the last two decades, group use of computer technology to assist group work in general and problem solving in particular has increased dramatically and become more sophisticated. The issue, as we pointed out in Chapter 1, is no longer whether a group meets entirely face-to-face or online: most groups use computer technology to some degree. For instance, face-to-face groups can use e-mail and chat rooms to keep in contact socially and discuss their work. They can upload written documents (such as agendas, minutes, notes, reports, and research) using a virtual Dropbox so geographically dispersed members can access and respond to the documents. Wikis, mentioned in Chapter 2, also permit multi-authored writing as members simultaneously create, write, analyze and edit documents.[36] We described in Chapter 8 a popular online tool called Wiggio (www. wiggio.com/) that can be used by both virtual and face-to-face groups for their work. In addition, some groups use computer technology as the *sole* means by which they interact with each other. Virtual groups exist because the sophisticated computer technology allows them to coordinate work even though they never meet face-to-face.

Groups use computer technology on two levels. First, as described earlier, groups use computer tools to conduct group business. Second, face-to-face and virtual groups use specially designed computer software for group problem solving. We now take a look at both uses, starting with basic tools.

General Tools

Instant messaging (IM), discussed in Chapter 8, is popular with virtual groups and allows members' rapid-fire messaging, compared to e-mail and voice mail messaging. An IM user clicks on the name of another user's IM handle to begin an immediate interchange. Instant messaging is used for fast, short messages and allows members to talk to each other during conference calls.[37] Kathy's brother manages a telephone command center for a major healthcare company. He related that during a recent conference call with another manager, a strange "pop" sounded during the call. Her brother was IM'd by another manager, during the call, asking him about the strange noise. They learned that another manager had been chewing and popping his gum during the call. Instant messaging gives members easy access to one another during conference calls, but interchanges are not documented, so group work cannot be archived. However, bulletin board and chat room messaging can be recorded and later retrieved.

Instructors use asynchronous electronic *bulletin board services (BBS)* and synchronous *chat room* environments, like the Internet Relay Chat (IRC), to facilitate classroom learning.[38] These tools are also a part of Blackboard platforms and services such as Wiggio (www.wiggio.com/). In the classroom context, these technological tools let teachers and students talk to each other, help them equalize participation, increase student self-responsibility, show differing perspectives, allow thoughtful consideration of message ideas, and train students to use these tools in their future professions.[39]

Pena-Shaff and associates compared both BBS and IRC in the classroom; their findings have important implications for small groups. BBS services allow group members to post asynchronous messages and are particularly useful when the group wishes to promote critical thinking and reflection.[40] BBS discussions are generally structured, reflective, and focused on the task and topic. The downside to BBS is that it does not promote collaboration and social interaction. Group members need to be motivated to use it. In contrast, the synchronous character of text-base "talk," such as IRC, does promote collaboration and works well for brainstorming.[41] IRC is more informal. Members feel more pressured to reach consensus, yet find it difficult to do so. The freewheeling nature of chat rooms, which helps members initially explore issues, also allows members to get offtrack easily. Once off track, it is hard to get the discussion back on track. Thus, although chat rooms allow for interaction in real time and provide immediate feedback, similar to face-to-face interaction, the talk can be confusing, with content and flow reflecting "messy" thinking.

Practically speaking, your group first needs to decide whether you want to use an electronic bulletin board service or a chat room. Your answer depends on whether you want free-wheeling discussion, as is appropriate during problem analysis, idea generation, brainstorming, and so forth, or critical evaluation, as is appropriate when a group is evaluating options and trying to decide something. Either way, effective use of bulletin boards and chat rooms is improved when members know the guidelines ahead of time and use them.[42] Table 10.14 offers some to consider and can be adapted to your own group.[43]

We introduced you to different forms of computer conferencing in Chapter 2. These netconferences (or teleconferences) are electronically mediated conferences that allow group members to meet while being located in different places within the same town or world. Your authors, Gloria (living in Missouri) and Kathy (living in California), conference by phone every two years with their editors (living in New York) in preparation for their revision of this text. Teleconferences are the most used technology tool for virtual group meetings.[44] Teleconferences take three popular forms: the *audio conference*, which lets members hear but not see each other; the videoconference, which let members see and hear each other; and the computer conference, which allow members to send messages

TABLE 10.14
Guidelines for
Bulletin Board and
Chat Room Use

1. Make sure everyone knows where the bulletin board or chat room is located and how to use it.
2. Guarantee that the bulletin board or chat room is private so outsiders cannot interrupt or see the discussion.
3. Select a group member as a moderator to help ensure discussion equity. This role can be rotated.
4. Moderators and group members should facilitate a climate of equitable participation both in asynchronous and synchronous environments.
5. Emoticons need to be used wisely because they can be misread or misunderstood.
6. Synchronous chatting needs to stay on task.

to each other that are displayed on computer monitors—like the IRC in classrooms and the tools found in a site like wiggio (www.wiggio.com/).

The audioconference includes telephone conference calls and is probably the most routine teleconference. Audioconferencing requires speakerphone equipment that has become readily available and inexpensive; it can be set up in any office. While easy and available, you need to keep in mind the lack of social presence in this kind of conferencing due to the lack of nonverbal cues.[45] If managed well, though, you can equalize participation.

The videoconference remains an expensive type of conferencing for companies, and it still requires specialized equipment. It is highly desired by groups because it most resembles face-to-face interaction, allowing members to see and hear each other. Members of virtual teams call for its use when it is important to see others' nonverbal (e.g., sensitive negotiations) but not for routine meeings.[46] Desktop videoconferencing is where the videoconference occurs via members' personal computers. This kind of conferencing remains expensive; however, with technological advances, some see it as the future of videoconferencing.

Computer conferences are becoming increasingly sophisticated and accessible, with a number of companies developing their own specialized software for employees linked to a network that lets them work simultaneously on a variety of tasks. Decisions made by computerized conference groups are just as good as ones made by face-to-face groups, but computer groups are less likely to come to agreement.[47] The *type* of computerized technique seems to make a difference. The window method, which permits each participant to see the responses of all other participants at once (which is more like face-to-face communicating), produced higher decision quality than a message system that required participants to complete a message before they could interact.[48] Some studies, in fact, have found that computer conferences can provide advantages over face-to-face meetings. Electronic mail conferences minimized inequalities due to status and expertise.[49] Computer programs permitting anonymity may help create greater and more equal participation.[50] On the other hand, computer-mediated group decision making leads to more delays, more outspoken advocacy, and more extreme decisions (i.e., group polarization) than face-to-face meetings.[51] Although research on the effectiveness of computer conferences may be mixed, it remains a very popular way for groups to conduct the business of problem solving. The mixed findings should not surprise you, given we have argued that computer-mediated communication is its own unique medium of communication with its advantages and disadvantages compared to face-to-face communication. In the first study of its kind, Jonassen and Kwon took a look at actual problem-solving processes in computer conferences and face-to-face meetings.[52] The computer conference problem-solving groups using asynchronous messaging actually rated their process higher and were more satisfied with it than when they problem solved face-to-face. Yes computer conference messages were longer, contained more ideas and perspectives, involved more agreements and disagreements, and their total process took four to six days compared to one hour for the face to face problem solving. However, the group members preferred computer conferencing because they could reflect on each other's messages, think about what to say next, and change their own comments in private before they sent out their comments. In an interesting way, although computer-mediated communication formats (like computer conferencing) do restrain users, those very restraints can actually foster greater critical reflection.

In general, teleconferences, like most computer tools, work best when you understand how they are meant to work best. For instance, instant messaging allows quick messaging to members of a group but is not meant for detailed messages that should be documented. It is still recommended, before going to teleconference, that you hold an extended face-to-face conference beforehand to form a sense of "groupness."[53] If you are in a virtual group, you have to find other ways to create this groupness, which can include directly asking for personal stories from members during the virtual meeting, including more personal touches in the instant messages and so forth.[54] Teleconferences benefit from the establishment of guidelines for participation before the conference and vigilant adherence to those rules. Rule creation and execution may be more potent in the virtual context than we have imagined.[55]

Computer Technology Designed for Group Problem Solving

Group support systems (GSS) or **group decision support systems (GDSS)** are computer-based hardware and software systems specifically designed to facilitate sound and efficient group problem solving. They also are called *groupware computer-supported cooperative work (CSCW) or electronic meeting systems (EMS)*.[56] Initially designed for use by face-to-face groups, these systems are available to virtual groups as well. For instance, one of us, in

Group Support Systems (GSS) or Group Decision Support Systems (GDSS)

Computer-based hardware and software systems designed to help groups improve a variety of group outcomes, such as creativity, problem solving, and decision making.

consultation with a local school board, recommended they use GSS technology to help them find closure on agenda items during regular meetings.

School board members met in a room designed for GSS meetings. Computers, all linked to each other, were configured in a U shape. A large overhead projection system was located at the open end of the U so that all board members could see the screen. Two faculty members served as trained facilitators for the meeting. One, working with the board's desires, mapped out which agenda items would be tackled: deciding which issues to focus on and what promotional strategies the board should use for the upcoming school bond levy. The other facilitator, positioned behind the operation desk, ran the GSS system for the meeting.

First the board members, at their stations, brainstormed about their first agenda item—which issues should be addressed during the bond campaign. Once generated, each sent their ideas to the central computer, and a master list of all anonymous ideas appeared on the overhead screen. Board members were allowed to comment on the items, anonymously, before a moderated, face-to-face discussion occurred. Board members then ranked the items and sent the rankings to the central computer, which produced overall rankings displayed in a bar graph to give the board a visual reinforcement for the members' opinions. A second face-to-face discussion followed, resulting in easy consensus. The board then proceeded, in similar fashion, to the next agenda item.

School board members reacted enthusiastically. Displaying the ratings and rankings for everyone anonymously showed more long-winded members that group consensus had already been achieved; so further discussion was not warranted. Their anonymity could have led to a lack of identification with each other and hollow decisions; however, in their case it worked for them.[57] When members are anonymous, they can be less inhibited, status differences can be reduced, quality of participation can be improved, and dominance by some members may be reduced.[58] These board members better analyzed and evaluated ideas while offering opportunities for everyone to contribute. GSS also provided them documentation of discussions so essential for the reflective assessment needed in good problem solving.

As you can see from this short example, GSS is designed to help groups perform the functions of effective problem solving reviewed in this chapter: generating ideas, organizing information, evaluating options, and making decisions.[59]

Different GSS address different problem-solving processes.[60] For example, some focus on just one step, such as the idea generation step of brainstorming. Others attempt to improve the entire decision-making process by providing structure for the overall process. Two of the most commonly known systems are GroupSystems and Software Assisted Meeting Management (SAMM); both include modules to help groups in every area of problem solving, such as group management, brainstorming, analysis, policy formation, evaluation and voting, exchanging comments on topics, and so forth.

GSS are an effective way for group members to consistently reflect on and adapt their problem-solving procedures. These systems have progressed so greatly over the years, becoming easier to use and requiring less direction by trained facilitators. They are designed to *support* group problem-solving and decision-making processes, not *replace* them. Used well, they help members focus on what they should do, but often don't do if groups are not vigilant enough on their own.

Jessup and Valacich, in their extensive review of GSS research, concluded that computer-supported decision making is as good as or better than traditional decision making.[61] However, given their advantages and disadvantages (see Table 10.15),[62] their effective use must take into consideration a variety of factors.

The first is the level of GSS support, which refers to how sophisticated a system is and how much intervention it provides into the group's natural problem-solving process. Simpler is not always better; sometimes systems with more sophisticated support produces better decisions and higher satisfaction.[63] The particular system used must be well matched to the task.[64] For example, some complex tasks require that information to be processed via many channels, including audio, video, and screen sharing. However, for other tasks, having an audio channel alone might be sufficient, as is the case with our audioconferences with our editors for this text.

Familiarity with the system is the second factor influencing GSS effectiveness. Hollingshead et al. observed that computer group members' poor initial performance seemed to be related to their unfamiliarity with using computer support, but those differences disappear over time.[65] They also noted that face-to-face groups are likely to outperform computer-mediated

TABLE 10.15
Advantages and Disadvantages of GSS

Advantages	Disadvantages
Provides anonymous reflection and evaluation of ideas diminishing status and dominance differences	GSS use is, overall, time consuming
Produces more ideas and alternative than face to face	Group members may not be comfortable nor trained in this type of computer use and may be resistant
Focuses members on problem solving steps	GSS structure can be experienced as too rigid
Organizes decision making discussions	Adaption to complex, cognitive tasks may not be suitable for GSS
Teaches members problem solving logistics in the doing of the GSS	
Focuses larger groups and shortens their meeting time	

groups on tasks, in which there is a correct answer, and negotiation tasks, in which members must reconcile their competing interests. These researchers warn managers planning to institute computer-mediated work groups that there may be initial declines in performance and dissatisfaction until members become comfortable with the technology.

The presence of a facilitator is the third factor affecting GSS performance. Poole et al. were surprised by their findings that, although groups using GSS exhibited more organized decision processes, they did not demonstrate improved critical thinking or more thorough evaluation of options.[66] However, the groups they studied had no facilitator support; these authors postulate that this, along with the level of GSS support as discussed earlier, were key factors hampering GSS effectiveness. Ideally, a facilitator should have a strong conceptual understanding of the technology and its capabilities, be able to make members comfortable with the technology and help them understand it, select the right technological system for the group, and have it prepared properly.[67] Skilled facilitation was a factor in the success of the school board meeting we described earlier. Today, with the increased user friendliness of these systems, the need for trained facilitators is lessening. However, the role facilitation can play in their use should always be considered.

To summarize, GSS are generally good for groups, although not useful in every circumstance.[68] Consistent assessment of GSS recommends that groups combine both modes of communication: computer and face-to-face.[69] When they are used consistently with their intended use, they can be very effective, but they don't eliminate the need for members knowledgeable about group processes and skilled in communication.

Recap: A Quick Review

Groups have many tools at their disposal and should use common sense in determining which tools to use.

1. The P-MOPS procedure is flexible; group members should tailor it by emphasizing some steps or eliminating others, depending on the type of problem facing the group.

2. Seven characteristics of problems help members decide which steps are essential and which are not. Task-related characteristics include task difficulty (how complex the task is) and solution multiplicity (how many possible solutions there are, potentially), and cooperative requirements (whether the task is a conjunctive one that requires substantial coordination among members).

3. Member characteristics include intrinsic interest (how genuinely interested members are in the issue) and population familiarity (whether the members have faced similar tasks in the past and are knowledgeable about how to approach the task).

(continued)

(continued)

4. Output characteristics include the acceptance requirements (whether the solution requires acceptance by those affected in order to succeed) and technical requirements (whether there are technical standards that must be met for the solution to be acceptable).

5. Several technologies are available to help groups, including instant messaging, e-mail, electronic bulletin boards, and interactive relay chat rooms.

6. When these technologies are used, it is important that members know how to use them and that guidelines encourage and motivate members to contribute and to use appropriate communication behaviors.

7. Teleconferences can include audio, video, and computer conferences. The effectiveness of these technologies is enhanced when members can meet face-to-face first to create a sense of "groupness."

8. Group support systems (or group decision support systems) are computer programs designed to help improve group problem solving. They may focus on one particular problem-solving step, such as idea generation, or may be designed to help the entire problem-solving process.

9. GSS groups generate more alternatives, make better decisions, and have more even member participation, but have difficulty with negotiation and complex tasks, take more time, have a harder time achieving consensus, and generally have lower member satisfaction.

QUESTIONS FOR REVIEW

 Go to self-quizzes on the Online Learning Center at mhhe.com/galanes14e to test your knowledge of the chapter concepts.

This chapter began with a description of a bad decision made by a university's Registration Staff regarding imposing fees for dropped and added classes; it also included a detailed description of a school board that used GSS to help decide two issues.

1. What do you see as the biggest problems with the way the decision was made by the Registration Staff? Which step or steps of P-MOPS seemed to have been handled most poorly?

2. What individuals or groups, in addition to the Registration Staff, could have participated in a RISK session before the drop-add decision was implemented? If you were in charge, whom would you have asked about possible risks?

3. What do you see as the characteristics of the problem regarding too many student drop-adds? How could the Registration Staff have modified P-MOPS to fit their problem?

4. Which procedure—P-MOPS, Single Question, or Ideal Solution—would you have used to discuss that issue?

5. Exactly how did the GSS process help the school board? Which features of GSS helped the board overcome its previous problems of not being able actually to decide anything?

KEY TERMS

 Test your knowledge of these key terms by visiting the Online Learning Center Web site at mhhe.com/galanes14e.

Acceptance requirements
Brainstorming
Brainwriting
Cooperative requirements
Electronic brainstorming
Group support systems (GSS)
   (group decision support
   systems (GDSS))
Ideal Solution Format

Intrinsic interest
Population familiarity
Problem census
Problem question
Procedural Model of Problem
   Solving (P-MOPS)
Program Evaluation and Review
   Technique (PERT)
RISK technique

Single Question Format
Solution multiplicity
Solution question
Task difficulty
Technical requirements

BIBLIOGRAPHY

Cathcart, Robert S., Larry A. Samovar, and Linda D. Henman, eds. *Small Group Communication: Theory and Practice.* 7th ed. Madison, WI: Brown & Benchmark, 1996, Section 3.

Hirokawa, Randy Y., and Marshall S. Poole, eds. *Communication and Group Decision Making.* Beverly Hills, CA: Sage, 1986, 81–111.

Jessup, Leonard M., and Joseph S. Valacich, eds. *Group Support Systems: New Perspectives.* New York: Macmillan, 1993.

Larson, Carl E., and Frank M. J. LaFasto. *TeamWork: What Must Go Right/What Can Go Wrong.* Newbury Park, CA: Sage, 1989.

McGrath, Joseph E., and Andrea Hollingshead. *Groups Interacting with Technology.* Thousand Oaks, CA: Sage, 1994.

Shaw, Marvin E. *Group Dynamics.* 3rd ed. New York: McGraw-Hill, 1981, Chapter 10.

NOTES

1. Carl E. Larson, "Forms of Analysis and Small Group Problem-Solving," *Speech Monographs,* 36 (1969): 452–55; Frank La Fasto and Carl Larson, *When Teams Work Best: 6,000 Team Members and Team Leaders Tell What It Takes to Succeed* (Thousand Oaks, CA: Sage, 2001): 84–90.

2. Carl E. Larson, "Forms of Analysis and Small Group Problem-Solving;" Alvin A. Goldberg and Carl E. Larson, *Group Communication: Discussion Processes and Applications* (Englewood Cliffs, NJ: Prentice-Hall, 1975).

3. Alvin A. Goldberg and Carl E. Larson, *Group Communication: Discussion Processes and Applications.*

4. For example, see Charles M. Kelly, Michael Jaffe, and Gregory V. Nelson, "Solving Problems," *Research Management,* 30 (1987): 20–23; Norman R. F. Maier and R. A. Maier, "An Experimental Test of the Effects of 'Developmental' vs. "Free' Discussions on the Quality of Group Decisions," *Journal of Applied Psychology,* 41 (1957): 320–23; and Randy Y. Hirokawa, "Group Communication

and Problem–Solving Effectiveness: An Investigation of Group Phases," *Human Communication Research,* 9 (1983): 291–305.

5. Alex Osborn, *Applied Imagination,* rev. ed. (New York: Scribner, 1975).

6. Paul Kirvan, "Brainstorming: It Is More Than You Think," *Communication News,* 28 (1991): 39–40.

7. Michael Schrage, "Meetings Don't Have to Be Dull," *The Wall Street Journal* (April 29, 1996): A22.

8. Vicky Putnam and Paul Paulus, "Brainstorming, Brainstorming Rules and Decision Making," *Journal of Creative Behavior,* 43 (2009): 23–39.

9. Graham Hitchings and Sara Cox, "Generating Ideas Using Randomized Search Methods: A Method of Managed Convergence," *Management Decision,* 30 (1992): 58.

10. R. Brent Gallupe, Alan R. Dennis, William H. Cooper, Joseph S. Valacich, Lane M. Bastianutti, and Jay Nunamaker, Jr. "Electronic Brainstorming and Group Size," *Academy of Management Journal,* 35 (June 1992): 350–70.

11. See also Joseph S. Valacich, Alan R. Dennis, and T. Connolly, "Idea Generation in Computer-Based Groups: A New Ending to an Old Story," *Organizational Behavior and Human Decision Processes,* 57 (1994): 448–68.

12. John Sosik and Bruce Avolio, "Inspiring Group Activity: Comparing Anonymous and Identified Electronic Brainstorming," *Small Group Research,* 29 (1998): 3–31.

13. Aaron Herman and Hussain G. Rammal, "The Grounding of the Flying Bank," *Management Decision,* 48 (2010): 1048–62.

14. Charles P. Koerber and Christopher P. Neck, "Groupthink and Sports: An Application of Whyte's Model," *International Journal of Contemporary Hospitality Management,* 15 (2003): 20–28.

15. Ibid.

16. Ibid.

17. Rebecca J. Welsh Cline, "Detecting Groupthink: Methods of Observing the Illusion of Unanimity," *Communication Quarterly,* 38 (1990): 112–26.

18. Carolyn J. Wood, "Challenging the Assumption Underlying the Use of Participatory Decision-Making Strategies: A Longitudinal Case Study," *Small Group Behavior,* 20 (1989): 428–48.

19. Ibid.

20. Anne Gero, "Conflict Avoidance in consensus Decision Processes," *Small Group Behavior,* 16 (1985): 487–99.

21. Koerber and Neck, "An Application of Whyte's Model."

22. Ibid.

23. Shaila M. Miranda, "Avoidance of Groupthink: Meeting Management Using Group Support Systems," *Small Group Research,* 25 (February 1994): 105–36.

24. Jay Hall, "Decisions, Decisions, Decisions," *Psychology Today* (November 1971): 51–54; 86–87.

25. Randy Y. Hirokawa, "Discussion Procedures and Decision-Making Performance: A Test of the Functional Perspective," *Human Communication Research,* 12 (1985): 203–24.

26. Randy Y. Hirokawa, "Group Decision-Making Performance: A Continued Test of the Functional Perspective," *Human Communication Research,* 14 (1988): 487–515.

27. Normal R. F. Maier, *Problem-Solving Discussions and Conferences: Leadership Methods and Skills* (New York: McGraw-Hill, 1963): 171–77.

28. Koerber and Neck, "An Application of Whyte's Model."

29. David R. Siebold, "Making Meetings More Successful: Plans, Formats, and Procedures for Group Problem Solving," in *Small Group Communication: A Reader,* 6th ed., eds. Robert S. Cathcart and Larry A. Samovar (Dubuque, IA: Wm. C. Brown, 1992): 187.

30. Annika Wiebow and Udo Konradt, "Two-dimensional Structure of Team Process Improvement: Team Reflection and Team Adaptation," *Small Group Research,* 42 (2011): 32–54.

31. Marvin E. Shaw, *Group Dynamics,* 3rd ed. (New York: McGraw-Hill, 1981): 364.

32. See, for example, John K. Brilhart and Lurene M. Jochem, "Effects of Different Patterns on

Outcomes of Problem-Solving Procedures," *Journal of Applied Psychology,* 48 (1964): 175–179; Ovid L. Bayless, "An Alternative Model for Problem-Solving Discussion," *Journal of Communication,* 17 (1967): 188–97; and Sidney J. Parnes and Arnold Meadow, "Effects of 'Brainstorming' Instruction on Creative Problem Solving by Trained and Untrained Subjects," *Journal of Educational Psychology,* 50 (1959): 171–76.

33. Shaw, *Group Dynamics,* 364.
34. Leonard Berkowitz, "Sharing Leadership in Small Decision-Making Groups," *Journal of Abnormal and Social Psychology,* 48 (1953): 231–38.
35. James H. Davis, *Group Performance* (Reading, MA: Addison-Wesley 1969).
36. Annette C. Easton, Nancy S. Eickelmann, and Marie E. Flatley, "Effects of an Electronic Meeting System Group Writing Tool on the Quality of Written Documents," *Journal of Business Communication,* 31 (1) (1994): 27–40.
37. Laura Hambley, Thomas O'Neill, and Theresa Kline, "Virtual Team Leadership: Perspectives From the Field," *International Journal of e-Collaboration,* 3 (January-March 2007): 40–64.
38. Judith Pena-Shaff, Wendy Martin, and Geraldine Gay, "An Epistemological Framework for Analyzing Student Interactions in Computer-Mediated Communication Environments," *Journal of Interactive Learning Research,* 12 (Spring 2001): 41–62.
39. Ibid.
40. Ibid.
41. Ibid.
42. Hambley, O'Neill, and Kline, "Virtual Team Leadership."
43. Tyrone Adams and Norman Clark, *The Internet: Effective Online Communication* (Fort Worth, TX: Harcourt, 2001): 105–07.
44. Hambley, O'Neill, and Kline, "Virtual Team Leadership."
45. John A. Short, Ederyn Williams, and Bruce Christie, *The Social Psychology of Telecommunications* (London: Wiley, 1976).
46. Hambley, O'Neill, and Kline, "Virtual Team Leadership."
47. Start Roxanne Hiltz, Kenneth Johnson, and Murray Turoff, "Experiments in Group Decision Making: Communication Process and Outcome in Face-to-Face versus Computerized Conferences," *Human Communication Research,* 13 (1986): 225–52.
48. Sharon L. Murrell, "The Impact of Communicating through Computers" (Unpublished doctoral dissertation, State University of New York at Stony Brook, 1983).
49. Vitaly J. Dubrovsky, Sara Kiesler, and Beheruz N. Sethna, "The Equalization Phenomenon: Status Effects in Computer-Mediated and Face-to-Face Decision-Making Groups, "*Human Computer Interaction,* 6 (1991): 119–46.
50. Start Roxanne Hiltz, Kenneth Johnson, and Murray Turoff, "Experiments in Group Decision Making, 3: Disinhibition, Deindividuation, and Group Process in Pen Name and Real Name Computer Conferences," *Decision Support Systems,* 5 (June 1989): 217–32.
51. Sara Keisler and Lee Sproull, "Group Decision Making and Computer Technology," *Organizational Behavior and Human Decision Processes,* 52 (June 1992): 96–123.
52. David H. Jonassen and Hyug II Kwon, "Communication Patterns in Computer Mediated Versus Face-to-Face Group Problem Solving," Educational *Technological Research and Development,* 49 (March 2001): 35–51.
53. Robert Johansen, Jacques Vallee, and Kathleen Spangler, *Electronic Meetings: Technical Alternatives and Social Choices* (Reading, MA: Addison-Wesley, 1979): 2.
54. Hambley, O;Neill, and Kline, "Virtual Team Leadership."
55. Joseph B. Walther and Ulla Bunz, "The Rules of Virtual Groups: Trust, Liking, and Performance in Computer-Mediated Communication," *Journal of Communication,* 55 (December 2005): 828–46.
56. Noshir S. Contractor and David R. Siebold, "Theoretical Frameworks for the Study of Structuring Processes in Group Decision Support Systems: Adaptive Structuration Theory and Self-Organizing Systems Theory," *Human Communication Research,* 19 (June 1993): 528–63.

57. Craig R. Scott, "The Impact of Physical and Discursive Anonymity on Group Members' Multiple Identifications during Computer-Supported Decision Making," *Western Journal of Communication, 63* (Fall 1999): 456–87.

58. Bolanle A. Olaniran, "Group Process Satisfaction and Decision Quality in Computer-Mediated Communication: An Examination of Contingent Relations," in *Small Group Communication: Theory and Practice,* 7th ed., eds. Robert S. Cathcart, Larry A. Samovar, and Linda D. Henman (Madison, WI: Brown & Benchmark, 1996): 134–46.

59. Marshall S. Poole, Michael Holmes, and Gerardine DeSanctis, "Conflict Management in a Computer-Supported Meeting Environment,"*Management Science, 37* (August 1991): 926–53; Leonard M. Jessup, Terry Connolly, and David A. Tansik, "Toward a Theory of Automated Group Work: The Deindividuation Effects of Anonymity," *Small Group Research, 21* (August 1990): 333–48; Hiltz et al., "Experiments in Group Decision Making."

60. For a more detailed description of these support systems, see Joseph E. McGrath and Andrea B. Hollingshead, *Groups Interaction with Technology* (Thousand Oaks, CA: Sage, 1994).

61. Leonard M. Jessup and Joseph S. Valacich, eds., *Group Support Systems: New Perspectives* (New York: Macmillan, 1993).

62. Susanna Opper and Henry Fresko-Weiss, *Technology for Teams: Enhancing Productivity in Networked Organizations* (New York: Van Nostrand Reinhold, 1992); Bolanle A. Olaniran, "Group Performance in Computer-Mediated and Face-to-Face Communication Media," *Management Communication Quarterly*, 7 (February 1994): 256–81; Marshall Scott Poole and Michael E. Holmes, "Decision Development in Computer-Assisted Group Decision Making," *Human Communication Research*, 22 (September 1995): 90–127; Marshall Scott Poole, Michael Holmes, Richard Watson, and Gerardine DeSanctis, "Group Decision Support Systems and Group Communication: A Comparison of Decision Making in Computer-Supported and Nonsupported Groups," *Communication Research*, 20 (April 1993): 176–213; Jessup and Valacich, eds., *Group Support Systems: New Perspectives.*

63. Izak Benbasat and Lai-Huat Lim, "The Effects of Group, Task, Contest, and Technology Variables on the Usefulness of Group Support Systems: A Meta-Analysis of Experimental Studies," *Small Group Research, 24* (November 1993): 430–62; V. Sambamurthy, Marshall Scott Poole, and Janet Kelly, "The Effects of Variations in GDSS Capabilities on Decision-Making Processes in Groups," *Small Group Research, 24* (November 1993): 523–46.

64. Steven M. Farmer and Charles W. Hyatt, "The Effects of Task Language Demands and Task Complexity on Computer-Mediated Work Groups," *Small Group Research, 25* (August 1994): 331–66.

65. Andrea B. Hollingshead, Joseph E. McGrath, and Kathleen M. O'Connor, "Group Task Performance and Communication Technology: A Longitudinal Study of Computer-Mediated versus Face-to-Face Work Groups," *Small Group Research, 24* (August 1993): 307–33.

66. Poole, Holmes, Watson, and DeSanctis, "Group Decision Support Systems and Group Communication."

67. Victoria K. Clawson, Robert P. Bostrom, and Rob Anson, "The Role of the Facilitator in Computer-Supported Meetings," *Small Group Research, 24* (November 1993): 547–74.

68. Poppy McLeod, "New Communication Technologies for Group Decision Making: Toward an Integrative Framework," in *Communication and Group Decision Making,* 2nd ed., eds. Randy Y. Hirokawa and Marshall Scott Poole (Thousand Oaks, CA: Sage, 1996): 426–61.

69. Scott, "The Impact of Physical and Discursive Anonymity on Group Members' Multiple Identifications during Computer-Supported Decision Making."

Managing Conflict in the Small Group

STUDY OBJECTIVES

As a result of studying Chapter 11, you should be able to:

1. Define conflict and explain both the positive and negative effects it can have on a group.

2. Describe a member who is an *innovative* or *opinion deviate* and explain how such a person can help a group improve its decision making.

3. Describe the four types of conflict that typically occur in small group interactions.

4. Describe the distributive (win–lose) and integrative (win–win) orientations and five specific conflict management styles and their tactics typically used to manage small group conflict.

5. Describe the ethical standards needed for dealing with conflict.

6. Explain how dimensions of culture affect how individuals perceive and manage conflict.

7. Explain the *principled negotiation procedure* for helping a group resolve conflict.

8. Explain three alternative methods for breaking a deadlock when negotiation fails, and describe a mediation procedure a group can use if it is deadlocked.

CENTRAL MESSAGE

If properly managed, the inevitable conflict during a small group's deliberations can improve problem solving and decision making by building cohesiveness and providing a variety of perspectives that promote critical thinking.

Student groups are a staple of university and college campuses and are often included in planning campus extracurricular activities, such as bringing in outside speakers to complement the learning that takes place in the classroom. On the surface, this kind of planning may appear straightforward and free of conflict, but often it is not. Lori, Kevin, Chris, Diedre, and Tony are members of a university Speaker Committee charged with planning their campus's speaker series. Kevin, Chris, Diedre, and Tony have volunteered for this group. Lori, as the elected student senator from the College of Arts and Humanities, chairs this committee.

Lori encouraged Tony to join the group because his interest in politics gives him access to numerous contacts locally and nationally. Tony talked her into encouraging his friend Kevin to volunteer after Chris and Diedre had volunteered. The group needed a fifth person and Kevin was eager to join. Lori hesitated because she questioned Kevin's commitment, but ultimately trusted Tony's judgment. Their first meeting did not begin well at all. Kevin, as Lori predicted, did not show up or contact anyone about his absence. Tony was quiet because he did not want to upset Lori any more than she already was and did not want to hurt his friendship with Kevin. When Lori asked for ideas for next year's speakers, she quickly learned that the rest of the members had different ideas about speakers than she did. Tony gently suggested that he and other students were tired of the same old "political" and education topics of national defense and terrorism issues. He thought it was time for some fun and hoped they could schedule entertaining speakers. Diedre confronted Tony directly by expressing a strong opinion that the speakers had to have educational value. Chris tried to mediate the conflicting opinions. Lori adjourned the meeting and called for everyone to bring more ideas to the next meeting. As she was leaving, she sarcastically remarked, "This is going to be fun!" Tony promised to get Kevin to the next meeting, after which Lori replied, "Good luck."

Small groups with different member qualities, affiliations, and viewpoints are ideally suited to produce the best decisions. However, the very characteristics that give the group diversity also provide the seeds of conflict. How to get along in this rapidly changing and diverse world is a topic on just about everyone's agenda. Pick up any popular general interest magazine and you will probably see an article about how to get along at work, at home, with friends. Sometimes, what you read may give you the impression that conflict should be avoided at all costs! The truth is that whenever individuals come together in any sort of social context, disagreement and conflict are inevitable. Trying to avoid conflict is futile and unwise.

Your cultural lens contributes to how you value, approach, and manage conflict.[1] Americans are ambivalent about conflict. Along with values that stress agreement and getting along, they say, "Stick to your guns." Americans have trouble reconciling the benefits of *both* harmony and conflict. Their more individualistic approach to conflict tends to emphasize the productive value of conflict and to directly confronting the issue at hand.

Individuals are encouraged to work it out in an open climate while sustaining individual dignity. Other cultures do not experience this tension to the same degree. Eastern cultures, in particular, see such apparently opposing concepts as harmony and conflict as yin and yang, sides of the same coin. Collectivist cultures like Japan and the Amish tend to see conflict as a threat to relational and community dignity; thus, they lean more toward avoiding open conflict and keeping silent. As you will see, different factors come into play and influence how group members manage the tension between harmony and conflict so that agreement *and* disagreement can contribute positively to a group's interaction.

Conflict is necessary to effective decision making and problem solving. By involving a group, you tacitly acknowledge the value of diversity, the same diversity that guarantees conflict. If your goal is simply understanding each others' diverse ideas, then that diversity is not problematic; however, if your goal is to solve a problem or make a choice, divergent ideas must be reconciled. Conflict *should* occur during group problem solving; if it doesn't, the group members aren't taking advantage of their diversity and are being swayed by their hidden profiles. Failure to express disagreement and avoiding discussion of conflict-producing issues leads directly to ineffective problem solving and poor decision making.[2]

Although too much conflict can hurt a group or even destroy it, our experience has been that groups of students have too little rather than too much conflict. Most of our students are afraid of disagreement and prefer groups with little or no conflict.[3] The more conflict members experience, the more negatively they view the group experience.[4] For that reason, this chapter stresses the benefits of conflict. We explain how to distinguish beneficial from detrimental conflict and how to manage conflicts to produce the best possible decision or solution.

A Definition of Conflict

A variety of definitions exist for **conflict.** We like Hocker and Wilmot's definition:

> *Conflict* is an expressed struggle between at least two interdependent parties who perceive incompatible goals, scarce resources, and interference from the other party in achieving their goals.[5]

This definition embodies several implications consistent with our emphasis on the central role that communication processes play in small group dynamics.

First, conflict as an *expressed struggle* indicates that conflict involves communicating. Although a group member may *feel* internal distress, this distress becomes interpersonal conflict *only when it is expressed,* whether verbally or in such subtle ways as not making eye contact or shifting nervously in one's chair.

Conflict

The expressed struggle that occurs when interdependent parties, such as group members, perceive incompatible goals or scarce resources and interference in achieving their goals.

Second, parties to a conflict must have an *interdependent* goal such that it is impossible for one person to attain the goal and not the others. Many secondary groups must produce something—a report, a proposal, a set of recommendations—that *all* group members must agree to. Such group members are interdependent; one cannot achieve the goal without the others. Therefore, they must find ways of reconciling diverse perspectives and beliefs affecting the decision. For example, Edd may detest Desha's views about what is appropriate treatment of laboratory animals, but that won't matter much unless both are in a group that is charged with recommending a university policy regarding treatment of laboratory animals. For the group to succeed fully, Edd and Desha must reconcile their views enough to collaborate on a policy each can support. However, their interdependence is accompanied by interference. Edd's disagreement with Desha interferes with Desha's having her way, and vice versa. This interference may take the form of Desha's trying to persuade the other group members to accept her view, Edd's trying to undercut Desha's credibility within the group, or Desha's sabotaging Edd's car so that he misses an important meeting.

Third, this definition suggests a number of things over which people conflict, such as *goals* and *scarce resources,* to which we add values, beliefs, and ways of achieving goals. We have observed numerous student groups whose members disagree on group goals. Maria's goal is to earn an A for a group presentation to the class, but Garry's goal is to do just enough to earn a C. Their divergent goals will cause a problem for the group. In contrast, assume that both Maria and Garry want to receive an A for the presentation, but Maria prefers to involve the class in an exercise followed by discussion, whereas Garry prefers to show and discuss a movie. In this instance, they agree on the goal, but differ on how to reach the goal. Suppose, instead, that Edd believes humans are superior to all other forms of life, which makes it appropriate for laboratory animals to serve human needs, but Desha values all animal life forms equally. This fundamental difference in values may make it impossible for their group to reach consensus on a policy regarding laboratory animals. It is also possible that Edd pushes for his idea because he is trying to be heard in a group where Desha's ideas are *always* supported—suggesting a conflict over perceived scarce resources—in this case, power.

Fourth, parties to a conflict must *perceive* that they are in conflict. This perceptual dimension is a very important one. There is nothing that automatically labels a situation as *conflict;* instead, conflict depends on how people perceive the situation. For instance, if Thomas disagrees with a proposal you have made, you have a *choice* about how to perceive Thomas's disagreement. You can say, "What a jerk! What makes him think he can do any better?" In this case, you have framed his disagreement as a conflict. However, you could also have said, "I wonder why Thomas disagrees. Maybe there's something in my proposal that I forgot to consider." In this latter case, you have framed his statement of disagreement as a possible attempt on Thomas's part to improve and strengthen your proposal. Thus, perception defines a situation as a conflict.

Perception of a situation is closely associated with emotions and behavior. To illustrate, your feelings can range from mild distress to out-of-control rage, depending on how you perceive the situation. If you think Thomas is a jerk for disagreeing with you or believe he disagreed just to make you look bad in some way, you will feel furious. Furthermore, you may be tempted to seek revenge or escalate the intensity of the conflict. On the other hand, if you perceive Thomas's disagreement to be motivated by a desire to strengthen your idea, then you may be only mildly hurt at his criticism, or even pleased that he cared enough to give your idea such a careful reading. In this latter case, you will behave cooperatively toward Thomas and collaborate to improve the proposal, not try to escalate the conflict. Thus, no perception of conflict, no conflict.

Your perceptions, emotions, and behavior merge with the other person's perceptions, emotions, and behavior to form a feedback loop (see Figure 11.1). Remember, you can't be in a conflict situation alone; your behaviors affect other people, as theirs affect you. Changing one of the elements will automatically change the others. Suppose you decide that Thomas is a jerk, so you rip his criticism of your proposal to shreds. That will certainly affect Thomas, who may now conclude that *you* are a jerk who just can't take constructive criticism. Thomas may now decide to

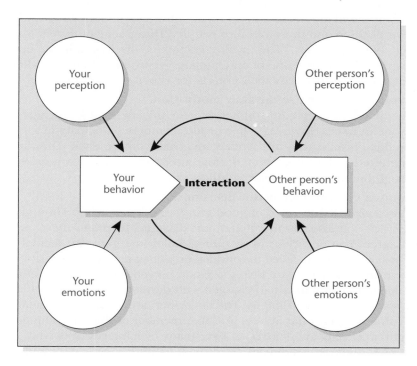

FIGURE 11.1
Perceptions, emotions, behavior, and interaction in a conflict

escalate the conflict or try to destroy your credibility within the group. On the other hand, if you indicate to Thomas that you genuinely want to know more about his criticism and the reasons for it, he may decide that you are an enlightened, cooperative group member whom he can trust and on whose good judgment he can rely. This may lead him to seek your opinions, support, and ideas in the future.

Positive and Negative Outcomes of Conflict

Communication scholars concur that conflict has both beneficial and harmful outcomes.[6] We will now examine some of these positive and negative effects.

Benefits of Conflict   Conflict can affect group decision making, teamwork, and satisfaction. Here are several potential benefits of conflict:

1. **Conflict can produce better understanding of both issues and people.**
    We often assume that most people see things as we do and feel as we do, and are often surprised to discover otherwise. When students discover others holding differing opinions on an issue, they become uncertain about their own positions, seek actively to get more information about the issue, are able to take the perspective of the other students, and are better able to retain information, both about their own position and those of other people.[7] Disagreement fosters learning about the issues.[8] The speaker committee discussion in the opening case about the value of entertaining versus educational speakers helped members clarify their criteria for choosing speakers.

2. **Conflict can increase member motivation.**
    People who do not care will not expend any energy disagreeing about an issue. However, when group members participate in a conflict episode, they are actively involved with the issue. They are interested and excited and pay close attention, so they learn more about the issue. Thus, some conflicts can be motivating.

3. **Conflict can produce better decisions.**
    This outcome is the goal of good *group* problem solving. Through conflict, you discover first that others disagree, then *why* they disagree. You find flaws in reasoning, holes in arguments, factors that other members failed to consider, or hidden profile biases that were ignored. Thus, you help the group prevent mistakes. One of us belonged to a campus staff charged with developing a plan for cutting costs at a commuter campus. The developer of the plan recommended closing the snack bar at 5 PM. Another member of the staff pointed out that closing at 5 PM would leave many evening students who came to the campus directly from work without food service and

might eventually lead to a drop in enrollment. After considerable debate, the committee decided to provide expanded vending machine service, which would accomplish the goal of cutting personnel and utility costs, but not leave the evening students without food.

4. **Conflict can produce greater cohesiveness among group members.**
   When a group experiences and resolves conflict successfully, the members learn that the ties holding the group together are strong enough to withstand disagreement. Most of us who have had serious arguments with significant others can recall the closeness we feel after we have "made up." Instead of driving us apart, the conflict serves as a catalyst to strengthen the bonds between us. So it is with groups. Disagreement that produces understanding and eventual consensus increases cohesiveness and improves the chance of success.[9]

Negative Effects of Conflict   Although conflict can be beneficial, we all have experienced its harmful consequences. If you have ever said to yourself after a group meeting, "I'll be glad when this project is finished; I hope I never have to work with these people again," you have experienced some of these harmful effects, which include hurt feelings, lowered cohesiveness, and even group dissolution. You will note, in the three negative effects of conflicts that we discuss below, a similarity to our previous points about defensive climates (Chapter 6) and unethical group behaviors (Chapter 1).

1. **Conflict can cause members to feel bad.**
   Most of us do not like to have others disagree with us. This is particularly true when others don't just disagree with an idea or proposal we give, but appear to devalue us as people. Their remarks feel caustic, even hostile. Members may be silent for fear of an attack, thereby depriving the group of valuable information and opinions. (We discuss later how you can deal with such an attack.) Moreover, even a conflict over issues and ideas can be carried on so long or turn into personal attacks that it increases tension and wears group members down to the point where they dread coming to meetings.

2. **Conflict can lower group cohesiveness.**
   If you believe that others in a group do not value your contributions, you will not be eager to spend time with that group. Prolonged conflict and attacks on one's self-concept loosen the bonds of attraction and cohesiveness, which can cause members to reduce the effort they put forth to achieve the group's objectives.

3. **Conflict can split a group apart.**
   A member who believes that a group dislikes his or her ideas, but finds support in other groups, will usually leave the group in which the conflict occurs. Conflict that goes on too long and too intensely tears members apart. One of us once observed a friendship group split up over a political issue. One side believed that busing was an

appropriate way to achieve racial equality; the other side disagreed. The two sides did not simply have an intellectual disagreement; they began to impugn each other's goodwill, ability to reason, and commitment to democratic values. Unkind things were said, a rift occurred, and the group died.

Expressing Disagreement in a Group

Deviate

A group member who differs in some important way from the rest of the group members; opinion or innovative deviates can help groups examine alternatives more thoroughly by forcing the group to take a closer look at something.

Many people are reluctant to express opinions that differ from a group's majority opinion because expressing such disagreement may cause such a person to be seen as a deviant member by the rest of the group. A **deviate** is a member who is viewed by the other members as substantially different in some *important* way from the others. Two common types of group deviates are members who do not participate and members who express incompatible views about the issues and test opinions of the group.[10] The second type is a potentially valuable one for a group, even though it may be uncomfortable for the deviate. Reluctant as you may be to express a deviant opinion, ethically you should do it for the good of the group. However, you do not want to rebelliously block or withdraw. Instead, you want to be an *innovative* or *opinion deviate,* someone who disagrees with a proposed action or decision of the group but who is strongly committed to the group and its goals. Diedre functions as an opinion deviate by stating the need for a speaker to have educational value.

Sometimes it is very hard for an opinion deviate to influence a group. Lindskold and Han found that it was nearly impossible for a single conciliatory member to influence a nonconciliatory group.[11] Thameling and Andrews also found that opinion deviates exerted little influence.[12] Other group members responded more emotionally to deviates than to conforming group members. A sex bias has also been observed: Members responded more cooperatively to male than to female deviates. Group members appeared to *perceive* male deviates as bright and well informed, and showed a willingness to work with them by asking for evidence, questions, additional information, and so forth; however, they were more likely to *perceive* female deviates as arrogant or overly confident.

However, even with all these caveats about the difficulty of being an opinion deviate, this kind of disagreement is valuable to the group, particularly for groups in the United States and other Western cultures. Innovative deviance has been found to account for one-fourth of group interaction, serving a critical thinking function.[13] Innovative deviance in the form of contradiction, challenging statements by other members, continuing a disagreement started by others, or agreeing with an assertion someone else had attacked was particularly helpful in the group's conflict and decision emergence phases. Furthermore, most innovative deviance occurred immediately prior to consensus, supporting the notion that conflicts can contribute to consensus.

A number of factors increase your chances of succeeding as an opinion deviate. First, express your opinion cautiously and carefully, as a loyal member of the group.[14] Members will trust your motives if you have already established your commitment to the group.

Social skill and timing are important, too. Diedre took a risk confronting Tony so directly at the very first meeting. Generally, opinion deviance is more accepted after a group has already built some cohesiveness and is at the stage when members expect direct expressions of opinion.

There is a high correlation between social skill and the use of verbal reasoning in conflict resolution, as well as a negative correlation of social skill with verbal aggression and physical violence.[15] Aggressive members are dominant and try to force ideas and practices on others compared to assertive members who respect self as well as others. Assertive innovative deviance is more beneficial than aggressive innovative deviance.

The quality and consistency of the argument matter, also. Garlick and Mongeau discovered that argument quality was the only factor that allowed a minority subgroup to influence majority attitudes.[16] Argument quality, not the number of members who support a position, seems to be a better predictor of group influence.[17] High-quality arguments provide a context for the argument ("It's in our charge that our speakers are supposed to supplement the educational component of classes.") and counteract potential objections ("I know that some students will not come if they think they're going to get another lecture, but with an educational speaker, many faculty will assign the lecture to their classes for extra credit.") In addition, successful minority subgroups are the most consistent in their arguments. This consistency allows them to maintain their initial stance and resist the arguments from the majority, especially if the majority presents an inconsistent line of reasoning. Deviant opinion, essential to a group, has to be skillfully and sensitively expressed.

Recap: A Quick Review

Groups should not avoid or suppress conflict. Conflict and harmony in groups are both beneficial and necessary aspects of group life. Conflict becomes an issue only when it is managed in anything but a constructive manner.

1. Cultural values offer a lens that can explain conflict differences. Individualistic cultures tend to have a hard time seeing both the benefits and disadvantages to conflict. They also prefer more directness in confronting conflict. Collectivist cultures have an easier time seeing the interdependence between harmony and conflict and prefer pacifist responses to conflict in an effort to preserve relationships.

2. Conflict is an expressed struggle between at least two interdependent parties who see incompatible goals, scarce resources, and interference from the other in reaching those goals.

(continued)

(continued)

3. Individuals or groups in conflict with each other are interdependent; the group goal cannot be reached for one and not the others.

4. Conflict is a communicative phenomenon emerging out of the perceptions of the parties. Group members can see, hear, and feel the conflict.

5. Constructively, conflict can help the group understand its members and issues better, improve member motivation, produce better decisions, and increase cohesiveness.

6. Destructive conflict makes members feel bad, lowers cohesiveness, and eventually splits the group apart.

7. Any member seen as significantly different from others in the group can emerge as a deviate. This can occur when disagreement is expressed.

8. Opinion deviates disagree significantly with one or more members, while showing commitment to the group goals.

9. Opinion deviancy should be done cautiously, in a climate of cohesiveness and trust. If opinion deviance is expressed assertively rather than aggressively, it can lead to effective decision making and management of conflict.

10. Group influence seems to depend on the quality and consistency of the arguments, the timing, and the social skill of the person expressing the argument.

Types of Conflict

As we have already shown, conflict in and of itself is neither necessarily helpful nor harmful to a group. What matters is what the conflict is about, how it is initiated, and how it is managed. Before we examine the primary types of conflict that can occur within a group and discuss the potential effects of each, we revisit a description of the conflict in our Speaker Committee. Every major type of conflict occurred in this group.

The Speaker Committee—Kevin, Lori, Chris, Diedre, and Tony—met several times, and still made little progress. Kevin either missed meetings or came late; the others were angry with him. The committee couldn't agree on anything. They continued to argue about whether they should select entertaining or educational speakers, whether they should book one major speaker or several lesser-known ones, whether they should decide by consensus or majority vote, and, most of all, what they should do about Kevin. Occasionally, one of the members would ask a question that encouraged the others to examine the criteria by which to make their decision, and occasionally a member would make a suggestion that received widespread support. In general, though, they exhibited problems in managing their conflicts. The conflicts in this group of students illustrate the four types of conflict described as follows.

Task Conflict   **Task conflict,** also called *substantive* or *intrinsic* conflict, is conflict over ideas, meanings, issues, and other matters pertinent (intrinsic) to the task of the group.[18] Task conflict, the *what* in small group conflict, and is the basis for effective decision making and problem solving. It provides the vehicle by which ideas, proposals, alternatives, evidence, and reasoning are challenged and critically examined, doubts are brought into the open, and the group works together to find the best solution. Opinion and innovative deviance described earlier are usually indicative of task conflict. In our example, the Speaker Committee debated whether an entertaining or educational speaker would be a better choice. The ensuing argument helped members clarify the purpose of the Speaker Series and presented good reasons for considering each type of speaker.

Relationship Conflict   **Relationship conflict,** also called *affective* or *extrinsic* conflict, is conflict that originates from interpersonal power clashes, likes and dislikes unrelated to the group's task.[19] It represents the *who* in small group conflict and is generally detrimental to the efficient functioning of any group. For example, Speaker Series committee members Lori and Kevin did not like each other and missed no opportunity to disagree or belittle each other. When Kevin agreed with Tony in preferring an entertaining rather than an educational speaker, Lori said, "I could have expected that from you. Let's not learn—let's party!" This statement revealed that Lori personalized the conflict with Kevin. Her dislike compounded the effects of disagreement over work procedures and ideas. She rarely failed to make sarcastic comments to Kevin throughout their meetings. Such conflict is both difficult to resolve and exceedingly harmful to the group.

Although the origin of this type of conflict is difficult to pin down, your coauthors' observations of numerous groups suggest that much of it is rooted in one person's acting as if he or she is superior, and another member's refusal to accept this difference in status or power. Most of this "I am better than you" signaling is nonverbal, projected by subtle patterns of vocal tones, postures, and head/body angles. Much of what is called interpersonal conflict emerges from a struggle for position and power, those scarce resources we mentioned in our definition of conflict. Research has indicated that group members are able to differentiate between personalized (relationship) and depersonalized (task) conflict.[20] Furthermore, the type of conflict affects group consensus. Because relationship conflict can impede resolution of task issues, Fisher and Brown recommend disentangling relationship and task goals and pursuing them independently.[21] This gives the parties a chance to resolve their task-related differences, even though they may never change their feelings about each other. We talk later about how you might do that.

Process Conflict   **Process conflict**, also called *procedural* conflict, is a third type of group conflict that involves both task and relationship dimensions.[22]

Task Conflict

Conflict resulting from disagreements over ideas, information, reasoning, or evidence.

Relationship Conflict

Conflict resulting from personality clashes, likes, dislikes, and competition for power.

Process Conflict

Conflict resulting from disagreement about how to do something and member contributions to the group.

The first dimension is *logistical*, a task-oriented dimension emerging out of issues related to the group's management of its charge, and represents the *how* of group problem solving. When group members disagree over how to distribute the work, scheduling, how to use their time best, which group tools are best for tracking their work, or whether they should make decisions by consensus or majority vote, they are struggling through logistics. In our Speaker Committee, Lori proposed splitting up the money available to the group and letting every member decide individually which speaker he or she would like to invite. Diedre countered with a more consensual way of selecting a speaker and provided a reason: "We should agree *as a group!* What if we all pick the same kind of speaker?" This disagreement over how members were to make their major decision is an example of process conflict with respect to logistics.

Conflict over Inequity The second process dimension involves *coordination*, a more relationally oriented dimension that emerges out of issues of distributing member responsibilities and workloads.[23] This category represents the *how much* of group work. We believe this kind of conflict is prevalent and serious enough to be identified as a separate conflict category. **Inequity conflict** occurs over perceived unfairness and workload inequity in the group. Group members do not seem to have equal workloads or contribute to the same degree or with the same quality. Inequity reduces satisfaction with the group and is associated with high levels of conflict.[24] In our Speaker Series Committee, Kevin's early behavior was perceived by Lori as irresponsible. His work and contributions came to be perceived as inadequate. Although Lori rode him the hardest about his lack of commitment, Chris, Diedre, and even his friend Tony mentioned Kevin's lack of follow-through and failure to complete assignments for the group. When Kevin showed up late again, Chris remarked, "I'm tired of waiting for the jerk. Let's get started." Later, Diedre directly confronted Kevin by describing his behaviors that indicated lack of commitment to the group ("You have missed two of the last four meetings and were late to the ones you did come to. You also didn't do what you said you were going to do."). Kevin's continued lack of commitment to the group also fed into Lori's dislike and her constant needling. She scrutinized Kevin's contributions more closely than those of other members and criticized comments he made while accepting the same comments from other members. Kevin's perceived inequity of effort created serious conflict with other members of the group and produced a situation where he was being required to measure up more perfectly to the group's performance norms.

As you can see the stress of inequity can lead to coalitions that in turn impact the management of group conflict.[25] **Coalitions** emerge in groups when members with access to few resources, minimal power, or little bargaining leverage seek out other members in an attempt to level the playing field. Kevin sought out his buddy Tony to side with him on the issue of

---

Inequity Conflict

Conflict about perceived unequal workloads or contributions to the group effort.

Coalition

Members who band together to pool their resources and power to try to increase their bargaining leverage.

bringing in more entertaining speakers. Lori, however, singled Kevin out for wanting to party rather than learn (although she also recognized "Tony's idea" as worth considering). Coalitions also form when group members come to identify more with a subgroup than with the group as a whole or when some members have tended to accommodate to others' ideas; those who accommodate may join forces in a coalition to try and get the upper hand. Low-status members or those who hold minority opinions sometimes have more success in being heard if they talk to one other group member rather than the entire group.[26]

While sometimes functional, coalitions can also be detrimental. As we mentioned, conflict involves perceptions, including how group members identify with each other. In mixed-sex groups with high sex dissimilarity, members with strong gender identifications tend to identify strongly with other members of the same sex, perceive more relationship conflict in the group, and act accordingly.[27] This is particularly true of men in mixed-sex work teams. Additionally, members may become willing to sacrifice their own goals in an effort to defeat the most popular member. If Kevin successfully unites with Tony and others against Lori, the group can self-destruct. However, if the members seek a common ground, producing the best speaker list for their university, they can help dissipate the negative impact of warring coalitions.

Computer-mediated (CMC) groups—whether they use simple e-mail to keep in contact or sophisticated group support systems to help them problem solve—tackle similar issues of conflict as face-to-face groups do. Early research comparing face-to-face to CMC groups found inconsistent results.[28] While CMC groups used more inflammatory, profane, and negative language compared to face-to-face groups, when groups used group support systems (GSS, discussed in Chapter 10) and adapted to them well, members exhibited *less* task and relationship conflict. This inconsistency suggests when CMC groups take time to get to know each other and to adapt appropriately to the computer technology, destructive conflict may be lessened.

A study comparing three types of conflict (task, relationship, and process) on both CMC and face-to-face groups found that CMC groups showed more relationship and process conflict at first, but the differences disappeared over time.[29] Both the CMC and face-to-face groups exhibited similar amounts of task conflict. Apparently, the anonymity of CMC groups suppresses the social norms people follow to support and maintain positive self-images. Conflict declines over time as members get to know each other. The early process conflict is explained by members' initial focus on how to use the computer technology. Groups using computer conferencing formats actually report liking the way the format allows them to focus on the task and manage their process needs.[30]

Essentially, CMC groups do not follow the same conflict patterns as face-to-face groups, but they do reach comparable levels over time. Groups that use any type of computer technology need to give themselves the time for social development. They should even consider meeting face-to-face, initially, giving themselves the opportunity to establish social and procedural norms acceptable to their group.[31]

Group members easily recognize all three types of group conflict.[32] Although described as distinct, they are not mutually exclusive. Process conflict, given its task and relationship dimensions, can be used to mask relationship or task conflict. For instance, group members can genuinely disagree over procedures, but sometimes use procedural conflict to side-step another task conflict another task conflict by forcing a vote or otherwise regulating the group's work.[33] Process conflict can seem to be a straightforward difference over how to logistically manage group work, but it may be rooted in differing member needs for structure versus freedom. Those high in needs for procedural order are more comfortable with linear procedures than those who prefer less structure.

These conflict types are dynamic, and all three involve human emotion.[34] One type can lead easily into another. Relationship conflict, in particular, is neither the cause of poorly managed task or process conflict or the consequence of poorly managed task and process conflict—it can be both. You can see this in our Speaker's Series Committee. Lori, whose dislike for Kevin (relationship) combined with Kevin's inequitable participation (process/contribution) and his disagreements with Lori (task) intensified Lori's dislike. She was most relieved when Kevin left the group. The dual dimensions of process conflict—that is, its task and relationship characteristics—explain why group members can be dissatisfied with perceptions of unfairness (process/contribution) yet not experience poor performance (process/logistical)—in the short term.[35] Process conflict, on the other hand, is problematic because its dual dimensions can render it more ambiguous than task or relationship. Studies of high-performance teams show that early process conflict, with its potential to become personal, can spill over into later stages of problem solving, leading to both task and relationship conflicts.[36] High levels of this conflict, especially if it is about the fairness of member contributions, if left unresolved, may so damage the group that later attempts to resolve it may be too late. These findings show us the importance of the early development of conflict management strategies.

Managing Conflict

We hope we have convinced you of the value of innovative, opinion deviance and task and process conflict during small group problem solving. Conflict is inevitable when people meet in groups. Avoiding it *circumvents the very reason for engaging in group discussion*—that the thinking of several people is likely to be more valid and thorough than the thinking of one person acting alone. Members' attitudes and the procedures they use to manage conflict affect the outcomes. Using further examples of the Speaker Committee, we discuss how to manage conflict so it is productive.

Basic Approaches Toward Conflict Management

Most people have a basic attitude or approach toward managing conflict, either *distributive* or *integrative*. The **distributive approach,** also called a *win–lose* attitude, assumes that what one person gains is at another's expense. Thus, there can be only one winning side; the others are losers. In the Speaker Committee, Tony and Kevin wanted to choose an entertaining speaker and Diedre and Lori wanted an educational one. The distributive orientation assumes that only one faction can win. *Either* Tony and Kevin get their entertaining speaker, *or* Lori and Diedre get their educational one. Whichever wins, the other side loses.

The **integrative approach** assumes that there is some way to manage the conflict so that all parties can end up winners; in other words, the main concerns of all parties can be integrated into a solution in which all involved receive what is most important to them. Someone with an integrative orientation would assume that a speaker could be found who is *both* entertaining *and* educational; thus, both factions can win. This approach has also been called a *win–win* attitude. A group may not be able to integrate the concerns of *all* members into its final solution or decision. Members' values may be so divergent that they cannot be merged, or resources are so scarce that needs cannot be fully met. In such cases, perhaps partial integration— *compromise*—is the best that can be achieved. However, even if a group cannot develop a fully integrative solution, it *certainly* will not develop one if members begin with the premise that integration is impossible. Without an integrative orientation, members will not spend any energy developing creative solutions, but will spend their time trying to beat the other side.

In a longitudinal study of 11 work groups in large American organizations, Kuhn and Poole discovered that the work groups that took the time and energy to create more integrative solutions to their problems, compared to those that merely confronted or avoided them, produced more effective decisions.[37] In addition, the work groups that used a more integrated conflict style also managed to fulfill other communicative functions effectively. They met the issues head on, worked through obstacles to their problem, and recognized that they needed to work together on the problem. These work groups used the difficult task of integration to develop group norms and rules that effectively guided them in future interaction.

Kuhn and Poole's study shows us that integrative solutions do not just happen, but take hard work and time. Schie and Rognes's exploration of member motivational orientations helps explain why.[38] Member characteristics are critical input variables to a group system. Such characteristics affect group processes, including conflict. For example, some members display individualistic orientations toward conflict by pursuing *their* goals, not group ones, and typically use distributive behaviors that are often defensive. In contrast, members with cooperative orientations pursue goals that integrate their personal goals with the group ones; they use integrative behaviors that are supportive to negotiate disagreement.

Distributive Approach

The conflict management approach that assumes fixed resources must be distributed among parties to the conflict; thus, whatever someone wins, someone else loses.

Integrative Approach

The conflict management approach that assumes that solutions can be created to satisfy every party to the conflict.

Schie and Rognes found that different member orientations influenced how members managed resources during disagreement and members' judgments of fairness. Individualists showed a willingness to exploit resources and use distributive behaviors to get their goals met. Groups composed of all cooperatively oriented members had the highest ratings of fairness compared to mixed groups. This suggests that using distributive behaviors may be effective on one level but may hurt perceptions about how fair the process was. Group members need to be prepared to deal with distributive approaches or risk being exploited or hurt by such approaches.

Labeling integrative group behaviors as all good and distributive as all bad oversimplifies these approaches and is misleading.[39] Members who come into task conflict with expectations the conflict will be competitive may experience integrative actions, initially, with suspicion because those actions violate their expectations. Group members who have high expectations of competiveness tend not to be dissatisfied with distributive

Recap: A Quick Review

Small group conflict comes in many forms and is managed in a variety of styles, all of which differ in their effectiveness and appropriateness.

1. When groups engage in task-related conflict, they are engaged in substantive conflict. This intrinsic conflict is beneficial to the group if managed well.

2. Affective conflict emerges over interpersonal clashes between members and is extrinsic to the task. This kind of conflict is rooted in power and status struggles between group members.

3. When group members engage in conflict over how to proceed, they are involved in procedural conflict. Procedural conflict can mask affective conflict.

4. Groups using computer-mediated communication should take time to get to know each other and the computer technology; this helps reduce the amount of affective and procedural conflict that can occur early in these groups compared to face-to-face groups.

5. The unequal distribution of work and member contributions to the task is fertile ground for small group conflict. The stress from the inequality often leads to the formation of coalitions that often battle each other and move the group away from its central task.

6. Conflict styles can be divided into two broad approaches: distributive and integrative.

7. Distributive approaches are grounded in win–lose criteria for managing the conflict and integrative ones are grounded in win–win criteria. Both affect the task and the socioemotional dimensions of group dynamics.

8. Member characteristics such as motivational orientations and task conflict expectations influence the use of distributive and integrative approaches. Integrative solutions do not just happen; they require reflection and adaptation.

behaviors—in the short term. This suggests that groups high in competitive expectations "shape" their behavior by initially being competitive, building trust, and then move into more collaborative actions.[40] Integrative and distributive approaches to conflict show us that dealing with conflict is, again, a complicated dynamic among perceptions, emotions, and behavior. We now turn to a discussion of more global conflict management styles.

Conflict Management Styles and Tactics

Your perception of the conflict situation is a major determinant of how you are likely to deal with the conflict.[41] Elements of the situation include your perceptions about whether the conflict is repetitive, the degree to which you and the other party have mutual goals, how certain you are about how to solve the problem, whether you believe the other party is the source of the conflict, and the degree of negative feelings you have for the other. These combine to influence your desire to cooperate. The specific management style you choose is likely to be a product both of how cooperative and how assertive you are, as illustrated in Figure 11.2.[42]

As you can see, each *style* represents a general pattern of behavior developed over time. Specific communication choices that people make in particular situations as they manage conflict will be referred to as conflict *tactics*. The key difference between a style and a tactic is the degree to which a person is aware of his or her behavior.[43] Generally, we are less

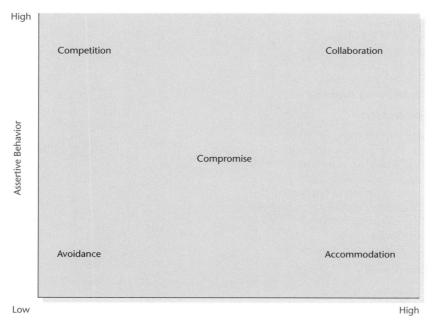

FIGURE 11.2
Your conflict management style depends in part on how assertive and cooperative you are

aware of our styles than our tactics, but competent group members are aware of not only their own preferred style and tactics but also those of other group members. This awareness is a key factor in changing unproductive patterns of conflict in a group. As we discuss each of the general conflict styles, we will also introduce you to common tactics that group members may use relevant to each style. These styles and representative tactics are summarized in Table 11.1.

Although no conflict style is always best, some conflict styles are perceived as more appropriate in certain circumstances. We recommend a

TABLE 11.1
Conflict styles and tactics

Avoidance

Denial
Topic changes
Noncommittal remarks
Irreverent remarks

Accommodation

Giving up/giving in
Disengagement
Denial of needs
Expression of desire for harmony

Competition

Personal criticism
Rejection
Hostile imperatives
Hostile jokes
Hostile questions
Presumptive remarks
Denial of responsibility

Collaboration

Analytic remarks
    Descriptive statements
    Qualifying statements
    Solicitation of disclosure
    Solicitation of criticism
Conciliatory remarks
    Support
    Concessions
    Acceptance of responsibility

Compromise

Appeal to fairness
Suggest a trade-off
Offer a quick, short-term solution

contingency view in which the most productive way for settling a conflict depends on time pressures, distribution of information and skills, group member values and needs, and other input variables, including culture, which we discuss later.

Each conflict style is appropriate under certain circumstances, but having an integrative orientation is preferred in most problem-solving discussions, especially for those task groups that have developed a history and thus must attend to both the task and social dimensions of their interactions. In practice, however, we sometimes find ourselves in temporary task groups with strangers who are asked to make relatively quick decisions that will have more of an impact on individuals outside the group than on the group itself.[44] For example, one of your coauthors chaired an academic department that underwent a self-study. An *ad hoc* committee was formed of members who did not know each other; they had three days to complete their task, after which they disbanded to go their separate ways. They did not have the usual time to build a strong cohesive climate; their decisions affected others (the department), but not themselves. How do you think this group's composition, time frame, and task influenced whether members used integrative, solution-oriented styles?

Group members generally perceive integrative styles as more competent, also. Integrative, solution-oriented, and less confrontational styles are related to group member satisfaction, improved productivity, increased decision quality, and are seen as more effective.[45] However, sometimes there is little time for collaborative decision making. In such cases, a group must balance passive tactics (e.g., giving in, avoiding the subject) with confrontational, controlling ones. Passive styles promote coming to an agreement too soon, without examining options carefully. Confrontational styles, while sometimes effective in the short term, risk harming member relationships. When you are in a temporary, short-term task group, steer clear of passive tactics and balance confrontational tactics with integrative ones whenever you can.

Avoidance   The **avoidance** style is a passive approach in which a person expends no energy discussing or exploring options. The member who disagrees privately but says nothing is avoiding conflict. Sometimes called *nonconfrontation,* conflict avoidance reduces satisfaction in groups.[46] As we stated earlier, avoiding is particularly detrimental to task groups that have a relatively short time to solve a problem. In addition, avoiding conflict over perceived inequity of member contributions only sets up the group for more conflict later. Such passive behavior is appropriate only when the problem is unimportant and the risks of making a poor decision are slight. For example, a committee to which one of us belonged was asked to develop a decorating plan for a student lounge/study area. The art instructor on the committee recommended a color scheme not particularly appealing to the chemistry professor on the committee. The students liked

Avoidance

The passive conflict management style that ignores a conflict.

the colors, so the chemistry professor kept his objections to himself. He reasoned that because he spent so little time in the lounge, color did not matter much to him.

Individuals avoid conflict by using tactics such as denying, managing the topic, and making noncommittal or irreverent remarks.[47] A group member expresses to you that another member, Kevin, is not doing his fair share of the work and something needs to be done. A response such as "I don't see that as a problem" can be construed as *denial*. Or "We are winding down our meeting and need to get to the next agenda item," effectively *shifts the topic* away from the potential issue. A *noncommittal remark* might be, "You know that is Kevin being Kevin." Replying with laughter to the concern is considered an *irreverent remark* that also tries to avoid conflict.

Accommodation

The conflict management style in which one person appeases or gives in to the other.

Accommodation **Accommodation,** also called *appeasement,* is a highly cooperative but passive approach that occurs when you give in to someone else. It may occur when the issue is not important to you, or when the relationship is more important to you than the outcome. For instance, in the Speaker Series Committee, after a brief discussion about educational versus entertaining speakers, Tony said, "I can go along with an educational speaker. I just want to avoid this arguing." Tony wanted to accommodate in order to end the arguments. Accommodation is appropriate only when the issue is relatively unimportant to you, the relationship is more important than the issue, or the other person's needs are genuinely more important to you. Don't accommodate just to end a fight, because the resentment you carry around with you may eventually poison the relationship anyway.

Tony's accommodating tactic is referred as an *expression of desire for harmony* tactic. Tony goes along with an educational speaker in a personal effort to curtail the arguing. Three other accommodating tactics include variations of *giving up/giving in, disengagement,* and *denial of needs.*[48] Had Tony responded with "Have it your way; let's bring in the educational speaker!" he would have given up the conflict. Disengagement would be characterized with a remark such as "You know, I will not even be here for the speaker, so do what you want." Denial of his needs can be found in "It's OK; go ahead with the speaker you want."

Competition

The uncooperative, aggressive conflict management style in which one person attempts to dominate or force the outcome to his or her advantage.

Competition **Competition** is a highly aggressive, uncooperative style in which one person tries to win over another. Sometimes called *dominating* or *forcing,* competition is appropriate when you have strong beliefs about something and you perceive that other approaches will not allow your needs to be acknowledged or accommodated. However, competitive approaches can damage relationships and may end up doing more harm than good. In the Speaker Series Committee, Lori and Kevin competed. Lori threatened to quit the group if only entertaining speakers were chosen, and Kevin told Tony not to accommodate so readily because he, Kevin, had plenty of good arguments left in support of entertaining speakers.

Both statements imply that the speaker will do whatever is necessary to get his or her way.

Competitive style tactics include such actions as personal criticism, hostile joking, rejection, and hostile questions.[49] These obviously denote a win–lose orientation and involve one-upping the other party. Lori's *hostile imperative* served as a threat to leave the group if Kevin got his way. Kevin, on the other hand, created a coalition with Tony to gang up on Lori. Competitiveness between Lori and Kevin can be expressed in other ways. Both may have *personally criticized* the other with remarks such as, "Lori, you are so selfish and unconcerned about the rest of us." Kevin could show *rejection* of Lori's hostile imperative by responding to her with, "Go ahead and quit—we don't need you," effectively dismissing her threat and attacking her personally. A *hostile question* that demeans another person could come in the form of a remark from Lori such as "Kevin, who does most of the work for this group?" Kevin, on the other hand, could attribute feelings to Lori that she has not acknowledged in a *presumptive remark* such as "Lori, you're just making yourself miserable threatening to quit." Parties in competition also have at their disposal tactics that are designed to *deny personal responsibility* for the conflict. How could Lori deny any personal responsibility for the conflict between her and Kevin?

Collaboration   Collaboration, also called *negotiating* or *problem solving,* is a cooperative and assertive style that stems from an integrative attitude. It encourages all parties to a conflict to work together in searching for a solution that meets everyone's needs. In the Speaker Series Committee, Diedre eventually suggested that the committee look for a speaker who was both entertaining and educational. In doing this, she assumed that both important needs of the factions could be met without either faction having to give up anything, that each faction's "must-have" point could be accommodated. Collaborative solutions can be ideal because all members of groups that arrive at collaborative solutions believe they have won without the others having lost. However, collaboration often takes more time than other approaches and certainly takes more energy. In addition, members with expectations for competitive task conflict may, initially, be suspicious of collaborative behaviors.

Compared to competitive tactics, collaborative ones focus on mutual rather than individual concerns and attempt to facilitate gains for all parties involved in the conflict.[50] They recognize the interdependence between parties. The first major category of collaborative tactics is *analytical remarks*. These facilitate collaboration by describing and disclosing important information as the parties try to maximize their gains. These kinds of statements are most like the kind you would expect in a supportive versus defensive group climate. Descriptive statements are nonevaluative remarks about events such as "We have confirmed the availability of individual speakers that fit both categories, including some that could be both educational

Collaboration

The assertive, cooperative conflict management style that assumes a solution can be found that fully meets the needs of all parties to a conflict.

and entertaining." *Qualifying remarks* from group members would define the nature of the conflict between members. For instance, Chris could say, "Lori and Kevin appear to disagree over the kind of speaker we could get, but I sense that both would entertain the idea of a speaker who could be both entertaining and educational." Group members can also *solicit both disclosure and criticism* in a nonhostile fashion. Tony could add to the discussion by soliciting from Lori what she meant by saying she would quit. Diedre could also solicit criticism of herself by asking for feedback from the group about her behaviors in the conflict between Lori and Kevin.

The second category of collaborative tactics involves those that are conciliatory; they demonstrate one's role in the conflict and display a willingness to work toward mutual gain.[51] For example, Kevin could back off his attacks of Lori and show *support* for her feelings: "I can see why you would want to quit, Lori." Lori, on the other hand, can reconcile with Kevin by showing a willingness to be flexible, offering a *concession,* rather than threatening to quit if she does not get her way. Important to collaboration is recognizing your role in the conflict and thus being accountable for the nature of the conflict. Kevin could show this *acceptance of responsibility* by acknowledging how he had let the group down by not doing his fair share.

Compromise

The conflict management style that assumes each party must give up something to get something.

Compromise   A **compromise,** also called a *shared outcome,* assumes that each party to the conflict will have to give up something in order to gain something more important. In the Speaker Series Committee, Chris suggested a compromise when he said: "Maybe we can get two speakers, less expensive—one educational and one entertaining." Each faction would have to agree to give up the idea of bringing in one very well-known speaker. Thus, compromises entail some losses for both parties. For this reason, we recommend attempting to find a collaborative, fully integrative solution when the decision is important to all group members. However, we think that compromise should *not* be considered a dirty word! When collaborative resolution is impossible or takes more time than is available, a compromise is a desirable and ethical outcome, especially if each group member feels that what he or she had to give up is fair in comparison with what others had to give up.

Chris's suggestion that they get two speakers by compromising their desires for one well-paid speaker is an example of a *suggested trade-off* tactic common to compromise.[52] He could have also *appealed to fairness* by remarking, "Lori and Kevin, you both got what you wanted last time, so this time let's go with two speakers." *Offering a quick short-term solution,* "We do not have time to complain about this; let's ask the educational speaker because we can get her immediately," is also an option for the group.

Expressing Disagreement Ethically

Ethical behaviors in conflict situations are those that promote the beneficial outcomes of conflict (e.g., greater understanding of issues, increased cohesiveness) while minimizing the destructive outcomes (e.g., hurt feelings, personal attacks). The following suggestions will help members behave with integrity and sensitivity during conflicts:

1. **Do express your disagreement.**
   Not confronting disagreements can reduce satisfaction with the group, and failure to express honest disagreement circumvents the decision-making and problem-solving process in a group. By not speaking up when you disagree, you deprive the group of potentially valuable information. In a sense you deceive, because your silence suggests that you agree.

2. **Stick with the issue at hand.**
   When you disagree, deal directly with the issue under discussion. Do not bring up side issues or allow hidden agenda items to motivate you.[53] Remember to separate process issues dealing with logistics from those dealing with fairness.

3. **Use rhetorical sensitivity.**
   Be sensitive and perceptive enough to select words that will not push others' emotional buttons. Be a high self-monitor, observing the effects of your statements on others and adjusting as appropriate. Use persuasion, not threats, to make your points.[54]

4. **Disagree with the idea but do not ever criticize the person.**
   Express disagreement so that it does not devalue the person with whom you disagree. Thus, "One flaw in your proposal to shut down the snack bar is that it does not consider the food service needs of evening students" is far superior to "You inconsiderate bozo! What are the evening students supposed to do for food?" Above all, no name-calling or personal attacks!

5. **Base your disagreement on evidence and reasoning.**
   Disagreements should be reasonable and substantive, based on evidence and reasoning.[55] They should not be based on rumor, innuendo, unsubstantiated information, or emotionalism. If you have no evidence or your reasoning is shown to be potentially faulty, *agree* instead of quarreling. As much as possible, keep the conflict issue based. This has the added advantage of being more likely to be persuasive.

6. **React to disagreement in a spirit of inquiry, not defensiveness.**
   Group members' reactions to argument are more important than the arguments themselves in creating group polarization.[56] If someone disagrees with you, do not react defensively as though you had been attacked personally. Keep your mind open to others' ideas, evaluations, and suggestions. Listen actively to your fellow member's remarks. Consider member motivations and expectations that might be "behind" their comments. Be certain that the person disagreeing has understood your position correctly, then clarify any

misunderstandings, and work together to search for the most effective solutions. In this way you can make conflict work *for* rather than *against* the group. This may not be easy! But it will benefit the group and you will have a clear conscience.

7. **If someone persists in attacking *you*, stay calm and speak reasonably.**
   One of the biggest challenges a group member has is to respond to a personal attack by another. The worst thing you can do is be bullied into being silent! Instead, confront the attacking member calmly and reasonably, explaining how you feel and what you want the other to do: "I resent your personal attacks, and I think they are inappropriate. I am willing to listen to your objections, but I want you to stop your attacks now." If the attacker was caught up in the heat of the moment, he or she may apologize and calm down. If your initial confrontation doesn't succeed, ask for the *group's* intervention: "Do we all think personal attacks are unacceptable behavior?" The other members, who probably are as uncomfortable as you, will now be encouraged to support you in confronting the attacker.

8. **Use an integrative rather than a distributive approach to solving the conflict.**
   Assume that there is a way to satisfy, at least partially, the important needs of all parties to the conflict. Use your energy to search for alternatives that integrate all parties' needs, not to destroy the other party. Act in ways that improve, not damage, the relationship. Principled negotiation, discussed later, helps you do that. Remember that a solution satisfying all parties will be more lasting than one leaving one party feeling disgruntled or mistreated. Also, consider the ethics of a person who gains pleasure from beating another in a way that damages the *group!*

Cultural Factors in Conflict

The tips we have given you about expressing conflict openly and directly apply in the United States but may not be appropriate for conflicts occurring in other cultures or for intercultural conflicts. Even in other Western cultures, people differ in their approaches to conflict, as Klopf and McCroskey explain:

> German negotiators are technically oriented, disciplined and orderly. The British want to get the job done properly in a civil and reserved manner. The French love to debate issues. In Spain, foreign negotiators need to be patient because the Spanish want to know and like with whom they interact.[57]

The dimensions along which cultures differ, described in Chapter 4, also affect how cultures perceive and deal with conflict. Two dimensions are particularly salient: individualism/collectivism and high and low context. Ting-Toomey and Oetzel note that in collectivist cultures, task and relational issues often blend, so that people are more likely to take person-ally what others might see as issue-related conflict.[58] Because the needs of the group predominate in collectivist cultures, conflict is perceived as threatening the harmony of the group. Openly expressing conflict—particularly in a loud or hostile way—is not considered appropriate. Con-flict is usually handled through avoidance, accommodation, and in indirect ways. In contrast, individualistic cultures value individuality; people are more likely to express conflict directly, to speak up for what they want and believe, and to try to *do something* about a conflict.

Facework, the communication strategies people use for preserving their own or others' self-esteem (or *face*), is emphasized differently in col-lectivist and individualistic cultures. People from individualistic cultures are more concerned with saving their own face, whereas people from collectiv-ist cultures are more concerned with saving the other person's face.[59] Indi-vidualistic people do not worry about backing someone else into a corner or forcing them to comply. Collectivist people will avoid backing another into a corner because that leaves the person with no way to save face.

The high- and low-context dimension also affects how people approach conflict.[60] In low-context cultures, such as that of the United States, the words convey the bulk of the meaning. In such cultures, individuals prefer straight talk and direct expression of conflict. Members of such cultures are advised to "go directly to the person you are in conflict with" to attempt to resolve the issue. In contrast, people from high-context cultures rely on the context and the nonverbal signals to understand what something means. They prefer subtle, ambiguous communication, nonverbal nuances, and tend to avoid direct expression of conflict. Conflict will be expressed indirectly, perhaps with the help of a third party.

We presented this brief discussion of intercultural conflict here sim-ply to alert you that how we handle conflict in the United States is not universal. We have oversimplified the discussion, and we remind you that there is great individual variation within all cultures. Individuals from the same culture will not all behave in the same way. For example, although collectivist cultures such as Japan's may prefer an integrative conflict style that values harmony, the style may change, depending on the context.[61] Japanese avoid conflicts over values and opinions with acquaintances but may disagree openly with close friends. In conflicts of interest, Japanese have no problem being confrontive and dominant with acquaintances.

Conflict is difficult enough to handle when the parties are from the same culture. When parties represent different cultures, including co-cultures such as race, gender, and age, the difficulties multiply. We urge you to wade into intercultural conflict waters carefully and with forethought.

No matter how skilled and ethical group members are at expressing disagreement, they can still crash on the rocks of conflict if their pro-cedures for handling conflict are poor. We next describe the principled negotiation procedure for managing conflict, then present five techniques if negotiation procedures fail.

Facework

Communication strategies used for preserving one's own or others' self-esteem (or *face*).

Recap: A Quick Review

General patterns of integrative and distributive behaviors used to manage conflict can be categorized into five conflict styles, with their related tactics. Effective conflict management can emerge out of the ethical expression of disagreement.

1. The integrative, solution-centered, and less confrontational styles are generally viewed as the most effective and appropriate; however, the more confrontational styles can be effective given certain contingencies.

2. The avoidance style is passive and nonconfrontational. The tactics of denial, topic changes, and irreverent remarks are especially detrimental to a task group with little time to solve the problem, but may be useful in long-standing groups.

3. The accommodation style is another passive style that is highly appeasing. Captured in tactics such as giving in and disengagement, it can be effective and even appropriate when dealing with certain affective conflicts or when the relationship is more important than fighting over a task issue.

4. Competition is highly confrontational and uncooperative and involves tactics such as hostile remarks and rejection. It may be effective in short-term task groups or when a member feels strongly about his or her positions; however, it rarely is judged appropriate because it harms the socioemotional dimensions of groups.

5. Collaboration is highly integrative, cooperative, and solution centered. It involves a win–win ethic and is expressed in analytical and conciliatory tactics. It is most consistently perceived as effective and appropriate by members, but takes time and effort.

6. Compromise is a moderate style also called *shared outcome*. It is captured in tradeoff tactics that are more appropriate when integrative approaches are not possible.

7. Disagreement should be expressed. Follow an integrative path; stay focused; consider your own needs and those of others; use evidence and reasoning; refute the idea, not the person offering the idea; and in the face of distributive tactics stay calm and do not reciprocate in kind.

8. Other cultures handle conflict differently from how people in the United States handle it. Individualistic and low-context cultures tend to be more direct, openly expressive, and concerned with self-face. Collectivist and high-context cultures value harmony and indirect, subtle expressions of conflict; they are more concerned with saving the other's face.

Principled Negotiation

A general strategy that enables parties in a conflict to express their needs openly and search for alternatives to meet the needs of all parties without damaging their relationships.

Negotiating Principled Agreement

Most task-oriented groups must resolve conflict for the group's goals to be met. A variety of techniques designed help groups manage conflict. We especially like the *principled negotiation* procedure because it is consistent with all the ethical principles we have outlined earlier, is extremely effective, and emphasizes good communication skills, especially listening. **Principled negotiation** is an all-purpose strategy that encourages all participants in a conflict situation to collaborate by expressing their needs and searching for alternatives that meet those needs.[62] It is called "principled" because it is based on ethical principles that encourage users to remain decent individuals and not act in ways that will damage the relationship among them. It puts the integrative approach into action.

Principled negotiation is an efficient and fair way to develop a solution meeting the legitimate needs of all parties; therefore, it is likely to produce lasting solutions. The guidelines in the principled negotiation procedure are consistent with communication behaviors that produce integrative outcomes.[63] Exchanging information, asking questions instead of making demands, and foregoing rigid, inflated positions helps bargainers attain integrative outcomes. *Appropriate communication techniques alone* help bargainers attain integrative outcomes regardless of their initial orientations. In addition, this type of negotiation will not harm the relationship among participants and frequently improves it. We particularly like it because it recognizes the major elements that enter into conflict—perceptions, emotions, behaviors, and interaction among individuals—and acknowledges that each must be considered.

The following description of principled negotiation shows how a group can incorporate the communication principles presented throughout this book, including such concepts as rhetorical sensitivity, active listening, and integrative conflict management, into a practical, effective technique for managing conflict. The group leader, an outside consultant, or members themselves can use the procedure. Here are the four steps:

1. **Separate the people from the problem.**

   In most conflicts, the content of the disagreement becomes tangled with the relationship among the participants. Each should be dealt with directly and separately. Give all parties the opportunity to explain, without interference, how they perceive the conflict and how they feel about it. Parties should share perceptions as they try to put themselves into each other's shoes. If emotions run high, allow them to be vented. Do not overreact to emotional outbursts, but listen actively and show by your actions as well as your words that you care about the needs of the other members with whom your interests conflict. The goal is not to become bosom buddies with the other party to a conflict (although that may happen), but to develop a good working relationship characterized by mutual respect.[64]

2. **Focus on interests, not positions.**

   When group members stake out certain positions ("I insist that we have an educational speaker!"), they become attached to those *positions* rather than the original *needs* the positions were designed to meet. However, rigidly adhering to initial positions prevents discovery of a solution.[65] When group members stick to their positions, decision quality is impaired, but when they exchange facts and reasons why, decision quality improves. For example, we discussed earlier the committee that debated closing the food service facility at 5 PM. One side's position was that the snack bar must be closed, but the other side's position was that the snack bar must be kept open. These two positions are incompatible, and there is no way to reconcile them—in their present form, one must win and one must lose. However, when group members started to explore the *interests* behind the positions (the desire to save money and the desire to meet needs of evening students), then an avenue opened whereby both parties could have their desires met by finding a way to do *both simultaneously*—provide the students with food without raising costs by expanding the vending service.

Understanding the difference between a person's position and their interest is key to principled negotiation. Your understanding of the difference can be helped by recognizing some important principles.[66] First, look for the possibility there is more than one interest underlying a position, especially a strongly held one. What other interests may have been behind closing the snack bar other than saving money? Second, others often misread interests. In conflict, we often assume what the other wants and are wrong. This is why listening is so important as well as directly asking for the interests—don't guess. Third, under what may very well be task issues, lurk potential relational issues. This relates to the importance of separating the issue from the person. How a comment is given or a look is portrayed can be read as somehow diminishing the self-worth of another. We talked earlier about how easy it is for group conflict to slip into relational issues of self-esteem and power.

3. **Invent options for mutual gain.**

The previous example illustrates how a new option, expanded vending service, was created that had not been apparent when the conflict started. Negotiators should assume that the interests of all parties can be integrated into the group's final solution and may use techniques like brainstorming to create options. The same committee that debated food service options for evening students also discussed how evening students could be served by the bookstore.[67] The evening student adviser on the committee noted that the campus bookstore was open in the evenings only during the first week of the quarter. Many evening students who drove directly to campus from work could not arrive early enough for the bookstore's regular hours, and so were unable to exchange books, purchase supplies, or even browse. The adviser proposed that the bookstore hours be extended to 8 PM every evening. The campus budget officer objected strongly, noting that the proposal would result in cost increases for personnel salaries unlikely to be recovered by purchases made by evening students.

The positions adopted by each person represented attempts to meet the legitimate needs of two important groups: the evening students and the budget watchdogs. However, through open discussion focused on the interests (not the positions) of each, a solution was invented that incorporated both sets of needs. The bookstore would remain open two evenings per week throughout the quarter, and would start business later in the morning the rest of the week. The total number of hours of bookstore operation remained the same, so costs were not increased, but the distribution of the hours changed to meet the needs of more students.

4. **Use objective criteria.**

Negotiations will be perceived as fairer if objective criteria *agreed upon by all parties* are established as the standard for judging alternatives. Group members will profit from establishing such criteria at the beginning of any problem-solving session, but they should *insist* on it in prolonged conflicts because such criteria make negotiation less likely to be a contest of wills and more likely to be settled upon principle instead of pressure. For example, the United Way organization of a major midwestern city nearly disintegrated as a result of arguments over which agencies should receive money. Finally, the *ad hoc* committee established a set of cost accounting procedures enabling each agency to determine how many people could be served for what amount. These procedures then served as relatively objective criteria for United Way to use in determining which agencies to fund.

Sometimes, despite a group's best intentions, even principled negotiation fails to bring about consensus, or a group is operating under a time deadline that forces members to use other methods.

When Negotiation Fails: Alternative Procedures

Settlements derived through negotiation by the group itself are preferable to solutions imposed by someone else because they tend to be more acceptable to all members. The first two of the four alternatives presented in the following section involve the group in breaking a deadlock. However, sometimes a group simply is not able to break a deadlock. In that case, when a decision *must* be made, the leader has the two remaining options.

Mediation by the Leader If a seemingly irreconcilable conflict emerges over goals or alternatives, the leader might suggest the following procedure, outlined in Table 11.2, which is an abbreviated form of that used by professional mediators for apparently deadlocked negotiations between a union and management. The procedure represents a last-chance group attempt to arrive at an acceptable decision without resorting to third-party arbitration.

TABLE 11.2
Steps to Mediation
by the Group's
Leader

Present the alternatives

    Side 1 presents its position: what it wants and why; Side 2 is silent.
    Side 2 can ask clarifying questions and additional explanations.
    Side 2 explains Side 1's position to the satisfaction of Side 1.
    The process is repeated for Side 2's position.

Chart the alternatives (see Figure 11.3)

    Group leader lists both positions on board or chart.
    Leader (with help from group) lists pros and cons for each position.
    Leader and group search for agreement and common ground on the charts.

Search for creative alternatives

    Leader reviews all elements of common ground.
    Leader asks group to look for solution acceptable to all; leader may propose such a solution.
    Leader asks members to compromise with a solution that meets minimum requirements of both sides.

Resolution occurs if and when a consensus or compromise is adopted.

If this procedure fails, other alternative procedures can be taken to resolve the conflict issue without producing consensus. Two-sided conflict is assumed for simplicity.

Generally, when the previously described procedure is followed out of a sincere desire to resolve the conflict, the group will find at least a compromise and will develop increased cohesiveness and team spirit. Lacking a consensus or compromise, other procedures will be needed to reach a decision.

Voting   *Voting* is one such alternative procedure. Naturally, some members are bound to dislike the outcome, but voting may be a necessary step

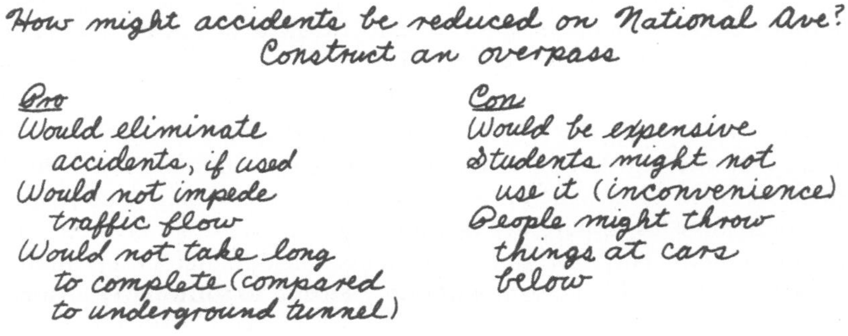

FIGURE 11.3
Example of a chart
of pros and cons

How might accidents be reduced on National Ave?
Construct an overpass

Pro
Would eliminate
   accidents, if used
Would not impede
   traffic flow
Would not take long
   to complete (compared
   to underground tunnel)

Con
Would be expensive
Students might not
   use it (inconvenience)
People might throw
   things at cars
   below

in overcoming an impasse. One danger with voting is that the group may arrive at premature closure on an issue. Be especially careful, if this is the option you select, that the group really is deadlocked.

Forcing Another option is *forcing*. Here, the leader breaks the deadlock and decides on behalf of the group. For example, in the U.S. Senate the presiding officer can break a tie. As with voting, several members are likely to be disappointed, but in instances in which an outside group, parent organization, or legitimate authority demands a report or when the group faces a deadline, a leader may have little choice.

Third-Party Arbitration *Third-party arbitration* occurs when the group brings in an outside negotiator to resolve its differences. This typically happens with joint labor–management disputes and some court-related cases. Arbitrators often have the power to resolve issues any way they please, from deciding entirely in favor of one party to splitting the difference between them. Sometimes, just the threat of bringing in a third-party arbitrator is enough to force conflict participants to negotiate with each other in good faith. Usually, all parties to the conflict end up feeling dissatisfied. Thus, third-party arbitration should be proposed only when the leader believes the group has reached an impasse and the cost of continuing the conflict, including resentment and the possibility of destroying the group, will exceed the cost of arbitration. Of course, group members must agree to such a resolution procedure.

Sometimes, no resolution about a group's issue is possible, but that does not automatically create a hopeless situation. Even when members cannot agree on basic values or goals, they often can find some areas in which they do agree. The group may find a way to come together on some issues and agree to disagree on others.

Recap: A Quick Review

Sometimes resolution of conflict within a group or between groups simply does not occur. When negotiation fails, there are alternatives.

1. The group leader can step in and with structured mediation try to show group members how they can select an alternative through compromise. If a stalemate still ensues, members are left with other alternatives.

2. When integrative solutions are not found after repeated attempts, then members can vote. Although not the best way to break a stalemate, it may be the only way to move on.

3. The group leader can step in and force an alternative by making the decision for the group.

4. Third-party arbitrators can be brought in to select an alternative. These individuals are brought in when the leader and the group believe that all else has failed.

QUESTIONS FOR REVIEW

Go to self-quizzes on the Online Learning Center at mhhe.com/galanes14e to test your knowledge of the chapter concepts.

Lori, Tony, Kevin, Diedre, and Chris worked through a lot of conflict to reach their goal of selecting their university's speaker series.

1. How can you apply the definition of conflict to their case? How was it expressed? How were they interdependent with each other? What were the scarce rewards and incompatible goals? Who is interfering with whom?

2. Who appear to be the innovative deviants? How could their conversation change to show better innovative deviance?

3. What are the substantive and affective conflicts between them? How are they interrelated?

4. How do their conflict styles clash? What are the patterns of their tactics? What kinds of consequences occur in light of these patterns?

5. How could each member better follow the ethical principles for disagreement?

6. How could you advise them to redirect their confrontational efforts along more principled negotiation?

7. If their negotiation failed to produce a speaker list, which alternative would be best to select in an effort to break their stalemate? Why?

KEY TERMS

Test your knowledge of these key terms by visiting the Online Learning Center Web site at mhhe.com/galanes14e.

Accommodation
Avoidance
Coalition
Collaboration
Competition
Compromise

Conflict
Deviate
Distributive approach
Facework
Inequity conflict

Integrative approach
Principled negotiation
Process conflict
Relationship Conflict
Task Conflict

BIBLIOGRAPHY

Cathcart, Robert S., Larry A. Samovar, and Linda D. Henman. *Small Group Communication: Theory and Practice.* 7th ed. Dubuque, IA: Brown & Benchmark, 1996, Section 4.

Fisher, Roger, and William Ury. *Getting to Yes: Negotiating Agreement Without Giving In.* 2nd ed. New York: Penguin Books, 1991.

Putnam, Linda L. "Conflict in Group Decision Making." In *Communication and Group Decision Making.* Randy Y. Hirokawa and Marshall Scott Poole, eds. Beverly Hills, CA: Sage 1986, 175–97.

Ting-Toomey, Stella, and John G. Oetzel, *Managing Intercultural Conflict Effectively* (Thousand Oaks, CA: Sage, 2001).

Wilmot, William W., and Joyce L. Hocker, *Interpersonal Conflict.* 7th ed. Boston: McGraw Hill, 2007.

NOTES

1. Judith Martin and Thomas K. Nakayama, *Experiencing Intercultural Communication: An Introduction,* 3rd ed. (Boston: McGraw-Hill, 2008): 171.
2. Carolyn J. Wood, "Challenging the Assumptions Underlying the Use of Participatory Decision-Making Strategies: A Longitudinal Case Study," *Small Group Behavior,* 20 (1989): 428–48.
3. Victor D. Wall, Jr., Gloria J. Galanes, and Susan B. Love, "Small, Task-Oriented Groups: Conflict, Conflict Management, Satisfaction, and Decision Quality," *Small Group Behavior,* 18 (1987): 31–55.
4. Kathleen M. O'Connor, Deborah H. Gruenfeld, and Joseph E. McGrath, "The Experience and Effects of Conflict in Continuing Work Groups," *Small Group Research,* 24 (August 1993): 362–82.
5. William W. Wilmot and Joyce L. Hocker *Interpersonal Conflict,* 7th ed. (Boston, MA: Boston: McGraw Hill, 2007): 8.
6. Morton Deutsch, "Conflicts: Productive and Destructive," *Journal of Social Issues,* 25 (1969): 7–41; Kenneth W. Thomas, "Conflict and Conflict Management," in *Handbook of Industrial and Organizational Psychology,* ed. M. Dunnette (Chicago: Rand McNally, 1976): 890–934; Louis B. Pondy, "Organizational Conflict: Concepts and Models," *Administrative Science Quarterly,* 12 (1976): 296–320; Brent D. Ruben, "Communication and Conflict: A System-Theoretic Perspective," *Quarterly Journal of Speech,* 64 (1978): 202–12; J. Guetzkow and J. Gyr, "An Analysis of Conflict in Decision-Making Groups," *Human Relations,* 7 (1954): 367–82; and E. P. Torrance, "Group Decision-Making and Disagreement," *Social Forces,* 35 (1957): 314–18.
7. Karl Smith, David W. Johnson, and Roger T. Johnson, "Can Conflict Be Constructive? Controversy versus Concurrence Seeking in Learning Groups," *Journal of Educational Psychology,* 73 (1981): 654–63.
8. Charles R. Franz and K. Gregory Jin, "The Structure of Group Conflict in a Collaborative Work Group during Information Systems Development," *Journal of Applied Communication Research,* 23 (May 1995): 108–27.
9. Ibid.
10. Sue D. Pendell, "Deviance and Conflict in Small Group Decision Making: An Exploratory Study," *Small Group Behavior,* 21 (1990): 393–403.
11. Svenn Lindskold and Gyuseog Han, "Group Resistance to Influence by a Conciliatory Member," *Small Group Behavior,* 19 (1988): 19–34.
12. Carl L. Thameling and Patricia H. Andrews, "Majority Responses to Opinion Deviates: A Communicative Analysis," *Small Group Research,* 23 (1992): 475–502.
13. Kristin B. Valentine and B. Aubrey Fisher, "An Interaction Analysis of Verbal Innovative Deviance in Small Groups," *Speech Monographs,* 41 (1974): 413–20.
14. Thameling and Andrews, "Majority Responses," 475–502.
15. Mark K. Covey, "The Relationship between Social Skill and Conflict Resolution Tactics" (Paper presented at the annual convention of the Rocky Mountain Psychological Association, Snowbird, Utah, 1983).
16. Rick Garlick and Paul A. Mongeau, "Argument Quality and Group Member Status as Determinants of Attitudinal Minority Influence," *Western Journal of Communication,* 57 (Summer 1993): 289–308.
17. Renee Meyers, Dale Brashers, and Jennifer Hanner, "Majority-Minority Influence: Identifying Argumentative Patterns and Predicting Argument-Outcome Links," *Journal of Communication,* 50 (2000): 3–30.
18. Guetzkow and Gyr, "An Analysis of Conflict," 367–82. ; Kristin J. Behfar, Elizabeth A. Mannix, Randall S. Peterson, and William M. Trochim, "Conflict in Small Groups: The Meaning and Consequences of Process Conflict," *Small Group Research,* 42 (2011): 127–76.
19. Ibid.

20. Roger C. Pace, "Personalized and Depersonalized Conflict in Small Group Discussions: An Examination of Differentiation," *Small Group Research,* 21 (1990): 79–96.

21. Roger Fisher and Scott Brown, *Getting Together: Building a Relationship That Gets to Yes* (Boston: Houghton-Mifflin, 1988): 16–23.

22. Behfar, Mannix, Peterson, and Trochim, "Conflict in Small Groups: The Meaning and Consequences of Process Conflict."

23. Ibid.

24. Victor D. Wall, Jr., and Linda L. Nolan, "Small Group Conflict: A Look at Equity, Satisfaction, and Styles of Conflict Management," *Small Group Behavior,* 18 (1987): 188–211.

25. Renee Meyers and Dale Brashers, "Influence Processes in Group Interaction," in *The Handbook of Group Communication Theory & Research,* ed. Lawrence Frey (Thousand Oaks: CA, 1999): 298.

26. Roderick I. Swaab, Katherine W. Phillips, Daniel Diermeier, and Victoria Husted Medvec, "The Pros and Cons of Dyadic Side Conversation in Small Groups: The Impact of Group Norms and Task Type," *Small Group Research*, 39 (2008): 372–90.

27. Amy E. Randel and Kimberly S. Jaussi, "Gender Social and Personal Identity, Sex Dissimilarity, Relationship Conflict, and Asymmetrical Effects," *Small Group Research*, 39 (2008): 468–91.

28. Elizabeth Hobman, Prashant Bordia, Bernd Irmer, and Artemis Chang, "The Expression of Conflict in Computer-Mediated and Face-to-Face Groups," *Small Group Research,* 33 (2002): 439–65.

29. Ibid.

30. David H. Jonassen and Hyug II Kwon, "Communication Patterns in Computer Mediated Versus Face-to-Face Group Problem Solving," *Educational Technological Research and Development*, 49 (March 2001): 35–51.

31. Ibid. Hobman, Bordia, Irmer, and Chang, "The Expression of Conflict in Computer-Mediated and Face-to-Face Groups."

32. Behfar, Mannix, Peterson, and Trochim, "Conflict in Small Groups: The Meaning and Consequences of Process Conflict."

33. Linda L. Putnam, "Conflict in Group Decision Making," in *Communication and Group Decision Making,* eds. Randy Y. Hirokawa and Marshall Scott Poole (Beverly Hills, CA: Sage, 1986): 175–96.

34. Behfar, Mannix, Peterson, and Trochim, "Conflict in Small Groups: The Meaning and Consequences of Process Conflict."

35. Ibid.

36. Lindred L. Greer, Karen A. Jehn, and Elizabeth A. Mannix, "Conflict Transformation: A Longitudinal Investigation of Intragroup Conflict and the Moderating Role of Conflict Resolution," 39 (2008): 278–302.

37. Tim Kuhn and Marshall Scott Poole, "Do Conflict Management Styles Affect Group Decision Making?: Evidence from a Longitudinal Field Study," *Human Communication Research,* 26 (2000): 558–90.

38. Vidar Schie and Jorn K. Rognes, "Small Group Negotiation: When Members Differ in Motivational Orientation," *Small Group Research,* 36 (June 2005): 289–320.

39. Kevin W. Rockmann and Gregory B. Northcraft, "Expecting the Worst? The Dynamic Role of Competitive Expectations in Team Member Satisfaction and Team Performance," *Small Group Research*, 41 (2010): 308–29.

40. Ibid.

41. R. H. Kilmann and K. Thomas, "Developing a Forced-Choice Measure of Conflict-Handling Behavior: The MODE Instrument," *Educational and Psychological Measurement,* 37 (1977): 309–25.

42. Hal Witteman, "Analyzing Interpersonal Conflict: Nature of Awareness, Type of Initiating Event, Situational Perceptions, and Management Styles," *Western Journal of Communication,* 56 (Summer 1992): 248–80.

43. Larry Erbert, "Conflict Management: Styles, Strategies, and Tactics," in *Small Group Communication: Theory and Practice,* 7th ed., eds. Robert Cathcart, Larry Samovar, and Linda Henman (Madison, WI: Brown & Benchmark, 1996): 213.

44. Michael A. Gross, Laura K. Guerrero, and Jess K. Alberts, "Perceptions of Conflict

Strategies and Communication Competence in Task-Oriented Dyads," *Journal of Applied Communication Research,* 32 (August 2004): 249–70.

45. Meyers and Brashers, "Influence Processes in Group Interaction," 297.

46. Hal Witteman, "Group Member Satisfaction: A Conflict-Related Account," *Small Group Behavior,* 22 (1991): 24–58.

47. Wilmot and Hocker, *Interpersonal Conflict,* 143.

48. Ibid., 162.

49. Ibid., 147.

50. Ibid., 165.

51. Ibid., 165.

52. Ibid., 159.

53. Gary L. Kreps, *Organizational Communication,* 2nd ed. (New York: Longman, 1990): 193.

54. Fisher and Brown, *Getting Together.*

55. Kreps, *Organizational Communication.*

56. Steven M. Alderton and Lawrence R. Frey, "Argumentation in Small Group Decision-Making," in *Communication and Group Decision Making,* eds. Randy Y. Hirokawa and Marshall Scott Poole (Beverly Hills, CA: Sage, 1986): 157–273.

57. Donald W. Klopf and James C. McCroskey, *Intercultural Communication Encounters* (Boston: Pearson Education, 2007): 166.

58. Stella Ting-Toomey and John G. Oetzel, *Managing Intercultural Conflict Effectively* (Thousand Oaks, CA: Sage, 2001).

59. Stella Ting-Toomey and John Oetzel, "Cross-Cultural Face Concerns and Conflict Styles: Current Status and Future Directions," in *Handbook of International and Intercultural Communication,* 2nd ed., eds. William B. Gudykunst and Bella Mody (Thousand Oaks, CA: Sage, 2002): 141–63.

60. Stella Ting-Toomey, "Intercultural Conflict Competence," in eds. Judith N. Martin, Thomas K. Nakayama, and Lisa A. Flores, *Readings in Cultural Contexts* (Mountain View, CA: Mayfield, 1998): 401–14.

61. Martin and Nakayama, *Experiencing Intercultural Communication,* 173–74.

62. Roger Fisher and William Ury, *Getting to Yes: Negotiating Agreement Without Giving In* (Boston: Houghton-Mifflin, 1981; Penguin Books, 1983).

63. Frank Tutzauer and Michael E. Roloff, "Communicative Processes Leading to Integrative Agreements," *Communication Research,* 15 (1988): 360–80.

64. Fisher and Ury, *Getting to Yes.*

65. Ichiro Innami, "The Quality of Group Decisions, Group Verbal Behavior, and Intervention," *Organizational Behavior and Human Decision Processes,* 60 (December 1994): 409–30.

66. Wilmot and Hocker, *Interpersonal Conflict,* 259-260.

67. A version of the discussion about this issue is depicted on the ancillary videotape, *Communicating Effectively in Small Groups* (Dubuque, IA: Wm. C. Brown, 1991). Segment 3 depicts an ineffective discussion, and segment 4 shows an effective discussion where this major issue of bookstore hours is resolved.

Group Observation and Evaluation Tools

Groups can often benefit from learning about themselves. Sometimes members can help a group evaluate itself. At other times, it is better to bring in an outside consultant to provide an objective perspective. Chapter 12 presents a variety of assessment and evaluation tools you can use to learn about yourself and your group or to conduct a systematic evaluation of another group.

PART

V

Tools for Assessing and Evaluating Groups

STUDY OBJECTIVES

As a result of studying Chapter 12, you should be able to:

1. Explain the benefits of assessing your own behavior as a group member and reflecting on it.

2. Explain the benefits of conducting regular group evaluations.

3. Explain the benefits of having a consultant observe and work with a group.

4. Prepare a consultant's observation guide appropriate for observing a small group.

5. Report observations in ways that are helpful to group members.

6. Devise and use instruments for assessing yourself, your fellow members, your group as a whole, and other groups for which you serve as a consultant.

CENTRAL MESSAGE

It is healthy for members periodically to evaluate themselves, their fellow members, and the group because information from such assessments can suggest specific areas for improvement. Sometimes a group can benefit from the observations of outside consultants, including students who understand group communication processes.

S am, the CEO of a small plant that manufactured specialized circuit boards, decided to hire a consultant to help his executive committee overcome several problems. The committee met weekly and consisted of the department managers: Roger, manufacturing; Elgin, quality assurance; Angela, sales and marketing; and Frank, the comptroller. The team had made several costly mistakes in the past several months, which Sam thought were caused by misunderstandings between members and made worse by the pressures due to an expanding business. In one instance, Angela had promised an early delivery to a customer on the basis of what she thought Roger had said, but the circuit boards weren't ready, and the company lost the customer. Things didn't seem to be improving, and Sam didn't know whether the problems were due to his leadership style, the competence of the members, ineffective communication at the weekly meetings, or something else.

Sam had already done what he knew to do. He found a rating scale on the Internet so that members could assess their own preference for procedural order. Group members had fun with this—they enjoyed learning that they were pretty low in preference for procedural order—but group meetings did not seem to improve. He also distributed brief questionnaires after one meeting to learn whether members thought the meetings were productive and worthwhile. He discovered that members didn't particularly think the meetings were worth their time, but they didn't give specific suggestions for improvement. Sam decided he needed the objective and informed opinion only an outsider could provide.

Enter Susanna, organizational trainer and consultant who specialized in team performance and teambuilding. First, she gathered all the information she could about the team by interviewing Sam and reading the group's memos and minutes. This didn't take her long because committee minutes were kept sporadically. She observed three meetings, which highlighted to her what some of the problems might be, and took extensive notes so that she could provide specific examples to the members. As a last step, she interviewed each group member to learn what they thought about the meetings and their own contributions.

Susanna prepared her feedback for the group carefully. She had a long list of things she could mention, but she didn't want to overwhelm or demoralize the team. She selected the few she thought were most problematic, beginning with "housekeeping." The team did not operate with an agenda, nor was anyone regularly assigned to take notes. She noted that the team met in an a noisy employee break room where other employees constantly wandered in and out. She observed that at each meeting, nearly every member was called away at least once by a secretary or subordinate to answer a question or take a phone call.

In her report, Susanna recommended that Sam provide members with an agenda at least a day or two before the meeting, and that if members didn't want to rotate the job of taking minutes, Sam's secretary could attend the meetings specifically for that function. She suggested that members find another place to meet—even if that had to be away from the plant, at a private meeting room in a restaurant over breakfast, for example. She also recommended that members not allow their secretaries or subordinates to interrupt the meeting, except for a dire emergency.

The next recommendations concerned the process of discussion itself. Susanna praised the group for its obvious dedication to the company and its creativity in solving problems. She noted, however, that because there had been several costly misunderstandings, members exhibited signs of distress and distrust, which she thought they could overcome. Susanna gave the group members several examples of how their discussion was disorganized, with members jumping from one topic to another without concluding a topic. At any given moment, there could be three different topics under discussion, and it was easy to mishear or misunderstand information. She affirmed that their problems were solvable and gave them several suggestions for how the group could monitor its own discussion process. She spoke privately with Sam about his somewhat lax leadership style and recommended that he keep firmer control of the meetings.

Finally, Susanna designed a training program for the group to take place during a weekend retreat. The program succeeded in improving the members' basic communication skills and featured several teambuilding activities to help the group begin to recover some of the trust eroded by recent mistakes.

This case study illustrates several points we want to make in this chapter. First, it is completely appropriate for members to conduct assessments of their own behavior. Most people like learning about themselves, with numerous surveys and scales designed to assess particular characteristics. Sometimes, such information is used only by each individual member. Often, that's enough to encourage members to reflect about how their own behavior contributes (or not) to the group. Sometimes, group members all take the same scale and want to discuss their findings within the group, as Sam's group did regarding their preference for procedural order.

Second, we have promoted the value of being a participant *and* an observer of group interaction. Experienced group leaders routinely conduct periodic "how are we doing" sessions in which the topic of the group discussion is the group itself and how well it functions. This information is usually shared with the group as a whole, but members want the safety of anonymity, so they may complete a group assessment survey that only the leader will see.

Finally, most groups can benefit from outside assessment. It is hard to split your attention between participating in the group at the same time you are observing the group process. You can't do both in the same instant; instead, your attention shifts back and forth between one and the other, which makes it likely that you'll miss something. Sometimes, you will know *exactly* what a group needs, but other times you won't have a clue—you just know it needs help! That was why Sam sought the services of an outside consultant who could be free just to observe without having to participate.

This chapter discusses all three of these processes: self-assessment, member and group assessment, and outside consultation. We also provide tools and instruments you can use for these kinds of assessments. All of these were designed for face-to-face groups. Groups, as you know by now, range from entirely face-to-face to entirely virtual. Most secondary groups are probably face-to-face groups that use one or more computer tools, such as e-mail, chat rooms, bulletin boards, etc. You may be in a group currently for a course that uses the Blackboard platform for your group's business. Every one of these tools and instruments can be adapted to your group's use of computer technology.

Platforms such as Blackboard and Wiggio (www.wiggio.com/) let you turn tools into surveys that can be filled out by group members or used by group leaders. SurveyMonkey (www.surveymonkey.com/) is a free Web-based tool that lets you create a survey without the hassle of downloading software—all you need is a browser. Even novice surveyors find it easy to use. Such platforms provide question types, question formats, and survey templates that can be customized to fit what your group needs. Your group can collect data via e-mail, Facebook, a Web link, or a survey link embedded on your group's site.

Assessment of virtual team performance has been an issue since the late 1990s, when virtual teams exploded onto the professional landscape.[1] Since then, systems such as Promus have been developed to provide ways to assess and give feedback to virtual team members and managers. Books, including *The Handbook of High-Performance Virtual Teams: A Toolkit for Collaborating Across Boundaries,*[2] provide information and tools to enhance virtual team performance.

Internal Assessment: Members Evaluate the Group

Knowledgeable group members can do a lot to make their groups effective. By now, you have an idea of what needs to improve and how you can contribute. Many resources are available for assessing yourself, one another, and your group.

Self-Assessment

Do you like learning about yourself? Most people do, and members of groups often enjoy taking personality and other assessments for that purpose. There are many such assessments available in textbooks and on the World Wide Web. You can use the information just to learn about yourself, but also to prompt group discussion about the effect a particular member characteristic has on the group as a whole. For example, members of a group we know answered questionnaires to learn their preferred conflict management styles. Their group leader then facilitated a discussion of their styles; the members used this opportunity to reflect and talk about how others perceived their behavior and how their actions influenced the group. Often, self-rating scales are easily changed to ones that can be used to rate the other participants.

Grouphate and Preference for Procedural Order were discussed in Chapter 5; Table 12.1 presents a short questionnaire to help you assess your level of grouphate, and Table 12.2 assesses how much you like group discussion to be orderly and organized. A self-rating of assertiveness is provided in Table 12.3; to change this scale from a self-rating scale to an other-rating scale, change the wording slightly: Instead of asking about your "best judgment of my own" degree of assertiveness, ask about your "best judgment of Sally's degree of assertiveness." Table 12.4, the Ross-DeWine Conflict Management Message Style Instrument, is the conflict styles assessment completed by the group mentioned above. When you score this instrument as indicated, you learn to what extent your conflict style is self-oriented (motivated to win, to get what you want), other-oriented (motivated to maintain the relationship with the other person), or issue-oriented (motivated to work with the other person to solve the problem or issue). Finally, Table 12.5 provides a self-rating scale that a discussion leader can use to evaluate his or her own performance. Had Sam completed this, he might have had an "ah ha!" reaction to realize where his leadership behaviors could have been modified to help the group.

TABLE 12.1   Grouphate

The following scale provides information about the extent to which you like or dislike working in groups. Indicate how much you agree or disagree with each statement by circling the appropriate response. Add the numbers you have circled. The higher the number, the more you experience grouphate.

Statement	Strongly Agree	Agree	Neither	Disagree	Strongly Disagree
1. I like working in groups.	1	2	3	4	5
2. I would rather work alone.	5	4	3	2	1
3. Group work is fun.	1	2	3	4	5
4. Groups are terrible.	5	4	3	2	1
5. I would prefer to work in an organization in which teams are used.	1	2	3	4	5
6. My ideal job is one in which I can be interdependent with others.	1	2	3	4	5
Total					

Adapted from Joann Keyton and Lawrence R. Frey, "The State of Traits: Predispositions and Group Communication," in Lawrence R. Frey, ed., *New Directions in Group Communication* (Thousand Oaks, CA: Sage, 2002): 109.

TABLE 12.2 Preference for procedural order

The following scale assesses your preference for procedural order. Indicate how much you agree or disagree with each statement by circling the appropriate response. Add the numbers you have circled. The higher the number, the more you prefer orderly, systematic group discussions.

Statement During Group Work, I	Strongly Agree			Neither			Strongly Disagree
1. Request or suggest deadlines for the group to follow.	7	6	5	4	3	2	1
2. Request or suggest agendas, task lists, or ranking of alternatives.	7	6	5	4	3	2	1
3. Request or make statements about group goals.	7	6	5	4	3	2	1
4. Suggest signposts to signal the start of group meetings.	7	6	5	4	3	2	1
5. Summarize/integrate contributions of members during a meeting.	7	6	5	4	3	2	1
6. Suggest or request division of labor among group members.	7	6	5	4	3	2	1
7. Suggest ways to implement a task or course of action.	7	6	5	4	3	2	1
8. Request direction about procedures for the group to follow.	7	6	5	4	3	2	1
9. Ask questions and make comments to clarify specific procedures.	7	6	5	4	3	2	1
10. Keep discussions task-related by following agenda topics.	7	6	5	4	3	2	1
Total							

Adapted from Linda L. Putnam, "Preference for Procedural Order in Task-Oriented Small Groups," *Communication Monographs, 16* (August 1979): 212.

Member and Group Assessment

One of the most effective group leaders we know conducts regular assessments of her group. Sometimes, she takes a few moments at the end of the meeting to ask members whether they thought the goals of the meeting were accomplished and what could have been done better. At other times, she distributes a more formal questionnaire asking for specific evaluation of some aspect of the group—problem solving, goal setting, or even her own performance as leader. Stopping to ask, "How are we doing?" can help a group completely change its direction or fine-tune an already effective process.

TABLE 12.3
Assertiveness rating scale

Name _____   Date _____

The check mark on each scale indicates my best judgment of my own degree of assertiveness as a participant in the discussion.

	Nonassertive	Assertive	Aggressive
Behavior			
Getting the floor			
	yielded easily	usually refused to let others take over or dominate	interrupted and cut others off
Expressing opinions			
	never expressed personal opinion	stated opinions, but open to others' opinions	insisted others should agree
Expressing personal desires (for meeting times, procedures, etc.)			
	never, or did so in a pleading way	stated openly, but willing to compromise	insisted on having my own way
Sharing information			
	none, or only if asked to do so	whenever information was relevant, concisely	whether relevant or not; long-winded, rambling
Manner			
Voice			
	weak, unduly soft	strong and clear	loud, strident
Posture and movements			
	withdrawn, restricted	animated, often leaning forward	unduly forceful "table pounding"
Eye contact			
	rare, even when speaking	direct but not staring or glaring	stared others down
Overall manner			
	nonassertive	assertive	aggressive

TABLE 12.4   Ross-DeWine Conflict Management Message Style instrument

Directions: Below you will find messages that have been delivered by persons in conflict situations. Consider each message separately and decide how closely this message resembles the ones that you have used in conflict settings. The language may not be exactly the same as yours, but consider the messages in terms of similarity to your messages in conflict. There are no right or wrong answers, nor are these messages designed to trick you. Answer in terms of responses you make, not what you think you should say. Give each message a 1–5 rating on the answer sheet provided according to the following scale. Mark one answer only.

In conflict situations, I

1	2	3	4	5
never say things like this	rarely say things like this	sometimes say things like this	often say things like this	usually say things like this

_____ 1.   "Can't you see how foolish you're being with that thinking?"

_____ 2.   "How can I make you feel happy again?"

_____ 3.   "I'm really bothered by some things that are happening here; can we talk about these?"

_____ 4.   "I really don't have any more to say on this . . . " (silence)

_____ 5.   "What possible solution can we come up with?"

_____ 6.   "I'm really sorry that your feelings are hurt—maybe you're right."

_____ 7.   "Let's talk this thing out and see how we can deal with this hassle."

_____ 8.   "Shut up! You are wrong! I don't want to hear any more of what you have to say."

_____ 9.   "It is your fault if I fail at this, and don't you ever expect any help from me when you're on the spot."

_____ 10.   "You can't do (say) that to me—it's either my way or forget it."

_____ 11.   "Let's try finding an answer that will give us both some of what we want."

_____ 12.   "This is something we have to work out; we're always arguing about it."

_____ 13.   "Whatever makes you feel happiest is OK by me."

_____ 14.   "Let's just leave well enough alone."

_____ 15.   "That's OK . . . it wasn't important anyway . . . You feeling OK now?"

_____ 16.   "If you're not going to cooperate, I'll just go to someone who will."

_____ 17.   "I think we need to try to understand the problem."

_____ 18.   "You might as well accept my decision; you can't do anything about it anyway."

Scoring:
 Self-oriented: Add items 1, 4, 8, 9, 10, 16, 18
 Other-oriented: Add items 2, 6, 13, 14, 15
 Issue-oriented: Add items 3, 5, 7, 11, 12, 17
 Roseanna G. Ross and Sue DeWine, "Assessing the Ross-DeWine Conflict Management Message Style (CMMS)," Management Communication Quarterly, 1 (February 1988): 389–413.

Almost any characteristic of individual behavior can be evaluated with an appropriate scale. Many different types of scales, surveys, and forms are available for this purpose; most of these instruments are easily modified. If a group cannot find a preexisting scale that suits its purpose, members or the leader should feel free to create a scale tailored specifically for what the

Instructions: Rate yourself on each item by putting a check mark in the "Yes" or "No" column. Your score is five times the number of items marked "Yes." Rating: *excellent,* 90 or higher; *good,* 80–85; *fair,* 70–75; *inadequate,* 65 or lower.

TABLE 12.5
Discussion leader
self-rating scale

		Yes	No
1.	I prepared all needed facilities.		
2.	I started the meeting promptly and ended on time.		
3.	I established an atmosphere of supportiveness and informality by being open and responsive to all ideas.		
4.	I clearly oriented the group to its goal and area of freedom.		
5.	I encouraged all members to participate and maintained equal opportunity for all to speak.		
6.	I listened actively, and (if needed) encouraged all members to do so.		
7.	My questions were clear and brief.		
8.	I saw to it that unclear statements were paraphrased or otherwise clarified.		
9.	I used a plan for leading the group in an organized consideration of all major phases of problem solving and all components of vigilant interaction.		
10.	I saw to it that the problem was discussed thoroughly before solutions were considered.		
11.	I actively encouraged creative thinking.		
12.	I encouraged thorough evaluation of all proposed solutions, both for effectiveness and negative consequences.		
13.	I integrated related ideas or suggestions and urged the group to arrive at consensus on a solution.		
14.	I prompted open discussion of substantive conflicts.		
15.	I maintained order and organization, promptly pointing out tangents, making transitions, and keeping track of the passage of time.		
16.	I saw to it that the meeting produced definite assignments or plans for action and that any subsequent meeting was arranged.		
17.	All important information, ideas, and decisions were promptly and accurately recorded.		
18.	I was able to remain neutral during constructive arguments, and otherwise encourage teamwork.		
19.	I suggested or urged establishment of needed ethical standards and procedural norms.		
20.	I encouraged members to discuss how they felt about group process and procedures.		

group needs to know. Examples of two participant rating scales are provided in Table 12.6 and Table 12.7. Table 12.6 is a simple rating form, originally designed by students, that can be given to each participant and quickly tallied. Participants can complete these scales anonymously about each other, then distribute them to the person being rated Web-based services like SurveyMonkey mentioned earlier can be used to distribute the survey and collect its data. We use something similar in our classes to help students in project groups understand how their behavior is perceived by others. In some cases, what students *think* they are doing and how they are *actually* coming across can be very different. One young woman perceived herself as being good at spotting potential problems with the group's plans; her group members dreaded working with her because she disagreed with *everything*— she didn't know when to turn it off. The participant reaction forms gave her

TABLE 12.6
Participant rating scale

Date _____

Observer_____

_____
(Name of participant)

1. Contributions to the *content of the discussion* (relevant information, issue-centered arguments, adequate reasoning, etc.).

5	4	3	2	1
outstanding in quality and quantity		fair share		few or none

2. Contributions to *efficient group procedures* (agenda planning, responding to prior comments, summaries).

5	4	3	2	1
always relevant, aided organization		relevant, no aid in order		sidetracked, confused group

3. Degree of *group orientation and cooperation* (listening to understand, responsible, agreeable, group centered, open-minded).

5	4	3	2	1
very responsible and constructive				self-centered

4. *Speaking competency* (clear, to group, one point at a time, concise).

5	4	3	2	1
brief, clear, to group				vague, indirect, wordy

5. *Overall value* to the group.

5	4	3	2	1
most valuable				least valuable

Suggestions:

Participant's name _____					

Instructions: Circle the number that best reflects your evaluation of the discussant's participation on each scale.

Superior   Poor

1	2	3	4	5	1. Was prepared and informed.
1	2	3	4	5	2. Contributions were brief and clear.
1	2	3	4	5	3. Comments relevant and well timed.
1	2	3	4	5	4. Spoke distinctly and audibly to all.
1	2	3	4	5	5. Willingness to communicate.
1	2	3	4	5	6. Frequency of participation [if poor, too low( ) or high( )].
1	2	3	4	5	7. Nonverbal responses were clear and constant.
1	2	3	4	5	8. Listened to understand and follow discussion.
1	2	3	4	5	9. Open-mindedness.
1	2	3	4	5	10. Cooperative, team orientation.
1	2	3	4	5	11. Helped keep discussion organized, followed outline.
1	2	3	4	5	12. Contributed to evaluation of information and ideas.
1	2	3	4	5	13. Respectful and tactful with others.
1	2	3	4	5	14. Encouraged others to participate.
1	2	3	4	5	15. Overall rating as participant.

Comments: Evaluator _____

TABLE 12.7
Discussion participant evaluation scale

an alternative "reading" of her behavior, which she was able to modify. The participant rating form in Table 12.7 has a similar purpose but is more comprehensive. The rating form in Table 12.8 is designed to evaluate the leader. Originally devised for rating Air Force personnel as discussion leaders, it has been modified substantially over the years and is quite thorough.

The rating forms discussed thus far look at the individual behaviors of members and leaders, but sometimes group members want to assess the performance of the group as a whole. Members can assess any aspect of a group and its discussion: group climate, norms, interpersonal relationships, speaking, listening, problem-solving effectiveness, and so forth. For example, the composite scale in Table 12.9, based on a similar one developed by Patton and Giffin, can identify deficiencies in problem-solving procedures.[3] The set of scales in Table 12.10 was developed by Larkey to allow members of a diverse work group to evaluate how well the group manages its diversity.[4]

TABLE 12.8
Comprehensive leader rating scale

Date _____   Leader _____

Time _____   Observer _____

Instructions: Draw a line through any item not applicable to the discussion you have just observed. Use the following scale to evaluate the designated leader's performance as discussion leader.

5—superior   4—above average   3—average   2—below average   1—poor

Personal Style and Communicative Competencies

To what degree did the leader:

_____ Show poise and confidence in speaking?

_____ Show enthusiasm and interest in the problem?

_____ Listen well to understand *all* participants?

_____ Manifest personal warmth and a sense of humor?

_____ Show an open mind toward all new information and ideas?

_____ Create an atmosphere of teamwork?

_____ Share functional leadership with other members?

_____ Behave democratically?

_____ Maintain perspective on problem and group process?

Preparation

To what degree:

_____ Were all needed physical arrangements cared for?

_____ Were members notified and given guidance in preparing to meet?

_____ Was the leader prepared on the problem or subject?

_____ Was a procedural sequence of questions prepared to guide discussion?

Leadership Techniques

To what degree did the leader:

_____ Put members at ease with each other?

_____ Equalize opportunity to speak?

_____ Introduce and explain the charge or problem so that it was clear to all?

_____ Control aggressive or dominant members with tact?

_____ Present an agenda and/or procedural outline for group problem solving?

_____ Encourage members to modify the procedural outline?

_____ State questions clearly to the group?

_____ Guide the group through a thorough analysis of the problem before discussing solutions?

_____ Stimulate imaginative and creative thinking about solutions?

_____ Encourage the group to evaluate all ideas and proposals thoroughly before accepting or rejecting them?

_____ See that plans were made to implement and follow up on all decisions?

_____ Keep discussion on one point at a time?

_____ Rebound questions asking for a personal opinion or solution to the group?

_____ Provide summaries needed to clarify, remind, and move group forward to next issue or agenda item?

_____ Test for consensus before moving to a new phase of problem solving?

_____ Keep complete and accurate notes, including visual chart of proposals, evaluations, and decisions?

_____ If needed, suggest compromise or integrative solutions to resolve conflict?

_____ (Other—please specify _____)

TABLE 12.9
Problem-solving
procedure scale

Instructions: On the basis of behaviors and interaction you observed, rate the degree to which the group measured up to each criterion.

Poor 1			Fair 2		Average 3	Good 4	Excellent 5

1	2	3	4	5	1. Concerns of all members were established regarding the problem.
1	2	3	4	5	2. Components of the undesirable situation and obstacles to change were clearly described.
1	2	3	4	5	3. The goal was clearly defined and agreed upon by all members.
1	2	3	4	5	4. Possible solutions were listed and clarified before extensive evaluation of them.
1	2	3	4	5	5. Criteria for evaluation were previously understood and accepted, or discussed and agreed upon by all members.
1	2	3	4	5	6. Based on facts and reasoning, predictions were made regarding the probable effectiveness and possible negative consequences of each proposed solution.
1	2	3	4	5	7. Consensus was achieved on the most desirable/acceptable solution.
1	2	3	4	5	8. A realistic plan was developed for implementing the solution and, if appropriate, for evaluating its effectiveness.
1	2	3	4	5	9. Overall, the problem-solving process was thorough, vigilant, and systematic.

One common type of assessment is the **postmeeting reaction (PMR) form,** which is a questionnaire given to participants at the end of a meeting to get objective feedback for improving future discussions. Usually anonymous, PMRs encourage candid and honest assessments. PMR forms are often handed out by a group's leader, but they can be planned by other group members. They can also be used by instructors, consultants, or planners of large conferences to evaluate a class, program, or conference. PMR results should be tallied and fed back to the group as soon as possible after members complete them; if a group has access to the right computer software, ratings can be entered and tallied simultaneously. The feedback provided by PMRs helps members and the leader adjust so they can be more effective in reaching their goals. Two examples of PMR forms are shown in Table 12.11 and Table 12.12. Although both are designed to be completed

Postmeeting Reaction (PMR) Form

A form, completed after a discussion, on which group members evaluate the discussion, the group, and/or the leader.

TABLE 12.10
Workplace diversity
questionnaire

Instructions: Answer each question on the basis of what you have observed and experienced in your workgroup.

Inclusion	Agree		Disagree		
1. If someone who is not included in the main-stream tries to get information or makes a request, others stall or avoid helping them out in subtle ways.	5	4	3	2	1
2. It seems that the real reason people are denied promotions or raises is that they are seen as not fitting in.	5	4	3	2	1
3. I have to prove myself more and work a lot harder to get into that next position because of my gender or ethnic background.	5	4	3	2	1
4. It's hard to get ahead here unless you are part of the old boys' network.	5	4	3	2	1

Ideation					
5. When people from different backgrounds work together in groups, some people feel slighted because their ideas are not acknowledged.	5	4	3	2	1
6. People are reluctant to get involved in a project that requires them to balance ideas from different gender and racial points of view.	5	4	3	2	1
7. Individuals with different backgrounds have a difficult time getting their ideas across.	5	4	3	2	1
8. Individuals in our group have a difficult time really listening with an open mind to the ideas presented by those of another culture or gender.	5	4	3	2	1

Understanding					
9. When people who are culturally different or of different genders work together in our group, there is always some amount of miscommunication.	5	4	3	2	1
10. Women and people of color are interpreted differently than white males, even when they say the same thing.	5	4	3	2	1
11. Whenever I've confronted someone for giving me a hard time because of my race or gender, they have denied the problem.	5	4	3	2	1

Treatment					
12. Some people in our group are "talked down to" because they are different.	5	4	3	2	1

13. People's different ways of talking or acting cause them to be treated as less competent or smart.	5	4	3	2	1
14. Performance evaluations seem to be biased against those who are different, because supervisors focus on very traditional ways of getting work done.	5	4	3	2	1
15. You can just feel a difference in the way some people are treated or talked to because they are different.	5	4	3	2	1

anonymously, groups can also set aside the last five or so minutes of a meeting for an open postmeeting discussion about how members felt about the meeting. Table 12.12, in particular, can guide such a discussion. These forms can also be completed electronically via a service such as Survey Monkey or embedded in your group's site.

TABLE 12.11
Postmeeting reaction (PMR) form

Instructions: Check the point on each scale that best represents your honest judgment. Add any comments you wish to make that are not covered by the questionnaire. Do not sign your name.

1. How clear were the *goals* of the discussion to you?

    very clear   somewhat vague   muddled

2. The *atmosphere* was

    cooperative and   apathetic   competitive
    cohesive

3. How well *organized and vigilant* was the discussion?

    disorderly   just right   to rigid

4. How effective was the *leadership* supplied by the chairperson?

    too autocratic   democratic   weak

5. *Preparation for this meeting* was

    thorough   adequate   poor

6. Did you find yourself *wanting to speak* when you didn't get a chance?

    almost never   occasionally   often

7. How satisfied are you with the *results* of the discussion?

    very satisfied   moderately satisfied   very satisfied

8. How do you feel about *working again* with this same group?

    eager   I will   reluctant

    Comments:

TABLE 12.12
Postmeeting
reaction (PMR) form

1. How do you feel about today's discussion?

    excellent _____ good _____ all right _____ not too good _____ bad _____

2. What were the strong points of the discussion?

3. What were the weaknesses?

4. What changes would you suggest for future meetings?

(You need not sign your name.)

Recap: A Quick Review

Groups can benefit when members take the time to assess themselves, each other, and the group as a whole.

1. Numerous instruments, such as personality inventories and rating scales, can help members learn about themselves; several examples were presented, but others can be found in textbooks and through the Internet.

2. Sometimes the information is given only to the member, but often members discuss within the group what they learned about themselves and how their behaviors affect the group.

3. Members can assess each other's behavior, thus providing valuable feedback to each other; any of the instruments and scales used for self-assessment can be modified to be used for assessing other members or the leader.

4. Groups should regularly evaluate their meetings and their processes so that they can make needed adjustments.

5. Any element of a group—its norms, decision making, leadership, and so forth—can be evaluated; questionnaires and rating scales can be specifically tailored to focus on the specific areas you most want to evaluate.

6. Postmeeting reaction forms are questionnaires used to evaluate specific meetings; they can be designed to evaluate specific areas of a meeting (such as the group's decision-making effectiveness) or can be more general (such as evaluating whether members thought a meeting was effective).

Calling for Outside Help: The Consultant

Sometimes, even the most knowledgeable group members or leaders may become so immersed in discussion of a particular issue that they lose sight of the process, or they just can't distance themselves enough to take an objective look. That's when a **consultant,** an observer who does *not* participate in the group's discussion, can be a real asset in spotting what might be wrong and helping a group fix its problems. Evaluating a group's process has been shown to be beneficial to both small groups and the organizations that created them.[5]

The consultant does not need to be a paid professional—our students can and have served as consultants to groups and organizations both on and off campus. By the time you finish this chapter, you will know how to plan and conduct an observation of a group.

In this section, we describe the functions consultants perform, suggest strategies for planning your consultation, and give you more examples of instruments that are particularly useful for observing and consulting. We also remind you that the scales and questionnaires already presented can be used by consultants, so don't forget about them when you put on your consultant hat.

Practice First

The best thing you can do to become an effective consultant is to practice. You need to train your eyes and ears in what to observe and how best to gather the information you need. There are many groups you can observe in their natural settings, such as most meetings of boards, councils, and government committees. Many groups will open their meetings to you if they know you are a student and you promise to maintain the confidentiality of the group's private business.

Observing as part of a team will increase your learning. A team can take in more than an individual can, and team members learn a lot from sharing and discussing their individual insights. An observation team may be able to arrange a fishbowl setup, with observers sitting in a circle outside the discussion group. Sometimes, all observers will focus on the same aspects of group discussion, such as leadership sharing; at other times, each member watches for and reports on a different phenomenon (e.g., Martha observes leadership sharing, Xiuchen concentrates on how the group uses information).

Consultants generally provide three functions for the groups they consult for: they *remind* a group of techniques or principles of discussion it has overlooked, they *teach* a group new procedures and techniques to improve the group's performance, and they *critique* a group's performance. Sometimes, consultants do all three of these at once.

Reminding   Often group members need only to be reminded of principles and techniques they already know but have temporarily overlooked in the excitement of a lively argument. A reminder is like a coach during pauses in a football game. Having a reminder can improve a group's decision quality. Schultz et al. trained certain group members to serve as reminders,

Consultant

A nonparticipant observer who works with a group to determine what it needs, then helps by providing information, special techniques, and procedures.

intervening whenever they observed symptoms of defective group decision making.[6] The reminders were instructed not to be aggressive but to remind the group by providing timely questions and suggestions: "Maybe we shouldn't make our final choice until we've looked at all the alternatives." Reminders, particularly those who were regular group members and not the emergent leaders of their groups, significantly affected decision quality.

Teaching   Sometimes a consultant can be a helpful teacher by providing basic information about small group processes. Many of the people who participate in groups of all kinds have never studied small group communication and don't know what is normal and what isn't. Just by taking a small group communication course, you are ahead of many group leaders and managers who may have been thrown into a group with no training.

A teaching consultant can provide specialized information or ideas for procedures and techniques designed to solve specific group difficulties. Examples of such procedures were provided throughout this text.

Critiquing   Many consultants, teachers, and trainers provide a group with **critique,** a descriptive analysis and evaluation of the group's strengths and weaknesses. Communication specialists on corporate training and development staffs are often called on to provide evaluations of both groups and individual members to managers, but even students can provide thoughtful critique. Evaluation is important! Greenbaum and associates claim that failure to evaluate adequately the procedures and output of the quality circles is often a major factor in the demise of quality circle programs.[7]

In general, a consultant's critique should cover at least four aspects of a group's discussion processes and culture: (1) inputs to and content of the problem-solving discussion; (2) the group process, including patterns of verbal interaction, member roles (including any ego-centered behavior and ethical lapses), communication process, decision making, and problem solving as a whole; (3) the group product, including how well it has been evaluated by the group, how appropriate it is to the goals or problem described by the group, and how committed members seem to be to making it work; and (4) leadership, especially the role of the designated leader and the sharing of leadership functions.[8]

Giving Feedback   No matter what consulting function you provide, there are guidelines you should follow when you deliver feedback. Following these guidelines will increase the chance that members will be willing to hear what you say instead of getting defensive.

1. Give the group a chance to correct itself first. Don't jump in right away when you observe a problem; see if the group will figure something out on its own.

Critique

Analysis and assessment of something, such as identification of strengths and weaknesses in a small group's process and interaction.

2. Focus on the most important issues or problems. Don't overwhelm a group by noting every single thing you think could be improved because that will bog members down and could demoralize them.

3. Stress the positive first; look for things to point out that the members and leader are doing well before you point out areas for improvement.

4. Focus on communication processes and procedures, not the *content* of discussion.

5. Don't give orders, try to force the group to change, or argue. Ultimately, it is up to the members whether they want to take your advice. Present your observations, back them up with specific examples, but leave members free to decide whether or how your feedback will be used.

6. Speak (or write) clearly, precisely, and briefly. If the group asks for an explanation, elaboration, or demonstration of a technique, prepare it carefully and don't ramble.

7. Phrase most of your remarks as descriptions of what you have observed, questions, and suggestions. Susanna did this for the executive team: "Did you notice that in the space of only four minutes, the team has discussed _____,_____ , and _____?"

8. If you need to correct a member's or leader's behavior, do so privately so that you don't embarrass that person in front of the group. To the group, focus on trends and tendencies rather than singling someone out (unless it is to praise them).

9. Don't bluff. If a group asks for information or procedures you aren't familiar with, admit it and explain that you will research these for the group and bring the information back at a subsequent meeting.

Planning the Consultation

Many new consultants feel overwhelmed by all that goes on. Planning your observation and consultation in advance will help you focus on variables most important to your purpose as a consultant. You may first want to talk with the group's leader for background material about the group, such as what its purpose is, the history of the group, how effective it is perceived to be, and so forth. One way to cope with information overload is to record the group's discussion on audio- or videotape (but only after obtaining permission from the group) for more detailed analysis at a later time. That way, you will worry less about missing something important and can make notes about parts of the discussion to review later. Services like Wiggio or Blackboard permit many of their interactions to be documented and accessible for analysis.

The questions in Table 12.13 can guide you in selecting a more limited list of questions for a specific observation. If you have been asked to consult, this list can help you decide what is going well so you can focus on what group members may want to change. Note also that most of the areas

TABLE 12.13 Questions to help guide your observation

Group Purpose/Goals

What is the group's purpose?
Do members clearly understand and accept the group's purpose?
Has the committee achieved a clear understanding of its charge?
Do members seem to know and accept limits on their area of freedom?
Can members describe what sort of output is needed?

Setting

How adequate are meeting facilities, such as seating arrangement, privacy, and comfort?
How adequate are facilities for recording and displaying group progress (information, ideas, evaluations, decisions, and so on)?

Communication Skills and Network

How competently do members encode verbally and nonverbally?
How carefully are members listening to understand each other?
How equally is participation spread among the members?
Is the network of verbal interaction all-channel or unduly restricted?

Group Culture, Norms, and Communication Climate

To what degree is the group climate characterized by openness, trust, and teamwork?
What attitudes toward each other and the content of information and ideas are members manifesting?
Are cultural, work style, or personality differences interfering with the group's effectiveness?
Are any self-centered hidden agenda items interfering with progress toward the goal?
Are any norms interfering with cohesiveness and progress?
Are arguments being expressed sensitively and being managed to test ideas and achieve consensus, or to win?

Role Structure

Is there a designated leader?
If so, how well is this person performing the role? With what style? Are others encouraged to share in leader functions?
If not, how is leadership distributed? Are any needed services missing?
Are all necessary functional roles being provided?
Are there any ego-centered behavioral roles?

Problem-Solving and Decision-Making Procedures

How vigilant are the group's problem-solving procedures?
Do members seem to be adequately informed or are they planning how to get needed information before reaching decisions?
Are information and ideas being evaluated thoroughly for effectiveness and possible negative consequences, or accepted without question?
Are criteria shared by all group members, or explicitly discussed and agreed upon?

Are there any tendencies toward groupthink?

Has some procedure or agenda for the discussion been accepted by the group? If so, how adequate is it and how well is it being used?

Are information, interpretations, proposals, and decisions being recorded?

Are these provided in some record visible to the entire group?

How creative is the group in finding alternatives?

How frequently are summaries being made and used to focus and move discussion toward the goal?

How are decisions being made?

If needed, is the group making adequate plans to implement its decisions? To evaluate the adequacy of its actual solution(s), and possibly make changes later?

Might procedural changes or special techniques such as brainstorming, committee procedural rules, Nominal Group Technique, or computer charting be beneficial to the group?

of focus in Table 12.13 include questions relevant to a group's computer use. In fact, you can assess a group's computer use by adding sections such as teleconferencing or electronic brainstorming.

Obviously, you cannot consider all these questions at the same time. Concentrate on the one or two factors that seem most important or most problematic. With increased experience you be able to pay attention to more factors.

Ethical Principles for Consultants

A consultant usually makes a detailed feedback statement to the group that assesses the group's strong and weak points. When you do so, respect both the individual members and the group as an entity. Don't poison the well for future observers and consultants. The ethical standards that apply to observers are analogous to those universities use when faculty and students conduct research involving human subjects. Group members, like research participants, deserve the same type of protections. As consultant, adhere to the following standards of personal conduct:

1. Do not harm group members either physically or psychologically by your feedback. Don't knowingly cause embarrassment, emotional upset, physical danger, and so forth. For example, it *would* be unethical for a consultant to make fun of a group member in front of the rest of the group, but it *would not* be unethical to speak with that member privately to describe the effect of the offending behavior on the group.

2. Tell the truth. It is unethical to tell a group that a critique will not be given to a superior when in fact it *will*. It is also unethical to tell a group that you think its decision-making procedures are thorough when in fact you think they are sloppy.

3. Make your criticism constructive. When you point out a problem, suggest what members might do to correct it, as Susanna did

when she recommended that the group find a different meeting room, that Sam provide an agenda, and that his secretary take minutes. You are there to help, not to judge.

4. Respect the privacy and confidentiality of group members at all times. It is not ethical to share with outsiders what you have observed in a specific group unless you told the group you were going to do so before observing and the group granted you permission to do so, or you so thoroughly disguise the identity of the group and its members (as in a statistical summary) that no one can possibly identify the group and members in your report. In addition, it is not ethical to receive confidential information from one member and share it with another without permission. Finally, unless a group meeting has been legally declared open to the public, you should not report details or the substance of group business to outsiders.

When you report findings of your observations (for instance, reporting to your teacher or class), you will need to get permission to do so from the group members *before* you do your observing. The members observed may be more willing to let you report if you offer to use pseudonyms instead of real names. In general, treat observed persons just as you would want to be treated if your roles were reversed.

More Instruments for Observing and Consulting

The final section of Chapter 12 is devoted to presenting more instruments and techniques for observing and evaluating groups. Just as the instruments presented early in the chapter can be used by observers and consultants, the instruments presented here can be used by group members themselves as part of a group's self-asssessment. Feel free to use the instruments as presented or adapt them to suit specific situations and needs.

Verbal Interaction Analysis

Verbal Interaction Analysis

An analysis of who talks to whom and how often during a discussion.

A diagram of a **verbal interaction analysis** reveals who talks to whom, how often each member participates orally, and whether the group has members who dominate or who do not speak up. The information at the top of Figure 12.1 identifies the group, time, and members involved, in this case the six members of the G.E. Tigers. Each circle represents a group member, and the arrows represent lines of communication connecting each member to every other member. The longer arrows pointing to the center of the circle represent communication to the group as a whole. The circles and arrows should be drawn in advance. Each time a member speaks, a short cross mark is made on the shaft of the appropriate arrow.

Verbal interaction diagrams are easier to interpret when the cross marks are represented as numbers and percentages in a chart, like the ones in Figure 12.2 and Figure 12.3. Judging from the numbers shown in this

Group___G.E. "Tiger"_____

Time_____

   Begin __1:03_____

   End ___1:54_____

Place _____Conf. Rm. 14____

Observer __Snow_____

FIGURE 12.1
Verbal interaction
diagram

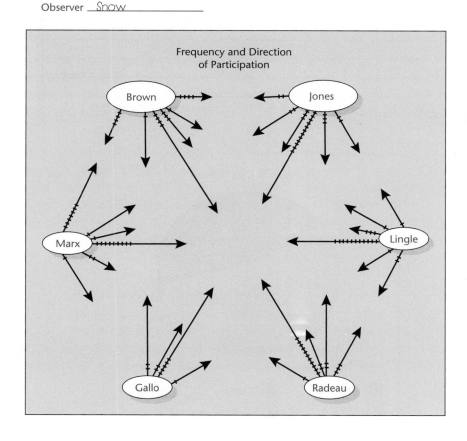

Frequency and Direction
of Participation

example, who do you think was discussion leader of the G.E. Tigers? Are there any other reasoned inferences you can make about this group from the data? You could modify this procedure and instrument to capture the frequency of some nonverbal behaviors such as eye contact and body angles. Obviously designed for face-to-face interaction, this instrument could become a message interaction analysis to track interaction in computer-mediated groups. Leaders of virtual teams sometimes use a method like this to track participation during teleconferences to ensure equitable contributions.

FIGURE 12.2
Displaying data from a verbal interaction diagram

Group _____ G.E. "Tigers" Q.C. _____ Place _____ Conf. Rm. 14 _____
Observer _____ Snow _____ Date _____ 5-3-12 _____
Beginning time _____ 1:03 _____ Ending time _____ 1:54 pm _____

TO:

FROM:	Brown	Jones	Lingle	Radeau	Gallo	Marx	Group	Total / Percent
Brown	–	5	2	4	2	5	5	23 / 16.1
Jones	3	–	3	4	4	3	13	30 / 21
Lingle	2	2	–	3	2	4	12	25 / 17.5
Radeau	3	3	4	–	0	2	12	24 / 16.8
Gallo	3	3	2	0	–	0	6	14 / 9.8
Marx	8	2	2	3	2	–	10	27 / 18.9
Total _number_	19	15	13	14	10	14	58	143
percent	13.3	10.5	9.1	9.8	7	9.8	40.6	100

FIGURE 12.3
Another way to display data from a verbal interaction diagram

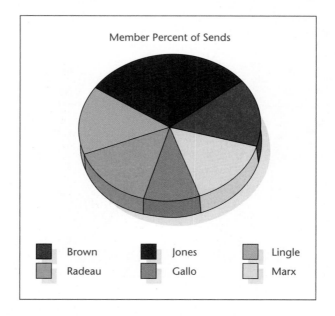

Member Percent of Sends

Brown   Jones   Lingle
Radeau   Gallo   Marx

Content Analysis

An analysis of the content (topics, behaviors, specific words or ideas, fantasy themes, etc.) of a group's discussion.

Content Analysis

Content analysis procedures examine the actual content of remarks (e.g., topics discussed, types of remarks) made during a discussion. One type of content analysis focuses on who performs what behaviors and how often. From such a descriptive analysis, members' roles can be described. The examples in Figure 12.4 and Figure 12.5 classify members' behaviors

Behavioral Functions	Participants' Names					
1. Initiating and orienting						
2. Information giving						
3. Information seeking						
4. Opinion giving						
5. Opinion seeking						
6. Clarifying and elaborating						
7. Evaluating						
8. Summarizing						
9. Coordinating						
10. Consensus testing						
11. Recording						
12. Suggesting procedure						
13. Gatekeeping						
14. Supporting						
15. Harmonizing						
16. Tension relieving						
17. Dramatizing						
18. Norming						
19. Withdrawing						
20. Blocking						
21. Status and recognition seeking						

Group_____ Place _____ Observer_____

Date_____ Beginning time _____ Ending time _____

FIGURE 12.4
Content analysis of behavioral functions of members

during the observed discussion. Specific behaviors are listed along the left side of the chart, and the participants' names in the cells at the head of each column. Each time a member speaks, the observer judges what the behavior was and places a tally mark in the appropriate cell of the chart.

The tally marks are then converted to numbers and percentages, as shown in Figure 12.5. They can also be converted to pie charts such as the one shown for Jodi in Figure 12.6. From this analysis, can you tell who is probably task leader of this group? Who is the social or maintenance leader? Do any individuals seem to be interfering with the group's progress toward its goal?

FIGURE 12.5
Displaying data from analysis of behavioral functions of members

Group EXECUTIVE COMMITTEE	Place CU LOBBY				
Observer ANDY	Date 3-21-12				
Beginning time 4:30 P.M.	Ending time 6:30 P.M.				

Behavioral Functions	Mary	John	Edna	Dave	Jodi	Total $\frac{number}{percent}$
1. Initiating and orienting	5	3				$\frac{8}{5.7}$
2. Information giving	6	5		2	3	$\frac{16}{11.4}$
3. Information seeking			3			$\frac{3}{2.1}$
4. Opinion giving	8	8	4	2	1	$\frac{23}{16.4}$
5. Opinion seeking			2			$\frac{2}{1.4}$
6. Clarifying and elaborating			3			$\frac{3}{2.1}$
7. Evaluating	2	4			1	$\frac{7}{5}$
8. Summarizing	2					$\frac{2}{1.4}$
9. Coordinating	8					$\frac{8}{5.7}$
10. Consensus testing				3		$\frac{3}{2.1}$
11. Recording			5			$\frac{5}{3.6}$
12. Suggesting procedure	3	6				$\frac{9}{6.4}$
13. Gatekeeping			1	5		$\frac{6}{4.3}$
14. Supporting	2		2	6		$\frac{10}{7.1}$
15. Harmonizing				3	2	$\frac{5}{3.6}$
16. Tension relieving					6	$\frac{6}{4.3}$
17. Dramatizing		5			3	$\frac{8}{5.7}$
18. Norming				4		$\frac{4}{2.9}$
19. Withdrawing		1				$\frac{1}{.7}$
20. Blocking	2	5				$\frac{7}{5}$
21. Status and recognition seeking		4				$\frac{4}{2.9}$
Total $\frac{number}{percent}$	$\frac{38}{27.1}$	$\frac{35}{25}$	$\frac{26}{18.6}$	$\frac{25}{17.9}$	$\frac{16}{11.4}$	$\frac{140}{100}$

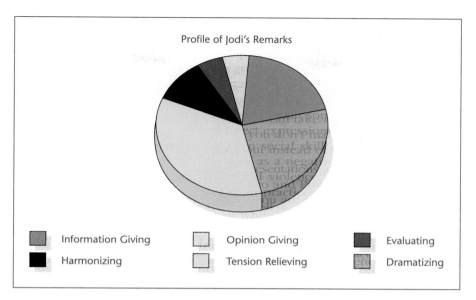

Profile of Jodi's Remarks

■ Information Giving □ Opinion Giving ■ Evaluating
■ Harmonizing □ Tension Relieving □ Dramatizing

FIGURE 12.6
Pie chart displaying Jodi's behavioral functions

A content analysis can be developed for virtually any set of categories that can be used to classify member behavior, including types of statements (e.g., questions, answers, opinions), styles of conflict management (e.g., self-oriented, other-oriented, issue-oriented), and so forth. It is important for the observers to classify the remarks consistently so that the same behavior is classified in the same way by two observers, or by one observer at two different times.

SYMLOG: Drawing a Snapshot of a Group

SYMLOG, which is an acronym for the System for the Multiple Level Observation of Groups, is both a theory and a methodology that permits a three-dimensional diagram to be constructed of a group.[9] Such diagrams can be constructed by outside observers and consultants or by the group members themselves. Examples of such diagrams are provided in Figure 12.7 and Figure 12.8. (Instructions for producing a simplified SYMLOG-like diagram are included in the *Instructor's Manual*.) You can see, even without detailed information about SYMLOG theory, that the first group (Figure 12.7) is fragmented and polarized, but the second (Figure 12.8) is unified and cohesive.

SYMLOG theory rests on the assumption that behavior of each group member in a group can be classified along each of three independent dimensions: dominant versus submissive; friendly versus unfriendly; and task-oriented versus emotionally expressive.[10] SYMLOG may be used in one of two ways. With the scoring method, external observers score the verbal and nonverbal behaviors of members as they interact in real time. The rating method is easier, requiring no special training; external observers or

SYMLOG

SYstem for the Multiple Level Observation of Groups, both a theory about member characteristics and effects on group interaction, and a methodology that produces a three-dimensional "snapshot" of a group at a given point in time.

FIGURE 12.7 SYMLOG diagram of a noncohesive group

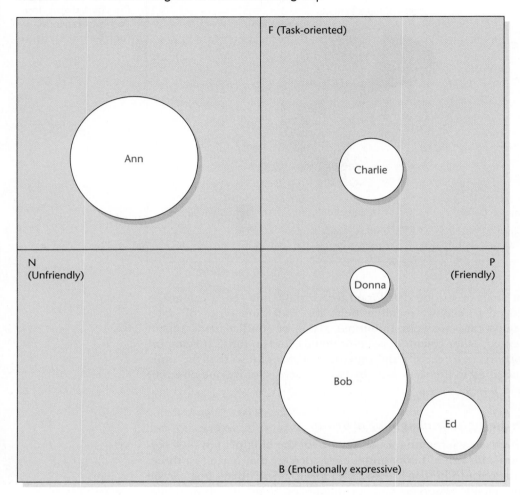

group members themselves complete a 26-question rating scale evaluating each member's behavior. The results are tallied in a particular way so each member can be placed on the SYMLOG diagram.

Each of the three dimensions is represented by a pair of letters that anchor the pole positions. For example, *P* (positive) stands for *friendly* and *N* (negative) stands for *unfriendly* behavior. On the diagram, the more friendly a member is toward the other members of the group, the farther the circle is placed to the right. The more unfriendly members are located farther to the left. (In Figure 12.7, Ed is the most friendly and Ann the most unfriendly.) Task orientation is represented by *F* (forward); the more task-oriented a member is, the closer he or she is to the top of the diagram.

FIGURE 12.8 SYMLOG diagram of a unified, productive group

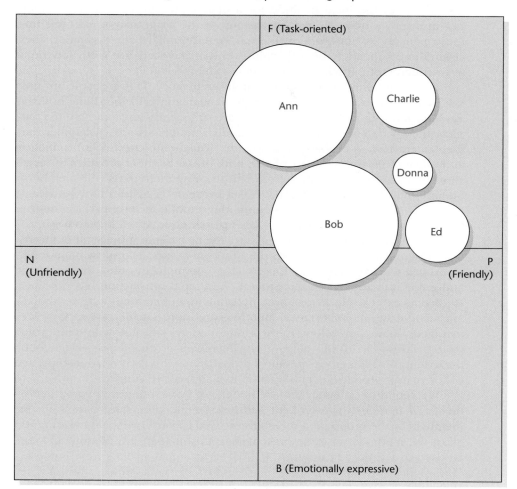

Emotional expressiveness is represented by *B* (backward); these members are closer to the bottom of the diagram. (In Figure 12.7, Ann is the most task-oriented, and Ed the most emotionally expressive.) The third dimension is depicted by the size of a member's circle; dominant members have larger circles than submissive ones. (In Figure 12.7, Ann and Bob are the most dominant, Donna the most submissive.)

You can readily see that the group shown in Figure 12.7 is not cohesive. Ann is dominant, task-oriented, and negative toward her fellow members. She tries to dictate what happens in the group. Bob is dominant, but friendly and emotionally expressive, which gets the group off track frequently; almost certainly, Bob's behavior clashes with Ann's desire to stick to the task. Charlie, who is moderately dominant, task-oriented, and friendly, is in the ideal position for a democratic, group-centered leader, but he's all by himself. Just by looking at the diagram you can tell that these people do not work well as a team. Members are dissimilar, they clash, there appears to be little cohesiveness, and there are wide variations in the degree of participation members exhibit.

The diagram in Figure 12.8 tells a different story. This group seems unified, with all members in the upper-right-hand quadrant (which Bales calls the *decision-making quadrant*). Members are sufficiently task-oriented to complete the group's assignment, but friendly enough toward each other that their interaction is probably harmonious. This is a picture of a productive and efficient group. As you can see, a SYMLOG analysis provides a "snapshot" of a group as a whole system whose component parts (the members) operate interdependently. SYMLOG is a particularly helpful tool because it so clearly displays such aspects as the degree of cohesiveness, the degree and type of member participation, group task orientation, and so forth.

Group work is not just about getting the task done. It is also about forming satisfying relationships with the other members. The most memorable teams you will experience are those with group members who do good work and enjoy one another in the process. Relational satisfaction has not been studied as extensively as task accomplishment, but communication scholars are recognizing its importance. Members are more satisfied when they feel involved, know they belong to the group, and are satisfied with their group relationships.[11] SYMLOG helps group members or outside observers "see" the extent to which group members are satisfied with their relationships, are cohesive and productive, and operate in a supportive climate.

We remind you again that, although we have suggested some instruments as particularly useful for self-assessment, others for assessing the members or the group, and others to be used by observers and consultants, all of the methods we have presented in this chapter are flexible and can be used in a variety of ways.

Recap: A Quick Review

Consultants can often provide the objective assessments a group needs:

1. Consultants, who are not group members, can serve the functions of reminding members of principles they have forgotten, teaching members procedures and techniques, and critiquing a group's performance.
2. Knowledgeable students can be effective consultants; their skills are enhanced through observation and practice.

3. Consultants must give feedback sensitively and cannot force a group to change; ultimately, the group decides whether and how to accept the consultant's feedback.

4. Consultants must plan their observations in advance because it is impossible to pay attention to every aspect of a group equally; they should focus on the most important or most problematic aspects of a group's interaction.

5. Consultants must treat members ethically, the way they would want to be treated; they can be guided by the procedures that universities have established for how to treat research participants.

6. Verbal interaction diagrams describe who talks to whom and how often.

7. Content analysis can be constructed to evaluate any type of content, including topic of discussion, types of questions, and style of managing conflict.

8. SYMLOG, which is both a theory and a methodology, can help members or consultants gain insight into how a group functions; it is especially useful for assessing the group's cohesiveness or lack of it.

QUESTIONS FOR REVIEW

 Go to self-quizzes on the Online Learning Center at mbhe.com/galanes14e to test your knowledge of the chapter concepts.

The case study that opened this chapter concerned Sam, who had tried several ways to assess and improve his executive committee's performance, but who elected to bring in Susanna as an outside consultant.

1. Do you think Sam's choice to ask members to assess their own preference for procedural order was a good choice? Why do you think he selected that scale? Were there better choices for him?

2. Sam also asked his group to assess how meetings were going. Given what you know about this group, what would you have done if you were Sam?

3. What were the specific issues that Susanna identified as problems for this group?

4. What do you think a verbal interaction diagram, content analysis, and SYMLOG diagram might have shown regarding the executive committee?

5. What would you have advised the group to do to improve performance?

KEY TERMS

 Test your knowledge of these key terms by visiting the Online Learning Center Web site at mbhe.com/galanes14e.

Consultant	Critique	SYMLOG
Content analysis	Postmeeting reaction (PMR) form	Verbal interaction analysis

BIBLIOGRAPHY

Bales, Robert F. *SYMLOG Case Study Kit*. New York: Free Press, 1980.

Schwarz, Roger M. *The Skilled Facilitator: Practical Wisdom for Developing Effective Groups*. San Francisco: Jossey-Bass, 1994.

Wheelan, Susan A. *Creating Effective Teams: A Guide for Members and Leaders*. Thousand Oaks, CA: Sage, 1999.

NOTES

1. Mauro Nunes and Henrique O'Neill, "The Promus Agent System, A Tool to Assess a Virtual Team's Performance," *Proceedings of the IADIS International Conference on Applied Computing*, in Algarve Portugal, 2 (February 2005): 417–24.

2. Jill Nemiro, Michael Beyerlein, Lori Bradley, and Susan Beyerlein, Eds., *The Handbook of High-Performance Virtual Teams: A Toolkit for Collaborating Across Boundaries* (San Francisco: Jossey-Bass, 2008): 439–568.

3. Bobby R. Patton and Kim Giffin, *Problem-Solving Group Interaction* (New York: Harper & Row, 1973): 213–14.

4. Linda K. Larkey, "The Development and Validation of the Workforce Diversity Questionnaire: An Instrument to Assess Interactions in Diverse Work Groups," *Management Communication Quarterly*, 9 (February 1996): 296–337.

5. Patricia M. Fandt, "The Relationship of Accountability and Interdependent Behavior to Enhancing Team Consequences," *Group & Organization Studies*, 16 (1991): 300–12; Harold H. Greenbaum, Ira T. Kaplan, and William Metlay, "Evaluation of Problem-Solving Groups," *Group & Organization Studies*, 13 (1988): 133–47.

6. Beatrice Schultz, Sandra M. Ketrow, and Daphne M. Urban, "Improving Decision Quality in the Small Group: The Role of the Reminder," *Small Group Research*, 26 (November 1995): 521–41.

7. Greenbaum et al., "Evaluation of Problem-Solving Groups."

8. Ibid., 137–39, 145.

9. Robert F. Bales and Stephen P. Cohen, *SYMLOG: A System for the Multiple Level Observation of Groups* (New York: Free Press, 1979). Space constraints prevent including a complete description of SYMLOG theory and methodology here; we refer readers who are interested in learning to construct a complete SYMLOG diagram for their groups to the following workbook: R. F. Bales, *SYMLOG Case Study Kit* (New York: Free Press, 1980). The *Instructor's Manual* for this text includes instructions and necessary forms for completing a simplified SYMLOG-like diagram so that students can have a better idea of what SYMLOG does.

10. Lynne Kelly and Robert L. Duran note that, in some recent writings, Bales refers to the third dimension as acceptance versus nonacceptance of authority, a designation that seems more appropriate when assessing group member values as opposed to behaviors; in "SYMLOG: Theory and Measurement of Small Group Interaction," *Small Group Communication: A Reader*, 6th ed., eds. Robert S. Cathcart and Larry A. Samovar (Dubuque, IA: Wm. C. Brown, 992): 220–33.

11. Carolyn M. Anderson, Matthew M. Martin, and Bruce L. Riddle, "Small Group Relational Satisfaction Scale: Development, Reliability, and Validity," *Communication Studies*, 52 (Fall 2001): 220–33.

Preparing for Problem-Solving Discussions: Informational Resources for the Group

A

A group's output can be only as good as its input and throughput allow. As with cooking or building a house, it's important to use the best possible materials, in this case, information. Groups that gather high-quality relevant information *before* they begin their problem-solving or decision-making procedures will produce better decisions, solutions, reports, and recommendations than groups that don't.

This appendix will help you improve your input resources by assessing the information you have, deciding what additional information you need, and then obtaining it, evaluating it, and organizing it for easy referencing by the group. The four steps, in order, are (1) review and organize your present stock of information and ideas, (2) gather additional information you need, (3) evaluate all the information and ideas you have collected, and (4) organize the information and ideas into a tentative outline. This comprehensive information-gathering procedure is especially useful for problems and decisions where making a mistake would be costly or worse. For less consequential problems, the group can adapt the procedure or focus on just the most relevant steps.

Review and Organize Your Present Stock of Information and Ideas

First, take a systematic inventory of the information you already have about your subject. This saves time and makes it easier for you to recall what you have when you need it.

1. **Place the problem or subject in perspective.**
   To what is it related? What will it affect, and what affects it? For example, when the church board mentioned in Chapter 3 decided on a new location for the church, it had to consider the financial condition of the church, long-range plans, the availability of public transportation and parking, types of activities planned for the church, and so forth.

2. **Make an inventory of information you have about the subject.**
   Each member needs to be on the same page as a group begins its
   problem-solving process. However, an advantage of group work is that
   members bring different perspectives, information, opinions, and so forth
   to the discussion. Members *should* represent different points of view;
   they should pool their collective knowledge and resources by sharing
   what they know, which they can do by mapping the problem thoroughly.

   In mapping, participants share all they know about a problem:
   facts, conditions, complaints, circumstances, factors, happenings,
   relationships, effects, and so forth. Someone—the group recorder or a
   volunteer—keeps track of the information that members share. Before
   the mapping process begins, as illustrated in Figure A.1, two or three
   members may have shared some information, but very little information was shared by all four. Some information was unknown by any
   of them. After the mapping process, four members share what they
   all know, ideally. Members are also in a better position to assess what
   they *don't* know and to plan a strategy for finding that information.

3. **Organize the information into a rough draft of a problem-solving
   outline.**
   Group together individual pieces of information, by topic, question,
   or issue. You may want to use the guidelines suggested in
   Chapters 9 and 10.

FIGURE A.1
Mapping
a problem

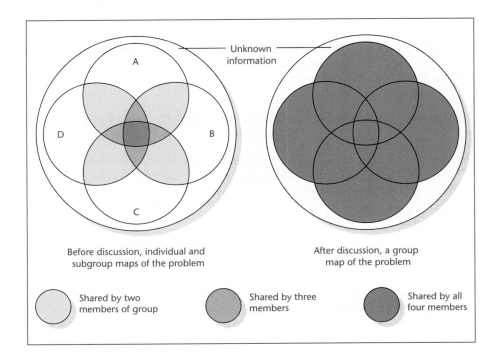

Unknown information

A

D   B

C

Before discussion, individual and
subgroup maps of the problem

After discussion, a group
map of the problem

Shared by two
members of group

Shared by three
members

Shared by all
four members

4. **Look for gaps.**
   The outline will reveal holes in the group's information and will suggest specific information needed.

Gather Information You Need

Now you can plan how to correct the gaps in your knowledge. *Planning* is important; otherwise, your information-gathering process will be haphazard.

For complex problems, expect to have several meetings. Even if members are familiar with the topic, they need time to think about it. The following two-step procedure helps ensure that the group overlooks nothing important:

1. **Identify and list all the major issues or topics, along with subtopics, that you need to explore further.**
   These issues were suggested by the rough outline produced during step 1 above. Add additional topics or deficiencies as they occur to you. Produce a list of all additional information needed.

2. **Assign research responsibilities to individual members.**
   Distribute items from the list produced in step 1 equitably to the members and establish deadlines to complete the research. This increases individual responsibility and involvement. Someone—the secretary or chair—should keep track of who has agreed to undertake what research.

Ideally, two or more members examine each major source for this common background study. This helps offset individual biases and helps prevent the group from relying on one "specialist" for each topic. However, time constraints often force members to work alone , which makes it especially important for each member to be conscientious and thorough.

Ways of gathering information are suggested below. We review it only briefly because you are likely to have learned this in other courses.

Note Taking

Information and ideas slip from memory or become distorted unless we make accurate and complete notes. Saying that a key piece of information appeared "in a book by some DNA researcher" is useless because fellow members cannot evaluate the credibility of the information or the source. The best system of note taking is to record each bit of information or data on a separate index card or directly into a database via a laptop computer, along with the topic heading and the full bibliographic reference, as shown in Table A.1.

Note cards and databases can be arranged in groups to help synthesize and interpret the evidence collected. They can be sorted in a variety of

TABLE A.1
A note card listing a topic heading, a specific subject, and exact details of the source

Self-Monitoring	Why related to leadership emergence

Robert J. Ellis and Steven F. Cronshaw, " Self-Monitoring and Leader Emergence: A Test of Moderator Effects," in *Small Group Research, 23* (February 1992): 113–129.

"It is possible that low and high self-monitors are equally effective at identifying the needs of a group, but only high self-monitors are proficient at modifying their behavior to respond to such needs." p. 124

ways and consulted with ease during a discussion without the researcher's having to leaf through a disorganized notebook.

Three important sources for gathering information useful to problem-solving discussions are direct observation, reading, and individual or group interviews.

Reading: Print and Electronic Sources

Often, a print or online encyclopedia, such as Wikipedia, can provide a helpful overview of a topic, although usually this overview will not provide much depth. Because, anyone can add items to Wikipedia, accuracy is questionable. However, Wikipedia is a good place to start for an overview of a topic.

For many topics and problems, the major source of information will be books, journals, newspapers, government documents, and other printed materials, whether in hard copy or online. First, compile a **bibliography**, which is a list of published sources on a particular topic or issue. For topics with many published sources, an abstract, or article summary, will help you narrow your sources to those most relevant. Internet sources are especially helpful here. Don't limit yourself to only one or two sources or to sources that support only one point of view. This will produce a bias in your information with no way to cross-check validity.

For efficiency, first prepare a list of key terms—descriptors—on the topic. For instance, a group investigating, "What type of lottery should our state conduct?" might use the following descriptors: *lottery, sweepstakes, gambling, crime, revenue,* and *betting.* Such descriptors provide the starting point for online searches. Once you start your search, you may encounter additional terms, such as *victimless* or *wagering.* A reference librarian's help is indispensable in using printed and electronic sources. The abstract sources are significant time savers because they provide brief summaries of articles or books to help you narrow your search.

Most sources are now accessible online, which can save you a lot of time. Computerized databases such as *ComAbstracts, Communication and Mass Media Complete, PsychINFO, SocINDEX, EBSCOhost,* and *Lexis-Nexis*

Bibliography

A list of sources of information about a topic; usually includes books, journal or magazine articles, newspaper stories, interviews, and so forth.

can be invaluable in locating information about a topic. Although some databases may entail a fee, they make it extremely easy for you to locate relevant items quickly, so they are usually worth the money.

Most online databases work the same way. Once you enter the database, often from your university or public library, you can search the database by key word, title, or author. For instance, in gathering information about capital punishment, key words such as *capital punishment, death penalty, death row, lethal injection,* or *electric chair* might be entered. If you know that John Smith has written a number of articles about capital punishment, you could search by author name, *John Smith.* Generally, this search will produce a list of articles pertinent to your topic. If your list is too long, you can refine it by adding additional key words: *capital punishment* and *Missouri,* for example. Often, in addition to the article's title, you can see the abstract, of the article. More and more often, articles are available full text online.

Even if you do not have access to specialized online databases, the World Wide Web itself serves as a giant online database. By using a **search engine** such as Yahoo.com, Google.com, AltaVista.com, or Infoseek.com, you can search the Web for items related to key words you enter. Many search engines attempt to rank-order the items they send you, so that the ones that seem most relevant appear first, but this process is not foolproof, so you may end up with information overload. Even so, you will want to try this to see what you do get.

Search Engine
Software that allows you to search the Web for items related to key words you enter.

In addition, seeking out the home page of organizations relevant to your topic can help. For instance, if your group is investigating the effects of drinking and driving, you may want to look at *Students Against Drunk Driving* to see what hits you get. If you do that, you will find that the first Web site listed is called *Students Against Destructive Decisions,* which is the name for SADD. Several buttons on that site link you to specific information helpful to your research.

Remember that when you cite research you obtained from the Web, you must provide the reader with enough information to locate the Web site you used. That means you need, at minimum, the Universal Resource Locator (URL) for the site, any links you clicked to get deeper into the site, the specific paragraph from which you obtained your specific information or your quoted material, and the date on which you accessed the material. In addition, many online documents now have unique digital object identifiers—doi—that you should reference in your bibliography.

Also helpful are bibliographies of bibliographies, such as *the Bibliography of Bibliographies.* Bibliographies are also found at the end of most books, doctoral dissertations, and research articles. Do not overlook indexes to periodicals, such as *The Readers Guide to Periodical Literature, The New York Times Index,* and *Education Index.* Federal and state government publications, in special sections of many libraries, also contain vast amounts of information. The *Monthly Catalog of U.S. Government Publications* and the *Monthly Checklist of State Publications* will help you locate relevant information in these publications. Other useful sources include the *Congressional Quarterly Weekly Report* and the *Congressional Digest*. Most of these are now online.

Begin reading even before you have completed your bibliography. A good strategy is for all members of the group to read some of the same things to provide a common background, then divide up the rest of the bibliography. When you evaluate a book for usefulness, read the index and table of contents for clues. Skim rapidly until you find something pertinent to your group, then read carefully. Take notes of the most important ideas and facts, and make copies of particularly valuable information for the rest of the group.

For controversial problems or topics, read as many contrasting interpretations and viewpoints as possible. For example, before developing a campus policy regarding use of laboratory animals for research, study the writings of those who favor and oppose using animals. Although it is easier to remember opinions that support your own, understanding other points of view is essential for effective group discussion and problem solving.

Direct Observation

Many times, needed information can come only from firsthand observation by group members, and often only direct observation can breathe life into a table of statistics or survey results. For example, a group of students trying to improve conditions at their student union's coffee shop spent time observing and recording how many customers did and did not bus their waste materials, the kinds of litter on the floor and tables, and the placement and condition of waste containers. In their final report, they were able to provide brief examples from their observations, which made their report more vivid and compelling.

Surveys

Sometimes a group may need more comprehensive or representative information than members can gather through observation alone. In that case, members may construct a survey. Entire courses are devoted to construction of valid and reliable surveys, and we can't provide details here. However, many student groups have designed simple, clear surveys to uncover additional information that they cannot get any other way. The student group investigating the coffee shop constructed an easy-to-take, short survey to learn who used the coffee shop, what time of day patrons were most likely to use it, what they liked best about it, and what they liked least. Patrons could pick up the one-page survey as they entered the shop, complete it in less than a minute or two, and drop it off in a specially designated box at the door. The students compiled the survey information and included it in their report. These days, it is easy to construct online surveys via software like Survey Monkey. Data from such surveys are easy to compile.

Individual and Group Interviews

Sometimes you need firsthand information or explanations by a knowledgeable individual; interviews can help you obtain information you cannot get in other ways. Members of the coffee shop group also interviewed a number of customers to determine how they felt about its condition and to ask their reasons for not busing their wastepaper and leftovers. They also interviewed the manager to determine why materials that contributed to litter were being used. Most people are flattered to be asked for their information and opinions, but remember that your interviewees are busy and would prefer that you read first, then interview them for clarification.

Interview questions may be open-ended ("Why do you eat in the snack shop?") or closed-ended ("If trash containers were more conveniently located, would you use them? Yes _____ No _____"). In-depth interviews using open-ended questions often yield unexpected information and provide richer data. However, answers to open-ended questions are more difficult and time-consuming to tally. In contrast, closed-ended questions can be asked of many people quickly and are easily tabulated if formulated properly. You may want to use both.

It is invalid to generalize findings from a casual or haphazard sample to a larger population. For example, interviews about location of a new sanitary landfill with 50 people who happen to enter a particular door of city hall will not provide an accurate picture of the beliefs of residents of that city, or even of people who go to city hall. A scientifically designed sample (a *representative* sample) must be taken if results of interviews are to be generalized to members of a larger population.

Focus Group Interviews   Individual interviews can be time-consuming; *Focus groups* allow several people to be interviewed at the same time. In a **focus group,** participants are encouraged to talk in an unstructured way about a topic presented to them by a trained facilitator, who often simply announces the topic and lets participants respond freely. This free-association discussion is usually tape-recorded for later content analysis. As an information-gathering technique, focus groups provide two advantages. They use researchers' time efficiently, and, because participants discuss issues in a group, they help spark ideas the focus group participants might not think of during an individual interview.

Focus group

A group procedure that encourages freewheeling discussion focusing on a specific topic or issue, often used to analyze people's interests and values for market research.

Focus groups have long been used in advertising and marketing research to discover potential markets and possible directions for innovation. Today, politicians use them to gauge voter reaction to issues; organizations, to identify problems, interests, and concerns of employees; and many different kinds of groups, to research particular issues.

Other Information Sources

Useful information may crop up anywhere, anytime. You may hear something relevant to your topic or problem while listening to the radio or watching television. You can sometimes access this information from the radio or TV station's Web site via podcast. Some televised material, such as the program content of C-SPAN, is cataloged and available for purchase or rent. Lectures or public speeches are another source of information. An idea may occur to you when you are not consciously thinking about the group's problem—for example, while riding to school, jogging, or talking with friends. Most of us find it helpful to keep a small notepad or a few note cards with us so that we can jot down ideas when they occur, lest we forget or distort them. The important thing is to be alert to unexpected information and record it promptly.

Evaluate the Information and Ideas You Have Collected

You must evaluate your information for accuracy and credibility. Many of your ideas may collapse in the presence of contradictory information, or some of your information may be from suspect sources, in direct contradiction to other evidence, or irrelevant. The group must know to cull the misleading, unsubstantiated, or wrong information so that your decision or solution will not be faulty.

In Chapter 10, we discussed ways you can evaluate information and reasoning, including information you get from the World Wide Web. For now, focus on the following questions:

1. **Are the sources believable?**
   Is the person a recognized expert? Is there anything—vested interest, known bias—that could have biased his or her opinion?

2. **Is a clear distinction made between facts and inferences?**
   Are opinions stated as though they are facts? Can the facts be verified by independent credible sources?

3. **Are statistical data validly gathered, analyzed, and explained?**
   Was the sample representative? Were appropriate statistical procedures used to analyze the data? Are the results appropriately generalized, or overgeneralized?

4. **Are conclusions (inferences) supported by good reasoning?**
   Are there any reasoning errors that call the conclusions into question? Can you draw different but equally valid conclusions from the same set of evidence?

Organize Your Information and Ideas

The most efficient way to organize the group's information is to write a tentative outline. Ask yourself, "What are the questions that must be answered by our group to understand the problem or subject fully?" Your answers can serve as tentative main points in your outline. In addition, your outline helps make the problem-solving process, discussed in Chapters 9 and 10, more systematic and less likely to omit something important.

Once you have decided on some tentative major issues or topic areas, arrange your notes into piles, one per issue or outline item. Some of the piles can be further divided into subheadings. For example, information concerning the nature of the problem might be arranged under such subheadings as "who is affected," "seriousness of the problem," "contributing causes," "previous attempts to solve the problem," and so forth. Organizing your information like this makes it easier for you to locate pertinent information when a topic arises during group discussion, helps you prepare questions the group needs to consider, and generally helps you and the group conduct an orderly and comprehensive discussion of a complex topic.

When you prepare for a problem-solving discussion, your outline is likely to contain some possible solutions you have found or thought of. You may have evidence or reasoning that shows how similar solutions were tried on a similar problem or even some suggestions about how to implement a plan. However, such thinking and planning should be *tentative*. It is easy to become attached to an issue after you have spent hours preparing to discuss it, but it is absolutely essential that your mind be open. Resist coming to a discussion prepared to defend your solution against all comers.

The information-gathering strategies we have suggested here can be modified to suit the particular needs of the group. For consequential decisions that will affect many people, something like this full procedure should be used. However, for relatively minor problems with few risks of making a mistake, the group can focus just on the parts most relevant to the group's problem. Use your common sense in applying any tools.

KEY TERMS

Bibliography	Focus group	Search engine

Making Public Presentations of the Group's Output

Often groups must make a public presentation of their output, which is, many times, a report of some kind. The group's leader or selected representatives may present the report to the parent organization, a political body, an open meeting of interested community representatives, or another type of public gathering. The audience members may themselves become participants who will discuss the report of the group. These public presentations involve three stages: planning, organizing, and presenting. In the discussion to follow, we will highlight the various decisions that your group must make at each stage. We follow this with information about group presentation at public meetings.

The Planning Stage

Start planning as soon as you know you must give a presentation. You must consider your group's audience, the occasion, your purpose, your topic, group member strengths and limitations, and logistics. Having an effective presentation rides on how well you initially assess what your presentation needs and how carefully you follow through.

Your Audience

Public presentations are not simply about what a group has to say to an audience. Successful presentations show audience members that *they* matter and are not just window dressing. Good audience analysis helps to create a comfortable speaking environment for both your group and the audience.

Audience analysis is a systematic approach to gathering as much information as possible about the audience. Audience members process material they hear in presentations through their own personal perspectives, as we discussed in Chapter 2. Understanding how your audience perceives the material you plan to cover helps you tailor how best to present it.[1] Engineers, for example, may give presentations to clients, fellow engineers, their staffs, local or federal agencies, and so forth. They must be able to communicate their main ideas in a multitude of different ways.[2] If your audience does not know anything about your topic, you need to stick with basic facts and clearly communicate background information. If audience members have some background with the topic, but your particular material is new to them, then you need to explain why your new information is relevant to them and why they should care about the topic. If audience members hold attitudes contrary to your topic, then you need to create common ground with them and relate your main ideas through the perspectives of the audience. For instance, if you plan to argue for the medical use of marijuana to an audience that is opposed to drug use, then you must connect to your listeners in some way. One way might be to talk about how much all of us value good healthcare for our loved ones, then relate your main points to those values. Audiences rarely think and feel exactly like the small group that prepared the presentation, so it is imperative that you learn something about their perspectives in order to craft your presentation accordingly.

Some audiences may not be there by choice. Your task still remains: Find out about your audience so you don't bore them or talk over their heads. Whether audience members are there by choice or are required to attend affects how you present your information and your level of enthusiasm. The more you know about the audience, the more you can connect them to your presentation and make them feel like they matter to you.

Your Occasion

Why have you been asked to present your group's final product? Who has asked you? Often, this person can help you understand both the audience and the specifics of the occasion. If it is a class presentation, clarify with your instructor the specific requirements for the presentation and what you can and can't do. If this is not a class presentation, try to visit the place to become comfortable with the setting. Ask about the number of people expected to attend. Will there be other speakers? How much control will you have over your setting? Clarify why you have been asked to speak and whether there are specific goals you will be expected to meet.

Your Purpose

Knowing clearly what you are trying to accomplish is an essential step in any effective presentation. If you do not know what you are doing and why, how can you get through to your audience? Many public group presentations are intended to educate and distribute information. For example, if your university's president has convened a student task force to investigate how best to improve student-community relations, then you may be asked to report your findings to the president and the city council. Your purpose is primarily informational. On the other hand, if you are charged with implementing a solution or presenting a recommendation, then your purpose becomes persuasive. Persuasive presentations involve explicit calls to action on the audience's part. Group presentations that are part of a small group discussion course often involve both informative and persuasive purposes.

Your Subject or Topic

Sometimes the most difficult part of planning is figuring out how to begin. The audience, the occasion, and your purpose help identify your specific subject and relevant subtopics. Often, you cannot present all the information you have gathered over the course of a project's life. Sometimes the person or agency that invited you to speak has an agenda that will guide your subject selection. You may be given a particular structure and time limit to follow or simply be told to "fill us in." Make the best of your parameters; novice presenters often present too much information and run out of time, which causes them to lose credibility with the audience or lose the audience altogether!

Member Strengths and Fears

Know and appreciate the difficulties your group members may have with oral presentations so you can organize and develop your presentation. Which members are knowledgeable about particular topics? What contacts and research did your group develop? What attitudes or feelings do members have about the topic and the presentation? Who are your better speakers? After assessing the strengths of group members, deciding who will present which topics is easier. In addition, if the presentation will be followed by a question and answer period, you can decide who is the best qualified to answer questions that are asked.

Your group also needs to talk about group member concerns. The best writer in the group may not be the best oral presenter. Someone who is quiet within the group may actually prefer to speak before larger audiences. On the other hand, a group member who is comfortable in smaller groups may feel threatened in larger settings. Leaders may not necessarily be the best ones to take the lead for the presentation. Anxiety is normal; group members experience it in different ways. Knowing and understanding a group member's difficulty with public communication can allow your group to plan presentation strategies , such as taking the focus off one person by having pairs present together. Oral public presentations also require a considerable behind-the-scenes work that can be done by members less inclined to speak.

Logistics

Near the end of the planning stage, your group should know what you need for the presentation: supplies, visual aids, equipment (laptop, projector, TV, etc.). Speakers often forget simple items such as tape and end up worrying more about the poster that keeps falling over than their presentation. You need to find out in advance what supplies you need and determine who will bring them. Don't assume your contact person will have what you need!

It also enhances your presentation if you go the extra mile to find current pamphlets, booklets, handouts, buttons, balloons, fact sheets, or any other items relevant to your presentation. Very likely, other community organizations mentioned in your recommendations will be happy to supply professional, updated information about your topic.

Types of Group Oral Presentations

After you have assessed your presentation situation, your group must decide which presentation format best fits that situation. A variety of formats allow for differing viewpoints to be expressed; these are often followed by audience comments and questions (see Table B.1).

Panel Discussion

A **panel discussion** is a public presentation in which a small group of people representing varying perspectives informally discusses issues relevant to an important question in front of a listening audience. For example, a panel might discuss abortion laws, solutions to congested parking on campus, what might be done to solve a community's solid waste problem, or the responsibility of society to the victims of crimes. Panel formats are often the format of choice for classroom presentations when your teacher asks you to present your group's final report to the class.

Groups may participate in panel discussions in a variety of ways. A group may be asked to plan and conduct an entire panel discussion, in which case the entire group must research and present fairly all relevant points of view about the issue. More typically, a group known to support a particular point of view will be asked to supply a representative to serve as a panelist with other panelists who represent different viewpoints. The **moderator** of a panel coordinates the discussion so that it does not ramble and so that all viewpoints are represented. Participants need to be

Panel Discussion

A small group whose members interact informally for the benefit of a listening audience.

Moderator

A person who controls the flow of communication during a public presentation such as a panel or forum discussion.

TABLE B.1 Types of group presentations

Panel: Conversation Among Experts	Symposium: Individual Uninterrupted Presentations	Forum: Questions and Comments from Audience
Topics outlined in advance.	Panelists discuss different aspects of topic.	Different viewpoints encouraged.
Controversy encouraged.	No interaction among panelists.	Questions directed at individuals or at entire group.
Moderator as traffic cop.	Moderator introduces topic and panelists.	Moderator selects audience participants.

both knowledgeable about the question under discussion and articulate in expressing their, or the group's, opinions. Panelists generally have an outline of questions to follow, but their speaking is relatively impromptu. Panelists need not agree on anything except which issues to discuss; the lively argument that often ensues can make for an intellectually stimulating program. The panel format is excellent for presenting an overview of different points of view on an issue of public concern.

Preparing for Panel Discussions   Panel and other public discussions call for special physical arrangements and other preparations. First, all discussants should be able to see each other and the audience at all times. Seat panelists in a semicircle in front of the audience with the moderator either at one end or in the center. Second, seat panelists behind a table, preferably with some sort of cover on the front. Two small tables in an open V make an excellent arrangement. Third, place a large name card in front of each panelist. Fourth, microphones, if needed, should be plentiful enough and unobtrusive. In a large assembly, if a floor microphone is required for questions from the audience, place it strategically and instruct audience members how to use it. Finally, visual displays , such as with a PowerPoint slide, of the topic or question under consideration help keep the discussion organized.

The panel discussion outline can follow one of several formats. The one described here is common. The moderator should ask panelists in advance to suggest questions and subquestions for the discussion. After these are compiled into a rough outline that the moderator intends to use, panelists should receive a copy in advance so that they have a chance to think of possible responses to each question.

The moderator's outline has an introduction, sequence of questions to be raised, and a planned conclusion format. The moderator acts as a conversational traffic officer directing the flow of the discussion. Moderators ask questions of the group of panelists, see that each panelist has an equal opportunity to speak, and clarify ambiguous remarks or ask panelists to do so. They do *not* participate directly in the arguments. They summarize each major topic and keep the discussion flowing.

Symposium

Symposium

One of three kinds of group public discussions in which participants deliver uninterrupted speeches on a selected topic.

A **symposium** is more structured than a panel discussion. Instead of a relatively free interchange of ideas, the topic is divided into segments, with each discussant presenting an uninterrupted speech on a portion of the topic. The purpose of a symposium is similar to that of panel: to enlighten an audience about an important subject. On September 11, 2001, after the attacks on the World Trade Center in New York City, Governor George Pataki, Mayor Rudolf Giuliani, and other New York dignitaries held a news conference in a symposium format to disseminate information to the public about the recent terrorist attacks. New York and the rest of the world needed information in a quick, controlled format. This symposium allowed each presenter to deliver information without interruption. Most symposiums and panels are usually followed by a forum, which allows the audience to question the symposium presenters or panelists and permits the discussants to answer these questions and comment on each other's presentations. After the press conference in New York City, reporters were allowed to ask questions of each presenter, who was given time to respond from his or her own area of expertise.

Symposiums typically present the history and background of their problem and are mostly informative in nature. Common procedures for a symposium involve three main steps. First, select a moderator to introduce the speakers and the topic and to offer a conclusion at the end of the symposium. Second, select a small group of experts to present different aspects of the issue. Because each individual presentation is uninterrupted, make sure there will not be much repetition among the speakers. Third, make appropriate physical arrangements as you would for a panel.

Forum Discussions

Sometimes when a group presents a report to a large gathering, members of the audience are permitted to ask questions or express opinions about the group's work. **Forum discussion** refers to this period of verbal interaction during which audience members interact in an organized way with the presenters. The term *forum* also refers to a discussion held by a large gathering of people, such as a university faculty meeting or a town meeting. Frequently, a forum follows a panel or symposium presentation. Audience members should be told in advance that a forum will follow the public presentation so that they can think of questions or comments. Microphones often are set up at strategic places for audience members to use. Sometimes, audience members are asked to supply their questions or comments in written form to a moderator, who reads them aloud for the entire gathering, followed by responses from panelists or interviewees.

Strict procedural control is needed for a successful forum. The moderator should control the forum so that the discussion is interesting and fair to all participants. The guidelines in Table B.2 will help you do that.

Forum Discussion

A large audience interacting orally, usually following some public presentation.

The Organizing Stage

The success of this stage depends on how well group members interact and listen to each other. Don't rely too much on one person to take the lead—share the leadership among group members. During the organizing state, focus on delegating duties, selecting appropriate verbal and visual materials, and organizing the presentation.

TABLE B.2
Guidelines for conducting a forum discussion

1. Announce the forum or question-and-answer period during the introduction to the presentation.
2. Just before the forum discussion begins, explain the rules, including:
   a. Whether only questions, or questions and comments, are allowed.
   b. How someone will be recognized: raising a hand, lining up behind a floor microphone, etc.
   c. Whether someone must address a specific panelist or the panel as a whole.
   d. How long a question or comment can be.
   e. That no one should speak a second time until everyone who wants to speak has first had a chance.
   f. Any other rules specific to your forum discussion.
3. Explain how long the forum will last, and hold to that time limit.
4. Restate questions if the entire audience cannot hear them.
5. Paraphrase unclear or long questions for clarity.
6. With a large audience, make sure to call on people from different parts of the room.
7. Encourage different viewpoints: "Does anyone want to present a *different* point of view from what we have just heard?"
8. Remind the audience when the allotted time is nearly up, and state that there is just enough time for one or two questions.
9. If no one seeks the floor, have a question or two prepared, or move on to the next agenda item.
10. After the last question, summarize briefly and thank everyone for their participation.

Delegate Duties

After assessing group member strengths and limitations, figure out how each member's abilities fit the needs of the presentation. Speak up, or you may be assigned to do something you are not prepared for or do not enjoy. Match subtopics of the presentation with member background and expertise. If you are organizing a presentation on campus parking problems, how might you select who speaks about what? For example, a math major can talk about funding issues and car-space ratios. A history major can provide a detailed history of the ongoing problem. A design major can prepare compelling visual aids, and a communication major might survey students and administrators for their feedback about your analysis.

After deciding speaker responsibilities, decide who will be responsible for obtaining verbal and visual aids. Who will set up the laptop projector? Who will control the lights and sound? Who will make sure the speaking environment is set up in a way that matches the needs of your presentation's format? Who will be responsible for contacting outside speakers if they are required? Who will be your moderator and will this person have other duties? If follow-up is required, who will be the contact person in the group? Every duty needs to be listed, with a group member identified as responsible for the duty. Delegation of duties is planned, not thrown together the day of the presentation!

Gather Verbal and Visual Materials

Verbal Materials   Once duties are delegated, work thoroughly on each area of discussion. Select how much of the information you have gathered to present. Don't rely too much on one person to take the lead—share the leadership among group members. You must organize the material so it flows clearly and logically. If you still have information gaps, figure out how to fill those. Then figure out what visual and verbal images will enhance your points. Listed below are common types of verbal supporting material often used during effective presentations.

- **Examples:** Examples can range from detailed factual ones (the story of a real victim of abuse complete with dialogue, names, and dates) to undeveloped factual examples (a list of the countries in the world with child labor laws) to hypothetical ones (how much the dollar would be worth in 10 years given a certain rate of inflation). You must decide the number and type of examples needed to make your case believable to your particular audience.

- **Statistics.** Statistics are numbers used to explain or support your claims. Audience members can be easily confused by statistics, so make your statistics clear and meaningful. It is hard to imagine how large a country is if the speaker only tells us that it is 200,000 square miles. More helpful is a comparison: about the size of California and Oregon combined.

- **Testimony.** Some people are recognized authorities on certain issues. To support your position, you may want to quote directly or paraphrase what these experts have said or written. Select the ones you believe will have the most impact on your audience. If your audience analysis has shown you that audience members believe in particular opinion leaders, make sure you incorporate quotes from these leaders in your presentation. You might also arrange to invite them as special guests.

    Testimony can come from famous people or ordinary people, so be creative. A group member's grandparents who have been married for 50 years might be the perfect people to get your point across about successful relationships, for example.

Visual Materials   What visual materials will enhance your presentation? Visual aids help your audience remember your main points and must be used carefully (see Table B.3). Lawyers are well aware that juries pay closer attention, understand technical points better, and remember more when oral testimony is coupled with a visual prop. The image of Johnnie Cochran

- Personally make sure that any equipment your group is using is in operating order before the presentation.
- Be prepared to give the presentation even if the audio and visual aids fail.
- Make sure the visual aid is large enough for all audience members to see.
- Make sure the visual aid is shown long enough to make your point.
- Practice using the visuals and know when you plan to use them.
- Do not pass anything out during your presentation. Materials are passed out before and after the presentation with specific instructions on how the audience is to use them.
- Do not get carried away with the bells and whistles of PowerPoint software. Keep it simple and do not let the slides do the presentation for you—they only complement your presentation.

slipping the leather glove onto the hand of O. J. Simpson while repeating, "If it doesn't fit, you must acquit" during his defense of O. J. Simpson is still talked about today. It was a powerful moment in the trial and probably influenced the jury's verdict. Visual imagery is important and your group has several options.

Objects: If what you are talking about is small enough, bring it with you. One of our students brought her two small dachshunds to demonstrate a typical veterinary exam. The dogs were well-behaved and effective visual aids. If what you are talking about is too large, bring in a model or a picture.

Models: A model can show the audience precisely what you are referring to. For example, one student used a small model of a skeleton to illustrate how bones are related to one another.

Pictures or videos: A photograph, CD, or YouTube video can focus the audience's attention on your topic. Doppler radar images can effectively show air pollution over California's highway 99 by using time-delayed images that let the audience actually observe the pollution's movement. All visual images must be rehearsed to ensure they appear correctly in the order you want.

Maps: Just because your small group knows where a city is, your audience may not know. Maps are quick references and can show comparative location.

Transparencies: Placing an outline of your presentation on a Power-Point slide allows you to talk to the audience while showing the image. Keep your images simple; do not overload them with information, fancy fonts, or special effects. Reveal the information as needed. Use these only as cues for your presentation—do NOT read material off them because you will bore the audience.

Charts: Charts are useful for showing statistics. They provide a concise way to present this kind of information. Different kinds of charts, such as pie or bar charts, can show comparisons. Make sure you explain how to interpret the chart images.

Handouts: Many visual aids can be placed on handouts. Often speakers give the audience a hard copy of slides of their PowerPoint presentation so that audience members can take notes during the presentation. Be careful, though—if you don't manage handouts well, the audience will focus on the handout instead of your presentation.

Chalkboards: These are still used in presentations, especially ones in class-rooms without the technology for video and PowerPoint presentations. Use them to illustrate something that you are saying at the same time. Audiences should not have to wait while you place information on the board. Also remember that writing on a chalkboard turns you away from the audience, whereas transparencies and PowerPoint slides let you show the information while you still face the audience.

Multimedia: Many different kinds of computer presentation software are available, such as Microsoft PowerPoint and Adobe Persuasion, which can make your presentation polished and professional. You can present verbal and visual material in any number of ways. In addition, you can access the Internet and show video clips. Make sure in advance that your speaking environment has the materials you need (television monitor, computer-projector table, or an LCD panel).

Organize Materials and Your Presentation

Map out your presentation. As with any road map, directions should be clear so that the audience understands how and why you are taking them through the chosen topic. If your presentation is based on a written group report, you can probably use the same organization used in the written report as a guide for your oral presentation. Typical organization—including an introduction, body, and conclusion—is provided in Table B.4.

Introduction An introduction has three essential elements: an attention step, a need step, and a thesis statement. First to motivate your audience to listen, get their attention in any number of ways: using humor, asking questions, making a striking statement, offering a striking quotation, or telling a short story (see Table B.5).

The need step follows the introduction and shows the audience why they need or can benefit from the information your group is about to give them. Speakers often state this directly. For example, if your topic is the outrageous prices in the campus bookstore, tell people how they can save money. Sometimes, this is handled indirectly, such as when the topic is so significant everyone should know something about it: "What happens to social security will affect all of us no matter how young or old we are today."

```
  I. Introduction
     A. Attention Material
        1. Striking statement
        2. Striking quotation
        3. Real question
        4. Rhetorical question
        5. Humor
        6. Story
     B. Need Step
        1. Direct
        2. Indirect
     C. Preview
 II. Body
     A. Chronological
     B. Spatial
     C. Cause-effect
     D. Problem-solution
     E. Topical
III. Conclusion
     A. Summary
     B. Appeal
```

The third element of a good introduction is the thesis statement and preview that tells the audience what you specifically will be talking about. Like a road map, the thesis shows your audience where you are going so they can follow your points. Use numbers (i.e., "first, second, third") so that they know how many points to expect.

Body   The main portion of your speech is the body, in which you actually discuss your main ideas. Present your ideas in an easily recognized

Humor	Tell a tasteful, relevant joke to get the audience to laugh.
Ask a Question	"How many of you have been late to class because you could not find a place to park?"
Striking Statement	"I can guarantee you an A in this course and in every other course you take this semester."
Striking Quotation	I have heard it said that "A theory is a thing of beauty, until it gets run over by a fact."
Tell a Story	People enjoy and can relate to stories about other people; such stories help capture an audience's attention.

pattern so that your audience hears the relationship among them. Use transition statements that help move your speech smoothly from point to point.

- **Problem-Solution:** This format follows the same kind of logic you used to analyze your group's problem (see Chapters 9 and 10). This kind of speech pattern is used most often when trying to persuade an audience to accept a recommendation. The problem is described, history discussed, and solution justified. You can also use this pattern to inform an audience about a problem that has already been solved.

- **Chronological:** This kind of organization follows a time pattern. It is useful for talking about how something is made, explaining a historical event, or listing the steps to a process.

- **Spatial:** This kind of pattern best describes locations in space. Showing an audience the best ski areas in California could be done by using a map and moving north to south.

- **Cause and effect or effect to cause:** This kind of pattern is useful for explaining why something has occurred. For example, it can be used to show how the Asian bird flu can move from birds to humans and then affect millions of people. You can reverse the pattern by talking about effects first, then explaining their causes.

- **Topical:** A topical organization follows the key parts of the topic. The U.S. system of government has three parts: executive, legislative, and judicial. You then discuss each component, in order.

No one organizational style is always correct and styles may be combined. Be careful, though; use styles to clarify, not confuse. Selecting the most effective pattern is a matter of matching the characteristics of your topic with those of the audience.

Conclusion   If your purpose was to inform, summarize your main points. What do you want the audience to remember? Your summary is similar to your introduction, but should be more concrete.

If your purpose was to persuade, this is your last chance to get the audience emotionally involved in your topic. Use this opportunity to reconnect with your audience, offer a challenge, or provide a call to action.

The Presenting Stage

Surveys show that many Americans fear public speaking more than they fear spiders, snakes, and even death.[3] You may be enrolled in a group communication class because you were trying to avoid the "dreaded speech." However, even as a group member, you may be faced with giving a public presentation. Many times in your professional career you may need to speak to a committee or larger audience, so it is wise to work through this fear now. We offer the following advice to help you do just that.

Check Your Language

Writing the speech is only half the battle; the delivery is just as important. Trying to engage your audience and take action requires an effective use of language. Speak to your audience in a conversational style, just as if you were giving the speech to good friends. Generally, speakers should strive for a style that is clear, vivid, and appropriate.

Clarity requires language that is concrete rather than vague and abstract. Note the difference between explaining that last night you saw Ed "coming down the street" and saying you saw Ed "staggering" or "crawling" or "stumbling" or "skipping down the street." Use terms the audience understands and avoid jargon.

Vivid language attracts attention. Using figurative language, repetition, and amplification will add vividness to your presentation and help your audience pay attention. Listen to Martin Luther King's "I Have a Dream" speech for effective use of repetition and figurative language.

Make sure your language choices are appropriate to the audience and the occasion. A formal classroom presentation probably should not be filled with expletives or street language unless they are being used to illustrate a point in your presentation.

Practice Aloud

There are four ways of delivering an oral presentation: manuscript, memorization, impromptu, and extemporaneous. Each has its own delivery style.

If you write out everything you want to say, word for word in a manuscript, you are less likely to leave something out when you present. Unfortunately, you can become too dependent on your manuscript and pay too little attention to the audience. You may not notice how your presentation resonates (or does not) with the audience. If you decide on a manuscript delivery, you must work with the material enough so that you can connect to the audience in a natural manner.

You can also memorize your presentation. This way you may not leave anything out and can maintain eye contact with the audience. However, you still must practice enough with the material so that you won't panic if you forget something. Also, you want your delivery to appear spontaneous and not robot-like. Remember that eye contact alone won't guarantee that you come across as interested in your material. You must be comfortable enough with your material that your delivery sounds conversational.

If you deliver material off-the-cuff, then you are using an impromptu style. You speak from your knowledge and expertise with minimal notes or specific preparation. Forum discussions often involve impromptu responses from group members as they answer questions from the audience. In addition, panel presentations may also be impromptu because the panelists are responding to moderator questions and may or may not have notes. Panelists are there because of their expertise, which is the basis for their responses. However, impromptu deliveries can sound incoherent if the speaker meanders from point to point. Even though there is no specific preparation for impromptu speeches, you can review for the presentation. In addition, good impromptu speakers have experience with this kind of speaking.

One of the most common kinds of speeches is one delivered extemporaneously. This is the kind of speech your instructor probably has in mind for classroom presentations. Instead of writing out a manuscript, you make an outline of the points you want to cover and use as few notes as possible. Experienced speakers can engage in a conversation with the audience, be flexible enough to alter the presentation, and yet deliver an effective presentation.

Once you have selected the method of delivery, practice your speech out loud. Going over the speech only in your head takes less time than actually saying it out loud. You also need to hear what the speech sounds like—something said easily in your head may be a tongue twister when you try to say it out loud. A colleague of ours was rather embarrassed when he wanted to say "needy student" but instead said, "nudey student." If this is a group presentation, then it will require both individual and group practice. Find the time to practice together, concentrating on transitions between speakers, how you will act while others are speaking, what members can do to help if someone forgets to say something, and so on. Showing continuity and togetherness during a group presentation is challenging and needs to be rehearsed. Also, plan for any spur-of-the-moment equipment failure! Anticipate problems and be ready to proceed anyway. Finally, have a Plan B in the event that a group member does not show up for your presentation.

Be a Good Listener

Public speaking events are not only about speaking—they are also about listening. Be respectful and engaged audience members when other presenters or groups are giving their presentations so the environment is comfortable for everyone.

Inviting Public Input Using a Buzz Group Session

Often, people who organize public presentations of a group's work decide to incorporate procedures that allow audience members to discuss what they have heard. A **buzz group session** allows a large audience to be

Buzz Group Session
A method that allows a large audience to be divided into many small groups of about six people to discuss the same question or issue, thereby permitting all participants in the large group to become actively involved in the discussion.

divided into many small groups that discuss the same question or issue, thereby permitting everyone to become actively involved in the discussion. Sometimes a buzz group session is used to generate a list of questions for panelists or symposium speakers to address; at other times, the audience members are asked to respond to what they have already heard as part of a public presentation. A colleague of ours participated with 500 educational leaders in Kentucky who met to work out techniques for promoting a Minimum Foundation Program for public education in that state. Organizers hoped the large group would identify ways to get the support of taxpayers for approving a statewide tax to help local schools based on need. This meant higher taxes and money flowing from richer to poorer districts. Several times, after audience members heard initial panel presentations, their work in buzz groups produced arguments in support of the program and inexpensive advertising and promotional techniques to be used. Instructions for the buzz group procedure are in Table B.6.
This versatile technique has many variations. Feel free to tweak it to suit your purposes.

TABLE B.6
Steps for the buzz group procedure

1. Present a focused, targeted question. Examples:
   a. What techniques can be used to publicize the Minimum foundation program to citizens in each county or city throughout the state?
   b. What new projects might our sorority undertake as service projects?
   c. What are arguments for (or against) charging students different fees depending on their majors?
2. Divide the large audience into groups of five or six, usually by seating arrangement. Give each group a copy of the question or post it up front, perhaps on a PowerPoint slide.
3. Have each group select a recorder.
4. Ask each group to brainstorm answers to the question in a fixed time period, usually 5 to 10 minutes. The recorder writes down *all* ideas presented.
5. Warn the groups when 1 minute remains.
6. Sometimes, you may ask the group to spend an additional minute or two rank-ordering the suggestions.
7. The organizers of the presentation have several options after the groups have discussed their suggestions, depending on the number of groups and the goals:
   a. Each recorder reports one idea, in round-robin fashion, until all unique ideas are presented, with one person serving as the overall recorder for the entire group. This may be followed by participants "voting" with stickers by the ideas they like best.
   b. Each recorder presents all the ideas orally to the entire group.
   c. The lists are collected and typed, after duplicates are eliminated, and a tally is kept of the most oft-mentioned ideas. The final list is often circulated to participants after the conference.

Public Meetings

One aspect of preparing for group presentations is understanding the occasion for the presentation. Public meetings come with their own challenges, both to the officials who call these meetings and to the public who attend them. Let's take a look at these special occasions for group presentations.

Public meetings or hearings are designed to allow the public or citizens to be a part of public policy making.[4] Public agencies are typically responsible for calling and managing these meetings. They occur at the local, state, or federal level and are called for several reasons: to discuss issues, evaluate options, provide and obtain information, create recommendations, review projects, and make decisions. They often have several different interested audiences, including citizen groups, planning committees, school boards, neighborhood associations, and zoning commissions. For example, a local school board in California held public meetings to discuss whether it should end the tradition of using Indian tribe names to refer to school athletic teams. On another occasion, a park system solicited public feedback regarding a proposed improvement to one of the parks.

Such meetings are part of our U.S. tradition of participatory government. They are intended to encourage the participation of local individuals in government decision making. Unfortunately, not only is there little research about public meetings, there is also a strong sense that they do not meet these ideals. The public often thinks that such meetings are held only to meet legally obligations, but that the agencies are not really interested in the public's feedback.

Public meetings are often conducted using the "DAD" model.[5] The agency in question makes its decision or creates policy (**d**ecides), advances a campaign to win support for the policy (**a**dvocates), and only then asks the citizens to comment and approve the policy (**d**efends). The public is invited to a meeting, given a forum to comment for a short time limit, and then asked to support the decision that has already been made. No wonder many citizen groups think that these meetings are held only as a formality. But you can improve such public meetings if you know how to make them more effective public problem-solving events.

When agency officials describe the attributes of a successful public meeting, their responses mirror many of the principles that we outlined in the three stages to an effective public presentation.[6]

- **Planning the public meeting.** Good planning entails selecting the right time and place to encourage participation and providing ample publicity in advance. Since the meetings are open to the public, officials may not always know who will be there and why. Knowing much about the audience is essential. The meeting must have a clear purpose and format. Visual aids must be prepared and scheduled. Any outside agencies need to be contacted and scheduled. Rehearsals have to be held and potential questions must be prepared for.

- **During the meeting.** A strong facilitator must keep the meeting focused and ensure that all sides of the issues are heard. The meeting must be run tightly but with enough flexibility to adapt to any contingencies during the meeting (a change in topic, larger than anticipated audiences, organized protests). Dialogue with those attending is necessary and should be encouraged even after the meeting. Agency officials have to try to encourage a representative number of citizens to attend the meeting.

- **Post meeting.** It is essential to show the citizens how their comments were heard and incorporated into future decisions. Officials should demonstrate a continued interest in keeping in contact with the citizens (setting up future meetings, getting phone lists, etc.). Audience members must be thanked for attending.

Generally, agency officials report more satisfaction with public meetings than the public does because the public gets the very real sense that a decision has already been made. It is no surprise that many citizens think their comments make no difference to the agency that called the meeting. In addition, audience members may not feel comfortable expressing their thoughts and feelings about the issue. They also may be there for multiple reasons.[7] Some come to see what their neighbors think about an issue and to offer support. Sometimes, just attending such a meeting may help the audience member feel that he or she has actually done something about an issue. Often, the issue is so controversial (e.g., police profiling and local crime) that going to such a meeting provides members of the public with information they desperately seek.

SHEDD is a model of public dialogue developed by communication scholars W. Barnett Pearce and Vernon Cronen to meet the public criticisms of public meetings.[8] This model uses a strong facilitator who helps members of the public to be heard and treats the public's comments as an important and an integral part of the total problem-solving process—it honors the public involvement in its own governance.

- Getting Started. Agency leaders commit to hearing all sides of the issue even if they do not want to. Trained facilitators actively listen and summarize participant comments so that divergent comments are validated.

- Hearing all viewpoints. The topic of the meeting should be compelling and of interest to many different factions of the community. The agency leaders need to work to make sure that those constituencies are invited and encouraged to attend the meeting(s).

- Enriching the conversation. Neither free-for-alls at open microphones nor strictly controlled events contribute to open discussion. Trained facilitators encourage open dialogue and help participants achieve that end.

■ **D**eliberating the options. Agency leaders recognize and use the comments they heard at the public meeting. They do not commit to solutions prior to meetings. Public meeting comments are summarized and provided to decision makers so that more informed decisions can occur.

■ **D**eciding and moving forward. A public whose opinions and insight are used by decision makers tends to be more committed to those decisions than a public whose members believe they have been ignored or dismissed.

Public meetings occur every day at all levels of government. As a future professional, you may attend one or more such meeting as an audience member or agency official. The skills you develop as a group member and your insight into group dynamics can help you organize and facilitate public presentations of all kinds. Poor public meetings do not have to occur. Meetings can be some of the most rewarding experiences of our lives and an integral part of public policy.

NOTES

1. Dan O'Hair, Rob Stewart, and Hannah Rubenstein, *A Speaker's Guidebook: Text and Reference* (Boston: Bedford/St. Martin's, 2004), Chapter 6.
2. Ann L. Darling and Deanna P. Daniels, "Practicing Engineers Talk About the Importance of Talk: A Report on the Role of Oral Communication in the Workplace," *Communication Education,* 52 (January 2003): 1–16.
3. George Kennedy (trans.), Aristotle, *On Rhetoric* (New York: Oxford, 1991): 181.
4. Katherine A. McComas, "Theory and Practice of Public Meetings," *Communication Theory,* 11 (February 2001): 36–55.
5. Randy K. Dillon and Gloria J. Galanes, "Public Dialogue: Communication Theory as Public Praxis," *The Journal of Public Affairs,* VI (1), (2002): 79–89.
6. McComas, "Theory and Practice of Public Meetings."
7. Katherine A. McComas, "Trivial Pursuits: Participant Views of Public Meetings," *Journal of Public Relations Research,* 15 (2003): 91–115.
8. Dillon and Galanes, "Public Dialogue: Communication Theory as Public Praxis."

KEY TERMS

Buzz group session
Forum discussion

Moderator
Panel discussion

Symposium

C Using Technology to Help Your Group

We introduced Chapter 1 with the story of the Artsfest Planning Committee, responsible for planning and executing an annual arts festival in Springfield, Missouri. In that opening case, we provided several examples of how the Planning Committee used technology to take care of committee business between meetings. Virtual groups meet primarily via technology, but even face-to-face groups these days use technology in a variety of ways. In this appendix, we expand on specific examples of how groups can use technology to enhance their work. We also refer you to McGraw-Hill's concise New Communication Technologies guide, available on the McGraw-Hill Web site, which provides descriptions and definitions of various technologies commonly used by groups: www.mhhe.com/socscience/comm/group/students/new_com.htm.

Keeping in Touch between Meetings

A number of old and new technologies help members touch base between meetings, including the *telephone, e-mail*, and *text or instant messages*. We have all used the telephone to make a quick contact or to explore issues in some depth. For example, when we (Kathy and Gloria) develop our writing plan for this text, we talk via telephone, sometimes for hours.

E-mailing is easy and popular. All that is needed is a device that allows a connection to the Internet, which may be a computer, smart phone, netbook, or something like an e-reader or electronic pad. Because e-mail is asynchronous, an advantage is that the receiver can access the message when it is convenient. Thus, e-mail conversations do not happen in real time. In addition, it is easy to send attachments, such as meeting notices and agendas, via e-mail. Also, issues that need to be dealt with immediately can be voted on by e-mail.

Texting and instant messaging, which also require a device (computer, smart phone, etc.) and access to a network (Internet), generally occur in real time. Often, these systems are excellent for short messages, such as "I will be 15 minutes late to the meeting because I am caught in traffic" or "Meeting location changed to second floor conference room." E-mails, texts, and instant messages can be sent to one person at a time or to a group of people.

Collaborative Work on Documents and Projects

Virtual groups and face-to-face groups often work collaboratively on documents and projects other than during regular meeting times. For example, the community group, described in Chapter 8, that produced the community report card wrote 11 sections of the report, with subcommittees working on specific sections and documents. It is inefficient to have an entire committee try to write a section of a report together, but it is very efficient for individual members to write, look at, comment on, and edit sections of the report. There are several ways to accomplish this, including such things as a *wiki* or a file-hosting service such as *Dropbox*.

A wiki is a type of software that allows multiple users to work on a single document. For example, a member of the community report card education subcommittee posted the initial draft of that section and the other members of the subcommittee accessed it. A wiki lets everyone know who contributed what sections and what changes to the document. Thus, members could be in different locations, working when it was convenient for them. The virtual wiki space needs to be set up, initially, by an administrator, and access can be controlled so that only group members have access. Most universities have the capability to do this for students.

A file-hosting service, such as Dropbox, allows virtual storage space to be set aside for specific users—similar to a virtual file cabinet. Often, a specified amount of storage can be set aside for free. A group member establishes the storage space and sends a link to others who need access; the rest of the members register to use the storage. Once the space is set up, users can upload documents, access and edit existing documents, and make everything accessible to all group members.

Comprehensive Group Management Systems

Many universities and organizations have online learning or course management software systems that help groups do a variety of tasks, including some of those mentioned earlier. For instance, Blackboard is one such system available at many universities. The university professor who chaired the community report card committee set up a Blackboard site at her university that the entire 27-member committee could access. With Blackboard and similar systems, announcements can be posted for everyone to see, and a calendar can be kept to help keep track of the group's work. E-mails can be sent to the entire group or to subgroups or individuals. Wikis can be set up for the entire group or subcommittees within a larger group, and document sharing can be provided. Discussion boards can be set up so members can access them asynchronously, and chats can be set up for real-time computer-based discussions. Thus, many different types of technological assistance are available within one comprehensive system. To use Blackboard, one of the group members must have access to an organization (often a university) that has the system. That member will work with the Blackboard administrator to set up a specific Blackboard site for a particular group.

Increasingly, easily accessible and often free Web sites are available for anyone to use. Examples include Wiggio and Enter the Group, both of which offer tools similar to Blackboard.[1] These tools include a calendar; task and to-do lists; group and individual e-mail, text, and voice mail capability; file sharing; both instant chats and asynchronous messaging; specific space set aside for subgroups; assignment tracking with deadline reminders; and the ability to poll group members. For example, if a group has produced two versions of a document, members can be polled to see which the majority prefers; if members are trying to find a convenient meeting time, they can be polled online. Wiggio provides the ability to host Web meetings, conference calls, and chat rooms. Enter the Group has video guides to help groups manage projects, resolve conflict, and so forth. With both systems, group members need access to the Internet and an e-mail address to be able to use them.

Real-time Meetings of Distributed Groups

As we have noted, some groups are always geographically distributed, but others may be temporarily distributed. Several technologies allow members to meet although they may not all be in the same place: *audioconferences* and *videoconferences*, both of which we have discussed throughout the text. Audioconferences are typically set up in advance, with members dialing in and providing a numeric passcode. When we recently conferred with our editors regarding this revision of our text, we used audioconference to connect Gloria in Missouri, Kathy in California, Janice in New York, and Deb in Iowa. Audioconferences can also allow a missing member to participate, as routinely happens at university Board of Governors meetings, when one or two members cannot physically attend but can participate via speaker phone.

Videoconferences add the ability for members not just to hear but to see one another, and their costs have been falling. For example, Skype allows two people—and up to a group of five—to connect via computer and conduct a real-time, face-to-face conference for free.[2] All participating individuals need broadband Internet access, a computer with a camera (which is built in to many newer computers), and a Skype account. Skype can also be used to conduct free audioconferences with more participants.

As you can see, groups today use technology in a variety of ways to make their work easier. Technology changes constantly, with methods being simplified and improved. We encourage you to browse the Web to keep up with the most current changes and get ideas for how technology can help your groups.

NOTES

1. http://wiggio.com/, accessed June 11, 2011; http://enterthegroup.com/, accessed June 11, 2011.

2. www.skype.com/intl/en-us/home, accessed June 11, 2011.

Glossary

A

Acceptance requirements: The degree to which the solution for a given problem must be accepted by the people it will affect.

Accommodation: The conflict management style, high in cooperativeness and low in assertiveness, in which one person appeases or gives in to the other.

Action-oriented listener: A listener who focuses on the task, remembers details, and prefers an organized presentation.

Active listening: Listening with the intent of understanding a speaker the way the speaker wishes to be understood and paraphrasing your understanding so that the speaker can confirm or correct the paraphrase.

Activity group: A group formed primarily for members to participate in an activity such as bridge, bowling, hunting, and so forth.

***Ad hominem* attack:** An attack on a person rather than his or her argument, often involving name-calling; distracts a group from careful examination of an issue or argument.

Adaptive structuration theory: The version of structuration theory that examines how the structures of computer technology get used during group decision making.

Agenda: A list of items to be discussed at a group meeting.

Agreeableness: The Big Five personality characteristic of being generally cooperative and compliant in a friendly way.

Aggressiveness: Behavior designed to win or dominate that fails to respect the rights or beliefs of others.

Antecedent phase: The preliminary phase in group socialization in which individual member characteristics influence member readiness and ability to engage in effective group socialization.

Anticipatory phase: The phase in group socialization in which members form initial expectations about each other and the socialization process.

Area of freedom: The scope of authority and responsibility of a group, including limits on the group's authority.

Assembly effect: A type of group synergy or nonsummativity whereby the decision of group members collectively is superior to adding together (summing) the wisdom, knowledge, experience, and skills of the members individually.

Assertiveness: Behavior that manifests respect both for your own and others' rights as opposed to aggressiveness and nonassertiveness.

Assimilation phase: The phase in group socialization in which the member and the group have worked out a comfortable fit.

Attitude: A network of beliefs and values, not directly measurable, that a person holds toward an object, person, or concept; produces a tendency to react in specific ways toward the object, person, or concept.

Autocratic leader: A leader who tries to dominate and control a group.

Avoidance: The passive conflict management style that ignores a conflict.

B

Backchannel: Nonverbal vocalizations such as mmhmm and uh-huh that are uttered while another is speaking; partly determined by one's culture; can indicate interest and active listening.

Behavior: Any observable action by a group member.

Behavioral function: The effect or function that a member's behavior has on the group as a whole.

Bibliography: A list of published sources about a topic or issue.

Bona fide group perspective: The perspective that focuses on naturally occurring groups that, in contrast to artificially created groups, are interdependent with their environments and have stable, although permeable, and boundaries and borders.

Boomer generation: Individuals born from 1946 to 1964; key experiences include the Vietnam war, the civil rights movement, and Watergate.

Boundary spanner: A group member who monitors the group's environment to import and export information relevant to the group's success.

Brainstorming: A small group technique for stimulating creative thinking by temporarily suspending evaluation.

Brainwriting: Individual brainstorming producing a written list.

Builder generation: Individuals born before 1945; key experiences include the Great Depression and World War II.

Buzz group session: Method whereby attendees at a large group meeting can participate actively; the large meeting is divided into groups of about six persons each who discuss a target question for a specified time, then report their answers to the entire large assembly.

C

Charge: The assignment or goal given to a group, usually by a parent organization or administrator of the parent organization.

Closed system: A system, such as a small group, with relatively impermeable boundaries, resulting in little interchange between the system and its environment.

Coalition: Members who band together to pool their resources and power to try to increase their bargaining leverage.

Co-culture: A grouping that sees itself as distinct but is also part of a larger grouping.

Cognitive complexity: The personal trait that refers to the level of development of a group member's construct system for interpreting signals; cognitively complex individuals are able to synthesize more information and think in more abstract and organized terms than are cognitively simple individuals.

Cohesiveness: The degree of attraction members feel for the group; unity.

Collaborating group: A group whose members come from different organizations to form a temporary alliance for a specific purpose.

Collaboration: The assertive, cooperative conflict management style that assumes a solution can be found that fully meets the needs of all parties to a conflict; a problem-solving conflict management style.

Collectivist culture: A culture in which the needs and wishes of the group predominate over the needs of any one individual; the idea of an individual following a path separate from the group is inconceivable.

Committee: A small group of people given an assigned task or responsibility by a larger group (parent organization) or person with authority.

　Ad hoc **committee:** A group that goes out of existence after its specific task has been completed.

　Standing committee: A group given an area of responsibility that includes many tasks and continues indefinitely.

Communication: A process in which people simultaneously create, interpret, and negotiate shared meaning through their interaction by sending verbal and nonverbal messages that are received, interpreted, and responded to by other people.

Communication apprehension (CA): Anxiety or fear of speaking in a variety of social situations; reticence; shyness.

Communicative competencies: The communication-related skills and abilities of members that help groups achieve their goals.

Communicative Competency Model: Model of leadership that assumes leadership involves performing behaviors that help a group overcome obstacles to goal achievement and communication skills (competencies) are how leaders actually lead.

Competition: The uncooperative, aggressive conflict management style in which one person attempts to dominate or force the outcome to his or her advantage.

Compromise: The conflict management style that assumes that each party must give up something to get something; a shared solution to a conflict situation.

Computer-mediated communication (CMC): Using computers to interact with others.

Conflict: The expressed struggle that occurs when interdependent parties (including group members) perceive incompatible goals or scarce resources and interference in achieving their goals.

Conformity: Following group norms and not deviating from them.

Conjunctive task: A type of group task in which each member possesses information relevant to the decision, but no one member alone has all the needed information, thus requiring a high level of coordination among members.

Conscientiousness: The Big Five personality characteristic of being reliable, diligent, and having a strong sense of responsibility.

Consensus decision: A choice that all group members agree is the best one that they all can accept.

Consultant: A nonparticipant observer who works with a group to determine what it needs, then attempts to help by providing inputs, such as special techniques, procedures, and information.

Content analysis: An analysis of the content (topics, behaviors, specific words or ideas, fantasy themes, etc.) of a group's discussion.

Content-oriented listener: A listener who enjoys analyzing information, dissecting others' arguments; can be seen as overly critical.

Contexts: The situations or environments that influence the dynamics of communication.

Contingency approaches: The study of leadership that assumes the appropriate leadership style in a given situation depends on factors such as members' skills and knowledge, time available, the type of task, and so forth.

Cooperative requirements: The degree to which members' efforts need to be coordinated for a group to complete its task successfully (see also Conjunctive task).

Criteria: Standards for judging among alternatives; may be absolute (must) or relative.

Critical thinking: The systematic examination of information and ideas on the basis of evidence and logic rather than intuition, hunch, or prejudgment.

Critique: Analysis and criticism of something, such as identification of strengths and weaknesses in a small group's process and interaction.

Culture: The patterns of values, beliefs, symbols, norms, procedures, and behaviors that have been historically transmitted to and are shared by a given group of persons.

D

Decision making: Choosing from among a set of alternatives.

Deep diversity: Member differences not due to visible characteristics such as sex and race but to factors that can affect a group more directly, such as how people approach work and solve problems.

Democratic leader: An egalitarian leader who coordinates and facilitates discussion in a small group, encouraging participation of all members.

Designated leader: A person appointed or elected to a position as leader of a small group.

Deviate: A group member who differs in some important way, such as degree of participation, values, or opinions, from the rest of the group members; opinion or innovative deviates help groups examine alternatives more thoroughly by expressing opinions different from those held by the majority, thus forcing the group to take a closer look.

Dialect: A regional variation in the pronunciation, vocabulary, and/or grammar of a language.

Disjunctive task: A type of group task in which members work on parts of the group problem independently, with little or no coordination of effort through discussion needed.

Distributed leadership: The concept that group leadership is the responsibility of the group as a whole, not just the designated leader; assumes that all members can and should provide needed leadership services to the group.

Distributive approach: The approach to managing conflict that assumes there are fixed resources to distribute among parties to the conflict; thus, whatever someone wins, someone else loses.

E

Electronic brainstorming: Brainstorming on computers linked to a large screen that display all responses, but no one knows who contributed which items.

Emergent leader: Member of an initially leaderless group who, by virtue of information and communication competencies, rises from within the group to enact leadership functions and is viewed as the leader by all or most members.

Emoticon: Typographical symbols used in computer-mediated communication to convey emotions in regular text, such as the smiley face :-).

Encounter phase: The phase in group socialization in which members' expectations meet with the actual behaviors and member and group goals become negotiated.

Environment: The context or setting in which a small group system exists; the larger systems of which a small group is a component.

Equifinality: The principle that different systems can reach the same outcome even if they have different starting places.

Ethics: The rules or standards that a person or group uses to determine whether conduct or behavior is right and appropriate.

Ethnocentrism: The belief that one's own culture is inherently superior to all others; tendency to view other cultures through the viewpoint of one's own culture.

Exit phase: The phase in group socialization in which the group disbands or a member leaves and the group must adapt.

Extraversion-Introversion Dimension: The Myers-Briggs Type Indicator® dimension concerned with whether one's focus is the external worlds (extraversion) or one's internal, subjective landscape (introversion).

F

Facework: The communication strategies people use to preserve their own and others' self-esteem (face).

Fact: A verifiable observed event; a descriptive statement that is true.

Fallacy: A reasoning error.

False dilemma: Either-or thinking that assumes, incorrectly, that only two choices or courses of action are possible.

Fantasy: A statement not pertaining to the here and now of the group that offers a creative and meaningful interpretation of events meeting a group's psychological or rhetorical need.

Fantasy chain: A series of statements by several or all group members in which a story is dramatized to help create a group's view of reality.

Fantasy theme: What the content of the dramatization of a fantasy or fantasy chain is about; the manifest theme is the overt, surface content, and the latent theme is the hidden, underlying meaning.

Faulty analogy: An incomplete comparison that stretches a similarity too far; assuming that because two things are similar in some respects, they are alike in others.

Feedback: A response to a system's output; it may come in the form of information or tangible resources and helps the system determine whether it needs to make adjustments in moving toward its goal.

Femininity (as applied to culture): The quality of cultures that value nurturing and caring for others.

Focus group: A special group procedure that encourages freewheeling discussion focusing on a specific topic or issue, often used to analyze people's interests and values for market research.

Formal role: Refers to a specific position within the group that carries a set of expectations for fulfilling that position, such as a group's chair or secretary.

Forum discussion: A large audience interacting orally, usually following some public presentation.

Functional Perspective: The approach to group problem solving that focuses on the necessary communicative functions group members must perform for the group to do an effective job of problem solving and decision making.

Functions approach: The study of functions performed by leaders; the theory that leadership is defined by the functions a group needs and can be supplied by any member.

G

Gatekeeper: Any member of a small group controlling who speaks during a discussion; any controller of the flow of messages among members.

Gender: Learned and culturally transmitted sex-role behavior of an individual.

Group: Three or more people with an interdependent goal who interact and influence each other.

Group charter: A written document that describes the purpose of the group, its specific charge, area of freedom, membership, deadlines, and required output.

Group climate: A group's emotional and relational atmosphere.

> **Defensive climate:** An atmosphere characterized by mistrust, in which members tear each other down.

> **Supportive climate:** An atmosphere of respect, in which members feel valued and appreciated.

Group culture: The pattern of values, beliefs, and norms shared by group members, developed through interaction and incorporating members' shared experiences in the group, patterns of interaction, and status relationships.

Group Decision Support Systems (GDSS) or group support systems (GSS): Computer-based software and hardware systems designed to help groups improve a variety of group outcomes, such as creativity, problem solving, and decision making.

Grouphate: The feeling of antipathy and hostility that many people have against working in a group, fostered by the many ineffective, time-wasting groups that exist.

Group polarization: The tendency for group members to make decisions that are more extreme (more risky or cautious) than they would make individually.

Group socialization: The process of learning to become part of a group, which involves reciprocal influence among members and between members and the group.

Groupthink: The tendency of some cohesive groups to fail to subject information, reasoning, and proposals to thorough critical analysis leading to faulty decisions.

H

Haptics: The study of the use of and perceptions of touch.

Hidden profile: When the information members hold collectively favors the best decision, but the information they hold in private, as individuals, favors a less effective solution.

High-context communication: Communication wherein the primary meaning of a message is conveyed by features of the situation or context instead of the verbal, explicit part of the message.

I

Ideal Solution Format: A problem-solving format that takes individual perspectives into account by asking a group to focus on what the ideal solution would do.

Idiosyncracy credit: Additional leeway in adhering to group norms, given to a member for valuable contributions to the group.

Individualistic culture: A culture in which the needs and wishes of the individual predominate over the needs of the group.

Inequity conflict: Conflict about perceived unequal workloads or contributions to the group effort.

Inference: A statement that includes more than a description of some event, thus going beyond fact; an inference involves some degree of uncertainty or probability and cannot be checked for accuracy by direct observation.

Informal role: Refers to a unique role that evolves through a member's behaviors and others' responses to those behaviors; reflects the traits, personality characteristics, habits, and preferences of the member.

Input variables: The energy, information, and raw material used by an open system, which is transformed into output by throughput processes.

Integrative approach: The approach to managing conflict that assumes that solutions can be found to satisfy every party to the conflict.

Intercultural communication: Interaction between and among individuals from different cultures or subcultures.

Interdependence: The property of a system such that all parts are interrelated and affect each other as well as the whole system.

Interdependent goal: An objective shared by members of a small group in such a way that one member cannot achieve the goal without the other members also achieving it.

Intracultural communication: Interaction between and· among individuals from the same culture or subculture.

Intrinsic interest: Extent to which the task itself is attractive and interesting to the participants.

K

Kinesics: Study of communication through movements.

L

Laissez-faire leader: A do-nothing designated leader who provides minimal services to the group.

Leader: A person who uses communication to influence others to meet group goals and needs; any person identified by members of a group as leader; a person designated as leader by election or appointment.

Leader as completer: A leader who determines which functions or behaviors are most needed for a group to perform optimally, then supplies them or encourages others to do so.

Leader-Member Exchange (LMX) model: The leadership model based on the finding that supervisors develop different kinds of leadership relationships with their subordinates, depending on characteristics of both the leader and members.

Leadership: Influence exerted through communication that helps a group achieve goals; performance of a leadership function by any member.

Learning group: A group conducting a learning discussion.

Least-sized group: The principle that the ideal group contains as few members as possible as long as all necessary perspectives and skills are represented.

Liaison: Communication between or among groups; interfacing; a person who performs the liaison function.

Listening: Receiving and interpreting oral and other signals from another person or source.

Low-context communication: Communication wherein the primary meaning of a message is carried by the verbal or explicit part of the message.

M

Maintenance function: Relationship-oriented member behavior that reduces tensions, increases solidarity, and facilitates teamwork.

Majority decision: Decision made by vote, with the winning alternative receiving more than half the members' votes.

Masculinity (as applied to culture): The quality of cultures that value assertiveness and dominance.

Meeting notice: A written message providing the time, place, purpose, and other information relevant to an upcoming meeting.

Message: Any action, sound, or word used in interactions.

Millennial generation: Individuals born from 1982 to 2000 ;the first truly "wired" generation, comfortable with technology in all forms.

Mindful communication: Communication that is open to multiple perspectives, shows a willingness to see the world from another's worldview, and shifts perspective if necessary.

Minutes: A written record of every relevant item dealt with during a group meeting, including a record of all decisions.

Moderator: A person who controls the flow of communication during a public presentation such as a panel or forum discussion.

Multifinality: The principle that systems starting out at the same place may reach different end points or outcomes.

Multiple causation: The principle that each change in a system is caused by numerous factors.

Myers-Briggs Type Indicator®: A personality measure, based on the work of Carl Jung, that categorizes people on the basis of how they relate to the world around them.

N

Net conference: A meeting that is electronically mediated by networked computers.

Nonassertive behavior: Passive behavior that allows one's own rights and beliefs to be ignored or dominated, often to avoid conflict, even at the expense of good decision making.

Nonsummativity: The property of a system that the whole is not the sum of its parts, but may be greater or lesser than the sum.

Nonverbal behavior: Messages other than words to which listeners react.

Norm: An unstated informal rule, enforced by peer pressure, that governs the behavior of members of a small group.

O

Open system: A system with relatively permeable boundaries, producing a high degree of interchange between the system and its environment.

Openness to experience: The Big Five personality characteristic of being imaginative, creative, and intellectually curious.

Output variables: Anything that is produced by the throughput processes of a system, such as a tangible product or a change in components of the system; in a small group, outputs are such things as reports, resolutions, changes in cohesiveness, and attitude changes in members.

Overgeneralization: Assumption that because something is true about one or a few items, it is true of all or most items of the same type.

P

Panel discussion: A small group whose members interact informally and in impromptu manner for the benefit of a listening audience.

Paralanguage: Nonverbal characteristics of voice and utterance, such as pitch, rate, tone of voice, fluency, pauses, and variations in dialect.

Paraphrase: Restatement in one's own words of what one understood a speaker to mean.

Participant–observer: An active participant in a small group who is at the same time observing and evaluating its processes and procedures.

Passive-aggressive behavior: Behavior that outwardly seems helpful but actually sabotages a group's work.

People-oriented listener: A listener who is sensitive to others, nonjudgmental, and concerned about how his or her behavior affects others; can become distracted from task by others' problems.

Perceiving-Judging Dimension: The Myers-Briggs Type Indicator® dimension concerning how people organize the worlds; perceivers are spontaneous and flexible whereas judgers are decisive and prefer structure.

Personal growth group: A group of people who come together to develop personal insights, overcome personality problems, and grow personally through feedback and support of others.

Phasic progression: The movement of a group through fairly predictable phases or stages, each of which is characterized by specific kinds of statements.

Population familiarity: The degree to which members of a group are familiar with the nature of a problem and experienced in solving similar problems or performing similar tasks.

Postmeeting reaction (PMR) form: A form, completed after a discussion, on which group members evaluate the discussion, the group, and/or the leader; PMR responses are usually tabulated and reported back to the group.

Power: The potential to influence behavior of others, derived from such bases as the ability to reward and punish, expertise, legitimate title or position, and personal attraction or charisma.

Power distance: The degree to which a culture emphasizes status and power differences among members of the culture; in low power-distance cultures, status differences are minimized, but in high power-distance cultures, they are highly emphasized.

Preference for procedural order: A trait characterized by need or desire to follow a clear, linear structure during problem solving and decision making.

Primary group: A group whose main purpose is to meet members' needs for inclusion and affection.

Primary tension: Tension and discomfort in members that stems from interpersonal (i.e., primary) sources, including the social unease that occurs when members of a new group first meet or during competition for power among members.

Principled negotiation: A general strategy that enables parties in a conflict to express their needs openly and search for alternatives that will meet the needs of all parties without damaging the relationship among parties.

Problem: The difference between what actually happens and what should be happening; components include an existing but undesired state of affairs, a goal, and obstacles to achieving the goal.

Problem census: A technique in which members of a small group are polled for topics and problems that are then posted, ranked by voting, and used to create agendas for future meetings.

Problem question: A question calling the attention of a group to a problem without suggesting any particular type of solution in the question.

Problem solving: A multistage procedure for moving from some unsatisfactory state to a more satisfactory one, or developing a plan for doing so.

Problem-solving group: A group that discusses to devise a course of action to solve a problem.

Procedural Model of Problem Solving (P-MOPS): A five-step general procedure, based on the scientific method, for structuring problem-solving discussions; P-MOPS is adaptable to any type of problem.

Process conflict: Conflict resulting from disagreement about how to do something.

Program Evaluation and Review Technique (PERT): A procedure for planning the details to implement a complex solution that involves many people and resources.

Proxemics: The study of uses of space and territory between and among people.

Q

Quality control circle: A group of employees meeting on company time to investigate work-related problems and to make recommendations for solving these problems.

Question of conjecture: A question that asks a group to speculate or make an educated guess about something.

Question of fact: A question that asks whether something is true or not, or actually happened or not.

Question of policy: A question that asks what course of action a group will take.

Question of value: A question that asks whether something is right, good, preferable, or acceptable.

R

Regulators: Nonverbal signals used to control who speaks during a discussion.

Relationship conflict: Conflict resulting from personality clashes, likes, dislikes, and competition for power.

Rhetorical sensitivity: Speaking and phrasing statements in such a way that the feelings and beliefs of the listener are considered; phrasing statements in order not to offend others or trigger emotional overreactions.

RISK technique: A small group procedure for communicating and dealing with all risks, fears, doubts, and worries that members have about a new policy or plan before it is implemented.

Role: A pattern of behavior displayed by and expected of a member of a small group; a composite of a group member's frequently performed behavioral functions.

Rule: A statement prescribing how members of a small group may, should, or must behave, which may be stated formally in writing, or informally as in the case of norms.

S

Search engine: Software that lets you search the Internet using key words.

Secondary group: A group whose major purpose is to complete a task, such as making a decision, solving a problem, writing a report, or providing recommendations to a parent organization.

Secondary tension: Tension and discomfort experienced by group members that stem from task-related (i.e., secondary) sources, including conflicts over values, points of view, or alternative solutions.

Self-centered function: Action of a small group member, motivated by personal needs, that serves the individual at the expense of the group.

Self-managed work group: A small group of peers who determine within prescribed limits their own work schedules and procedures.

Sensing-Intuiting Dimension: The Myers-Briggs Type Indicator® dimension concerned with the type of information individuals use; sensers prefer facts and figures whereas intuiters prefer to dream about possibilities.

Sex: Biologically determined femaleness or maleness.

Single Question Format: A special procedure for structuring problem-solving discussions that facilitates critical thinking and systematic problem solving, but is more suitable for members low in preference for procedural order than more highly structured linear procedures.

Small group: A group of at least three, but few enough members for each to perceive all others as individuals, who meet face-to-face, share some identity or common purpose, and share standards for governing their activities as members.

Small group discussion: A small group of people communicating with each other to achieve some interdependent goal, such as increased understanding, coordination of activity, or solution to a shared problem.

Social loafer: A person who makes a minimal contribution to the group and assumes the other members will take up the slack.

Social presence: The extent to which participants perceive that a communication medium is like face-to-face communication emotionally and socially.

Solution multiplicity: Extent to which there are many different possible alternatives for solving a particular problem.

Solution question: A question directed to a group in which the solution to a problem is suggested or implied.

Status: The position of a member in the hierarchy of power, influence, and prestige within a small group.

Ascribed status: Status due to characteristics external to the group, such as wealth, level of education, position, physical attractiveness, and so forth; status given on the basis of a member's input characteristics.

Earned status: Status earned by a member's valued contributions to the group, such as working hard for the group, providing needed expertise, being especially communicatively competent, and so forth; status that comes from performance during a group's throughput processes.

Structuration: The concept that a group creates and continuously re-creates itself through members' communicative behaviors; the group's communication both establishes and limits how the group develops.

Styles approach: The leadership approach that studies the interrelationship between leader style and member behaviors.

Symbol: An arbitrary, human-created signal used to represent something with which it has no inherent relationship; all words are symbols.

Symbolic convergence: The theory that humans create and share meaning through talk and storytelling, producing an overlapping (convergence) of private symbolic worlds of individuals during interaction.

SYMLOG: System for the Multiple-Level Observation of Groups, both a theory about member characteristics and effects on group interaction, and a methodology that produces a three-dimensional "snapshot" of a group at a given point in time.

Symposium: One of three kinds of group public discussions in which participants deliver uninterrupted speeches on a selected topic.

System: An entity made up of components patterned in interdependent relationship to each other, requiring constant adaptation among its parts to maintain organic wholeness and balance.

T

Task conflict: Conflict resulting from disagreements over ideas, information, reasoning, and evidence.

Task difficulty: Degree of problem complexity and effort required.

Task function: Task-oriented member behavior that contributes primarily to accomplishing the goals of a group.

Teambuilding: A set of planned activities designed to increase teamwork, cohesiveness, or other aspects of group performance.

Technical requirements: The degree to which the solution for a given problem is technically feasible or must meet standards of technical excellence.

Teleconference: A meeting of participants who communicate via mediated channels such as television, telephone, or computer rather than face-to-face.

Thinking-Feeling Dimension: The Myers-Briggs Type Indicator® dimension concerned with how individuals prefer to make decisions; thinkers are objective and fact-based whereas feelers are subjective and emotion-based.

Throughput variables: The actual functioning of a system, or how the system transforms inputs into outputs.

Time-oriented listener: A listener sensitive to time; may be impatient or try to move the group prematurely to closure.

Top management teams: Teams composed of upper-level executives responsible for strategic planning and leading an organization.

Trait: Relatively enduring, consistent pattern of behavior or other observable characteristic.

Traits approach: The approach to leadership that assumes leaders have certain traits that distinguish them from followers or members of a group.

Transactional process: All interactants mutually and simultaneously create meaning during communication.

Transformational leadership: Leadership that empowers group members to exceed expectations by rhetorically creating an inspiring and motivating vision.

U

Uncertainty avoidance: The degree to which members of a culture avoid or embrace uncertainty and ambiguity; cultures high in uncertainty avoidance prefer clear rules for interaction, whereas cultures low in uncertainty avoidance are comfortable without guidelines.

V

Variable: An observable characteristic that can change in magnitude or quality from time to time.

Verbal interaction analysis: An analysis of who talks to whom and how often during a discussion.

Virtual team: A group in which the members' interactions take place primarily through some combination of electronic systems, such as computers, telephones, and videoconferences, instead of face-to-face.

X

X generation: Individuals born from 1965 to 1981; key experience includes divorce on a massive scale.

Photo Credits

Chapter 1

Part Opener I: Stockbyte/Getty Images; Chapter Openers: Alistair Berg/Getty Images; p. 13: Digital Vision/Getty Images

Chapter 2

Page 40: Stockbyte/Punchstock Images; p. 40: (c) moodboard/Corbis

Chapter 4

Part Opener II: Royalty-Free/CORBIS; p. 85: C Squared Studios/Getty Images

Chapter 5

Page 117: Digital Vision/Getty Images

Chapter 6

Part Opener III: Jack Hollingsworth/Getty Images; p. 169: © Purestock/PunchStock

Chapter 7

Page 183: Royalty-Free/CORBIS

Chapter 9

Part Opener IV: Javier Larrea/age fotostock

Chapter 12

Part Opener V: Getty Images

Name Index

Subject Index